Ben Klassen, P.M.

NATURE'S ETERNAL RELIGION

BOOK I

The Unavenged Outrage

***

BOOK II

The Salvation

Dedication

Dedicated to MY PEOPLE, the Noble White Race, the finest Creation in Nature's realm. May this book be an inspiration to unite the White Race, to find its racial soul and propel it forward to the manifest destiny decreed by Nature herself. In so doing, may it expand, advance and populate all the good lands of this planet Earth.

First Printing 1973

Copyrights, 1973

By Ben Klassen

Library of Congress

421113

This Edition 2014

CONTENTS

The Unavenged Outrage

The Laws of Nature are Eternal 1
The White Race: Nature's Greatest Miracle..19
Lessons from the Laboratory of India 33
The White Race - Creators of Chinese, Mexican and Aztec Civilizations..........37
The Black Plague in our Midst...40
Masters of Deceit A Short History of the Jews 52
The Kehilla..77
A Few Examples of Jewish Atrocities..81
Five Jewish Books..93
The Old Testament 95
The Book Of Esther..117
The Incongruity of the Jewish God 121
The New Testament...131
Revelation: A Jewish Nightmare in Technicolor......................................150
Getting to Heaven Project impossible: Or, Everybody is Going to Hell 158
Christ's Existence Not Substantiated By Historical Evidence 166
A Closer Look At The Judeo-Christian Hoax 174
The Talmud...186
The Protocols of the Elders of Zion 191
The Text Of The Protocols 196
Marxism: The Modern Poisonous Brew 218

The Salvation

Nature and Religion 234
Your Loyalty— A Sacred Trust 239
The Purpose of Life..248
The Sixteen Commandments 252
Germany, Adolf Hitler, and National Socialism.......................................272
Racial Socialism...296
The Leadership Principle 305
Foundations of Our White Society..308

The Importance of Land and Territory	313
Manifest Destiny	320
Mohammedanism - The Power of a Militant Religion	329
Queen Isabella— The Inspired Crusader	333
Mormonism — A Better Fraud	347
Christianity and Communism - Jewish Twins	353
Creativity vs. Christianity	360
Christianity Peculiarly Vulnerable	368
False Leadership	373
False Ideas Disseminated by Jews	378
Respect for Whose Law and Order?	406
Facts, Myths and Lies	412
Evidence, Judgment, Conclusions and Decisions	417
My Own Spiritual Awakening	422
Guideposts Along the Path of Life	430
The Advantages of Being Self-Employed	444
Horatius at the Bridge	450
Latin— Civilization's Foremost Language	453
Road to Greatness	457
Our Brilliant Future	467

FOREWORD

The principles and creed set forth in this book constitute the Articles of Faith of the Church of the Creator.

Our beliefs are strongly reinforced by an overwhelming mass of substantiated evidence. They are based on the eternal Laws of Nature; they are based on the lessons and experience of history; furthermore; they are based on logic, common sense and reality, not myth and fantasy. No other religion can honestly make this claim.

We furthermore believe that in 6000 years of recorded history, Nature's Eternal Religion is the most profound and meaningful religious book ever written for the survival of the White Race. It is a fundamental creed, based on the eternal Laws of Nature for the survival, expansion and advancement of the White Race, the noblest creation in Nature's realm. We are confident that the White Race will soon return to reality, embrace our power religion, regain control of its own destiny, and advance forward to new heights never before dreamed of.

It is towards this noble objective, the survival, expansion and advancement of the White Race, that Nature's Eternal Religion is dedicated. It is for this reason our dynamic religion was founded. We call our religion Creativity, and members thereof, Creators, because, we believe these words, in essence, best describe the characteristic soul of the White Race.

We completely reject the Judeo-democratic-Marxist values of today, and supplant them with new and basic values, of which race is the foundation. We take a new, revolutionary and dynamic approach to the problems that face the White Race today in its desperate struggle for survival.

Although our religion is new, the laws embodied in our religion are not new, nor are they something we have invented. On the contrary, we have only observed and put into words that which Nature in her eternal wisdom has decreed for the survival of all her creatures from the beginning of time.

Nor is it at all remarkable that we should have observed these laws and based our religion on them. What is most strange is that the creative White Race has not done so centuries ago. In fact, it is amazing that the Romans and the Greeks failed to do so in their time. Going back even further, it is hard to understand why the highly gifted Egyptians failed to do so in their great White civilization 5000 years ago. Had the White Race done so in its earlier history, it would not now be trapped in the idiotic and precarious struggle for survival in which in now finds itself ensnared.

We believe that reality is more important than "believing" in the unsubstantiated ramblings of a wild and over-stimulated imagination. We believe that facts substantiated by massive evidence are a thousand times more valid and meaningful than supernatural claims that not only are unsubstantiated, but fly in the face of reason. We refuse to accept on "faith" ludicrous claims that repudiate historical evidence, geological evidence, scientific evidence; and fallacious claims that repudiate every other kind of evidence. We believe that evidence and judgment are basic in forming conclusions and decisions in all the vital matters pertaining to our lives.

We believe a religion that is detrimental to the survival of a race is a bad religion. A religion that helps a race to survive, expand and advance is a good religion for that race. Our creed is such a religion, and will have the most profound and far-reaching implications for the benefit and welfare of the White Race.

It is not our intention to make the White Race less religious. On the contrary, it is our intention to have the White Race become much more strongly devoted to religion than it is today, and above all, it is our objective to give the White Race a far superior religion than the self-destructive, suicidal religion with which it is now burdened.

We believe that the highest Law of Nature is the right of any species to survival, expansion and advancement of its own kind. We deem that for the White Race, the right to survival, expansion and advancement of its own people is not only the highest Law of Nature, but also the foundation of our religious creed.

It is overwhelmingly clear that unless the White Race in this generation changes the suicidal course on which it is now embarked it will miserably perish from the face of the earth, overrun and inundated by a flood-tide of colored mongrels.

We are confident that in the near future the White Race will rally, unite, and embrace the Creativity program for its own survival.

Furthermore, we are convinced that if only one-tenth of the time, energy, and money, were spent on propagating our dynamic religion as is spent on keeping alive the sick and morbid religions now undermining our race, that Creativity would spread like wild-fire. We mean to organize all our good people and expend that energy—and more. United and organized the White Race is ten times more powerful than the rest of the world put together. We predict that our religion, Creativity, will be the supreme religion of the future. We predict that it will not only spread to all the corners of the earth, but will eventually supplant all other religions, barring none. We believe that such is inevitable.

Ben Klassen, P.M. 1973

BOOK I
THE UNAVENGED OUTRAGE

CHAPTER ONE

THE LAWS OF NATURE ARE ETERNAL

When we look at the natural world about us, we are awed at the beauty and the majesty of Nature. We view the delicate rosy sunsets reflected in the wispy clouds, we view the massive splendor of the mountains, gleaming and shining in their white coats of snow in the winter, bursting with greenery and the color of flowers in the spring and in the summer, painted with endless coats of yellow and red with the changing leaves in the autumn. We can view about us the vast expanse of the oceans sweeping endlessly, wave upon wave, and finally beating upon some distant rocky shore or some sandy beach. We are deeply impressed with the clear, crisp, tingling air of the desert at sunrise and the coral, pink beauty of it all as the first rays of the sun strike the dry, wind- eroded crags of the mountain. As we wander through an endless field of brightly colored flowers on the prairie hillsides in the springtime, we are overwhelmed with the profusion of colors and beauty and variety with which Nature has surrounded us.

As we drink in the beauty of the flowers, of the blue skies, the green trees, the mountains and the rippling streams, we are glad to be alive. We don't understand it all, we have no idea how long Nature has been putting on her bountiful displays. We just know that year after year Nature rolls through her seasons of winter, spring, summer and fall. We just know that Nature is always the same, yet always changing. We see as spring approaches flowers come forth out of the ground and later begin to bloom in their profuse colors, only to wither and wilt during the summer, produce their seed in the fall, and go to sleep under a blanket of snow during the winter. Then comes spring again, and seeds burst forth into a new generation of flowers and the same cycle is repeated again.

If we are observant there is one outstanding fact that cannot possibly escape our attention, nor can it fail to impress us, and that is the over-riding fact that Nature is governed by laws. The landscape may change, the face of Nature upon any particular area of the earth may change, but the laws of Nature never change.

They are eternal, they have always been thus and they always will be thus; they are immutable.

For example, the laws of gravity have been as they are today for untold eons. They will be the same tomorrow and they will be the same all eternity. Not only are the laws of gravity fixed and permanent on the face of our planet, the earth, but they are the same on the planet Mars, Jupiter and Venus. They operate on exactly the same basis in and around that huge star from which we derive all life and energy, which we call our Sun. Not only that but, the laws of gravity operate in the same fashion and in the same manner, exactly and precisely, on all the other suns of our constellation, and without a doubt on all the millions of constellations that reach distances that are completely unfathomable by the human mind, distances that reach as far away as billions of light years.

We have mentioned the laws of gravity. Nature has millions of other laws, such as the laws of governing electricity, laws of governing the activity of chemicals. There are myriad of laws governing the relationship between light, heat and energy. There are laws governing the interaction of electricity and magnetism. There are mathematical laws.

Woven through all the laws of Nature is a fantastic astounding interrelationship, a meshing of all the intricate gears that make Nature function endlessly and perpetually in her inexorable drive forward through the eons of time, forever changing, but her laws forever fixed, stable and unbending. There is not one shred of evidence that a single one of Nature's laws has ever changed or been broken.

* * *

What is Nature? The broad answer is not too difficult. Simply, Nature is the whole cosmos, the total universe, including its millions of natural laws through space and time.

These laws are eternal. Man has already unveiled millions of Nature's mysteries. Today man is discovering more of Nature's eternal laws at an increasing rate. Through technology he is increasingly benefiting by his understanding of Nature's mysteries. It is fairly safe to say that although mankind will continue to rapidly expand his knowledge of Nature's laws, that it will never, never solve more than a small fraction of them.

When we consider the vastness of our own constellation known as the Milky Way, and realize that it is only one constellation out off millions that can now be detected by our powerful telescopes, our imagination is staggered by the vastness of Nature's universe. We come to realize that our own little world is only a tiny speck in the vastness of space, and our own lifetime only a fleeting moment in the framework of eternity.

We observe that whereas the mass of Nature is inanimate, Nature is also teeming with life. Life itself is subdivided into many, many groups. It can roughly be divided into the field of flowers, trees, grasses, vegetables, etc., belonging in the filed of botany. Then we also have the immensely diverse and interesting group of birds and animals, fishes, and insects, roughly classified as in the field of zoology. Further we find that whereas the diversity of each on of these fields is immense, beyond our imagination, that each species can be subdivided into many, often hundreds, of sub-species. For example, there are thousands of species and sub-species of birds. There are thousands of species and sub-species of fish, there are thousands of species and sub-species of birds. When we come to the insect world it seems that we will never get through classifying all the species and sub-species that exist on the face of the earth. Scientists have classified one million species of insects, estimated

to be only 10 per cent of the total existing. It is interesting to note that there are over 320 species of humming birds alone.

If we look at ourselves we find that we, of the human race, too, are a creature of Nature. Furthermore, we observe that he human race, now numbering approximately 3.6 billion, too, is sub-divided into many species and sub-species, with hundreds of differences in their physical, mental, emotional and psychic makeup. Many of these differences are of major importance, but all of them are significant. Of all the species of mankind, we, the proud members of the White Race, feel that Nature, in her creation of our race over the millions of years, has up to this time, reached the pinnacle of her creation. We believe this, and we believe it because there is a great amount of substantial evidence to corroborate this conclusion. I am proud to be a member of the White Race and I am thankful to Nature that she has allowed me the privilege of being a member of her most outstanding and most advanced species.

I will have more to say about the White Race later, but it is my objective here and now to delve further into the phenomena of Nature and her myriad of wonderful laws as pertains to the survival and propagation of life itself. There are some people who contend that we have now conquered Nature. They contend that man with all his scientific inventions is now above the laws of Nature. This, of course, is plain foolishness and completely untrue. At best, we have partially lifted the veil on some of Nature's secrets and discovered what some of her laws are.

Understanding a fraction of what these laws and then putting them to our own use for our survival is all that we can really claim. The overwhelming fact is that we are subject to the laws of Nature in her totality just as is any other living creature. We ourselves are a creature of Nature, as are all others, and furthermore we either obey the laws of Nature and work in harmony with those laws, or Nature will phase us out just as surely as she has so many other species, just as the dodo bird and the dinosaur have been relegated to the scrap heap of antiquity.

In each species Nature has implanted a strong urge for the survival and perpetuation of its own kind. It is over-abundantly apparent that Nature urges the inner segregation of each species. Among birds there are, for instance, 87 species of king-fishers; there are 175 species of woodpeckers; there are 265 species of fly-catchers; there are 75 species of larks; there are also 75 species of swallows; there are approximately 100 species in the jay, magpie and crow family; in the vast realm of fishes, there are for instance, 250 known species of sharks and so on. Furthermore, once a species is firmly established, it will practically never interbreed with that of another species of the same family. For example, canvasback ducks may be swimming and feeding in the same pond as a flock of pintail ducks, but they will not interbreed. They will strictly mate only with their own kind, the pintail duck with the pintail duck, and the canvasbacks with the canvas backs.

The brown bears may live in the same forest with the black bears, but they, too, instinctively know enough not to interbreed. They will stay strictly with their own kind. There may be 175 species of woodpeckers, but they, too, strictly stay with their own kind and do not interbreed.

The 75 species of swallows may all have originally descended from one species a long time back in their evolution, but they do not retrogress and interbreed amongst each other and become again one mixed-up species of swallows. No, Nature does not plan it that way.

If this were not so, then all the species would soon be mongrelized into one mixed-up species. Furthermore, the mongrelized swallow would soon breed with the 75 species of larks and we would soon have a swallark. The mongrelized swallark would soon breed with mongrelized cardinals and bluebirds and the whole process would degenerate into a mongrelized bird. The end result would soon be that birds would lose their own innate, peculiar characteristics that enabled them to survive all these thousands of years.

Much to our disgust and detriment, something unnatural like this has been going on amongst the human races in recent years. If it is not stopped, we, the White Race, will be paying a heavy price for our criminal perversion of Nature's laws.

Why does Nature urge the inner segregation of the species? There is a very good reason for this and it is in pursuit of the law of the Survival of the Fittest. Nature is continually striving to upgrade, to improve, and to find a better breed, a better species, a better specimen. Let us repeat this: Nature is continually trying to upgrade the species by segregating the woodpeckers, for instance, into 175 species. It has 175 different entries in that one particular species, each of them with its own peculiarities and particular means of survival and propagation. Some of them are better than others. Some of these species are not going to survive. Others are better fitted to cope with the environment, their natural enemies, the food situation, propagation, etc., are not only going to survive, but multiply in great numbers. So the answer is obvious, Nature is continually producing new species which will be able to better compete the hostile arena of life against all others. If some are better adapted than the others in coping with their environment, they will survive and prosper. If they are less capable, they will survive for a time and then be relegated to the scrap heap of evolution. In so doing, Nature is ever evolving to a higher plane.

Nature further endows each particular species and sub-species with its own peculiar attributes for its propagation, for its defense, and for gathering its food supply— in short— as a means for survival and multiplying itself.

Some animals, like the tiger for instance, have a number of remarkable attributes in their favor, both offensively and defensively. Tigers have ferocious claws and sharp teeth; they can run fast; they are physically strong and savage fighters. The elephant on the other hand has no teeth at all, and no claws, but he is a big brute of an animal with a tough hide and one of the heaviest land mammals existing. It is therefore extremely difficult for any animal to attack and kill it because of its huge bulk, its powerful build, its tough hide, and the fact that it can, and often does, trample other animals to death.

The rabbit, on the other hand, is a small, light animal. It has none of the defenses of either the elephant or the tiger, but it seems to exist in large numbers anyway because it has other peculiar attributes that more than compensate. It is not a fighter like the lion or the tiger. On the contrary, it is a very timid animal, but Nature has endowed it too with a means of defense, and that is its ability to run fast. Nature has also compensated the rabbit in various other ways, and not the least of which is its ability to breed and multiply prolifically. During the same period of time that has passed between an elephant cow giving birth to one calf and the time she gives birth to the next calf, a rabbit will have had many litters of half a dozen or more, and several generations on the way.

And so it goes. As far as Nature is concerned, there are no good guys or bad guys, there are no heroes or villains. There is only one immutable law: the Law of Survival. Perpetuate your own kind.

There is no such thing amongst its creatures as righteousness, or morality, or a sense of fair play. Nature tells each creature: you are endowed with certain characteristics, peculiarities and attributes, to propagate and perpetuate your species and defend it against all others, no holds barred. Whether deception, trickery, cunning, robbery, or whatever is used, it is all part of the game. For instance, it may seem grossly unfair and terribly cruel that a big mountain lion should pull down and kill a beautiful little baby doe. But it happens every day and this is completely in line with the laws of Nature. One species feeds on another and in order to do so, it kills and destroys. The fact that they may not be evenly matched is completely beside the point and Nature is totally indifferent.

It may also seem exceedingly treacherous that a rattlesnake, armed with poisonous venom in its fangs, may be able to sneak up on a rabbit and strike it with a poisonous hypodermic, something against which the rabbit has no defense whatsoever. It may seem unfair fair and cruel that a fish hawk may spot a fish under water, scoop down from the heavens and impale it for its dinner. Nevertheless, that is the natural course of Nature and completely in keeping with Nature's laws. It's a matter of the big fish eating the little fish and the lion eating the lamb, contrary to anything we may read in some mythical fable about the lion and the lamb peacefully sleeping together. It just isn't so, that is just not the way the laws of Nature work.

Implanted within each creature, whether it be bird or mammal, fish or insect, there is a strong instinct driving it onward to perpetuate its species and its species alone. This instinctive urge is the basis of the continuation of all life and it is something that we want to place a great deal of emphasis upon. It is something that we, the White Race, also possess, but are in great danger of having obliterated through artificial, alien influences. In order to see just how strong that urge is, we will examine the life cycle of a few species of birds, animals, plants and insects.

* * *

One of the most interesting is the study of the life cycle of the sockeye salmon. Probably in no other species is the urge to propagate their own kind stronger than in this fish. The ending of its life cycle is filled with drama and pathos.

The Adam's River is one of the vast network of the Fraser River system in British Columbia, Canada. There, on the gravelly beds of the Adam's River, 150 miles away from the ocean, are some of the spawning grounds of the sockeye salmon. Another big spawning ground is the Brooks River, feeding into Bristol Bay, Alaska.

Let us start the cycle with the female having laid her eggs in a nest called a "redd" in a gravelly bottom of the river. Here the eggs may lie for many weeks under as much as 16 inches of gravel. Eventually the dark spots that are eyes shine through the transparent cells. Late in this "eyed-egg" stage the unborn little fish can be seen wriggling around, preparing to burst forth. Sometime in the winter the eggs hatch. The "alevin," as fishery men call the hatchling that emerges, is an ungainly creature with a massive orange colored yolk sack attached to its underside. The sack supplies food for the little fish while it waits in the gravel, developing. Then on a dark night it wriggles forth, an inch long, beginning life in the open world.

It is a cruel world upon it emerges. Flooding, drought and temperature changes in the water can be deadly. The young salmon are the prey to sculpin, trout, yearlings of their own species, birds, even the aquatic immature stages of dragonflies.

The attrition is terrible— out of some eggs of a female sockeye, only 30 to 100 salmon will reach fingerling size.

The young pink and chum salmon move directly to sea. Other species remain in lakes or rivers for a year or two, sometimes growing as long as 5 to 6 inches before traveling downstream.

Once in the ocean, they are hard to trace, but intensive tagging experiments have given us much information. Salmon swarm over much of the north Pacific Ocean. During the earlier stages, while still in the estuaries, they swim in enormous schools. As they grow larger, the sockeyes make an annual circuit in the Pacific Ocean of more than 2,000 miles for each of 3 years in a row. Then, after 3 or 4 years in the ocean, when Nature has programmed them to return, they head for the home rivers on an amazingly precise schedule.

So exact is the timing of Alaska's Bristol Bay sockeye run, for example, that all the fish, numbering as many as five million, arrive in the estuary within 3 weeks in late June and early July— despite the fact that individuals approach it from at least half the directions of the compass and from a distance of 1,200 miles or more. They gather with such uncanny accuracy that the peak of the run, occurring about July 5th, never varied by more than 8 days in the 10 years covered by the recent scientific survey.

Consider the problem the salmon faces in getting home. When its reproductive urge tells it to head back for spawning, it can follow no trails worn into the ocean by long lines of ancestral fish. There are only shifting currents, slight differences in saltiness, and subtle variations in the temperature of the water, none of which seem patterned enough to be useful in steering a migration course.

It is still a mystery to scientists just what the mechanism in the salmon is that enables it to navigate with such uncanny accuracy through the uncharted waters of the ocean. Whatever the mechanism is, Nature has endowed it with an infallible means of not only getting back to the mouth of the same river from which it entered the ocean years before, but to swim upstream to navigate its way through the different channels, tributaries and branches and arrive back precisely in the same spawning grounds where it originally hatched. For some salmon the trip up river is short. Pinks and chums usually spawn closer to sea, sometimes right in the intertidal zone. Other species travel hundreds of miles inland; some battle upstream for months journeying as far as 2,000 miles from the coast.

Let us consider the sockeye salmon going up the Adam's River in B.C. The inland migration is a Herculean ordeal. The salmon arrive at the river mouth in prime condition, their flesh often tinged red from the shrimp-like crustaceans on which they have fed at sea, and oil-laden from a diet of herring and other fatty fishes.

But once headed upstream they stop eating altogether. The stomachs of both sexes shrivel. Through their long struggles against the current and waterfalls, the fish live on body stored fat alone, becoming mere carriers for the sex products which they will deposit before they die. In the case of the Adam's River salmon, the fish will make their run in approximately 18 days, traveling 300 miles upstream.

During this 18 days remarkable biological changes occur in the salmon on their trip up the river. Their bodies turn a vivid scarlet and the males jaws become grotesquely hooked and deformed and develop teeth. Eventually he cannot close his mouth. Also the males develop a hump on their back that they did not have at the time they left the ocean.

Finally they arrive in large numbers at their spawning grounds, gravelly shoals where they were born. Immediately the female begins to dig a pit a "redd" to lay her eggs in. This she does by slapping her tail against the gravelly bottom of the stream. After depositing a portion of her eggs in a spawning ritual with the male, who fertilizes the eggs, she moves slightly upstream to spawn again. Gravel from the second egg pit washes down to cover the first. Over a period of several days and nights of digging and resting she may have dug several such pits and deposited in all or more eggs, each time a male standing by, ready to fertilize them as soon as they are deposited.

And so the sockeye salmon, in framing red dress glide together in courtship ritual over their spawning nests, or "redd". Driven by one of the strongest instincts in Nature, the salmon found their way across the tractless Pacific, eluded fishermen, battled up the river and leaped waterfalls and man made obstructions. Finally, reaching their native waters and having reproduced, with life draining from them, they die. They have fulfilled their mission. They have assured a new generation will be born to again repeat the cycle. This they do year after year, generation after generation, following the distinctive pattern that Nature has designed particularly for them.

* * *

What can we learn from the previous life history of the sockeye salmon? We can observe the working of several of Nature's fundamental laws:

1) Nature has endowed each species with a strong instinctive drive to

perpetuate its own species to the exclusion of all others.

2) Nature has a peculiar and particular program ingrained in the instinct of each creature which it faithfully follows in its life's program to bring in the generation. If for any reasons, such as natural disasters or whatever, the species deviates from that program, it suffers tremendous losses. In some cases, if unable to cope with the change thrust upon it, it suffers extinction.

3) Death is a natural sequence in the everlasting chain of life, and Nature is never interested in preserving the individual, but only in preserving the species.

4) The percentage of loss and attrition before the species reaches the mating stage may be extremely high, but the strongest, the healthiest, the most alert survive to reproduce the next generation. The weaker and the less aggressive are culled out and fall by the wayside.

5) Practically the whole life cycle of the species is spent in surviving and growing to the mating stage. Then the culmination of life's whole effort reaches its climax in reproducing and bringing in the next generation, and thereby continuing the endless chain of life.

* * *

A great many of Nature's creatures are predatory, meaning that their main means of survival is to kill and eat some other form of life other than plants. Under this category in the animal kingdom, we can list lions, wolves, coyotes, leopards, foxes, and hundreds of others. In the bird kingdom we have eagles, hawks, vultures and many others. In the kingdom of fishes practically all the large fish eat smaller fish and in many cases they even eat the fingerlings of their own kind.

Man, himself, is predatory to a large extent in the fact that he eats meat. He kills cattle, sheep, pigs, chickens, fish, wild game, or eats the products of animals and fowls, such as milk from cows, eggs from chickens, etc. However, man does not like to regard himself as being predatory since he takes a hand in raising most of the animals and birds that he consumes. Nevertheless, this in no way changes the fact that he is predatory and does kill and eat other creatures of Nature.

Some of the lower, inferior species man, such as the blacks of Africa, are even cannibalistic and eat each other.

A distinctive category from that of the predatory class is the group of parasites that infest this world. We have such creatures as mosquitoes, lice, fleas, bedbugs, ticks, and thousands of others that live on the bodies of other creatures, and generally without killing them, manage to get their food and sustenance by sucking out the blood and life juices of their unhappy hosts.

Some parasites, as we will see later, exist among the human species itself.

We now want to take a more detailed look at two predatory creatures, one in the bird kingdom and one in the animal kingdom and see how they cope with the problems of survival and perpetuating their species.

* * *

One majestic bird, indeed, is the eagle. Its emblem has graced the heroic standards of Rome's far-flung legions of ancient history. Its emblem also stood proudly on the standards and banners of Hitler's heroic Germany. Many other peoples and countries have used the eagle as the symbol of pride and power. It is as noble a bird as ever spread its wings across the azure skies. It is the king of the birds.

The golden eagle is a predator. The range and habitat of the golden eagle spreads over most of North America, a large part of Asia, a very small fraction of Africa and Europe bordering immediately around the Mediterranean.

This king of the birds, so famous in story and fable, is now also a vanishing species, or at least it is now declining in numbers. There are only approximately 10,000 left on the North American Continent, we are told in an authoritative study of the golden eagle.

This bird may be one of the greatest hunters in the bird kingdom, but it may have to range as much as 100 square miles in order to feed its family. The adult itself consumes approximately a pound of meat a day. In the mountains of Montana, 18 pair of nesting eagles were counted over a large area and it was estimated that the average pair took unto itself a territory of 70 square miles. The golden eagle will nest in the same area and often in the same site, season after season.

In the study of eagles in this given area it was found that the average nesting female laid two eggs per year from which hatched an average of 1.8 eaglets. Of those hatched, 87 percent survived to leave the nest.

Despite being king of the birds, eagles face many perils. Before they even leave the nest many fledglings take a fatal tumble from the nest located on some high aerie. Adult eagles' most dangerous enemy is man himself and many eagles are either shot or poisoned, or even hit by moving cars. In fact half of all eagle deaths are caused by man, the main reason for the eagle now being a shrinking species.

Eagles work hard to supply their family with the food necessary for them to survive. Jack rabbits provide 37 per cent of their fare and desert and mountain cottontails make up another third. Other birds make up 12 per cent of its fare.

The Laws of Nature are Eternal

The other 18 per cent consists of a variety of prey, including some domestic sheep. Altogether, the golden eagle of this Montana area consumes 32 species of prey, ranging from ground squirrels to young deer, from the great horned owl to rattlesnakes.

The birds generally mate for life. If one dies, the survivor soon takes a new mate. What can be learned from this short life history of the golden eagle? There are a few additional observations here

about the operation of Nature's laws. One obvious fact is that despite it being the king of the birds, it is not necessarily holding its own in the fight for survival of its species. The White Race, above all, should take good note of this lesson.

Although the eagle is an excellent hunter, it has to work hard in order to feed itself and its family. We note furthermore that the bird, like the early homesteader, stakes out a definite given territory for its very own. It knows that one family needs a minimum amount of territory in order to be able to provide for itself and feed its young. In the case of the eagles, this amounts to approximately 70 square miles.

The most important lesson that we can learn from the eagle is despite the fact that it is a great hunter, is a brave and courageous fighter, its species is vanishing from the face of the earth because of its low reproductive rate. It is obvious that even with its admirable qualities— keen eyes, great wings and sharp talons, this is not enough. They also must have a more prolific rate of reproduction in order for its species to survive. Although the morality rate of the sockeye salmon is much, much greater, the salmon does much better in proliferating its species, because, unlike the golden eagle, which only lays two eggs, the female salmon lays 3,000 eggs and therefore has a much better multiplication factor in its favor.

Rabbits on the other hand have numerous natural enemies— coyotes, badgers, hawks, eagles, snakes, and a host of others. Not the least of these is man himself, who certainly shoots and kills hundreds of times as many rabbits as he does eagles. Yet the rabbit, because of its fecundity, has no trouble holding its own against man and the rest of its natural enemies.

Obviously survival of the species entails a high degree of fertility.

* * *

The Canadian timber wolf, too, is a predator, but in the animal kingdom. We have an interesting account of their habits and life pattern from a writer and a naturalist, who went up into the Labrador area of Northern Canada to watch the wolf population in general, and a wolf family of three adults in particular.

Nature's Eternal Religion

Wolves are very interesting and much misunderstood animals.

They are nomadic roamers as is commonly believed, but are settled beasts, having large permanent estates.

The naturalist found that this family of three adults had a territory well staked out for themselves and it consisted of approximately 100 square miles. The boundaries were staked out by urinating on certain markers around the whole circumference of their territory. Once a week, more or less, they made the rounds of the family estates and freshened up the boundary markers. Their territory abutted two other adjoining wolf estates, but there was no evidence of any disagreements or bickering over boundaries and each clan respected that of the other.

This again points up that even birds, like the eagle, and animals like the wolf, realize the importance of having space and territory within which to roam and provide for their families, and that a certain minimum amount of territory is needed in order to support their families.

Wolves are fairly orderly and lead a well-regulated life. Although not adherent to a fixed schedule, they do follow a fairly well planned pattern. Males hunt at night but stay within the limits of their territory. Females usually stay in the den with their cubs except for short trips perhaps outside for water or a visit to a meat cache.

Wolves are monogamous. They mate only once and that is for life. The mating period itself usually lasts for only two or three weeks in early spring. Their home is a den and very often generations of wolves use the same den for raising their families. During the summer the wolves will pull down grown caribou, usually weak specimens in the herd, or calves. During the period when the caribou go further north the wolves will eat and feed their young on mice, ground squirrels, and anything else they can catch.

Although wolves are usually looked upon as being a mean and fierce animal, they are very affectionate and lovable to their own families and take excellent care in providing for their young. They are, furthermore, loyal to their mates and stick with them for life.

A litter of four pups is a good average.

From the wolf species we can learn two outstanding characteristics: the wolf importance of land and territory, and unswerving loyalty to its own kind.

* * *

One of the most remarkable little creatures is the honeybee. It is particularly interesting to our study because it has every well- organized and highly developed social structure. The productivity and activity that goes on within the beehive and outside of it is extremely interesting and amazing to behold.

Bees and flowers are two parts of the same life, like heads and tails of a coin. This amazing creature-and-plant team, coordinated to an almost unbelievable degree, is one of Nature's most wonderful creations.

A bee is the only flying creature built to carry heavy freight. It has storage space and lifting power to transport syrup, pollen, and varnish. Whereas man's freight planes carry a planeload of perhaps 25 per cent of their own weight, a bee can carry almost 100 per cent. Whereas the bee has short wings on a fat body and cannot glide, it can nevertheless move up, down, or stand still in mid-air. Its short wide wings beat at a high rate of speed with a weaving figure-eight motion. By changing the figure eight the bee can drive itself forward, or stand still in mid air in front of a flower and look it over.

This flying machine has three places for storing cargo. One is a tank inside, which fills by sucking up nectar syrup through a long tube from inside the flower's body. The other two are the baskets on its hind legs for carrying pollen.

Mostly the bee carries freight only in one direction. Outward bound, it needs only a speck of honey for fuel, enough to reach the goal, where it can find plentiful stores of honey, and refuel. Honey is so powerful that a pin-head sized speck of it will whirl the bees wings for about a quarter of a mile.

The bee is an intensely social creature. The hive in which it lives is like one unit, like one animal, living in a beautiful home, with rows of six-sided rooms built of wax that look like marble. A small hive will have 20,000 bees, whereas a middle sized hive will probably have 75,000 and a big hive even 200,000 members. The whole hive throbs as a single life, one unit. One extra large bee that lives in the heart of it all has produced all the bees that are in the hive. This is the queen bee, who slaves to lay up one or two thousand eggs per day.

The work is all very well organized. The beehive, which consists of combs and their six- sided cells, are built by the younger bees under seventeen days old, which have not yet reached the flying stage. Honeybees enjoy quite a reputation of being architects and engineers because they build many rows of little rooms the same size, each one with three pairs of walls facing each other, so that they are hexagon shaped. Without drawing boards, compasses or rulers they perform a job that is well measured, strongly made and is very precise throughout. The cell walls are only 1/350th of an inch thick.

There is only one queen bee in the hive. Except for a few drones who fertilize the queen, the rest of the colony consists entirely of workers. These workers are forever busy collecting from flowers, building their wax homes, storing up honey and pollen and passing around food.

The queen is a special invention. Other bees work so hard that they don't have time to have any offspring, so Nature invented the queen, who is different from all the others and who lays all the eggs.

To keep a hive of many thousands of bees strong and healthy, several thousand baby bees must be born every day. For although the queen may live for five years, worker bees live only 41 days, and it is the endless job of the queen to replace them as they die off. She spends most of her time walking across the face of the comb, and as she passes one six sided cell after another she pauses for a few seconds and drops in an egg. Her job takes so much energy that she must have attendants to feed her constantly.

When the queen bee is busy laying eggs, she is surrounded by a retinue of 22 bees making royal jelly. They face her, surrounding her like spokes of a wheel. Their entire job is to keep feeding her royal jelly. As they pass the twelve-day-old mark, they are replaced with younger bees, probably six days old, for this remarkable food can be made only in the heads of adolescent bees.

The queen bee has a fine pair of wings but she uses them only about twice in her long life; once to fly off on a mating flight, and again to fly away from her hive forever with a swarm to start a new home. She can lay no eggs until after she has flown up into the sky with the drones and returned home from her mating flight.

When drones return to the hive, demanding honey, the workers refuse to feed them and they starve. They are no longer needed for the life of the colony, and are discarded.

Worker bees do not spend the night among the flowers. They wait in the hive until sunrise. Since they do not know which flowers will open pollen boxes and gush nectar the following morning, or where they will be located, these intelligent little creatures don't send out tens of thousands of flying freight cars on a wild goose chase. They have scouts who do reconnaissance work first thing in the morning.

Perhaps a dozen bees go out in different directions and scout the countryside. They fly around in the vicinity of the hive in ever widening circles. If there is an apple orchard, a field of poppies or alfalfa, or a garden of beans or peas close by, or a meadow blooming with clover, great is the excitement in the hive and a whole army will be on the wing and ready to travel in a few minutes.

But the day's plunder may be some distance away. The scouts may have to search across miles of countryside. When one of these returns, it will tell the others exactly what kind of flowers are open, and give them a compass bearing for the direction and announce the distance to the spot. Many other creatures can communicate, but few can equal in clarity and usefulness the language that

The Laws of Nature are Eternal

the honeybee has developed and uses to communicate with its fellow workers.

We have often heard the expression "busy as a bee" and we like to compare the productivity and organization of the bee colony of that of the White Man in his organization and his productivity. If there is one thing that we can learn from Nature's social structure in the beehive, it is that (a) the whole colony functions because of its organized social structure, (b) in order to function colony must have a leader, in this case the queen bee, (c) each one has their particular function in the survival of the colony and when that function is no longer useful (such as the drones) no further food or effort is wasted on them.

* * *

Another most interesting creature, who is Nature's finest engineer in the kingdom, is the beaver.

Beavers weigh 30 to 68 pounds, and reach 43 inches in length, including their sixteen-inch broad, flat, scaly tail. The hind feet are webbed. Beavers live in the water, and construct dams several hundred feet in length and as much as 15 feet high, creating ponds in which they live, and in which they are protected from their enemies.

Their houses are large structures of poles and mud having under water entrances. Beavers eat the bark and twigs of trees, particularly of aspens, which they gnaw down with their large, incisor teeth. Occasionally they will build canals up to 2,000 feet long, in which to float sections of feed trees to their ponds.

Like the bees, beavers, too, are engineers and builders and are busy little productive workers. They further prove that man is certainly not the only engineer. In fact, their ability to be able to scout and size up proper streams for their dam building and then to build substantial lasting dams is more advanced than that say, for instance, of the African natives, whose tribes have never been known to build a dam. In fact the house that the beaver builds is probably in every way as well constructed as are the mud huts that are built by the natives of the jungle tribes of Africa.

* * *

These abilities, that the bees have in constructing their hives and their combs and their cells, and the abilities that the beavers have in constructing their dams and their homes are ingrained and imbedded in their instinct and are peculiar to themselves and are their very own. They are further examples of the marvelous way in which Nature has given each creature a unique, built-in instinct and programmed them to perform miraculously and flawlessly generation after generation. Not only is it most miraculous that this instinct,

Nature's Eternal Religion

with all the detailed information must be passed on through the microscopically small genes through a never ending chain of generations. Nature is marvelous indeed.

Bees are not the only creature in Nature whose communal life revolves around a leader. There are many animals with a herd instinct who live together in social groups and whose group has a definite leader. Wolf packs, for instance, usually follow a leader. Herds of buffalo usually follow a leading bull who blazes a trail.

A herd of wild horses out in the west is usually led by a stallion who takes care of his herd and keeps an eye open for danger. Flocks of geese, flying south for the winter, are usually led by a lead goose who charts the way. The leadership principle manifests itself in the animal kingdom, bird kingdom, and in the insect world just as obviously as in the human social structure. It is implanted there by Nature.

* * *

In the above we have cited the life patterns of several species in particular and several more we have touched on in general. In summation to what we have briefly covered in the foregoing, we can form the following conclusions:

1) The universe is governed by the laws of Nature.

2) The laws of Nature are fixed, rigid and eternal.

3) The laws of Nature apply to living creatures just as firmly and relentless as they do to inanimate objects.

4) The human race, too, is a creature of Nature.

5) Nature is interested only in survival of the species, and not the individual.

6) Only those species survive that can complete in the hostile face of all others and either hold their own or increase.

7) Nature continually tries to upgrade the species by the law of the "Survival of the Fittest." It ruthlessly culls out, generally before reproduction, all the misfits, the sickly and the weak.

8) In the struggle for the survival of the species Nature shows that she is completely devoid of any compassion, morality, or sense of fair play, as far as any other species is concerned. The only yard stick is survival.

9) Nature favors and promotes the inner segregation of each species and causes the sub-species to compete against each other.

10) Nature frowns upon mongrelization, cross-breeding or miscegenation. She has given not only each species, but each sub-species, the instinctive drive to mate only with its own kind.

11) Nature has evolved for each particular species a particular pattern in its life cycle which that species must follow. This is called instinct, a very important and vital part of its makeup. Any deviation, deadening or dulling of its instincts, usually results in the extinction of that particular species. The White Race should note this well.

12) Not only has Nature usually assigned a particular lifecycle for each species, but usually also a certain type of environment that the species is limited to, such as fish can only live in water, polar bears in the Arctic regions, etc.

13) Nature is completely impartial as to which species survives, each being on its own, in the hostile faces of all others.

14) Each species is completely indifferent to the survival of any other species, and Nature tells each species to expand and multiply to the limit of its abilities. Love and tenderness are reserved exclusively to its own kind.

15) There are many species that realize the importance of territory and stake out limits of the territory that they need for the survival and raising of their families.

16) Many animals, birds, insects, and other categories have a well developed social structure.

17) The leadership principle is instinctively ingrained and utilized by many species of animals, birds, and insects as well as the human race.

18) One species, for example a flock of gulls, will sometimes wage wholesale war against another species, such as a plague of locusts. A pack of wolves will attack a herd of musk oxen.

19) However, fratricidal wars among the species against its own kind are unknown in Nature, except for some misguided human species.

20) Nowhere in the realm of Nature does a stronger, superior species hold back its own advancement and expansion in deference to weaker, inferior species. There is no compassion between one species and another, only life and death competition.

21) Species themselves are continuously changing and evolving over the millenniums of time. This can even be greatly speeded up by means of deliberate selection, as in the breeding of dogs and horses. Some species die out. New species evolve. None remain static, but

all, including the human species, are forever changing and evolving. Evolution is a continuous process.

22) Eternal struggle is the price of survival.

23) Nature has given each creature a strong natural instinct whose basic drive is the perpetuation of its own kind. Ingrained in this instinct is a complete blueprint for its whole life pattern that will propagate its own kind, generation after generation. A species must follow its ingrained instinctive pattern or perish.

24) Last, but not least, Nature clearly indicates that is her plan that each species continuously improve and upgrade itself, or be ruthlessly phased out of existence.

*　*　*

With these ground rules in mind, rules ordained by Nature herself, we will now take a fresh look at ourselves. We will observe how these same laws apply just as relentlessly to the human species in general, and to us, the White Race, in particular. We will explore whether the White Race has been complying with the laws of Nature, to transgressing those laws; and finally, whether the White Race, at this stage of its history, is on its way up, or on its way out.

CHAPTER TWO

THE WHITE RACE: NATURE'S GREATEST MIRACLE

If there is one thing in this wonderful world of ours that is worth preserving, defending, and promoting, it is the White Race. Nature looked fondly upon the White Race and lavished special loving care in its growth. Of all the millions of creatures who have inhabited the face of this planet over the eons of time, none has ever quite equaled that of the White Race. Nature endowed her Elite with a greater abundance of intelligence and creativity, of energy and productivity than she endowed unto any other creature, now or in the millenniums past.

It has been the White Race who has been the world builder, the makers of cities and commerce and continents. It is the White Man who is the sole builder of civilizations. It was he who built the Egyptian civilization, the great unsurpassed Roman civilization, the Greek civilization of beauty and culture, and who, after having been dealt a serious blow by a new Semitic religion, wallowed through the Dark Ages, finally extricated himself, and then built the great European civilization.

These European White Men, then, with civilization in their blood and in their destiny, crossed the Atlantic and set up a new civilization on a bleak and rock bound coast. It was the White Men who drove north to Alaska and west to California; the men who opened up the tropics and subdued the Arctics; the men who mastered the African Veldts; the men who peopled Australia and seized the gates of the world at Suez, Gibraltar and Panama.

It was the White Race who produced men like Columbus who crossed the unknown Atlantic; men like Magellan who first circumnavigated the globe; men like Michelangelo, Leonardo da Vinci, Rembrandt, Velazquez, Bernini, Rubens, Raphael and thousands of other geniuses who created beautiful and exquisite productions in the fields of sculpture and painting; geniuses like Beethoven, Bach, Wagner and Verdi who created beautiful music; men like James Watt who invented the steam engine; men like Daimler who invented and built the reciprocating internal combustion engine; production geniuses like Henry Ford, inventors like Thomas Edison; such a prodigal genius as Nikola Tesla in the field of physics and electricity; literary geniuses like Shakespeare, Goethe and thousands of others, untold geniuses in the fields of mathematics, in the fields of chemistry and physics.

It was the White Man who spanned the continents of the world with railroads and super highways and electrical power lines. It was the White Man who created the miraculous world of electronics, ushering in the telephone, the radio and television. It was the White Race, who in a combined burst of energy and genius sent rockets to the moon and planted the feet of the White Man on extra-terrestrial territory in the last decade.

The brilliant accomplishments of the White Race are endless and rapidly expanding even as this is being written. All one has to do is leaf through the pages of an encyclopedia to appreciate the magnificent legacy of achievements wrought by the White Race through the centuries.

What other race can even come close to this remarkable record of creativity, achievement and productivity? The answer is none. None whatsoever. None can even come close. In contrast, the black man of Africa never so much as even invented the wheel.

Yes, it is the White Man, with his inborn and inbred genius, that has given form to every government and a livelihood to every other people, and above all, great ideals to every century. Yes, we are the ones, racial comrades, who were especially endowed by Nature and chosen to be the ruling Elite of the world. Indeed, we were chosen by Nature to be masters of the world by building it ever better and better. We were destined to be fruitful and to multiply and to inhabit the entire hospitable face of this planet.

This is our Manifest Destiny as ordained by Nature herself.

We, the White Race, have such a glorious heritage and such an illustrious history that every member of the White Race should be bursting with pride to be part of it. Each and every one of us must dedicate ourselves to the great mission that Nature has set for us, but have not yet fulfilled, namely: to rule and to populate all the good earth of this planet.

It is not my objective here to retrace the history of the White Race in these few pages, nor is it my purpose to make a scientific study of the races of mankind. I want to show and remind my White Racial Comrades of something that at this time in history they are sadly unaware of: the greatness of our history in the past; the noble mission that Nature has set for us in the future. Also I want to set forth in stark profile the danger that we are now in and the enemies that are determined to engulf and destroy us.

When we reflect on the source of all our knowledge, we find that the only real truths are in Nature and in Nature's laws. All that we know is rooted in the natural laws that surround us. It is the White Man's uncanny ability to observe, to reason and to organize his knowledge of that small part of Nature's secrets from which he has lifted the veil.

One of the first major observations man has made is that Nature is governed by law. The laws of Nature are unchanging, unbending and unyielding. They are eternal. One of the inexorable laws of Nature is the survival of the fittest. We have seen from the previous chapter that Nature is continually striving to upgrade each of the species by dividing them into sub- species and having each one of the sub-species compete against each other. Those who cannot compete fall by the wayside and forever fade into oblivion. Those that are superior prosper and multiply. Nowhere in Nature do we see the superior fleeing before the inferior, nor do we observe where a superior charitably tries to help sustain or uplift an inferior species.

Nature evidently wishes the inner segregation of the species. For instance, if we look at the bird kingdom we find that hummingbirds have been segregated into some 320 different species, sparrows have been segregated into some 263 species, wrens into over 60 species, and so on. In the animal kingdom we find the same phenomenon being revealed before our eyes.

Whether we look at the species of mice or rabbits or cats in their natural habitat, we find that they have been segregated into dozens of different species, each following its own pattern for its survival, propagation and multiplication in competition with its own subspecies and the other creatures of the earth. Each has its peculiar means of protection, of mating, of propagation. Each has its natural enemies.

Man, too, is a creation of, and a creature of Nature. He, too, has been endowed by Nature with a special program for survival and propagation. He, too, has his natural enemies and it is a cold hard fact of Nature that the White Man's most deadly enemies are other species of mankind, namely the Jews and the other colored races.

We further observe about Nature that she abhors mongrelization and bastardization. Nowhere in Nature's natural kingdom do we find a fraternization or mongrelization of the different species, nor do we find them inter-breeding and mixing their genes. Not only do we find that the different species of birds, for instance, do not inter-breed, but we find that the sub-species do not inter-breed, although they may live in the same forest or in the same environment. For instance, we do not find crows, who are birds, mating with white egrets who are also birds. We do not even find that any of the 60 species of wren mix or inter-breed with each other.

Nor do we find any inter-breeding among the different sub-species of the jay. For instance, a blue jay will not mate with a grey jay or a Mexican jay, or a Stellar's jay, or a scrap jay, or a green jay.

If this were not one of the prime objectives and laws of Nature we would soon find that not only would all the sub-species be mongrelized into one species, but all the birds would be mongrelized into one type of bird only and all the fish with all their thousands and thousands of species would be mongrelized into one type of fish. There would soon be no such a thing as a beautiful

blue jay or a beautiful cardinal or a wonderful little hummingbird or a delightful meadowlark. No, the black bear and the grizzly bear may live in the same forest, but they do not commune with each other, nor do they socialize with each other, nor do they mongrelize or mate with each other. This is one of the inexorable laws of Nature. Nature frowns upon bastards, and usually punishes them by extinction.

The species of mankind, too, have been endowed with a natural instinct to segregate, mate and socialize only within its own narrow sub-species. Each has a natural instinct to preserve its own kind by protecting it, fighting for it, and defending it against all other races which it deems hostile to its own. Despite all the Jewish propaganda we have been inoculated with, this instinct is still there. All this false, unnatural propaganda may heap such derogatory terms as racist, bigot, etc., upon its victims, but the fact still remains that the White Race prefers to live, socialize with, and marry within its own kind, the Chinese among their own kind, the blacks among theirs, and so on. The fact that the color line is being broken down, mongrelization is taking place and has taken place, is an abomination against Nature. It is unnatural and Nature does not wait long to heap retribution upon those who violate her laws.

Unfortunately, the White Race, which has the most to lose, has in its past history been most criminally careless in safeguarding that most precious gift endowed by Nature in its genes. Where it has been so marvelously illustrious in learning the laws of physics, botany, zoology and technology, it has for some strange reason been most criminally blind and careless in applying those laws of genetics in its own propagation for its own preservation. Whereas the White Man nurtures proudly the thoroughbred breeding of horses, dogs and cats, he is strangely blind about his own breeding. He still does not seem to have fully grasped that Nature always extinguishes those forms of life which fail to abide by her laws.

In the twentieth century, the race issue is becoming overwhelmingly clear and ominous. It will soon become impossible to confuse it with semantics, or economic theories, or Marxist jargon, or humanitarian garbage, or "religious" double talk. The issue will soon be so sharp that the final choice will be overwhelmingly obvious. However, as this is being written, most of the white people of America, and elsewhere, are still most tragically confused and sadly deluded. They seem to be stricken with a strange blindness about the race issue, a blindness that is almost criminally insane. It is the purpose of the following pages to briefly look into the White Man's history and throw a glaring spotlight upon the crimes and errors he has committed in not safeguarding the purity of his blood.

Whereas at any time in history it is dangerous to make an accurate prediction of the future, it is especially so regarding anything that pertains to the White Race. Contradicting all the obnoxious and erroneous ideas about race that have been implanted into the minds of the mob, and despite all the delusions now prevalent, I will nevertheless make the following prediction: the White Race will either rally and unite in the very near future and possess for its very own the strategic idea of winning the world for its own peoples, or it will be miserably and savagely destroyed by the colored peoples of the world. We must now either make this planet forever secure for our race, or miserably perish. We must either populate all the continents with our own, or be over-run by the inferior coloreds.

One of the truisms of contemporary history is the fact that those Whites who know least about the niggers and have the least amount of contact with them, always seem to bear against those Whites who are thrown in contact with the niggers, an unreasonable hatred. Such insanity against their own White brothers is unnatural, contrary to their inner-most natural instincts, and artificially planted by the diabolically cunning propaganda of the perfidious Jew. Without a doubt the most difficult obstacle in the White Man's struggle to save himself from destruction and mongrelization by the colored races is the strange and perverted attitude of the White Man towards himself. The main problem now is not overcoming the Jews or the blacks, but strictly a matter of straightening out the White Man's thinking.

* * *

Throughout this book I am going to use the non-scientific term, the "White Race" and for good reasons. I am well aware of the fact that various anthropologists have divided, sub-divided, classified and reclassified the White Race into many branches, and subbranches. I am well aware of some arbitrary major sub-divisions as Aryan or Nordic, Mediterranean and Alpine. These are then reclassified into a multitude of further branches and mixtures.

Purposely I am avoiding this whole hassle like the plague. To here argue anthropological divisions and sub-divisions is to fall into a vicious Jewish trap. To even use the word Nordic or Aryan in this book is highly divisive. This book was not designed to start the White people arguing among themselves but to unite the whole White Race in the battle against the Jews in particular, and all the colored races in general.

Therefore, the term, White Race, is broad enough to encompass all good members of our race without nit-picking as to which branches are best, or who belongs where. I am well aware that the White Race has some mongrelized fringes. It has many mixtures in its own inner groups, such as Nordic mixed with Alpine, Alpine with Mediterranean, etc. However, it serves no purpose whatsoever to differentiate and create caste systems within the White Race itself. On the contrary, it would be highly destructive and divisive.

Even to use the term Aryan would be harmful to our creed, since this term, too, is widely misunderstood by most members of the White Race itself. To most Americans this term would relate (although incorrectly) to Germans only and something that belonged to Hitler's movement. Although Hitler was undoubtedly a great White leader, this term, nevertheless, would be an obstacle, rather than an aid, in uniting the White Race and promoting our new religion.

Our first objective in this battle is, and must be, to unite the White Man, and straighten out his thinking. United and organized the White Race is ten times as powerful as the rest of the world combined.

Once we have done this, the Jew and the nigger problem is as good as solved. Once we are again in control of our own destiny, then we can proceed with more meaningful programs in advancing and upgrading our own race. This can easily be done without coercive methods. We can accomplish this by promoting and encouraging the reproduction of the better elements amongst the White Race and discouraging the lesser elements. As explained in more detail in Commandment No. 12, this can easily be done through education, financial encouragement, religious creed and several other methods, without the necessity of using coercion.

In any case, to unite the White Race and win the coming battle against the Jews and the colored, we must rally the White Race.

We must unite and we must organize. For this reason the term "White Race" will be used throughout this book and in our religion. On this broad base we can unite all the good members of our race, rather than divide and fragment them with divisive and confusing technical terms.

Having laid these ground rules, we are going to take a brief look at the history of our race and see what we can learn from it. We hope to do this so that we may prevent in the future those disastrous mistakes we have made in the past.

* * *

In reviewing the long history of the White Race and white civilizations in contact with the colored races, especially the negroid races, we see over and over again these lessons being hammered home to us: First, that the racial destruction of the White Race is inescapable in time whenever there is substantial presence of a colored race amongst it, and secondly, that civilization itself never survives the destruction of the White Race, even where its civilization has been implanted for thousands of years.

This, in essence, puts in a nutshell the greatest problem that the White Race has ever faced, and faces today.

Today, more than ever before, with ever increasing rapidity the choice is being presented to us in cold and stark outline, namely, the continuation of our present human level and also the possibility of further evolution to even higher planes, or, on the other hand, devolution, retrogression, mongrelization, and finally, utter decay.

The fact is that for the White Man it is not even going to be a slow or gradual retrogression, but one that will flare into a horrible massacre that will make the slaughter of the 20 million White Russians by the Jews pale into insignificance.

One thing is certain, the White Race will either unite and fight for its survival soon, or it will be exterminated. This is a certainty from which the White Man cannot flee— the Jew has done too thorough a job of inflaming the colored races of the world with hatred for the White Race, just waiting for the time and opportunity to make the big kill.

Madison Grant, in his classic, The Passing of the Great Race, put it this way in regards to the race situation in America, "If the purity of the two races is to be maintained, they cannot continue to live side by side, and this is a problem from which there can be no escape." Alexis de Tocqueville phrased it this way: "There are two alternatives for the future of the negroes and the Whites. They must either wholly part or wholly mingle." The Jews have misquoted Thomas Jefferson most criminally in his famous passage by quoting only half of it and leaving off the rest of it, even on the Jefferson Memorial in Washington. Here is what Jefferson said: "Nothing is more certainly written in the book of fate than that these people are to be free: nor is it less certain that the two races, equally free, cannot live in the same government." The last part the Jewish press suppresses.

The history of the world is a never-ending history of racial movement and migration. Great people wanderings are the warp and woof of history. The fact is historic and prehistoric. However, we are not particularly interested at this point about the wanderings of the Turks, or the Magyars, or how the Indians crossed The Bering Strait and came to inhabit America. We are here primarily interested in the history of the White Race, the civilizations it has created throughout the world, and how the White Man failed miserably in preserving the purity of his blood; how he was submerged and diluted amongst the inferior races which he had conquered and partially civilized; how he lost his identity, lost his culture and, indeed, lost the hard won civilization which he had created.

The White Race conquered and civilized India, Persia and Greece. This is well known. Not so well known is the fact that he also invaded the islands of Japan and created a civilization there and also entered into, conquered, and created a great civilization in China approximately 4,000 years ago.

* * *

Let us now look at the first great White civilization in that cradle of civilization in the Delta of the Nile. Here, due to unusual climatic conditions and the sands of the Nile, have been preserved so many artifacts, monuments and creative archaeological treasures that the history of Egypt can be read like an open book, stretching back as far as 6,000 years of their exciting history. Furthermore, Egypt offers a classical lesson in history for us to study the contacts between a culture-creating, energetic White Race, and the negroid masses immediately to the south of it with whom the Egyptians were continually intermingling.

From the time of the consolidation of the kingdoms of upper and lower Egypt by Menes (3,400 B.C.) to the final decay and overthrow of the kingdom of the Pharaohs, is a period of approximately 3,000 years, and this period is divided into possibly 30 dynasties. Between the ascent of Menes to the throne of Egypt as the first Pharaoh at approximately

B.C. and the ascent of Teharka, a mulatto to that same throne in 688 B.C., we see the span of Egyptian history unraveled from the first great heights it achieved, to its mongrelization and slow decay and final stagnation from which it never recovered. We can regard the ascent of Teharka as the death and the end of Egyptian civilization.

However, this White civilization did last for almost 3,000 years, and that is a long time. We can learn from this span a great deal about the genius of the White Man and the results of blood poisoning that occur when he is in contact with the negroid race. The one thing we see in the survey of this ancient civilization is that its great achievements were in the earlier centuries, that is, when the White Race was still pure. There was a prolonged period of decline. The inhabitants lost initiative and ingenuity. When the Assyrians came, the Egyptians could offer but feeble resistance.

We can best understand this situation if we grasp the fact that Egyptian civilization was not overthrown. It was mongrelized and it decayed like a rotten apple. The trouble was internal. It was in the poisoning of its blood by intermingling with the blacks.

Already in the forty-third century B.C. the men of the Delta, who were White, had discovered the year of 365 days and they introduced a calendar of this length. It was the civilization of the Delta, therefore, that furnished us with

The White Race: Nature's Greatest Miracle

the earliest fixed dates in the history of the world. It was the northern kingdom of the Delta region, farthest removed from the Nubians to the south, and in close contact with the other White peoples of north Africa and Asia Minor, that was the most advanced. At the time of the consolidation of the upper and lower kingdoms under Menes in

B.C. the kingdoms of the north and the south were expanded. Of this time Breasted in his History of Egypt says, that Menes, the first Pharaoh "carried his arms southward against northern Nubia, which then extended below the first cataract as far northward as the Nome of Edfu and built a dam above the city of Memphis to divert the waters of the Nile to gain more room for that city. The swamp lands of the Delta were being reclaimed as before the consolidation of the two kingdoms, and the rich lands obtained drew to the Delta a rapidly increasing population."

So we see that the first Pharaoh reigned over a people already able to divert the waters of the Nile, reclaim the swamp land of the Delta, and important for our consideration, to wage warfare against the negroid peoples of Nubia. In addition to these attainments the people under the first Pharaoh are known to have used not only the hieroglyphic, but a cursive hand as well, and thus have to its credit the invention and use of alphabetic signs at least 2,500 years earlier than any other people.

The second dynasty erected stone temples. Namar, an early king, took 120,000 Libyans captive and of their herds "1,420,000 small and 4,000 large cattle." There is evidence that the kings of this time maintained foreign relations with far remote peoples, and that they were in commercial relations with the peoples of the northern Mediterranean in the fourth millennium B.C.

The third to the sixth dynasties inclusive have formed the period known as the Old Kingdom and encompassed the time span from 2,928 to 2,475 B.C. In religion, government, society, industry, and art, the Old Kingdom is revealed as a well constituted state, exhibiting rapidly developing culture, physical and spiritual, superior to the culture of the dynasties to follow.

The Egyptians were a religious people, who at this remote date devoutly believed in the resurrection of the body after death and in the immortality of the soul. Osiris was their God of the dead,

"King of the Glorified." Of a just man they said, "As Osiris lives, so shall he live; as Osiris died not, so shall he also not die; as Osiris perished not, so shall he also not perish." They believed that a praying man would roll the departed to the land of the glorified, but that this praying man would receive only those of whom it was said, "There is no evil which he has done."

This is the earliest record of an ethical test at the close of life making the life after dependent upon the moral quality of the life lived in this world. The animal worship which is usually associated with ancient Egypt, as a cult, is a later product brought forward in the decline of that nation as it became more intermingled and mongrelized with the blacks, bringing about a decline of its religion at the tragic closing of its history.

Not only were the ancient Egyptians highly advanced in their spiritual conception, but they had also achieved a surprisingly high level in their social and material culture as well. Within the home, the wife was in every respect the equal of the husband, and was treated as such. Affection among the immediate brothers and sisters and obedience to their parents was religiously taught to all youths. A favorite inscription upon a tomb was "I was one beloved of his Father, praised of his Mother, whom his brothers and sisters loved."

Probably the most outstanding achievement of the early Egyptians was their use of metal tools, which date back to such early times that some authorities claim that the Egyptians initiated the age of metals.

We can hardly overestimate the importance of this step in the history of man. Prior to the invention of metal implements, the tools used in the industries and arts were those made from stone, reeds and bones. This placed a tremendous limitation upon the advancement of any people or nation so handicapped. With the use of metals, however, industry could take a rapid course in war as well as in the arts of peace. We owe, therefore, to Egypt a great debt for the contributions to the progress of mankind, and not the least of these was their invention of the use of metal tools.

With their creative genius awakened and conscious of their constructive talent, the Egyptians sought yet greater triumphs. As the dynasties followed each other, and the Pharaohs reigned and died, these hardy individuals wished to build for themselves imperishable monuments to their power. This desire to live in the eyes of posterity gradually found expression in the pyramid tomb. Each succeeding Pharaoh, viewing the tombs of his predecessors, would wish for a yet greater expression of his power and his glory in the building of an ever larger pyramid. And so the age of mighty pyramids was ushered in. These are undoubtedly the most conspicuous evidence of Egyptian greatness; and in the ability of the engineers in planning and overseeing, and the organized power of the Pharaohs in bringing them to perfection, we catch a glimpse of the White civilizers of Egypt which must further impress us with the magnitude of their power.

Zoser, the first Pharaoh of the Old Kingdom (2,980 to 2,475 B.C.) made his capital at Memphis. It was the Old Kingdom in which art and mechanics reached a level of unprecedented excellence never later surpassed. With Zoser, as with Menes (3,400 B.C.) we have a record of the extension of the Egyptian influence over the mulatto tribes of Nubia. During the reign of Zoser, Egyptian conquest had quelled the turbulent mongrel tribes of northern Nubia and peaceful navigation of the Nile was possible for a distance of 75 miles south of the first cataract. From Menes to Zoser intervened more than 400 years. Within these four centuries the southern frontier had been extended but little. Sesostris III of the 12th dynasty, who came to the throne in 1887 B.C., completed the conquest of Nubia.

Between Menes and Sesostris III there is a period of 1,500 years. This evidence of the slow conquest and absorption of the negroids to the south of Egypt is worthy of our attention. These centuries cover the period of Egypt's greatness. Egypt was still White.

Before the time of Zoser the royal tombs were constructed of sun-dried brick. However, with the arrival of Zoser, who, desiring a more permanent memorial for himself, built a terraced pyramid of stone 195 feet in height. He became the first pyramid builder.

Later kings of this dynasty erected the great pyramids of Dashur and Sneferu, and the last king constructed vessels 170 feet long for traffic on the Nile.

Across the Nile from modern Cairo, which was ancient Gizeh, the tourists who visit Egypt today will get their first glimpse of the might and power of the civilization that has perished. There they can see among others the great pyramid build by Khufu (Cheops). To properly appreciate how strong and effective must have been the organization of Khufu's government, we must realize that this pyramid contains some 2,300,000 blocks, each weighing on the average two and a half tons.

Furthermore, the sculpture of the Old Kingdom exhibits the highest technical skill and compares favorably with the work of modem artists. Egypt at the close of the fourth millennium B.C. had solved the fundamental problems of great architecture, developing with the most refined artistic sense and the greatest mechanical skill the treatment of voids. The art of weaving was also highly developed. So much so that their fabrics are a source of wonder to the modern beholder, while the goldsmiths were capable of producing the most exquisite ornaments, many of which have survived to the present day.

Toward the close of the Old Kingdom, that is around 2,475 B.C., there is evidence of the weakening of the central power, but Egyptian culture did not suffer. Race is more than politics, religion or art. These are but the expressions of race. The sixth dynasty, the last of the Old Kingdom, marks a foreign policy of increasing vigor. The negro tribes of the south were compelled to contribute quotas to the Egyptian army; and the use of these levies against the White neighbors with whom the Egyptians were at war marks an unsavory epoch in the history of the contact of races.

The non-creative black races, compelled to rely upon their own resources in war or peace are insignificant competitors with the White Man. But armed with the White Man's inventions they are transformed into formidable competitors, immediately attaining rank which evolutionary forces have not conferred upon them, and assuming an influence which they are incapable of maintaining.

The Pharaoh's use of multitudes of negro troops against the enemies of Egypt had much to do with the final decay of Egyptian civilization. In it we see the seed leading to its final decay.

Let us now proceed approximately another thousand years in the history of Egypt in the search for light upon the Egyptian-negro problem. This will bring us approximately to the year 1,500 B.C.

Astonishingly, we find the negro policy of the Egyptian Empire of this time not to be radically different from that of the White nations now ruling Africa. Egyptian temples had now sprung up at every large town and the Egyptian Gods were worshipped therein. The Egyptian's arts were learned by Nubian craftsmen and everywhere the rude barbarism of the upper Nile, which was black territory, was receiving the stamp of Egyptian culture. Nevertheless, the native chieftains, under the surveillance of the Viceroys, were still permitted to retain their titles and honors, and doubtless continued to enjoy at least a nominal share in the government. The annual landing of the Viceroy of Thebes, who was black, and the bringing of the yearly tribute from all the Nubian lands, was now a long established custom in Egypt.

The gradual diffusion of White culture and the utilization of native chiefs, under the direction of White colonial governors was characteristic of the first attempt to implant civilization in negroid Africa, as it is of the present effort on the part of modern White nations.

The earliest period of Egyptian history reveals only a very slight negroid mixture in the population of southern Egypt, and Egyptian art, civilization and culture flourished. At the period we are now considering, namely 1,500 B.C., there is no way in which we can possibly tell the exact extension of negro blood, but as Egyptians were constantly going into the south and peoples from the south constantly coming into Egypt proper, it is not likely that more than half of the population of the southern half of Egypt was still White. Blood admixture has without exception been the inevitable result of long continued race contact.

From pre-historic times, the negro had sifted into the country.

Many thousands came as soldiers for the Pharaohs of old.

Countless numbers had come as slaves— many included in the yearly tribute of the southern dependencies— others as captives taken in war; while the large levies for purposes of labor, even though they were not necessarily kept by Egyptian authorities, would find that the Egyptian environment was better than their own squalid settlements, and decided to remain in Egypt.

The Egyptians were not entirely unaware of the degenerating influence of the blacks among their civilization. Certain of the Pharaohs tried to prevent the mongrelization of Egypt by restricting negro immigration, even to the extent of inflicting the death penalty upon the immigrant. But the negro was a docile subservient workman and soldier, and these characteristics created a demand to the influence of which less enlightened Pharaohs succumbed. So they came for centuries; not by force of arms and battle array, but as subjugated and enslaved people. With the result of all this mongrelization we now arrive at the end of the line. In the 25th dynasty in the year 688 B.C. the ascent of Teharka, a mulatto, to the throne of once proud Egypt, marked for all practical purposes, the end of Egyptian civilization. Teharka was the son of a Nubian woman and his features as preserved in contemporary sculpture show unmistakenably negroid characteristics. As the mulatto inherited the throne of the once powerful Pharaohs, his sister became the divine head of Egyptian religion, which in these centuries had become so grossly debased that the mulatto king's Nubian mother became a Queen Mother before whom all bowed down. For a period prior to the ascent of the mulatto Pharaoh, Teharka, the civilization of Egypt had become stagnant, while those dynasties succeeding Teharka's reign were imposed by foreigners, who were now easy conquerors of Egypt.

And so ends tragically a once proud and beautiful civilization. We have many lessons to learn from the degradation and decay of Egypt— lessons that evidently have not penetrated our minds even to this day. Yet the lessons are clear and they are plain. One of the lessons that we can learn is that a civilization can live for thousands of years. In fact there is no reason why it cannot live forever if the blood of its creators remains pure and uncontaminated.

Secondly, we learn that no matter what civil or religious laws are inaugurated, the very presence of the black race in contact with the White Race will produce mongrelization, and mongrelization will inevitably result in the destruction and decay of that civilization. We also see that the nigger, who makes a docile and pliable slave, is a temptation that the aggressive but short-sighted White overlords have found impossible to resist for use as cheap labor.

It is this very characteristic of the nigger— the face that he makes a docile and easily manageable slave— that has made him the deadly conqueror of the White Race wherever this poison was so conveniently, but short-sightedly, put to use.

We must also learn that no enforcement of civil laws, of social taboos, of religious practices, or any other practice yet conceived in the history of mankind, has been able to prevent the mongrelization of the White Race when it had the black non- creative race in its midst.

We can quite succinctly sum up the whole moral of Egyptian history in saying that there is no way in the world that we can save ourselves from the destruction of the black racial plague other than by expelling them far from our shores as quickly as we possibly can.

For the White people of America the lesson is overwhelmingly plain— in fact it screams to high heaven: we must ship the niggers from out of our midst, back to Africa, as soon as possible.

CHAPTER THREE

LESSONS FROM THE LABORATORY OF INDIA

Whereas the Egyptian civilization started off with a relatively pure White Race that was slowly mongrelized over a period of 3,000 years by the White Egyptians of themselves voluntarily dragging in the black barbarians, India, on the other hand, has a different history. Emerging from the hill country of Afghanistan and the slopes of the Hindu Kush, the White Warriors by conquest took possession of that extremely desirable portion of India known as the Punjab. A look at the map will show that the Punjab is a well- watered northern province and that it comprises but a small portion of the present Indian Empire. This took place approximately 4,000 years ago and the height of the White Man's civilization held sway approximately between the years 2,000 B.C. and 1,400 B.C.

From their base in the Punjab these blond, tall, heroic White warriors expanded their conquests and imposed themselves by force and influence of superior culture upon the mixed- breeds who infested the country in countless numbers then as they do now.

The natives they conquered were mixed-breeds of ancient Negroid stock and black, yellow and other Asiatic mixtures. The conquerors made no attempt to expel or exterminate their inferiors, but on the contrary brought to them culture and civilization which they then imposed upon their subjects. They set themselves up strictly as aristocrats and rulers and utilized the slave labor of the subjugated people they ruled.

It is noteworthy that throughout the history of his conquests the White Man has not expelled a subjugated people whom he could profitably enslave. The modern White conquerors of North America did expel the red man, but they imported the black. The former would not work, the latter could be made to work.

The ancient literature of the White Man in India is embodied in the Rig-

Veda and the Epics. The Veda times cover approximately 600 years between 2,000 B.C. and 1,400 B.C., the high noon of White

culture in India. From these writings we get a fairly good picture of White Society of the times and they reveal a vigorous White conquering people, well organized, respecting their women, already in possession of ancient laws, glorying in agriculture, passionately religious, imposing their faith and culture upon the surrounding colored populations to whom they refer in terms of contempt. They refer to themselves as a people of fair complexion and term those whom they have subdued as "colored," and ridicule them, calling them monkeys. Similarly, the White Man 4,000 years later has gone into Africa, Asia, Oceania, and the Americas, and has boasted of his White complexion and vigorous mentality, and has accredited the dark races of these lands with close relationship to chimpanzees and gorillas.

As we look backward over a span of 40 centuries and take a closer look at these White invaders of northern India we find from their records that they were of fair complexion, with straight well bridged noses. This latter feature, as well as the complexion, marks them as a separate people. They so impressed their social ideas in the conquered territory that even to the present day, a man's social position varies in inverse ratio to the width of his nose: that is to say the nasal index, as it is called, is a safe guide to the amount of White blood, as distinguished from aboriginal blood, in his veins.

Being constantly outnumbered by his black and mongrel inferiors, the White conquerors realized in short order their problems of maintaining their racial purity. It is highly interesting to observe and study the ingenious methods and means they used to try to preserve their racial bloodlines. The White conquerors by reason of race and culture, came as aristocrats. They looked upon the mongrel and black multitudes as inferiors and treated them as such. Nevertheless, how to preserve their own race, and at the same time utilize inferior peoples to do their labor, was the problem confronting the Whites. Their answer to the problem was, "Caste, enforced by law and religion."

The priests were the scientists and philosophers, and they devised a system of social control designed to meet the requirements of the native problem. This extraordinary scheme has been classed among the greatest expressions of human ingenuity. Caste, as originally instituted, divided the population into four divisions—(a) warriors, (b) priests, (c) agriculturists and merchants, and (d) laborers. The first group was composed of those of the purest White blood, while the last was made up mainly of the subjugated mix-breeds with whom the White Man was in immediate contact. There were also large groups of the subjugated population whom the Whites did not honor with cast at all. These were referred to collectively as outcasts and considered as barely human.

The superior White Race, realizing the problem, and intent upon retaining

Lessons from the Laboratory of India

their racial purity, were yet unable to restrain men of their race from unions with colored women. In most instances, unable to discover the guilty White, they turned with a terrible wrath upon the helpless mix-breed. The half-castes were not permitted to reside within the limits of the city. They were reviled by all, both black and White, and finally the Aryan laws provided that under certain conditions the soldiers may slay them without mercy.

Nevertheless, the caste system, with all the severe laws, with all the religious taboos barring the mixing of the races, what with legal statutes preventing inter-racial marriages, was incapable of preventing illegitimate unions. It failed in the end to prevent the amalgamation of the races primarily because of the fact that all these means could not be permanently enforced. In spite of legal and religious restrictions, the mix-breeds increased. Whereas caste prolonged race purity, it did not preserve it. The modern "Aryan" in India is just such a mixture as the ancient Aryan was authorized to kill. We should heed well the lessons of this tragic experiment.

The White people of the United States, unlike their early kinsmen in India, are not nearly as well fortified against this situation as were the ancient White Men of India, who supplemented legal prohibition of marriage with non-Whites by his religious teaching and by caste, which was perfect in ideal and enforceable by law.

Whereas, in the United States, most of the States had laws prohibiting inter-racial marriages, these have now been completely destroyed by the Jewish controlled Supreme Court. Whereas the ancient Indian religion prohibited and opposed inter-breeding with the colored races, we have a so-called Christian religion, which is interpreted in such manner as to minimize or abolish the color line. Add to this the fanatical propaganda barrage, the heavy hand of government pushing integration, and we find ourselves in a headlong rush to bring about that tragic catastrophe as soon as possible, instead of later, as history would lead us to expect.

We find in India, as in Egypt, amalgamation and mongrelization destroyed the White Race, and with it the beautiful culture and civilization that it had wrought. Whereas the Egyptian civilization survived some 3,000 years, the Hindu civilization survived barely more than 600 years, despite the ingenious and valiant efforts of the White conquerors to prevent that mongrelization.

Nevertheless, the odds were against them, and being out-numbered amongst the colored races, mongrelization came about much faster than among the Egyptians, who started out with a relatively pure White Race.

We have many valuable lessons to learn from the history of White civilization in India. The story of civilization is in the main the story of the White Race and its culture. History tells us that White conquerors coming in and dominating a colored race will not, over a period of time, be saved from being conquered by their colored subjects. This is well illustrated in India. Nor do we find that as in Egypt, where the blacks and Nubians were brought in as slaves, was it possible to save the masters from being destroyed by their subjects.

As in India, as in Egypt, as in America, the lesson is quite plain that laws and religion cannot stop inter-breeding. The problem is not so much legal inter-breeding of the races. Today, as it was in ancient times, it is, and was, the illegitimate mix-breed who threatens the purity of the White Race. There has been always a deplorable freedom between the White and non-White races, which has resulted in an increasing number of mix-breeds.

No, indeed, the answer is not legal separation nor even religious taboo, nor is segregation the answer. On this point history speaks loud and clear. The only answer is expulsion and geographic separation. Yes, the lesson is overwhelmingly clear to even the most naive student of history and that is: if America is to be saved from mongrelization and destruction by the black cancer that is within our midst the only answer is to ship the niggers back to Africa from whence they were dragged by their Jewish slave traders.

CHAPTER FOUR

THE WHITE RACE - CREATORS OF CHINESE, MEXICAN AND AZTEC CIVILIZATIONS

During the last century popular thought in Great Britain, cleverly nurtured by the unseen Jewish hand, reached a high pitch of insanity in regards to the racial facts of life. The abolitionists, philanthropists and the negrophiles conceived the colored races to be child races in the process of development. The colored problem was considered to be a problem solely of color and not one of mentality. The abolitionists taught that the nigger was, for all effects, like a White child. He, therefore, should be treated as such, they said, for before long he would reach maturity. The color problem would then vanish as a result of religious instruction, and training in the sciences and arts.

Since this same misguided thinking is still prevalent today and some of these perverted race- mixers point with pride to some of the other civilizations that have seemingly emerged from some of the colored races, we want to treat briefly here the vanished civilizations of China, Mexico and Peru. Whereas we do not have the space here to go into the full history of these erstwhile civilizations, we just need to touch briefly here to show that the history of higher cultures reveal that all those which are popularly called civilizations can be traced in origin to the White Race.

Early Chinese records refer to blonde tribes and there yet remain tall, fair skinned, blue-eyed individuals in Manchuria and Korea, which represent the racial outcroppings of the early White Caucasian. The presence of the early White Man in central and east central Asia is now well recognized by ethnologists. Early Chinese civilization so nearly resembled that of Babylon as to cause some scientists to even believe that the Chinese moved en masse from the regions adjacent to Babylon. This, of course, they did not do. But evidence is overwhelming that the Babylonians moved into China in a history similar to the White invasion of India but antedating it by a considerable period of time.

Some of these movements were probably of a prehistoric date. In any case, in a history similar to that of India we find the White Man conquering and taking over as the ruling class of China.

Again we find that the White conquerors interbred with the inferior yellow Chinese, producing a hybrid race. The rulers of China, however, constituted the upper class and it is from this class that Chinese higher culture issued. We find that the White element in China did for that people what it has done for other colored races and that is: impart unto them a culture which in its first stages was progressive and in its later stages was dwarfed as the White blood became submerged. This will account for the fact that Chinese civilization was more creative in its earlier stages. In fact, the Chinese were a more progressive people 20 centuries ago than when the modern Europeans first reached East Asia.

The important issue here is that it was the White element that imparted unto China its early civilization and the higher culture was imparted in the early period, as at present, through the influence of the White Race. Secondly, it is important to note that the blood of the White Man has not in China, as it has not in other instances, raised the mongrel to the level of progressive culture.

The Chinese seem in some respects to be almost as incapable of progress as the niggers themselves, the only essential difference being that the arrest of mental development comes later in life for the yellow than for the black. Furthermore, it may be pointed out that Chinese culture has been stagnant since the early historic period, despite impulses from within and without to shake off the chronic state of lethargy in which the nation seems to vegetate.

And so we find another perished civilization, a civilization that was first created by the civilized White Akkads of Babylonia.

These people, when they reached China, were already a somewhat cultured people, with a knowledge of letters, astronomy, and various industrial arts. In their new environment they continued the development up to a certain point, after which, when engulfed in mongrelization, they have mostly remained at a standstill and are to this day in a hopeless quagmire of stagnation. To this day this inert mass of semi-civilized savagery offers a dead resistance to all outward pressure. Their astronomy has scarcely advanced beyond the astrological state, while their medical art continues to be a hopeless mixture of superstitious practices, absurd nostrums, and a few grains of common sense.

* * *

Let us herewith leave the Chinese and now turn to the civilizations of Mexico and Peru, which the Europeans found in a slow state of decay when they explored these countries four centuries ago.

There are even today some ethnologists, mostly American, chiefly promoted by Jewish propaganda, who confidently assert that the cultures of

Mexico and Peru were of independent origin. Let us, however, at this point again restate a basic truth: behind every culture there is race. The cultures of Mexico and Peru were Caucasian like.

Stone Age migrations of the White Man had carried him across northern Asia to Japan and across southern Asia to Polynesia. All will admit that the American Indian is derived in whole, or in part, from Asia. There is an unquestioned Mongolian strain in the Indian. The question is, is the Indian only Mongolian or is he partly White?

Whereas the early movements of peoples is lost in antiquity, there is great probability that the more aggressive Whites of China could as easily have managed to cover the route to America as did the less capable Mongolians. The way before the White Race was easy and enticing. The path that lured him onward was peopled by inferiors that the White Race's long history had taught him he could subdue and enslave, and so the White Man followed the colored to America in prehistoric times as he did to central Africa and southern Asia, and everywhere eventually interbred with those with whom he had conquered.

The evidence is therefore weighted toward the supposition that cultures in the New World were indeed created by the leadership of the White Man who had followed the Mongoloid Indians.

These civilizations stagnated and decayed as his numbers became fewer and his blood was finally submerged amongst his inferiors.

CHAPTER FIVE

THE BLACK PLAGUE IN OUR MIDST

When I was a youngster I used to refer to the black man by the term of "nigger." At the time this seemed like the natural, uninhibited term to use. As I became older, went through college, and was exposed to a liberal education and the mass media brain pollution programs, I changed to the more "respectable" term of "negro." Today, I am most emphatically again using the term nigger.

In so doing I have been rebuked and criticized by some people that this is being low-brow, uneducated, crude.

Nothing could be further from the truth. The fact is that I have passed through the "nigger" stage, the respectable "negro" stage, and have finally advanced to the "nigger" designation again, because I have found, from a lifetime of experience and from a lengthy study of the subject, that the term nigger is by far the most correct and proper term to use.

Furthermore, in looking up the word in Webster's dictionary I found the term "nigger" very descriptive: "a vulgar, offensive term of hostility and contempt for the black man." I can't think of anything that defines better and more accurately what our position toward the nigger should be than what the dictionary said. If we are going to be for racial integrity and racial purity and for supremacy of the White Man, we should and we must take a hostile position toward the nigger. We must give him nothing but contempt.

The black man is without a doubt the most dangerous creature on the face of the earth to the further survival of the White Race. He is a danger that rivals that of the Jew himself, although for different reasons. Granted, the Jew is by far the greater overall danger in manipulating and destroying the White Race. He could, however, never completely destroy the White Race without the help of the nigger without completely exterminating the White Race. This, of course, the Jew does not want to do, because he would then be deprived of a productive slave element to furnish him with all the better essentials of a plush standard of living. The central aim and objective of the Jewish conspiracy in destroying past White civilizations always has been, and always will be, and is today: the

40

The Black Plague in our Midst

pulling down of the White Race; poisoning its blood and mongrelizing it to become a mulatto race of bastards, one which he can easily control. He knows very well that as long as the White Race remains pure, there is always the danger that a sleeping giant can awaken, turn on him, and destroy him.

One of the most infuriating con games the Jews play on the Whites is to parade a mulatto, perhaps 7/8 White, on the TV screens as a "typical black." Whereas any intelligence such a miserable mixed- breed may have, undoubtedly comes from its predominantly White ancestry, total credit is allotted to the mulatto as being black. In picking and choosing an unusual mulatto that is able to make a halfway decent presentation, the Jews thereby take the talent and ability derived from the White blood and use it to boost the stock of the niggers. A most shabby and treacherous deception, but most Whites unfortunately have not caught on.

If they were to expose a pure black African nigger he would, undoubtedly, be too repulsive to sell to the American public. The Jews therefore use mulattos extensively— not only half and half— but mulattos with predominantly White ancestry. Most of the "professional" blacks such as the late Congressman Adam Clayton Powell, have very little nigger blood in them— just enough to darken their skin. Thus equipped they then become professional nigger promoters, displaying themselves as a typical nigger. The only reason they get away with this, of course, is because they have the full support of the Jewish news media behind them, giving them ample favorable exposure in a thousand different ways.

The black African represents the lowest scale in the human ladder. Throughout recorded history over the last 6,000 years the African has invented nothing. He has not even so much as invented the wheel, although he has had plenty of opportunity to observe from other nearby races the use of it. He has never domesticated a single animal. His only means of transporting goods has been the human head as a means of cartage. He has never progressed beyond the common mud hut as a means of shelter. He has never learned to read or write on his own. He has never produced a written language. Practically the only trade he has ever indulged in is the trading of ivory, beads and slaves, in other words, the sale and trading of his own kinsmen.

He is shiftless, lazy and dumb. The average pure black African nigger has an I.Q. about 40 points lower than the average White. This puts his average well below the moron class. The average American nigger, having assimilated a large quantity of White blood and actually being a mulatto, has a somewhat higher I.Q., somewhere at approximately 80, a good 20 points below the average White. This puts him just on the borderline of the moron classification, with a large percentage being actually in the moron category.

The nigger is, however, tough, and he is prolific in producing more

NIGGERS.

For all the above reasons mentioned he has been well adapted for slave labor under the direction of a superior race. But for the same reasons he is a very useful and dangerous tool in the hands of the Jew, and an extremely dangerous threat to the White Race.

The Founding Fathers, when they wrote the Declaration of Independence, inserted in it a glaring error, an error that has lived to haunt us ever since. In a burst of generosity that was exceeded perhaps only by stupidity, they magnanimously inserted into the Declaration that much heralded phrase, "All men are created equal." We can be sure that the hand of the Jew was involved in this perversion of the facts of life. We can be sure the founding fathers themselves did not believe it. They themselves owned numerous slaves, and when a dozen years later they wrote the

Constitution, they gave the coloreds a voting "value" of three-fifths. But even this they did not give to the niggers themselves, but to each State as a whole in calculating their respective representation in Congress.

The Jew has made much of that treacherous phrase, ignoring the fact that the Founding Fathers did not grant citizenship nor voting rights to the niggers. They owned them as slaves and considered them as chattel.

Today we hear that same statement, that "all men are created equal," dinned into our ears again and again over television, over radio, and in the newspapers, and by means of every other Jewish communication medium. Being hammered into our brains day after day, the young people especially, are beginning to believe it. The objective of the Jews, of course, is to get us to accept the niggers as our equal, get us to inter-marry. They want to mongrelize the White Race, and to pull it down to somewhere near the shameful level of the jungle dwelling cannibals themselves.

It has been said, and rightfully so, "You can take the nigger out of the jungle, but you can't take the jungle out of the nigger." This is an eternal truth of Nature. Every species is designed to live in its own rightful element. A fish out of water would be as much out of place as a polar bear transplanted to the jungles of the tropics. A beaver is an expert at building dams but it cannot fly like an eagle nor build a nest like an eagle. Conversely, an eagle cannot possibly live the life of a beaver. So it is with each species in Nature. To each his own, and to each his own pattern of living and his own peculiar environment.

The nigger, taken out of the jungle and transplanted into the middle of a White Man's civilization is as much out of his element as a fish out of water. The harm that was done in forcibly tearing the black man away from Africa and transplanting him into the middle of White America, was not nearly as great to the nigger himself as in future years it was to the White civilization.

The Black Plague in our Midst

The foul act of tearing the black man from the shores of Africa and injecting him into the New World that was to be the future home of the White Man was a major catastrophe for White civilization. It planted the seeds for the future disintegration of a great and beautiful civilization that was flowering in the New World.

And who was it that indulged in the slave trade almost to a monopoly? Why, it was the Jew, in overwhelming numbers, carrying on one of his favorite rackets— that of dealing in human flesh for a profit. The Jew had been famous for indulging in the slave trade not only for centuries, but for thousands of years. In fact, he was indulging in one of his prime activities, that of dealing in human commodities, or should we say, sub-human commodities, and commercializing on it at the same time. In so doing, he was furthering his master plan in two ways: one, he was making money and thereby strengthening his financial monopoly, and two, he was implanting the black jungle blood of Africa into the veins of White America where it could fester and grow until it would finally destroy White America.

If we are to save ourselves from the black scourge here in America we must first of all redirect the thinking of the White Man. We must destroy the shameful lie that "all men are created equal." We must not only again make the White Man aware of his great heritage and his wonderful gift of blood, but we must make the idea of racial purity the first and foremost passion of our new creed. We must, therefore, make every man, woman and child realize the immensity of the gulf that exists between the great White civilization, the great White Race versus the black inhabitants of the jungle. We must make them realize that there is a far greater gap between the great intellect of our leading White geniuses and that of the nigger than there is between the nigger and the next highest ape. We must guard our precious bloodlines at all costs.

Therefore, when we think of the black man we must think of his natural habitat being that of the jungle of Africa. We must realize and think of him as a creature whose natural level of existence is more closely related to that of animals than it is to the great and high civilization of the White Race. We must counteract the Jewish propaganda that is poisoning the minds and the natural instincts of the White people. We can best do this by looking at the nigger for what he is, by thinking of him in terms of hostility and contempt. We must never refer to him in such a respectful term as "negro" but heap contempt and derision upon his head, and call him what he is at all times— a nigger.

Our proper attitude towards the nigger at all times must be one of hostility and contempt.

We must speed the day when we are ready to expel this racial poison from the body of White America. In order to do this we must re-orient the White Man's thinking until he is ready to do the job that he should have done a long time ago— and that is to cleanse America of the black poison that is within us, to forcibly if necessary, ship the nigger back to Africa from whence he was torn.

* * *

As I have stated repeatedly, the White Man's main problem is not overcoming the black man, or even the perfidious Jew. The main problem is to straighten out the White Man's thinking and get him back to sanity. Once we have accomplished that much, the rest of the battle will be child's play. Once we have restored the White Man's sanity to where his natural instincts will again be performing in accordance with Nature's laws, the battle will be as good as won.

The White Man, brought back to sanity, and freed from the clutches of Jewish propaganda, is the most powerful force on the face of the earth. In fact, the White Man, united and organized, is ten times more powerful than all the rest of humanity put together.

It is the objective of this book to bring about this situation.

* * *

When the Jews dragged the black man from the shores of Africa and planted him on American soil, they already had integrated into their master plan the means of using the black blood of Africa to destroy the burgeoning White civilization in the New World. Not only was the trading in slaves highly profitable to the Jew, but 300 years ago he already knew how he was going to use this African poison to destroy the White Race.

During the aftermath of the Civil War the Jew launched a tremendous power drive to mongrelize the White blood of the South. In this he failed mainly due to the rallying battle of the Ku Klux Klan. By the 1880's the southern states had driven the nigger from power and reclaimed his courts, legislatures and government.

In the early 1900's the Jew launched a new program for the mongrelization of the White Man, under the guise of the communist party. This time it was aimed at the entire United States with the spearhead being launched from the Deep South.

Here is the blueprint as laid down by Jew Israel Cohen in his book entitled *A Racial Programme for the Twentieth Century:*

"We must realize that our party's most powerful weapon is racial tension. By propounding into the consciousness of the dark races that for centuries they have been oppressed by the Whites, we can mould them to the program of the Communist party. In America, we will aim for subtle victory. While inflaming the Negro minority against the Whites, we will endeavor to instill in the Whites a guilt complex for their exploitation of the Negroes, we will aid the Negroes to rise in prominence in every walk of life, in the professions and in the world of sports and entertainment. With this prestige the Negro will be able to intermarry with the Whites and begin a process which will deliver America to our cause."

Basically the program is to instill hatred among the niggers for the Whites— the "Kill Whitey" obsession; at the same time promote "love" and "brotherhood" among the Whites; instill a paralyzing guilt complex in the Whites to the point they would do anything to placate the nigger.

With government, money and the weapons of propaganda in the hands of the Jews, the battle is on.

A ferocious onslaught is being made by the Jews to mongrelize the races in America in this generation. Everything possible has already been done to mix and integrate housing, but even this is not fast enough. The Jews know that in order to get interracial marriages accepted and get them in progress, they have to start with the school children at an early age.

In order to do this, they have done everything possible to push and promote the abominable crime of forced busing of our school children. Although this is completely contrary to the Constitution, completely contrary even to the vicious Civil Rights Laws that have been passed in the 1960's, the Jewish judges everywhere have handed down verdicts of forced busing. To anybody in their right mind these verdicts are the most vicious, abominable, hideous crimes that anybody could possibly dream up. Nevertheless, with the sugar coating and smoothing over by the Jewish-directed news media and propaganda networks, they have made it seem almost reasonable.

The result is that White school boards and county governments have shamefully abdicated their duty to their electors and to their citizens. They have bowed to these scoundrels of Jewish judges. Not only have they bowed to them, but in a most abject and shameful manner, have cow-towed to them. The consequence of this abomination is clear to everyone. Schools have become hotbeds of crime, of knifings, of beatings, of lawlessness, and anarchy. The Jewish press blandly goes on its way and acts as if, "Well there are inconveniences, but My! Look at the rewards. We must make the Constitution work. We must make equal opportunity for everyone." What garbage.

The obvious facts stand out that none of these idiotic arguments are valid. Busing little black savages into White neighborhoods, and conversely busing innocent little White children into the crime ridden blackboard jungles of the nigger districts has not achieved any of these so-called noble objectives. The fact is that the schools have downgraded education for both the blacks and the Whites. They are not any longer even semblances of educational institutions, but crime ridden penal colonies. They are slave labor camps in which our lamentable White children are the victims of a heinous Jewish crime.

Even the dirty, black niggers don't want to have their children bused, but a few of the Jew- promoted black spokesmen act like this is a must so that they can get "equal opportunities." In all cases, it is the Jewish financed and controlled "Legal Defense Fund," always with some Jewish kike lawyer at its head, that brings suits before the courts, before a Jewish judge. This Jewish judge then hands down an almost unbelievably ridiculous verdict, forcing large-scale busing of White children into the jungles of the black territories, and the fierce little black animals into White suburbs.

A great deal of opposition has sprung up. It must be our objective to capitalize on such opposition, organize it, and introduce these White Racial Comrades to our new creed.

In Pontiac, Michigan, for instance, a group of White parents calling themselves the National Action Group has organized boycotts that kept 35 percent of Pontiac's White children home on the first day of school. Immediately the Jewish controlled police were put into action to make sure that those few White traitors that violated this boycott were protected to the hilt to try and break these boycotts. The slogan of the White group was "Bus Judges, not children." Probably a better slogan would be "Boating, not busing". The implication of this slogan, of course, is that we should put the niggers on boats and send them back to Africa instead of busing our poor innocent children.

It is rather ironical that the most determined opposition to busing has come not from the White people and the White parents who have the most to lose, but from the Chinese racial group in San Francisco. Although they live in a country that is not their own and a country in which they are a small minority, these Chinese at least have enough racial loyalty and enough racial pride to stick together. Outwardly they claim that their concern is that the children will lose a part of the close-knit community's ancient cultural heritage. However, one Chinese American teacher admits, "At least that is what they say to you, but if you could speak Chinese, you'd learn they just don't want their children going to school with blacks." Even the colored Chinese, whose cultural heritage is much less than that of the magnificent White Race, have enough racial solidarity and loyalty to stick together and know when they are being debauched and debased by mixing with a bunch of inferior black animals. As this is being written at least

Chinese children were still boycotting the schools in San Francisco.

In reading the reviews about the so-called "problems" of busing such Jewish propaganda pieces as Time Magazine, Life Magazine, and others present the picture as "yes, there is a problem, but we will overcome all these obstacles and everybody will be better off," and an endless collection of similar drivel. The cunning Jew never argues the question: is busing really good for our country?

The Black Plague in our Midst

Is it really achieving any positive results? It is always presented in a manner that, of course everybody knows that we need to have integration, everybody is agreed that this is a highly desirable objective. All the while he is preaching this kind of monstrous lie, the Jew knows very well what he is doing. He knows that it is completely devastating and ruining our public schools for which the White parents are paying tremendous sums of money in taxation. He knows that the net results of this operation will be a mongrelization of the blacks and Whites in the next generation, and that it will pull down, degrade and debauch, destroy and mongrelize the White Race.

All this time he is deceitfully promoting the idea on a (seemingly) most high level plane, as if this were the American dream; as if this were the law of the land; as if this is what our Founding Fathers meant by the term "democracy." They are vigorously promoting the idea that if we could only have this country's races integrated, everything would be just lovely, and a whole flood of similar criminal propaganda.

Let's just examine some of these treacherous and fallacious ideas that the Jews are putting forth and promoting.

Let's look at the claim that this is the law of the land. In the first place nowhere in the Constitution is it stated or even implied that schools must be integrated. According to the 10th Amendment, which plainly states that all other rights not delegated to the Federal Government are reserved to the states respectively, or to the people, there is no question that schools and education are completely outside of the prerogative and the jurisdiction of the Federal Government. It belongs wholly within the jurisdiction of the state governments and the county governments. Furthermore, the Founding Fathers never did consider race mixing as a constitutional right. In fact, most of the Founding Fathers who wrote the Constitution were themselves owners of slaves, including such people as Jefferson, George Washington and others, who did not necessarily write the Constitution but were rightly considered as our Founding Fathers. They never did consider the black niggers as being the equal of the White founders of this nation. They considered them all as a chattel property, who were given neither rights of citizenship, nor were they given any voting rights. For these Jewish propagandists now to prattle that it was the will of our Founding Fathers that we should forcefully mix the races and bus our White children about like a bunch of cattle is a foul lie of the lowest order.

Let us further consider that fallacious Jewish argument that this is the law of the land. Even the most vicious laws that the Jewish controlled congress has passed in the last decade does not state anywhere that our children must be bused about like a bunch of cattle in order to achieve racial mixture and integration. In fact, the notorious and vicious civil rights laws of the 1960's specifically state that federal funds cannot in any case be used for busing to achieve racial integration. For these contemptible Jewish judges now to come along and say that this is the law of the land is a lie, and a vicious contemptible lie at that.

It is neither embodied in the Constitution, nor is it the law of the land. In fact even as far back as in 1896 the Supreme Court ruled that separate but equal facilities were constitutional, and in all our past Anglo-Saxon jurisprudence it has always been an established axiom that once a decision was handed down, that future decisions would be governed thereby. The presently Jewish-controlled Supreme Court has raped and violated this established jurisprudence and stakes out decisions that are in complete violation of precedent, in complete violation of the laws passed by Congress, and in complete violation of the Constitution itself. In any case, I say to you, White Brothers and White Sisters, even if such a vicious code was the law of the land, was imbedded in the Constitution and had been accepted by our courts, there is a higher law that supersedes all these— and that is the law of survival.

There comes a time when the highest law of Nature must be invoked by whatever means available and this law is the law of preservation of your own species.

It is therefore one of the holiest causes to which we can dedicate ourselves to expel this racial black poison from out of our national blood stream; to ship the niggers back to Africa as quickly as possible and cleanse and keep pure our racial integrity.

We must point out again and again to our White Racial Comrades the horrible facts of present day history, namely: in 1920 the White Race was outnumbered only two to one in the world. Today it is outnumbered seven to one, and the Jewish United Nations gleefully predicts that in another 20 years we will be outnumbered to 1 by the hostile colored hordes. It does not take a great deal of imagination as to what the fate of the White Race will be when the colored, agitated and controlled by the Jews, have enough physical power to slaughter us.

The facts of history and the facts of Nature are plain: The White Race must dominate the earth or miserably perish at the hands of the inferior coloreds.

* * *

The first step in the White Man's struggle to save himself must be made right here in America— and that first step is to expel the niggers from our midst and ship them back to Africa. It must not be our objective to "help" the nigger "improve" himself. We have no interest whatsoever in "improving" and assimilating the nigger into our White society. It is the most stupid thing we could possibly do. The only thing niggers produce when they get outside help is— more niggers.

The only answer is boating— ship them out. This is the only real solution. When it comes to implementing the real solution of the nigger problem in America, namely that of shipping the niggers back to Africa, people generally parrot two starkly negative answers, implanted in their brains by Jewish propaganda: (a) How can we possibly afford it? (b) Yes, it would be the sensible thing to do, but you'll never get the American people to do it.

Both attitudes (a) and (b) are, of course, intensely negative, just as the Jew tailored them to be. He is promoting these ideas along the lines of a sound maxim as old as the strategy of warfare itself— namely, if you can get your enemies to think they are defeated before the battle starts, then they are as good as defeated.

Let us examine (a) Can we afford it? And the answer is so overwhelmingly yes, we can. In fact, we can't afford not to.

Practically all normal White people in the U.S. agree that the niggers do not fit into our society. Most are aware of the facts of life— that niggers cause 85 percent of all crimes of violence— despite the fact that they reputedly only constitute 12 percent of the population; that most of the welfare money is going to niggers, that welfare is becoming an ever-increasingly expensive burden, taking increasingly greater amounts of our earnings each year; that the inner core of practically all the large cities in the U.S. are rotting from the effects of the nigger problem; that school busing and mongrelization are a frightening evil caused by the niggers in our midst. Most normal White Americans are aware of these facts, and with the exception of the idiotic hypocrites in our midst, the average American is well aware that our racial policy is going to destroy our country, our race and our nation. Nevertheless, the idea of taking 30 million niggers and transporting them back across the ocean to the continent from which their ancestors were torn, seems somewhat staggering to them. Again, this is so because the Jews have implanted these negative ideas in their minds.

However, when we consider this on the basis of economics and racial logic, it is the best bargain we could possibly buy for ourselves, if we did ship them over to Africa as quickly as possible. Let's look at the figures.

If we assume that we were to ship every one of the 30 million blacks back to Africa, and even sent them over in style at a cost of $1,000 per head, the total sum would come to only $30 billion, a fraction of the total U.S. national budget for only one year. And this would only be a one-time expense. How can we afford it? For one thing, we could take all the money now being wasted on foreign aid to countries which hate and despise us, and spend it on transporting American niggers back to Africa. We could take all the money that we are now wasting on breeding and proliferating niggers in this country today, niggers that are polluting our Race with the black blood of Africa, and use that money to ship these same niggers back to Africa.

When you think of all the increasing billions and billions that are being spent on hundreds of idiotic welfare programs to breed and proliferate blacks, money being spent on foreign aid, money being spent on armaments that are not really defending us at all, and all the rest of the $200,000,000,000 a year (plus) budget, that for the largest part is being entirely wasted, and being appropriated by the Jews, we come to the conclusion that the question has been entirely misstated.

It should be: How can we afford to keep the niggers here? How can we afford to keep coming up with billions and billions for one black hand-out program after another, year after year after year, with no end in sight?

With all the billions now being poured out for black welfare, black crime, black "capitalism," and black slum programs, we could have shipped this alien black population back to Africa dozens of times over.

As to part (b), that the American people will never do it— this becomes the more difficult part of the program. It is here that we need an intensive program of re-educating, not so much the blacks, but re-educating the Whites. It is entirely a matter of willpower.

Again, it is a matter of straightening out the White man's thinking.

If we have the will to live, the will to survive, we must and shall have the will to reject and to repel the pollution and proliferation of the black blood from our national White body.

When we look at recent history, we find that the Jews had no particular compunction about driving fourteen million Germans from their native soil in Prussia and East Germany, land they had occupied for the last several thousand years, and driving them westward. Nor did the Jews feel particularly conscience-stricken when they drove one and a half million Arabs from their native lands in Palestine and appropriated all their farms and property and left the Arabs to starve out in the hot, dry desert.

Why should we Americans, who evidently had no compunction about killing millions of our White Brothers in Germany during World Wars I and II; of bombing Hamburg and killing 50,000 men women and children in one night; of fire-bombing Dresden and killing 300,000 of our White brethren there; why should we suddenly be struck dumb with tenderness when it comes to dealing with the nigger problem?

Certainly the niggers are a real and present threat to our survival, which the Germans are not, and never were. In fact, approximately 30 percent of all White Americans have German blood in their veins and it was, of course, one of the great travesties of history that we should have ever taken up arms against the courageous Germans, a people who were fighting OUR battle against the Jews for us and all White mankind.

We are only quoting history to show that the problem of shipping the niggers back to Africa is neither an economic problem, nor really a problem of morals, but purely a problem of racial attitude. Once we get our thinking straight, the problem of shipping the niggers back to Africa is as good as solved. When we think of how many niggers we could ship over there by employing a fleet of 747's, or even as in wartime, using Liberty Ships, which we built in short order, it can readily be seen that the economic and physical problem is no problem at all. We can do it, we must do it. We can't afford not to.

I repeat, the real problem is to get our thinking straightened out, and that is what this book and the Creativity religion is all about. And the key to straightening out the White Man's thinking is propaganda and enlightenment, organization, and more propaganda. Remember, organized and united, the White Race is ten times as powerful as all the other races combined.

It is towards achieving this exalted and lofty goal that this book is dedicated. It is the predominant aim of our new religion to achieve this magnificent goal.

CHAPTER SIX

MASTERS OF DECEIT A SHORT HISTORY OF THE JEWS

Nature in her infinite wisdom has put the highest premium on survival of the species. In her profuse variety Nature has brought forth creatures of all kinds, fish and fowl, animal and vegetable, insect and bacteria. Some creatures like the cardinal and bluebird are beautiful to behold. Others like the scorpion fish and the lizard are not. Some creatures are flesh eating. Others are herbivorous. Some animals, like cows, forage on the grass of the meadows. Others like the coyote, the wolf and the tiger are predatory. Other creatures like cockroaches, mosquitoes and maggots are parasitic. Each creature has its means of existence and survival and its means of perpetuating its species. In all, the will to live and perpetuate its own kind is intensely strong. If it were not, the species would soon have died out.

In the human species there is one race that stands out above all others in the intensity and fierceness in its will to survive— that is the Jewish race. How this one race has survived and stayed intact through all the convulsions and upheavals of history for 5,000 years is something remarkable to behold.

Whereas some of the ancient races of recorded history such as the Babylonians, the Romans, the Phoenicians, the Egyptians, as a race, have all gone down the sinkhole of history— the Jew has survived. Not only has he survived, but he has become the slave-master of all the other races of the world, although he only numbers a small percentage of the world's population.

Whereas the glorious White Race has been a builder, explorer and creator of civilizations, of governments and nations, the Jew has been none of these. On the contrary, he has been the very antithesis of the noble White Man. Throughout his history, which goes back more than 5,000 years, during which he has remained united as a race, the Jew has been the parasite and predator on the backs of those nations who have been his unwilling hosts. The Jew has never been a creator, nor a builder, nor a producer, like the members of the White Race. On the contrary, he has been a destroyer of civilizations, a plunderer of nations, and a killer who invented the very idea of genocide in the earliest stages of his own history. All we have to do is read their own Old Testament to find that in page after page after page they slew, killed and plundered one tribe after another. One nation after another was put to the sword, man, woman and child.

Yes, indeed, the Jews are a blood-thirsty race. They have survived over a long period of time, although they have been scattered throughout the other nations of the world. They have been a plague on the body of mankind from the earliest dawn of recorded history. Nor has that plague abated in modern times. In fact, today it is more deadly than ever, and since we, the White Race, are the chief target and the chief victims marked for destruction, it behooves us to take a close look, and study our destroyer.

It is a fascinating and horror-filled history. It is an ugly story. But study it we must, and understand it we must, if we are to extricate ourselves from our plight and fulfill the obligation that Nature has placed upon us: namely, the survival of our very own species, the noblest creation on the face of the earth: the White Race.

The history of mankind is filled with wars and conflict, but of all the conflicts that have ensued between the different nations and the different races, there is only one race that has aroused the most violent antagonisms no matter where they settled— that race is the Jewish race.

Throughout all the turmoil of history and all the wars, conflicts and massacres, sooner or later the two conflicting parties settled down and either reconciled their differences, and lived peacefully together, or they went elsewhere to live. Not so with the Jews, however. The Jew has never been reconciled with the host nation upon whose back he feeds. Nor have the Jews peacefully migrated to other countries. The history of the Jews demonstrates two things: first, that there has never been a reconciliation between them and their hosts, and second, that no nation has ever succeeded in barring them permanently. Furthermore, as the Jews bored into their host nations and became more and more reprehensible and intolerable, the host nation generally has turned on them and tried to expel them from their national body. However, in no case has a victimized nation been successful in expelling them permanently. In fact, it is surprising that in every case where Jews were expelled from a nation, often under conditions of humiliation and suffering, within a few years the Jews have returned. Not only have they usually returned, but they then set about with increased viciousness to destroy the host nation upon whom they had previously fed like a parasite. The Jews have since time immemorial been culture destroyers and civilization destroyers. The Jewish problem has been on the back of all nations for at least the past 5,000 years.

Whereas the White Race, with its creativity and restless energy, has moved to the various areas of the world and created civilizations, the Jew invariably followed, bored into their very vitals and sooner or later destroyed those civilizations. They helped to destroy the Egyptian civilization, the Greek civilization, and were the prime cause in the destruction of the great Roman civilization. When Europe slowly again picked up the threads of civilization from Rome, the Jew was already there and has lain like a cancer upon the body of Europe from the time of the Romans.

However, the main center of power of the Jewish world-wide conspiracy now resides in the New World. In fact, in New York is the largest center of Jewish population in the world, and New York is the central financial powerhouse, not only of the United States, but also the rest of the world. Since the United States is now also the last great stronghold of the White Race, it is the untiring and current goal of the Jew to not only destroy the United States as a country, but to destroy White America, mongrelize it, and pump the black blood of Africa into the veins of White America.

Why is it that the Jewish Race has survived through all the upheavals of over 5,000 years of history, whereas more powerful races like the Romans have perished? Is it because the Jew is tough? We find that the Jew is tough, but other races, such as the Romans, have been even tougher and they have not survived. Is it because he is a good fighter? No, he is, in fact, a physical coward and in open combat he is certainly one of the lesser and more cowardly warriors. Is it because he is more treacherous and deceitful? Perhaps, since in this characteristic he undoubtedly excels all other peoples. But this is not the sole reason why he has survived either. The reason for his survival lies in his unique religion.

Early in their history the Jews realized the tremendous potency of religion as a weapon— a weapon to either unite their own race, or a weapon to disintegrate and destroy their enemies. For thousands of years they have capitalized upon this knowledge to the hilt. In a masterful fashion, they have manipulated religion to their advantage with a devilish cunning that no other people seems to have even suspected— least of all the White Race.

If we could briefly look at the wars between Rome and Carthage, and the brief siege and destruction of Jerusalem during the rise and expansion of the Roman Empire, I think we can find the answer to the Jews' survival.

As Roman power increased and expanded, it was inevitable that it should soon come into conflict with the increasing power of Carthage. For over 100 years these two great rival powers fought battles of attrition and annihilation. Finally Rome emerged the victor, and when they had Carthage at its mercy, they leveled the city, killed all the male population and sold the women and children into slavery. Carthage was no more. It was gone forever.

Now let us contrast this with what happened to Jerusalem in the year 70 A.D.

Masters of Deceit A Short History of the Jews

During the rule of Emperor Vespasian, the Jews in Judea became rebellious. Emperor Vespasian sent General Titus down there and after a 139-day siege of Jerusalem, the city was sacked, leveled to the ground, and the Jews were either killed or dispersed. It would seem that in a fate similar to that of Carthage, this would be the end of the Jews, But not so.

The Jews had one extraordinary thing going for them: and that was the unique religion that bound their race together. Far from being destroyed, the Jews in their cunning and resourcefulness, with their religion uniting and binding them together, planned revenge on the Romans. And revenge they did get. They inflected on the Romans a religion that undermined the will of the Romans to survive as a race and as a nation.

With tremendous zeal the Jews propagated among the Romans a new religion with such suicidal ideas as "turn the other cheek, love your enemies, resist not evil" and other self- destructive philosophies that sapped the strength of the Romans and left them naked and defenseless before their enemies. In a few centuries the great Roman civilization completely disintegrated and was defenseless against the marauding vandals who finally sacked Rome in the year 476 A.D. and Rome was no more.

However, with his tenacity and zeal for preserving the Jewish race as embodied in his fanatic religion, the Jew did not go down with Rome. No, on the contrary, he fed on the corpse and went from the Roman corpse to scatter and infect the incipient and growing new cultures that were emerging in Western Europe, cultures and civilizations that were blighted from the very beginning with the handicap of the new religion with which the Jew had destroyed Rome.

It is true that the Jew is tough. He is cunning and he is treacherous. He is also tenacious and he is persistent. All these qualities fit him well to be the foremost predator and parasite on the body of mankind. But even with all these qualities he would not have survived had it not been for his Mosaic religion. It is the basic ingredients of his religion that bind him together in a holy brotherhood hostile to all mankind, striving, pushing, clawing, always and forever for the good of his race, for the survival of his race, and exhibiting in its raw form one of the strongest laws of

Nature: the propagation and survival of its own species.

The Jews learned one other significant fact early in their history: There is nothing as powerful in uniting a group (any group) as having a common enemy. Based on this premise, they have seen to it that they have always been at war with other races. In fact, all other peoples are their enemies at all times. It is only a matter of strategy as to who is the prime enemy at any given time.

This theory has worked wonders. It has kept the Jews united and fighting. Their solidarity has destroyed all enemies before them.

It is destroying the White Race today.

The central theme of the Jewish religion is hatred, hatred for the Gentiles, that is all other races. The other overwhelmingly powerful facet of the Jewish religion is racial loyalty, loyalty to its own kind. Whereas to the average White Gentile, sadly enough, it matters very little with whom he does business, whether it is another White Man or not. Nor is the average White Gentile too interested in whether the person next door or the person he meets is one of his own kind. But to a Jew, whether he is doing business with a Jew, living next door to a Jew, or meets a Jew, this means everything. Let us keep this in mind, this factor of racial loyalty, as we go about searching for a better religion for the White Race.

That the Judaic religion has been the rock of strength around which the Jewish race has rallied for the last 5,000 years is without question. The Jews do not believe in God nor are they foolish enough to put their efforts or beliefs centered in a hereafter. Golda Meir, the present Prime Minister of Israel, stated succinctly when she said in her speech from the Knesset, the Israel Parliament in Yiddish, "I am a non-believer, yet no one will be able to root from the heart and mind the conviction that without the Jewish religion we would have been like all other nations, who once existed and disappeared." From the earliest glimmerings of childhood the Jewish parents inculcate into their offspring the idea of racial loyalty, the idea that the survival of the Jewish race is everything, the idea that all other peoples are their enemies to be either exploited or destroyed.

The Jewish Old Testament is crammed full of make-believe of Jewish history, very little of it true. But interwoven through all this fantasy the idea of racial survival is driven into their brains, advice on how to survive. It and the Talmud are full of advice and wisdom binding the Jewish race together in an indestructible unit of purpose.

In Prov. 29:18 is spelled out the idea of a long term program, "where there is no vision, a people perish." If we contrast this with the advice the Jews foisted on the White Race in the New Testament, for instance: Matt. 6:34 where it says, "take therefore no thought for the morrow: for the morrow shall take thought for the things of itself." Here we see clearly spelled out that it is essential for the Jews to have vision for the long term, a long-term plan. In reality, their religion is a perpetual conspiracy which is essential for their survival as a parasitic race. But in order to weaken and soften their victims for aggression, conquest and slavery, the White Race has had its brains polluted with all kinds of bad Jewish advice of which, "take no thought for tomorrow" is one of the many, and that is exactly the position of the white Race today. The Jews have laid their long-term plans, going back thousands of years, for the mastery and enslavement of the world.

The White Race, in contrast has no plan, no program for survival. It has no religion to rally around or to unite its White Brothers. It is just fumbling, bumbling and stumbling along with absolutely no defense against the Jew, whose historical mission it has been over thousands of years to destroy or enslave the White Race.

Whereas the noble White Race is creative, productive and self- sustaining, the Jews instinctively decided far back in their early history that the best means of survival was to choose the role of a parasite on the bodies of other productive nations. Over the thousands of years this decision has hardened and has become so permanently ingrained and inbred into the Jewish character that he could not now do otherwise, no more than a maggot could fend for itself without devouring the body of its host. This being so, the Jew has planned and planned and prepared.

He has a far-reaching and all-encompassing program for the control, domination and exploitation of his host, for whom he nurtures a terrible, pathological hatred. The driving force of his whole religion is hatred for his host. He has always hated his host nation with a terrible passion. How many times have we heard the expression ingrained in Jewish controlled books about the "whore of Babylon." The fact is that the Babylonian people were a good White people, a productive people, a creative people, who were finally destroyed by the Jews in their midst. Throughout history the Jews have propagated a vicious lying propaganda about degeneracy of the Babylonian people; a monstrous lie.

When the Jews poured into the Roman civilization and finally destroyed it with the new suicidal religion they foisted upon the Romans, they then pictured the Romans as being cruel, degenerate and immoral. Even to this day, the Jewish movies coming out of Hollywood depict the Romans as a debauched and degenerate people. Even lying Jewish propagandists like Billy Graham perpetually denounce the Romans as cruel, debauched and tyrannical. Another terrible Jewish lie.

Having chosen to play the role of a parasite far back in their history, the die is now long cast and they can do no other than to roam the civilized world seeking any spot where they can settle down in the midst of an established community, where they can remain and prosper at the expense of others. As a parasitic people the Jews can only survive by living on that which others produce. When they come into a community they bring nothing with them but their cunning and their treachery. The Jew knows when he enters the Gentile community that sooner or later he will be discovered and there will be violence and retribution. The thing the Jew fears more than anything else is open detection and the ensuing physical violence. One of his phrases throughout the centuries has been "Oy, gewalt!" This old Yiddish phrase translates "Oh, violence."

Knowing that his parasitic activities of fleecing, robbing and plundering the Gentile community will eventually result in violence against his person, he prepares for it in advance. We go back to the quotation from Proverbs in which the Jews are advised "where there is no vision, a people perish." So as he sinks his tentacles deeply into the body of the community that he is about to ravish, he prepares in advance to nullify, neutralize and minimize the opposition from the Gentile community that he knows sooner or later will develop into hostility against him. In this respect the Jew is very similar to other parasitic creatures of Nature. When a wood tick crawls up the leg of an individual he does so very stealthily and usually completely unnoticed. The wood tick is searching for an appropriate place on the body of the host he can dig into and suck its blood for its own nourishment. The wood tick knows that when he digs in, normally it would be painful to the host, therefore attract its attention and result in its being picked off and destroyed. But the wood tick has a remedy for this. Before digging in he carefully anesthetizes the skin surface of the victim host. Having done this, it then carefully begins to chew and suck, all this time anesthetizing the area so that the host will feel no pain. Meanwhile, the head bores in deeper and deeper and the parasite begins to bloat itself on the blood of its victim without the host having felt any pain whatsoever, or even being aware of its presence. By the time the victim finally discovers the tick, it is thoroughly rooted into its flesh. The host is no longer in a position to remove it without causing pain and infection to himself and the death and destruction of the parasitic tick. Even though the victim now tries to remove the parasite, he cannot do so. He can pull off the bloated body and destroy part of the tick but the head will remain imbedded and cause infection and perhaps blood poisoning. At this stage it becomes a major operation to remove the infectious tick, which he could have easily flicked off with a finger at the beginning, had he realized that the parasite had designs upon his blood. The parasitic operation of the Jew upon the body of his unfortunate host is very similar.

Being a non-productive parasite, the Jew has less than nothing to offer to the host community or nation which he enters and into which forthwith he beings to sink deep his tentacles. Remember the title of this chapter that the Jews are masters of deceit. His main commodity is deceit and lies on a massive scale. Having chosen to be a professional parasite this characteristic is now so deeply and instinctively ingrained in his very nature that he knows by instinct what he must do to protect himself and what the weaknesses of his Gentile host are. He therefore chooses to concentrate on all the nerve centers of power in his productive and creative host. In short order, he has control of the main functions that determine the destiny and welfare of a people and a nation.

The Jew does not farm, he does not labor in the fields, he does not work in the factories. He concentrates on placing himself in control of the money of a nation, of the news media of that country, of its educational facilities, and of its government. He labors diligently and skillfully to manipulate, confuse and confound the minds of his victims. Like the wood tick, he anesthetizes the brain of the Gentile nation in whose midst he has settled. He sinks his tentacles deep and prepares to counter any efforts to dislodge him.

Today, throughout the world in general, and in America in particular, we therefore find the Jew in charge of the nation's finances. He has complete control of the Federal Reserve System about which most Americans understand nothing, but believe that it is a department of the Federal Government. Many books have been written about Jewish ownership of the Federal Reserve System and we do not have space here to treat this subject in detail. But suffice it to say here that the Federal Reserve Board is not a government function, but a completely private system of banks owned, controlled and manipulated by the international Jewish bankers and completely beyond the reach and control of the Federal Government. Not that this would make much difference in any case, because the Federal Government also is controlled by the Jews, but it is significant to make this distinction.

Through manipulation, through the floating of Government bonds, the Federal Reserve can have billions printed for its own aggrandizement and pay nothing more for the billions of dollars that go into its coffers than the cost of the paper and ink involved. This usually costs about 7/10 of a cent per paper note, whether that note is a $10.00 bill or a $1000.00 bill. The actual printing is done by the U.S. Bureau of Engraving and Printing, but the notes are then transferred to the international Jewish bankers under the guise of the Federal Reserve System. The only expense to the bankers is the cost of the paper and ink.

Not only do the Jewish bankers get the money virtually free, but the U.S. Government is then obligated to issue U.S. Government Bonds as security for the loan involved. The American people are then shackled with not only paying off the principal of the Government Bonds over a period of years but also the interest thereon. These debts are never paid off, but on the contrary, as the history of the last 40 years shows, they increase from year to year. And so the American taxpayer is increasingly enslaved in debts, paying interest in this generation and the next and the next to the international Jewish bankers, who, by and large, acquired the loan money free of charge from the Government Printing Office itself.

The Jews have been manipulators of money and usurpers of the nation's treasuries of the world from time immemorial. Their Bible speaks of the money changers in their temples. They were all, of course, Jews. The Jewish monopoly of money goes back as far as the history of money itself. The fraud of the Federal Reserve System is by no means new and it has evolved over the thousands of years from the ancient practice of the goldsmiths being safe keepers of the gold of wealthy individuals.

Gold has had a special and fascinating attraction to the Jews in particular from the earliest of times. From the early beginnings of money, gold has been used as a means of exchange and from the earliest beginnings, the Jews have gravitated around the occupation of being safe keepers of other peoples' gold. They soon found that as they had a number of clients who kept gold in their vaults, that at no time did they all withdraw their gold at the same time. They then hit upon the secondary idea of loaning out some of the gold that belonged to somebody else at a rate of interest, which means they could loan out somebody else's gold and have the borrower use it for a limited period of time with an additional amount of gold coming back as a premium. As the number of clients increased they found out that they could loan out practically 90 percent of all the gold they held and still have enough reserve on hand to cover any withdrawals. This then developed into the business of banking and this became a tremendously powerful tool for the benefit of the Jew in accumulating the wealth of the productive traders and merchants in whose midst they operated.

From this basic beginning all foundations of banking have evolved. Today the Jews have added to this tricky arrangement thousands of further embellishments, and through the payments of interest, through the Federal Reserve System, through international loans and manipulations, they now exclusively control the money of the world.

Not only do they control the banking systems but they also control the stock markets of the world. Anyone examining the roster of those who own seats on the N.Y. Stock Exchange, or the other stock exchanges throughout the nation, will find that by and large they're all Jews, and a few associates of Jews. By also controlling the stock market, which they can manipulate up or down at will, they can and do skim all the benefits of the hard working, productive and creative White Americans off the top into their own coffers. Not only that, but by withholding credit at any time they choose, they can throw this nation (or any other nation) or the whole world economy, into a depression. Since these are planned and the Jews know in advance when they are going to do these things, they can, of course, again reap tremendous benefits and fleece the unsuspecting goyim forever and endlessly.

The Jew could never maintain such a stranglehold and such vicious control over his victims for any period of time were it not for the fact that he is also completely in control of the means of communications, the means of information, and the means of propaganda. Few people realize how powerful a tool propaganda is. Adolf Hitler has said correctly that by the use of propaganda the Jews can make heaven look like hell, and hell look like heaven. This is only too true, and the Jews have done this skillfully and artistically. Because they control the money, they have the means wherewith to acquire control of all newspapers, all radio networks, all television networks, all television stations, all leading national magazines, and moreover, the news wires themselves, such as United Press International, the Associated Press, and every other news wire network. Thus they can control every piece of news that goes nationwide, or worldwide for that matter. They can just as easily also suppress and reject any story that comes into their news gathering headquarters and withhold it from the world, and this is even more important.

Also in their arsenal of propaganda, and a very important one, is the movie industry— again completely controlled by the Jews. In fact, so thoroughly is Hollywood and the movie industry controlled by the Jews that Hollywood has often been referred to as Kosher Valley. The movie industry in the last 50 years has undoubtedly developed into one of the most powerful means of propaganda and brain pollution to the White Race the world has ever seen. It is only in recent years that it has been equaled, and perhaps excelled by the Jewish controlled television industry. You can be sure that the movie industry was not left unexploited in promoting the interests of the Jews and in promoting their program for the destruction of the White Race.

During the war years the Jewish movie industry in Hollywood was busy cranking out one anti-German, anti-Hitler, anti-Nazi propaganda film after another. Being naive and gullible as we are, many of our white brothers swallowed this poisonous bait and was enlisted in the Jewish snare of having the White Americans join in the vicious Jewish program of having White brothers kill White brothers in order to save the neck of the perfidious Jew. At the same time the communist countries were lauded to the skies. By treacherous lying propaganda it was made to seem plausible that we, the United States of America, could join forces with Jewish controlled communist Russia in waging a suicidal war of destruction against the heroic defenders of the White Race, namely the German people.

Not only have the movies been used as instruments for getting us involved in suicidal wars, but they have also been used as a means of setting the tone of our morals and our mores. Basically they have been used to undermine and degenerate the moral climate of our youth and of our country as a whole. During the 1920's the movies had become debauched and degenerate to the point where they were threatening their own survival. Strangely enough, during the 30's the moral tone improved somewhat. Many of the best stories that have been put out by Hollywood originated during the 1930's and people were lured back into the movie theatres in large numbers. Then the Jew cleverly began to interject the anti- German, anti-Nazi propaganda into his revitalized movie industry and began to inflame and pollute the minds of the White people of America towards hatred and a willingness to accept the idea of war against their own White brothers.

During the war itself the movies went into high gear. Nearly every production was viciously slanted to enhance the war effort in destroying Germany. At the same time, injected into the theme was the idea of racial

Nature's Eternal Religion

integration. When the war was over the idea of co-existence and collaboration with Russia was promoted along with an intensification of the idea of one world, one-world government, and the United Nations.

By the 1950's the idea of racial tolerance for the Jews broadened towards acceptance of the nigger as an equal in our society and as being the downtrodden victim of the White Man's greed and cruelty. The suicidal idea of the nigger being a permanent and vital equal part in our American society has been progressively promoted ever since. To find a movie today that doesn't in one way or another promote racial mongrelization is hard to come by. The Jew today in movies, the press and in television, is driving at a vicious and frightening pace for full mongrelization of the American people. All opposition has been effectively clobbered and destroyed.

In the 1950's and the 1960's two new elements were injected into the movie propaganda campaign. One is the use of drugs as an ever-increasing problem. It is made to seem that the people themselves are promoting drugs without any inside or outside influence. To the young people it is made to seem like everybody is doing it, and why shouldn't they try it, too. The other factor is the ever-increasing outright filth and pornography being injected into our movies, thereby undermining our morals and polluting the thinking of all the people, especially our up- and-coming younger generation.

The television industry, which went into high gear shortly after the end of World War II, now rivals, and undoubtedly excels, the effectiveness and the viciousness of the movie industry itself in polluting the minds of the American people.

So thoroughly polluted have the minds of the American viewing audience become with the obsession of watching television that in many families, if their television set were taken away, they would be left absolutely helpless in knowing what to do with their time. Some mothers shunt their youngsters off into a room with the television set on, full blast, using the Jewish idiot box as a baby sitter for their youngsters. Little do they realize that while these impressionable young minds sit in front of these Jewish boob- tubes, they are absorbing degenerate Jewish ideas. Nor do they realize that they are allowing their most precious possessions to become polluted with poison that will be hard to eliminate from the minds of their offspring for the rest of their lives.

And so with the Jews in full control of all the propaganda networks, the news wires, the newspapers, the radio networks, television networks, the movies, magazines and every other form of propaganda, America and the world is being deluged with the Jewish poison. It is being deluged and overwhelmed with the idea of intermarriage with the blacks, with the idea that Jews are sacred, immune and untouchable; with the idea that filth and pornography are the normal state of things in entertainment; with the idea that drugs are the coming thing and that everybody should try to go on a trip.

Above all, the idea of racial loyalty is being portrayed as the most heinous crime a person could ever entertain in his thoughts. Not one constructive idea comes out of all these hours and days and months and years of brain pollution that the Jew is promoting. But everything that is destructive for the White Race is being pushed and promoted: everything that is good for the niggers, the blacks, the coloreds and the Jews is being highlighted and promoted. The list of the confusing, destructive and suicidal ideas that are being slopped upon the American people, like so much garbage, is endless. In another chapter entitled, "False Ideas Disseminated by the Jews" we will discuss a few dozen more ideas with which the American people's minds are being polluted. However, these are only a few dozen out of thousands that are continuously, forever, perpetually, and unendingly being rained upon the American people.

In their propaganda tactics the Jews are fond of always labeling something just the opposite to what it is and one of the labels they use for mind contamination is "brain washing." I reject this term, and throughout this book I prefer to use the term "brain pollution" instead, because I believe it more correctly portrays what is actually being done. To wash one's brain would mean to cleanse it of all impurities and pollutants. But this is not what the Jews are doing. They are actually taking normal healthy brains, that is the brains of the Gentiles, and infecting them with a lot of filth, pornography and pollutants of wrong ideas. Hence, I believe that the term "brain pollution" much more correctly signifies what the Jew is doing than does the term "brain washing."

In aggressive pursuit of his vicious program of brain pollution, the minds of our young people are the initial and main target. In order to capture the brains of our youth, the field of education is of vital importance and the Jews have completely monopolized our educational facilities for many, many decades.

Henry Ford wrote his excellent book The International Jew over 50 years ago. Here is what he says about the Jewry in schools and colleges: "Colleges are being constantly invaded by the Jewish idea." "The sons of the Anglo-Saxons are being attacked in their very heredity." "The sons of the builders, the makers, are being subverted to the philosophy of the destroyers."

"Young men in the first exhilarating months of intellectual freedom are being seized with promissory doctrines, the source and consequences of which they do not see...." "The central group of Red philosophers in every university is a Jewish group, with often enough a 'Gentile front' in the shape of a deluded professor. Some of these professors are in the pay of outside Red organizations. There are Intercollegiate Socialist Societies, swarming with Jews and Jewish influences, and toting Jewish professors around the country, addressing fraternities under the patronage of the best civic and university auspices."

In suggesting what to do about it, Henry Ford said, "Simply identify the source and nature of the influence which has overrun our schools and universities. Let the students know that their choice is between the Anglo-Saxon and the Tribe of Judah. ... The only absolute antidote to the Jewish influence is to call college students back to a pride of race."

Remember Henry Ford, the great American, wrote these lines back in 1921, over 50 years ago. Since then the Jewish avalanche in our educational systems, starting with kindergarten, running through grade school, high school, and through the colleges, has turned these institutions for learning into absolute insane asylums in which the young, fertile, creative mind of the White child is polluted and perverted into an instrument for its own destruction and for the destruction of its country, nation and race. What with compulsory laws compelling the parents to send their impressionable young children to school through the age of 16 today, it invariably amounts to becoming the inmate of a penitentiary for five days a week during school hours, and, whether they like it or not, then having the young brains polluted with Jewish trash and garbage for the destruction of their race.

Henry Ford's idea of merely identifying the source today is no longer possible or practical. Much more fundamental and drastic measures must be taken. The White Man as a whole needs a completely new outlook on life and religion. He needs a completely new philosophy and, in fact, he needs a new religion that will give him goal and purpose, an identity and ideology that are his own. The fact is the White Race needs a new religion polarized around the value of his race, the greatest value on the face of the earth. This idea and this ideology must be impregnated into the minds of our young offspring from the time they begin to talk.

There is hardly a phase in any sphere of activity that controls the destiny of this nation that the Jews don't directly or indirectly control. With two powerful segments in their hands, namely control of the means of propaganda, and control of the money, the government of the United States is a captive puppet going through the motions of being a democracy representing all the people. But in truth, it is a powerful instrument in the hands of the Jews used to exploit, tyrannize and destroy the White Race, whose government it only seems to be.

There is hardly a public official in office of any importance today who is a free man. Almost every one of them has been placed in office or has obtained his position through Jewish manipulation and Jewish design. Having arrived where they are through the beneficence of the Jews, they then in turn must answer to the Jewish conspiracy. Behind a man like President Nixon is a Jewish boss like Henry Kissinger, born in Germany of a Jewish Rabbi.

Not only does Nixon have one Jewish "advisor," but two. The other is the Jew Arthur Burns, born Bernstein, in Austria, also the son of a Rabbi. In fact,

Nixon's whole political career was originally launched back in 1946 by a Jew named Murray Chotiner. He has continuously guided Nixon's career and been the pimp between the Jewish community and Nixon.

President Lyndon B. Johnson had the notorious Abe Fortas and Walter Rostoff, both Jews. President Kennedy had Walter Rostoff and Arthur Schlesinger, Jr. President Roosevelt had as his real boss the head of the Kehilla, the tough, no-nonsense Jew, Bernard Baruch, as well as several lesser Jewish advisors. And, so it goes.

The same kind of Jewish control, of Jewish background, of advising and controlling, is found all the way down to the local municipal level. Many Jews themselves are elected to office, but preferably they like to have some White Gentile stooge fronting for them with the Jews pulling the strings in the background, directing, manipulating, giving orders.

Should any honest, natural leader of the White Race try to run for office and make it on his own, the gigantic propaganda machines that the Jews have at their disposal are immediately set in motion. Such a man is then smeared and attacked and vilified. Or sometimes the reverse tactic is used and he is completely blacked out so that the voters hardly know that he is even running. Should such a natural White leader make it despite all these handicaps, then the full power of the propaganda apparatus is brought into play to smear, besmirch and slander him, and downgrade him before the gullible public. The full resources of their money power is also brought into play and in the next election his opponent is well financed, given a tremendous build-up by the news media.

Usually the Jews like to select as their front stooges, men who have a fatal weakness in their character and a shameful episode in their past, one not generally known to the public. Because of their weakness of character in general and their vulnerability to blackmail, such people are easy to manipulate. What with bribery and financial assistance, they are easily enticed into becoming traitors to their own race and doing the bidding of the Jews. They are easily kept in line by threat of exposure of their disgraceful past.

I have mentioned the means of communications as being in the hands of the Jews. I have mentioned control of money and international banking, control of education and control of government as all being in the hands of the Jews. By no means does this cover the whole territory. In fact, there is hardly an activity of any significance in this country that is not directly or indirectly controlled by the "chosen" race. This also includes the law enforcement agencies, the courts and even the White Man's religions. Of the latter we will have more to say in another chapter. I do want to mention here, however, the fact that most of the businesses, especially the significant big businesses, are all in the hands of the Jews.

Over 50 years ago Henry Ford wrote the following: "To make a list of the lines of businesses controlled by the Jews of the United States would be to touch most of the vital industries of the country— those which are really vital, and those which cultivated habits have been made to seem vital. The theatrical business is exclusively Jewish: play producing, booking, theatre operations are all in the hands of the Jews. This accounts for the fact that in almost every production today can be detected propaganda, sometimes glaringly commercial advertisement, sometimes direct political construction."

"The motion picture industry; the sugar industry; the tobacco industry; 50 percent or more of the meat packing industry; over 60 percent of the shoe making industry; most of the musical purveying done in the country; jewelry; grain; cotton, oil; steel; magazine authorship; news distribution; liquor business; the loan business; these, to name only the industries with national and international sweep, are in control of the Jews of the United States, either alone or in association with Jews overseas."

This is what Henry Ford observed over 50 years ago. This great, creative and productive genius of the White Race, who built one of the world's biggest empires with his bare hands from the ground up, should know a little something about who controlled the business of the United States during his time.

Having built the mighty Ford empire he found that some mysterious forces were trying to steal it from him through trickery and cunning. He suspected that these manipulators were being engineered by powerful Jewish financiers. Being an intelligent and resourceful man, Mr. Ford set about to find the culprits back of this maneuver. He called into his office the most intelligent research men within his acquaintance. He commissioned them to make a thorough study of the International Jew and published their findings in The Dearborn Independent which, at that time, was the official organ of the Ford Motor Company. The results of those findings, published in 1921, were a bombshell, not only to the White Gentiles, but to the Jewish conspiracy itself, because it exposed their nefarious tactics in their world-wide conspiracy. The information compiled was a valuable contribution to the White Gentiles of America and is recommended reading for everyone who wishes to learn more about the background of the International Jewish Conspiracy.

* * *

Since the Jews have had such a deadly impact upon the White civilizations over the last several thousand years, it behooves us to study intensely the nature of our Nemesis. It is also fundamental to our survival to develop a cure for this plague. This we are endeavoring to do throughout this book.

* * *

Masters of Deceit A Short History of the Jews

Who are these strange, peculiar people who have been able to survive longer than any other race in recorded history? Who are these people that have been destroyers of such great civilizations as Rome, Babylon and Egypt? What peculiarities in their make-up is it that has enabled them to destroy a highly wealthy country such as Russia in modern times and turn it into a Jewish slave labor camp? How, in fact, have they been able to capture the wealth of the world into their hands and turn the world into a Jewish dictatorship? How have they been able to do all this without us, the great White Race of America, even being able to discuss the question intelligently without fear and trembling?

It is of utmost importance that we study this creature biologically, psychologically, economically and also from a standpoint of race and religion.

Most White people are terribly confused about the Jewish race.

One of the sorriest notions most Gentiles have fallen for is the mistaken idea that Jews are members of the White Race. This is a most treacherous deception the Jews themselves have promoted among our people, but to their own they have made it abundantly clear that they have nothing in common with the White Race.

The Jews are forever Semitics, originating out of Asia from prehistoric times.

Jewish Professor Leonard J. Fine, makes the racial point crystal clear to his own people: "We are not White symbolically, and we are not White literally. We should not permit ourselves to be lumped together with White America, for that is not where we belong."

Much time is wasted among the White Gentiles in arguing whether the Jews are a race, or whether they are a religion, or whether they are a nation. The fact is they are all three, and it matters little in what proportion you want to attribute the importance of any of these three factors.

From ancient times, they have constituted a race that has been the plague of the civilized world. This they have been able to do because of the uniqueness of their religion. It was primarily designed to perpetuate and preserve the race by being a parasite on the body of productive nations. They are a world-wide nation and form a nation within a nation in each country on which they have fastened their tentacles. This includes just about every country in the world. If there is one factor that has bound the Jews together and made them the most tenacious, persistent race in the world it is their Mosaic religion, and the resultant racial loyalty that it has imbued upon every Jew member. It is this racial-religious unity that makes them powerful and it is something that we should take heed of in thinking about the preservation of the White Race.

The early origins of the Jewish race are lost in antiquity. The Jewish shibboleths as set forth in the story about Abraham, Isaac and Jacob are, of

Nature's Eternal Religion

course, so many Jewish lies which make a good story around which they can rally their ideology, but it has absolutely no basis in fact or history.

The Jews themselves have never bothered about really tracing their origins in history, which origins remain shrouded in mystery.

They simply come out with a claim that they are the chosen people of God, a very special people, and they also claim the longest historical record of any people of earth. Whereas the former claim about Abraham, Isaac and Jacob is a basic tenet in their religion, one that has built the Jewish race, the second claim about having the longest historical record is hard to dispute.

The Jews appear and reappear in histories of other nations for

years. Being basically a predator and a parasite, they were either never able to, nor have they ever been willing to establish a nation in their own right. This is rather a sorry record for such a strange and virulent race, and incredible when one considers that they claim to be the favorite "chosen" of God.

The word Jew is of fairly modern usage and derives from the word Judah and Judaic. In ancient history the Jews were known as Hebrews which derives from the Aramaic word "Ebri," which in turn derives from the Hebrew word "Ibhri" meaning "one who is from across the river." Hebrew in all ancient literature was written as "Habiru" and appears as such frequently in the Bible and in Egyptian literature. In the Bible, Habiru is used interchangeably with "Sagaz" meaning cutthroat. Thus the Egyptians always wrote of the Jews as "the cut-throat bandits from across the river."

Since Palestine was the crossroads of the ancient world, most of the wealthy trade routes crossed in this area. This, of course, made it a natural habitat for bands of cutthroats and robbers. The fact that deserts and mountains were part of the natural landscape further attributed to making this area the natural habitat for the development of a nation of bandits, cutthroats, robbers and parasites. This is exactly what developed, and this is as far as historical facts can show the early origin of the Jewish race.

A German Jew, Kastein, who shortened his name from Katzenstein, is recognized as an outstanding scholar of Jewish and Biblical history. In his History of the Jews, Kastein identifies many of the great names in Jewish history as bandits. He mentions Jepthah as one of the saviors of the Jewish people and identifies him as the robber chief of Gilead. Of the great Jewish hero David, he says, "At the time of Saul's death, we find David the leader of a band of free-booters, living in Ziklag... On hearing that the throne was vacant, David immediately hastened to Hebron in Judea. Nobody had summoned him, but he put forward his claim to the kingship, declaring that Samuel had secretly appointed him."

About the great and wise Solomon, Kastein has this to say, "Shelmo,

Solomon the Peaceable, inaugurated his rule by committing three murders which cleared his path and got rid of his only brother, and did so without the slightest qualms of conscience."

The fact that Solomon, David and Jepthah were all blood-thirsty bandits is typical of all Jewish leaders. Whereas the Jews have been a part of history since the dawn of civilization, theirs has always been a history of treachery, of bloodshed, murder, robbery and crime.

Despite the fact that this peculiar race has persisted longer than any other on the face of the earth, two rather strange facts stand out. One is that over these thousands of years they never tried to form a country or nation of their own, and even today's bandit state of Israel is no exception to that statement. Israel is intended only to become the headquarters for the Jewish dictatorship of the world, not a gathering place for all the Jews of the world. The second strange fact is that this tough and persistent people has never developed a civilization or a culture of their own, all their claims to the contrary notwithstanding.

One of the outstanding fortes of the Jews is the skillful manipulation of propaganda. However, the record of the Hebrews and their history shows that all the Jewish claims of culture are entirely without foundation. The Horizon Book of Christianity, a standard reference work, says "The Jews began as an agglomeration of small tribes who later attained independence only in the interlude between the rise and fall of great empires. They have bequeathed no monuments testifying to magnificence. There are no tombs of Hebrew kings with chaplets of gold and chariots studded with jewels. Palestine archeology has unearthed no statues of David or Solomon, but only water pots like the one from which Rebecca watered the camels of Abraham's servants."

The Oriental Institute of Chicago contains one of the world's most outstanding collections of the fine arts, specializing in Egyptian, Syrian and other cultures of the Near East, in the area which the Jews claim as that of their origin. One would expect to find the Jewish contribution to civilization well represented there. After walking through vast halls filled with great works of art, splendid statues, exquisite jewels, and other artifacts from the tombs of Egyptian and Assyrian conquerors, we come to the Jewish exhibit. Here we find a glass case filled with broken bits of clay pots, crude, undecorated, and unglazed utensils which might have come down to us from the Stone Age. This is the great Jewish "culture" about which the Jews brag so flagrantly and it is about all they have to offer.

The fact is that the Jews were known throughout ancient history only as destroyers. They produced no art, founded no dynasties, built no great cities, and, alone of all the ancient peoples, had no talent for the finer things of culture or civilized life. Yet today we will hear the Jews boast loud and long about how they are the sole torchbearers of civilization.

The noted historian, Arnold Toynbee, defined the Jews for all time a few years ago, when he described them as a "fossil" people. By this he meant that they were a people who had failed to develop since the Stone Age, as their primitive clay pots prove to us. They were never able to master agriculture, animal husbandry, architecture, or any of the civilized arts. Even as a bandit nation the Jews were not too successful, and eked out a precarious living in Palestine where they were often on the verge of starvation.

Kastein says further of the Jews: "Some remained within the confines of Canaan, others settled down along the great military highway of the East, and in the neighboring deserts and wildernesses, where they led a nomadic existence, while a smaller section, driven by hunger, finally succeeded in reaching Egypt, where the Pharaohs took them under their protection." The Egyptians, who built one of the earliest and one of the great civilizations of all time, failed to recognize their own greatest asset: the innate, inborn value of their racial lines which produced the civilization in their midst. We have already discussed how one of their greatest mistakes was to allow the entry of the blacks from the lower Nile to come into their country and intermingle, defile and bastardize their bloodlines. Of all the races in ancient Egypt that intermingled, the Jews alone held themselves apart.

The Pharaohs, having allowed the Jews to come in through sheer sympathy for their starved and miserable existence, were soon to learn the virulent and destructive nature of the parasite that they had allowed to enter. The Jews soon rose to high positions in the land of the Pharaohs, and, simultaneously, as was to happen in so many other countries, the Empire began to disintegrate. The parasites the Egyptians had taken in through sympathy, in short order began to manifest their outstanding characteristics, namely that of tearing down a civilization from within. Gangs of bandits soon sprang up and began to harass and plunder the trade routes.

They became bolder in the outposts of the Empire. They seemed to know just when to strike and which of the towns were poorly guarded.

With the Jews acting as leaders and catalysts, the process of trading in black slaves was increased and the mongrelization of the White Egyptian nation was hastened. The Empire began to decay from within. Its leadership became apathetic, the race became more and more tinged with black blood and the morale of the people was undermined. Here is what Alan H. Gardiner translates from an ancient papyrus in Leiden: "Egypt was in distress, the social system had become disorganized; violence filled the land. Invaders preyed upon the defenseless population; the rich were stripped of everything and slept in the open, and the poor took their possessions. It is no merely local disturbance that is here described, but a great and overwhelming national disaster. The Pharaoh was strangely inactive."

Here we have a typical description of the Jewish virulence in spreading disintegration, and destroying a great nation upon which they had fastened their tentacles. We saw the same thing happen in the downfall of Babylon. In studying the French Revolution and the Russian communist revolution we find a similar and parallel occurrence.

By 2,100 B.C. the Egyptian nation was so demoralized and divided that they were unable to resist conquest from outside. And as usual the Jews paved the way for the conquerors. They paved the way for the Hyksos, or Shepherd Kings, who won Egypt without a battle and maintained an iron dictatorship over the people for 511 years. The Hyksos were known as the protectors of the Jews. During this period of five centuries the Jews were princes in Egypt, taking what they wanted from the enslaved Egyptians, and incurring their enmity by their vicious arrogance over the betrayed population. Finally, the native leaders of the Egyptians led a successful revolt, and expelled the Hyksos forever. After the Egyptians regained control of their own country and their own destiny they punished the Jews for their treachery, and enslaved them for a life of hard labor.

This brings us to the period of Moses, when the Jews complained about their hard lot in Egypt. Before they betrayed the nation to the Hyksos, they had enjoyed every freedom in Egypt, and it was only natural that they should now be punished for their treason.

Rather than endure this slavery, they petitioned the Pharaoh to let them return to Palestine, and resume their life of nomadic banditry. But the outraged Egyptian people demanded that they serve out their punishment, and the Pharaoh was forced to agree. Now the Jews used every device to obtain their freedom, bringing plagues upon the Egyptian people through the use of poisons and contaminating the water.

They were finally allowed to depart from Egypt. It is during this period that their religion became more solidified and the bandit race began to develop a more distinct character.

From here on out they scattered into the midsts of other nations such as the Babylonian civilization, the Greek civilization, and the Persian civilization, there to infect and infest the body of these nations and spell their destruction.

A leading businessman, J. J. Cavanaugh, has compared the dispersion of the Jews to the physiological effects of cancer. He says, "The Jews can be best understood as a disease of civilization. They can be likened to the spread of cancer throughout the human system. Just as the Jews spread out through the civilized world, following the trade routes, so cancer cells spread through the body, traveling along the arteries and veins to every part of the system. And just as the Jews gather in critical areas of the world and begin to multiply, and strangle and poison whole communities and nations, so cancer cells gather and multiply and destroy the organs of the body, and finally, the body itself."

Many historians of the ancient world noted the Jewish phenomenon, and commented upon it, but most of these works have since been destroyed. When Julius Caesar arrived in Alexandria, one of the first acts that he had his soldiers perform was to burn the great libraries that the Egyptians had accumulated in Alexandria. Since Julius Caesar was a defender of the Jews and one of their agents, this is easily understood. If we still had these libraries, these books and this information available to us today, we would undoubtedly be able to focus a lot more light on the influence of Jewish infestation on the ancient civilizations.

Among the few comments on Jews which have survived the Jewish destruction of libraries are those of Philo and Strabo. Philo, an important historian, wrote that "Jewish communities have spread out over all the continents and islands."

Strabo's comments upon the Jews, written in the time of the Emperor Augustus of Rome, is even more revealing. He wrote, "This people (the Jews) has already made its way into every city, and it is not easy to find any place in the habitable world which has not received this nation and in which it has not made its power felt."

So we see that as the Roman civilization developed the Jews were there. By the time of Julius Caesar the Jews were a powerful and controlling influence on the financial structure of Rome and the government of Rome itself. Julius Caesar was one of their agents, as in modern times were Roosevelt and Churchill. By this time the Romans themselves were becoming well aware of the evil and destructive influence that the Jews heaped upon their nation and there began a reaction against the Jews. The Romans, like so many other peoples who were infested with this parasite, made attempt after attempt to get the Jews out of Rome, but they always came back. Rome, at the time of Julius Caesar, was operating under a republican-democratic form of government made up of many opposing political parties and groups, a situation similar to what we find in America today. In order to win, a politician needed the support of one group which would stick by him without fail and, thus, influence other groups to support him. In Roman times, as in the present day democracies, the one solidified, unified group who knew their purpose in politics were the Jews. They would guarantee their support to any politician who, in turn, would become their stooge.

Julius Caesar discovered this simple fact of life. He sought out the Jews and won their support. With the Jews behind him, Caesar soon became the dictator of Rome and the unchallenged ruler of the world. Alarmed by his increasing subservience to the Jews, a group of loyal senators, led by Brutus, a former friend of Caesar's in his pre-Jewish period, resolved to assassinate him. We have all heard of the famous assassination of Julius Caesar, but few have heard of the central fact in the case, namely that Julius Caesar was assassinated because he was a stooge for the Jews. Emperor Augustus, who inherited the Empire after Caesar's generals fell out among themselves, again restored special privileges to the Jews. This explains why he emerged stronger than the other factions which divided Rome after Caesar's death.

Despite the strong Jewish influence, one factor emerged that helped strengthen the Roman position. The democratic-republican form of government changed to the Empire form, with an Emperor as head of the nation. The Romans had finally found from experience that the multi- party system, with the powers split among several divisive factions, was a weak and ineffective method of government. When they changed over to the leadership principle, the Empire for 200 years progressed amidst peace and prosperity. In fact, Pax Romana, a period from the time of Emperor Augustus to approximately 200 A.D., was the longest period of peace in the history of civilized nations of the world and in the history of the White Race. We must remember that this was accomplished despite the Jewish influence and because some of the Emperors had the intestinal fortitude to resist the Jewish power.

This they could never have done under the democratic-republican system of government. We find, therefore, under Emperor Vespasian, that when the Jews in Jerusalem and Judea rebelled, he sent General Titus down there to lay siege to the city. In short order the city was conquered, the inhabitants were either slain or sold into captivity and the city itself was leveled to the ground.

Roman justice was tough and final but the Jews were far from finished. It was at this time that Jewish hatred for the Romans reached its peak intensity. They hated the Romans with a vengeance as they had the Babylonians, whom they had destroyed earlier. This is a key characteristic of the Jews: to hate with a fierce passion the host upon whom they are feeding and whom they have marked for destruction. The fact that the host has been their main means of sustenance makes no difference. Like a true parasite they will pursue the destruction of their host to the bitter end, although this might mean their own destruction.

Having learned the lesson in the destruction of Jerusalem that they were no match for the Romans in open combat, the treacherous and cunning mind of the Jews conceived a means of pulling down and destroying the Roman Empire. It was during this period, shortly after the destruction of Jerusalem that the Jews feverishly began propagating the Christian ideology which implanted in the minds of the Romans such suicidal ideas as "turn the other cheek", "love thine enemy", "sell all thou hast and give it to the poor", "resist not evil", "judge not", "think not of the morrow", "lay up treasures in heaven."

The new religion that the Jews foisted upon the Romans promised them that if they would do all these suicidal things, they would get their reward in the hereafter, eternal salvation, etc. The Romans fell for this suicidal advice with the bait of a promised reward in the hereafter. Shortly thereupon the Roman Empire went into rapid decline.

When the Roman Empire collapsed, one of the primary reasons for its fall was the declining birth rate of White Roman children. History records that eventually there was virtually no one left to rule Rome but mongrelized minority groups who had bred themselves into the majority and formed the mindless mob that brought death and destruction to the Roman Empire. Today the same thing is happening in America as young people of White racial ancestry are being taught and bombarded with the idea that it is a sin to bring children into the world and that if they wish to have children, they should adopt some poor underprivileged children of a minority race (meaning niggers).

After the death of Emperor Domitian in 96 A.D., the emperors of Rome were no longer of Roman birth; from there on they were all foreigners influenced by Jewish "advisors" in the background. By the year 313 A.D., Emperor Constantine, in the Edict of Milan proclaimed Christianity as the official religion of the Roman Empire. From there on out, under the influence of the Jewish ideology imposed on the Roman people, history shows that Rome began to disintegrate rapidly. By the year 476 A.D. the barbarians from the West had conquered Rome with hardly any opposition. The will of the now mongrelized and Christianized people of Rome to defend their nation and homes was gone. Rome was no more.

In all our history books, and especially in religious circles, we are told that Christianity and the Jews were in opposition; that Christ denounced the Jews; that the Jews crucified Christ. Even today we are being told in Kosher Konservative circles that the main objective of the Jews is to destroy Christianity. This is, of course, one of the biggest hoaxes in the history of the world. The facts are plainly there for everyone to see. The Jews concocted Christianity as their special poison to unhinge the minds of the Romans so that they would no longer be able to maintain their civilization. This was the Jews' revenge for the destruction of Jerusalem and the biological manifestation of the intense Jewish hatred for the host nation upon which they prey.

The Jewish historian, Kastein, frankly admits this extraordinary characteristic of the Jews. He says, "To the Jews, Rome constituted the quintessence of all that was odious and should be swept away from off the face of the earth. They hated Rome and her device, arma et leges, with an inhuman hatred." We have seen other examples of how the Jew continues to hate the people he has destroyed. Centuries after Babylon was no more the Jew fulminates again and again about "the whore of Babylon." But of all the nations, the Jews hated Rome the most, probably because Rome represented one of the finest examples of what a beautiful and powerful civilization the creative and productive White Race can produce.

Masters of Deceit A Short History of the Jews

So terrible is the hatred that the parasitic Jew has for the host upon whom he feeds, that it is most important for the Jew to mask his true feelings. Consequently, he always appears bearing an olive branch. His first word is "shalom," or peace. It is this necessity to conceal his true feelings which leads the Jew to conduct his affairs and his meetings in secret.

We, the White people of the globe, have much to learn from the history of Rome. Roman history probably is the greatest teacher mankind will ever have, for all time. They built a wonderful civilization, an achievement that has never been equaled. On the negative side the lessons we can learn are even stronger.

Let Us Examine What These Lessons Are, First On the Positive Side:

1) The civilization the Romans created was a result of what the Romans themselves were— a blonde, tall, blue-eyed White Race, endowed by Nature with beauty, creativity and intelligence.

2) They were— during their rise and development— a pure and unadulterated race. Their rise continued as long as they remained a pure race. It halted, declined and decayed as they became mongrelized through the mixture of races injected in their national bloodstream.

3) They were manly, brave, courageous and outstanding warriors. In a few centuries they conquered most of the then known world.

4) They were systematic, well organized, and had a penchant for law, order and organization. They were the greatest law-givers that the world has ever seen. Most of the laws of the civilized Western world is based originally on Roman law.

5) They developed the most expressive and orderly language in the history of mankind. Today, 2,000 years later, the Latin language has still not been equaled.

6) They had an inborn sense of responsibility towards their homes, their family and their country.

7) They were a creative, culture loving people and developed language, literature, art and sculpture to heights never before attained and, perhaps, in some respects not equaled today.

8) They could be hard and decisive when dealing with their enemies, as for example the complete destruction of Carthage and Jerusalem.

On the Negative Side We Can Learn the Following:

1) The Romans failed to realize that their empire, their civilization, and their greatness were due to the inherent quality of their outstanding racial stock.

2) They imported blacks and other inferior peoples into their Empire,

and took no decisive measures to prevent the contamination of their precious bloodlines.

3) The Romans had a useless and pointless religion that was a copy of, and a modification of, the Greek mythologies and their Gods. The essence of their religion consisted of a number of Gods and semi-Gods, cavorting and clowning from one mischievous affair to another. It did absolutely nothing to give the Romans purpose or unity. It contributed nothing toward any racial or national goals, nor did it teach them the value of their marvelous race. In summation, it failed to protect them from racial destruction.

4) They were completely unable to cope with the treacherous and cunning Jew in their midst. Because they allowed the mongrelization of their racial stock; the infiltration of the Jew into their finances, education and government; and because they then succumbed to the suicidal "new" Christian religion, they perished miserably.

5) If they had had a strong sense of racial loyalty, rather than "national" loyalty to Rome, and embodied this as their national religion, they would neither have been mongrelized, nor would they have succumbed to the poisonous new religion the Jew injected into their thinking, a religion which unhinged their reasoning and brought about their destruction.

6) Had the Romans had such a religion, instead of the silly, superficial religion they copied from the Greeks, Roman civilization would undoubtedly have survived to this day and for many thousands of years thereafter. In fact, civilizations do not die except when their racial blood becomes contaminated and the progeny is no longer the same as the forefathers who created the original civilization and culture.

7) If Roman civilization had prevailed, what a blessing for this world it would have been! Instead of a Jew-ridden world racked by revolution, dissension and anarchy, teeming with increasing floods of mongrels and coloreds, we would today have a beautiful White world in every part of every continent, prosperous, peaceful, orderly, and productive. We would have a world minus the colored and inferior scum that infests so much of the good real estate of the globe today, and undoubtedly minus that destroyer of all civilizations— the parasitic Jew.

CHAPTER SEVEN

THE KEHILLA

It has taken the Jews a long time and a great deal of planning to reach the tremendous power that they now wield all over the world. At the root of all their power is their religion, the bond that ties them together and gives them racial loyalty. From this springboard they have acquired the other attributes with which they have conquered the world. Three of the main attributes may be briefly listed as propaganda, money, and organization.

The Jews are organized to the hilt. They not only have their own organizations but they have the Gentiles organized, they have the niggers organized, they have the Arabs organized, they have the Christians organized and they have just about everybody else organized as well.

Among their own people some of the leading ones are the B'nai B'rith, which is strictly Jewish, the Anti-Defamation League, which is the Jewish Secret Police, and thousands of others. For the niggers they have the N.A.A.C.P., The Urban League, Southern Christian Educational Conference, and dozens of others, all Jewish controlled and used to inflame hatred against the Whites amongst the American niggers. For the White people or the Goyim, as they call us, they have the Masonic Lodges, Americans for Democratic Action, they have the Communist Party, they have The Council on Foreign Relations, the Republican Party and the Democratic Party, and hundreds of others, all Jewish controlled.

To control the White Man's religion they have innumerable organizations set up to do that also. The Jews organized and control the World Council of Churches and the National Council of Churches, which is a branch of the World Council. They have the Conference of Christians and Jews, and a myriad of other organizations all there for the control of the White Man's religion, which, incidentally, is Jewish Christianity, and was founded by Jews nearly two thousand years ago.

Whereas the Jews have many powerful organizations limited to their own people only, such as the American Jewish Congress and the others already mentioned, the key organization of all these is a little known and little understood secret organization called The Kehillah. The Kehillah takes precedence over all other organizations and is controlled by a board of 300 directors who meet every few years to determine the policies to be carried out in their program of world dictatorship. These orders are then relayed to the Jewish leaders in control of this myriad of organizations, including the governments of the world.

In order to become a Kehillah Director a Jew must be at least sixty years of age and must have shown in his life's work that he has been an ardent contributor to the cause of the Jewish Race. On becoming a Kehillah Director he is honored by being called a Jewish "Patriarch". He is permitted and expected to wear a full beard.

For more efficient control they have divided the world into two sections, the Eastern hemisphere and the Western hemisphere. The headquarters for the Western Hemisphere is in New York and that for the Eastern hemisphere is in London, England. Over the entire world is their "King of the Jews" called ACHAD HA'AM. Over each hemisphere there is a "Prince" of Jewry known as a "Sponsor". Until his recent death, Bernard Baruch was "The Prince", the head of The Kehillah for the Western Hemisphere. Baruch, as we all know, was advisor to several Presidents from Woodrow Wilson to Herbert Hoover, to Franklin D. Roosevelt, to Harry S. Truman.

The Kehillah is a very efficient organization and is organized around the number seven. It is based strictly on the leadership principle, which I have described more fully elsewhere in this book. As I stated, the top leader of each Hemisphere is known as the "Sponsor". He has seven prominent Western Hemisphere Jews under him as his subordinates. This is the first echelon of leaders and each one of these seven knows each other and, of course, their leader. The first echelon of seven is known as the 7th Kehillah degree and each one in the first echelon is known as an "ArchCensor".

Each one of these seven leaders has seven men under him, making 49 in the second echelon or the 6th degree. Each one of these is called a "Minister".

Each one of these 49 has seven men under him making 343 in the third echelon or the 5th degree. Each one of these men is called a "Herald".

Each one of these 343 has seven men under him making 2,401 in the fourth echelon or the 4th degree. Each one of these men is called a "Courtier".

Each one of these 2,401 members has seven men under him making 16,807 in the fifth echelon or in the third degree. Each one of these is called a "Scrivener".

Each one of these 16,807 members has seven men under him, making 117,649 in the sixth echelon or the second degree. Each one of these is called an "Auditor".

The Kehilla

Each one of these 117,649 members has seven men under him making 824,543 in the seventh echelon or the first degree. Each one of these is called a "Mute".

If you add up all the members of the various seven echelons we find that there are nearly one million members in each Hemisphere, all fanatically loyal and dedicated to carry out the Jewish program of subversion and intrigue in order to create the Jewish dictatorship for which the race has so ardently strived and connived during the last several thousand years. They are all sworn to carry out the secret program as is set forth in The Protocols of the Learned Elders of Zion, although the Jews vehemently deny its existence over and over again.

The Kehillah is such a secret network that outside of the first echelon or the seventh degree of the seven Hemisphere leaders none of the rest of the Kehillah members know who the others are.

With a secret, dedicated, fanatically loyal organization, with this kind of structure, it is easy to see how orders can be communicated and carried out with a minimum of delay or red-tape. When the Hemispheric head of The Kehillah gives orders to his seven, from there on there are only six steps down the line of command in order to have every one of the one million Kehillah members notified in short order. All that is necessary is to make seven sets of telephone calls down the chain of command. Remember, each man only has to make seven calls to the seven men below him and in a matter of minutes the whole network of one million members has been given their marching orders. That is how the Jews manage to set in motion strikes, agitations, student riots, or whatever is the order of the day, all over the world at the same time. This is the leadership principle at work.

Among other things, Kehillah members are taught to infiltrate the management of our schools, colleges and universities in order to indoctrinate our younger and rising leaders with their false philosophies. If you wonder why we have so many Hippies and Revolutionaries come out of our colleges, there is the answer. It is also the answer as to how such vast student organizations "simultaneously" flare up in student riots on our college and university campuses across the land. These Kehillah members also infiltrate and take control of civic clubs, patriotic societies, business organizations, labor unions, farm organizations, women's clubs, church organizations, debating societies, fraternal societies, including the Masonic Lodges and other lodges. Radio and TV networks have all come under the control of Jewish Kehillah members who carry out the Jewish program for the enslavement of the world.

We could go on and on as to the organizations that are under their control; the medical profession, newspaper publishing houses, the newspapers themselves, magazines of national scope such as Time,

Life, Look, etc., are all under their control. It is interesting to note how far back this infiltration, organization and control by the Jews goes and many devout Catholics will be surprised to learn that the Jesuit Order of Monks was set up by Loyola, a Spanish Jew, to further control the Catholic hierarchy, and through it the Catholic Church. We want to add, however, that the Catholic Church and the Christian Church as such already were under Jewish control long before that.

CHAPTER EIGHT

A FEW EXAMPLES OF JEWISH ATROCITIES

Throughout their history the Jews have committed millions of atrocities, most of which will never be recorded and most of which are intentionally covered up and lost to history. Not only have they committed millions of atrocities throughout their history, flagrantly, and constantly, but they are perpetrating atrocities today, in Russia, in China, in Cuba, in Hungary, and in Germany, both East and West. In fact they are committing atrocities today in every country of the world, including these, our United States. Therefore, to list a few paltry examples does not do the subject justice. However, since so many people are so completely unfamiliar with the nature of these atrocities, I believe that reciting a few examples of Jewish atrocities will at least partially serve to shed some light on the fierceness of the Jewish nature, the vast immensity of their satanic program, and the diabolical cruelty perpetrated by the Jews upon the host nations amongst whom they have lived and grown fat.

The Jewish religion itself is based on hatred, deception, and the destruction of all other nations. In the Old Testament, starting with Deuteronomy 20:10, we find the policy of deceit and destruction spelled out by the Jewish scriptwriters: "When thou comest nigh unto a city to fight against it, then proclaim peace unto it And it shall be, if it make thee answer of peace, and open unto thee, then it shall be, that all the people that is found therein shall be tributaries unto thee, and they shall serve thee. And if it will make no peace with thee, but will make war against thee, then thou shalt besiege it: and when the Lord, they God, hath delivered it into thine hands, thou shalt smite every male thereof with the edge of the sword: but the women, and the little ones and the cattle, and all that is in the city, even all the spoil thereof, shalt thou take unto thyself: and thou shalt eat the spoil of thine enemies, which the Lord thy God hath given thee... But of the cities of these people, which the Lord thy God doth give thee for an inheritance, thou shalt save alive nothing that breatheth."

There we have the crux of the Jewish religion which we, the White people, have foolishly been partners in worship. By cunning, by treachery, by deceit, the Jews claim they have an inherent God given right to destroy, kill and obliterate all other peoples and nations that they may choose to victimize. After all, "the Lord" commanded it. At least so the Jewish scriptwriters say, and hundreds of millions of White Gentiles have been stupid enough and gullible enough to support them in this philosophy.

The stupidity, the gullibility, and the cooperation of the Gentiles as a whole and the White Gentiles in particular in this respect has been, and is today, a key factor in the Jew's ability to divide, conquer and destroy vast numbers of their enemies far in excess of their own numbers. The Jews' diabolical cunning in being able to pervert the minds of their victims so that the victims themselves will help in their own destruction is a paramount factor in the Jewish program of world conquest and world destruction. The old saying that "whom the Gods would destroy they first made mad" should really read, whom the Jews would destroy, they first proceed to unhinge their minds to the point where their victims will then help to destroy themselves.

Let us now look at a few examples of Jewish atrocities in action. Let us also remember the Jewish axiom to always kill the best, thereby forever destroying any leadership that a people or nation might have, or might develop in the future.

The Murder Of Dresden

Before World War II the City of Dresden was one of the most beautiful in the world. In fact the word Dresden was synonymous with culture, beauty and art. Like so many other cities in Germany, this city in particular was rich in German culture and the heritage of its people. The Castle, the Opera, the Hofkirche, the Frauen Kirche, to name a few amongst thousands of other buildings, were beautiful and outstanding examples of German (and White) culture. Many of these beautiful buildings dated back a thousand years or more.

The normal population of Dresden was about 600,000. In February of 1945, as the refugees from the Eastern countries were fleeing before the Red Army, and seeking safety in the west, a large number of them fled to the apparent safety of Dresden and swelled the population of that city to over 1,200,000 people. These were people who had fought the Communists and were strongly anti-Communist. We must remember that at this period of history World War II was practically over and Dresden was by no stretch of the imagination a military objective. In judging what follows we must also keep in mind that Dresden represented the finest examples of German art and culture, that it was not a military objective, and that it was swollen at this time with refugees fleeing before the Red Army, the barbarians of the East.

On the night of February 13, 1945 at 10:13 p.m., British bombers started dropping hundreds of thousands of firebombs on the poor, helpless refugees

A Few Examples of Jewish Atrocities

and citizens of Dresden who were only trying to escape the butchery of the Red Army. These raids were carefully planned by these heinous and diabolical Jews to reap the maximum in death and destruction. The timing was such that it would hit the citizens of Dresden at a time when they were out on the streets celebrating a Christian religious holiday. Thousands were burned alive.

When the first raid was over and the survivors came out of their shelters to begin rescue operations and when thousands of fire fighters arrived from other cities to help in the rescue, the treacherous Jews struck again. At 1:30 a.m., February 14th, only three hours after the first attack, a second and larger force of British bombers rained down more death and destruction on the helpless White men, women and children below. So many firebombs had been concentrated on this once beautiful old city of Dresden that a firestorm of hurricane proportions engulfed the whole city. The heat was so intense that once live people were shriveled into corpses reduced to half their size. Thousands of people hiding in air raid shelters were melted into one pool of liquid. A mother with her baby in her arms was found melted into the pavement forming a small tar statue. In a furious, fiendish effort to incinerate this beautiful City of Dresden, the city of art and culture, more than 650,000 firebombs were dropped on it during the raids.

As if this were not enough, the next day, which was Ash Wednesday, while Dresden was still burning furiously from the two attacks of the night before, a huge force of American B-17's started pounding on what was left of the magnificent city.

The great shame and tragedy of it all was that the pilots who were dropping these bombs were White Gentiles killing their own brothers in a battle that the Germans had been fighting for the preservation of the White Race. What these White pilots, with their mentality deranged by Jewish brain pollution, did not know, but their Jewish bosses did, was the fact that 26,260 Allied prisoners of war were in this same area! Just another example of Jewish evilness and treachery. Even though the American and British soldiers were fighting to save these Jewish parasites from their just dues, the Jews themselves didn't mind at all having the White prisoners killed as well!

But this was still not the end of Jewish fiendishness and barbarity. A final touch of Jewish treachery was added when after the B-17's had left, 37 B-51 American fighters were ordered to fly low over the city and kill anything that moved! This they did by shooting and machine-gunning people trying to escape along the roads out of Dresden or people who were trying to save themselves along the banks of the River Elbe. These B-51 fighters flew low along the banks of the river and killed everything in sight.

Does this sound familiar? Remember the vicious ideology of the Jews as laid out in Deuteronomy 20:16 "thou shalt save alive nothing that breatheth"?

Let us remember that this is the vicious Jewish religion, a religion that they have been practicing for thousands of years; a religion that they have swindled the White Man into as making it part of his own, in order to worship, idolize and protect the Jew. After the war, the world was lied to and told that only 35,000 people were killed during the raids, but as the years passed they finally admitted to 135,000 deaths. This still was a big lie. The actual number of people killed between February 13th and 14th was 350,000 to 400,000!

To add a further insult to treachery, when the war was over the Jews invented a huge hoax accusing the Germans of killing and incinerating six million Jews in order to heap hatred on the Germans and create sympathy for the treacherous Jews who had started the war in the first place. In order to try to "substantiate" this colossal hoax, the Jews showed photograph after photograph of heaps of burned corpses. But the corpses they were showing were not Jews at all, but Germans that had been burned in the once beautiful City of Dresden.

We White Brothers and Sisters have a tremendously powerful lesson to learn from this horrible event. The overwhelming lesson is that the Jews regard all White people as their enemies and that it is only a matter of time when they will try to incinerate the cities and people of America just as they did Dresden, provided we will let them do it. The second lesson that we can learn is that it took the willing cooperation of White pilots, the British Air Force and the American Air Force to do this treacherous deed - the killing of their own White Brothers. This illustrates again and again how powerful is propaganda!

The third lesson that we must learn is that there is no compromising, no negotiating, and no co-existence with the treacherous and diabolical Jew. Their religion and their inbred parasitic nature drives them on to destroy all that is good in this world. There is no peace, no co-existence with this vicious evil. It is either them, or it is us. Being a member of the great White Race, I would rather we survive than this evil parasite.

As I have said before, the Jews have committed millions of atrocities throughout their history, and these atrocities are continuing into an ever-increasing crescendo today. It is not my purpose to re-capitulate them all her by any means, since this would take a whole encyclopedia. I am only going to mention briefly a few more, since I do not want to take the space.

The Red Terror In Russia

In 1917 the Russian revolution broke out and overthrew the Czarist government. This was done by a hard core of Jewish terrorists, trained by the Jew, Leon Trotsky, in New York's East Side. In large part it was financed by Jacob Schiff, a Jewish multimillionaire at the head of the Wall Street banking firm of Kuhn, Loeb & Co. Among other Jews, he contributed $20,000,000.00 toward the success of the Russian revolution.

On August 30, 1918 the Jew, Uritzky, who was then head of the Cheka, the Jewish secret police in Russia, was assassinated and Lenin was wounded. The Bolsheviks used this as an excuse for instituting the Red Terror, which began the following day, and which in a sense has continued nor for more than 50 years. The entire membership of the Communist Party, which in

1918 numbered perhaps no more than 100,000, was turned into a Jewish instrument of murder. Its purpose was two-fold: to inspire dread and horror among the Russian masses, and to exterminate the middle and upper classes, namely the best of the leadership. This leadership formerly consisted almost entirely of the White Russians.

Men and women were executed or imprisoned not because of any offense, but simply because they belonged to what the Jews considered as potential leadership class. This category came to include just about every merchant, professional person, and landowner. The Jews not only murdered these upper and middle class White productive citizens, but members of their families were murdered as well.

Little time was wasted in sifting evidence and classifying people as they rounded them up in nightly raids. The prisoners were generally hustled to the old police station not far from the Winter Palace. Here, with or without perfunctory interrogation, they were stood up against a courtyard wall and shot. The staccato sounds of death were muffled by the roar of truck motors kept going for the purpose. This was the Red Terror in action.

This kind of terror was going on throughout the cities of Russia. Soon every factory, every government bureau, every school district and every army unit would function under the gimlet eye of a Jewish commissar. Soon the blood of human beings would be oozing from under the doors of communist execution chambers as tens of thousands of White men and women were butchered like cattle in a slaughter house. Soon five million landowners were deliberately starved to death as part of a premeditated plan. I might add that one of my earliest childhood recollections is when I personally lived through the famine in Russia in 1922.

The Jews moved rapidly to exterminate the Gentile leader class of the entire nation by murdering every White factory owner, lawyer, and government leader, army officer, and every other person who had been, or might be, a potential leader. Every church and cathedral was gutted and every priest and teacher became a criminal in his own community. The standing population of the slave labor camps soon reached an excess of 15,000,000.

It is a long, grisly story, but in summation some 20,000,000 of the White Russian leadership class were butchered and murdered, in accordance with the directives of the Jewish Talmud. Today Russia is a zombie-like proletariat slave state, under the heel of the Jewish dictators. The population is docile, hungry, willing to work, easily controlled, without leadership and completely incapable of revolt. The Jewish ritual of murder goes on and on, and some 20,000,000 more of these pitiable slaves are the inmates of bestial internment camps, tortured and goaded by their Jewish slave masters.

Bela Kun In Hungary

The Jew, Bela Kun, whose real name was Cohen, had participated in the Bolshevik revolution in Russia. Following the armistice, he and a group of Jewish revolutionaries, using forged passports, moved into Hungary. Well supplied with finances by the Soviet government, and aided by the pro-communist resident Jewish population, Bela Kun soon became the dictator of all Hungary.

Bela Kun's program was to arm at once and forcibly transfer every industry and all landed property without reservation into the hands of the proletariat. He nationalized all banks, all concerns with over 200 employees, all landed property over 1000 acres, every building other than workmen's dwellings. All jewelry, all private property above the minimum which consisted of two suits, four shirts, two pairs of boots and four socks, was seized.

The result of this program was, as in Russia, economic and social chaos. The land, buildings and industries of a nation cannot be nationalized over night without creating havoc. Therefore, as in Russia, such a program could only be enforced by resorting to the Red Terror. The communization of the country's industrial and agricultural resources produced a famine in the cities, and this, combined with the peasants' hatred for the Jews, resulted in Kun's eventual overthrow. Nevertheless, during his three-month reign of terror, tens of thousands of people, priests, army officers, merchants, landowners, and professional people were butchered with a sadistic frenzy that was characteristic of Bela Kun and his band of Jewish cutthroats.

It is interesting to note that it was the peasants on the farms who had little education but had enough instinct to realize that the culprits were the Jews who took the appropriate measures to revolt against them and bring them to heel.

The Civil War

One of the most destructive atrocities that the Jews inflict upon the young American republic was the perpetrating of the War Between the States, raging between 1861 and 1865. The cause of that fratricidal war was neither the issue of slavery, nor was it the desire of the Southern states to secede. It was something altogether different, something our history books have never, never mentioned.

A Few Examples of Jewish Atrocities

Between the decades of 1820 and 1860, due to climate, soil, the cotton economy and other factors, a tremendous economic expansion was taking place in the Southern states. Led by the plantation owners, a significant new aristocracy of landowners and millionaires was evolving at a healthy growth in this area. Along with this tremendous expansion, a genuine American tradition, a way of life was being established. It embodied all the best aspects of the classical civilizations of Rome and Greece, and in fact much of the architecture was fashioned after the Classical era. Many of the cities such as Athens, Rome, Atlanta, Augusta, Alexandria and others were named after their counterparts in classical ancient history. A fine new culture was developing, the best of its kind, in the New World.

With it a large new group of millionaires was suddenly being created. Even a small city like Natchez, Mississippi had more millionaires than any other city in the United States except for New York and a few others. A similar situation existed in Atlanta, Richmond, New Orleans, and in general, spread over most of the Southern states. They were in fact, extremely prosperous. At the bottom of most of the newly created millionaires was the cotton economy.

The most significant fact about these newly rich millionaires was that they were mostly all Anglo-Saxon. It took a spirit of brash adventure, a tremendous amount of energy and work to blaze new trails in the virgin lands and build a large and profitable cotton plantation. This the White Man did with a zeal. It was the White

Man at his best. In this the Jew did not participate, since pioneering and blazing a wilderness is not his stock-in-trade.

With the tremendous amount of new wealth that was created by the White Anglo-Saxons of the South also came financial power and political power that foreboded a serious threat to the Jewish financial power of the Eastern seaboard. And herein lies the real cause of the Civil War.

The Jew foresaw in the new White Anglo-Saxon aristocracy of the South a serious potential threat to his financial and political stranglehold, not only over America, but over England and the rest of the world as well. The Jew determined that this power must not only be broken, but it must be demolished. The best way to do it, as usual, was to divide up the White Race into two factions, invent some idiotic, spurious issue, incite them to war, and have them slaughter each other. This the Jew did with a fury unmatched in American history.

Whereas neither the Whites of the North, nor of the South really cared a whit about the black man as such, nevertheless, through clever manipulation of propaganda and the levers of government, a war that the Jews had planned for years was actually brought about.

It was a ghastly, vicious and cruel war. On the Union side, the men killed in battle, dying from wounds, disease, and from other causes added up to a total of 359,528 dead. The Union side also had another 281,881 wounded and maimed. On the Confederate side a total of over

were killed and the number wounded was never even recorded. Altogether this amounted to almost 1,000,000 casualties in a young nation that in the 60's had a population of only approximately 32,000,000. This is a ghastly toll, but it only tells part of the story.

While the flower of America's young manhood was being slaughtered and maimed, the Jews were financing both the North and the South with huge loans. The House of Rothschild, then, as now, the aristocrats of worldwide Jewish banking, had their agents strongly implanted in both the governments of the North and of the South. In the North they had their man, August Belmont, a Jew, who, in league with Samuel B. Chase, the Secretary of the Treasury, was in charge of the Rothschild interests. In the South the Rothschild's had Juda P. Benjamin, a Jew and a relative of the Rothschild family, as Secretary of the Treasury for the Confederacy.

Abraham Lincoln tried to by-pass the Jewish bankers and issued 346,000,000 dollars of interest free national currency called "greenbacks." This the Jewish banking houses viewed with great alarm. They knew that should this become an established precedent that the government could furnish its own money without interest, this would be followed by other countries and they would be out of business. They brought to bear all their tremendous power to have this stopped, and for this reason, they had Lincoln assassinated by another Jew whose family name was not Booth but Botha.

The end of the Civil War was by no means the end of this horrible exercise in self- destruction. The Jews were determined to smash the South once and for all and they went about it with a vengeance. Even before the war was over, but the South was already defeated, they engaged in a wanton program of destruction that had absolutely no necessity in military strategy whatsoever. They had Sherman cut a swath 60 miles wide from Atlanta to the sea, the heart of the wealth of the Southern Confederacy, and burn, pillage and demolish every piece of physical asset that the White Man had built over the years. From there the destroyers turned north into South Carolina and continued to cut a broad swath of destruction, terror and wanton annihilation.

When the War was over the destruction was pursued with an intensified fury. The South's commerce and financial structure had been utterly demolished. Northern carpetbagger Jews came in and bought up properties and plantations that were worth hundreds of thousands before the War, now due to the bankruptcy of the Southern economy, could now be bought up in many cases for a couple of hundred dollars. Just as in Germany after World War I, when the Jews had brought that country to its knees in bankruptcy, the Jews now swarmed into

A Few Examples of Jewish Atrocities

the South, and for a few cents on the dollar they bought up all the valuable properties that were formerly owned by the Anglo-Saxon White Man.

Nor was this the end of their diabolical program of destruction. With Union army bayonets to back them up, they were now determined to not only make the newly liberated nigger the equal of the white Southerner, but they were determined to make him his overlord. The White male population was completely disenfranchised (women still couldn't vote in any case), under the excuse that it had been in rebellion to the American government. Under the leadership of carpetbagger Jews, the niggers were now the only ones who had the right to vote and they became legislators, senators, governors, judges, and in short, were the Jews' stooges for political power in the South. White women were molested and attacked by the newly released savage mob of black animals, and the White Man had absolutely no governmental protection whatsoever. The Jew, then as now, launched a massive drive to promote the mongrelization of the races in the former Confederate States.

It was through the heroic efforts of the White Man organizing through the newly formed Ku Klux Klan that he finally regained freedom and political power again. One of the most shameful and miserable periods in the history of America was endured by the South during its so-called reconstruction days, a period that was not really so much devoted to reconstruction as it was to looting the White population, and consolidating the power of the Jews in an area that had previously been dominated by the creative and prosperous White Man.

It took some states 15 to 20 years to again free themselves from under the heel of the Jewish tyranny. When they finally did drive the niggers from power and gained control of their own

Legislatures again, the South was still a broken and impoverished area. Even today, after one hundred years, the South has never regained the financial or political position that it had previous to the Civil War. Even today, the South, still being the stronghold of White resistance against mongrelization, is the hated target of the Jewish conspiracy. It is against the South that the Jews are directing their most vicious programs of school-busing, and the most persistent attacks against the White Man himself.

Jewish Use of Wars to Further Consolidate Their Power

We have seen from the above short summary of the Civil War how the Jews use wars to smash their enemies, and to consolidate their financial and political power. There is nothing new about this in the long treacherous history of the Jews. They have done this from time immemorial, and it behooves us to analyze just how powerful tool-instigated wars are in the hands of the Jews.

Some of the goals they achieve through instigating wars are as follows:

a) They induce the White Man to commit fratricide, brother killing brother, thereby decimating and weakening the White Race as a whole.

b) In wars like Korea and Viet Nam they use the colored races to kill the White Man, but the results are the same, namely the best of the young White population is killed, crippled and maimed.

c) Through war the Jews smash a potential stronghold of the White Race such as, for example, the threat the Southern aristocracy posed to the power of the Jews, or as, for instance, the growing, thriving German nation posed to the Jews before World War I and World War II. Today the strength of the United States as a whole is a threat to the Jews and their total worldwide efforts are now bent towards smashing the United States, the foremost stronghold of the White Race.

d) By impoverishing both sides of the warring nations or factions and lending money to them, the Jews thereby usually, when the war is over, have both sides ensnared in financial bondage, a miserable situation from which the victims are then unable to extricate themselves for decades.

e) Not only are the Jews involved in financing the wars and reaping tremendous profits thereby, but usually they have in control their own agents in government that are doling out tremendously lucrative war contracts that enriches new hordes of Jews. When the war is over the consolidation of their financial power and their stranglehold over the economy of the victim nations is greatly enhanced.

f) Without exception, wars incite and inflame hatreds between factions of the White Race that will persist for generations in many instances. The Civil War is a good example. The Jews see to it that these hatreds are kept alive and are often used to instigate a second war of the same type a generation later.

g) Wars are always accompanied by a breakdown of moral standards, and are very useful in the Jewish program of destroying the morals and established traditions of the White Man.

h) By sending our young American boys all over the world to foreign colored countries like Japan, Korea and Viet Nam, many of them come back with colored wives. This is directly in line with the Jewish program of mongrelizing the White Race.

In general, every war that the Jews push the White Race into, the White Race emerges weaker financially, morally, politically and genetically. The Jew always emerges stronger financially, politically, and has dramatically advanced his program of destroying, mongrelizing and enslaving the White Race.

Other Jewish Atrocities

I would like to list many more of their vicious atrocities that have been perpetrated on the White Man over the last several thousand years, but I cannot take the space.

I would like to mention the Thirty Years War in Germany from 1618 to 1648 during which five-sixths of all the property was destroyed and one third of all the people killed. This was purely instigated by the Jews over the idiotic issue of religion. I would like to mention the St. Bartholomew's Day Massacre in France when 50,000 Protestants were murdered; I would like to mention the operation "Keelhaul" in which White traitor Eisenhower collaborated with the Russian Jews and Stalin to extradite two to three million nationals from all countries who had fought on the Allied side. They were forcefully rounded up and shipped back to Russia where Stalin then wreaked vengeance upon them by either executing them or sending them to their death in Siberia.

I could cite innumerable other instances of Jewish atrocities perpetrated upon the White Race, but we just do not have the space. So in summation, just let me say that the atrocities are boundless and endless, they are going on today as relentlessly as ever in the diabolical Jewish program aimed at the destruction of the White Race.

There is one last atrocity, however, that I must bring to the attention of my White racial comrades. One of the most sinister atrocities of all time is being perpetrated upon White America today. Yet very few people know it is going on. I am referring to the diabolical Jewish program of mongrelizing the White Race here in America.

This fiendish program is being pursued relentlessly and furiously with every ounce of energy and with every weapon at their command. Yet the majority of the White people of America are completely asleep and befuddled on this issue. Very few are aware that this is the real Jewish objective of all their civil rights gibberish. Let us make no mistake about it, it is their real objective. It is the unswerving goal of world Jewry to make America a mongrel brown, and, in fact, phase out the magnificent White Race from the face of this planet.

This is without a doubt the most damaging, the most permanent, and the most fiendish catastrophe that the Jews could possibly perpetrate on Nature's crowning glory, the noble White Race. If all buildings were smashed, as in Germany, and our highways and railways were wrecked, we would suffer a severe blow, but we could rebuild them, as have the Germans. If our cities were destroyed, as the niggers and the Jews have done in the heart of some of our great cities in America today, we can and will erect newer and better ones. We could be defeated in war, we could suffer every other kind of catastrophe, but we could raise new sons who would redeem our power.

But let us never forget, that if the blood of our White Race should become mingled and mongrelized with the black blood of Africa, then the White Race has, for all purposes, been destroyed forever, and all hope for the future would be forever gone. We would be much better off dead than have the magnificent, noble White Race corrupted into an abysmal brown scum, to be enslaved by the Jews.

It is the avowed aim of this book and our new religion to awaken the White people of America and of the world. It is our goal to organize them, to give them a fighting creed, and for us to again regain absolute and unconditional control of our Manifest Destiny.

CHAPTER NINE

FIVE JEWISH BOOKS

As we have seen from the history of the White Race and of the Jewish race, the Jews throughout their long and tortuous history have been the supreme masters of deceit. Whereas the Egyptians are no more, the Babylonians have disappeared, the (original) Greeks were mongrelized, the Romans perished, the Jews, on the other hand, are alive today, and going strong. They are, in fact, now in control of the world.

Why is it that this miserable race, which could never even found a culture or a civilization, or manage to build a country of their own, has nevertheless come out on top?

If we analyze Jewish history, the answers are not too hard to come by. There are hundreds of reasons that could be listed, but basically they are these few:

1) Early in their history they recognized what a powerful weapon was religion— a weapon with which to unite their own race, and a weapon with which to destroy their enemies.

2) They learned that in racial unity there is strength. They have been fanatically dedicated to their own race.

3) They found that there is nothing more potent in unifying a group, nation or race than hating a common enemy. As a consequence all non-Jewish peoples have perpetually been their enemies, and always will be.

4) The Jews mastered the tricky technique of confuse, divide and conquer as a key in overcoming their enemies.

5) They have relentlessly organized - they have organized their own people into thousands of effective and all encompassing groups. They have also organized their enemies for their own destruction.

6) They have been diabolically clever at propaganda. They have grasped

early in their history what a powerful tool was propaganda with which to manipulate their enemies.

It is this last aspect we want to examine more thoroughly.

Whereas the Jews are in complete control of today's propaganda and "news" media— radio, television, motion pictures, newspapers, magazines, etc., they were already extremely adept at using propaganda before the modern means were even invented.

Manipulation of the word has been their specialty as Masters of Deceit. In St. John 1:1 the Jewish Bible says: "In the beginning was the Word, and the Word was with God, and the word was God." A strange claim indeed, but one loaded with meaning— a meaning that escaped most Gentiles, especially the preachers.

What this strange bit of hocus-pocus really means in Jew- language is that with words they can create Gods, and conversely words can become as powerful as a God in controlling and directing the minds and destinies of people.

The Jews have used words and propaganda profusely and relentlessly to their advantage and to the White Man's detriment. They have specifically written five books that have had a catastrophic effect on the history of mankind, and the White Race in particular.

These books are:

1) The Old Testament. It has been a powerful instrument in uniting the Jewish race.

2) The New Testament. It was written to confuse and confound the Romans in particular, and the White Race in general. It has been devastatingly effective.

3) The Talmud. It was compiled over several centuries to give the Jews a Code of Laws to live by and a formula by which they could successfully destroy the "Goyim", e., the White Race.

4) The Protocols of the Elders of Zion. This was a modern distilled-essence of the principles scattered throughout the Talmud but concentrated and brought up to date.

5) Karl Marx's Das Kapital and The Communist Manifesto. Together these two are the foundation and program for turning the Gentile peoples of the world into an organized Jewish slave labor camp. This program has already been successfully executed in Russia, Cuba, China and dozens of other countries now under the Jewish heel.

In the next several chapters we are going to examine each of these Jewish books in more detail.

CHAPTER TEN

THE OLD TESTAMENT

For the last several thousand years we have been told again and again by the Jewish propaganda networks that the Jews are God's chosen people. We have been told again and again that God is racist, that he dispenses favors, that he discriminates and that he made a special covenant with Abraham, Isaac, Jacob and their seed. We are told that their offspring and future generations were blessed, especially blessed by God. No matter how many crimes they committed, they had a special sacred niche in the eyes of God, we are told. Reading the Old Testament, we can't escape the conclusion that God cared not a wit about all the other peoples of the world, all the other creatures he had created. No matter how brutally the Israelites murdered other tribes and nations and how want only they destroyed the cities and properties of other people, God looked favorably upon their actions, we are led to believe.

Not only have the Jews and the Jewish religion with their propaganda networks been promoting this line ad nauseam, but the Christian churches, who are Gentile, and evidently outside the favors of this same God of Abraham, Isaac and Jacob, have been promoting this line of nonsense to their followers again and again and again.

We might divide the Christian churches into two classifications: the Liberal churches and the Fundamentalist churches. The liberal churches are completely under the domination of the Jews and spend most of their fervor and energy telling the White people that they must integrate, mongrelize with the niggers. They keep pounding away at the theme of integration. According to them, we, the White people owe the nigger everything, our daughters, our properties, our money and, yes, our very blood. We must make them whiter and us blacker.

The Fundamentalist churches, while pretending they are in the opposite camp to the liberal churches, in fact attack them, nevertheless strongly promoting the line that the Jews are God's chosen people and that we must not criticize the Jews, we must not lift a finger against them. They resurrect and latch on to some quotations from the Old Testament that the Jew wrote, of course, such as, "I will bless them that bless thee, I will curse them that curse thee," thereby giving complete immunity to the treacherous Jew, who is destroying the White Race.

The claim that the Jews are special in the eyes of God, is, of course, one of the biggest and most profitable lies they have invented. Why any God, who had an ounce of sense, and even a mere smattering of justice, would want to lavish special sweetheart arrangements with such a band of cutthroats and scoundrels, is just too much for anybody to swallow. Why a wise and righteous God would want to choose a race whose progenitors, Abraham and Sarah, were a pimp and a whore respectively, is just too fantastic even for the gullible.

Whereas it is doubtful whether the Jews themselves believe such trash, they have gotten tremendous mileage from this invention. Millions of White people have been taken in by this hoax and defend it even more vigorously than the Jews themselves. It has given the Jew a mantle of holiness and immunity from retribution that has worked wonders. It has worked wonders only because the White Christians have been silly enough to swallow such garbage.

So much for the "Chosen People" hoax. It is one of their biggest lies from which they have derived a fantastic advantage for themselves.

There are three other religious claims that the Jews have bragged about for centuries. They are equally phony and should be laid to rest for all time.

1) The first claim is that they invented the idea of monotheism. This is not true. The Egyptians were espousing this idea long before the Jews infiltrated Egypt and began the mongrelization and disintegration of their host.

   Not that there is anything so outstanding about the "One God" idea. Christians who also claim to worship one God, are really worshipping three Gods, the Holy Trinity, in a sort of confused "now you see it, now you don't" fashion. On the other hand, many other religions such as the Roman's, had many Gods. Nobody has ever rationally explained to me why one is superior or inferior to the other.

   In any case, the Jews have made a big to-do about this spurious issue, an idea they stole in the first place, and has no particular merit in the second place.

2) The second claim is that they originated the idea of immortality of the soul. This idea they, too, stole from the Egyptians. As I mentioned in a previous chapter, the Egyptians had already conceived this idea long before the Jews copies it in the ensuing 5,000 years since the Egyptians originated this idea, there has not been one shred of evidence to confirm it, and it too has little or no merit.

The Old Testament

3) Their third claim is the highly touted "Ten Commandments." In the first place, these "laws," compared to the comprehensive system of laws the Romans devised, are so elementary and primitive, that to even compare the two is a rank injustice. In the second place, no people has violated the killing, stealing and lying part of it more flagrantly than the Jews themselves. Thirdly, even these primitive ideas the Jews did not originate but stole from the earlier Code of Hammurabi. This Code was one of the earliest known to be put down in writing, and was codified in stone by the Babylonian King whose name it bears during the era of the 20th century B.C. It was from this code in stone that the Jews stole the mythical idea of Moses' Ten Commandments in stone.

The first part of the "Commandments" really have little meaning for the White Race in the first place, but place emphasis on the special relationship between the Jews, their God and their Sabbath.

We can hardly claim that the Ten Commandments have much significance for the White Race, in any case, since we are specifically excluded right from the start in Commandment No. I, which says "I am the Lord, they God, who brought you out of the land of Egypt, out of the house of bondage."

Since we never fled from Egypt, (in fact, the White Egyptians are our racial brothers) this whole affair evidently does not include the White Race, but is, again, as the Jews claim, part of their special "covenant" with God.

An Impartial Look at the Patriarchs and So-Called Heroes of the Old Testament

It behooves us now to take a close, impartial, yet critical look at the Patriarchs and so-called heroes of the Jewish race and see just what kind of men they were; to quote and judge them by the self- righteous standards as presumably set up by the Bible itself.

According to the Jewish story, as told in the Old Testament, the Jews claim that they are descendants of a tribe founded by Abraham, Isaac and Jacob some 3,700 years ago. According to this story Jacob had 12 sons, 10 by his first wife, and two, Joseph and Benjamin, by his second wife. Of these sons, Judah figures prominently and we hear of the wonderful line of Judah and his descendants. In fact, the word Judah is almost synonymous with the word Jew, and whereas there is a story of the lost tribes of Israel, supposedly lost somewhere in obscurity, most of the Jews pride themselves as being descendants of Judah. The word "Judaize" has been used in this and other books with considerable frequency and has as its meaning the implication to make something Jewish.

Some 14 generations after Abraham, there arises the most outstanding and famous King of the Jews, namely King David.

From him is derived the Jewish symbol, the Star of David, and David himself plays a very prominent part in the Jewish bible and also present day Jewish worship.

The first chapter of Matthew, Verse 17 says "All generations from Abraham to David are 14 generations; and from David until the carrying away into Babylon are 14 generations; and from the carrying away into Babylon unto Christ are 14 generations." In the previous 16 verses it lists the generations of Jesus Christ, Son of David, the Son of Abraham and in the 16th verse it says that "And Jacob begat Joseph, the husband of Mary, of whom was born Jesus, who is called Christ." So there is the implication, loud and clear, that Christ was descended through his father, Joseph, who was a descendant from Abraham, David and all the rest of the lineage. The fact that this contradicts the claim that Jesus was not the son of Joseph, but the Son of God, is another contradiction, another non sequitur, that the Jews throw at the Christians. I, therefore, do not need to rationalize their lies, but you might ask your preacher for his version. It is always interesting to see them try to squirm out of an obvious contradiction. I am not going to discuss this inconsistency here, but merely want to also list Joseph, the father of Jesus, as one of the prominent people in the Jewish hierarchy.

Of these people I want to review only a few of the outstanding "Patriarchs" and "heroes" of Jewish lineage as described in the bible itself, by the Jewish scriptwriters themselves. Let us examine what kind of scoundrels we have been revering, adoring and holding up to our children as great examples, as "Men of God."

Our brains have become so polluted with the persistent and long enduring propaganda of how wonderful are the "Chosen People of God" that there are many White preachers going around twisting the bible so that it will fit their most ardent wish, until they come to the strange conclusion that we, the White people, are the "real" children of Israel. They go to great lengths to invent and contrive explanations of how the Germans are descendants of Judah; the Americans are descendants of the tribe of Manasseh; Great Britain the tribe of Ephraim; Spain, the tribe of Simeon; and so on down the Jewish line. What colossal nonsense! Just a little bit of common sense would tell us that the American people, who are a mixture of many European races (and others), could not possibly be designated as being the "pure" descendants of Manasseh or anybody else.

Not only that, but when we study the kind of character, for instance, Judah was, the question is: who would want to be a descendant of Judah? What

The Old Testament

White person in their right mind would want to be the descendant of any of this treacherous tribe?

In fact, most White people would rather be the descendants of a horse thief than be a descendant of Judah after reading all the treacherous and lecherous details of his life as set forth in the "Good Book" itself.

The Story of Judah

Genesis 38 is subtitled "Judah's Houschold Troubles." It tells more about Judah than any other chapter in the bible. It is a rather lurid story. In fact, it is rather pornographic and would do credit to such present-day Jewish pornographers as Ralph Ginsberg.

The story starts out with Judah leaving his brethren and going to a certain Adullamite whose name is Hirah. There Judah saw a daughter of a certain Canaanite whose name was Shuah.

"And he took her and went into her." Just like that. It doesn't say anything about him marrying her.

In any case, they had three sons. The first-born was called Er.

The story then evidently skips a generation of time and says that "Judah took a wife for Er, his first born, whose name was Tamar." However, Er evidently was wicked in the sight of the Lord and the Lord slew him. Judah then went to his second son who was called Onan, and said to him, "Go into they brother's wife and marry her, raise up seed by they brother." Onan didn't like the idea too well, but in an attempt to obey his father "when he went into his brother's wife, he spilled it on the ground, lest that he should give seed to his brother."

This evidently also displeased the Lord, and he thereupon slew Onan, Judah's second son.

(The Lord evidently didn't fool around— they displeased him— he slew them, it says.)

Judah then went to Tamar, his daughter-in-law, and told her to remain a widow at her father's house till his third son, Shelah, was grown. Tamar did as she was told and went to live in her father's house.

Time passed on, and Shuah, Judah's wife, died. Then Judah, with his old friend Hirah, the Abdullamite, went to his sheepshearers to a place called Timnath. This is where Tamar had resided all these years during her widowhood. We will remember that the Lord had slain both her husbands, Er and Onan, who had respectively been the first and second sons of Judah.

When Tamar heard that Judah was coming to visit her area, she put her

Nature's Eternal Religion

widow's garments away and covered herself with a veil, and wrapped herself, and sat in an open place by the road. In the meantime, Judah had apparently forgotten about his promise to give to Tamar his third son when he was grown. Anyway, Tamar was waiting for Judah on the side of the road with her face veiled.

When Judah saw her, he thought she was a common harlot, because she had her face covered. Being a typical Jew and making sure that he took advantage of every opportunity, he propositioned her, without recognizing who she was. Thereupon Tamar asked him "What wilt thou give me, that thou mayest come in unto me?" Judah offered a kid from his flock. Tamar, on the other hand, demanded some kind of pledge until she received the kid and specifically demanded his signet and his bracelets and the staff that was in his hand. Judah complied and "he gave it her, and came in unto her, and she conceived by him."

Tamar arose, went away, and put back on the garments of her widowhood.

When Judah sent the kid in repayment by means of his friend the Adullamite to receive in return the pledges from the woman, she could not be found. Upon further inquiry about the harlot by the side of the road, he was told that there was no harlot in that place.

About three months later Judah was told that Tamar, his daughter-in-law, had played the role of the harlot and that she was pregnant "by whoredom." This evidently incensed Judah and he said "bring her forth, and let her be burnt."

And here we see typical Jewish justice. Judah had been as guilty as his daughter-in-law, but whereas he considered his actions without reproach, she, on the other hand, was to be burned for participating in his debauchery.

When Tamar was brought before Judah she told her father-in-law that he was the one that had gotten her pregnant. She showed him his own signet, bracelets and staff he had given her.

At this point Judah confesses that she had been more righteous than he, because he had not given her his son Shelah. But "he knew her no more" after that.

The story is lurid enough up to this point, but it ends on an even more lurid note as it describes how Tamar gave birth to twins. In fact, it is so disgusting that we refrain from recapitulating it here. You can read the whole story for yourself in Genesis, Chapter 38. It's all there and it's part of the "Holy Book" that we are supposed to look up to with such sacred reverence. There are many, many other instances of pornographic stories scattered throughout the Jewish "Holy Book."

One significant sidelight of this story is that twins were born of this sordid affair, namely Pharez and Zarah. If you look up the "proud," "glorious," "purebred" ancestry of David, Solomon and Jesus Christ in Matt. I, you will find they all descended through the whoremonger Judah, and his bastard offspring, Pharez.

The question arises, however, why in the world would anyone want to choose a lecherous whoremonger like Judah to be the champion of his people and the revered and lionized Patriarch of his lineage? Why would the righteous and sin-hating heavenly Father want to pick these kinds of people as the Patriarchs of his "chosen" people? The characteristics of Judah as described in the so-called "Holy Book" consist of nothing but lechery, deceit and treachery. No self-respecting White Man would want to have such a tricky, philandering reprobate for his ancestor. Yet the Jews hold this man up as a great hero in the history of their race and have sold the White people on the idea that his descendants are God's favored and chosen people. We are told that this scum has finagled for itself a sweetheart arrangement with God. Why millions of White Christians should be gullible enough to believe such bilge water over these thousands of years is hard to understand.

The Story of David

Whereas the lurid and pornographic story of Judah is not too familiar to the average, church going, White Christian, most of them are thoroughly familiar with the story of King David.

David is undoubtedly regarded by the Jews as the greatest hero of all, in their long and torturous history. In fact, the very insignia of the Jews is the Star of David.

Most White Christians are fairly familiar with the story of the teenage David who slew Goliath with a sling shot and thereby won an important battle against the Philistines and for the Jews, so it is claimed.

The adult life of David seems to be continually preoccupied with killing and waging war. He is credited probably more than any other character in the Jewish mythology of building up Judea and therewith the Jewish nation. The stories recited in the bible are full of killing, of blood, of murder, and especially racial genocide of the enemies of Israel. Since the Old Testament seems to condone this wholesale slaying, murdering and killing of rival tribes, David doesn't seem to be too different from many of the other Jewish perpetrators of genocide. In his moral, or shall we say, immoral character, he also seems to run true to form of the Jewish mentality.

In Second Samuel, Chapter 11, we have a story about David's more private life that reflects on his morals and his character.

David arose from his bed in the evening, so the story goes, and walked upon the roof of the King's house. From the roof he saw a woman bathing herself. She was evidently rather beautiful. Thereupon David lost no time checking out who she was and found her name was Bathsheba, the wife of Uriah, the Hittite.

Next "David sent messengers and took her; and she came in unto him, and he lay with her."

Not too long thereafter Bathsheba broke the news to David that she was pregnant. This worried David somewhat because her husband had been off to wage his wars for him during the last several months, so something had to be done.

He hit upon the idea of sending immediately for Uriah, her husband, so that he could spend some time at home with his wife and David could thereby escape the responsibility of his adultery. However, a little hitch developed. Uriah would not go home to his wife, but being such a dedicated and loyal subject of his "great" King, he slept at the door of the King's house with all the servants and would not go home.

When this was reported to David, he sent for Uriah, and had a personal conference with him. He urged him to go home to his sweet loving wife and spend some time with her. But evidently all to no effect. Next David pulled a typically Jewish trick and invited him to eat and drink with him and got him roaring drunk, hoping to get Uriah into his own bed with his wife. But all to no avail.

Uriah would not go home and he slept in the beds with David's servants in the King's quarters.

David then resorted to more drastic measures. He wrote a letter to Joab, who was Uriah's Commanding General, and had the audacity to send it by messenger through Uriah himself. In the letter he told Joab to put Uriah in the forefront of the hottest battle so that he would be sure to be killed. Joab carried out David's instructions to the letter. He put him in the suicidal part of the battle, and Uriah, in fact, was killed.

And therewith ends another sleazy, treacherous chapter of a reprobate Jew, whom the Jews to this day hold up as the greatest of all of their kinsmen. The sad part of it is that millions and millions of White people, who should know better, have fallen for the story that David was a great and wonderful "servant of God."

There are more reprehensible chapters in David's life and one of them has to do with his immediate offspring.

It seems that David had many wives and many sons. One son's name was Amnon and another son's name was Absalom. Amnon had a sister named

Tamar.

It seems that Amnon became extremely enamored and infatuated with his sister who was reputedly a virgin. He was determined to have sexual relations with her and so forthwith propositioned her. When she refused and tried to talk him out of it, he contrived to have her abducted and then raped her.

Word of this soon reached her other brother by the name of Absalom, who had a more normal brotherly affection for her. Absalom was so enraged that he forthwith went to Amnon and murdered him. Herewith ends another chapter in the normal life of the chosen people as set forth in the "Holy Book."

The Jews have not only kept on admiring David through all these thousands of years but recently they made a great movie of the story of David and Bathsheba. The parts, of course, are played by White Gentiles. In the story David is portrayed with great tenderness and the fact that he later seems to repent is portrayed with a great deal of sympathy.

The story in the "Holy Bible" goes on. There is more treachery between David and his son, Absalom.

After Absalom had murdered his brother he fled from the country. Nevertheless, David had a special place in his heart for Absalom and he loved him above all his other sons. He entreated him to come back to Jerusalem.

Absalom coveted David's throne and after many years, as David was growing older, he conspired to wage war against his father and drive him from the throne. After much maneuvering he gathered an army and set David and the people of Jerusalem to flight. Eventually Joab, who was David's general, defeated Absalom. In flight, Absalom got hung up by his hair under an oak tree. Joab, when he learned of this, hurried to where Absalom was hanging, still alive, and ran three darts through his heart, and thereby ends the story of Absalom.

Remember, this is all part of the story of the royal house of David, the great King of the Jews, as told in the "Holy Bode."

I ask you, dear White Brothers, you who have a proud and noble heritage, are these kinds of people worthy of anything other than our utter contempt?

The Story of Lot

In Genesis, Chapter 19, we have a rather unsavory story of how Sodom was destroyed, but Lot was saved. In case you might wonder who Lot is, why, he is the nephew of Abraham, that great Patriarch of all Patriarchs of the Jewish race, the one with whom God made a special covenant that he would bless his seed and multiply it like the sands upon the beach. He made a very special

Nature's Eternal Religion

sweetheart arrangement with Abraham, so the Jews claim at least, and we will have more about that in another story. Suffice it here to say that Lot was the nephew of Abraham who left Egypt with Abraham and his wife and went south.

Apparently Lot went to live in the city of Sodom, which was a very wicked city, so Chapter 19 says. Evidently God had a very special interest in this Jew Lot also, and he sent two angels to Sodom one evening as Lot sat at the gate of that city. Apparently they were disguised as two men.

Lot invited them to stay in his house overnight. He baked unleavened bread and had a feast with them.

Evidently, (and I am following Chapter 19) so this lurid story goes, that when these two strange men came into Lot's house, it aroused the interest of all those wicked homosexuals that lived in that city to the extent that "The men of the city, even the men of Sodom, compassed the house round, both young and old, all the people from every quarter; and they called unto Lot, and said unto him, where are the men which came into thee this night? Bring them out unto us, that we may know them."

It does seem rather strange that Lot, who was the nephew of this great "chosen" one of God, and who himself had attracted the special interest and blessing of God, should be living in a city that is so overrun with homosexuals that as soon as two strange men come to visit him, the whole city should flock around his house to get at them. Anyway, it seems that Lot kept them out and instead offered them his two daughters to "let me, I pray you, bring them out unto you, and do, ye to them as is good in your eyes."

Can you think of a more depraved and idiotic situation? Can you think of a more irresponsible and abominable father, one who would throw his daughters to a savage gang of deviates, offering them willingly to such a mob?

In any case, there is a lot of hocus-pocus. The mob is smitten with blindness and other things that frustrated their lecherous intentions and the angels are saved from the ravages of the mob of homosexuals.

The "angels" then advise him that the Lord is going to destroy Sodom and Gomorrah and that he had better get out of this wicked place and take his wife, daughters and in-laws with him, with the rest of them evidently not being convinced and staying in the city.

As this small group is on their way out, the Lord rains fire and brimstone on Sodom and Gomorrah.

They are told not to look around as they are leaving. Lot's wife makes the fatal mistake of doing just that and she is turned into a pillar of salt. Rather a weird and unusual punishment to receive for looking around at a rather catastrophic event behind her, something almost anybody would compulsively do.

However, this bizarre story goes on. Lot and his two daughters went on to dwell up in the mountains, to live in a cave. Here this queer story further continues to expose the depraved and grotesque meanderings of the Jewish mind, as usual, running to pornography.

It seems that his two daughters, thinking that there were no further men available to them on the face of the earth, decided they would play a little trick on their father, so that they would not die without preserving his seed. So it seems the first-born said to the younger one, let's get our father drunk and then lie with him. This act of incest was evidently completely successful and she jubilantly told her younger sister to do the same thing with her father the next night.

This she did, and both of them conceived. Evidently Lot, however, was blameless in this whole thing, according to the story (if you can believe it) because he was evidently too drunk to know what he was doing with his two daughters. A very improbable story, but this is the way the Jewish "Holy Bible" tells it. Now remember, I did not make this up, it's all there in Chapter 19 of Genesis.

As the Jews like to tell it, each one of these bastards became the father of a race of people. The first born, having a son by the name of Moab was the father of the Moabites, and the second daughter also had a son, and he was the father of the children of Amnon unto this day. At least, that's what it says in Genesis 19.

Here we have another glaring example of what kind of people were the Lord's "chosen." The Lord evidently did look with great special favor upon Lot as being the finest of the city of Sodom, and being the nephew of that great Patriarch Abraham, the Lord must have approved his getting drunk and committing incest with his two surviving daughters. Or else why did he pick these kinds to be his "chosen?"

How anybody can hold up this kind of a book as being "Holy"; as being the type of trash that we should hold up to our children; as being the "Good Book"; as something we should all study and obtain "wisdom" from, is completely beyond me.

The Story of Abraham

Let us now look at the story of Abraham himself: that great, great Patriarch with whom God was so terribly smitten that he made all kinds of special concessions and sweetheart arrangements over and above all the other people; giving him all kinds of land that had already been settled by other tribes;

and all kinds of promises that were extremely far-reaching. Evidently, he must have been regarded as being something extra special, regarded by the Lord as being an extra ordinarily "good man." Let's take a look at just how "good" Abraham was and what it was that he did that should earn him such a special preference in the eyes of God.

Again, we find a rather strange and a weird story in which the events certainly do not bear out the idea of the Lord choosing a reprobate like Abraham to warrant all these untold special favors and making him the Patriarch of the "Chosen Race." If all these things seem unusually bizarre and strange, not to say queer, we should remember that this is the story according to the way the Jews tell it, and are really only the reflections of the innermost meanderings of the collective, perverted Jewish mind.

In Genesis 6:12, God was impelled (for reasons unknown) to make a special call on Abram.

(He started out with the name of Abram.) The Lord makes some rather extravagant, magnanimous, and far-reaching promises to Abram. Why he should pick this fellow is hard to understand, but anyway, this is what the Jewish Bible tells us in Chapter 12, "And

I will bless them that bless thee, and curse him that curseth thee: and in thee shall all families of the earth be blessed." And in the previous verse, "I will make of thee a great nation, and I will bless thee and make thy name great; and thou shall be a blessing."

When we look at some of the rather shady and immoral activities this character Abram carried off, we find it rather hard to believe that God, of all people, should choose this particular sleazy reprobate. However, we have to remember that this is the story the Jewish Bible tells us, written by the Jews, and for the benefit of the Jews.

It evidently makes a good story for them. On the basis of this covenant they have formed the powerful society called the B'nai B'rith, which means "The Sons of the Covenant." If we are to believe this story, then the Jews are specially blessed and chosen by the Lord, and we are on the outside looking in. According to the Jews, they are the blessed ones and the rest of us are just plain Goyim, a bunch of cattle, who are there to be robbed and looted and exploited. Whereas this might be a good story for the Jews, it is a little more than idiotic for the White Race to fall for this kind of trash, and be subjugated and subdued into such submissive thinking.

Anyway, to look a little further into the story of what kind of a fellow Abraham was, we find that Abram took Sarai (these were their names before the Lord changed them) for his wife, and they and Lot and some more of that tribe moved on to Canaan. An interesting side note is the fact that Sarah (or Sarai) was Abraham's (or Abram's) half-sister, being the daughter of his father. Yet in Leviticus 20:17, the Lord lays down the law to Moses: "And if a man shall take his sister, his father's daughter, or his mother's daughter, and see her nakedness; it is a wicked thing; and they shall be cut off in the sight of their people." That's the law laid down by the Lord, and at the same time he picks this very kind of a pair to be the progenitors of his "Chosen People." Some Jewish story!

To continue the story— evidently the pickings weren't too good in Canaan and they were faced with famine. Abram and his wife then went to Egypt, where evidently the pickings looked better. He had a little scheme up his sleeve. It says that his wife was a real good-looking woman and he was going to cash in on this fact. He planned to palm off his wife (and sister) as a whore to the Egyptian Pharaoh for profit. Normally, this would make him a pimp and her a whore.

He, therefore, told his wife that when they got to Egypt they were to pretend that they are not man and wife, but that she was his sister. When they arrived in Egypt, the Egyptians agreed with him that she was a pretty good looker. The Princes of Pharaoh saw her and recommended her to the Pharaoh himself. She was forthwith taken to the Pharaoh and he evidently fell for her. It next says. Genesis 12:16, "And he entreated Abram well for her sake: and he had sheep, and oxen, and he asses, and menservants, and maidservants, and camels."

So we see that Abraham with his sleazy act of passing off his good-looking wife to the Pharaoh was cashing in pretty handsomely and had conned the Pharaoh out of wealth and property. In ordinary language, this would be called pimping or pandering.

Now a strange thing happens. Our just and righteous God, who had the sweetheart arrangement with Abraham, instead of chastising him for pulling such a depraved and deceitful con game on the Pharaoh, on the contrary, heaped upon the Pharaoh and his house all kinds of nasty plagues. Evidently in all his righteousness this was supposed to be a lesson to the Pharaoh not to play around with Abram's wife, when in fact, Abram had deceitfully offered her to him as a sister. Anyway, it seems that the Pharaoh found out it was his wife and rebuked Abram for deceiving him. He sent both of them on their way, Abram evidently taking all his ill-begotten loot with him, for it says at the beginning of Genesis 13, "And Abram went up out of Egypt, he, and his wife, and all that he had, and Lot with him into the south. And Abram was very rich in cattle, in silver, and in gold."

Pretty good pickings for a panderer that had arrived there strictly from hunger.

Here we have a typical Jewish trick, Abram stoops to pawn off his wife like a prostitute to the Pharaoh, deceiving him that she was only his sister. He cashes in with a lot of loot and then he and his Jewish God blame the Pharaoh for being the villain. As usual, the Jews get driven out, but they take with them all the loot that they have swindled from the Pharaoh. The Pharaoh, according to this Jewish story, is cursed and our tricky little hero, Abram, is blessed. It further says that "Lot also went with Abram and had flocks and herds and tents." Remember they went to Egypt starving and strictly empty handed and here they leave after their skullduggery, trickery and deceit with all kinds of gold and silver, flocks and herds and tents, having executed a successful pimping operation.

Abram had no sooner left Egypt, but he built an altar to the Lord and called upon the name of the Lord. Having done that, as usually happens among thieves, there was a falling out between Lot and his herdsmen and Abram and his herdsmen. Having escaped with their ill-begotten loot, they decided to split up and part company.

The story goes on and on. The Lord having this special sweetheart arrangement with Abram, named him Abraham and Sarai was renamed Sarah. However, a small obstacle developed to Abram's becoming the father of a nation whose numbers would be as great as the stars in the heavens. It seems that his wife, Sarah, was barren. So when Abraham was in his eighties, Sarah proposed to him that he should go into her maid by the name of Hagar, which he did, and she conceived.

At this point it seems that Sarah had a change of heart and drove Hagar from the household. Then we have some hocus-pocus about the angel of the Lord appearing to Hagar and induced her to return

to the house and Hagar bore a son by the name of Ishmael, to Abraham. He was 86 years old at this time.

We should be done with this lurid story, but it continues. Again I want to remind the reader that I am not making up this fantastic story. It is all in Genesis, chapters 20-25.

After we get through with the lurid story of Lot and his daughters in Genesis 19, the story of Abram, now renamed Abraham, is picked up again in Chapter 20. I should add that in Genesis 18 God renewed his binding covenant with Abraham, and for reasons hard to understand, heaped further extravagant promises of land and kingdoms and nations upon him, although in man's judgment, Abraham would by now have revealed himself to be a scoundrel, a pimp, and a con- man, not to mention his whore-mongering with his maid. In any case, God promised him when he was 99 years old and his wife Sarah, (who at this stage was 90 years old and had evidently not only been barren all these years, but was long past her child bearing stage), that next year they were going to have a son and he was going to be called Isaac. It was this son that was going to be the patriarch of the coming Chosen Race.

The Old Testament

To continue to Chapter 20. Whereas before it seems it had been established that Abraham had lived in the land of Canaan and had all this wealth that he had apparently swindled from the King of Egypt, we now Find him journeying from "thence toward the south country" wherever that is, and "sojourned in Gerar." Since this is two chapters after God had already told them that they are going to have their son Isaac and since evidently they are past the age of 99 and 90 respectively, Abraham and his partner in the con game, Sarah, approached the King of Gerar. They pulled this same "sister" trick again that they pulled on the King of Egypt.

Anyway, according to the Jewish scriptwriters, it says, "And Abimelech, King of Gerar, sent and took Sarah." Why any King would be smitten by a Jewish hag who is at least 90 years old and evidently pregnant with Isaac, is rather hazy, but anyway, this is what it says in Chapter 20. Can you imagine anything more ridiculous?

Now you would think that our righteous Jewish God, as described by these same Jewish scriptwriters, would be very angry with Abraham and Sarah for pulling such a sleazy, dirty trick again and again. But no. Instead it says God came to Abimelech in a dream by night, and said to him, "Behold, thou art but a dead man, for the woman whom thou hast taken; for she is a man's wife."

Notice the double standards. When, for instance, David knowingly took another man's wife and had her husband murdered, he received no such dire threats. In the case of Abraham and Sarah who were the real scoundrels in this con game, and played the role of pimp and prostitute respectively, it was not they who were reproved, but King Abimelech. Not only was God going to punish King Abimelech for unknowingly taking Sarah for his wife, whom, after all, Abraham had offered to him as his sister, but he was also going to punish all the other people in Abimelech's household, his servants and who knows how many more. Not only that, but the rest of the people of his kingdom were going to be sterile and it says, "The Lord had fast closed up all the wombs of the house of Abimelech, because of Sarah, Abraham's wife."

Again I want to remind the reader that I am not making up this idiotic story. It is all there in the 20th chapter of Genesis. In any case, to continue this bizarre story, not only did Abimelech, who is now scared to death of Abraham's God, give back his wife Sarah to Abraham, but furthermore it says "Abimelech took sheep, and oxen, and men-servants, and women-servants, and gave them unto Abraham, and restored him Sarah, his wife." That wasn't the end of the King's generosity to Abraham for having pulled a nasty, dirty, shameful trick on him. It also says further, "Behold, my land is before thee: dwell where it pleaseth thee." So evidently he also gave him his land for his conniving. And he further said to Sarah that he had given her brother, Abraham, a thousand pieces of silver as an extra bonus.

Where does this brother act come from? When Abimelech takes Abraham to task for being so deceitful and tricky, Abraham explains that if he hadn't pulled that trick he would probably have been killed "for his wife's sake," which is really a silly argument, because he didn't have to come there in the first place. But then he goes on to explain that Sarah was indeed his sister;

"She is the daughter of my father, but not the daughter of my mother." So here we evidently have Abraham and Sarah indulging in incest, in pimping and in prostitution, but God was really overjoyed with their "goodness."

There is much more, but let me just add that in Genesis 25:6, it mentions that after Sarah died, Abraham had a number of concubines and a number of sons by them. He got rid of these sons, however, gave them a few gifts and sent them on their way, reserving all his stolen wealth for his favorite son, Isaac.

So here we further see the amazingly perverted morals of these Jews: we Find that Abraham indulges in incest and marries his half sister, and his nephew Lot gets drunk and fornicates with his own daughters.

These are the kind of people that the Jews hold up to us as being the greatest patriarchs of their race and those specially "chosen" by God, and "beloved" by God. Because they were such "fine" people he just lavished all kinds of extravagant promises upon them. All I can say is it reminds me of General Grant's remark that anybody stupid enough to believe that would believe anything.

We are not going to take up any more space with the story of this conniving and morally depraved reprobate and pimp. There is much more, but certainly as far as I am concerned this would suffice that I would be ashamed to have this kind of a depraved profligate as the patriarch of my family line. Nevertheless, this is the kind of trash that we are being fed. It is the basis of that great and "blessed" Jewish race with whom God made a special sweetheart arrangement and a special covenant, "to bless them that bless thee and curse him that curseth thee." I can't understand anyone worshipping and regarding holy this kind of trash, and I reject it in total as being the depraved ravings of the collective

Jewish mind, and certainly unworthy of the respect and reverence of the noble White Race.

The Story of Isaac

There follows a long cock-and-bull story about how Isaac obtained his wife, Rebecca, and that Abraham finally died at the age of 175. In Genesis 26, we then have a strange replay of the tricks that Abraham pulled about passing his wife off to King Abimelech of Gerar, with Isaac playing the con man. However, the time schedule doesn't seem to fit the picture unless one again is willing to

The Old Testament

believe just a about anything.

If we figure back that Isaac was born at the time Abraham was 100 years old and that Abraham died at the age of 175, it seems very strange that Isaac could now, after Abraham was dead, go to the same King Abimelech of Gerar, who would be long dead by this time. Like his conniving father Abraham, he too told the King that his wife Rebecca was his sister. She, too, being fair to look upon, Isaac gave the excuse that if he didn't lie about her that he too might be killed. Again we come to the question: why then did he bring her there in the first place? Be that as it may, after he had been there a long time. King Abimelech looked out the window and saw that Isaac was sporting Rebecca, whom he believed to be his, the King's wife.

In any case, we have a similar re-play. The King is very much upset about being deceived, and you would think that if Isaac had been in danger of being killed as he claimed he was (had he been honest) the King would certainly have had as good a reason to kill him now for being dishonest However, he didn't do that.

Strangely, instead we find that Isaac was sowing his land and received in the same year a hundred fold. The Lord again was blessing him and it says next "the man waxed great, and sent forward, and grew until he became very great: For he had possession of flocks, and possession of herds, and great store of servants." It says in the beginning of Chapter 26 of Genesis that Isaac came there because there was again famine in the land. So it seems rather odd that he could come to the same King Abimelech of Gerar, arrive there strictly from hunger, pull this same trick about his wife being his sister, and again, like his father, end up with possession of a lot of land, great herds and great flocks and a store of servants. With all this loot in hand King Abimelech then again sent him on his way. Of course, if we add up all these years undoubtedly King Abimelech must have been completely senile from old age, having reigned at least some 80 or 90 years.

Like father, like son. Here we have the first two generations of "the chosen" (by God) engaged in whoring and procuring, in pimping and pandering as the basis of deriving their loot. Abraham and Sarah, according to the story, played the roles of pimp and whore, respectively, not only once, but at two major periods of their lives. Isaac and Rebecca, too, followed the route of indulging in pandering and whoredom as a means of livelihood.

Pimps and whores— this is the sleazy foundation on which the Jewish race was built. And we are supposed to believe that this is the kind of scum God was so wildly infatuated with to make them his favorites, his "special people."

No matter how you look at it, it is a ridiculous story. But that again is the way the Jewish scriptwriters wrote it and millions of people believe this trash and drool over it with reverence and awe.

111

Nature's Eternal Religion
The Story of Jacob

It seems that Isaac then moved on to parts unknown and Rebecca had twin sons named Esau and Jacob. Evidently this already happened before the caper with King Abimelech. In any case, God renewed his covenant with Isaac and told his wife that of the twins that were in her womb, the first-born shall be served by the younger.

As Isaac grew old and his eyes grew dim and he was about to die, he arranged to give his blessing to Esau, the first-born. Rebecca, hearing of this, got together with Jacob, her favorite, and connived to beat Esau out of his blessing. We have all heard the story of how Rebecca then took some goatskins and put them on Jacob's hands and his neck (since Esau was a hairy character) and how Jacob went to his blind father and lied to him.

Isaac, suspecting that it might not be Esau since his voice sounded like Jacob's, felt his hands and neck and fell for the ruse and gave the blessing to Jacob instead. So here we see another example of a lying Jew deceiving his dying blind father and beating his own brother out of his birthright.

Jacob soon thereafter married two daughters of a man by the name of Laban, also related to Abraham. A lot of hocus-pocus and finagling went on before this marriage was settled, but the conniving Jacob, before long, beat his father-in-law out of herds and flocks. As so often happens to swindling Jews, we find Jacob fleeing before the wrath of Laban, with Laban in hot pursuit. According to this long, drawn out story that the Jews have given us, it is from the 12 sons of Jacob by his two wives, Leah and Rachael, that the whole tribe of Judah owes its existence. All I can say if this is true, then they have some real sorry swindling ancestors upon which their foundation is supposed to rest.

It seems very strange, very odd, and very unlikely indeed that a supernatural being from outer space would make such far reaching and extravagant agreements and covenants with a motley crew of swindlers and con-men, adulterers, pimps, prostitutes, and thieves, as are described in these various chapters of Genesis.

I don't believe all this trash for one minute. Much more plausible are the Egyptian histories that tell about the Jews being a bunch of cutthroats and thieves from way back. This, I believe, is much more in line with the facts of history.

That these con-artists then wrote themselves a complicated history and mythology around which to unite their band of thieves seems much more likely. Invoking then the blessing of their God of Abraham, Isaac and Jacob, and claiming that they had a special covenant, no matter how treacherous and murderous and thieving they were, that God was always with them, helped not only to tie this band of thieves together, but also helped to confuse and confound their enemies. It helped pave the way for the exploitation and the appropriation of the properties of the peoples whom they then further victimized. As a prime example of how they deceived, exploited, and then destroyed nations, let us refer to the story of Esther, recited later in this book.

The Story of King Solomon

We now turn to the first book of the Kings which tells the story of King Solomon, whom, as we all have heard a thousand times over, has been so highly touted as being the wisest and noblest of kings. In fact, the Jews have boasted over and over again of what a wise man Solomon was, of the Wisdom of Solomon, and on and on, until we are practically lead to believe that he invented the idea of wisdom.

From reading the story of this lustful Jewish derelict with 700 wives and 300 concubines at his disposal, it seems that his claim to fame is based on one rather unimportant incident. When at the beginning of his reign two prostitutes (probably some of his own) came before him, each claiming the possession of a child, he ordered the child to be sliced in half with the sword and each woman be given half the child. Whereupon, as we all know, the first woman relinquished the child to the other in order to save its life and Solomon awarded the child to the first woman. However, I can find very little in his whole story that indicates he had any great wisdom. In fact, the total story indicates, to the contrary, that he was a treacherous, murderous, lecherous and lustful man, greedy for gold and treasure, and acquiring as many whores, wives and concubines of all creeds as he could possibly lay his hands on. In other words he was a typical Jew.

In the beginning of The First Book of the Kings it tells of David becoming old and stricken in years. David felt cold, it says "but he gat no heat." Whereupon his servants went out scouting to find him the finest looking virgin that they could possibly get and "let her stand before the King and let her cherish him, and let her lie in thy bosom, that my Lord the King may get heat." They searched throughout all the coasts of Israel and found a fair damsel by the name of Abishag, the Shunamite, and brought her to the King. She thereupon duly tried to do her duty.

Evidently it didn't have too much effect on the old codger, for he became more feeble day by day. At this point his son Adonijah claimed the throne and "prepared his chariots and horsemen, and fifty men to run before him." Most of the high priests and other important ministers supported Adonijah and everything seemed to be going pretty well for him. He was the legitimate heir to the throne.

However, we will remember from the story of David and Bathsheba that the whore- mongering old King David had an adulterous affair with the wife of Uriah, got her pregnant, and sent Uriah, who had been tremendously faithful to his King, into the thick of battle to be killed. The product of this sordid and illegitimate affair was Solomon. It seems the Jews have a penchant for making the illegitimate and the lurid later come to life as the exalted and highly touted leaders of their race. And so it was with Solomon.

After Adonijah had become King, it seems that the prophet Nathan went to Bathsheba and had her prevail upon the aging King David. Bathsheba went into the King's chamber while Abishag the Shunamite was ministering unto the King and "Bathsheba bowed, and did obeisance unto the King." She reminded the old codger he had promised her that her son, Solomon, would reign after him and now Adonijah sat on the throne. David, in this case being true to his concubine, and being half out of his mind with feebleness and old age, got all wrought up and assured Bathsheba that Solomon, her son, would reign after him.

After much Jewish finagling and conniving it did come to pass that Solomon, not Adonijah, inherited the throne of Israel.

When this became an established fact, Adonijah was afraid for his life and the lives of his followers, for good reason, and asked for mercy. King Solomon assured his half-brother that if he would show himself to be a worthy man there would not be a hair on his head touched. They then brought Adonijah before Solomon, who bowed to his king and Solomon said unto him "Go to thine house." For the time being, this seemed fair enough.

Not too long after that King David died. Before passing to the great Jewish beyond, he called Solomon in and charged him with the following "Keep the charge of the Lord they God, to walk in his ways, to keep his statutes, and his commandments, and his judgments, and his testimonies as it is written in the law of Moses."

Soon after David had died and Solomon sat upon the throne of his father, Adonijah the son of Haggith, came to Bathsheba, the mother of Solomon. After much haranguing he admitted that he would like to have her petition the king that he, Adonijah, might marry Abishag, the Shunammite, who, we remember, was the fair damsel that was procured to warm up the aging King David.

Bathsheba did go to her son and ask this favor for Adonijah. Solomon evidently flew into a rage at this, for apparently he wanted to keep this bed-warmer for himself. Invoking the name of the Lord he said "now therefore as the Lord liveth,... Adonijah shall be put to death this day." He thereupon duly dispatched his executioner and had him slay his half-brother Adonijah. This was one of the first and early acts of our newly crowned King Solomon, that great, wise and beloved king of whom the Jews are so proud.

Evidently slaying his half-brother for a trifling reason was no problem

The Old Testament

at all to King Solomon. He next slew some of the priests and military captains that had surrounded the court of his father and had favored his half-brother Adonijah.

The next "wise" thing that Solomon did was to take the daughter of Pharaoh, the King of Egypt, for his wife. We hear so much garbage about how the Israelites kept their race pure, but we continually read about how they are taking an Egyptian's daughter for their wife or daughters of every other conceivable tribe. This we read again and again throughout the Old Testament.

In any case, this was only a small beginning of a long parade of wives, of all kinds, of all different nationalities, that Solomon dragged into his court to make up his harem of some 700 wives and 300 concubines. He was certainly a busy boy.

We then come to Chapter 3 where it says very piously "and Solomon loved the Lord, walking in the statutes of David his father." Evidently the treacherous slaying of his own half-brother didn't phase the Lord very much, because he soon appeared before Solomon in a dream and asked Solomon "Ask what I shall give thee." A blank check from the Lord.

Solomon asked for wisdom. "And the speech pleased the Lord, that Solomon had asked this thing." He forthwith made a sweetheart arrangement with Solomon because he was so pleased with this man. The Lord said to him "Lo I have given thee a wise and an understanding heart: so that there was none like thee before thee, nor after thee shall any arise like unto thee."

Let us now read on further and see how wise the Lord was in conferring this great gift upon his humble servant King Solomon, and how faithful this humble servant was in carrying on with the tremendous amount of wisdom that he had been given by the Lord. Since he has been touted all these thousands of years as the wisest man that ever lived, let us look closely.

We will now skip many pages and chapters about how Solomon built the great Jewish temple, which was lined with gold covered walls and the whole house was overlaid with pure gold. In fact, the whole thing was just a Jewish dream of opulence that could only be exceeded by the New Jerusalem as described in the last chapter of the Revelation.

Evidently this building of the temple pleased the Lord a great deal for he appeared to Solomon the second time and said unto him "I have heard thy prayer and they supplication, that thou has made before me: I have hallowed this house, which thou hast built, to put my name forever: and mine eyes and mine heart shall be there perpetually." The Lord was evidently all with him. The Lord overlooked all of Solomon's whores and concubines. Let's see what he did next

Over his 40 year reign Solomon evidently gathered together all the riches and precious stones and gold and silver that he could possibly lay his hands on. His court was the most lavish and extravagant that Israel had ever seen and even the Queen of Sheba came to visit him to see if it was really as great as it had been advertised. She was evidently fully convinced and left him a lot of precious gifts to further enhance his holdings.

Not only did Solomon collect a lot of wealth and gold, but he evidently started in collecting a vast harem of women for his amusement. In Chapter 11 it says "But King Solomon loved many strange women, together with the daughter of Pharaoh, women of the Moabites, Ammonites, Edomites, Zidonians, and Hittites; and he had 700 wives, princesses, and 300 concubines: and his wives turned away his heart."

Now evidently the Lord didn't hold it against him that he had all these women and concubines in his harem, but the thing that the Lord was very displeased about was that he was taking women from all these foreign tribes and they were evidently strange women. This was contrary to the law the Lord had lain down to the Israelites, namely to keep their race pure. Not only did he take in all these strange women, but the next thing we know we find that he also began worshipping their Gods, and in Kings 11:33 we find he worshipped "Ashtoreth, the goddess of the Zidonians, Chemosh the god of the Moabites, and Milcom the god of the children of Ammon."

For such a wise king who was supposed to have a monopoly on all the wisdom of the world and who now had the benefits of 40 years experience as a reigning king, this seems like a rather stupid thing to do. In fact, after reading all these pages of his perambulations and antics, we can hardly detect where he showed such great wisdom, if, in fact, any at all. In any case, God must have been grievously deceived by this "great king" upon whom he had presumably heaped such a great deal of wisdom, so he was going to punish him for it.

He did so in a rather strange way.

He was going to bring his kingdom down in ruin, but not while his death. This should be a real good lesson to this wisest of all men that ever lived. Let him have his lavish court, let him have all the wealth and gold and silver and pomp and luxury; let him have his seven hundred wives and 300 concubines; let him worship strange gods and forget all his vows; but we'll get even with him. We'll punish his son when he gets to be king. How do you like that?

Now I didn't make up this story. It is all there, written in the "Holy Book" in I Kings, set down in all its lurid detail. And thus ends the story of another of the "great" patriarchs of Jewish History, King Solomon himself, as told by the Jews in the Old Testament.

CHAPTER ELEVEN

THE BOOK OF ESTHER

In the King James Version of the bible I have, there are a total of 39 "books" in the Old Testament. One of the most revealing of all these is the Book of Esther, which, more than any other, lays bare the essence of the Jewish program, and the workings of the Jewish mind. It is the favorite book of the Jews. Nowhere throughout this book does the name of God even appear. The story starts out with King Ahasuerus of Persia giving a great feast to all his princes, nobles and servants from all the 127 provinces in his kingdom. In order to display the riches of his glorious kingdom, the event was evidently protracted over a period of 180 days. It was a magnificent and opulent affair.

It seems that on the seventh day when the King was somewhat Imbued with wine, he commanded his seven chamberlains to bring before him the Queen, whose name was Vashti, so that he could show off her beauty to the people and the princes. However, somewhat of a problem developed, for Queen Vashti refused to come at the Kings command. This made the King very wroth.

On holding council with his seven topmost Princes, it was decided that Queen Vashti was to be punished and deprived of her position, and be replaced by another. This was also done as an object lesson to all the wives in the kingdom, so they would not be encouraged by her example in disobeying and defying their husbands. A search was to be made throughout the land for the fairest young virgins, to be brought unto Shushan Palace, so that the King could choose the best of them as his Queen.

Now in Shushan Palace there lurked a certain Jew by the name of Mordecai. He brought with him a girl named Esther, who was his cousin. According to the Jewish scriptwriters, she was "fair and beautiful", and when her mother and father died, he took her for his own daughter. Seeking to get an entree into the manipulation of the King's court, Mordecai entered Esther into the sweepstakes. In so doing, he told her to keep her identity as a jewess a secret, and he himself remained in the background.

After a duly elapsed period of twelve months, during which the

Nature's Eternal Religion

prospective brides went through much formality and protocol, lo and behold, "the King loved Esther above all the women" and "so that he set the royal crown upon her head, and made her Queen instead of Vashti."

King Ahasuerus then gave another great feast with Esther as the Queen and Mordecai sitting in the King's gate, biding hid time. At the same time he was continuously coaching and advising Esther and telling her not to reveal her Jewish identity.

Mordecai furthermore trumped up some story of two of the King's chamberlains allegedly plotting to kill the King. He then told this story to Esther and asked her to inform the King, making sure that she gave him, Mordecai, full credit for having brought this "vital information" and "saved" the King's life. The King believed it, and had the two men hanged.

Here we have a typical Jewish trick being demonstrated before us. Mordecai connived to accuse two innocent men of some dastardly act, informed on them, had them destroyed, and then sure that he got full credit for being the hero of this despicable plot.

The story now shifts to the King's Prime Minister whose name was Haman. It seems that all the King's servants and all those that were at court bowed and showed reverence to Haman, for the King had so commanded them concerning his First Minister. That is, everybody bowed except Mordecai, who on the contrary, showed hostility towards Haman. This information was soon brought to Haman and he was also informed that Mordecai was a Jew.

This made Haman very angry, and instead of laying hands on Mordecai alone it says,

"Haman sought to destroy all the Jews that were throughout the whole kingdom."

Haman thereupon went to the King and said to him "there is a certain people scattered abroad and dispersed among the people in all the provinces of they kingdom; and their laws are diverse from all people; neither keep they the King's laws: therefore it is not for the King's decree in writing that these people be destroyed and that talents of silver be given to those that have charge of carrying this out.

The King so decreed and the orders in writing went out to every province of the kingdom, sealed with the King's ring. The order read that upon a certain day to destroy, to kill, and to cause perish, all Jews and to confiscate their property.

When Mordecai heard of this "he rent his clothes... there was Great mourning among the Jews, and fasting, and weeping, and Wailing."

Mordecai decided to play his trump card, namely, his cousin Esther who

The Book Of Esther

he had shrewdly placed in an extremely intimate and delicate position next to the center of power, namely, the throne, and the King himself. To make a long story short, between the manipulations and connivings, with Esther coached and directed by Mordecai, the King became so confused, submissive, servile that between the two of them, Mordecai and Esther, they were able to manipulate him easily as the present day Jew, Henry Kissinger, manipulates Richard Nixon. The result was that King Ahasuerus completely reversed his order, turned against Haman, and had him hanged.

He went further than this. According to the Jewish scriptwriters, the King set Mordecai over the position that Haman had occupied, naming him as his First Minister, and furthermore gave him his ring, which was the final seal of the King's orders. Esther was given the house of Haman. According to the story, they had King Ahasuerus so befuddled that not only did he give them the ring and seal, but the King asked Mordecai to write to the Jews in all the provinces, giving him blanket authorization to order anything he wanted, all in the Kings name, and seal it with the Kings ring.

Now that he was in complete control, Mordecai got the King's scribes together and had them write orders that the Jews "which were in every city to gather themselves together, and to stand for their life, to destroy, to slay, and to cause to perish all the power of the people and province that would assault them, both little ones and women, and to take the spoil of them for a prey." Mordecai then had riders on mules and camels and dromedaries ride out to all provinces of the land, distributing the King's orders to the Jews in every city of the land.

It says the "Jews gathered themselves together in their cities throughout all the provinces of King Ahasuerus, to lay hand on such as sought their hurt: and no man could withstand them; for the fear of them fell upon all the people."

How often this has happened in the ensuing centuries, as one people after another have become enslaved by the Jews! The first prerequisite is that the fear of the Jews falls upon the people.

It next says that "Thus the Jews smote all their enemies with the stroke of the sword, and slaughter, and destruction, and did what they would unto those that hated them." Undoubtedly the King's lieutenants, following the order of their government, namely the King, were a great aid in helping the Jews do their murderous dirty work. We should remember that when the Jews came to power in Russia, in one of the bloodiest massacres in history, they killed 20 million of the best White Russians and thereby destroyed for all time any leadership or resistance that the Russian people might have had. We must also remember that it was White pilots who burned and slaughtered 300,000 White people of Dresden, related elsewhere in this book.

It says they slew 75,000 of their foes. Esther also asked the King that

Nature's Eternal Religion

Haman's ten sons be hanged upon the gallows. The King commanded it so be done and they were hanged.

After it was all over the Jews celebrated and made it "a day of feasting and gladness." To this day the Jews celebrate the feast of

Purim every year on the same day of the Jewish calendar month, which falls either in February or March.

The Jews just love the book of Esther. Why? Because Esther was typically Jewish. She deceived and betrayed her husband, the King, who had raised her to great heights and made her Queen.

She betrayed the people of Persia over which she had deceitfully connived her way to become Queen. She betrayed her husband, her King and her country. But she was fanatically loyal to her race— the ultimate virtue in the eyes of the Jews— and rightfully so. The Jews love her because she was the epitome of Jewishness.

As with practically everything else in the bible, there is a wide difference of opinion among biblical scholars regarding the Book of Esther. Some scholars have regarded with this view, finding flaws with the books portrayal of Persian life and pointing out there is no historical evidence of a Jewish Queen of Persia. These scholars regard the Book of Esther as a romance reflecting their times, written possibly to explain the festival of Purim, which was already in existence.

I tend to agree with the latter group. I believe that the story of Esther is, again, purely a figment of the Jewish mind to help bind their people together, in giving them a sense of mission, and above all, forever portraying the Jews as triumphant over their enemies. Furthermore, the master blueprint of how to destroy a nation is clearly spelled out in this book for all future Jewish generations. The program is pretty clear: to attach Jewish whores to the King's and leaders of the various kingdoms of the White Race; to inveigle the Jewish advisors into the confidence of those in power in government; and then, with their Jewish network of conspirators spread throughout the land, to gain control of the people of that country. When they have brought that country to a position where they can then turn on the opposition, to kill such opposition and to destroy every last vestige of leadership that may then, or anytime in the future, oppose them. This the Jews have done in country after country over the last several thousand years, and brought their host countries down to destruction. One of the grizzliest examples of recent times is the history of Russia.

And so we see another book of the Old Testament devoted to uniting the Jewish people, sharpening their parasitic instincts, and further laying the blueprint for the destruction of whole nations on which Jews have fastened their tentacles.

CHAPTER TWELVE

THE INCONGRUITY OF THE JEWISH GOD

Throughout the bible, and especially in the New Testament, we are continuously urged to become more perfect, more God-like. We are continuously told that we are a collection of no- good, worthless sinners. We are told that our shortcomings and our weaknesses are as numberless as the stars in the heavens. In contrast to this, we are reminded again and again how perfect is the Jewish God as portrayed in the Scriptures.

We are told that God is kind, he is loving, he is gracious, he is the incorporation of all wisdom; he knows everything that has happened and everything that will happen and not a hair falls from our head but that God wills it. We are told he is merciful and forgiving.

In the Sermon on the Mount we are told that we must be humble, that we must be meek, that our mind must become simple like a little child, above all, gullible, to the extreme. We are continuously told that we should forgive others their trespasses.

We are told that we must be forgiving, and that everybody is our brother. Above all we are told again and again that our main purpose in life is to amplify the greater glory of God, in other words, praise God continuously, fervently and endlessly. What scanty information we have about our activities in heaven, in fact, seems to be concerned mostly with the endless praising of the Lord. If we are to believe the Jewish scriptwriters, then, in fact, the only purpose that the Lord created us for was to harvest everlasting praise from our automated lips into all eternity. We, on the other hand, are told that pride and vanity are a dastardly sin.

Having laid these few ground rules, let us examine how ridiculous is the Jewish conception of their God, compared to those qualities that we are told we must strive for to become more perfect, more God-like. In so doing, let us remember that we are not really examining any real God of which we find a shred of evidence in the realm of Nature or in the realm of facts, but merely a conception of a God as set forth by a passel of Jewish scriptwriters.

Let us first of all examine the quality of kindness. We are told that we must, of course, be kind and gentle and loving. If these are godly attributes, just how kind and gentle and loving is this Jewish God?

When we ask that question the whole Jewish conception of creation and philosophy of life breaks down and becomes a ridiculous shamble. In the first place, before he even created man and mankind (according to the Jewish scriptwriters) he created heaven and earth. Evidently at the same time he also created hell, because it is the counter-part of heaven. He also, at this time, must have created the devil. Christian apologists lamely explain that he, the devil, was actually created a lovely angel, but he "fell." This is, of course, a silly and ludicrous explanation. For a God who knows all, sees all, creates all, can destroy all, to accidentally have created something he thought was a lovely angel but turned out to be a vicious devil is too ridiculous for anybody to believe. It is a lame-brained explanation indeed, and one would have to be an idiot to swallow that kind of a preposterous and laughable explanation.

According to the Jewish scriptwriters, we evidently have a God there that before he even created the human race had already created a huge, fiery, hot, torture chamber into which he would confine most of us poor miserable creatures for all time to come, into all eternity. By any standards, by any line of reasoning, by any evaluation whatsoever, this is about the most monstrous, the most heinous, the most cruel, planned torture operation that could possibly be conceived by God or man. When we compare this long-lasting torture, which is not even mitigated by the mercy of ending it all by death, then all other ghastly crimes of history fade into pale insignificance. When we compare it to what the savage Indians did in scalping and torturing their prisoners; when we compare it to the beastly killings of the Jewish communists of 20 million White Russians; when we compare it to the murder and slaughter of 50 million victims in China by the Chinese communists; when we compare it to all the ghastly crimes of humanity put together in all history, that of our most wonderful "loving" God as described by the Jewish scriptwriters surpasses all a million times over.

No, a kind and loving God he is not When we examine what the bible says he has in store for us poor miserable human beings that he himself created, then he is one of the most fiendish, tortuous and ghastly sadists that could possibly be conceived by anybody.

Then we are told that our God is just. We are told that justice is a godly attribute. We are told that we are all equal in the eyes of the Lord. Let us examine exactly how just is our Jewish God.

According to the Jewish scriptwriters, in the Old Testament we are told again and again that the Jews are God's "Chosen People." We are reminded throughout the various chapters that Abraham, Isaac and Jacob had special sweetheart agreements with this Jewish God. The sweetheart arrangement

The Incongruity of the Jewish God

wasn't just merely limited to promises made to Abraham, Isaac and Jacob, but was repeated again and again to people like David and Solomon and other murderous whoremongers.

If we read Chapters of Exodus, Leviticus, Numbers, Joshua, Isaiah, Kings, Chronicles and many other books and chapters throughout the Old Testament, we find nothing but bloody murders, slaying, killing, genocide, vengeance and retribution inflicted by the Jews upon their enemies. Always the Jews are victorious, and their enemies are slaughtered.

No matter how beastly the Jews are, how many tribes they invade, rob of their land, kill their men, women and children, the Lord is always with them, the Lord is always blessing them, the Lord is always looking with a kindly favor upon their murderous and treacherous acts. The Israelites can violate every law set forth in the Ten Commandments or anywhere else, but the Lord blesses them. They can kill, murder, lie, steal, cheat, deceive, commit untold treacheries, but the Lord is all for them. After all, he tells them again and again they are his special people and he is all for them.

If by any stretch of the imagination a gullible fool can be brought to believe that condoning and promoting this kind of murder and treachery is justice dispensed by a wise and just God, then any further claim we might have to an ounce of reasoning goes completely out the window. How this can be reconciled with the claim that we are all equal in the eyes of the Lord and that he is kind and just is about as stupid and ridiculous as anything that has ever been set down on paper by Jewish scriptwriters or anybody else.

To substantiate the above all anybody has to do is read the Old Testament, especially the books that I mentioned above. The evidence is so overwhelming and so massive that I need hardly waste any further space in quoting page after page, chapter after chapter.

Nor should the White Race have any misconceptions about the God the Jews concoct as also being "our" God, i.e., a White Man's God. As described by the Jews, he is strictly a Jewish God. He is eternally and forever on their side, helping them slay, murder and mutilate their enemies. And who are the Jew's enemies? His most dire hate is directed at the White Man. He hates the White Race with an unreasonable, pathological hate.

Exodus 29:45, 46 says (and this is the Lord speaking) "And I will dwell among the children of Israel and I will be their God." In Exodus 34:11 God says: "Behold I drive out before thee the Ammonite, and the Canaanite, and the Hittite, and the Perizzite, and the Hivite, and the Jebusite." And further, verse 13: "But ye shall destroy their altars, break their images, and cut down their groves."

In other words kill, ravage and destroy. Exterminate all other races to make room for the Jews. God himself will lead the way for these pirates, robbers and murderers.

Where did we ever get the idea he was on our side? Where did we get the idea we are all equal in the eyes of the Lord?

In Deut. 7:6, again God speaking: "for thou art a holy people unto the Lord thy God: the Lord thy God hath chosen thee to be a special people unto himself, above all people that are upon the face of the earth."

If that isn't abundantly clear, I don't know what is. He is saying again and again that he is all for this murderous tribe— the Jews. He will lead them, he will fight for them, he will help them kill, murder, loot, ravage, pillage and destroy. And who is on the receiving end of all this mayhem? Why, we, the Gentiles are. Plainly, we are God's (and the Jew's) enemies and plainly he is our enemy.

This is the way the bible tells it. This is the way the Jewish scriptwriters wrote it. We should have no illusions about it. This is neither the White Man's God, nor is this any part of the White Man's religion, nor is the bible the White Man's "Holy Book."

On the contrary, that book was written by our most deadly enemies for our destruction.

So far we have seen overwhelmingly that the Jewish conception of God is neither kind, nor is it loving, nor is such a God a just God.

Let us examine the idea that he is so all embracingly wise, and that, to quote "not a hair falls from our head, nor a sparrow from the roof" but he is there, and wills it, and knows it, and it only happens because he wants it to happen.

In the first place, for such an all-wise and all-knowing God to choose a treacherous and perfidious race like the Jews as his favorites is neither just, nor is it wise. Not only is it utterly stupid, but it is a treacherous betrayal of the overwhelming majority of mankind, a vast humanity which he himself has created, according to the bible. By their own account in the Old Testament, the Jews are deceitful, treacherous, and almost their entire history abounds with murder, warfare, killing, and thievery. Any God that would ally himself with this kind of criminal element certainly has not earned our love or our respect, nor can such a God have any claim to justice, wisdom, reverence, or fair play.

I must again remind the reader that we are not really considering any real God in coming to these conclusions, but we are examining the irrational ramblings of the Jewish scriptwriters who wrote the Old Testament. When we do start examining this mess of garbage we find it is pretty sad merchandise.

Pursuing further the idea of the Jewish God as portrayed by these

The Incongruity of the Jewish God

scriptwriters being all wise, we find it rather peculiar that he should have picked such associates as Abraham, Isaac and Jacob, whom we have found in the previous chapters to be deceitful, treacherous, immoral and most despicable. We find it hard to believe that he would pick as his "chosen" such lecherous whoremongers as Judah, who fornicated with his daughter-in-law, thinking she was just an ordinary roadside whore. We find it hard to believe that such a God would be particularly enamored by such profligates as David, who betrayed one of his most loyal warriors, Uriah, stole his wife, and then sent him to the front lines of battle to be murdered. How such a wise and just God could be enamored of such a scoundrel, bless him, and heap special favors upon him, is beyond anybody's comprehension of wisdom and justice.

We read the story of Abraham and Sarah, whom the Jewish God chose specially to be the progenitors of his "chosen-race." We find that Abraham was a pimp of the worst kind, pawning off his wife (who was also his sister) as a prostitute for loot. This makes Abraham a pimp and Sarah a whore in the full sense of these words. That a wise and righteous God would choose such a foul and reprehensible couple as his special chosen to be the founders of a special and favored race is inconceivable. That they should bear their first son when they were 99 and 90 respectively would be laughable if it were not so idiotic. That they were brother and sister heaps incest and crime against Nature further upon an already foul and lurid story.

Why should the noble White Man worship such trash?

We go further to King Solomon. We find that this scurrilous panderer and whoremaster accumulated unto himself 700 wives and 300 concubines of many strange races. Reading through the Jewish scriptwriters gibberish, we find that the wise and just God heaped upon this man another special covenant, another sweetheart agreement, blessing him and his seed. On reading further we find that Solomon was endowed with great wisdom by the good Lord himself. Reading on, we find that Solomon not only indulged in acquiring as many women as he could get his hands on, but he forsook the religion and worship of his own God and turned to the worship of the strange Gods of the heathen whores and concubines that he had assembled. This would certainly seem to indicate that the Jewish God's choice of favorites was not only in bad taste but it was utterly stupid. Yet we are to believe that these kinds of villains, seducers, scoundrels and reprobates were the exclusive choice of a just and wise God.

Again, I must repeat that this is not at all relevant to any real phenomenon in Nature, but merely the gibberish and drivel of a passel of Jewish scriptwriters, exact identity unknown.

Examining further how wise this Jewish God was, we find that throughout the Old Testament this Jewish God seems to stumble from one bad blunder into the next. In the first place he created Adam and Eve, whom we are led to believe were to live forever in the Garden of Eden. Hardly a day had passed but the programs and plans of this all-knowing, all-wise God ran into trouble. According to the Jewish scriptwriters, Adam and Eve turned out badly and were driven out of the Garden of Eden. Nor is that all. Their offspring, as they multiplied, (with whom did Cain mate?) were such a bad lot that the good Lord, who had created them all, saw fit to kill and execute them all by drowning, except for one family.

One might well ask at this point, if God is so wise and allknowing, if he knows everything forwards and backwards, how does it happen he didn't foresee how his creation would turn out?

Or, if everything turns out exactly the way God wills it, then isn't it logical to assume that God had created man in such a manner that he would turn out bad? And, hadn't he planned to drown them later? Hadn't he further planned to send most of them into his fiery torture chamber which he created even before he created Man?

In following further the story of mankind as set forth by the Jewish scriptwriters in the Old Testament, we find that this is not the end of the tragic torment imposed upon a long suffering mankind by their Creator. We are then told that this Jewish God, in a desperate attempt to "save mankind" resorted to an attempted solution that surpasses all. We are told by the Jewish scriptwriters that this God then descended upon a Jewish woman, who, although being married, was claimed to be a virgin, got her pregnant, and she bore him a son. All this was done only so that this son could grow up, be nailed to the cross, and die for all the "sinners."

This is, of course, an extremely ridiculous story when we relate the whole episode to the enormity of the universe itself; the timelessness with which the universe has existed over the billions of years and time eternal; the long history and development of mankind itself, spanning a period of hundreds of thousands, if not millions, of years. But even taking the Jewish scriptwriters at their word, this caper evidently also turned out to be a disastrous blooper. So evidently the Jewish God had blundered again. Two thousand years after this episode supposedly is to have happened, we find that most of the world doesn't believe this cock-and- bull story, that we have more wars, crime and killings than the world has ever known before, that Christianity itself is virulently sick.

We find that the Jews and the Communists are winning the world and that neither one of these two (or shall we say one) believes in Christianity itself.

So we find that seemingly God has consistently chosen the worst of the criminal element people as his "chosen," and has made far- reaching sweetheart agreements with this kind of people in reference to the rest of mankind. Certainly this is neither wise nor is it just. We find that he has continually blundered from one idiotic and tragic catastrophe to another in guiding the human race which he supposedly created. We find further, much to our horror, that he has planned to send the overwhelming majority of his creation into an eternal hell, a fiery torture chamber, in which these poor miserable victims are to be burned and tortured for time everlasting. We find that although the Jews wrote the New Testament and sold the idea of Christianity to the White Race, they themselves don't believe a word of it.

For many years, long before I ever even saw through the Jewish-Christian hoax, I had been puzzled by the one-sided phenomena of thanking God, from whom presumably, all blessings flowed. I was not only puzzled but irritated.

If a man worked hard all his life, used relatively good judgment, kept out of trouble, and built up a comfortable nest egg, why, then he should be thankful to God, because God "gave" him everything he had. No credit at all to the productive, responsible individual.

If on the other hand, he was unfortunate enough to be beset by fire, flood, famine, disease, pestilence, war, death and disaster, why, then God was completely absolved of any responsibility. This is the way it is presented by the organized churches.

Having committed the "crime" of being successful and prosperous, a productive citizen is then beset by these Jesus people to give! give! and give some more. And no matter how generously such a deluded victim gives, it is never enough. He is denounced as a greedy miser and urged to give more.

According to the Christian creed, God does not bear any responsibility for all the evils and disasters that have plagued mankind throughout the ages. Usually the preachers will add insult to injury by implicating those unfortunate souls stricken with disaster by charging they deserved it. They will imply that somehow they were justly being "punished for their sins." How strange! How idiotic!

It seems to me if God is to be given credit for all the good things in life, then he should also be held responsible for all the evils and disasters that befall mankind. If we must credit him for a productive rain then he must also bear the blame for a disastrous flood. If we should credit him for health, then we must also blame him for sickness and death. If he is responsible for a bountiful crop, then he is also responsible for famine and starvation. If we are to thank him for peace and plenty, then we must also charge him for plaguing us with war, revolution, communism, murder, famine and starvation.

Again this is another one of these inconsistent incongruities palmed off on the gullible. This, too, tends to destroy your own self-confidence and strengthen the idea of "blind faith."

So in summation, we find that the story as set forth by the Jewish scriptwriters in the Old Testament and the New Testament breaks down miserably when exposed to the light of reason and examination. We find that the conception of the Jewish God as portrayed by these deceitful scriptwriters is completely incongruous, it contradicts itself, and is so absurd and preposterous that a person would have to take leave of his senses to swallow such Jewish gibberish.

We find that their conception of a God is not at all kind and loving, but on the contrary, he is most viciously cruel. We find that he is not at all just, but on the contrary, is criminally prejudiced towards a murderous and treacherous race of people, namely the Jews. Nor can we conclude that he is very wise as is evidenced by one blunder after another through which he leads a long-suffering mankind. Significantly, all these blunders tend to heap suffering and misery upon us, the human race.

Nor can we say that he is a forgiving God. We read continuously in the Old Testament about the Lord threatening that "vengeance is mine." When someone "displeased" him, (such as two of Judah's sons) "he slew him," much as a gangster would get rid of his enemy. Yet we are told that if we employed such tactics we would be committing the gravest of all crimes. What an idiotic set of double standards! We are told we should become more God-like, but if we follow any of these "God-like' examples, we are condemned as the worst of criminals. No matter which way we turn we are wrong. No matter what criminal acts God commits, he's perfect how can we ever win with a set of rules like that?

Not only are most of his actions criminal, but are also viciously cruel.

In the end we find that not only is he not forgiving, but all the great majority of the "beloved" humanity he created is destined to suffer eternal agony in hellfire, a miserable suffering from which there is no reprieve, from which there is no escape, and to which there is no end.

We find further that whereas we are admonished not to have pride, whereas we are told to be humble, the Jewish God himself is the most vainglorious and conceited phenomenon that anybody could possibly imagine. In fact, these Jewish scriptwriters tell us that our main purpose in being created at all is so that the Creator himself could utilize us in harvesting eternal praise from our automated lips. Whether we like it or not, we are supposed to sing eternal praise to this Jewish God because he is wise, because he is loving, because he is kind, because he is just. Since, as we have seen, he is none of these things, we are evidently supposed to be manipulated like a herd of stooges or robots to heap praise on an impossible and cruel tyrant.

There is one other serious credibility gap in this whole Jewish story that no preacher has ever explained to me. If the devil is such a bad character, why did God create him in the first place? Why did he let this polished con artist loose on naive, newly created Adam and Eve? Or having created him, and having made the most monumental blooper of all time, why didn't he quickly rectify his mistake? Why didn't he just simply kill the devil, as he did to Judah's two sons?

Why prolong this endlessly drawn out cat-and-mouse game where we poor human beings are the pawns? Why is God taking such a severe trouncing from his own creation? Since most people are going to hell evidently God is losing badly. Does this make any sense? It does not.

One other thing. If the eternal destiny of millions of poor souls is at stake, why is God so obscure, so coy, so terribly confusing about the issues? We have seventeen versions of the Bible, we have the book of Mormon; we have Confucius' teachings, we have the Mohammedan Koran. In fact we have a thousand and one different stories being circulated as to what is the "true religion."

If the issues are a thousand times more important than life itself you would think God would reveal himself to the four billion people living today and make the issues crystal clear before sending them into the fiery furnace in all eternity. If he were real, he would owe mankind that, to say the very least. If in the days of the Israelites, he could come down to earth and indulge in such nonsense as wrestling with Jacob all night, you would think the very least he could do would be to reveal himself to the four billion inhabitants of the earth today.

In any case, such is the story of the demented ramblings of the Jewish scriptwriters, identity unknown. It is their story, not mine.

I didn't write it. They did.

They are rambling about a God as unreal and imaginary as are Zeus, Mars, Jupiter and a thousand others concocted by the imaginary meanderings of the human fantasy.

After you have backed these Jesus people against the wall with their own incongruous and contradictory claims, they will make one desperate, last-ditch stand. They will come back at you with this non sequitur: "But surely you believe in a Supreme Being? Surely you believe in a Creator? Somebody had to make all this.

If God didn't, who did?

The answer to this old trick question is so obvious it would occur even to a ten year old. If "somebody" had to make everything first, then it is just as logical to assume "somebody" first had to create God. So, who created God? But, oh! They then abandon that line of reasoning and say, "God always existed." Very well, if you want to go that route. Then it is also logical to assume the universe could always have existed.

In fact it seems more logical to me that it always did exist, rather than just pop up out of nothing 6,000 years ago, as these Jewish scriptwriters would have you believe. Certainly, the evidence is massive and overwhelming that the universe has existed for billions of years, if not eternally. But how it ever "started," if there ever was a start, nobody has the answer to this mystery of the universe, least of all these perfidious Jewish scriptwriters.

The fact is, there are millions of mysteries in the realm of Nature the human mind has not solved, and the beginning of the universe, if there was a beginning, is one of those unsolved mysteries. In this regard I will venture two fairly safe predictions, (a) The human mind never will solve all the myriads of Nature's mysteries, (b) The White Race of the future will solve more of Nature's mysterious laws than have been solved in all past history. In fact our accumulation of knowledge is accelerating at such a fantastic rate that it is hard to comprehend. Whereas during a thousand years of the Dark Ages it progressed hardly at all, it is now doubling and redoubling in an ever shorter time span, such interval of doubling now being less than a decade.

Be that as it may, certainly the cock-and-bull story as related in Genesis is no explanation at all. It creates nothing but a mass of confusion and explains nothing.

Nor is it of utmost importance that we over preoccupy ourselves with this pointless pontification of "how it all started."

This is about as useless a speculation as when during the Dark Ages the clerics indulged in the argument as to how many angels could dance on the head of a pin.

We have more urgent and immediate problems to solve, and the most urgent is the preservation of our own species— the Crowning Glory of Nature— namely the White Race. This is what Nature tells us to do, and this is what we must do, and this is what we will do.

We, of the CHURCH OF THE CREATOR, categorically reject this Jewish conception of such an impossible and contradictory conglomeration. Again, I reiterate that all the truths that we have accumulated over the ages derive from our observation of the laws of Nature and the phenomena of Nature itself. Any conceptions or misconceptions that we might entertain in contradiction to the laws of Nature and the truths we have derived from the observation of Nature, can be rejected as the irrational ramblings of an unhinged mind. In this category we might well place the conception of the Jewish God as set forth by the Jewish scriptwriters of unknown identity.

CHAPTER THIRTEEN

THE NEW TESTAMENT

The Old Testament was designed to unite the Jewish race and give them a binding creed. Its objective was to give the race a united solidarity such as none has ever achieved before or after, and to give them purpose, direction, and a program to conquer and plunder the rest of the world. Early in their history the Jews realized an astounding fact of human nature. They discovered what an amazingly powerful weapon was religion, defensively and offensively, constructively and destructively.

They have capitalized upon this discovery to the ultimate throughout their long and tortuous history.

By skillful use and manipulation of religions, they have not only survived but prospered; they have built a solidarity of race no other people has accomplished; they have demolished all enemies (and all other peoples are their enemies) though these enemies might be a hundred times more powerful than themselves.

This they have done through the fantastically skillful use of religion. It is high time that we, the White Race, too, grasp this powerful weapon into our own hands, for our own benefit.

Whereas Judaism was designed to unite the Jews into a solid ramrod, Christianity, on the other hand, also a Jewish creation, was designed to do just the opposite to their enemies— divide, confuse and destroy them. The New Testament was also written by the Jews— it supposedly revolves around the character of Jesus Christ, who is identified in the very first chapter of the New Testament (Matthew 1) as being a direct descendant of Abraham, Isaac and Jacob, through David and through Joseph and Mary, with great emphasis being placed upon him being a purebred Jew. In Luke 2:21 it reads Christ was a circumcised Jew. Christianity was designed not for the Jews, but was designed to destroy the great White power of the times— in particular, the Romans, and in general, the White Race. It was designed not to unite and solidify, as the Old Testament had done for the Jews, but designed to divide, confuse and destroy the White Race.

We, therefore, list the New Testament as a second book of major importance, undoubtedly of the greatest importance, produced by the Jews, in their program to destroy the White Race.

Not only was Christ himself a circumcised Jew, but so were Matthew, Mark, John, Peter, and all the rest of the so-called apostles, with the probable exception of Luke. Nevertheless, Luke ran around with Paul, who was a Jew, and who purportedly wrote practically half of the New Testament and was, therefore, under his complete influence. So, regardless of what angle we approach it from, the New Testament was written by the Jews and is a Jewish production.

The adherents of Christianity are continuously being told over and over again, thousands of times, that the New Testament and its prime spokesman, Jesus Christ, brought "Glad Tidings" to the world. We hear so much about it bringing "Peace on Earth, Good Will to Men." This, the spokesmen of Christianity, known as preachers, pastors, ministers, reverends, priests, etc., keep repeating over and over again. It is imbedded in a multitude of hymns and songs and sermons and speeches and slogans until their adherents are so mesmerized by the idea, they take it for granted.

The trouble with most people who profess to be Christians is that they have never taken the trouble to really read the New Testament to which they claim to be so dedicated. Those who have read smatterings of it have not put the pieces together and understood what it is all about. While they are devoutly meandering and laboring through a labyrinth of impossible contradictions and meaningless generalities, they never suspect that the whole purpose of the book is to confuse, divide and demoralize the White Race.

However, it shouldn't be so hard to understand Luke 12:51 through 53, where Christ purportedly says, "Suppose ye that I am come to give peace on earth? I tell you, Nay; but rather division; for from henceforth there shall be five in one house divided, three against two, and two against three. The father shall be divided against the son, and the son against the father; the mother against the daughter, and the daughter against the mother; the mother-in-law against her daughter-in-law, and the daughter-in-law against her mother-in- law." Does that sound like Peace on Earth and Good Will to Men? If you ask your preacher to explain that, he will give you about an hour's worth of double-talk, and when you come out of there, he will have so browbeaten you that you think, well, he probably has the answer, although you don't understand it. The fact is he doesn't have any answer. The fact is that this passage states the intent and purpose of the New Testament more clearly than any other quotation.

We must remember that the New Testament is the basis of Christianity, and Christianity has only flourished among the peoples of the White Race. It was, of course, rejected by the Jews, and two thousand years later it is still rejected by the Jews. (This, despite the fact that Christ and

his disciples were a completely Jewish group, we are told by the New Testament.) Just how does the New Testament go about accomplishing this divisiveness and this breaking up of the family, of the individual, of the nation, and of the White Race itself?

This is most clearly spelled out in the Sermon on the Mount, which anyone can read in Chapters 5, 6 and 7 of Matthew. Most of the suicidal advice and teaching that is given to the White people is contained in those brief chapters, but not all of it. More of the disintegrating advice and philosophy that brought down the Roman Empire is sprinkled throughout the rest of the chapters of Matthew, Mark, Luke and John and much of the so called "new teaching" is repeated over and over again throughout the entirety of the New Testament, but particularly the Gospels of Matthew, Mark, Luke and John. These four Gospels are regarded by the church as being the cornerstones of the Christian Creed.

But before we go into the suicidal teachings embodied in the Sermon on the Mount, I want to once and for all refute the lying claim that Christianity brought "Good Tidings" or "Glad News." It is, on the contrary, a teaching and philosophy of gloom and doom.

Undoubtedly the most terrible indictment that can be brought against Christianity is that it has introduced into the minds of millions and perhaps billions of people from their earliest tender childhood, the most vicious and hideous concept that was ever invented by the depraved mind of man. I am speaking about the very idea of HELL. Only by dredging up from the very lowest depths of a perverted collective Jewish mind could such a heinous concept originate.

Can you think of a more hideous, depraved, and hateful idea than that of sending people into confinement, setting fire to them and having them burn forever and ever in all eternity without even allowing the mercy of death? I would certainly never want my grandchildren to have their minds polluted with such an abominable and terrible idea. No where else in human history has a more despicable and atrocious concept ever been dreamed up and promoted as the idea of hell in the so called "New Teaching" of Christ that was supposedly bringing Peace and Love to a waiting world.

If ever a depraved sadistic human perpetually practiced this kind of torture on animals, i.e., slowly torturing them by burning them in a cage but keeping them alive as long as possible, what would you think? The outrage that would ensue would cause such a person to be strung up from the nearest lamppost. Yet how much worse is hell— to pursue such vindictive torture into all eternity by the Lord himself on the very creatures he designed and created. How hideous! How depraved! And this is the kind, loving God we should worship? Only the tormented, twisted mind of a Jew could dream up such a ghoulish monstrosity. And to think the White

Gentiles were stupid enough to fall for such depravity and teach it to their children!

We think about how abominable the savages are in their warfare in torturing their prisoners. We think of the Indians' depravity of scalping their prisoners and perhaps torturing them for a day or two before killing them. Vicious and uncivilized as this may be, it is a thousand times more kind and merciful than casting them into hell, a superheated confined torture chamber, the millions and billions of poor human souls that are supposedly earmarked for this everlasting torture.

And who prepared this cozy bit of red hot coals "into the fire that never shall be quenched; where there worm dieth not, and the fire is not quenched?" Why, our good gracious, kind and loving God, that's who, of course.

And for what reasons would our good, kind, loving God heap such vengeance upon us? Why, the reasons for him doing that are almost endless, perhaps you didn't eat the right apple, it was a forbidden fruit, but you weren't too clear on that. Or maybe in your thinking you're honest, and you came to conclusions that weren't exactly like those you were supposed to think and believe, so therefore you would be relegated to the eternal hell fire. Or perhaps somebody was thirsty and you didn't bring him a glass of water just at the right time, so that would entitle you to eternal damnation; or perhaps you were a devoted follower of Mohammed and hadn't heard too much about Christ, so you believed in Mohammed; that too would reap upon you the vengeance of the Lord; or perhaps sometime in a moment of distraction, you "blasphemed" the Holy Ghost; that, being a "cardinal" sin and is never forgiven, would surely land you in the eternal hot coals. In any case, there are thousands of reasons why you should be tortured forever and ever in a hot fire that is never quenched, and there are almost no means of escaping it that is what the "Good Book" says.

So what are the "Glad Tidings" and the "Good News" that Christianity brought to the world? They are not "Good News" at all. They are the harbingers of doom. The supposedly "Good News" is that there is an everlasting hell to which you will almost surely be relegated, and even should you escape it, undoubtedly by the law of averages and by the law of percentages, most of your relatives, your brothers, your sisters, your children, your parents— most of them would most surely end up in hell. Those are the "Glad Tidings" that Christianity brought to the world.

I can't think of anything more gloomy and more depressing than such a message.

Of course the "Good News" message is supposed to be now that you

The New Testament

know there is a hell and that you're almost surely going to it, Christ came along to intercede with his Father, who, being rather vengeful, demanded a blood sacrifice, that his son be nailed on the cross, and his blood flow from his sides, and this was to "atone" for your "sins." Of course, until you were told that you were a no good, low down, dirty sinner, committing sins all the time, you didn't know that you were a sinner, so there is some more "Good News" for you.

So the whole sleazy argument of the "Good News" that was brought to you adds up to something like this. You're brought the "Good News" that there is a terrible place called hell waiting for you in the hereafter; that you are a dirty low down "sinner," born in sin and will most surely go to this terrible place that is prepared for you "where the worm dieth not and the fire is not quenched"; that you have to completely remake and remodel yourself from the form in which Nature created you, and all the healthy instincts that Nature implanted in you for your own self- preservation are all bad and all wrong; you have to be born again and "believe unto the Lord," whatever that means, so that he and his "Grace," whatever that means, will save you from this eternal damnation. There in a nutshell is the "Good News" that Christianity brought to the world, the most outstanding feature of which is fear— fear of this horrible new monster— HELL— that they suddenly filled you full of. The outstanding characteristic of this whole shabby teaching is a horrible psychology of fear— it drove those who believed this trash almost insane with fear, ready to comply and do just about anything that their "shepherds" of the church would urge them to do.

On the other side, of course, if you did completely subjugate yourself to the will of the church, then there was a reward, a nebulous place called heaven, but the description of that place was not nearly as specific or as dramatic as that of hell. In any case, with these two psychological weapons— the carrot and the stick— heaven and hell— Christianity set about to conquer the Roman Empire and dismantle it, and plunge the greatest civilization of classical history into the abyss of the Dark Ages.

History shows us that these two psychological weapons did work, and Rome did fall to pieces.

Of these two psychological weapons, fear— the monstrous fear of hell— was by far the most powerful.

Having firmly established these two concepts of heaven and hell (and especially hell) the "New Teaching" set about to put a high premium on belief— faith in that which you do not see. Simply put, this means— believe in what we tell you to believe in, although we don't have a shred of evidence to offer. No matter how ridiculous the teaching, if you could only make people believe it, it was as good as real, lack of evidence notwithstanding.

This, the whole Jewish network set about to propagate amongst the Romans with a vengeance. Unfortunately, the Romans were stupid enough to buy this bag of garbage and with it came the teachings that really tore them apart— namely the bad suicidal advice embodied in the "Sermon on the Mount."

Whereas the concepts of heaven and hell were already mentioned in the Old Testament, they were of minor importance, and certainly were not as dramatically portrayed and spotlighted as they are in the New Testament The Jews were primarily interested in overcoming their enemies, committing genocide on all the tribes and cities that they could get their hands on, and marching forward with the blessings of their Lord, Jehovah. All this tended to unify and mold the Jewish Race.

With the Sermon on the Mount in the New Testament we have an altogether different story, however. We find here that Christ is dispensing a new kind of advice and it's the kind of advice that if you do follow it, you would most surely tear yourself apart, destroy yourself, destroy your family and destroy your nation.

And this my dear White friend, is exactly what it was designed to do— not to destroy the Jews, who were immune to it and were perpetrating it on the White Race, but to destroy their enemies— the whole Roman Civilization of that time in particular, and the White Race in general, thereafter.

When you mention the Sermon on the Mount to the average person he doesn't have the foggiest idea what it's all about and thinks that it is a collection of nice, idealistic platitudes which, perhaps are not easy to accomplish, but wouldn't it be nice if everyone did do those things?

And the answer is, no, it would not be nice if everyone did those things.

It would destroy us and it would also destroy our civilization and our Race. The concepts contained in the Sermon on the Mount are not idealistic— they are downright stupid and in complete contradiction to all the laws of Nature, in contradiction to the good, healthy, clean natural instincts that Nature imbued you with for your own self-preservation, and in general, in complete contradiction to all the sensible, good laws that civilization has built up over the thousands of years.

Most of the Sermon on the Mount is contained in Matthew, Chapters 5, 6 and 7 but it is again repeated in other places. Additional similar ideas are sprinkled throughout the four Gospels in particular and some of it throughout the rest of the New Testament.

We're now going to examine most of the outstanding ideas incorporated in the Sermon on the Mount and see just how "wonderful," "beautiful," and "idealistic" they really are. In so doing, we must at all times keep in mind what would happen, if, for instance, one group, namely the White Race, adopted these rules of playing the game, and the other side, namely the Jews, did not adopt them, but stuck with the eternal laws of Nature in fighting for their own self-

The New Testament

preservation. If we look at it from this point of view, the results are disastrous for the White Race.

In Matthew 5:3, Christ says, "Blessed are the poor in spirit; for theirs is the kingdom of heaven," and verse 5 "Blessed are the meek; for they shall inherit the earth." Once the ideas of heaven and hell are thoroughly soaked into your mind as being real, then, of course, everyone would want to be "blessed." Therefore, if you want to be "blessed," you'd want to be "poor in spirit" and "meek." Whereas, this kind of person would ordinarily be the village idiot and the clown, he is now upgraded to where he is the future inheritor of the earth, and he's also going to get the kingdom of heaven, and not only that, but above all, he is blessed. We all know what the words "poor in spirit" mean— they indicate that a person is dumb, stupid and ignorant. Now the word "meek" is not quite so well defined in the average person's mind, so let us go to Webster's Dictionary and see what it means. Webster gives three shades of meaning for the word (1) "manifesting patience and long suffering; enduring injury without resentment; mild" (2) "deficient in spirit and courage; submissive, tame" (3) "not violent or strong; gentle, moderate, weak." Then it also gives us the synonym— the word "humble."

And there you have a description of the type of person that is now most desirable in the eyes of the Lord. Since we are not all born that way, i.e., stupid, ignorant, dumb, submissive and meek, we should all, of course, try out utmost to become such village idiots, because, of course, we all want to be "blessed," don't we?

Of course, we must always again keep in mind that this is what the Jew is telling the White Man to be. Isn't that kind of a cowed, submissive person so much easier to subdue and plunder, to ravish and to enslave, than a strong, bold, intelligent, courageous and aggressive individual who knows what his rights are and has the courage to defend his life, his property, his family and his country?

This concept of voluntarily becoming submissive is, of course, completely a contradiction and a perversion of Nature's laws. Everywhere in Nature it is the strong, the bold, the quick and the intelligent that survive, whereas the weak and the slow fall by the wayside.

In Matt. 5:12, Christ says, "for great is your reward in heaven" and in Matt. 6:19, "lay not up for yourselves treasures upon the earth, where moth and rust doth corrupt, and where thieves break through and steal: but lay up for yourselves treasures in heaven, where neither moth nor rust doth corrupt, and where thieves do not break through nor steal." The implications of this advice are, of course, catastrophic for the White Race, if we again consider that the Jews would have no part of this idiotic advice and it would only apply to the White Gentiles.

You are being told that it is completely pointless to be industrious and

Nature's Eternal Religion

thrifty and be a builder such as is instinctively characteristic of the White Man. You are urged to forget about providing for your family, or planning a future, or building a business, or creating an enterprise or any other constructive effort that you would naturally apply yourself to. If you have already made the mistake and acquired some property in the past, why, undo this quickly, and get rid of it. Of course, this is an extremely good deal for the Jew, who will be right there waiting to grab it as soon as you are ready to let it go. Whereas the Jew makes sure that he gets his in the here and now, he wants to make sure he gets yours also in the here and now by having you keep your eye on the hereafter and meekly submit to his plunder on this earth, the only place where man has ever been known to exist, spiritually or otherwise.

We notice in this case, as happens time and again throughout the bible, the use of the non sequitur argument. Non sequitur in Latin means, "it does not follow." In this case the clinching argument is supposed to be that there is no point in trying to get ahead in this world, or trying to save anything, or lay up any treasures, because here you have two obstacles presumably insurmountable— namely we have rust, and we have thieves, and in heaven you don't have rust and you don't have thieves. So, therefore, forget about it, as far as trying to build anything, or save anything, or produce anything, or lay anything aside or plan for the future. This is, of course, a silly, non sequitur argument. If the worst things in this world we had to worry about were rust and thieves it would most certainly be easy sailing. Personally, I don't know whether I've lost much in the way of substance from rust and so far very little from thieves. So far, therefore, I am completely unconvinced that these two obstacles are insurmountable. I am not at all convinced that I should make no effort to build, or plan, or acquire anything.

Now that we have mentioned the non sequitur argument which is used time and again throughout the Bible, we will be using that term again wherever it applies.

The non sequitur argument goes something like this— it is raining, therefore it must be Tuesday. Of course, anyone knows that it does not necessarily follow that it is Tuesday because it is raining, because we know that it has also sometimes rained on Wednesday, Thursday, Friday, Saturday, Sunday and Monday, and furthermore, there have been any number of Tuesdays that it hasn't rained.

That, in essence is the non sequitur argument and it is used to ad nauseum throughout the bible.

In Matt. 5:25, Christ dispenses to us this choice piece of advice, "agree with thine adversary quickly, while thou art in the way with him, lest that anytime the adversary deliver thee to the Judge, and the Judge deliver thee to the Officer, and thou be cast in prison." And in v. 40 of the same Chapter he

The New Testament

advises us, "and if any man will sue thee at law and take away thy coat. Let him have thy cloak also." These two in essence say the same thing and were a man to follow this kind of dumb advice he would in short order be walked over by just about anyone that came along, especially the rapacious, plundering Jew.

It says in essence that no matter whether you are right ex wrong, don't put up any fight to protect your property—just let anybody come along and run over you and walk away with anything you have.

This is, of course, wonderful for the other fellow—especially the Jew, but it is pretty disastrous for yourself. In no time at all you would be bereft of anything you ever strived and worked for, including your home, your money, your business, and any assets you might ever have had. This is, of course, completely in line again with the concept of being the village idiot and being "poor in spirit" and being "meek" as described earlier. A more sensible and more fitting answer to this would be the old saying, "A fool and his money are soon parted."

We note again that the idiotic non sequitur argument is used as to why you should do this, namely, that if you should defend yourself in court, why, the judge might have you thrown in jail so naturally (or is it?) you would not defend yourself.

In the same Chapter 5:29 and 30, this gem of advice is dispensed in the Sermon on the Mount, "if thy right eye offend thee, pluck it out, if they right hand offend thee, cut it off..." Evidently this means that if your eyes or your hands have caused you to sin, destroy and mutilate those parts of the body. This is the non sequitur argument again raised to its ultimate idiocy. In the first place neither the eye nor the hand have any particular part in the decision making. If we were to follow this stupid bit of advice this country would be overrun with hordes of one eyed, one-armed helpless nitwits who would have of their own volition, mutilated parts of their body in order to comply with the requirements of this idiotic piece of advice from the Sermon on the Mount. As an indication of how few people really follow any of this kind of utterly impossible advice, I have never seen anyone nor heard of anyone that has plucked out their eye or cut off their hand just to make sure that the eye or the hand did not induce them to repeat some alleged sin.

To make unswervingly sure that you will not miss the point, and that you will set yourself up like the proverbial sitting duck for the rapacious Jew, in Matt. 5:39 Christ says, "Resist not evil" and "Turn the other cheek." In a world where Nature has put supreme emphasis on survival, and only the fittest survive, this advice is so obviously suicidal that we can hardly mistake its malicious intent. If we understand the English language correctly this means that any crook, gangster or criminal who wants to come along and rob you, plunder you, commit mayhem and do you in, why, be a good Christian chump and let him. Don't fight back, don't resist, in fact encourage him, and turn the other cheek in case he missed the fact that you had two cheeks to smash into pulp, rather than just one.

If we were to follow this kind of suicidal advice, we would do away with all our law enforcement organizations, such as the police force, the sheriffs department, the highway patrol, the FBI, and we would not only let the criminals run rampant, but encourage them by "turning the other cheek." We would also do away with our Army, Navy and Air Force, in fact our whole military establishment, and let, for instance, the Russians, the Chinese or any other aggressive enemy, or anybody else, run all over us.

What idiotic, suicidal advice! This is so completely contrary to all that experience and history has taught us, and completely contrary to all the laws of Nature in the animal kingdom. Every animal, every bird, every other species when threatened with assault, will instinctively defend itself. Even the most timid, such as a rabbit, when cornered will defend itself. Even the most timid nesting mother bird will do its utmost to defend its nest and its young when in danger by trying to lure away the threat with a feigned broken wing, should danger appear.

The pattern of self-destruction continues. In Matt. 5:42 we are told, "Give to him that asketh of thee and from him that would borrow of thee turn thou not away." This, of course, is wonderful advice if you want to create a whole nation of freeloaders. Unfortunately, a whole nation of freeloaders can't survive, since freeloaders have to have a substantial group of productive workers upon whom they can freeload. In today's world, where more and more people are holding out their hand and expecting the other man to support them, anybody who would follow this silly advice would soon be depleted of all his resources and would soon find himself among the destitute.

Of course, there is nothing novel about today's army of freeloaders. In all periods of history there have been parasites, leaches, and freeloaders, even in Roman times, and the obvious lesson of history is the more that is given to the freeloaders the bigger such an army becomes. The easier it is to freeload, the more of the otherwise respectable people who would work for a living soon also become leaches. So the whole impact of this kind of philosophy is to tear down the productive, working, creative citizen and breed a generation of parasites. To give to everybody that asks of you, or to lend money to everybody that asks you, is about the most miserable, silly, destructive advice anybody could possibly give you, and, of course, nobody would continue practicing this for very long. It would be impossible because soon such a person would simply be left with nothing to give. As the saying goes, "A fool and his money are soon parted," and a person would have to be a fool to give everything away just for the asking. But as this is right in line with the great "new teaching" as taught

The New Testament

by Jesus Christ, this silly advice, too, is part of the much-ballyhooed Sermon on the Mount.

The program for our self-destruction continues in Matthew 5:43 where we are further given this bit of generous advice, "Ye have heard that it hath been said, thou shall love they neighbor and hate thine enemy, but I say unto you, love your enemies, bless them that curse you, do good to them that hate you and pray for them that despitefully use you and persecute you." Now, dear friends, aren't you just being too, too sweet in helping your enemies help you commit hari-kari? If some burglars, armed to the teeth with knives and pistols, were to break into your house and assault you and your family, why should you love them, and bless them, and do them good? While you're loving them, they would be robbing you and assaulting you and your family. But you don't really mind that, do you? Or do you?

Most Kosher Konservatives will profess that they "believe" in the Sermon on the Mount and that they also believe in the Constitution of the United States. Before we go into these completely contradictory and untenable positions, let us see what Webster's definition of the word "enemy" is. Here are some of the things Webster says: "Enemy: one that seeks the injury, overthrow or failure of a person or thing to which he is opposed; something injurious, harmful, or deadly." There is more, but I think we have sufficiently demarcated that which we are so foolishly told to love and do good.

Now what does the United States Constitution say about treatment of the enemy? It plainly spells it out: Giving aid and comfort to the enemy is treason. It has been regarded as a capital crime. The punishment for treason throughout history has been most severe— it has been death— until very recently when the laws for our own protection have been completely dismantled by the treasonous Jews in our midst. Even as late as the 1950's the Jewish atom spies, Julius and Ethel Rosenberg, were dealt the death penalty. Certainly "loving" your enemies and doing them good would be considered treason as defined in the Constitution itself. It is therefore, of course, ridiculous and contradictory for anyone to claim they believe in the Constitution of the United States and also in the Christian teachings. Of the two, despite its many flaws, the Constitution, on this issue makes a thousand times more sense than "loving your enemies."

In fact, throughout the history of White civilization, traitors have been looked upon as being more despised and more contemptible than murderers or any other foul criminal. And rightfully so.

When a person is engaged in a life and death struggle and is betrayed by one of its own kind, the consequences can be disastrous and far-reaching.

We, of the CHURCH OF THE CREATOR, are putting new emphasis on the punishment of traitors and treason. Whereas we agree with the established historic concept that treason to the country is punishable by death, we regard racial loyalty as a higher virtue than loyalty to the country. We regard a race traitor as a more abominable criminal than any other. We regard treason to the White Race as the most contemptible crime any member can commit and will institute punishment to fit the crime. Let the race traitors of today, traitors betraying the White Race with impunity, take heed.

This kind of suicidal response is contrary to all the laws of Nature and also completely contrary to all the laws of common sense and past experience. I don't know of anyone who professes Christianity who has the slightest notion or intention of practicing such a stupid piece of advice. This, of course, is again justified by one of these nonsensical non sequitur arguments and the reasoning could hardly be more thin, to say the least. Christ says you should do these stupid things "that ye may be the children of your Father which is in heaven for he maketh his sun to rise on the evil and on the good and sendeth the rain on he just and on the unjust." Now, with such a clincher of a convincing argument, aren't you just simply overwhelmed with the logic of it all?

In case you aren't, we'll repeat it again. Here is how it goes: it rains on the criminals just like on the good people. For this overwhelming reason you should, by all means, let the criminals assault you, rob you, plunder you, or whatever it is that they want to do to you, because, and we'll repeat it if you missed it the first time: because it rains on them the same way as it does on the good people.

In case you didn't quite follow that argument, it is followed by a real clincher that reinforces it in v. 46, where the great "Teacher of Righteousness" says, "For if you love them which love you what reward have ye? Do not even the Publicans do the same?" Here the non sequitur argument is that evidently in no case should you be like the Publicans, whoever they are, and who are evidently using good sense.

If the Publicans, whoever they are, eat three meals a day, in no case should you do the same, even if it makes good sense, because you don't want to be like the Publicans. If the Publicans wear clothes, live in houses, go to work, get married, raise children, why, don't you do any of those things, because you don't want to be like the Publicans, whoever they are. In other words, if a Publican has enough sense to get in out of the rain, you don't want to get in out of the rain, because you don't want to be like a Publican.

In case at this point you still have not been persuaded to part with your hard earned possessions and all the worldly goods that you have accumulated over a lifetime and neither giving them away nor loaning them appeals to you, you are advised that there is another way that you can get rid of your possessions. In Matt. 19:21 Jesus says, "Go and sell that thou hast, and give to the poor, and thou shall have treasure in heaven." Certainly we can conclude that all this advice is consistent— it keeps telling you again and again— get rid

The New Testament

of everything you have. If you don't want to just simply give your possessions away, do it in a more roundabout way— sell your goods and then give the money away. Of course, you'll end up the same as before— with nothing— but that's all right, because that way you'll be "laying up treasures in heaven."

Here we come to another bit of strange, non sequitur reasoning. If it's such a ghastly crime to have possessions and treasures in this world, actually the only world in which man has ever been known to exist, why is it such a beautiful and righteous thing to lay up treasures in the next world? If it's wrong to lay up treasures in this world, surely it must be wrong to lay up treasures for the next world. If it's a good thing to lay up treasures in the next world, then it must be equally good to lay up treasures in this world. Of course, the big trick is that if you get rid of your treasures in this world, the Jew will get them, and he is not the least bit concerned about who has them in the probably non-existent next world. All that he is really concerned with, of course, is laying his grubby hands on your goods as easily as possible in the here and now.

We proceed on to Matthew, Chapter 6. The Sermon on the Mount and the dispensing of bad advice continue merrily on their way, hand in hand, unabated. The first four verses make much to do with giving alms in secret. Make sure that "thine alms may be in secret and thy Father which seeth in secret himself shall reward you openly." In other words, you're only giving alms so that you will get a better payoff and that you'll get a better reward for it one way or another, but— you are to do it in secret. This is, of course, completely contrary to what the Jews do. Any time they even pretend to do something charitable, they make sure that it is highly advertised, and that the whole country knows about it. But you, being a Gentile, are supposed to give and give and give, and never, ever get any credit for it.

This brings up the whole subject of giving alms, or in other words, giving charity, which is, in itself, a questionable practice.

The whole subject of charity in today's world has become a huge reprehensible racket. So many different ways and means and devious practices have sprung up with charities, that today's good, honest, big-hearted citizen, who is not too bright about where his money is going, is being fleeced and robbed and swindled by a band of professionals.

Before anyone gives his hard warned money to anyone, he should investigate and make doubly sure just what the money is going to be used for. He should be unequivocally certain it is not going to be actually used to promote those that are hostile to him, that it will not be used to aid people who are completely alien and a threat to his own existence and to that of his own family. We are being continuously asked to send money to help the Korean children, money to buy food packages to be shipped to people in India, money to help the Indians in New Mexico, and who knows where else. We are being

Nature's Eternal Religion

robbed of billions in the form of foreign aid, which is being used to promote our Communist enemies, to promote the colored races, and, in fact, to promote and propagate blacks, the colored and all kinds of people on the face of the earth who are a threat to our very existence, and would, at their First opportunity, destroy us.

We next go through about a dozen verses which make a great deal to do about praying in secret The reasons are not very clear except that "thy Father which seeth in secret shall reward thee openly."

We are again looking for rewards that will exceed our investments, which is rather hypocritical and in open contradiction to the admonition of "lay not up for yourselves treasures upon earth, where moth and rust doth corrupt and where thieves break through and steal." We are again being torn two ways—we are continually being told that we must not work for any gains, or reward, or any profits, or goods, or any of the good things of life here on earth, but then we are told that if we pray in secret and give alms in secret, our heavenly Father will reward us, in other words we'll reap some handsome dividends, presumably in the here and now.

As far as being rewarded in the hereafter, we may or may not get to this hereafter, if there actually is one. Even if there is one, the chances are a thousand to one, even according to the rules laid down in the "Good Book" that we will never get to heaven at all, but will end up in eternal hell fire. Therefore, playing all these chances (a) that there is no such a place in the first instance, and (b) that the chances are a thousand to one that we won't make it, then it is rather a bad investment to forego all the rewards on this earth and defer them to "laying up treasures in heaven." It is rather ridiculous to concentrate on "laying up treasures in heaven," if chances are extremely remote that you will ever get there in the first place. It certainly does seem strange and contradictory that it's such a good policy to have all these treasures waiting for you in the next life when there is little or no assurance of getting there, but it's terrible to work for honest rewards for yourself and your family in this life.

If it's such a crime to lay up treasures, in other words accumulate wealth in this world, why is it such a virtue to lay up treasures in the next world? If accumulating wealth is a crime per se then it certainly must be a crime in the hereafter.

In Matthew 6, v. 25, Christ certainly goes all out to destroy any sense of responsibility the good honest citizen may have acquired from a good upbringing by his parents. He says, "therefore I say unto you, take no thought for your life, what ye shall eat or what ye shall drink, nor yet for your body, what ye shall put on." And in v. 26 he says, "behold the fowls of the air for they sow not neither do they reap nor gather into barns, yet your heavenly Father feedeth them. Are ye not much better than they?" If we take a good hard look at this piece of

The New Testament

suicidal advice, then it is not difficult to understand why the whole Roman Civilization fell apart and disintegrated after it embraced Christianity. Here is a most contemptible piece of advice designed to undermine the responsibility that a father might have in providing for his family, or the citizen's responsibility towards his country, or that of the soldier in defending his empire. In fact, it would even prevent you from so much as taking care of your own sustenance and taking care of your own body.

The parable about beholding the fowls of the air that sow not nor reap is completely contrary to the facts of life. In the first chapter of this book we studied about the life cycle of that great bird, the eagle, one of Nature's great hunters. We found that the eagle worked hard and consistently in covering his territory of approximately a hundred square miles in order to forage for game and food to bring home to his family. Practically most of the birds' waking hours are spent either hunting for food or building a nest and raising its young. And so it goes with practically every bird you observe in Nature. It goes out and beats the bushes and scurries around working through most of the day, gathering food for itself and for the offspring in its nest. Squirrels will lay up nuts for the winter, bees gather honey for the next generation as well as food for its whole colony. Beavers build dams and build houses in order that their group will have shelter and be able to accumulate food for their own survival. Every plant and every flower that grows is in competition with other plants and weeds and forms of life struggling to sink down their roots and gather moisture and food in order that they can grow and produce seed and bring in the next generation. Any species of life that is too sluggish to put forth the most strenuous effort for its own survival in competition with all others, is mercilessly phased out by Nature.

Human beings have the most advanced intellect, are the most responsible and are the most capable of planning and building a society. To advise them that they should give no thought for tomorrow, nor give any thought for their life, for what they eat, or what they wear, or what they provide for their children, is most fantastic, to say the least. In any case, it is just about the most irresponsible type of advice you could give to anyone.

We proceed further to v. 31 where Christ says, "therefore take no thought saying what shall we eat or what shall we drink for after all these things do the Gentiles seek." Here Christ again slyly indulges in his non sequitur type of argument and reverts to the silly insupportable argument that if the Publicans do it, we must do it differently. If the Gentiles do these things, it must be wrong. If the Gentiles live in houses, it must be wrong. If the Gentiles work for their living, it must be wrong. If the Gentiles eat three meals a day, it must be wrong. If the Gentiles get into their pants one leg at a time, you've got to do it differently— jump in with both legs at the same time.

Chapter 6 ends with v. 34, which says, "take therefore no thought for tomorrow, for tomorrow will take thought for the things of itself." In other words, don't think, don't work, don't plan, don't do anything, everything will take care of itself. If you can think of any better advice for the destruction of a society, of a country, of a family, and, in fact of our race, I certainly don't know what it would be.

Contrast this kind of advice with the advice the Jews retain for themselves in the Old Testament where they admonish "where there is no vision the people perish." (Prov. 29, v. 18.) Let us now proceed on to the third chapter of the Sermon on the Mount, namely Matthew, Chapter 7, which has, right in the first verse, a piece of advice that, if followed, would make a person a candidate for a mental institution. The first verse says, "judge not that ye be not judged." Now we are all given by a benevolent Nature an intelligence which sets us apart from the rest of the creatures of this world. One of the finest attributes that a man can develop over the years by the use of this intelligence is good sound judgment. The average, intelligent, normal person uses judgment at least at least hundreds at least hundreds of times a day, probably thousands of times a day. If he were about to abandon that judgment, he would in effect be abandoning his senses, he would be abandoning the good common sense that he was born with, and in fact, negating and destroying all that he had learned over the years ever since the day he was born. To abandon one's judgment is to abandon one's senses and is to become, in effect, a hopeless imbecile.

Again in the second verse we are being subjected to a real clincher of a non sequitur argument to back up why we should not judge, saying that, "for what judgment ye judge ye shall be judged." The answer is, so what? Of course, we're going to be judged by others regardless of what we do and the more idiotic we are in refraining from using our judgment the more harshly we are going to be judged by others who observe this, and will most certainly exercise their judgment. Anyone knows that, in any case, in order to live at all, in order to meet the responsibilities of life, we certainly not only must use judgment, but we are continually compelled to use our very best possible judgment.

In the seventh verse Christ says, "ask and it shall be given unto you." This, of course, is not true. If all a person had to do was ask and everything was given to him, who would do the work that would create all those things that everyone is asking for? Was this great country of America built by just the asking? Was the winning of the west and the building of ranches, farms, roads and railroads accomplished by just the asking, or was it accomplished by strenuous hard work and sacrifice? This theory and philosophy is completely in contradiction to all the good experience of history and only a shiftless idiot could accept it as an excuse for getting out of earning an honest living.

Of course, this is exactly in line with the suicidal philosophy that the Jewish controlled welfare government is pursuing in America today. It is continually telling the shifty, the freeloaders, the lazy, the blacks, the niggers, those who will not work, that all they have to do is apply for relief, apply for welfare, pretend that they are destitute, pretend that they can't work, in fact just about any pretext will do; raise large numbers of illegitimates and the government will come to the rescue with money and welfare, with food and clothing, shelter and all the other goodies.

Now the government doesn't really produce any of these things. What it does is rob and steal these by force from the creative, responsible, productive citizens that do produce and do work. It takes these from the productive elements by force of law and threat of reprisals. The government punishes the productive citizens and rewards the shiftless and the freeloaders. This is, of course, exactly in line with Jesus' teachings, "ask and it shall be given," "think not of tomorrow for tomorrow will take care of itself," and all the other destructive advice that is so highly lauded in the Sermon on the Mount

So far I have only basically quoted from the Sermon on the Mount and a few other dovetailing adjuncts and we have come up with a persistent pattern of nothing but real bad suicidal, destructive advice. Most of the Sermon on the Mount is contained in Matthew, Chapters 5, 6 and 7. However, the same bad advice is repeated again in Mark and also in Luke and also in John and then further amplified throughout the rest of the New Testament. I believe that the evidence by now is overwhelmingly clear that the whole intent was at the time of the Romans, and is today, to give the White Man such bad advice that if he even halfway tried to follow it, he would destroy himself and tear apart the fabric of his society. I could go on and further pile evidence upon evidence, but I believe the point has been made, and to proceed further would be just a matter of overkill.

Having examined it in the light of cold reason, it is hard to understand why anyone would place so much value on such a collection of trash, or why they would buy such a bag of garbage. Nevertheless, it should prove to us how effectively a well-laid plan of propaganda and brain pollution can work if applied skillfully and persistently. The fact is that the Jews did apply their deception skillfully and persistently, and they did sell it to the Romans. By the fourth century A.D., the Romans were engulfed by it and destroyed by it. The White Race thereafter was plunged into a thousand years of the Dark Ages. Now that we have properly analyzed what the inherent poison of Christianity is, we can easily understand why.

In summation, Christianity is a teaching designed to confuse, divide and destroy the White Race by not only tearing apart the fabric of society itself, but by also setting an individual at odds with himself by destroying the natural instincts given to him by Nature for his own self- preservation.

Let us pursue this last indictment further: how does it tear the individual apart?

We have already noted that the Christian teachings, if they are believed and practiced, dull and stifle all the good instincts that Nature gave us for our own self-preservation, thereby leaving us frustrated and torn apart. We are told that all those things that we would naturally do, are bad, and we must follow these new artificial teachings that are completely contrary to the laws of Nature. We are told to do this in order to gain salvation. Here is the crux of the thing, either you believe and follow the idiotic, selfdestructive, suicidal advice— or you are doomed to eternal hell fire. You are naturally born bad, we are told. All those Fine instincts Nature gave you are bad— so the argument goes— and, therefore, along comes Christ to save you from all your wicked natural desires and to save you from going to hell. This is called "salvation."

Before the New Testament was written and before Christianity appeared on the scene to plague the Romans in particular and the White Race in general, the good people of Rome where not aware that their souls were in jeopardy of being damned to "hell." They had never heard of "hell." They were not particularly concerned with the multitude of problems they might have in a "hereafter" which to them was, after all, more or less just a dim fairy tale. The Romans were good, industrious, law abiding people. They had enough real problems to cope with that were with them in the here and now, and they took care of them rather well. They built a network of roads throughout Italy and much of Europe. They built aqueducts and cities, they brought law and order to the uncivilized tribes of Western Europe. At the height of the glory that was Rome and the splendor that was Greece, Christianity hit the Roman citizens like a plague and Rome began to crumble.

As Christianity spread, the obsession with "saving their souls" became the main preoccupation of these new converts. Instead of taking care of their duties in the here and now, the only real world that has ever been known, their minds became unhinged and were increasingly preoccupied with what would happen to them in the "hereafter," a place no one had ever been, no one had ever come back from, and no one really had the slightest inkling of its existence. Despite the fact that there was not the slightest proof of any "hereafter," this became the overwhelming obsession of the Romans, to the detriment of their responsibilities and duties to their families, to their country, and to their race.

The idea that they needed "salvation," which up to that time nobody was particularly aware of or concerned about, is very similar to the Chicago gangsters coming around to different store

owners and selling them on the need for "protection." Until the gangsters came around and told them that they needed protection or else their store windows would most surely be smashed by flying objects, the store owners were totally unaware of any need for "protection." But the gangsters, selling

The New Testament

their "protection," presented it to them as a threat, that either they pay them extortion money, or their store windows would be broken. And the threat was only thinly veiled.

The selling of "salvation" is very similar. If you don't buy "salvation," the threat is that you will go to hell and burn forever and ever. As I have said before, the very word "hell" sums up the most depraved, vicious, horrible, vengeful idea that only the very depths of the collective depraved Jewish mind could conjure. On the other hand, in contrast to hell, the image of heaven was dreamed up as the very epitome of bliss and eternal happiness. By using the carrot and the stick method to the most ultimate extremes the human imagination could conceive— with these psychological weapons— they deceived, bludgeoned and euchred the White people of Rome into destroying themselves.

CHAPTER FOURTEEN

REVELATION: A JEWISH NIGHTMARE IN TECHNICOLOR

For years I had heard all these fabulous claims about the Revelation, the last book of the Jewish bible. In this "miraculous" book, I had heard our whole future was prophesied, revealed, and laid out for all to see. A high-powered radio commentator by the name of Armstrong was on the air, night after night, for years on end, telling us all the great things that are foretold in Revelation.

In the meantime, he was taking in something like 40 million dollars a year in order to broadcast his souped-up message to all the gullible who were waiting with baited breath to hear what the future next held in store for us. I had also heard so much garbage about how the bible must undoubtedly be divinely inspired, because it had foretold so much of what was to be that had already been fulfilled. Only a divinely inspired book could so such a thing, I had been told.

It was only recently that I decided to read Revelation again and find out for myself. I was truly amazed at the collection of confused garbage that I encountered. If a Hollywood director had instructed some of his Jewish scriptwriters to let their imagination run rampant and come up with the wildest scenario that they could possibly concoct. I am sure that they could not have come up with anything weirder than those Jewish scriptwriters did nearly 18 centuries ago.

It is like a grotesque honor movie, minus a plot, without rhyme or reason. In sheer ghastly horror, killing, pain and torture, it exceeds anything Hollywood has ever put on the screen in all its perverted Jewish history.

It is hard to believe that such an abominable piece of writing could be accepted by so many millions as being sacrosanct, holy, and untouchable. To be frank, it is the most bizarre, wild and psychedelic piece of writing that I have seen in many a moon. The best description that I can think of is that it is something the depraved mind of a Jew would come up with in a real wild nightmare.

There is no use in trying to cover the story of that which is contained in Revelation. There is no story. It is just one unconnected, unrelated piece of unmitigated honor after another. Nevertheless, the images portrayed are most decidedly vivid and graphic. To cast it in anything less than Technicolor would be to do it a great disservice. I am not, therefore, going to try and review it. It is pointless. There is no coherent story. Instead, let us just lake a look at the cast of characters that are portrayed in this wild rampage of somebody's unbalanced imagination.

Revelation is evidently supposed to be a pulling back of the curtains to show St. John "a servant of Christ," what is in store for us poor mortals. What is in store for us is really a horrible, tragic and tremendously painful mess. John, being the faithful servant that he was, with pencil in hand, quickly took notes of the whole Revelation that was spread before him. At least, so we are told.

Here is a list of the bizarre characters that we encounter in these 18 pages consisting of 22 chapters.

To begin with, the way John tells it, "and I turned to see the voice that spake with me. And being turned, I saw seven golden candlesticks; and in the midst of the seven candlesticks one like unto the Son of Man, clothed with the garment down to the foot, and gird about the paps with a golden girdle. His head and his hairs were white like wool, as white as snow; and his eyes were as a flame of fire; and his voice as the sound of many waters."

The next set of characters we have are four beasts full of eyes before and behind. "And the first beast was like a lion, and the second beast like a calf, and the third beast had a face as a man and the fourth beast was like a flying eagle. And the four beasts had each of them six wings about him; and they were full of eyes within: and they rest not day and night..."

Next we have a scene where there is a great book sealed with seven seals on the right hand of him that sat on the throne. A strong angel proclaimed in a loud voice, "Who is worthy to open the book, and to loose the seals thereof?"

It seems there was no one worthy and great enough to do so and John wept much because no man was found worthy to open and read the book, neither to look thereon.

However, lo and behold, suddenly someone came forth that was great enough to do this powerful, high and mighty deed. And guess who it was?

Remember way back in Genesis 38 that old, whore-mongering reprobate, Judah, who fornicated with his daughter-in-law, thinking she was just an ordinary whore on the roadside? Well, now in heaven, this circumcised Jew has been upgraded (by the Jewish scriptwriters) to be the greatest of the four and twenty elders who are sitting on the throne. In fact, he is one of the first and foremost now and he is the "Lion of the tribe of Judah, the root of David," and it is he who "hath prevailed to open the book, and loose the seven seals thereof."

As we proceed to have the seals opened, we find as the First seal was opened there appeared a white horse. As the second seal was opened there appeared a red horse. As the third seal was opened there appeared a black horse, and as the fourth seal was opened there appeared a pale horse. Anyway, sitting on the pale horse was something that sat on him and his name was Death, and Hell followed him.

As we go into Revelation 9 we have a great deal of torment and torture, and on the scene to do the job appear some weird forms of locusts who are to torment men without killing them. The torment is to be something like that of a scorpion when he strikes a man. The shape of the locusts were like "unto horses prepared unto battle; and on their heads were as it were crowns like gold, and their faces were as the faces of men. And they had hair as the hair of women, and their teeth were as the teeth of a lion's. And they had breast plates, as it were breastplates of iron; and the sound of their wings was as the sound of chariots of many horses running to battle. And they had tails like unto scorpions, and there were slings in their tails: and their power was to hurt men Five months." How many locusts just like that have you seen in your lifetime? Weird, real weird.

Next we have an army of horsemen consisting of two hundred thousand. That would be an army of 200 million horsemen. I never knew there were so many horses in existence at any lime. How John could count them all in short order is a mystery. Anyway, it says, "And thus I saw the horses in the vision, and them that sat on them, having breast plates of fire, and of a jacinth, and brimstone; and the heads of the horses were as the heads of lions; and out of their mouths issued fire and smoke and brimstone." Not only did I not know there were two hundred million horses around, but what horses!

As we move on to Chapter 12, it is a real weirdie. In the First verse we find "A woman clothed with the sun, and the moon under her feet, and upon her head a crown of twelve stars: and she being with child, cried, travailing in birth, and pained to be delivered."

As an overwhelming threat to this unusual woman about to give birth to a child was a fierce and strange great red dragon "having seven heads and ten horns, and seven crowns upon his head. And his tail drew the third part of the stars of heaven, and did cast them to the earth." Can you imagine a Hollywood screenwriter coming up with a more weird abortion than this? Anyway, here was this dragon with all those heads and horns and crowns ready to devour her child as soon as it was born.

The story goes on. The child somehow escaped, but the dragon was wroth with the woman and went to make war with the remnant of her seed. We never

Revelation: A Jewish Nightmare in Technicolor

do find out whether or not he got the woman too.

There seems to be no end to the strange, odd beasts that parade through the fast changing scenario. In Chapter 13 we have a beast rise up out of the sea again, having seven heads and ten horns, and upon his horns ten crowns. He looked "like unto a leopard, and his feet were as the feet of a bear, and his mouth, as the mouth of a lion: and the dragon gave him his power, and his seat, and great authority." In the sump chapter we have another beast coming up out of the earth and he has two horns like a lamb and, "he spake as a dragon."

We next come to the purple clothed woman on the seven hills In Chapter 17. One of the seven angels said to John, "come hither; I will shew unto thee the judgment of the great whore that sitteth upon many waters:" "...and the woman was arrayed in purple and scarlet colour and decked with gold and precious stones and pearls, having a golden cup in her hand..." In any case, this woman had drunken the blood of the saints and the martyrs, and she, too, encountered the beast with the seven heads and ten horns. In the end this beast "shall make her desolate .mil naked, and shall eat her flesh, and bum her with fire." Now I ask you just what would you think of a hopped up Hollywood scriptwriter who came out with a story like that?

There are more characters, however less grotesque and mangled, such as foxes and serpents and dragons. There are also great armies of men on white horses, seven angels with vials, filled with plagues, "full of the wrath of God," and there is a bizarre description of the great city, the holy Jerusalem. This, too, is something to behold.

After having told us in the first four gospels how wicked it is to lay up treasures on earth and that a rich man could never get to heaven, and that you should "Sell all thou hast, and give it to the poor" we get a very good description of what the Jew's version of eternal

bliss and heaven really is, and what his conception of the new city of Jerusalem is, evidently his idea of heaven.

Here is the description in Revelation 21. It is quite a city. It is twelve thousand furlongs wide and twelve thousand furlongs in length and evidently the height is the same, twelve thousand furlongs. In checking a furlong in the dictionary, I find it is 1/8 of a mile. Therefore this New Jerusalem would be 1,500 miles square and also 1,500 miles high, if you can conceive such a city. The wall evidently was 144 cubits, and looking up a cubit, it is 18 inches, which would make the wall 216 feet high. However, it just told us that the city was 1,500 miles high. Don't ask me to explain the inconsistency. The Jewish scriptwriters wrote it, I didn't. Anyway, the wall itself was of jasper and the city was of pure gold, "like unto clear glass." Then it gives a detailed description of the twelve foundations of the city, each of which consisted of precious stones. The first foundation was of jasper; the second, sapphire; the third, a chalcedony;

153

Nature's Eternal Religion

the fourth, an emerald. Then it goes on through the other eight foundations each of which are of precious stone. The twelve gates were twelve pearls. The street of the city was pure gold. "As it were transparent glass."

As you are undoubtedly aware, Jews have always been just wild at the sight of gold and have an insatiable desire to get their hands on all the gold and precious stones possible. Therefore, when they wrote the script for the Holy City, the New Jerusalem, it was just chuck full of gold in the streets, with emeralds, diamonds and precious stones in the foundations, and pearls in the gates. It is just about the most lavish extravaganza one could concoct, one that would make a Hollywood screenwriter just boil over green with envy.

But remember the Sermon on the Mount? You are told to get rid of all you have, "Sell all thou hast."

The other most outstanding characteristic about Revelation is the constant referral to vengeance and horror and pain and suffering and agony. It seems just about every chapter is laden with the vengeance of God, exercising itself without letup upon us poor and long-suffering earthlings. We are all aware of how many people get killed on the Jewish television screen by the hour, but the agony and suffering of the people that are slaughtered in Revelation is something else again. Anyone with a real sadistic bent would really have a field day reading Revelation.

We have so much of this "Glad Tidings" and "Good News" spread throughout Revelation that it is hard to know where to start. We are not going to give all of them but just a scattered sampling of the different sadistic ways there are of doing in us poor human creatures and making us suffer without end.

In Chapter 8 we have, for instance, the seven angels opening the seventh seal and sounding the seven trumpets.

As the first angel sounded its trumpet, "there followed hail and fire mingled with blood, and they were cast upon the earth; and the third pan of trees was burnt up, and all green grass was burned up." This was followed by the second angel sounding its trumpet and "as it were a great mountain burning with fire was cast into the sea: and the third pan of the sea became blood." Naturally the third of all the creatures in the sea died and the third pan of the ships were destroyed. And so we go on down the line through the 3rd, 4th, 5th, 6th and 7th angel, each sounding its trumpet and each one creating a major catastrophe upon us poor human inhabitants of the earth.

Then in the next Chapter we have those terrible locusts that we described earlier and here is what they do for us, "And to them it was given that they should not kill them, but that they should be tormented five months: and their torment was as the torment of a scorpion, when he striketh a man. And in those days shall men seek death, and shall not find it; and shall desire to die, and death shall flee from them." Here again we have the Jewish obsession with torturing their enemies, not only to death, but depriving them of the mercy of dying so that they can torture them longer and more relentlessly.

We then have one catastrophe and torment following another, nil this calamity raining down upon the so-called "wicked," until you would think there were no more people left to kill and torture. But you are wrong, there seems to be a new fresh crop in each chapter, again in torment and mutilate, to kill, and to torture.

Finally we come to Chapters 15 and 16 where we have the seven angels bearing seven vials of the "Wrath of God." Here is what happens as they pour forth their vials of the wrath of god upon the earth.

As the first one poured out his vial upon the earth, "there fell a noisome and grievous sore upon the men which had the mark of the beast." As the second angel poured out his vial upon the sea, "it became as the blood of a dead man: and every living soul died in the sea."

Since the earth and the sea had been taken care of, the third angel had to find a different outlet for his deadly vial. It poured its wrath upon the rivers and fountains of waters, "And they became blood."

What a bloody, idiotic mess!

Where could now the fourth angel pour his vial? Well, he poured it upon the sun and, "power was given unto him to scorch men with fins. And men were scorched with great heal, and blasphemed the name of God." Can you wonder why they would blaspheme him instead of loving him?

The fifth angel poured his vial upon the seal of the beast. "And his kingdom was full of darkness: and they gnawed their tongues for pain." Evidently it was the poor miserable human beings that were in his kingdom that gnawed their tongues for pain.

The sixth angel poured out his vial upon the great river Euphrates which dried up the water of that river and three unclean spirits like frogs came out of the mouth of the dragon, and out of the mouth of the beast, and out of the mouth of the false prophet. It is somewhat unclear as to what all these spirits were about to do, except they are evidently to gather together and do battle at a place called Armageddon against the great and almighty God.

The seventh angel poured out his vial into the air. This evidently caused a great deal of thunder and lightning and great earthquakes. And the great city (evidently it refers to Babylon here) was thereby divided into three parts. And every island fled away, and "the mountains were not found." That is not all. And there fell upon men a great hail out of heaven, every stone about the weight of a talent. "And men blasphemed God because of the plague of the hail; for the plague thereof was exceeding great." Anyway, after all this was done the seventh angel proclaimed with a great voice out of the temple of heaven, "From the throne, saying, it is done."

Thank God for small mercies.

This is by no means the end of all the bizarre and ridiculous tortures and torments that were inflected upon the helpless people of Earth. We have other choice phrases such as "And whosoever was not found written in the book of life was cast into the lake of fire." Further on it mentions a group of sinners. Then it says this is what will happen to them: "They shall have their part in the lake which burneth with fire and brimstone: which is the second death." Kill them again! "And fire came down from God out of the heaven and devoured them." And here is more: "By these three was the third part of men killed, by the fire, and by the smoke, and by the brimstone, which issued out of their mouths."

Well, there is much more ghoulish, bloody and grotesque detail, but I think we have covered enough. I find nothing very uplifting in this whole sorry, wild and psychedelic mess. Certainly it is nothing that I would want to have my grandchildren read and pollute their minds with— all these weird aberrations conjured by the minds of depraved Jews. Nor do I find anything in there that has correctly foretold and prophesied the future, which has now come to pass. The whole thing is a garbled and incomprehensive collection of atrocities, but it certainly does not spell out any rational forecast of events to come.

It is something like looking into a cup of tealeaves. Anybody can make of it whatever they want to. They can cite this and that phrase as meaning such and such, and the seven headed monster being such and such a country or such and such an event, or whatever. In any case it is absolutely meaningless and about as relevant as the tea leaves in the cup. Therefore, when these preachers come along and say that they have the inside track as to what all these things mean, they are actually lying to you. They don't have any more information about it than you or I do. What all this means. Christ only knows, and he did not leave any codebook wherewith to decipher this ridiculous and bizarre collection of catastrophes. In one place it says that they will finally lie up the devil and cast him into the bottomless pit and that Christ will then reign for a thousand years with a select group. Then, however, the devil is to be let loose again and who knows from there on out what will happen next.

A great deal to do has been made about this idea of the thousand- year kingdom coming up. We have high-powered programs on radio, we have mailing organizations calling themselves

"The Second Coming," etc., and all kinds of hopped-up preachers spouting about the second coming of Christ.

Christ says, "Behold, I come quickly." The apostles understood he was

Revelation: A Jewish Nightmare in Technicolor

coming in their lifetime. After 2000 years, the "Believers" are still wailing. After 80 generations, nature goes on as in the millions of years before, and, as it will, millions of year's hereafter. After 80 generations, the dupes are still holding the bag, worried, paralyzed, waiting.

All this has a very neutralizing and disastrous affect upon the deceived and deluded White Man who is thereby hypnotized and paralyzed into inaction, waiting for the second coming of Christ. After all, if he believes all this garbage, and if everything is programmed anyway, and it is going to get worse and worse, and the devil is in complete control, why, there is nothing the White Man can do but just fold his hands, let everything go by and

resignedly wait for the second coming of Christ. It is high time we exposed all this treacherous brain pollution flooded upon the minds of the White Race, and get back to reality. The last thing in the world we need is the idea of impending disaster, of gloom and doom. Instead, we need some good clear thinking, a new realization of the value of our Race, a common bond to tie our Race together, and then the united will to fight and survive.

CHAPTER FIFTEEN

GETTING TO HEAVEN PROJECT IMPOSSIBLE: OR, EVERYBODY IS GOING TO HELL

Most Christians are under the impression that if you only believe, then getting to heaven is pretty straight forward. Most preachers and the various churches will tell you how simple it is to have "salvation," and it is all for free! All you have to do is— just simply believe— so they tell us.

But, as you read the fuzzy details as spelled out in the bible you apprehensively find it is not at all that simple. In fact, the more you read the bible and try to find out just how you can gel to that there "salvation" the more confusing, the more complicated, the more ambiguous, and the more difficult it gets. In fact, there are so many ambiguous and contradictory quotations by Christ saying that because of such and such you cannot get into the kingdom of heaven, that instead of it being so simple, we find there are so many conflicting stipulations, all of which say that you can't get salvation, say that you can't get to heaven.

By the lime you get through examining and finding all the road blocks that are placed in your way, you find out that you just can't gel there— which means that practically everyone is condemned to go to hell and bum forever and ever. Evidently, there are only two camps. If you can't get to heaven, you're going to go to hell.

These are the supposedly "Glad Tidings" and "Good News" that Christianity brought.

Let us now examine the different roadblocks. In Matt. 7:21 Christ says, "Not everyone that says to me. Lord, Lord, shall enter into the kingdom of heaven, but he that doeth the will of my Father, which is in heaven. Many will say to me in that day Lord, Lord, have we not prophesied in thy name and in thy name cast out devils, and, in thy name, done many wonderful works? And then I will profess unto them, I never knew you: depart from me, ye that work iniquity." In other words, despite your efforts, despite your good deeds, despite your loyalty, Christ says: you can go to hell.

In Matt. 8:10 he says, "Verily I say unto you, I have not found so great faith, no, not in Israel. And I say unto you that many shall come from the East and West and shall sit down with Abraham, and Isaac, and Jacob, in the kingdom of heaven. But the children of the kingdom shall be cast out into the outer darkness: there shall be weeping and gnashing of teeth..." Pretty fuzzy, but if the "children of the kingdom" are going to hell, you can be sure the rest aren't going to heaven either.

We are just starting but already we are beginning to see the exclusions pile up, one after another, and they all add up to this: the majority of these people are excluded from entering the kingdom of heaven, and of course, therefore they are programmed, planned, and scheduled to go to hell. There is no middle road. But let us go further.

In Matt. 10:37 Christ says, "He that loveth father or mother more than me is not worthy of me: And he that loveth son or daughter more than me is not worthy of me. And he that taketh not his cross, and followed, after me, is not worthy of me." We can most assuredly assume that those who are further relegated to this category and are not worthy of him are most certainly not going to get into the kingdom of heaven, so add these millions further to the list. They, too, are going to hell. How many people do you know that have categorically come out and made the commitment that they love Christ more than they do their father or mother or their son or daughter? How many people do you know that have taken up their cross and followed him, especially since crosses are rather hard to come by, and since it is most confusingly unclear just what it is that you must do to follow him?

In Matt. 12:31 Christ says, "Wherefore I say unto you, all manner of sin and blasphemy shall be forgiven unto men: but the blasphemy against the Holy Ghost shall not be forgiven unto men. And whosoever speaketh a word against the Son of man, it shall be forgiven him: but whosoever speaketh against the Holy Ghost, it shall not be forgiven him, neither in this world, neither in the world to come." So there, if you have blasphemed against the Holy Ghost, whatever that is, you've had it. You have no further chance of any forgiveness or redemption or the slightest chance of mercy. From that point on you are going straight to hell no matter what and there is no further court of appeal.

In Matt. 12:36 he says, "But I say unto you. That every idle word that men shall speak, they shall give account thereof in the Day of Judgment. For by thy words thou shall be justified, and by thy words thou shall be condemned." If such are the rules of the game, everybody would be in just about continuous jeopardy, because who knows, any word you might say might be the one by which you will be condemned. Isn't that a comforting thought? This is some more of that real "Good News" that Christianity brought to you.

Let us proceed further with Matt. 13:41. "The Son of man shall send forth his angels, and they shall gather out of his kingdom all things that offend, and them which do iniquity: And shall cast them into a furnace of fire: there shall be wailing and gnashing of teeth." This is, of course, rather fuzzy but undoubtedly here goes another shipload of poor souls destined for the fiery furnace.

It isn't really so simple to get to heaven after all, is it? In fact, we have already piled up enough categories that would embrace just about every living human being. But let us proceed.

In Matt. 15:4 Christ says, "For God commanded, saying. Honor thy father and mother: and. He that curseth father or mother, let him die the death." Chalk up another transgression that will doom the offender to the fiery pit.

Matt. 15:22,23 and 24 give the following story: "And, behold, a woman of Canaan came out of the same coasts, and cried unto him, saying, have mercy on me, O Lord, Thou son of David; my daughter is grievously vexed with a devil. But he answered her not a word. And his disciples came and besought him, saying, Send her away; for she crieth after us. But he answered and said, 'I am not sent but unto the lost sheep of the house of Israel."

So here, evidently, we have a new development. We find that the only people Christ claims he was sent to bring salvation to was the House of Israel. Apparently that would completely wash out the rest of us that are Gentiles and not Jews. Then we have the further perplexing situation that none of the Jews believe in Christ and therefore would be excluded from salvation also. So who is there left? Confusing as all this may be, and undoubtedly is meant to be, this is further confirmed by John 4:22 where Christ is speaking to the women of Samaria and says to her, "Ye worship ye know not what: we know what we worship: for salvation is of the Jews." Evidently he is spelling it out to the Gentiles: salvation is a Jewish thing and the Gentiles are so confused they don't know what they're worshipping. With this I heartily agree.

But let us continue. Then Jesus said unto his disciples, "If any man will come after me, let him deny himself, and take up his cross, and follow me. For whosoever will save his life shall lose it: and whosoever will lose his life for my sake shall find it." (Matt. 16:24.) This is one of those confusing pieces of double talk where you don't know whether you're coming or going, but in any case, those of you who would try to save your life are going to lose it and evidently will not get to heaven.

Proceeding in the same book, Chapter 18:3, Christ further admonishes and excludes, "Verily I say unto you, except ye be converted, and become as little children, ye shall not enter into the kingdom of heaven. Whosoever therefore shall humble himself as this little child, the same is greatest in the kingdom of heaven." Proceeding to v.6, "But who so shall offend one of these little ones which believe in me, it were better for him that a millstone were hanged about his neck, and that he were drowned in the depth of the sea," From this we may gather that we are to act humble and become simple minded as little children again, and forget all the experiences and judgment that we have acquired through all our years of maturity, or else we are not qualified to enter the kingdom of heaven. Furthermore, if we have offended any of these little ones, those people, too, are better off if they had a millstone hanged about their necks and were drowned. Evidently these, too, are disqualified from entering the kingdom of heaven and destined to perdition. They, too, are going to hell.

We are finding that it is harder and harder to get into the kingdom of heaven. The list of those who are not going to get there becomes greater and greater, and in the same chapter v. 34, Christ says, "And his lord was wroth, and delivered him to the tormentors, till he should pay all that was due unto him. So likewise shall my heavenly Father do also unto you, if ye from your hearts forgive not every one of his brother their trespasses." Add a further huge multitude of those that did not forgive their brothers their trespasses. They, too, shall be chalked off and "delivered" to the tormentors. They, too, are going to hell.

The list is growing and the obstacles are piling up. In Matt. 19:20, it says, "The young man saith unto him, 'All these things have I kept from my youth up: what lack I yet?'" and Jesus said unto him, "If thou wilt be perfect, go and sell that thou hast, and give to the poor, and thou shall have treasure in heaven: and come and follow me." When the young man went away "sorrowful," Jesus said to his disciples, "Verily I say unto you, that a rich man shall hardly enter into the kingdom of heaven. Again I say unto you, it is easier for a camel to go through the eye of a needle, than for a rich man to enter into the kingdom of God." Now here we have added to the exclusion, which is now growing by leaps and bounds, all those people who have "riches." It says further in v. 25, "When his disciples heard it, they were exceedingly amazed, saying who then can be saved?" A real good question. Jesus blandly gave them this reassuring double-talk, "With men this is impossible; but with God all things are possible." This is typical. If you can't explain things in a sensible and logical way, just say, "Well, we operate in the field of magic, anything goes, and it doesn't have to make sense."

The doom and damnation continues. We are to be booby-trapped and caught with our pants down at the moment when we least expect. This is thrown at us just so that we will be nervous and on edge at all times, never knowing when [he boom is going to be lowered. "The Lord of that servant shall come in a day when he looked) not for him, and in an hour that he is not aware of, and shall cut him asunder, and appoint him his portion with the hypocrites: There shall be weeping and gnashing of teeth." (Matt. 24:50, 51)

Vengeance and damnation proceed unabated. "Then shall he say also unto them on the left hand, depart from me, ye cursed, into everlasting fire, prepared for the devil and his angels."

"For I was an hungered, and ye gave me no meat: I was thirsty, and ye gave me no drink."

"I was a stranger, and ye took me not in: naked, and ye clothed me not: sick, and in prison, and ye visited me not."

"Then shall they also answer him, saying, Lord, when saw we thee an hungered, or a thirst, or a stranger, or naked, or sick, or in prison, and did not minister unto thee?"

"Then shall he answer them, saying, Verily I say unto you, inasmuch as ye did it not to one of the least of these, ye did it not to me." "And these shall go away into everlasting punishment." Matt. 25:14-46.

Do you still think it is as simple as "just believing?" Far from being simple, it is getting extremely complicated and the odds are mounting not only a hundred to one but a thousand to one that nobody, but nobody, can hurdle all the booby-traps that are put in the way of getting to "heaven." On the other hand there is no middle road. Those that don't go to heaven all go to eternal damnation and hell fire.

But there is more, much more. There are many repetitions in the chapters in Mark, also Luke, and also John, with various embellishments and variations thereof. We are not going to belabor the subject much further. In Mark 11:26 Christ says, "But if ye do not forgive, neither will your Father which is in heaven forgive your trespasses." In Luke 6:24,25, He goes after those terrible rich again and says, "But woe unto you that are rich, for ye have received your consolation. Woe unto you that are full, for ye shall hunger. Woe unto you that laugh now, for ye shall mourn and weep." The moral here is supposed to be that if you have things pretty well under control, worry anyway, just worry, worry, and worry. See nothing but doom and gloom ahead. These, after all, are "Good Tidings," you know. Your reward shall be in the hereafter, and the chances are a thousand to one your reward shall be eternal hell fire.

We skip over the rest of Mark and Luke and so that we won't entirely neglect John, we quote from John 3:3 where Christ says, "Verily, verily, I say unto thee, except a man be born again, he cannot see the kingdom of God." And in v. 5, "Verily, verily, I say unto thee, except a man be born of water and the spirit, he cannot enter into the I kingdom of God."

So there we have it, hell fire and damnation. Wailing, weeping and gnashing of teeth. Eternal damnation. Woe unto you. Better a millstone were hanged around your neck and you were cast into the furnace of fire. Ye shall be cast into the utter darkness.

The Gospels are just full of doom and damnation throughout their entirety. This is supposed to be "Good Tidings" that Christ brought to the world. The salvation that your preacher keeps dangling in front of you, even by their own rules, is so ridiculous and so impossible to overcome that nobody, just about nobody, is going to qualify to be one of those that go into the "Kingdom of Heaven."

Speaking of heaven, let us just examine what kind of a place it is supposed to be. Whereas hell is described in most graphic and frightening terms, the descriptions of heaven are most sketchy and to say the least, very fuzzy. In Matt. 13:31, Christ says, "The kingdom of heaven is like to a grain of mustard seed, which a man took, and sowed in his field: which indeed is the least of all seeds: but when it is grown, it is the greatest among herbs, and becometh a tree, so that the birds of the air come and lodge in the branches thereof." v. 33, "The kingdom of heaven is like unto leaven, which a woman took, and hid in three measures of meal, till the whole was leavened." Does that give you any kind of a picture of a place you would just break your neck to get to?

In the next chapter we find a few more tidbits and morsels that are not too descriptive but they are the best we could find. In Matt. 14 starting with v. 44, Christ says further. "Again, the kingdom of heaven is like unto treasure hid in a field: the which when a man hath found, he hideth, and for joy thereof goeth and selleth all that he hath, and buyeth that field. Again, the kingdom of heaven is like unto a merchant man, seeking goodly pearls: Who, when he had found one pearl of great price, went and sold all that he had, and bought it. Again, the kingdom of heaven is like unto a net, that was cast into the sea, and gathered of every kind: which, when it was full, they drew to shore, and sat down, and gathered the good into vessels, but cast the bad away. So shall it be at the end of the world: the angels shall come forth, and sever the wicked from among the just."

Does that give you any kind of a picture of heaven, or are you still puzzled about the nature of "your reward in the hereafter?" As far as I can see, this doesn't present much of a picture of anything but a lot of double-talk, and frankly I am not at all the type that would want to go to such a nebulous and ill-described place. But just to make sure that you don't miss the point that the other alternative is pretty horrible, the 50th verse follows the 49th which we just quoted previously and Christ there says, "And shall cast them into the furnace of fire: there shall be wailing and gnashing of teeth."

Can you get to Heaven? Not likely in any case, and especially not so if Christ can help it. After Christ had laid down his creed and spelled out all the suicidal advice for the destruction of those who would embrace his creed, he supposedly then organized a campaign to disseminate this teaching further into all the world. Purportedly, he then gathered around him 12 Disciples, rank

Nature's Eternal Religion

amateurs, which are named in Chapter 10 of Mildew. These 12 blundering accomplices, who evidently were not too bright and couldn't seem to understand what it was he was saying. Jesus then sent forth and commanded them saying, "Go not thou in the way of the Gentiles and into any other cities of the Samaritans enter ye not, I'm go rather to the lost sheep of the house of Israel." (Matt. 10:5) Now there is a very contradictory passage here. Jesus was commanding his disciples not to spread the word for the new teaching to the Samaritans or the Gentiles, but to give it exclusively to the Jews. It is rather strange, therefore, that it was the Jews who rejected his teachings, but the Gentiles who embraced it. We suspect that it was undoubtedly planned the way it happened, but that's what it says in Matt. 10:5, 6, namely for his disciples not to teach it to the Gentiles or the Samaritans, but only to the Jews.

In Matt. 10:21, he openly predicts what the divisive effect of his teachings will be and says, "And the brother shall deliver up the brother lo death, and the father the child: and the children shall rise up against their parents, and cause them to be put to death. And ye shall be hated of all men for my name's sake."

When we see all the destructive wars that were fought in the name of Christianity, such as, for instance, the Thirty Years War from 1618 to 1648, we can see what he means by this prediction.

During that war, along with hundreds of others, brother did rise up against brother and deliver him unto death, and in fact, about one third of all the Germans were decimated in that bloody, fratricidal religious war, with brother killing brother, and 5/6 of all the housing in the land was destroyed. By no means was this the only war that was fought in the name of Christianity, but throughout

Europe, brother fought brother, Protestant fought Catholic, and the White Man destroyed himself with a vengeance, all in the name of Christ. Today, in Ireland, this is still going on. Christianity, in fact, is an exercise in self-destruction.

An interesting question about all this "believing" business is this: Why should anyone be coerced into believing anything? If you are not freely convinced about a situation on the strength of the evidence presented, or the lack of it, why must you be threatened with torture, vengeance and retribution?

Isn't this the method used by tyrants and gangsters? Isn't this the same method used by the Communists? Either accept communism or we'll shoot you— that is also the code of Jewish communism in Russia, China and elsewhere.

Any belief arrived at under threat or coercion is, in any case, a dishonest one. It is a "belief one might be stampeded into temporarily under the influence of panic or fear, but it is neither a rational conviction, nor can it be an honest belief.

Yet throughout the bible, this gangster method of threat, coercion, and fear is used to get people to believe: either you believe in Christ and all his hocus-pocus or you are going to hell, he says, or better, the Jewish scriptwriters say. What a sleazy operation!

In Matt. 10:34 he says further, "Think not that I am come to send peace on earth; I came not to send peace, but a sword. For I am come to set a man at variance against his father, and the daughter against her mother, and the daughter-in-law against her mother-in- law. And a man's foes shall be they of his own household."

In Matt. 12:25, Jesus really spells out the crux of the Jewish technique for destroying the Gentiles, when he says, "Every kingdom divided against itself is brought to desolation; and every city or house divided against itself shall not stand."

We see in the previous teachings he has already said that he has come to divide, and divide he did. The more these nefarious teachings spread throughout Rome, and the Roman Empire itself, the more the process of dissolution and the ferment of disintegration set in. As these teachings spread and the Roman citizens, good people that they were, fell for all this bad advice, they became confused, they became confounded, and they became divided. They forsook the good judgment that they had built up over the centuries and they abandoned their good senses. They lost all sense of responsibility to their family. Their patriotism was completely undermined, and we know the rest is history. The Roman Empire and the White civilization that it embodied, crumbled, and fell to ruin.

CHAPTER SIXTEEN

CHRIST'S EXISTENCE NOT SUBSTANTIATED BY HISTORICAL EVIDENCE

In the previous material it has been fairly well proven beyond a shadow of a doubt that Christianity is a suicidal philosophy or teaching. If taken seriously enough by its followers it will destroy them, and if a whole race or nation takes it seriously enough and faithfully attempts to follow the teachings of the The Sermon on the Mount then that whole nation will destroy itself.

The great Roman nation, the finest civilization produced by the White Race in classical times, in the first few centuries A.D., did take Christianity seriously, and it did destroy itself, never to rise again.

Where did Christianity originate? If we read the Jewish Bible, the Old Testament and the New Testament, we will not get the correct answers. The fact is Christianity is, and was, a Jewish creation, dreamed up, composed, and promoted by the hierarchy of the Jewish Race, undoubtedly, by the Elders of the Sanhedrin itself.

It is, in fact, an unholy teaching designed to unhinge and derange the White Gentile intellect and to cause him to abandon his real responsibilities of doing that for which Nature created him. It is an unnatural and completely perverted attitude towards the natural surroundings with which Nature has provided us.

Whereas the full impact of it completely destroyed the Roman Empire within less than two centuries after it became the adopted religion of Rome, it is today still an overriding influence hanging like a shadow over affairs and thinking of the White Race throughout the world. It is, therefore, important that we trace its origin, despite the fact that much evidence has been deliberately destroyed and many roadblocks have been placed in the way of objectively even considering the evidence that still survives.

Anyone recapturing his senses and looking at that evidence will find hat its origin is much different from what our church fathers today would have

Christ's Existence Not Substantiated By Historical Evidence

us believe. However, let us take at face value what the church fathers and the "Holy" bible are teaching us today. The first page of the New Testament, Matthew 1, immediately makes it clear that Jesus was a Jew and it traces his genealogy all the way from Abraham through David through Joseph to Christ.

At another place it gives the genealogy of Mary, and makes sure that we are fully aware that she, too, is a Jew.

Here, immediately, the first major contradiction is revealed, glaringly revealed, that is, if Jesus was the Son of God how could he also be the son of Joseph?

Anyway, be that as it may, we now look at the disciples of Jesus and the apostles and we find that Matthew, who supposedly wrote the first book in the New Testament, was also called Levi, son of Altheus and was, as so many Jews are, a tax collector in Capernaum. We find that the Apostle Mark, who wrote the second book of the New Testament, was also called John Mark, he son of Mary, in whose home in Jerusalem the early Christians gathered and he was a cousin of Barnabas. We find, that above all, Mark was also a Jew. We now come to St. Luke, who was probably the only Gentile in the group of twelve. Historians regard him as a Gentile physician. However, he was under the complete dominance of Paul, who was a proselyte Jew, and Luke spent most of his life as a disciple traveling around in the company of Paul, the Jew.

We now come to Apostle John whom we find is also a Jew, along with his brothers Peter and James.

We now come to the Apostle Paul, who changed his name from the real name of Saul, born in tarsus, of Jewish parents, and a man who was reared strictly in the Jewish tradition of the Pharisees of his time. Of the 27 books of the New Testament, it was Paul who is credited with writing 14 of them and credited with writing well over half of the New Testament itself.

And so it goes. Of the 12 disciples that Christ supposedly had, all of them Jews with the possible exception of Luke and as we noted he was completely under the influence of Paul. It is more than passing strange that, according to the New Testament itself, the writers, preachers, and apostles of this "New Teaching," as well as the supposed founder himself, are all Jews with very little exception. It is more than passing strange also that the Jews themselves never accepted this highly suicidal teaching but were tremendously active in promoting and foisting it on the White Gentiles in general, and the great Roman nation in particular.

We do not doubt that these Jewish characters were fanatically active in promoting the suicidal new teaching of Christianity, nor do we doubt that they had not only hundreds but thousands of Jewish helpers that were the "Hidden Hand" that promoted the spread of this teaching among the Romans and

Gentiles in the Roman Empire. There is, however, serious doubt that such a character as Jesus Christ ever lived at all, and there is, however, overwhelming evidence to indicate he did not exist, but was figment of the Jewish of the Jewish imagination.

The beginning of the Christian era found Rome near the height of her civilization. Her supremacy, in the then known world, was pretty much unchallenged and it was the beginning of a long period of peace. To be specific, Pax Romana (Roman Peace) lasted approximately 200 years beginning with the reign of Caesar Augustus. Rome was highly literate; there were many great writers, scholars, historians, sculptors and painters, not to mention other outstanding men of philosophy and learning.

Yet it is highly strange that despite the great commotion and fanfare that supposedly heralded the birth of Christ and also his crucifixion (according to the bible), we find not a single historian nor a single writer of the era who found time to tale note of it in their writings. Outside of the fabricated biblical writings, no Roman historian, no Roman writer, and no Roman play-writer, has left the slightest hint that he had the faintest awareness that this supposedly greatest of all greats was in their very midst and preaching what is claimed the greatest of all the new gospels.

Whereas Caesar left voluminous writings that are still extant today and can be studied by our high school boys and girls, Christ himself, who had supposedly the greatest message to deliver to posterity that the world has ever known, left not the slightest scrap of paper on which he had written a single word. This, in fact, the biblical literature itself confirms and mentions only that once he did write in the sand.

Today we can still study Cicero's great orations and writings. He has left over 800 letters behind that we can study to this day. We can study whole books of what Marcus Aurelius wrote, we can study what Aristotle wrote, what Plato wrote, and scores of others wrote that were contemporary with the first beginning of the Christian era, or preceded it. But strangely there is not a word that is in writing hat can be attributed to Jesus Christ himself.

Furthermore, the Greeks and the Romans of that era, and even previously and afterwards, had developed the art of sculpturing to a fine state. We can find busts of Cicero, of Caesar, Of Marcus Aurelius and innumerable other Greek and Roman dignitaries and lesser lights, but nor one seemed to think it important enough to sculpture a likeness of Jesus Christ. And the reason undoubtedly is there was none to model at the time. There were undoubtedly numerous skilled artists and painters at that time, but again strangely enough none took the time or the interest to paint a likeness of this purportedly greatest of all teachers, who in fact was proclaimed the Son of God come to earth. But no painting was ever made of this man, who, we are told, gathered great multitudes around him and caused great consternation and fear even to King Herod of Judea himself.

Now all of this is very, very strange, when, if, as the Bible claims, the birth of Jesus Christ was ushered in with great fanfare and great proclamations. Angels proclaimed his birth. An exceedingly bright star pointed to his place of birth. In Matt. 2:3, it says, "When Herod, the king, had heard of these things he was troubled and all Jerusalem with him." We can hardly gather from this that no one was aware of the fact that the King of the Jews, the great Messiah, was born, for we are told in the preceding verse that the Wise Men came to King Herod himself saying, "Where is he that is born King of the Jews, for we have seen his star in the East and we are come to worship him." Evidently the event was even lit up with a bright star from heaven. In any case, King Herod, we are told in Matt. 3, was so worried that he sent the Wise Men to Bethlehem to search diligently for the young child to bring it to him so he undoubtedly could have him put to death. As the story further unfolds we learn that Joseph heard of this and quietly slipped out in the night taking with him his wife, the young child and a donkey and departed for Egypt. When Herod found out that he had been tricked it says that he "was exceedingly wroth and sent forth and slew all children that were in Bethlehem, and in all the coasts thereof, from two years old and under."

Now this is a tremendously drastic act for a King to take, that is, to have murdered all the children in the land that were under two years of age. Again we can hardly say that the birth of Jesus was unheralded, unannounced and unobserved, according to the story in the bible. However, it is very, very strange that this act of Herod, as drastic and criminally harsh as it is, is nowhere else recorded in the histories or writings of any of the other numerous writers of the times. All we have is the claims of those people who wrote the New Testament. In fact, whoever wrote the New Testament invented so many claims that are inconsistent with the facts that they even made a rather glaring error by pulling King Herod into the story. History tells us that in the year 1 A.D., when Christ was supposedly born, Herod had already been dead for four years. He could hardly have been disturbed or very wroth about the birth of anybody in the year 1 A.D.

There is further great evidence that Matthew, Mark, Luke and John never wrote any of those chapters that are supposedly attributed to them. What historical evidence can be dug up reveals that they were written much later, not at the time that Jesus supposedly said all those things, but somewhere around 30 to 50 years later by a person or persons unknown. Furthermore, when we compare the first four books of the gospel with each other, which supposedly tell more or less the same story, we find that they contradict each other in so many details that one need only read them for himself to pick them out. I neither have the time, the space, not the inclination to go into all these contradictions. They are too numerous.

I do not contend that it really makes a great deal of difference whether there ever was a Jewish character by the name of Jesus Christ that led to the creation of a new religion to be foisted on the White Race for their destruction. The point is that, in any case, it was the Jews collectively who created and promoted this new teaching upon the White Race and it did destroy the Roman civilization.

Nevertheless, the evidence is overwhelming that these ideas long preceded the Christian era and it was not Christ who came out with them but a Jewish sect called the Essenes who lived on the border of the Dead Sea. It was they who had already evolved the ideas contained in the Sermon on the Mount but have been attributed to Christ. Not only had they evolved the same ideas as set forth in Matthew, Mark, Luke and John, but the wording, the phraseology and the sentences were the same and they preceded the supposed time of the Sermon on the Mount by anywhere from 50 to 150 years.

The Essenes were a Jewish religious group living in approximately the first century B.C. and the first century A.D. We have important sources of their contemporary writings in the historian Josephus and also in the philosopher Philo. They are also mentioned by various other Roman and Greek writers of those times in which their religious teachings are revealed in considerable detail. However, in the last twenty years the thousands of Dead Sea Scrolls, many of which were written by the Essenes themselves, reveal a tremendous amount of insight into their religious teachings, and above all, reveal that they preceded and preempted the Sermon on the Mount word for word, so that the so-called "new" teachings of a figure supposedly appearing from heaven in the year 1 A.D., and preaching during the years 30 to 33 A.D., were neither original nor were they new.

Furthermore, we learn that the Essenes were notable for their communistic society, their extreme piety and purity and their practice of celibacy. They possessed all their worldly goods in common and looked upon private property as an evil which might divert them from sanctity. They engaged in agriculture and handicrafts, considering these occupations less sinful than others. They also practiced baptism, and this practice preceded the Christian era by at least one hundred. So the Christian apostles can hardly be credited with having instituted the ritual of baptism, as is claimed.

Why, the average reader might ask, haven't we been told more about the Essenes if they were the original practitioners of Christianity? There are two good and overriding answers for that. The Christians on their part, although the early Christian fathers were well aware of the Essene teachings and writings, took every measure possible to destroy them and purge them from circulation. The reason being they did not want their presence known because it would undermine their dogma that Christ was the originator of the New teaching. It would make impossible the claim that this was a great new revelation sent forth by God himself amid the hosannas and singing of angels. The Jews, on the other hand, did not want to reveal the presence of the Essenes because they wish to completely hide any connection between the Jews and the new religious teaching that they were about to administer unto the Gentiles. They even went to great lengths to appear hostile to it.

Before I go further into the highly illuminating and highly interesting Dead Sea Scrolls I want to make just one further point that is that the original manuscripts on which the New Testament supposedly based is always alluded to being translated from the "Original Greek." Since the New Testament repeats over and over again and again that Paul spoke to his flock in Jewish and that Jesus spoke in Jewish and that the Apostles were Jewish, why, then, is it that the manuscripts were all in Greek?

The historical facts add up to this: the Jewish hierarchy and undoubtedly the whole conspiracy was well coordinated and had many, many members and co-workers. It was not written at the time of Christ at all, but the movement was given great promotion by the combined efforts of the Jewish nation. As they organized and promoted their ideas further, these were reduced to writing considerably later than the years 30 to 33 A.D., when Christ supposedly came out with these startlingly and "new" revelations. The conclusions are that they were written by Jewish persons whose identity we shall never know and were written by collectively by many authors, were revised from time to time and not only in their original formation and formulation but have been revised time and time again throughout the centuries to become more effective and persuasive propaganda. However, we want to go further into the teachings of the Essenes and who they were and why their particular teachings were pounced upon by the Jews to be formulated into a well distilled poisonous brew and then fed to the Gentiles.

The Dead Sea Scrolls, which are more numerous and much more revealing than the Jewish press of today has informed us tell us much about the teachings and the life of the Essenes. One of the important things that they tell us about the Essenes is that they vanished from the face of the earth after about two centuries of existence and the termination date being somewhere around the year 100 A.D. They were, needless to say, only a very small sect of the Jewish tribes and not a part of the Jewish conspiracy as such. Being outside of the mainstream of Jewish activity and thought, the Jews nevertheless observed from them that this kind of teaching could ruin and destroy a people. The Jews, looking for a way to destroy the Roman nation, who in the year 70 A.D. had destroyed and leveled Jerusalem to the ground, noted well what these teachings were and decided to perpetuate them on the Romans.

Essenism was really a revolutionary new form of social order, an ideal cooperative commonwealth in miniature. Instead of the Messiah, the ideal of the Essenes was the "Teacher of Righteousness." They established a new cooperative communitarian brotherhood and they were the first religious society to establish and observe the sacraments of baptism and the eucharistic meal. Most important of all they were the firs group to condemn and abolish the age-old institution of human slavery. Furthermore, the "Teacher of Righteousness" as promulgated by the Essenes may not have been the first pacifist in history, but he was the first to implement his pacifist theories with an overall practical measure, which if generally adopted, would abolish war. This, of course, was a wonderful religion for the Jews to sell to the Romans, for if they convert the Romans into submissive pacifists they could certainly soon thereafter dominate them in full. And this they did.

The Essenes lived in the area of Qumran near the Dead Sea and according to Philo, the Jewish Philosopher and writer contemporary of that age, "the Essene brotherhood would not allow the manufacture of any weapons or allow within their community any maker of arrows, spears, swords or any manufacture of engines of war, nor any man occupied with a military avocation, or even with peaceful practices which might easily be converted to mischief." Not only does Philo tell us about the Essenes, but also Josephus and Pliny, both contemporary historians, tell us much about the Essenes.

As mentioned before, much is emerging also from the study of the Dead Sea Scrolls. The overriding fact that emerges from the study of the writings of the historians of that time and the Dead Sea Scrolls is this tremendously significant fact: namely that the beliefs, teachings, and practices attributed to Jesus Christ, although not exactly identical in all respects with those of the Essene school, were nevertheless, closer to those of the Essenes than to those of the Bishops of the Ecumenical Council which determined the Nicene Creed of orthodox Christianity.

So we can come to the obvious conclusion that the Christian beliefs and doctrines as supposedly enunciated by Christ in the Sermon on the Mount did not originate at all at that time but at least 100 years earlier from a Jewish sect called the Essenes living near the Dead Sea; that the Elders of Sanhedrin recognized this teaching as being deadly and suicidal; that they further took this doctrine and distilled and refined it into a working creed; the Jews then, with a great deal of energy and tremendous amounts of propaganda (in which they excel), promoted and distributed this poisonous doctrine among the Romans.

Setting this creed down in writing in what is now called the New Testament evolved over the next several centuries. It was written by persons unknown to us today but undoubtedly of Jewish origin. Furthermore, to give it a mystical and heavenly sent deification, they invented the person of Jesus Christ, and claimed that he was the Son of God. Then, having laid the groundwork for this new church, they consolidated that power at a meeting in Nicene, where the creation of the new church was solidified, the creed formalized and given official sanctification.

Thus, in short, was launched the new church and the new religion of "Jesus Christ" which was fabricated out of thin air. Not a single trace of the Jesus Christ personage can be found in authentic history. Nevertheless, this newly fabricated hoax of Jesus Christ, the Son of God this idea, with all its suicidal doctrines, was soon to pull down in ruins the great Roman Empire and the great White civilization that went with it.

Never again did the White Race shake off the control if the Jews. Never again did the White Man regain control of his own thinking, of his own religion, his own finances, nor his own government. Unto this day the White Race has not regained control of its own destiny.

It is the unalterable goal of our new religion, Creativity, and the CHURCH OF THE CREATOR, to again have the White Man regain unconditional control of his own destiny and his own future.

To do this we, first of all, have to straighten out the White Man's thinking. That is what this book is all about.

CHAPTER SEVENTEEN

A CLOSER LOOK AT THE JUDEO-CHRISTIAN HOAX

We have reviewed the Old Testament and found it to be basically a collection of dirty stories about dirty, whore-mongering Jews, such as Abraham, Judah, David, Solomon and many others. We have taken a closer look at the New Testament and found that it, too, was written by a passel of Jews. Whereas the Old Testament served as a rallying creed for the unification of the Jewish race, we find that the New Testament doing just the opposite for the White Race, namely it was designed to confuse, confound, divide and disintegrate the White Race by overwhelming it with so much drivel and with such a multitude of bad advice as to leave the White Race naked and defenseless before the rapacious Jew.

In this chapter I want to examine further the old Judeo-Christian hoax as set forth in both the Old and the New Testament, since combined, they constitute the White Man's bible. The bible in turn is the foundation of his religion, called Christianity, which has been such an unfortunate catastrophe for the White Man during the last 2,000 years of his history.

The last thing the White Race needs for its survival is a collection of bad advice. This, however, is exactly what the Christian religion does give the White Man a multitude of just outright bad and suicidal advice that if followed, will most surely destroy those that embrace it. Christianity despises facts, it despises evidence and reasoning. It despises thinking men. It wants "believing" sheep. It loves gullible fools. Christ is quoted as saying, "Unless ye become like little children, ye shall not enter into the kingdom of heaven." It wants to reduce everyone to a simple childlike condition where they are easily duped and misled to believe just about anything. It wants to reduce the creative, productive, heroic and energetic White Race down to where they are meek and submissive fools, easily managed, easily controlled and easily enslaved.

Christianity is a treacherous mental snare. It rapes the minds of otherwise intelligent men. Once it has the majority under its control it then resorts to force,

A Closer Look At The Judeo-Christian Hoax

if necessary, to break and destroy those who will still insist upon thinking for themselves.

When that great early scientist, Galileo, in 1632 brought logical evidence to show that the earth revolved around the sun and that the sun itself was part of a vast inter-stellar system, it was the Christian church which immediately was aroused to stop this advance in scientific thinking. In the following year Galileo was summoned to Rome, where he was examined by the Inquisition, humiliated and forced to kneel before a vast assembly and renounce his findings. This is only one of the thousands of cases where the Christian religion used force and terror to stifle and paralyze the minds of thinking men.

Christianity thrives on lies. It has built a whole network of lies, one lay parlayed upon another, one lie designed to seemingly substantiate another, in and endless chain, until the average person is confused and so overwhelmed by the massiveness of it all that his is psychologically browbeaten into accepting the whole carload of lies as being God's unalterable truth.

Here is one of the first and most obvious lies— one that even a child can see through— namely that every word in the bible was God's unalterable word, being exactly as he has set it down and not a letter having been changed. It is obvious to even the most simple-minded person that the bible has been changed continuously and repeatedly. For instance, we have the Vulgate Edition of the bible for the Catholics, we have the King James Version for the "Fundamentalist" Christians, we have the Revised Standard Version for the more modern Christians, and just the other day I went to the bookstore and bought the New English bible which throws all the others overboard and puts it into a "more readable prose." In going back to the encyclopedia I find that the bible has been translated from the Greek into the Latin, from the Latin into English, German, and a multitude of other languages. Whatever version these translations came out as was completely dependent upon the whim and interpretation of the translator.

In fact, the encyclopedia says further that the bible has, over the last 1,000 and some years of its existence, had more that 100,000 changes made in it, but then adds quickly and apologetically that only five percent of these were "significant." It would seem to me that any changes in the "unalterable word of God" would be significant and 100,000 changes would render it a completely different animal, to say the least. But even taking the five percent figure as such, that would still make 5,000 significant changes spread over approximately 1,000 pages of the bible. That would leave 95 so-called "insignificant" changes and five significant changes per page. It doesn't take a great deal of brains to conclude that the bible has certainly been changed continuously and significantly and to claim it has been unaltered from the very beginning is only one major lie in the whole chain to follow.

The whole network of the bible itself is shot through with contradictions and inconsistencies of what it says in itself, one part with another. In other words, the bible is continually contradicting itself and making a liar of itself. Not only that, but the whole story is so illogical and ludicrous that even as a teen-ager a number of perplexing questions arose in my mind.

One of the first of these was that why, if God was such a kind and loving God, were most of the people that he had made with such tender loving care, were these people, by and large, all going to hell? It is still a good question, basic and fundamental, and it is one that no preacher, no matter how much double-talk he has given me, has ever successfully answered.

When we examine the whole story structure as set forth in the Old Testament we find something like the following, if we're gullible enough to believe the Jewish scriptwriters who wrote it:

In the beginning everything was void and God was evidently just floating around in this void with nothing to do, nothing to think about, nothing to see (there was no light). After being in suspended animation for billions and billions and billions of years like that, suddenly only about

6,000 years ago he got the idea of creating heaven and earth. It didn't say that he created hell, but evidently he must have created it at the same time, with the idea of putting somebody in it in the future. Since that is where most people were destined to go, he must have created an extra large hell, comparatively.

In any case, on the sixth day he created man in his own image, blessed him, and put him in the Garden of Eden. We get the impression that it was God's original intention to have man live in the Garden of Eden forever. However, then a curious thing happened. Adam and Eve hadn't been in this garden for more than a day when they were booby-trapped into eating some forbidden fruit. Why the tree was there in the first place, why it was such a crime to eat its fruit, why the Lord put the serpent there to encourage and persuade them into eating the fruit, why the good Lord didn't give Adam and Eve more sense to be taken in by the serpent, no one has ever explained to me.

In any case, for this "horrible" crime of eating the fruit from this particular tree, evidently the Lord's whole place for the human race changed instantly, we are being led to believe by the Jewish scriptwriters. He was angry with Adam and Eve for this little blunder, and no longer was he a forgiving and loving God, but instead in anger he drove them out of the Garden of Eden, and cursed them "to earn their bread by the sweat of their brow". From this little insignificant incident, we are told, the whole human race is now cursed with the "original sin" of Adam and Eve.

As ludicrous as this story is, a multitude of logical questions arise. Since, we are told, the Lord knows all, sees all, knows the future as well as the past,

A Closer Look At The Judeo-Christian Hoax

and not a hair falls from our head nor a sparrow from the roof without him knowing it, how does it happen that he didn't know long in advance that Adam and Eve were going to do just what they did do, and that he was going to drive them out of the Garden of Eden? He must have known this and planned it that way before he even created them, or anything else. If he did know all this in advance, and in fact, he constructed the whole universe, including the creatures of mankind, God cannot very well escape the responsibility of having planned it that way. After all, mankind was a creation of God himself, who knows all, sees all, knows everything in the future, forward and backward. If man turned out to be such a dastardly sinner, then we must also assume that God designed him that way and intended him to be that way.

As mankind multiplied, so the story continues, he became exceedingly "sinful" and God decided that he would drown them all except for one family, namely that of Noah. The kind and loving God, the one we are told loves us all, then set about to drown all these people like a miserable bunch of rats. This, according to one version of the Bible that I have (that places dates on everything) occurred in the year 2,348 B.C., in a deluge that lasted 40 days and 40 nights.

According to the Jewish scriptwriters that wrote this ridiculous story, Noah being forewarned by the Lord, built an ark and took into it every living thing "of all flesh, both of fowl, and of cattle, and of every creeping thing that creepeth upon the earth." When we consider that there are 10 million species of insects alone, not to mention the number of reptiles, birds, animals and what have you, this story certainly becomes more implausible than the story of Alice-in- Wonderland.

Nor does the fact that there is absolutely no evidence that the whole earth was covered with water in the year 2,348 B.C. or thereabouts particularly bother these Jewish scriptwriters, nor all these preachers that go about spouting these claims. Contemporary Egyptian history mentions no such floods.

How contradictory all this is with the evidence of Nature before us! When we look at the Grand Canyon, for instance, that has been eroding in its channels for many millions of years, when we look at the glaciers that have been around for hundreds of thousands of years, when we look at the evolvement of the different species such as horses, mastodons, or the saber-tooth tiger, or the more recent historical development of man himself that goes back far beyond the 2,348 B.C., a person just has to simply take leave of his senses, become gullible like a child, in order to believe such nonsense.

The story then goes on, and soon Abraham, Isaac and Jacob, the Patriarchs of the Jewish race appear upon the scene. According to their own stories these people were all a bunch of moral profligates as we have read about in the chapters previously. But according to the Jewish scriptwriters, God took a special fancy to this group and made all kinds of lavish far-reaching, and overly generous promises to them and to their seed. He made a special sweetheart arrangement with them. The Jews therewith claim that they have a special covenant with God, that they are the chosen people and that they have the inside track with the Lord himself. One of their major organizations, the B'nai B'rith means "Sons of the Covenant."

Again he question arises, why would the Lord, who is supposed to be so righteous, so just, and so wise, make a special sweetheart arrangement with such a s group of perfidious cutthroats, scoundrels, whoremongers, pimps and prostitutes, such as, e.g. Abraham and Sarah?

It's a great story for the Jews, but a pretty stupid story for us Gentiles to incorporate into "our" religion.

So far we find that God has made a bad mistake with Adam and Eve and has driven them out of the Garden of Eden. Their seed evidently turned out badly. He tried to correct this second mistake by drowning all except for one family.

Evidently that was a bad choice also, because Noah's progeny turned out so badly that the Lord decided something drastic had to be done again, short of drowning them all the second time. Since mankind was so bad, so wicked and so sinful he decided to do something really meaningful.

In the second part of the bible (which is the New Testament) it says that the Holy Ghost descended upon the Virgin Mary and she became pregnant. She conceived "God's only begotten Son" who was to save mankind from this horrible fate, evidently going to hell. This is indeed a droll and fantastic story. To think that this all powerful Creator, who could create the earth, and the sun, and the milky way, and galaxies billions of light years away, a universe so vast in which the earth is only a mere speck, and man upon it is more like an atom, that such a supernatural being would have to stoop to the idea of having intercourse with an earthly creature, and a married Jewish woman at that. All this so that she could raise up his son, only to have him nailed to the cross, seems so fantastically farfetched and idiotic that you sometimes wonder about the sanity of the human race as a whole.

In any case, that is the story, as set forth by the Jewish scriptwriters of unknown origin, and hundreds of millions of people have been gullible enough to swallow it.

The whole idea of "he died for own sins" in itself is not a very reasonable one. It is something as if for an instance, a bunch of niggers commit a number of murders, thefts and crimes, and burn down the city of Detroit, and then you took a good upstanding White citizen, humiliated him, spat upon him, mailed him to the cross, and then drove a spear into his side to make his blood run, and this was to "atone" those niggers having committed all those crimes. What kind of justice is that? How would this atone for their crimes? How would that teach those niggers a lesson in any way, shape or form? This whole story about "He died for our sins" is about as ridiculous and as idiotic as the example I just quoted.

In any case, evidently 2,000 years later, looking back on it now, we certainly can't say that this strange humiliating act that the Lord condescended to in order "to save mankind" has worked, and evidently we can chalk up another blooper and failure against the workings of God.

It seems as though throughout the thread and story of the bible, our Creator is just blundering from one bad mistake to another, and none of the programs seem to work out the way they should.

When we contrast this with the real world and the laws of Nature, how completely in conflict this is with what our common sense, our eyes and our ears tell us. It s completely unthinkable that any of the laws of Nature have ever broken down, or have ever failed, or have ever been in conflict with each other, We know of no case where the law of gravity was suspended, not the laws of light, nor the laws of electricity, or he laws of magnetism, nor were any other laws of Nature ever in conflict with each other, nor did they fail to work. In fact, Nature's laws have been performing flawlessly, immutably and inexorably from time immemorial, and will undoubtedly continue to do so in all eternity.

In any case, if we just use an ounce of common sense and use the intelligence with which Nature has so gratuitously endowed us, we can't help but come to the conclusion that Christ's appearance on earth and being nailed to the cross did not do any great wonders for mankind. An overwhelming contradiction that manifests itself here is that the Jews (who wrote the New Testament) sold this story to the White people only, and the Jewish race, who are supposedly God's chosen and God's favored, never did believe in Christ. Ask some preacher to explain this idiotic contradiction to you, and he'll give you an hour's worth of double talk.

Therefore another obvious contradiction looms before our eyes, and that is, why would the Jew's be God's chosen people, why would Christ, who is God's son, be made to die on the cross, in order to "save mankind" and yet at the same time fail to convince the Jews, God's chosen people? The whole thing doesn't make sense. Furthermore, in the first chapter of Matthew it makes it abundantly clear that Christ was a direct descendant from Abraham, Isaac and Jacob through those whore-mongering kings of David and Solomon and right on through to Joseph, Christ's father. Furthermore, it makes it quite clear that Christ was a circumcised Jew (in Luke 2:21). It says, "when eight days were accomplished for circumcising the child, his name was called Jesus." We, therefore, have the New Testament saying that Christ was a Jew, descendant in the long lineage from Abraham, Isaac and Jacob. At the same time we are told, however, that he was called the son of God. At the same time God's "chosen" didn't believe it. A rather contradictory and a most ridiculous story, to say the least.

So here is the White Man, saddled with a religion that is in the first part overwhelming about Jews and God's infatuation with that perfidious parasitic race; and in the second part, of God's impregnating and fertilizing a Jewish married woman, who has a son, supposedly the Son of God, but at the same time he is the son of Joseph, and proudly having his male lineage listed all the way back to Abraham, Isaac and Jacob. Then we have the situation where the Jews themselves don't believe the second part of the story, namely the New Testament, but by a huge concerted effort that lasted approximately 300 years they finally convinced the White Roman civilization that this was to be their new religion. And the White Man bought it.

How silly can you get?

Preachers and missionaries will make a big to-do about how Christ gave us "everlasting life." We are supposed to be so eternally and forever grateful for this great magnanimous gift. This again is completely contrary to what we see in Nature. We know of no species, of no individual that Nature has ever given "everlasting life" anywhere, at any time. There just isn't a single shred of evidence to back up any of this nonsense. Most plants live only one season, produce their seed and die, only to have a new generation come up in the following spring. Most mammals like deer, rabbits, coyotes, etc., live only a matter of one to two to perhaps six years on average, and die. During their life period they have produced enough offspring to carry on the species. There is not a shred of evidence that man fares differently.

In any case, who said that we would want everlasting life, even if we could have the choice, especially if there might be a dismal and torturous hell waiting for us and we can't terminate the period of our torture? Or even if there was such a place as heaven to go to, who says that we are especially fond of playing the harp forever and praising the Lord?

It would seem to me that such indulgence could get awfully boring after a relatively short time. Furthermore, with the bible telling us most of us are going to go to hell anyway, probably about 99 percent, what is so great about everlasting life? The answer is nothing, of course, and it is a great big Jewish hoax. There just isn't a single shred of evidence to back it up. It is contrary to all observations that we have witnessed in Nature, and we can chalk this down, too, as another one of the Jewish network of lies.

When it comes to frightening and terrorizing the minds of his victims with the fiendish and hideous characteristics of hell, the details are brutal and vivid. The great "loving" God who created us all, had evidently planned from the beginning to send 99 percent of us to a confined torture chamber where we could be forever tortured in a blazing fire from which there is no escape.

When it comes to heaven, however, the details are completely missing, in fact the description, except for how it's lined with gold and precious stones and all that, are pretty nebulous. Evidently our main preoccupation will be praising the Lord. I can't think of anything more boring and more ungodlike than to have a huge herd of captive subjects rendering praise day and night to their master. How tyrannical!

We are continually told in the bible that we should be meek and not vain and that any pride that we might have is sinful. Yet how vainglorious is our supposed Creator? Here he is, creating a huge herd, a captive audience, that will spend the next millions of years doing practically nothing but mouthing praise. If this is a Godlike attribute then it contradicts all the other values that are proscribed in the bible.

On the other hand, it then pictures us as angels playing a harp, perhaps. Frankly, I have never looked forward with any great anticipation towards playing a harp. If that were such a wonderful and joyous pastime I would have purchased one a long time ago, but I don't see very many other people particularly enraptured about playing a harp. So, what else is there to do in heaven? Do we eat? Do we wear clothes? Do we sleep? Are we solid? Are we a bunch of spirits flitting through the ether? Do we have wings? The only answer is we don't know any of these things. It is all very vague, very hazy, very nebulous.

And as to the location of this wonderful heaven that we're supposed to be knocking ourselves out for, just where is it located? Is it a thousand miles above the earth? A million miles below the earth? A hundred million miles away? Is it near the sun? Is it in this galaxy? Is it really anywhere? And again the answer is vague and nebulous.

Jesus is quoted as saying, "Heaven and earth shall pass away, but my word shall never pass away." Are we then to understand that heaven is only temporary? Well, some say there is a second heaven. So, is it also temporary, or what? It is all very sketchy, very mysterious, very muddy and very dubious. It has all come down to us from a hundred hand downs of second hand hearsay that has been revised and rewritten and repatched a hundred thousand times, and we are supposed to take it all as "the Gospel truth."

It would seem to me that if the difference between doing the right thing and the wrong thing would mean between going to heaven and eternal hellfire that God would have made it abundantly clear what it is that he wants us to do. If I had a hired man and gave him the alternatives, that by doing the right thing he would be rewarded with a million dollars, but if he did the wrong thing, I would shoot him, then the least thing I could do would be to make it crystal

Nature's Eternal Religion

clear what it is he must do and what he must not do.

Similarly, if what the bible says has any validity at all (and it does not) then God would certainly not have confused us with a thousand differing religions, Mohammedanism, Judaism, Mormonism, Confucianism, Christianity and a host of lesser creeds. He most certainly would not have splintered the Christian religion into a thousand different branches, such as Catholics, Unitarians, Methodists, Holy Rollers, and what have you, all of which denounce and discredit each other. Even if you wanted to do the right thing, who is on the right track? The Mohammedans? The Jews who don't believe in Christianity? From such a mass of confusion, how could you possibly ever tell?

The whole mess of garbage, of course, breaks down miserably.

We return to our senses, take a breath of cool clean air and go back to the laws of Nature, which are real, which are in harmony, which are eternal. All truth and all knowledge originates from our observations of the laws of Nature.

What these "born again" Christians will try to trap you with is: "How do you explain all the universe around you? Somebody had to make all this." If they are a more sophisticated philosopher, they will phrase it this way: "There has to be a first cause and this first cause is God." This is a lame assumption and a most unwarranted presumption. We have no evidence whatsoever that this presumption has any basis in fact. We don't know but that the universe has not been here forever and will be here forever in the future. Whereas the scenes of Nature are eternally changing, it is nevertheless always the same and the laws of Nature itself have never changed. They are eternal.

In fact, as far as "time" is concerned we don't even know what the term itself means except as it is related to the movements of the planets or some other moving object. It can be argued just as effectively that the universe has always been here, as to say that God has always been here. In answer to the argument that somebody had to create all this, it can just as validly be argued that well, then somebody else had to create God in the first place. It is just as reasonable to assume that the universe, constantly changing as it is, could not suddenly spring into existence out of nothing as that the Creator sprang out of nothing. It makes just as much sense to argue that somebody first had to create God as it does to argue that somebody first had to create the universe.

So we are left with the obvious. The answer is simply we don't know how it all started if there ever was a beginning. The universe, as far as we know, has always been here. About the mystery of a God, or Gods, we have no evidence, we know nothing, and as far as anyone can tell there are thousands of myths and stories and fairy tales about Gods and Goddesses, Spirits and Angels, and Devils and Fairies and Ghosts and Gremlins, but as far as any evidence is concerned, all we know is that they are only a product of man's fertile imagination.

To succumb to the Christian philosophy is to indulge in a cowardly flight from reality, to escape to an Alice-in-Wonderland fantasy world, and to destroy reason and common sense. We repeat: Christianity despises fact, evidence and reasoning. Christianity despises logic. To become a Christian is to succumb to the perversion of one's mind by Jewish mind manipulation. A "born again" Christian is a pervert. He has had his instincts warped, his mind unhinged, and his total outlook on life, outlook on sex, and on the survival of his kind, completely perverted from that, which, as a natural human being, he was originally created by Nature. He becomes a destroyer of his own race.

Although the matter of becoming a Christian is a matter of degree, and very few people of the White Race actually take it seriously, nevertheless, everybody pretty well passively consents to its domination of our outlook and our society. This in itself is a very significant concession and one that has had catastrophic effects on the culture, government, and outlook of the White Race over the last 2,000 years. And herein lies the White Man's dilemma.

In politics, in business, in warfare, and in all his other actions, he uses the instincts and common sense with which Nature endowed him so richly. He invokes the laws of survival, the laws of Nature, and those of his own experience. Then he goes to church on Sunday and has his brains re-manipulated to repudiate all his common sense. He goes off into orbit into an unreal, nebulous world. His brain slips a cog and completely derails from reality.

He comes out confused and conscience stricken, betwixt and between, his brain in limbo, to again tackle the problems of the world on Monday. He remains torn, betwixt and between two incompatible worlds the world of reality and an unreal world as prescribed by a bunch of Jewish scriptwriters of unknown identity. His mind is paralyzed with the fear of hell, that fiery pit, that ghastly confined torture chamber prepared by your kind, loving, merciful, gracious (and Jewish) God, for 99 percent of his "beloved" victims.

At this time we might as well also raise the question: just when did God, "in his great wisdom", create hell and the devil? Was it on the first day when he created heaven and earth? Did Christ, one of the Holy Trinity, "who always was," and undoubtedly must have existed at the time hell was created, did he also participate in the designing and creation of hell? Since God knows all, sees all, both forwards and backwards, did he not therefore plan sending all these human beings that he was creating into hell sometime in the future so that he could torture them at will?

Taking a closer look at the devil, we are given to understand that this also was an accident, that God really created him as an angel but that "he fell." As a result of this unexplained little accident we have a serious antagonist on the other side from God, who is vying, it seems, in a game of cat and mouse to corral more of us poor unfortunate pawns into his side of the fence than God is able to get on his side of the fence. The way the story is told to us it would seem that God is desperately trying to save us all for heaven, but the devil is more clever and more devious and more successful ion inveigling us into hell. It would seem obvious that God is losing and his "accident" is winning.

What a preposterous and droll situation this is! Here we are led to believe that God is infallible, all knowing, not a hair falls from our

head but what he is in control and in charge, yet in all the major points he seems to have goofed, all to our, the human beings, detriment.

First of all Adam and Eve went wrong on the first day and fell into a booby trap that God had evidently set. Secondly he had to drown all the millions of offspring that ensued, except for one family. Then they all went badly anyway. This droll story then goes on to tell us that he had to father a son from a married Jewess by the name of Mary and had him nailed to the cross and bled dry because that was supposed to save us miserable sinners from going to hell. But after 2,000 years that evidently went far wrong also, since today we find fewer people than ever believing in Christianity anymore, and the Jews and communists are taking over the world. But in any case, the proposition that here is this all-knowing infallible God, who, by a quirk of an accident, has created a devil instead of an angel. This devil is now a hot competitor of his, and according to the story ion the bible, is going to win the game, crowding human beings into his hell (created by God) way beyond anything that the original Creator will be able to salvage for his heaven. Can you think of anything more ludicrous? As a famous general once said, anyone that will believe that kind of cock-and-bull story will believe anything.

Nevertheless, we find that the bible has been written, and hundreds of millions of members of the White Race have succumbed to it. There certainly must be some motive behind it other than telling silly stories, and there is.

The answer becomes fairly obvious when we look at (a) who wrote both the Old and the New Testaments and (b) who benefited thereby. When we consider that the Old and the New Testament were both written by a passel of slimy Jews, then the whole nefarious conspiracy begins to make sense.

We have already reviewed the treacherous and conspiratorial nature of the Jewish Race over the thousands of years. We have also reviewed their history and how, when the Romans destroyed

Jerusalem, they came back on the Romans, not by force of arms, but by treachery, trickery, conniving. By foisting upon the once proud and powerful Roman Empire the suicidal Christian religion, they destroyed Rome. We all know that a thousand years of the Dark Ages followed the collapse of Rome, during which the White Race wallowed in ignorance, poverty and superstition. We know that when the White Race did finally extricate itself (partially) from this perversion of the mind, (during the Renaissance) the Jew was there in his midst, still in control of the White Man's finances, his government and his religion.

We know that the Romans, who produced the greatest civilization of ancient times, and probably of all time, 2,000 years ago were dominant without competition in the then known world. We know that this was one of the fines manifestations of the energetic and productive characteristics of the White Race. We are also aware of the fact that once this great proud race succumbed to the perfidious and treacherous Christian teaching, it was never again the same, and that the White Race has never been in charge of its destiny.

The parasitic Jew has been in charge of the world ever since.

The answer is therefore quite obvious that Christianity has been, and is today, a powerful tool used by the conniving and conspiratorial Jewish race to overcome, disintegrate, and destroy the great White Race. It is being used more flagrantly than ever today to mongrelize and hasten the White Man's destruction to that he can be more permanently enslaved and thereby become a meek and humble and yet productive beast of burden for the parasitic Jew.

In short: the Jew invented Christianity, perpetuated it upon the White Race in order that he could turn him into a perfect "goyim," his term for submissive cattle.

Yes, that is my conclusion and that is my verdict. It is the only conclusion that makes any sense.

The time is long overripe for the White Man to have a religion of his own, one that was formulated by White Men, and one that was designed for the survival, expansion and advancement of the White Race. It is the overriding purpose of this book to lay the groundwork for such a religion.

CHAPTER EIGHTEEN

THE TALMUD

The real essence of the Jewish creed is not the Old Testament as such, not the Pentateuch, or the Book of Moses, but the basic creed as set forth in the Talmud. To the outside world, the Jews profess to be attached to the Old Testament. Again, this is partial deception and also a partial smoke screen for their real program. When Jewish boys and girls reach the age of thirteen, it is not the Old Testament that they pursue, look to for guidance, but by this time they have a completed a thorough study and indoctrination course of the Talmud. It is their real Bible.

The Jews claim that whereas Moses received the written law from God on Mount Sinai on tables of stone, he also received interpretations of it, or the "oral law," at the same time. They claim this is the reason why Moses remained so long on the mountain, since God could have given him the written law in one day. Whereas all this again is so much fiction and Jewish invention, nevertheless it is significant to note their explanation of the origin of their creed.

Moses is said in turn to have transmitted this oral law to Joshua; Joshua in turn supposedly transmitted it to the seventy Elders; these Elders then passed it on to the Prophets, and the Prophets to the Great Synagogue. The Jews then claim it was later transmitted successively to certain Rabbis until it was no longer possible to retain it orally and they began to put it down in writing.

This again is their mythical explanation of the origin of their sacred creed. It is, of course, not based on any fact. Like the rest of their self-concocted history, it is pure myth. It is very doubtful whether characters such as Moses or Joshua even existed. Nevertheless, going back to historical sources, it is well know that before the advent of Christianity, schools existed in Palestine in which "sacred: Jewish literature was taught. The commentaries of the doctors of law were noted down on charts and lists as an aid to memory, and these collected together formed the beginnings of the Jewish Talmud.

There is a long history from here on out as to its compilation and its growth to the present day Talmud. I do not want to take up the space to go into

The Talmud

all the complicated machinations that took place in order to build it up to its present huge volumes.

Suffice it to say that the Mischnah is the foundation and the principle part of the whole Talmud. This book was accepted by the Jews everywhere and was recognized as their authentic code of law. With the passing of time, the interpretations of this code increased and disputations and decisions of the doctors of the law concerning the Mischnah were written down. These writings, which were interpretations of the law, constitute another part of the Talmud called the Gemarah. In total therefore, these two parts, namely the Mischnah, which serves as the text of the Jewish law, followed by the Gemarah which serves as an analysis and interpretation of that law, constitute the Jewish Talmud.

By the year 500 A.D. the Talmud was more or less compiled in its present form. Even at that time there were two main Talmuds used by the Jews, one was the Palestinian Talmud, and the other was the Babylonian Talmud, of which the latter, the Babylonian Talmud, was the more comprehensive. It was not compiled by any one person nor at any one time, but many prominent Jewish leaders labored over it for many years.

The Babylonian Talmud is the one that is today accepted by the majority of Jews, but not all. When we refer to the Talmud in this chapter, we will be talking basically about the Babylonian Talmud.

Thus the Mischnah, the Gemarah, Tosephoth, and the Perusch Hamischnaioth of Maimonides, all collected into, constitute a vast work which is called the Talmud. The complete Talmud contains sixty-three books in five hundred and twenty-four chapters.

It is this vast piece of literature, which contains much trash and also much filth, that has nevertheless woven into, and throughout the length of it, the basic Jewish teaching. It lays down the line for the destruction of the Gentile peoples of the world with all its wealth, the enslavement of all peoples. It basically contains all the Jewish laws in their relationships between each other, and also in relationship of the Jews towards the Gentiles.

The Talmud also contains much detailed advice about the use of fruits, seeds, herbs, trees, etc. It goes into much detail about Jewish festivals, about when they are to begin, when they are to be ended and how they are to be celebrated. It has a voluminous amount of law treating the subject op marriage, and repudiation of wives, their duties, relationships, sickness and many other subjects in this field.

The fields that it covers is almost unlimited. It takes in the penalties and compensations in regards to damages. It makes a big to do about sacrifices and sacred rites and holy days. It also goes into the subject of purifications in great detail.

Nature's Eternal Religion

The Talmud further goes into great length about the laws themselves. It has a treatment of laws concerning buying and selling, laws concerning real estate and commerce. It goes into the treatment of courts and their proceedings and the punishment of capital crimes. It also deals the different kinds of oaths and the breaking thereof. It has a collection of traditional laws and decisions gathered from the testimonies of their distinguished scholars and Jewish teachers.

The books go on and on. There is hardly a subject that is not covered as far as the life of a Jew is concerned. Much of it is trivial, much of its tremendously boring. Nevertheless, threaded throughout the Talmud is the basic philosophy and creed of the Jew himself that makes such a dangerous parasite to every society he bores into.

It is not my purpose to spend too much time on the massive detail embodied in the compendium of the books of the Talmud. Suffice it to say that this work has always been regarded by the Jews as holy. They have also held it, and still hold it, as more important

that the so-called sacred scriptures. The Talmud itself shows this very clearly. In one part it says "Those who devote themselves to reading the Bible exercise a certain virtue, but nor very much; those who study the Mischnah exercise virtue for which they will receive a reward; those, however, who take upon themselves to study the Gemarah exercise the highest virtue."

In another part of the Talmud it says "The Sacred Scripture is like water, the Mischnah wine, and the Gemarah aromatic wine."

The following is a well-known and highly praised opinion in the writings of the Rabbis: "My son, give heed to the words of the scribes rather than to the words of the law." In other words, the young Jew being trained for his prospective role and part in the Jewish world conspiracy is told over and over again that he musty pay close attention to the teachings of the Talmud rather than the written law of the Old Testament itself. Whereas both are part of their underlying religious creed, the teachings of the Talmud prevail and are predominant.

Throughout the Talmud the word Goi is used in referring to the Gentiles and in particular to the White Gentiles and the Romans. This is their derogatory term for the word cattle, or beast, and is sometimes spelled Goyim. From early childhood the Jews are taught that a Gentile, any Gentile, is a beast and is to be treated the same as they would treat cattle. Interwoven throughout the teaching of the Talmud is the idea of hostility and hatred towards the Goyim.

Although the Talmud was not compiled until the year 500 A.D., much of it was written before the Christian era and at the time when Rome was at its height. The policy of the parasitic Jews from time immemorial has always

188

The Talmud

been to vent their fiercest hate against the dominant and prevailing White power structure. It is therefore not surprising that much of the hate in the Talmud is directed against Rome directly.

When Babylon was at its height their most violent hatred was directed against Babylon. After they had destroyed Babylon their most vehement hatred was directed against the Romans. As always the Jews invade and disperse themselves throughout a healthy White productive society. Then they scream persecution. They called the Romans tyrants. They claimed that the Romans held captive the children of Israel. The Jews frantically exhorted their people that only by the destruction of the Romans would the Jews be freed from what they call their fourth captivity. They urged therefore, that every Jew was bound to do all that he could to destroy this impious kingdom of the Edomites (Rome), which ruled the whole world.

Since, however, it is not always and everywhere possible to effect this extermination of the Goyim, the Talmud orders that they should be attacked at least indirectly, namely by injuring them in every possible way, and by thus lessening their power, help towards their ultimate destruction. Wherever possible, a Jew should kill the Goyim, and do so without mercy, the Talmud says.

Their hatred for Rome knew no bounds. They say that the Princetom, whose chief city is Rome, is the one to be hated most of all by the Jews. They call it the Kingdom of Esau, and of the Edomites, the Kingdom of Pride, the Wicked Kingdom, Impious Rome. The Turkish Empire is called the Kingdom of the Ismaeklites which they do not wish to destroy. The Kingdom of Rome, however, must b exterminated, because when corrupt Rome is destroyed, salvation and freedom will come to God's Chosen People. So says the Talmud.

As we all know, destroy Rome they did. The weapon that was instrumental in destroying Rome was the suicidal Christian teachings that the Jews perpetuated upon the White Roman civilization.

The Talmud further says "Immediately after Rome is destroyed we shall be redeemed." Translated from the Jewish jargon this means that as soon as they have destroyed Rome that they will be supreme. History shows that after the Jews destroyed and disintegrated Rome with their suicidal teachings, the White Man has never regained control of his own destiny.

The destruction of Rome was not the end of the Jewish program by any means, of course. A Jew, by the fact that he belongs to the Chosen People and is circumcised, possesses so great a dignity that no one, not even an angel can share equality with him, so says the Talmud. In fact he is considered almost the equal of God. "He who strikes an Israelite" says Rabbi Chanina "acts as if he slaps the face of God's Divine Majesty." A Jew is always considered good, in spite of unlimited sins he may commit; nor can his sins contaminate him, any

Nature's Eternal Religion

more than dirt contaminates the kernel in a nut, but only soils its shell. A Jew is always looked upon as a man; the whole world is his and all things serve him, especially "animals which have the form of men."

In legal matters "A goi or a servant is not capable of acting as a witness." Furthermore, a Jew may lie and perjure himself to condemn a Goyim. About this the Talmud says further "Our teaching is as follows: When a Jew and a Goi come in to court, absolve the Jew, if you can, according to the laws of Israel. If the Goi wins, tell him that is what our laws require. If, however, the Jew can be absolved according to the Gentile law, absolve him and say it is due to our laws. If this cannot be done, proceed callously against the Goi, as Rabbi Ischmael advises."

In any case, their war against the Goyim is relentless. They quote the Proverbs 24:6 "By wise counsel thou shalt war against them" and the Talmud then asks the question further by what kind of war? "The kin do war that every son of man must fight against his enemies, which Jacob used against Esau by deceit and trickery whenever possible. They must be fought against without ceasing, until proper order can be restored. (Restoring order to the Jews means the final Jewish tyranny over the world.) Thus it is with satisfaction that I say we should free ourselves from them and rule over them."

So much for quoting from the Talmud. By its sheer length of volume it hides most of the vicious and insidious material from the eyes of the Goyim. It is only by the intense and lengthy study followed by the Jewish teaching that the whole import f the deadly program is revealed. It is not my intention to even partially review such a lengthy volume of books.

Suffice it to say it is a detailed program for binding the Jews together under a code of laws and a long-term program fro the destruction of the White Race. The final aim is the complete destruction of the Gentiles and the domination of the Gentile world of which the White Race is their most hated enemy.

I will further expose the contents of the Talmud by going into more detail in the chapter on the Protocols of the Elders of Zion. Since the Protocols spell out more clearly and in concise essence the teachings of the Talmud, more space will be devoted to them.

In summation, outside of what I have already quoted about the Talmud, the Protocols and the Communist Manifesto pretty well cover the entire ground of the Jewish program for the enslavement of the world. The protocols and the Communist Manifesto themselves are nothing more than a distillation of the teachings of the Talmud. The Talmud came first, and it is in itself the supreme Jewish master plan overshadowing all other Jewish books.

CHAPTER NINETEEN

THE PROTOCOLS OF THE ELDERS OF ZION

I have said previously that the Jews wrote five major books that have been of overwhelming importance in their program for the destruction of the White Race. The first two were the Old Testament and the New Testament. The third was the Talmud.

The fourth is the Protocols of the Elders of Zion.

The Protocols are undoubtedly the most deadly, the most vicious, the most diabolic program for the subjugation and destruction of mankind that was ever conceived by the collective depraved minds of man, they constitute the secret program of the inner circle of the powerful Jewish insiders that rule the world. It is thought that this circle, these powerful insiders, are composed of approximately 300 men, all Jews, all of whom know each other but are unknown to the rest of the world, They are also unknown to the Jewish following whose support they demand and whose support they enjoy. These Elders, the supreme nerve center of power of the Jewish dictatorship, have for centuries usurped unto themselves the supreme power of the world. They are also the governing body of the Kehilla, and the Jewish race.

The program that is set forth in the Protocols is a very concentrated program and it defies summarization, because it is in itself a summarization of the hidden programs that the Jews have interlaced in the complex and shifting volumes of the Talmud. Its program is also the distilled concentrated poison set forth in Karl Marx's Das Capital and Communist Manifesto. It is also an extension of the philosophy set forth in the Old Testament and the New Testament of the Jewish bible. However, whereas the Old Testament is for the consumption for the Jewish membership at large and the New Testament especially designed to confuse and confound the Gentiles, the Protocols are a secret compilation. In no event, were they ever to be seen by the eyes of the Gentiles.

Note even was the Jewish membership at large ever to know the exact details of what the leadership had in mind.

The fact that the Protocols are now available to the Gentiles and to the White Race in particular is one of the great accidents of history. They were first published by Professor Sergyei Nilus, who was a priest in the Orthodox Church in Russia. He published the first Russian language edition in 1905. In his introduction he says that a manuscript had been handed to him about four years earlier by a friend, who vouched that it was a true translation of an original document stolen by a woman from one of the most influential and highly initiated leaders of Free Masonry, at the end of a meeting of the "initiated" in France, that "nest of Jewish- Masonic conspiracy." Professor Nilus added that the Protocols are not exactly minutes of meetings, but a report, with a part apparently missing, made by some powerful person inside the Jewish conspiracy.

The Protocols were published in book form by Sergyei Nilus in Russia in 1905. A copy of this is in the British Museum bearing the date of its inception, August 10, 1906.

The publication of this book was a very serious threat to the Jewish conspiracy and Adolph Hitler says that whenever this book becomes the common property of a nation the Jewish threat can pretty well be deemed as broken. This goes to show just how important this document is. The Jews realized this, and all copies that were known to exist in Russia in the Kerenski regime just after the revolution were destroyed and under his successors the possession of a copy of the Protocols by anyone in Soviet Russia was deemed a crime to insure the owner being shot on sight. It is highly recommended that every White man and woman study this ferocious and deadly document for themselves, and convince themselves of its genuineness and get a better understanding of the Jewish conspiracy.

Naturally the Jews keep screaming again and again that they are forgeries, but what they are forgeries of they do not say, since a forgery implies that there is a genuine article to be forged. In any case, the Jewish program of subversion and conquest of the world has followed this plan so faithfully that the events of history speak for themselves. They are the best proof that the Protocols are genuine.

Mr. Henry Ford, in an interview published in the New York World, February 17, 1921, put the case for Nilus tersely and convincingly thus: "the only statement I care to make about the Protocols is that they fit in with what is going on. They are 16 years old and they have fitted the world situation up to this time. They fit it now."

Since Mr. Henry Ford made that statement, more than 50 years have gone by. Today we can see with our own eyes the world picture that has unfolded in the meantime. We can see more precisely the confirmation of the program contained in the Protocols. Practically all of the world is now under Jewish control, and so much more of the deadly program has been unraveled before our eyes that a person has to be either a Jewish agent, or a complete idiot to deny the authenticity of the Protocols of the Elders of Zion.

Meanwhile, the Jews consistently keep denying that the Protocols are genuine. In fact, they have even set up a committee in the Senate to investigate them and issue a report that they were forged. Naturally this was done under the leadership of such Jewish senators as Senator Javits and others, with a goodly support of pro- Jewish lackeys. In any case, the claim of the Jews that the Protocols are forgeries and the fact that the Jews are the world's greatest liars and masters of deceit, is the best proof of their genuineness. Strangely, the Jews never attempt to answer the facts corresponding to the threats which the Protocols contain, and indeed, the correlation between the prophesy of the Protocols and the fulfillment that has already been brought about is just too obvious to be argued away. This the Jews know only too well and therefore they never argue about the material contained in the Protocols itself and the obvious unraveling of the conspiracy before our eyes.

In any case, the diabolical plans spelled out in the Protocols of the Elders of Zion is not new to Jewish history. They reveal the concerted plan of action of the Jewish nation that has developed through the ages and edited by the Elders themselves up to that date. According to the records of the secret Jewish Zionism, King Solomon and other Jewish learned men, in 929 B.C., already had thought out a scheme in theory for a peaceful conquest of the whole universe of Zion.

As history developed, this scheme was worked out in detail and completed by men who were subsequently initiated into this program. These learned men decided, by any means whatsoever, to conquer the world for Zion with the slyness of the Symbolic Snake, whose head was to represent those who have been initiated into the plans of the Jewish administration, and the body of the snake to represent the Jewish people. The administration was always to be kept secret, even from the Jewish nation itself. As this Snake penetrated into the hearts of the nations it encountered, it undermined and devoured all the non-Jewish power of these states. It is foretold that the Snake has still to finish its work, strictly adhering to the designed plan, until the course which it has to run is closed by the return of its head Zion and until, by this means, the Snake has completed its round of Europe, it will then encompass the whole world. This it is to accomplish by using every means possible, subduing countries by economic conquest, by propaganda, by cunning, by trickery, by deceit, by war, by finance, by force, or by any necessary means whatever.

Anyone studying the Talmud will find imbedded in much chaff and other long winded diatribe the essence of the program prescribed in the Protocols. To show that the diabolical conspiracy embodied in the Protocols is not new, we have the same principles and morality of the latter day Protocols (which are really as old as the tribe itself) set forth in the 15th century program which was printed in a French journal financed by the Rothschilds and published in 1889. Four hundred years earlier, on January 13, 1489, Chemor, Jewish Rabbi of Arles, in Provence, France, wrote to the grand Sanhedrin, which then had its seat in Constantinople, for advice, as the people of Arles were threatening the synagogues. What should the Jews do? This was the reply:

"Dear Beloved Brethren in Moses,

We have received your letter in which you tell us of the anxieties and the misfortunes which you are enduring. We are pierced by a great pain to hear it as yourselves.

The advice of the Grand Satraps and Rabbis is the following:

1) As for what you say that the King of France obliges you to become Christians: do it, since you cannot do otherwise, but let the Law of Moses be kept in your hearts.

2) As for what you say about the command to despoil you of your goods (the law was that on becoming converted, Jews gave up their possessions): make your sons merchants that little by little they may despoil the Christians of theirs.

3) As for what you say about their making attempts on your lives: make your sons doctors and apothecaries, that they may take away Christian lives.

4) As for what you say of their destroying your synagogues: make your sons Canons and Clerics in order that they may destroy their churches.

5) As for the many other vexations you complain of: arrange that your sons become advocates and lawyers and see that they always mix themselves up with the affairs of the state, in order that by putting Christians under your yoke you may dominate the world and be avenged on them.

6) Do not swerve from this order that we give you, because you will find by experience that humiliated as you are, you will reach the actuality of power.

Signed V.S.S.V.F.F., Prince of the Jews, 21st Caslue (November, 1489)"

In the year 1844 just before the Jewish revolutions of 1848 swept most of Europe, Benjamin Disraeli, whose real name was Israel, and who was a damped or baptized Jew, published his novel Conningsby, in which he revealed the following: "the world is governed by very different personages from what is imagined by those who are not behind the scenes." He even went on to show that all these personages were Jews.

A map of the course of the Symbolic Snake is shown as follows: its first stage in Europe was in 429 B.C. in Greece, where at the time of Pericles, the Snake first started eating into the power of that unfortunate country. The second stage was in Rome at approximately the time of Julius Caesar. It may come as a surprise to many readers that Julius Caesar, who has probably received more fame and publicity than any other Roman, was a valuable agent of the Jews. It was for this reason that he was murdered by a small group of patriotic Romans who risked their lives in order to try to avert the destruction of the Roman Republic. The Jews wept and cried around the body of Julius Caesar as they always do when one of their own agents has been killed.

The third stage takes place in Madrid in the time of Charles V, in 1552. The fourth in Paris about 1790 at the time of Louis XVI and the French Revolution. The fifth movement of the Symbolic Snake is designated in London from 1814 onwards after the downfall of Napoleon. The next and sixth stage, the Symbolic Snake moves on to Berlin in 1871 after the Franco- Prussian War. The seventh stage takes place in St. Petersburg over which is drawn the head of the Snake under the date 1881. All these states which the Snake has traversed have had their foundations and their constitutions shaken to the roots.

There are 24 Protocols all together and each one of them is loaded with deadly concentrated poison. The term "Goyim" is used throughout and it is a Jewish term for Gentiles or non-Jews. It is a derogatory term and is synonymous with the word cattle. In other words, they view the Gentiles (including the White race) as so many cattle to be maneuvered, herded about, and finally slaughtered, or enslaved for the benefit of the Jews.

As stated previously, a par of the protocols is deemed to be missing. I strongly suspect that the matter dealing with the tremendously powerful part the Judeo-Christian hoax has played in subjugating the "Goyim" is what is missing. Since Professor Nilus was also a priest, he himself might have deleted or destroyed this part, feeling it was harmful to his church.

In any case, the Protocols as we have them are incomplete. Nevertheless, in their 70 short pages they contain so much that is basic in the Jewish program that it is imperative for us to study them. They are vital for our understanding of the Jewish thanking and their tactics.

In the next chapter I am therefore reviewing the text of the 24 Protocols in abridged form.

CHAPTER TWENTY

THE TEXT OF THE PROTOCOLS

The following is an abridgement of the 24 Protocols. In summarizing them, much had to be left out.

The ideas expressed are implicitly those of the Jews themselves, not mine.

We should keep in mind that these Protocols were written at least 70 years ago, and formulated centuries earlier.

Protocol No. 1

This Protocol is a concentrated treatise on the ABC's of political power. It deals with all the naive fantasies about democracy, about self-determination, and many other illusions that we have cherished over all these years, and depicts them as a mere sham.

It contends that political freedom is an idea only, but never an actual fact. The idea of freedom can be used as a bait to attract the masses of the people to one's party for the sole purpose of crushing another party who is in power. The conclusion is drawn that, by the law of Nature, right lies in force and right lies in might. It is pointed out that the blind might of a nation cannot for one single day exist without guidance. In order to grasp this power the task is rendered easier if the opponent has himself been infected with the idea of freedom or so-called liberalism and for the sake of an idea it is willing to yield some of his power. In any case, the whole idea of self-government is a hoax and a fraud and has been used as an illusion wherewith to capture the mobs, who when left to their own devices invariably end up in havoc.

Anarchy is something that the Jew promotes relentlessly. While in complete control of the financial powers of the state, they promote internecine strife, which they soon aggravate into battles between classes, in the midst of which states burn down and their importance is reduced to that of a heap of ashes.

When a state has been exhausted itself in its own convulsions, whether its internal discord brings it under the power of external foes, or by civil warfare, it can then, in any case, be accounted as irretrievably lost and in the power of the Jews.

They then rationalize that there is nothing immoral about using trickery, cunning, treachery or any other device to bring a state within their power. They say, after all, it a state is fighting an external enemy they will use the same means of treachery, cunning, deceit or any other device in order to win a war and overcome that enemy's state. Therefore, what is the difference about waging war internally against that state if the powers that stand in their way are their enemies?

They then go on to show that despotism is the only possible kind of government, the mob is a blind man, a blind force, without possible leadership. Even if a leader emerges from the mob, he has no program, he has no idea of the principles of political guidance. There is no possible success of guiding these crowds by the aid of reasonable councils and arguments. For any objection, a contradiction, senseless though it may be, can be made. Such senseless objection may find more favor with the people than reason. The peoples' powers of reasoning are, after all, purely superficial. Masses are guided solely by petty passions, paltry beliefs, customs, traditions and sentimental theorism. As a result they fall prey to party dissensions, which hinders any kind of an agreement, even on the basis of a perfectly reasonable argument.

Politics has nothing to do with morals. Any ruler who is governed by morals is an unskilled politician and, therefore, is very vulnerable and unstable on his throne. Anyone who wishes to rule must have recourse to both cunning and to deceit. The result justifies the means. Therefore, the Jews say, their intentions are directed not so to what is good and what is moral, but to that which is necessary and useful.

They, therefore, contend that no people is capable of ruling itself that thinks they can rule with the common consent of the majority

and for the good of all. They have, therefore, trained their own men from childhood for independent rule who understand the mechanics of ruling mobs and ruling nations. "It is unthinkable," (they say, for the mob to rule themselves) "for a plan broken up into as many parts as there are heads in the mob loses all homogeneity and thereby becomes unintelligible and impossible of execution." Consequently, they point out, that the only means of government is by the application of the leadership principle. The conclusion is inevitable that a satisfactory form of government for any country is one that is concentrated in the hands of a responsible person. Without an absolute despotism there can be no existence for civilization, which is carried on not by the masses, but by their leader, whosoever that person may be. The mob is a savage and displays savagery at every opportunity.

They therefore feel, that without a doubt, they are entitled to rule not only one nation, but all nations, and that they must not stop at bribery, deceit and treachery when they should serve towards the attainment of their ends. Their countersign is Force and Make Believe.

Rather than conquer states by force of arms they want to march along the path of peaceful conquest and replace the horrors of war by less forceful and more satisfactory sentences of death which they deal out to anyone who stands in their way of grabbing power. In fact, they place great emphasis on the necessity of maintaining the terror which tends to produce blind submission. Just, but merciless severity, is the greatest factor in the strength of the state, "by the doctrine of severity we shall triumph and bring all government into subjection to our super- government."

They admit that already far back in ancient times, they, the Jews, were the first to cry among the masses of the people the words, "Liberty, Equality, Fraternity." They have used these words, or their equivalent, innumerable times since and have had them repeated by stupid parrots, who from all sides flew down upon these baits and with them carried away the well-being of the world, carried away the true freedom of the individual, which formerly was so well guarded against the pressures of the mob. They point out that the Goyim did not note the contradiction of the meaning of these words and did not see that in Nature there is no equality, there cannot be freedom; that Nature herself has established inequality of minds, of characters and capacities just as immutably as she has established subordination of her laws.

The Jews show that the White Man, whom they call the Goyim, has ruled through his nobility only by dynasties. In these, the father passed on to the son a knowledge of the course of political affairs in such a way that none should know it but members of the dynasty and none should know it but members of the dynasty and none could betray it to those that were governed. As time went on and the Jewish ideas of democracy penetrated further and further into the thinking and government of the White people, the true position of the ruling dynasties became confused and their political skills were lost. This was a great aid to the success of the Jewish cause in taking over these nations.

Therefore, in shouting the words, "Liberty, Equality and Fraternity" they brought to the Jewish ranks, thanks to their own agents, whole legions who bore their banners with enthusiasm. All the time these words were canker worms at work, boring into the well-being of the Goyim, putting an end everywhere to peace, quiet, solidarity and destroying all the foundations of the Goyim states.

The Jews show that their triumph was rendered much easier by the fact that in their relations with the men whom they wanted to have, they always worked upon the most sensitive chords of the human mind, namely, upon their lust for money, upon heir stupidity, and upon the insatiability of material needs for man. Whereas each of these human weaknesses taken alone is sufficient to paralyze initiative, taken together it hands over lock, stock and barrel the will of men to the disposition of those who have been paid for their treachery and treason.

By using the power of their gold, their financial forces, and by using cunning deceit and treachery they have made it possible to replace the representatives of he people and put in their place instead their lackeys and their agents.

Protocol No. 2

The Jews, herein, reveal the tremendous importance of instigating and waging economic wars and military wars between Goyim states. Wars have been referred to as "the Jewish Harvest." It is by means of wars that the Jews reap and lay the foundations of Jewish predominance. When the wars are over both sides are devastated and at the mercy of international Jewish finance. They say, "our international rights will wipe out national rights." While wiping out huge assets, laying waste large sections of both sides of the Gentile nations, when the war is over both sides find themselves in financial distress and overwhelmingly in debt. Thus we find the Jews reaping a three-fold harvest from wars: first they make a huge profit form munitions manufacturing and other financial sinews of war, secondly they are therewith able to weaken the racial stamina of the White Race by sending forth into battle the flower of manhood of the White nations of both sides, thirdly, when the war is over, and both sides are prostrate, the Jews then further ensnare the Gentile nations by chaining them with huge indebtedness and collecting interest upon interest. Thereby the White nations (and the White Race) are further ensnared into bondage and the Jewish stranglehold is progressively tightened.

The Jews then boast how they choose Goyim administrators for public office, people who will front for them and whose loyalty as stooges they can count upon. Naturally these will be people who are willing to be traitors to the White Race and who know very little about the art of government. Back of these lackeys will be their own Jewish advisors, who, they claim, are men of learning and genius, specially bred and reared from early childhood to rule the affairs of the whole world.

The last part tells about the powerful part played by the press in the hands of the Jews, "through the press we have gained the power to influence while remaining ourselves in the shade; thanks to the press we now have the gold in our hands, notwithstanding that we have had to gather it out of the oceans of

Nature's Eternal Religion

blood and tears."

They sum it up by saying that the triumph of the Jewish system will fail of success if the practical application of it is not based upon a summing up of the lessons of the past in the light of the present.

Thus, we see the gathering of the reins of power into the hands of the Jews by their treacherous devices. These are: by the use of wars; by plunging the ravaged nations into indebtedness; by the control of stooges to front in positions of power; by the skillful use of the press to keep pointing our requirements are supposedly indispensable, to give voice to the complaints of the people, to express and create discontent. And last but least the power of gold.

Protocol No. 3

With overbearing arrogance and supreme confidence the Jews tell us: "that out goal is now only a few steps off. The old, long path we have trodden is now ready of close its cycle of the Symbolic Snake, by which we symbolize our people. When this ring is closes, will the states of Europe will be locked in its coil as in a powerful vise."

They reveal further how they are going to lock us, the Goyim, in their powerful vise. Whereas the Goyim think that they have constitutions that are sufficiently strong to keep the ship of state on an even keel, the Jews have our kings, rulers and representatives surrounded with their advisors who "advise" them into one foolish, irresponsible move after another. By stirring up a host of confused issues, they increasingly widen the gulf between the rulers and the people. With the power of the press in the hands of the Jews, they encourage abuses of power by the rulers on the one hand. By agitating and stirring the up mob on the other hand they "will put the final touch in preparing all institutions for their overthrow and everything will fly skyward under the blows of the maddened mob."

In the meantime, by continually worsening and bringing about financial and economic crises all the people are chained down to heavy toil by poverty more firmly than they ever were chained by slavery and serfdom. "Our power is in the shortness of food and physical weakness of the worker because by all that this implies he is made a slave of our will." Thereby they further promote the hate and the envy that will move the mobs to turn upon those and wipe out all those who are an obstacle in the way of the Jews and their take-over of power. "When the hour strikes for our Sovereign Lord of all the World (in other words the Jewish Dictator) to be crowned, it is these same hands which will sweep away everything that might be a hindrance thereto." As these mobs then rage and destroy, the Jews have made sure that they will not touch their property, because the moment of attack will be known to the Jews only, and they have prepared to take measures to protect their own.

They frankly admit that they engineered the French Revolution and that the secrets of its preparations were well known to them for "it was wholly the works of our hands."

They mock at the word "freedom," saying that it means absolutely nothing but is a useful tool for them to use to inflame the mobs and bring out whole communities of men to fight against every kind of force, against every kind of authority. The mobs, under the Jews control, will then kill the last visages of Gentile leadership and acquit the criminals so that in the end the mob will unwittingly help the Jews to enthrone the "King-Despot of the blood of Zion, whom we are preparing for the world."

Protocol No. 4

Here the Jews reveal to us frankly that they have organized Gentiles into Masonic Orders which are one of their most powerful tools for controlling the world and for driving the Gentile states into destruction for their total Jewish take-over of the world. "Gentile Masonry blindly serves as a screen for us and our objects, but the plan of action of our force, even its very abiding-place, remains for the whole people an unknown mystery."

To further move the conspiracy to its ultimate conclusion it is necessary for the Jews to destroy all the foundations upon which the Goyim society has been built. They will furthermore keep the Goyim so busy earning a living that he will have no time to think or take note of what is going on. While the Goyim is working and earning a living and pursuing industry and trade the Jew will be pursuing a speculation. This will result in everything that is produced from the land, or by industry, to slip through their hands and pass into speculation and pass into the hands of the

Jews. Having destroyed all moral principles among the Gentiles, that is the White people, having turned their minds completely towards industry and trade and earning a living, they will bring them to a stage where "their only guide is gain, that is Gold, which they will erect into a veritable cult, for the sake of those material delights which it can give, not even to win wealth, but solely out of hatred towards the privileged, the lower classes of the Goyim will follow our lead against out rivals for power, the intellectuals of the Goyim," in order to destroy them.

Again the stupidity of the Goyim will be used to destroy their own.

Protocol No. 5

Creation of an intensified centralization of government. Methods of seizing power by Masonry. Causes of the impossibility of agreement between States. The state of predestination" of the Jews. Gold the engine of the machinery of the States.

Significance of criticism. "Show" institutions. Weariness from word-spinning. How to take a grip of public opinion. Significance of personal initiative. The Super-Government.

Protocol No. 6

The establishment of huge Jewish financial monopolies, containing reservoirs of colossal riches is hereby spelled out. These monopolies will be so powerful that the fortunes of any Gentile will depend upon them to such an extent that the non-Jewish fortunes will not be able to exist outside of the control and manipulation of these Jewish monopolies. Today we see these as an established fact. No matter what business you look into whether it be oil, sugar, movies, television networks, steel, railways, automobile manufacturing and a hundred other lines of endeavor, they are all in the hands of the Jews.

While they are garnering all the riches of the land into huge Jewish monopolies they still say that in every possible way them must develop the significance of their super government by representing it as the Protector and Benefactor of all those who voluntarily submit to them.

The next section deals with the means of depriving the Goyim of their land, and, they say, frankly, this must be done, whatever the cost. The best way to bring this about is to load land and property with debts and thereby keep it in a state of humble, continuous and unconditional submission.

A further way to deprive the White people of their hard earned money and property is first and foremost for the Jews to engage in speculation and monopolize it. In this way they drain off from industry and from labor and capital and from the land and transfer into Jewish hands all the money of the world. "Then the Goyim will bow down before us, if for no other reason but to get the right to exist."

In order to bring further ruin to the Goyim they will promote and encourage by propaganda a greedy demand for luxury which will swallow up any earnings that they might have left over.

"We shall raise the rate of wages, which, however, will not bring any disadvantage to the workers, for, at the same time, we shall produce a rise in prices of the first necessities of life, alleging that it arises from the decline of agriculture." On top of this they will further encourage and accustom workers to anarchy and to drunkenness. At the same time they will take all measures possible to exterminate from the face of the earth all the educated forces of the Goyim.

While they are doing all this they will mask their heinous destruction of the White Race under an alleged ardent desire to serve the working classes and the great principles of political economy.

Protocol No. 7

To back up and enforce all these viscous programs of economic strangulation of the Goyim, the Jews plan the intensification of armaments, the increase of police forces and the sowing of ferment discord and hostility all over the world. When they get through, all that will be left in all the different countries of the world will be the masses of the proletariat, a few millionaires devoted to Jewish interests, and police and soldiers.

By having Jewish agents in the governments of all the countries in the world; by economic treaties; by loan obligations; by the ferments and hostilities they have created; they will, with their intrigues, have so entangled all the threads of the governments of the world that none of them will be able to act without the Jews manipulating the levers of power.

If any country dares to oppose them, the Jews will then collectively organize their neighbors into a joint venture to stand collectively together against that country and destroy that country by universal war. How frightful and real this power is was shown in World War II when Germany, through courage and strength, shook off the Jew, then immediately through vicious propaganda, intrigue, financial means and other levers of power the Jews organized the surrounding neighbors into a beastly war of annihilation.

This they can do because as they say. "We must compel the governments of the Goyim to take action in the direction favored by our widely-conceived plan, already approaching the desired consummation, by what we shall represent as public opinion, secretly promoted by us through the means of that so-called "Great

Power"—the Press, which, with a few exceptions that may be disregarded, is already entirely in our hands."

Should Europe get out of their control, then the Jews are determined to show their strength by responding with the guns of America, or China, or Japan, to smash Europe, if necessary.

Protocol No. 8

The manipulation of the courts is herewith discussed. Their plan is to destroy the White Man's courts of law and degrade and degenerate it into a legal jungle. Further, to hamstring and harass honest citizens, the Jews first of all plan to heavily staff the whole legal system with their own breed. If we look around us today it is hardly possible to ignore how heavily Jew-infested our legal system is. The majority of the judges are Jews. The number of attorneys is heavily weighted with Jews.

But in order to b ring about their contrived and perverted decisions and justify them to the public they make it a fine science to cover their idiotic decisions with the most high-sounding, exalted moral principles passed into legal form. To train their breed of lawyers for all this intricate treachery and finagling, they have schools which prepare their selected personnel by a special super- educational training course in their special Jewish schools. With their special training they will be "made acquainted with the whole underside of human nature, with all its sensitive chords in which they will have to play."

The Jews go heavily into the study of economics, not to clarify the issues, but the better therewith to confuse them. Around their government, that is the Jewish government, there will be a whole constellation of bankers, industrialists, capitalists and above all millionaires, because, as they say, everything will be settled by the question of money. The Jews will install Gentile stooges to had up government departments but they will be people and persons whose past and reputation are such that have criminal involvement, people who have some dark, murky hidden past, and are easily blackmailed. Such people never represent the interests of their own race, but are outright traitors to the White Race, and this, as the Jews say, "on order to make them defend our interests to their last gasp."

Protocol No. 9

The Jews make a full and detailed study of the character of the people of the country which they intend to destroy. By cautious application of this principle, "you will see that a decade will pass before the most stubborn character will change and we shall add new people to the ranks of those already subdued by us."

They confide that the Masonic watchwords of "Liberty, Equality, Fraternity" have been a powerful tool for the destruction of the different nations of the world. Whereas these words express a meaningless and impossible idealism, that is beside the point. It has been tremendously useful and has worked.

A short discussion then ensues about the use of artificially controlled anti-

Semitism being tremendously useful to them for the management "of our lesser brethren." In other words, controlled anti-Semitism is a very useful tool to unite and bring all the Jews in line in cooperation with their worldwide master plan.

For the Jews there are no checks or limits to the range of their activities. Their Super-Government is not limited by any laws or conditions. "At the proper time, we, the law givers, shall execute judgment and sentence, we shall slay and we shall spare, we, as head of all our troops, are mounted on the steed of the leader."

They have enmeshed into their network the service of persons of all opinions, of all doctrines, demagogues, socialists, communists, and Utopian dreamers of every kind. Each of them has been given a task. Each of them, on his own account is boring away at the last remnants of authority, striving to overthrow all established forms of order. "By these acts all States are in torture— but we will not give them peace until they openly acknowledge our international Super-Government, and with submissiveness."

Remembering that these Protocols were written over 70 years ago, even then the Jews openly bragged that they already had in their hands the administration of the law, the conduct of elections, the press, the liberty of person, but above all, education and training of the young people. They further brag that they have fooled, used, and corrupted the youth of the Goyim by rearing them in principles and theories which are known to the Jews to be false.

They further openly brag that they have in the Western countries a means and a maneuver of such appalling terror that even the very stoutest hearts will quail. They have undergrounds called Metropolitans "those subterranean corridors which, before the time comes, will be driven under all the capitals and from whence those capitals will be blown into the air with all their organizations and archives."

Protocol No. 10

Illustrating how easy it is to fool the Goyim, the Jews state point blank that the people are perfectly content with the outside appearances of their governments and don't have the faintest understanding of the underlying meaning of things or the actions going on behind the scenes. In order to keep it that way it is important that all questions ought not to be touched upon directly and openly before the people. By not naming a principle the Jews leave themselves free for any action they choose. A political scoundrel, who is a rascal but clever, will be admired by the mob for his impudent audacity.

The Jewish hierarchy has drawn up a master plan for erecting a new fundamental structure embracing all the nations of the earth (United Nations).

They mean to bring all the peoples under their one despotic Jewish dictator by first subjecting the peoples of the world to such terrible suffering, confusion and torment that they will throw up their hands in desperation. The Jews will then offer them the solution to all their problems. By a coup d'etat that they will then bring about, they will set themselves on the throne of the world.

Some of the tools for accomplishing this are to give everybody a vote without distinction of classes or without qualifications; by destroying among the Goyim the importance of the family and its educational value; by creating of the mob a blind mighty force which will never be in a position to move in any direction without the guidance of the Jewish agents set at the head as leaders of the mob.

The Jews are well aware of the leadership principle and have utilized it from the beginning of their history to bring them to the present state of power. They realize that a scheme of government must come ready made from one brain and must not be split into fractional parts from the minds of the many. Whereas it is allowable for a select company of their hierarchy to have knowledge of the general scheme of action, they must not discuss the details because it would destroy its artful design, the interdependence of its component parts, and the secret meaning of each clause.

They take a very dim view of the usefulness of a constitution as a means of protecting the people from their conspiracy. They state openly "a constitution, as you well know, is nothing else but a school of discords, misunderstandings, quarrels, disagreements, fruitless party agitations, party whims— in a word, a school of everything that serves to destroy the personality of State activity." Democracies and Republics with everybody having a vote down to the last scum and rabble provides the Jew with the finest element with which to destroy the State, and the people within that State.

In order that they can best manipulate such a State they arrange to elect Presidents and other officials which have in their past some dark undiscovered stain. These agents will then do their bidding without any fear of revelation on the part of the Jews.

Finally, by means of creating discord, by plundering the people blind by taxation, by bungling, by a breakdown of law and order, by dissension, hatred, struggle, envy and even by the sue of torture, by starvation, by the inoculation of diseases, by want, finally the people will be so exhausted and so desperate that they will see no other choice but to take refuge in the Jewish leadership. The people will submit and surrender to their unconditional Jewish sovereignty.

Protocol No. 11

"The Goyim (White Gentiles) are a flock of sheep and we are their wolves. And you know what happens when the wolves get hold of the flock?"

In this Protocol they go into further detail about destroying the last vestiges of our type of government and replacing it with their Jewish world order which will come in the form of a revolution of the State. As a precondition to this new world order, many combinations of concepts which we now accept, such as freedom of the press, right of association, freedom of conscience, the voting principle, and many others must disappear forever from the memory of man. The Jews want to make sure that when they spring the final closing of the jaws on the Goyim, such victims must recognize once and for all that they the Jews, are so strong, so super- abundantly filled with power, that in no case will they take account of any protest, nor will they pay any attention whatsoever to the opinions or wishes of the Goyim, and they want to impress upon us that they are ready and able to crush with irresistible power all expressions of such protest at any moment and al every place. In fear and trembling the Goyim will close his eyes to everything and be content to wait and see how it will all end. In the meantime, the Jews will keep the Goyim Gentiles pacified by promising to give back to them all the liberties they have taken away as soon as they have quelled "the enemies of peace."

Why are they doing this? In order to obtain in a roundabout way that which their scattered tribe would be unable to obtain by direct methods. That is why they have organized an army of Masonic lodges— to throw a smoke screen over their real aims which are not even so much as suspected by "these Goy cattle."

"God has granted to us, His Chosen People, the gift of dispersion, and in this, which appears in all eyes to be our weakness, has come forth all our strength, which has now brought us to the threshold of sovereignty over all the world."

Literature and journalism are regarded by the Jews as the two most important educative forces and therefore they what to make sure that their government will become the sole proprietor of the majority of all journals. They regard freedom of the press, or freedom as such, as the right to do only that which the law allows. Since they are going to create or abolish such laws as are desirable to them, all freedom will be in their hands.

Propaganda and the press which creates it are therefore regarded as a key to control over the Goyim. "We shall saddle and bridle it with a tight curb: we shall do the same also with all productions of the printing press: anybody in the printing business will be required to have a stamp tax and deposits of caution-money. If anybody attacks the Jews, if such is still possible, we will inflict fines without mercy." They intend to so straddle the press that no one shall with impunity lift a finger on the correctness and infallibility of their government.

They will also establish magazines and papers of their own that will make phony attacks upon their Jewish establishment, but, of course, they will be limited to such trivial points that will cause t hem no problem. They will belabor a hundred sides of every point but never bringing up any real issues until they have the public so confused that they won't know where they stand or what a valid opinion even is. In any case, not a single announcement will reach the public without going through the control of the Jews. The Goyim will look upon events of the world through the colored spectacles "which we are setting astride their noses." They brag that even now (and this was written over 70 years ago) there is no State secret that the Jews don't have access to. Now, 70 years later, we can imagine how much further they are in control.

The future despotic Jewish State will have three classes of journals that they will control. In the front rank will stand the organs of an official character. These journals will always stand guard over the

Jewish interests and they admit that, therefore, their influence will be comparatively small. In the second rank will be the semiofficial organs whose part it will be to attract the tepid and indifferent Goyim. In the third rank they will set up their own papers, but to all appearances they will be in opposition to their regime. This will (a) trap their real opponents to accept this simulated opposition as their own. (b) They can lead the opposition opinion into the very channels to which they then desire, and thereby neutralize them.

In this way they will carry on their own sham fights which will confound and confuse the Goyim. At the same time the Goyim will still be under the illusion that he is enjoying freedom of the press.

Even at the time that the Protocols were written the Jews bragged that with the French press all organs of the press are bound together by professional secrecy. No journalist would venture to betray this secret, because not one of them has ever admitted to practice literature unless his past has some disgraceful episode with which the Jews could thereby blackmail and control that member of the press. When the Jews have finally accomplished their world goal and have the despotic regime in full control, they intend to make sure that there will be no revelations by the press of any public dishonesty. The new regime must be thought of to have so perfectly satisfied everybody that even criminality will seem to have disappeared.

The Text Of The Protocols

Protocol No. 12

(Subject headings only)

This chapter is rather long and deals with the tremendously important role of the Jewish-created Masonic Orders and Masonic Lodges play in control of the press, government and the Gentiles as a whole.

Masonic interpretation of the word "freedom." Future of the press in the Masonic kingdom. Control of the press. Correspondence agencies. What is progress as understood by Masonry? More about the press. Masonic solidarity in the press of today. The arousing of "public" demands in the provinces. Infallibility of the new regime.

Protocol No. 13

The need for our daily bread will be the most powerful club the Jews intend to wield over the head of the Goyim to keep him in silence as their humble servant. They will use their Gentile agents of the press to discuss those issues that are inconvenient for their official journals to mention. The Jewish controlled regime will then simply take and carry through such measures as they wish and then offer them to the public as an accomplished fact. Once done, no one will dare to demand a change in the matter, and all the more so, since the Jewish press will then represent their new measures as a great improvement. Immediately thereafter the press will distract the current thought towards new and frivolous questions.

As the Goyim people become more and more enslaved, the Jews intend to further distract them with amusements, games, pastimes, passions, people's palaces and many other distractions such as competitions in art and sports of all kinds. The Jewish controlled press alone will guide the people to any and all forms of opinion which the people will then regard as their own, because they, the Jews, will have all monopoly in offering them any new directions for thought.

Liberals and Utopian dreamers will play their part in wrecking the remnants of the Goy government until the Jews take over. After that these liberals will be of absolutely no value to them. In fact, they may even be dangerous and they have to be set aside. Although they will upset our whole White civilization and turn society upside down, their orators will expound at great length on how they have now enslaved us. "Who will ever suspect then that all these peoples were stage-managed by us according to a political plan which no one has so much guessed at in the course of many centuries?"

When the Jews have established their despotic kingdom they intend to make sure that no other religion will exist than their religion, the religion of Moses, in which they will stand out as the chosen people. All other forms of belief will be swept away. They will then delude the Goyim that in their religion there exists a mystical rite on which all educational power is based.

After they have enslaved all the peoples of the world and imposed their tyrannical regime upon them they will then at every possible opportunity publish articles and make comparisons between their benevolent rule and those of the past ages. They will extol the blessings of tranquility, although that tranquility was forcibly brought about by centuries of Jewish agitation. The eras of the previous Goyim governments will be denounced by the Jews in the most forceful language.

All the useless changes of forms of government through which they have run the goyim when they were undermining their State's structures, will so have wearied the peoples, that finally they will prefer to suffer anything under the Jews rather than run the risk of enduring again all those agitations and miseries. When they are in full power they will further emphasize again all the historical mistakes that their previous Goy government made for so many centuries by their lack of understanding of everything that constitutes the true good of humanity. In contrast they will expound to them how fortunate the people now are in contrast to the dead and decomposed old order of things. In countries known as progressive and enlightened the Jews admit that it was they themselves that created a senseless, filthy and abominable literature. Yet this will later be brought out as a charge and discredit to the old order.

No one will ever be allowed to bring under discussion their Jewish faith from its true point of view. No one but the Jews will be fully instructed and fully learned of its contents. None of the "chosen" will ever dare to betray any of its secrets nor how it was used to enslave the rest of humanity.

Protocol No. 15

(Subject headings only)

One-day coup d'etat (revolution) over all the world. Executions. Future lot of the Goyim- Masons. Mysticism of authority. Multiplication of Masonic lodges. Central governing board of Masonic Elders. The "Azev-tactics." Masonry as leader and guide of all secret societies. Significance of public applause.

Collectivism. Victims. Executions of Masons. Fall of the prestige of laws and authority. Our position as the Chosen People. Brevity and clarity of the laws of our kingdom of the future. Obedience to orders. Measures against abuse of authority. Severity of penalties. Age-limit for judges. Liberalism of judges and authorities. The money of all the world. Absolutism of Masonry. Right of appeal. Patriarchal "outside appearance" of the power of the one and only right. The King of Israel. Patriarch of all the world.

Protocol No. 16

Realizing that the universities are the key institutions forming and molding the thought of the people, the Jews plan to emasculate the universities by re-orienting them in a new direction, one that is useful to the Jews. All officials and professors will have detailed programs prepared for them from which they will proceed to teach and not be allowed to diverge in the slightest. They will be selected with care and be put into such a position they will be wholly dependent upon the government.

No meaningful courses in the study of state law or political questions will be given except to a few dozen carefully selected persons chosen for their special abilities and coming from the ranks of their Jewish brethren. During the transitional period while they are still struggling for absolute despotism, the Jews will introduce into the educational programs all those divisive principles that have been used so brilliantly to break upon the order of the Goyim governments. But once they are completely in power they plan to remove every kind of disturbing subject from the course of education. Instead they will make the young people obedient children of authority, loving him who rules, giving him support and hoping for peace and quiet.

The study of Classics, the study of Ancient History and the lessons of past experience will be replaced with theoretical studies of programs for the future. "We shall erase from the memory of men all facts of previous centuries which are undesirable to us and leave only those which depict all the errors of the government of the Goyim." Special emphasis will be placed on the study of practical life, the obligations of the people to the State, and to law and order. Each different trade and faction will be given a special and different treatment.

In order that the despotic Jewish King will be more firmly seated in control, it will be necessary that all his activities be relayed to the nation as a whole, in the schools, and on the market places in such a manner that he people will have a clear understanding of all his acts and his many and great benevolent accomplishments.

There will be no such thing as freedom of instruction. Special groups will be taught in the philosophy of new theories which have not been declared to the rest of the world. These theories will be in the nature of a dogma of faith and used as a transitional stage in initiating the people towards their faith, i.e., the Jewish faith.

They observe that the experience of many centuries has taught them that people live and are guided by ideas and that these ideas are absorbed by people only through education. All different ages are equally receptive to ideas. The end result strived for in the so- called system of teaching will be to turn the Goyim into unthinking, submissive brutes, waiting for things to be presented before their eyes in order to form any idea at all.

Protocol No. 17

(Subject headings only)

Special training of their own attorneys. Future attorneys paid by state. Information used by attorneys limited to that provided by state. King of the Jews will be the real Pope of the universe, the patriarch of the international church. Destruction of existing church when it has served its purpose. Function of the contemporary press. Organization of police. Volunteer police. Espionage on the pattern of Cabal espionage. Abusing and degrading Goyim authority.

Protocol No. 18

Realizing that nothing damages the prestige of authority more that it obviously being surrounded by a mass of secret police forces for its own protection, they plan to protect their Jewish despotism by more devious means. They will set up conspiracies of their own among the people led by brilliant speakers who will gather around them all those sympathetic to their protest of opposition against the regime. In this way they will be able to remove weak and wavering members among their own police force and also be able to round up the potential opposition that might develop by natural means. This way they will be able to nip in the bud and root out any conspiracies before they even get started.

It is a measure of weakness for too many conspiracies to be known among the people and to compel rulers to acknowledge their weakness in advertising their secret measures of defense.

Similarly, if several attempts upon the lives of the rulers are known, this, too, weakens their prestige and their authority over those being ruled. The Jews frankly admit that they have instigated any number of assassinations and attempts at assassinations of kings and rulers in the past. They thereby helped to destroy the authority of the whole Goyim government by undermining the idea of absolute authority and encouraging the idea that underneath lies a vast opposition.

When their supreme Jewish King of the World is in power they plan to reinforce his protection by creating such an aura of power and mystical Deity about him that the poor stupid Goyim will think of him as being next to a God. The Goyim will then do everything possible to protect him and to inform authorities of any opposition that might lie anywhere among his subjects.

Political criminals will be dealt with extreme cruelty. They will be arrest on the first suspicion whether it's well grounded or not. No opportunity will be given of escape of people even suspected of political crime and in these matters they intend to be completely merciless. Why, anybody even thinking about political ideas is already guilty of a crime, for he should have no understanding of it in the first place, and secondly, he should not be occupying himself with such matters.

Protocol No. 19

No dabbling in political affairs that will have any meaning whatsoever will be allowed among the subjects or, shall we say, the victims of the Jewish regime. The Jews point out that under a well organized, powerful government, for any individual, or groups of individuals, to make any attempt at what they call "Sedition-mongering," is about as significant as a lap dog yapping at an elephant.

So no individual will get the idea of being a hero and leading the people to opposition, all individuals who make such attempts will be put to trial in the same category as thieving, murder, or any other kind of abominable and filthy crime. This will disgrace these heroic people in the eyes of the public and they will be branded with the same contempt as they might hold for any low criminal.

In any case, everything will be done to completely wipe out any possibility of sedition or opposition. In the past, to break down Goyim regimes, they have inserted into history books the idea of heroism and martyrdom of those who have opposed the Goyim governments. This will be completely changed and wiped out when their Jewish regime has been established. The average citizen will have no more influence or control in the affairs of politics than will a herd of cattle.

Protocol No. 20

"The sum total of our actions is settled by the question of figures." By this the Jews mean money and that money controls everything. Protocol No. 20 is a long and complicated one having mostly to do with money, taxation and interest.

It lays out the blueprint for their fiscal policies when the King of the

World rules supreme. In the first place the Jewish King will enjoy the legal fiction that everything in his State belongs to him. They state in parenthesis this "may very well be a fact." He will then, therefore, have the legal power to confiscate any and every kind of sums on whatever pretext he may choose.

The Jews blatantly boast that economic crises have been produced by them for the destruction of the Goyim by very simple means: the withdrawal of money from circulation. They admit that they have burdened the finances of the State with huge loans on which they obtain huge sums of interest and made them the bond slaves of their international bankers. They further boast that the concentration of all industry in the hands of their Jewish capitalists and out of the hands of the small masters has drained away all the strength of the peoples, along with the strength of the State.

The Jews point with pride to the fact they the gold standard has been the ruin of the States which have adopted it, for it has not been able to satisfy the demands for money, the more so as they drained the gold from circulation. The reader should remember that this was written prior to 1900 and then recall that in 1933 the Jews first of all took all the gold away from the American public and made it a crime of an American citizen to own gold. By now, they have shipped practically all the gold we had in Fort Knox out of the country. The little that the United States has left is now over-committed, and over obligated. We are now completely plundered and devoid of any gold.

They pat themselves on the back for their ingenuity and cunning compared to the "purely brute brains of the Goyim." They boast that with their clever banking system the Goyim has been borrowing from them with payment of interest without ever thinking that, all the same, all the money that they have been paying interest on had to come from their own State pockets in order to pay them these huge amounts of interest. As long as the loans were internal the Goyim really shuffled their money from the pockets of the poor to those of the very rich. But this changed when it came to borrowing from foreign sources. What it then amounted to was that the wealth of this country flowed into the cash boxes of the Jews and the Goyim was really paying tribute to the Jews as subjects or slaves.

This is all part of their master plan. "Without a definite plan it is impossible to rule. Marching along on an undetermined road and with undetermined resources brings to ruin by the way heroes and demigods." And so, in accordance with the plan, the poor Goyim hardly realizes what a state of financial disaster he is now in, despite the astonishing industry and productivity of their people.

Protocol No. 21

Having grasped absolute control of all the money systems of the different

States of the world and having a monopoly on banking and credit, the Jews now brag that they get their money twice, three times and more times over by lending it to the Goy government. They frankly admit that most of the time the Goy governments have no business and no need for making these loans. However, by means of bribery of the state officials, and the slackness of the Goy rulers themselves, they have now lured them into the position where they are al hopelessly deluged with an overwhelming sum of debt. Not only do they have to borrow more money every year but they have to borrow money to even pay the interest on the mountains of debts that they have piled upon the stupid Goy.

But when the Jews ascend the throne of the world, all these financial shifts that do not served their interests will be swept aside so as not to leave a trace. Money markets will be destroyed and they will not allow the prestige of their power to be shaken by any fluctuations of prices, but they, the Jews, shall announce by law values and prices.

They shall replace the money markets by grandiose government credit institutions, the object of which will be to fix the price of industrial values in accordance with whatever the government determines. This will make all industrial undertakings become completely dependent upon the Jews and they arrogantly add, "you may imagine for yourselves what immense power we shall thereby secure for ourselves."

Protocol No. 22

The ultimate goal for which the Jews are striving is further defined and clarified in this Protocol.

"In our hands is the greatest power of our day— gold." When we consider that these words were written at least 70 years ago and look at the picture today of how they have plundered and looted the reservoirs of gold of the different peoples of the world today, we are beginning to get a pretty fair idea of the success of their master plan.

Arrogantly, they then point to the fact that, having accumulated all this wealth, isn't this surely proof that their rule is predestined by God? Though much violence will be necessary, nevertheless, they are determined that their fiendish and diabolical rule will be established. Having once done so, they will contrive to prove that they are the benefactors who have restored freedom, order and tranquility to a confused and strife torn world.

"Our authority will be glorious because it will be all-powerful, will rule and guide, and not muddle along after leaders and orators shrieking themselves hoarse with senseless words which they call great principles." Their authority, they vow, will be the crown of order and will have about it an aura of Deity that will inspire a mystical bowing of the knee before it and a reverent fear before it of all the peoples. "True force makes no terms with any right, not even with that of God: none dare come near to it so as to take so much as a span from it away."

Protocol No. 23

Reducing all people to abject slavery and bending them to their supreme authority is the main thread that runs through all the Protocols. One more way is to inculcate lessons of humility, that is make people more humble and, therefore, they will be more obedient. (Remember the Sermon on the Mount?) By reducing the production of luxury articles and depriving the people of all forms of luxuries they will force them to become more humble and, therefore, more obedient. Furthermore, they will undermine and reduce large manufacturers to a people of small masters and small units. This is a return back to the middle ages. Drunkenness will also be prohibited by law and will be punishable as a crime.

Whereas the Jews have stirred up dissension, revolution and the fire of anarchy all over the world, when the chosen one of God, that is, their Jewish King, is on he throne, then all these agitators will have played their parts. Having served their usefulness they will then be liquidated. "Then it will be necessary to sweep them away from his path, on which must be left no knot, no splinter."

All this to bring about ruin, and to erect on those ruins, finally, the throne of the King of the Jews.

Protocol No. 24

The coming King of the World and the King of the Jews must have his ancestral lineage confirmed in the dynastic roots of King David. He will evidently be selected and sponsored by three of the highest Elders of Zion. He will be most carefully selected, not by any right of heritage, but by sheer, outstanding ability. Then follows a most intensive and rigorous training (of their future King) by those Elders that are on the inside, to familiarize him

with all their secrets of the Jewish Zionist program. The King will then be inducted into the most secret mysteries of the political, into the schemes of government, and into the whole program. All these secrets, nevertheless, will be strictly kept within a very limited inner circle.

The King will no necessarily be followed by direct heirs, but his heirs will be screened for ability. Only those who are unconditionally capable of firm, even though it be cruel, direct rule, will be allowed to take over the reins of government from the Learned Elders. In case the King falls sick, or displays weakness of will, or any other form of incapacity, he must, by law, hand over the reins of rule to new and capable hands.

Once he is on the throne only the King and the three Elders who stood sponsor for him will know what the program for the future will be. "None will know what the King wishes to attain by his disposition, and therefore none will dare stand across an unknown path." The King of the Jews must be devoid of all feelings and passion and must exercise the cold reasoning power of his superior mind. "The prop of humanity in the person of the supreme lord of all the world of the holy seed of David must sacrifice to his people all personal inclinations."

CHAPTER TWENTY-ONE

MARXISM: THE MODERN POISONOUS BREW

By no recognized standard may Karl Marx be considered a great writer, nor even a great thinker. His famous production Das Kapital is so dull and so boring that it is almost impossible to read. Despite the fact that it has been highly touted by the Jewish propaganda networks and tremendously promoted by international Jewry, this book has been read very little, and is still, today, very seldom read by anybody. In fact, the book was not even written by Marx alone but was compiled with a great deal of help from Friederich Engels, his Jewish collaborator and his financial angel. Engels revised and re-arranged Marx's notes in a more readable form, but even so, the whole production is as difficult to wade through as to wade up stream in a river of cold molasses.

Nor does this book contain any really intrinsic new theories. Marx borrowed most of his socialist theories from Condorcet, Saint- Simon, Auguste Compte and others. The theory of Thesis, Antithesis and Synthesis, which he calls Dialectical Materialism, was lifted from the works of G. W. Friederich Hegel. It is a useless and unproductive theory that is no more than a play on words and can best be described as Semitic semantic casuistry.

Nevertheless Marx's writings have been able to permeate and poison the minds of most of today's world, and it therefore behooves us to analyze and study why it did so and just what it was that Marx wrote.

It must be added here that the spread of Marx's teachings has not taken place because of their brilliance, or because of their persuasiveness, nor because of their eloquence, nor because they had something constructive to offer, nor even because there was anything particularly new in his writings and his thinking. The reason they have attained worldwide dissemination is because they have been fervently promoted by the Jewish propaganda network and by force of all the power and influence of the total Jewish conspiracy, just as Christianity was. I repeat, Marxism has not spread because it was a saleable product, nor was it wrapped in an attractive and desirable package— no, it was spread and disseminated and perpetrated solely by the force of the Jewish worldwide organized conspiracy with thousands of speakers in union halls, on radio, on television, injecting the poisons distilled by Marx down the throats of millions and billions of unwitting victims. Like the Sermon on the Mount, it did not offer new solutions, nor did it offer new hope, nor did it offer any constructive doctrine, but on the contrary, like the Sermon on the Mount, it offered a suicidal program for the destruction of our White civilization.

The other work that Karl Marx wrote in collaboration with Friederich Engels is the Communist Manifesto. It is shorter and was written considerably earlier than Das Kapital. It is much more widely read and is considered as the basis of communist doctrine.

Marx was born in Trier, Prussia in 1818. His real name was Moses Mordecai Levy, son of a Jewish rabbi. His father was a proselyte Jew who seemingly left the Jewish religion and turned to Christianity in 1824 when young Marx was six years old. We need not really take this conversion seriously, since the Jews have a habit of parading under false colors, and like the chameleon, merge into the environment they are trying to infiltrate. Since in retrospect we can now see the momentous role that the Jews have bestowed upon Karl Marx, it is not only possible, but highly probable, that the hidden hand of Jewry helped Engels and Marx write their poisonous diatribe. They further, undoubtedly, especially picked Marx as the author so that it could seemingly be attributed as originating from a non-Jew. Then having compiled this assembled doctrine designed to poison the mind of the Gentile, the whole Jewish network worked feverishly to promote and distribute these revolutionary ideas, all in the service of the Jewish race.

* * * *

Let us digress at this point and get our bearings straight in regards to Socialism vs. Communism. Although most people confuse the two as being closely related, we beg to differ vigorously.

Socialism is not an evil as such, any more than is capitalism or money or government or organization, or education, or many other essential building blocks of our civilization. In fact the progress of mankind can be measured by the degree in which mankind was able to live together, institute government and law, organize the subdivision of labor, and form a social community which as it grew, became nations and countries. There is nothing wrong with this. In fact, this is all constructive, and all of these activities are socialistic activities or collectivism in its truest sense.

In fact, the very idea of a group of people living under an organized government is a socialistic endeavor as such, there is no question about it. When we get together to build national highways, to build airports, to create an Army and Navy for the defense of our country, when we join together in common efforts to build a school or schools to educate our children, we are definitely engaging in a socialistic enterprise. All of this means that people collaborate in a common or collectivist effort for their collective good and achieve a benefit far beyond anything that they could do if they acted solely as selfish individuals, each going their own individual path. Socialism, in short, is organized society.

It can truly be said that the measure of human progress can be directly computed by the willingness of the individual to sacrifice his own interests for that of the common good, and this is the essence of socialism. There is absolutely nothing wrong, we repeat, with socialism, per se, or collectivism, and during Hitler's short peacetime period in Germany from 1933 to 1939 under National Socialism, Germany built and created and progressed at an astounding rate never before seen by any other nation in history. That was a White Man's Socialism under the leadership of a great White Man and, we repeat, the results were tremendously constructive, creative and productive.

It is a different matter with communism, a Jewish perversion of socialism designed not to build for the common effort, but designed to destroy the White Man's nation, the White Man's country and the White Man's civilization. Out of the ruins the Jews then forge a hellish Jewish dictatorship. That is what communism is designed to do and that is what the Jew means when he talks about socialism.

Again it is like every other tool that the Jew uses in his program for world conquest: there is nothing wrong with money, but when he uses money, he uses it for the destruction of the White Race and for the creation of a Jewish world dictatorship; there is nothing wrong with government as such, but when the Jew gets a hold of government he uses it to destroy the White Gentiles and help to forge the chains for their enslavement; there is nothing wrong with education as such, but when the Jew gets a hold of it he uses it to pervert the minds of our children, and turn them into hateful enemies of their own culture, of their own civilization, of their own people, and of their own country; there is nothing wrong with labor unions as such, except when the Jew gets in control of them, which he has, he turns them into shock troops to tear down our economic and national structure; and so it goes with everything that the Jew touches and everything that the Jew controls.

Unfortunately, most of the White intellectuals have not been able to distinguish between socialism as such, and the form which the Jews have perverted and converted it into, namely Jewish communism. Unfortunately, in their ignorance the White Race has lumped communism and socialism together as twin evils divided only by degree, and if you are a socialist you must therefore be a blood brother to the communists. This is patently false and deceptive. On the contrary, socialism is the basic fabric of civilization. It is the foundation of organized society. It is the basis of any possible government, and the underlying ingredient of all the progress that the civilized White Race has ever made. It does not take a great deal of thought to come to the conclusion that if every man labored only in his own selfish interests, in other words was completely immersed in "individual enterprise" as the Conservatives are so eager to espouse, humanity would still be back in the caveman stage. In fact he would not even be able to build the basic unit of society— which is the family— because that, too, takes cooperative sacrifice of the individual for the good of the group, small though it may be.

Communism, on the other hand, is an altogether different animal. In fact it is a grizzly beast. Whereas National Socialism under Germany retained private property for the individual; it retained private enterprise as such; it not only retained but promoted family building and family life; it promoted the idea of patriotism and the idea of the loyalty to one's race; communism does none of these things but seeks viciously to wipe them all from the face of the earth. Under the aegis of National Socialism in Germany, during six short years Hitler rebuilt a bankrupt and broken nation, a nation broken morally, financially and spiritually. He built it and forged it into one of the most progressive and productive nations that the astounded eyes of the world had ever seen. The fact that the Jews later through lying, connivery and conspiracy managed to corral the rest of the White nations of the world together to smash Germany from the outside is another story. Nevertheless the accomplishments of Nation Socialism, which was a socialist government, during the six peaceful years in Hitler's Germany is something that no amount of lying Jewish propaganda can erase from the history of our times.

* * * *

Now that we have drawn a distinguishing line between the creative and constructive idea of socialism as such and separated it from communism, let us examine just what some of the concepts of Jewish communism were, as belched up by this Jew, Karl Marx.

The Jews are great dividers, and the theory of divide and conquer has been developed by them to a treacherously fine art. There are a number of ways of dividing humanity— by sexes, by age groups, by religions, and by nations, and various other ways. But Karl Marx chose to divide them into "Bourgeois and Proletarians." Whereas he did not exactly invent these words, he, for all practical purposes, pulled them out of a hat and made them the fighting words they are today, with the help, of course, of the total worldwide conspiracy.

By "Bourgeois" he meant the people in the class of modern capitalists, or owners of the means of production and employers of workers. In fact, just about anybody in the middle class who owned even a small store or a small shop would be classified as "Bourgeois." As we all know, the middle class is the real strength and backbone of a nation, but it was even against these, and especially these, that Marx turned his full invective and his wrath, that as a class they must be destroyed.

"Bourgeoisie" had originally meant the inhabitants of cities, but by the Romantic Age the term had come to mean the middle classes whether they lived in cities or not. Businessmen from the greatest textile magnates down to the smallest hole-in-the-wall shopkeepers, doctors, lawyers, teachers and other educated and professional people, all the groups that we now call

"White Collar workers" were part of the "Bourgeois" according to Marx, and must all be wiped out. Marx's own definition was a new economic definition of the Bourgeois "the owners of the means of capitalist production." And he used this definition to include the middle class in its entirety.

Marx professed to be the great champion of the working class, for whom he coined the word "Proletarians." For this word he reached far back into ancient Roman history, for the Proletarians had originally been the poverty-stricken class (of minor import) of ancient Rome, who had no property save their children (proles). Although the Roman poor had nothing whatsoever to do with factories, Marx liked the term because he believed it had a grand romantic historical sweep. Under the Proletarians he included not only the factory workers but all the urban poor, whether they worked in factories or not, as well as the peasants, who, he was sure, would be drawn into the city sooner or later by economic necessity. The Bourgeois, too, would sooner or later become Proletarians because they would bankrupt themselves by capitalistic competition and would sink into the mass of the Proletariat. The fact that a hundred years later this has not happened, but on the contrary, the middle class has immensely grown and prospered far beyond anything envisioned in the middle of the nineteenth century, doesn't trouble the Jewish propagandist of today in the least. They just keep espousing the same Marxist- Jewish doctrine, forging forward towards enslavement of the world. We might add that this is only one of many of the theories and predictions of Karl Marx that time has proven completely wrong and fallacious.

Marx further wrote in the Communist Manifesto, "The working men have no country. National differences and antagonisms are vanishing gradually from day to day, owing to the development of the Bourgeois, to freedom of commerce, to the world market."

This also was patently false, probably more obviously and stupidly false than many of the other things that he wrote in his treatise— and he wrote many things that were stupid and false. Since the Communist Manifesto was written on the eve of the series of Jewish revolutions unleashed in

1848, Marx judged that nationalistic feelings were on the way out. He

Marxism: The Modern Poisonous Brew

couldn't have been more wrong. It was the beginning of a great resurgence of nationalistic feeling among the working man, just at a time when Marx declared that the working man had no country.

Marx was a master of delineating cleavage between two classes that he had practically invented. In the first chapter of the Communist Manifesto, Marx pictured Europe as being in the throes of a tremendous struggle for "the upper hand between the rising Bourgeois and the developing Proletariat." He pictured the future struggle was to be marked by strikes, lockouts, sabotage, wage slashes, bankruptcies, business crises, the simultaneous rise of industrial combines and trade unions, increasing Proletarian "class consciousness," and violence. He thereby drew the blueprint for tearing apart a country and a nation which the powerful hidden hand of the Jew was to promote with great zeal and energy, was to be used to smash several of the great nations of the world, and is today undermining those that have not yet fallen. He saw this as a vast dramatic clash between two irreconcilable and hostile classes of society who could pursue no other course but fight to the death. As a follower of Hegel, he too believed that progress came through "the fruitful struggle of opposite principles," and to this process Hegel and Marx gave the celebrated name of "dialectics." By this he described the struggle between two opposites, the thesis and the antithesis, finally merging into a synthesis. The synthesis then became the new thesis which soon developed an antithesis which then would again evolve into a new synthesis and so on and on ad nauseum. This pointless theory was then given a fancy name, called "dialectical materialism."

In the second chapter of the Communist Manifesto entitled Proletarians and Communists he presents an argument with Bourgeois critics of Communism as to whether Communism is good or not. When he asks the question "in what relation do the communists stand to the Proletarians as a whole?" an honest answer would have been that there was no relationship since there wasn't really any Communist Party at this stage. However, Marx being as deceptive as he was arrogant,

(a trait very common to his race), blatantly strode forth as if his party and the impending destruction of the Bourgeois was already an established fact in this chapter he sets forth the communist program of the abolition of private property and then goes on to abuse and vilify the Bourgeois. He pictures them as thieving, bloated, stupid villains of some vulgar horse opera, a stance that has since been followed by his Jewish supporters over the past century.

In this second chapter Marx steps up his invective, and the attack against the Bourgeois becomes more vindictive and vicious. He defends the communist program and its aims and objectives to annihilate the state, to destroy culture, religion and the family, claiming, of course, the Bourgeois have already done all this.

Nature's Eternal Religion

He claims there is nothing wrong with the Bourgeois losing their private property since they have already stolen all their property from the hard working heroic Proletarians and farmers that produced it. According to Marx, back in 1848 everything had already been destroyed by the Bourgeois and this included culture, the state itself, religion, family life, private property and on such an insane basis he justifies the communist aims of suicidal annihilation for the nation, arguing that everything would be wonderful as soon as everything was smashed and the working class was in control. These charges are so ridiculous and so detached from the real world that the average person might wonder if Marx had not already lost his mental facilities, and if he hadn't, that he most certainly could not have believed what he himself wrote.

The answer to this, of course, is that certainly he did not believe what he wrote, certainly he did not think that the working class would benefit by what he was advocating. He had no intention of the working class benefiting from anything. We must keep in mind one hard and fast fact, Karl Marx was a Jew, dedicated to his race in the pursuit of the destruction of the White Race. Like the Sermon on the Mount, which advocates "love your enemies, turn the other cheek, sell all thou hast and give it to the poor, resist not evil," Marx's ideas were pure destruction, annihilation and suicide. Nobody was too interested and nobody really bought them. But it was with the tremendous propaganda program of International Jewry behind these ideas that foisted them on the world as they had done previously nearly two thousand years ago when the Jews promoted the suicidal ideas of the New Testament upon the then supreme Roman White world.

Marx then goes on to advocate the abolition of the family unit as such. He defends this suicidal proposal (which certainly has no support from the working class or anybody else) by launching another vicious attack on the "Bourgeois." We must keep in mind that the term

"Bourgeois" meant nothing until Marx and the Jewish propaganda network made it a household word, and it still means nothing, since there are people in all walks of life with different sizes of incomes and all kinds of variations in the amount of their net worth. Nevertheless, Marx continues to hammer the "Bourgeois" as if they were the devil personified and asks the question "on what foundation is the present family, the Bourgeois family, based?" Then he gives a non sequitur (it does not at all follow) answer and says, "on capital, on private gain." He further states that 9/10 of all the people presumably in Europe don't own any property. When these two statements are taken together, they, of course, contradict each other, since the Proletarians he claims make up 90 percent of the people, also have families, in fact, they probably, on the whole, have larger families than the so-called "Bourgeois." According to his ridiculous line of reasoning, those 9/10 (since they don't have any capital and since the family is based on capital) shouldn't be having any family at all. And so it goes.

He jumps from one non sequitur argument to another ridiculous and unfounded argument, but nevertheless he keeps justifying his brew for the destruction of society, that is White society.

He then goes on in this vein of idiocy and advocates that women are to be "freed" and are to be the objects of "free love." He defends this by saying that there is no need for the communists really to introduce this as such, since in any case "it has existed almost from time immemorial." Therefore, all his good little communists want to do is "to introduce, in substitution for a hypocritically concealed, an openly legalized system of free love."

He goes on. Destroy, destroy, destroy. All the known values that previous civilization has set up, Marx wants to destroy.

It is very strange that the whole program and the whole book is consumed with how to destroy the present "Bourgeois" system, how to promote a revolution, how to overthrow, how to annihilate. When one looks beyond the revolution and beyond the tearing down and beyond the destruction, we find very few, if any, constructive ideas about how to build something to take its place, or, in fact, how to build anything. It is the old Jewish program of tear down, tear down, destroy, annihilate. And the next communist plank is the abolition of countries and nationality, arguing that the workmen have no country, a treacherous lie! He then states that national differences and antagonisms between peoples are daily vanishing, a statement that back in the 1840's was completely contrary to fact and history. Very seldom has nationalist feeling been as high as during that period, and not only was it not diminishing, but it continued to grow even stronger over the next half century.

Marx continues on in this kind of idiotic drivel, completely out of contact with fact, history or reality, the main theme being destroy everything, down with everything. The end result will be "the Proletariat will use its political supremacy to wrest, by degrees, all capital from the Bourgeois, to centralize all instruments of production in the hands of the state, i.e., of the Proletariat organized as the ruling class." The thing that he fails to mention is whose hands the state will really be in. What he really has in mind is that it will be concentrated in the hands of the Jews themselves, as history has shown over the last 50 some years of Jewish communist tyranny in Russia.

The end and culmination of the second chapter then winds up with setting forth the famous ten points of the Communist Manifesto and they are famous not because of any intrinsic wisdom contained in them, but again, only because the Jewish worldwide conspiracy has taken hold of them and foisted and propagated them on the rest of the world, much to the sorrow of the unfortunate inhabitants thereof.

We herewith set forth the ten points verbatim in order that we may examine how much progress the Jews have already made in implementing them, not only in the communist countries where they now rule supreme, but also in the so-called "free" Western countries like the United States where they are rapidly tearing down the frameworks of these nations and the foundations of the White Race itself.

Here is the gibberish that the Jews have made so spectacularly famous:

The Communist Manifesto

1) Abolition of property in land and application of all rents of land to public purposes.

2) A heavy progressive or graduated income tax.

3) Abolition of all right of inheritance.

4) Confiscation of the property of all emigrants and rebels.

5) Centralization of credit in the hands of the state, by means of a national bank with state capital and an exclusive monopoly.

6) Centralization of the means of communication and transport in the hands of the state.

7) Extension of factories and instruments of production owned by the state; the bringing into cultivation of wastelands, and the improvement of the soil generally in accordance with a common plan.

8) Equal liability of all to labor. Establishment of industrial armies, especially for agriculture.

9) Combination of agriculture with manufacturing industries; gradual abolition of the distinction between town and country, by a more equitable distribution of the population over the country.

10) Free education for all children in public schools. Abolition of children's factory labor in its present form. Combination of education with industrial production, etc., etc.

Not that there is any great logic attached to the above program, nor is there evident any over-riding need for such changes. Nevertheless, when we consider how much progress the Jews have made in instituting and making this diabolical program become a reality, it is gruesome to behold. It is fantastic to consider that the Jews have created two seemingly antagonistic groups, have artificially divided them, have synthetically labeled them as "Bourgeois" and

"Proletarians," and built on this unsubstantiated and flimsy proposition a program for world conquest. Nevertheless, as fantastic as it seems, with the power of money, propaganda, and organization in their hands, this the Jews have done.

In the third chapter Marx has no new material or ideas that are worth mentioning. He spends most of the chapter justifying with little substantiation and much twisted logic, trying to shore up that which he has already said before. Mostly it is a case of further trying to make a bogey man out of what he prefers to call the "Bourgeois" and trying to whip up the hostile opposing group which he calls "Proletariat."

One point that he does make that is rather interesting and significant, although not in the manner he intended, is that communism and Christianity have a great deal in common. He says,

"Nothing is easier than to give Christian asceticism a socialist tinge. Has not Christianity declaimed against private property, against marriage, against the state? Has it not preached in the place of these, charity and poverty, celibacy and mortification of the flesh, monastic life, and Mother Church? Christian socialism is but the Holy Water with which the Priest consecrates the vexation of the aristocrat."

Whereas Marx did not at all state the case correctly, he inadvertently brought up a point that needs emphasizing, and that is the similarity between Jewish Christianity and Jewish communism, which, we contend, are amazingly similar, although neither the communists nor the Christians would ever admit this. Nevertheless, they are extremely alike and we are going to make a comparison of the two.

One of the main planks of the communist program is the abolition of private property. Christianity, too, promotes such, in fact it castigates again and again against those productive members of society who have the energy and the foresight to provide for their families. The New Testament says again and again, "sell all thou hast and give it to the poor." "It shall be harder for a rich man to enter the kingdom of heaven than for a camel to walk through the eye of a needle." "My kingdom is not of this world." "Lay not up treasures on this earth but lay up treasures in heaven. "Behold the lily in the field, it toils not yet your heavenly Father cares for it." And so on and on. The theme is repeated again and again that anybody that is energetic and ambitious enough to work for a living and provide for his family is an extremely poor candidate to enter into the kingdom of heaven.

Then we come to the matter of family life. On this we find that Jesus is quoted as saying,

(Matt. 10, v. 34) "Think not that I am come to send peace on earth: I came not to send peace but a sword. For I am come to set man at variance against his Father and the daughter against her mother and the daughter-in-law against her mother-in-law. And a man's foes shall be they of his own household. For he that loveth father or mother more than me is not worthy of me and he that loveth son or daughter more than me is not worthy of me." Here we have clear evidence as quoted by Christ himself that the objective of the new Christian religion is to divide— divide the household, divide the family, destroy the family.

We may have other manifestations of the Christian church pulling down the family and stifling the procreation of its members. For nearly 2,000 years the Catholic Church has been promoting celibacy amongst its people. Priests were, and still are, forbidden to marry. It has set up numerous monasteries, the members of which, namely Monks, are dedicated to living out their life in an unmarried state'. The best and the most devoted of the young women are deluded into joining a convent and becoming a Nun and stripping themselves of any form of womanly appeal that they might have originally had. They are then rigidly regulated by the "Mother Superior," spending the rest of their lives in a bleak Nunnery, finally withering away and dying, unproductive and childless, having destroyed their hereditary line with their religious perversion.

Another major similarity between Jewish communism and Jewish Christianity is the philosophy with which both of them attack the productive, creative leaders of society. We have already well covered the vicious attacks that communism makes on the so- called "Bourgeois," and how it extols the virtues of the "Proletarians," that is, these people who have not managed to acquire anything. That the reason therefore might be due to their own lack of ambition, is not mentioned.

In the same way the New Testament continuously denounces the rich man or the man who has acquired any property or any assets. Whether he did so by dint of his own hard work and perseverance is ignored. It keeps repeating again and again that he is completely disqualified from ever getting to heaven and it says, "For what shall it profit a man, if he shall gain the whole world, and lose his own soul?" Then in the Sermon on the Mount it extols the virtues of the shiftless, the unambitious and the lazy. It says, "blessed are the poor in spirit," "blessed are the meek," and so on and on.

These concepts are completely contradictory to the ideals and virtues of the White Man, who has always held such virtues as productivity, creativity, ambition, progress, in high esteem.

In a later chapter, in Part II of this book, I will go more fully into a detailed comparison between communism and Christianity.

Suffice it here to say that Marxism is a Jewish creation, designed to undermine and disintegrate the White Man's society, to tear it asunder, and lay it wide open like a dead carcass for the parasitic Jew to feast upon.

Continuing on to the third and fourth chapters of the Communist Manifesto, we find (a) a scattered and confused review of history at large, with

Marx doing much violence to history, trying to justify his idiotic arguments (b) his appraisal of the then existing and competing socialist parties. He has very little good to say about any of them, and predicts their early demise. He insisted that he was right and that every other group that called itself socialist was inadequate, unscientific, wrong, and vile. Right or wrong, all those groups soon disappeared, as Marx had predicted.

However, it is important to point out here that it was not due to the fact that Marx's ideas, if they can be called such, had any superior merits to these others. No, on the contrary, they were probably more inadequate, more unscientific, more wrong, and more vile than any of those that he denounced. The success of Marx's ideas is solely due to the fact that it was his ideology that the huge Jewish conspiratorial apparatus selected to make their vehicle for their program of the destruction of the White Race.

This is what the whole program is aimed at. He insists on the "forcible overthrow of all existing social conditions," with the reckless abandon of a pyromaniac. He ends the last chapter with the fiery appeal to the workers, "Let the ruling classes tremble at a communist revolution. The proletarians have nothing to lose but their chains. They have a world to win. Working men of all countries, unite!"

And there we have a summation of the highly touted Communist Manifesto. In short, Marx pulls out of ancient history two terms, the Proletariats and the Bourgeois, twists them, gives them new meaning, and uses them as a divisive wedge to create two antagonistic groups where none existed before. He then unleashes a campaign of vilification, slander and hatred to stir up the working group to destroy just about anybody who has acquired any property during their lifetime of productive work. On this flimsy "theory," if it can be called such, is launched a whole program to destroy society, to destroy the family, to destroy the state, and in short, as he himself says, to destroy "all existing social conditions."

Das Kapital

We now turn to that monumental one thousand-page production that is revered as his masterpiece, namely, Das Kapital. We are not, however, going to waste much time on it because it is not worth it. In all those thousand pages of garbage there is very little grain to glean.

Mostly it is all chaff. In fact, it is very dull, dry chaff, at that. He tries to amalgamate and blend economic theory and political theory with history, sociology and his own Utopian thinking. The result is one unholy disaster. He makes a great to do about his theory of "surplus value," something he really did not invent, but derived from classical British economic doctrine of the time.

Marx's whole method was not that of observation and logical deduction of that which he had observed. Rather, he had some very fixed conceptions— namely that society should be destroyed— and then went to work to drag together a mass of fallacious "evidence" that he twisted in such a fashion that it would seem to support his untenable theories. Even at this he fails miserably. However, after 1,000 pages of this kind of trash, he seems to have convinced many people (although they haven't really read it and although they really don't understand it) that somehow there must be something to it. Even so, it has convinced hardly anyone who was not already tinged with the ideas of Revolutionary Marxism previously. Economists, historians, and philosophers have long since ceased to take it as a serious contribution to any of their fields. It is so long and so dull a book that even very few Marxists can stand to read it, or can understand it.

The best function of the book, Das Kapital, to the world of Marxist Socialism is to sit on the shelf, looking heavy and impressive, and to be pointed to as evidence that somewhere in all those hundreds of pages there must be some deep intellectual proof of anything that any given Marxist may happen to feel at any given moment

The Communist Manifesto was published in 1848. Volume I of Marx's Kapital was published in 1867, nearly two decades later. This amounted to approximately 800 pages. When Marx died in 1883, Volumes II and III were no more than a confused mass of notes, references and outline. It was Engels' lot to put them together in final form and prepare them for publication. These appeared in 1885 and 1894, respectively, bringing this massive accumulation of trash to more than a thousand pages.

Most of Marx's organizational activities involved him in prolonged quarrels with other socialist leaders, notably the German Trade Unionist Ferdinand Lassalle and the Russian Anarchist Mikhail Bakunin. He helped found an abortive working man's association in 1864, which is known in socialist history as the "First International." However, his struggle to keep Bakunin from taking over that organization helped wreck it in the early 1870's. When he died there was no communist organization as such to speak of.

The greater development of the organizations that profess Marxist doctrines came only after his death. From the 1880's on, the International Jewish apparatus really took hold of his theories which they had helped to propound and built them into parties of major importance in most continental European countries, especially Germany, France, and Italy. By 1889 they formed an international coordinating committee called the "Second International."

Whereas Marx had tailored his program with the idea of Germany being the first victim, history turned out somewhat differently. It remained for Nikolai Lenin, another Jew, to found the important Russian Marxist party.

The Bolsheviki, between 1909 and 1913. These later renamed themselves "communists" after Marx's term in the Communist Manifesto.

Lenin's party, however, was very different from the theories propounded by Karl Marx and could scarcely be called Marxist at all. In fact, Lenin picked up most of his doctrine of "dialectical materialism" from other Russian revolutionaries, particularly N.G. Chernyshevskii rather than from Marx. He formed his plans for the Bolshevik Party, a tiny, well disciplined, conspiratorial, elite group in a vast backward peasant country, from earlier Russian revolutionary theory and practice, and not from Marx, who had rejected such ideas as "unscientific adventurism." The only thing that Lenin really adopted from Marx was the "scientific" idea of the "inevitability" of a socialist revolution and the emphasis on the Proletariat.

Whereas we neither have the time nor the space to concern ourselves with the history of the Russian Revolution, let us not, however, delude ourselves that it was the attraction of either Marx's "brilliant" theories, nor those of Lenin's. The grizzly story of the destruction of the Russian people is something altogether different.

Russia for centuries had been infested with more Jews than any other country in the world. These Jews had been conspiring, agitating and planning anarchy and revolution for a long time.

Leon Trotsky, another Jew, had been trained along with 3,000 other cutthroat Jewish revolutionaries in East Side New York to do the strong-arm job for the overthrow of the Russian government. Jacob Schiff, a Jewish financier of New York, contributed 20 million dollars to this cause. When the proper time came, Trotsky and his band of revolutionary cut-throats were shipped to Russia, and along with their Jewish brethren they managed to pull a bloody coup d'etat. It was strictly an example of Jewish conspiratorial tactics at their best. The Russian people and the Russian "Proletariat" couldn't have understood less as to what was going on. The Jewish propaganda network both in Russia and in the outside world then loudly proclaimed the triumph of the "poor, down-trodden" Russian workers over the "tyrannical" regime of the Tsar.

Both of these representations were overwhelming, atrocious lies.

If the Russian Tsar had any faults they were not on the side of tyranny, but rather on the side of tolerance, weakness and vacillation. The Russian workers neither understood what was going on nor did they have any conception of the ghastly fate that was in store for them.

Once the Jews were in power in Russia they quickly seized all the strategic posts in government and in propaganda. They immediately launched a massive campaign to slaughter 20 million White Russians.

It must here be pointed out that it was the Nordic White Russians, who for centuries had been the intellectual and creative leaders of the Russian people, in fact, had built modern Russia. It was, therefore, this select group of elite White Russians that was the prime target of the Jewish takeover immediately after they had the revolutionary government in their hands. They proceeded on a reign of terror the likes of which the world had never before seen, a reign of terror that continues even to this day. In a few years they miserably slaughtered 20 million White Russians, the cream and leadership of the Russian population, leaving the Russian Slavs and Kulaks as a mass of slaves in the hands of their Jewish masters. These now became the hewers of wood and the drawers of water for their Jewish masters— who had promised them a worker's paradise.

Thus we witnessed the death of the Russian nation and the establishment of Jewish communism with a worldwide operating base in the largest country on the face of the earth, and with it, control of its enormous natural resources.

BOOK II
THE SALVATION

CHAPTER ONE

NATURE AND RELIGION

In studying the creatures of Nature, we have observed with increasing clarity that each creature has its own peculiar means of survival, of propagation, of gathering food, of defense, and of ushering in the next generation. Not only does each creature have its particular pattern for survival, but in this pattern are imbedded many peculiarities that are to each creature inherently its own. For example, a beaver instinctively knows how to build dams and this provides a useful means for its survival. A cat instinctively knows how to catch mice and this also is a great aid in its survival. A cat can do many other things that are inherently peculiar to a cat, but certainly building dams is not one of them. Furthermore, we could never hope to teach a cat to swim like a beaver, to build dams like a beaver, cut trees like a beaver, and to act like a beaver. The instinctive inbred peculiarities of a beaver are its own, and those of a cat are its own.

Similarly, in observing the peculiarities of the human race, we find an inherent characteristic that is universal and peculiar to the human races, and that is the pursuit of some religion or other.

When we study the history of the different civilizations, of the different peoples that have lived on the face of the earth, of the different races, we find almost without exception that each and every one of them had some kind of a religion. Whether it was one of the highly developed civilizations of the Egyptians, or the Greeks, or the Romans, or whether it was some backward colored tribe like the Indians in the Amazon region of South America, or on the great plains of North America, or whether the Hottentots in Africa, no matter how primitive they are, or how primitive they were, they all have had a religion, and they all have some kind of a religion today.

The fact is that the human races, from the most primitive to the most highly developed nations of the world today, have been infested with thousands of religions, all different from each other. Even within the different religions, they have divided and subdivided themselves into a multiplicity of sub-religions such as the Christian religion, for instance, until just about every walking

Nature and Religion

Christian has a belief that differs from his co-religionists, each one wandering around in the belief that he has the ultimate key to knowledge and wisdom and that everybody, but everybody, that differs from him is wrong in so far as he differs from his own religion.

Little does such beguiled Christian realize what deceptive and flimsy tenets are the basis of his creed, nor does he realize its true origin.

In no religion has the splintering, fragmentation, internal bickering, squabbling and disagreement been more manifest than in the Christian religion itself. We can be sure the Jew planned it that way.

Nevertheless, from all the foregoing we must conclude that religion and the affinity of mankind for religion is an inborn trait with which Nature has endowed us, and is inbred in our genes. We apparently need religion for our survival, one way or another.

And the fact is, we do. As the Old Testament says, a people without vision perish. All people in order to survive and flourish, need a religion, a creed, a life-philosophy. They urgently need a religion to give them direction, goal and purpose. We need a sense of belonging.

Without it mankind flounders, withers and dies like a fish out of water. Furthermore, the more closely a people's religion is rooted to their racial soul, the more healthy and dynamic it is for that particular race. Fortunate is that race whose religion has found its own racial soul.

Many religions have been notoriously bad for the races that have embraced them, as for example the White Race having embraced Christianity, or, should we say, having had it foisted upon them by the Jews. Some religions were neither good nor bad, but were utterly ridiculous and nonsensical. Such an example is the religion with the multiple Gods that the Romans and Greeks had, Gods that cavorted around in the heavens committing all kinds of infidelities, adulteries and trivial nonsense.

There are a few, a very few, that have been good for the race which embraced the religion they created. One notorious example is the Judaic religion of the Jews, which was tailor-made for a parasitic race. It has been the greatest thing that they have produced and it has sustained them for the last several thousand years.

In sum total, we can safely conclude that most religions have been notoriously bad, and it has been the unfortunate lot of the White Race to be cursed with one of the worst of them in the last 2,000 years.

I feel extremely blessed and fortunate to be a member of the great creative White Race. I am very proud to be a member of the White Race and I love the White Race more than anything in the world. Nature has endowed the

White Race with a deep instinctive loyalty to its own kind - Racial Loyalty. We have been endowed with this instinctive characteristic for our own survival by a gratuitous Nature. This healthy instinct has been atrociously smothered by an outrageous alien religion that we are cursed with and seem to be unable to shake off.

Yes, we are cursed with the Jewish religion of Christianity, whether we like it or not. It is a sick religion, a death-oriented religion, a religion that is destroying us. It is smothering every healthy instinct with which Nature has endowed us and is blunting and perverting all the best attributes with which Nature has so generously blessed the White Race. What we most desperately need is a new religion, a religion of our own, a religion that was created by the creative genius of the White Race itself, not foisted upon us by the treacherous Jew. We desperately need a good religion.

But what is a good religion?

This is really not too hard to answer. A good religion is one that helps to promote and advance the race which embraces it. If it helps the particular race, it is a good religion. If it neither helps nor hurts, it is a useless religion and is more of a nuisance than anything else. If it hinders the race that embraces it in its fight for survival, then it is a bad religion and harmful to its adherents.

We have heard countless numbers of times people say, "well you have to believe in something." This is true to the extent that everyone does need a life philosophy that relates to and reconciles us with the natural world in which we find ourselves, one that helps us to have a realistic and rational view of our struggle for survival in a competitive and hostile world. The closer this philosophy or religion or creed, whatever we may choose to call it, harmonizes with the laws of Nature, the more beneficial, realistic and useful such a creed will be. The more it departs from the natural laws and indulges in a flight from reality into a dream world of fantasy and superstition, the more artificial, unrealistic and dangerously harmful such a creed will become.

Since I am addressing myself solely and exclusively to the membership of the White Race, I can say without hesitation that the only thing we are really interested in is a creed that will help to propagate, protect, promote, preserve, advance and expand the White Race. We are interested in a religion that will aid and benefit the White Race in its struggle for survival in a competitive and hostile world. We are not interested in a creed for the Papuans of New Guinea; we are not interested in a creed for the American Indians; we are not interested in a creed for the niggers, neither here in America, nor the niggers of Africa; we are not interested in a religion for the Hindus, nor for the Chinese. Nor are we interested in a universal religion for the "salvation" of all mankind. Not at all. We are interested purely and simply in a religion for the survival of the White Race and the White Race alone, and helping that race advance to heights greater than have ever been dreamed of before.

When we put it on this plain and simple basis, namely of the two concepts enunciated, one, that a religion is good if it helps to benefit the race that embraces it, and two, that we are only and exclusively interested in a religion for the White Race, then the solution becomes fairly simple. In fact, the formulation of a creed for the White Race can now be basically summed up in one sentence—the guiding principle of our new religion should be: will it benefit the White Race?

Whereas the formulation of a new creed is relatively simple and relatively basic, we are faced with a much more gigantic problem of clearing the ground of all the rubble, rubbish and debris of the present religion that we are now stuck with. As is so often the case in building a beautiful new edifice where all the ground has already been pre-empted by trash and slums, clearing the required area often presents more of a problem than building the new structure itself. So it is with our own plight. Building the new religion is not nearly as difficult as clearing away the rubbish and confusion impregnated in the brains of our White kinsmen. Our greatest task is exposing the monstrosities of the Christian teachings and bringing our White Brothers and our White Sisters back to their senses to clearly see what is good for us, good for our children, good for our future generations, and good for our race. We are faced with the task of clearing up the aberrations that have unhinged the minds of the White Race for the last two millenniums and have nearly brought about the wreckage of our race. Our foremost task is: to straighten out the White Man's thinking.

The first and most urgent question which the White Man must come to grips with is the matter of finding himself and following the brilliant destiny Nature has mapped out for him. All other problems such as food supply, pollution, traffic congestion, overpopulation, finances, etc., will become child's play as soon as the White Man regains full control of his faculties and of his own destiny. If he does not solve this prime and urgent problem, all others will never be solved, nor will they really matter. If the White Man remains entrapped within the Jewish framework of ideas he will fumble and flounder in confusion until he is obliterated from the face of the earth and all the other problems will become utterly meaningless.

Nor is our major problem overcoming the Jews, the niggers and the other colored scum of the world. No, not at all. Our major problem first and foremost is to straighten out the White Man's thinking. We must reorient his thinking to basic values. Once we have cleared his brain of the Jewish poison, clearing the Jews and the niggers from our midst, too, will be child's play. It is to this noble objective that our new religion is dedicated.

The White Man must be brought back to his senses. Before we can even begin to straighten out the White Man's thinking, there are a few basic prerequisites that we must be crystal clear about The first one is, just where does the While Man's loyalty lie? And, secondly, what is the purpose of his life here on this earth?

In answering the first question we must realize that we, the White Race, are now in a desperate battle for survival. It is being waged by a treacherous and cunning enemy who has so befuddled the minds of the White Race that the overwhelming majority of White people don't even know who the enemy is, and, in fact, most of them don't even know that they are in a bitter war in which they are the victim marked for extinction. The White Man's mortal enemy, the International Jewish apparatus, has so confused and scrambled the brains of the White Man that he is now not even putting up the least bit of a fight, or the slightest resistance. In fact, the White Man's brains are so polluted with the wrong concepts and the wrong ideas that he has actually joined with the Jew in his own destruction.

In any battle it is of paramount importance lo know who your enemy is; what are his weapons; what is his strength; what is his method of operation, and many other vital facts that can be gleaned from intelligence. Know your enemy. The more you know about your enemy and the more you know about your own strength and weaknesses the better prepared you are.

Not only must you know the strength, the weaknesses of your enemy, and that of your own, you must also know who is on your side and know what it is you are fighting for. Furthermore, you must have a specific detailed aggressive plan of battle that will inspire confidence for a victory. You must have a specific program. You must have a goal.

One of the most powerful weapons the Jew has in his favor is his masterful manipulation of confusion into the minds of the White Race. He spreads confusion as a farmer spreads fertilizer on his fields, and the Jew's harvest in war and destruction of our people is even a thousand fold more productive than the farmer's fertilizer. The one area that most White people are desperately confused about is— just where does their loyalty lie?

The other major question is: What is our purpose in life?

In the next two chapters I want to discuss these two vital questions— questions that have confused the White Race to no end. It is my purpose to explicitly set forth the position of the CHURCH OF THE CREATOR on these basic issues of life.

CHAPTER TWO

YOUR LOYALTY— A SACRED TRUST

Where does your loyalty lie?

If you belong to one of the Kosher Konservative groups, they will have pounded into you over and over again that you must be loyal to your country, loyal to your flag, and above all, loyal to that great, great American Constitution. "Patriotism" is the great virtue, they say. Even the Jewish controlled newspapers will tell you the same thing, although they then will immediately proceed to desecrate and befoul all of these with the most scurrilous trash and garbage that they generally heap upon all of the White Man's institutions and emblems.

The fact is that a man's loyalty belongs to none of these. A man's loyalty is first and foremost to his racial family, which is an immediate extension of his own family. In other words, a White Man's first and foremost loyalty belongs to the White Race. Every other race knows instinctively that their loyalty lies with their own race. The Jews know it, the niggers know it, and every other race knows it except the average White American, who it so happens, is the basic target for destruction in this treacherous and tricky war we are now enmeshed, whether we like it or not, whether we know it or not.

The Jew may be a citizen of France, or England, or Germany, or the United States. He is completely unconcerned about the welfare of his host country. He acknowledges no loyalty to any such country. On the contrary, he usually is actively engaged in pulling down the framework of the country in which he lives, plundering and ransacking the remains in the process. He has only one loyalty— the Jewish race. Let some country threaten to harm a Jew anywhere in the world— such as the recent Russian hijackers, or the Rosenberg atomic spies of a few decades ago— and all the Jews of the world rise to a man and scream to high heaven: "Save the Rosenbergs!" "Let our people go!" The fact that the condemned Jews are guilty criminals is irrelevant as far as they are concerned. Save them at any cost! Scream persecution! Scream loud and long!

Anything to save any Jew no matter how guilty, no matter how criminal

Let us never forget that it is this racial loyalty and solidarity that has made the Jews the world power they are today.

Racial loyalty is a fundamental instinct given us by Nature for the preservation of each race. The healthier this instinct is and the more a race exercises this healthy instinct, the more likely it is to survive. The more it is smothered by deception or brain pollution, the more vulnerable such a race is to destruction from those who utilize their native instincts of racial loyalty.

The black man has it and the Jew finds it easy to promote racial loyalty among the niggers, to organize it and utilize if for the destruction of the White Race. He has the niggers talking about

"Black Culture" where none exists. He has them talking about "Black Pride" where there is very little to be proud of. The Jew, through his skillful manipulation of propaganda has the black man screaming "Kill Whitey." He fans an emotional hatred for the White Race not only among the blacks and mulattos of America, but among all the colored peoples of the world. His plans call for the deployment of the inferior colored races of the world as shock troops to mongrelize the superior White Race and kill and exterminate those that will not mongrelize.

This program of mongrelization or extermination is taking place before our eyes in America today. Forced school busing, a dastardly outrage and a shameful insult to the White Race, is a major part of the program to mongrelize the next generation. It is their objective to pump the black blood of Africa into the veins of White Americans. Nobody need deceive themselves that the Jewish program of "togetherness" and "intermingling" during the school years, fortified with a massive brain pollution program in the schools, on television and in the news media, that this is not going to end up in mixed marriages and race mixing. In fact, mongrelization is the overwhelming massive drive that the Jews have in store for us today. They're going to use every power play, every trick of propaganda, and every unconstitutional law that they can force upon us to achieve this, their goal, the mongrelization of the White Race.

Just today I read about a Jewess by the name of Cohen lecturing a group of "Christian" White women about where their "Christian" duty lay. According to this Mrs. Cohen, the White families were living in an artificial world and they better get with it and start adopting black babies, because there was a surplus of black babies for adoption and it was their "Christian duty" to give them a home. She added ominously that if this wasn't pursued with vigor and enthusiasm, there were already laws in the making that would force them to adopt these little black jungle bunnies. And, again, let us not deceive ourselves, unless we put a stop to this outrage, the Jews will successfully perpetrate this and other hideous programs upon us to obliterate and mongrelize us.

Another part of the program to reduce and cut down the cream of America's White youth is the present senseless war in Vietnam where every week something like 50 or more young White Americans in the prime of their manhood are killed in the jungles of Vietnam, Cambodia, Korea and elsewhere. Several hundred more are maimed and crippled for life. Thousands return from these jungle wars addicted to dope, their lives tragically ruined and not only useless, but many have been turned into dangerous criminals when they return to American soil.

Let us repeat: the Jew knows where his loyalty lies, and every other colored race knows where their loyalty lies, namely with their own race. It is only the White Race that is confused— strange to say— that very race that Nature has crowned as the pinnacle of her creation and destined to rule the world.

Thanks to the Jews' overwhelming control of the instruments of propaganda, the White Man is now so filled with a zeal to be a do- gooder and to save every worthless scum and parasite on the face of the earth, that he doesn't even realize that the parasites are multiplying rapidly while the White Race is declining, and that the parasites intend to destroy him as soon as they have the power.

This is racial suicide.

So we, members of the great White Race, must come to our senses and discard such an idiotic, self-destructive philosophy. It is contrary to all reason. It is contrary to all the good, healthy instincts given to us by Nature for our own self-preservation. It is contrary to all common sense. We must believe first and foremost in practicing racial loyalty— loyalty to the White Race and the White Race alone.

We must abandon the idiotic suicidal attitude we have pursued in the past and turn to a sane, realistic course as prescribed by Nature herself. Of all the millions of species in Nature, I know of none that says: "In deference to a weaker and inferior species, we will hold back in the expansion of our own, in fairness to the underprivileged we will render aid to the scum so that they can multiply, outbreed us, and push us from the face of the earth."

No, none of them practice this idiotic program of compassion for the scum, the weaker and the inferior. None, that is, except the White Race.

We of the CHURCH OF THE CREATOR, therefore, completely reject the Kosher Konservatives' idea that loyalty to country, to the flag and to the Constitution comes first.

Who could be loyal to an America when it has become completely niggerized and Judaized and whose prime national objective is the mongrelization and extermination of the White Race? Certainly any good intelligent member of the White Race is bound to realize that such a country is his enemy, whether he likes it or not, and he owes it no loyalty whatsoever. In this respect, too, we must realize that it is not the country itself that is the culprit, but the traitorous structure that has usurped power over the country, led by the Jew.

If I saw an American nigger beating up a White Canadian, I would not be on the side of the nigger because he was an American, but I would rush to the aid of the Canadian because he was White. I find it impossible to owe any loyalty whatsoever to a government when such government is continually proving by its deeds that it is promoting the welfare and multiplication of the blacks and promoting the destruction of the White population. No thoughtful White parents would care to stay and bring up their family in a country that had become niggerized, as Haiti, for instance. Since many parents see this happening in the big city jungles of the United States, a number of them are planning to leave this country and move to Australia, or elsewhere, where there are no niggers. Many have already done so. This shows that when the chips are down a responsible parent will think first of his family and its racial future— not the real estate upon which he resides.

While I commend such parents for their loyalty to their race, I cannot approve of running. I believe White Americans must stay in America and fight to regain control of our destiny. This land is ours. We must be determined to stay here and fight for what is ours. We should be pursuing, not fleeing.

The United States of America now is the only reservoir of White power left in the world strong enough to overcome the treacherous Jew. The White people of America must rise up to a man, as did the White people in Germany a generation ago. When this happens in America, fortunately then the massive productive power of this great country will be aligned on the side of the interests of the White Race and not against it, as in World War II.

I repeat, the solution is not for the White Man to run to Australia, or any place else. The solution is to move the niggers out— back to Africa where they belong— before they drag this great land of ours into the sump hole of history.

We must change our stance. We should be pursuing, not fleeing.

Let us now consider loyalty to the flag as a paramount virtue. The fact is, the flag is only a symbol, one that has been changed many times in our past history. In fact, it changes every time we take in a new state, such as Hawaii or Alaska. But more important, the flag is a symbol only as honorable as the country that flies it. It flew with the Union Army when the Jews had White Americans organized to kill another group of White Americans. They called one group of Whites "The North" and the other group of Whites "The South." This dastardly fratricidal war was a Jewish harvest in which the Jews got rich and fat, but was a most shameful and destructive episode in the history of the White Race. World Wars I and II again had White brothers killing White brothers, and again, the

Jews reaped a rich harvest in spoils and White blood spilled. White Americans marched into these Jewish arranged slaughters under the banner of the Stars and Stripes, but it is not something we can be proud of. Until we cleanse our country and our history and the flag that flies over it of Jews and niggers we do not have a flag of which we can be particularly proud.

When we, the White people, again have control of our own destiny we will undoubtedly want to mark this even with a new flag, an unsullied flag that is truly a symbol of the White Race. It will be one which we can be proud of indeed.

Our neighbor to the north, Canada, recently discarded their hundred-year-old flag and designed a new one— predominantly red— a fitting color considering the direction that country has taken. In any case, we can always design a flag without any great pain, but once the White Race is destroyed, it is gone forever and nothing can bring it back.

No! Our loyalty is not with our country, nor our flag, but our people— our own race. Then we have the Constitutionalists who remind us of our "great" Constitution, the Bill of Rights, and proclaim that it alone is responsible for the greatness America has achieved. They tell us that it is because of our unique and wonderful Constitution that we in American have a standard of living higher than that of any other country in the world. It is because of our Constitution— the "greatest freedom document conceived by the mind of man"— they tell us that we enjoy our many "freedoms."

That is a lot of bosh. There are several serious flaws in the reasoning that "we owe it all to our wonderful Constitution." The Constitution has inherent in it many serious defects, some of which indeed, are fatal. In any case, we now know that it has not, and will not, save us from a Bolshevized Jewish take-over.

Some of the serious defects that it has are:

a) It did not base the formation of this great country on the issue of race. It failed to do this at a time when the White Man was building America and was unusually race conscious and united in fighting the red man. Furthermore, the opportunity at this time was great since the Jewish infestation was still relatively small, although growing.

b) Instead of incorporating the Leadership Principle, the only real basis for building a permanent and lasting society, it chose instead to base it on the fragmentation of authority which is the so-called principle of democracy. It then eulogized their wonderful principle of "divided powers," "check and balance system" and called it a "republican" form of government as if they had created something new. Actually this was nothing new.

The Romans had a republican form of government more than 2,000 years earlier and finally discarded it for a better form when they changed to the Empire form with an Emperor at the head commanding absolute authority and incorporating the Leadership Principle.

c) Foolishly, and contrary to all common sense, they incorporated in the Declaration of Independence the "heroic" proclamation that "all men are created equal." This is a fraudulent lie in the face of history, Nature and experience. Although the

Declaration of Independence is not part of our Constitution, the importance of that proclamation has really given the liberals, the Jews and the bleeding hearts a field day in perverting our sense of reality, in promoting the inferior races and in thwarting and punishing the better elements of the White Race. A whole network of harmful lies has been spawned from this unfortunate and most deceitful statement.

d) It has the further inherent weakness of dividing Church and State. Whereas the ideology of the Church promotes the ideas of "Resist not evil," "Love your enemies," "Turn the other cheek," etc., the fundamental basis of any state is authority, law and order.

A much more harmonious relationship is achieved when the government, church and religion are ideally harmonized on the same principles. Of course, we cannot blame the Founding Fathers for not being able to achieve this at that time since they had no good racial religion to work with, but unfortunately were stuck with the suicidal ideology of Christianity. Unfortunately, too many of them were themselves over imbued with this Jewish hoax.

e) Lastly and most important of all, the Constitution did not keep out the Jews and keep this parasitic race from contaminating this great new land of promise. Had the Founding Fathers heeded Benjamin Franklin's advice and just put in that one stipulation - to exclude the Jews - it would have done more good than all of the rest of the Constitution and the Bill of Rights put together.

Here is what Benjamin Franklin said at the first Constitutional Convention of the United States in 1778, almost 200 years ago:

"In whatever country Jews have settled in any great numbers, they have lowered its moral tone; depreciated its commercial integrity; have segregated themselves and have not been assimilated; have sneered at and tried to undermine the Christian religion upon which that nation is founded by objecting to its restrictions; have built up a state within a state; and when opposed have tried to strangle that country to death financially, as in the case of Spain and Portugal.

"For over 1,700 years the Jews have been bewailing their sad fate in that they have been exiled from their homeland, as they call Palestine. But, gentlemen, did the world today give it to them in fee simple, they would at once find some cogent reason for not returning. Why? Because they are vampires, and vampires do not live on vampires. They cannot live only among themselves. They must subsist on Christians and other peoples not of their race.

"If you do not exclude them from these United States, in this Constitution, in less than 200 years they will have swarmed in such great numbers that they will dominate and devour the land, and change our form of government, for which we Americans have shed our blood, given our lives, our substance and jeopardized our liberty.

"If you do not exclude them, in less than 200 years our descendants will be working in the fields to furnish them substance, while they will be in the counting houses rubbing their hands. I warn you, gentlemen, if you do not exclude the Jews for all time, your children will curse you in your graves.

"Jews, gentlemen, are Asiatics, let them be born where they will, or how many generations they are away from Asia, they never will be otherwise. Their ideas do not conform to an American's, and will not, even though they live among us ten generations. A leopard cannot change its spots. Jews are Asiatics, are a menace to this country if permitted entrance, and should be excluded by the Constitution."

In the first place America owes her success to her racial stock— the fact that the initial immigrants were of the great White Race— the good English, Irish, Scots, Germans, Swedes and other White European races. Secondly, unlike the Spaniards of South America, they had the good sense not to mongrelize with the savage natives— they kept their bloodlines pure. They drove back the inferior savage and built a great empire from the Atlantic to the Pacific— an era that is the most dramatic saga and most productive epoch in the history of the great White Race. Their standard of living soon exceeded those of their European forbearers because they had, and have today, a more ample supply of land and natural resources to work with.

Our forbearers did not make the same mistake that the Spaniards did who colonized South America. Whereas the Spaniards who were more strongly religious and under the influence of the Catholic Church, intermarried and interbred with the inferior native Indians and poisoned the blood of their future generations, we now see the difference in the pages of history. In mongrelized South America and Mexico, we see perennial revolutions, poverty, backwardness, and a future written in dissolution and anarchy. We White Americans are now (stupidly) subsidizing the mongrelized bastard offspring of these Spaniards to the tune of billions of dollars.

As further evidence that the much ballyhooed American Constitution had little to do with America's pre-eminent success, we only need to be reminded that when the Latin American countries became independent from Spain, each and every one of them copied the United States Constitution almost to the letter.

Did this insure their success and greatness? Most decidedly not. South America and Central America have been racked by turmoil, revolution, instability, poverty and inflation almost constantly.

Having the same "wonderful" Constitution, why did they then not achieve the same success as the United States? The answer is clear and simple: It lies in race and in the blood. They are a mongrelized conglomerate, whereas the United States was built by

the White Race. Therein lies the answer, and not in constitution, flag or territory, for certainly. South American is equally rich in the natural resources of its territory, if not more so.

No, our success in America was not due to our "wonderful" Constitution. It was due to the good White racial stock and the wealth and bounty of our land. The Constitution had little to do with it. Today, as the Jew is working full time for the destruction of America and the White Men who built it, our Constitution is not going to save either our freedoms, our country, or our race. We are no longer free. In fact through trickery, deceit and betrayal, due to lack of racial loyalty among the offspring of the founders of America, we are an occupied country— we are at the power and the mercy of the International Jew. We are economically enslaved. We are culturally being Judaized. Our children are being bused around like cattle in order to mongrelize future generations and liquidate the White Race.

The biggest mistake the Founding Fathers made in writing the Constitution of the United States was failing to heed the advice of Benjamin Franklin— one of our greatest of the White statesmen.

It is an important part of our creed to correct this fatal mistake made in the writing of the Constitution. We must drive the Jew from power and drive him from our shores in order to reclaim the government of these United States and ensure the destiny of the White Race. We mean to take it back into the hands of the White people and disfranchise the Jew, render him harmless so that never again will the White Race be placed in the shame and the peril in which it now finds itself.

No, my White Racial Comrades, our first loyalty is neither to country nor to flag nor to the Constitution, all of which are transient and subject to change. Our first loyalty lies in our blood, to our own people, to the great and wonderful White racial family.

Let us never forget this overwhelmingly important fact, it is the basic building block on which our new religion is founded— the

religion which will not only restore the independence of the White Race, but make it great beyond our fondest dreams.

We are herewith founding a new religion for the White Race. We are calling the new religion Creativity. Our church is called The CHURCH OF THE CREATOR. Members of our religion are called Creators.

In the next chapter, we will examine our purpose and our mission. We will examine the reason for our existence and the meaning of life itself.

CHAPTER THREE

THE PURPOSE OF LIFE

    For millennia mankind in general, and philosophers in particular, have been pondering the meaning of life. This question has undoubtedly troubled and concerned practically every thoughtful human being. Few have arrived at any conclusion during their lifetime, leaving the question unanswered at the time of their demise. Certainly this question has concerned me, more or less, during many phases of my life, beginning with early adolescence. Although I searched the scriptures, the religions, the philosophies of various notables throughout history, none of these seemed to give me a satisfactory answer. Finally I concluded that there was no meaning to life, that there was no purpose to it, that our stay here was a meaningless, useless pursuit which might well have been left better undone. In fact, ten years ago I was so convinced of the futility of our existence here on earth that I began to write a book on the subject called The Rat Race to Oblivion.

    But the fact kept persisting that we are here, and we are going to be here, and our offspring are going to be here for generations and centuries and millenniums to come. Obviously, the kind of people that were going to be living here in the centuries and millenniums to come would be largely determined by each generation as to what they did, what their outlook on life was, what their mating habits were, and what their philosophies and religions were. Also it was obvious that the conditions under which our future offspring were going to be living would largely be determined by what we now did, just as the conditions under which we are now living had been determined by what our forefathers had done, or had not done.

    The more I studied history the more it became obvious that throughout the threads of history was woven the interminable and overriding factor of race. The most obvious of all factors began to emerge— that one race and one race along had built and blossomed and flowered all civilizations— and that was the White Race. Furthermore, it became more and more obvious that the decline of each civilization had been the poisoning of the blood of the creative White Race and its downfall had always been preceded and caused by the negligence of the

White Race to guard and protect the purity of its bloodlines.

Further studying, examining and probing the facts of history, it became obvious that mankind as a whole followed the same evolutionary patterns as did every other species, and that the evolution of every species followed the rigid and immutable laws of Nature. Man was no exception whatsoever, although in his conceit and stupidity he so often tried to tell himself that he was above and beyond the laws of Nature and, in fact, had conquered Nature.

So he thought. However, nothing could be further from the truth.

A cold, critical analysis of history, and the laws of Nature, shows that the development of mankind follows the laws of Nature just as faithfully and just as rigidly as the development of, say, the bluebird or the dinosaur. Furthermore, man's decline and extinction is just as possible as the vanishing of the dinosaur from the face of the earth.

From all this studying, certain most obvious conclusions began to emerge. No. 1, that man is a species whose evolvement and stay on the face of this earth is subject to the organized laws of Nature. No. 2, that one of Nature's most inexorable laws is the survival of the Fittest. No. 3, that Nature, in order to improve the species, promotes and favors the segregation of the species in which one species competes against that of another and the better equipped survive. Those that go down channels which do not fit them for the fierce competition, those species to not survive, but perish.

Apparently it became obvious that Nature is not concerned about the survival of the individual, but has wisely placed and inbred into each individual of the species the means and the will to propagate and promote and perpetuate the species itself, and in so doing, in the fierce competition for survival, it forces the species to improve and upgrade itself, or else perish.

It is in this third law of Nature that we find overwhelmingly the purpose in life and the purpose for which we are placed upon this earth. We are here to perpetuate and advance our own kind. Not only is this the purpose of the human species, but the purpose of every other species that we see around us, be it the bluebird or deer, or the fishes of the sea, or the fowl of the air. The whole sum of their efforts and the complete time span of their life is devoted to this great purpose that Nature has set forth for the individual: To promote, propagate, and perpetuate the species, and in so doing, improve it as it goes along. It is either that or extinction. Nature is neither kind nor unkind, neither merciful nor unmerciful, in the enforcement of her laws. She makes no exceptions and tolerates no excuses. Only a pompous, conceited fool can imagine himself as being above and beyond the laws of Nature.

Every bird and every animal knows what its purpose is. As soon as they are mature enough to do so, they start propagating their own kind, and raising their families to maturity. It is their main preoccupation throughout their adult lifetime. They clearly seem to know their purpose. Only the White Race seems to be sorely confused about their purpose-Nature has decided our purpose for us, whether we realize it or not. Man, like every other creature, leads the most rewarding life following the path Nature has decreed for him: propagating his own kind, raising his family, and perpetuating his race.

And so we have come upon the great and final answer as to what our purpose in life is: The purpose set before us by nature herself, for us, the White Race, is, namely, to propagate, advance and expand the White Race, the highest pinnacle reached in the handiwork of Nature.

We, the White Race, are that supreme species. We are Nature's Crowning Glory. We bear a great honor and a tremendously important burden. It has taken millions of years for the White

Race to evolve as a species to its present high pinnacle. It is up to us to carry on the promotion, propagation, perpetuation, advancement and expansion of this most elite of all of Nature's wondrous species. Not only is it up to us to carry on, but also it is up to us to lift ever higher, to advance the development of this most marvelous of all creations, and improve from generation to generation. It is possible at this juncture in history to greatly accelerate and speed up the improvement of the White Race, and it is equally possible to destroy the White Race in short order and undo this marvelous phenomenon in the history of creation.

Yes, these are the indisputable lessons of history and the inescapable conclusions to be drawn from the laws of Nature herself. Some people will spend their lives searching for the truth. In the process they can run head-on into the very truth they have been searching for, without recognizing it, stumble over it, pick themselves up and keep on searching forever. There are some truths that are so overwhelmingly obvious that they escape the attention of the over-sophisticated searchers. And this very truth we are here speaking about is one of the most outstanding of all the obvious truths that has been ignored and overlooked, stumbled over and finally bypassed.

This does not change by one iota the laws of Nature anymore than stupidly ignoring the laws of gravity will change that rigid and inexorable law. It is plainly there for all to see— Nature wants you to perpetuate and carry on your species and improve it you will either do that or your kind will be wiped from the face of the earth. Nature cares little whether you accept or reject that fact, her laws will be obeyed, regardless. It is this fact that our whole philosophy is based upon. It is upon this law of Nature that our whole religion is founded.

This being so, we are convinced that any philosophy of life or any religion, that is in harmony with the laws of Nature is a good religion for such race. Any religion that does not mesh in harmony with the laws of Nature is an unnatural

The Purpose of Life

religion, is an artificial religion, and is a harmful religion that will destroy the race or the people that embrace such an artificial and unnatural religion.

Our religion is, therefore, designed to be in harmony with that which Nature wants us to do. Our religion is designed to help promote, propagate, expand and advance the White Race in all perpetuity. We can think of no higher goal, nor a more lofty religion than that which helps to perpetuate and improve Nature's finest handiwork— the White Race.

We believe that in the process of propagating our own kind, the individual finds the highest meaning in life. In so doing he obtains the greatest satisfaction and enjoyment of his earthly span for the years that Nature has placed him upon the face of this planet. In mating, in building a family, in having children, and providing for their welfare and in watching their healthy growth and development, the man and the woman find their highest fulfillment and the most lasting satisfaction. All other activities gravitate around this grand central purpose— to raise the children to adulthood to where they again in turn will mate with the opposite sex of their own species, form a family, propagate their own kind, raise them to be stronger, healthier, more intelligent, more beautiful, more capable. In short, they, too, will improve the next generation and send it on its way to again bring in the succeeding generation. This is the great goal in life that Nature in her eternal wisdom has set before us, whether it be the White Race or any other species of this huge and varied universe.

Any activity that hampers or imperils this noble objective is unnatural, and, therefore, a violation of Nature's laws. We all clearly recognize, for instance, that homosexuality is unnatural and that such people are called deviates. We must also recognize that Nature harshly punishes deviates and extinguishes them from the face of the earth. It is quite clear, for instance, that a society of sexual deviates would be short-lived and Nature would wipe them from the face of the earth.

Not so clear to the present day thinking is that one of the prime laws of Nature is keeping the species pure, and in our case, keeping our race pure and unpolluted from the blood of that of other races. Nature hates bastards. She despises mongrelization. And since Nature has selected us, the White Race, as the peak and pinnacle of her highest development, it is more than ever our holy duty to safeguard this honor at all costs.

It is for this purpose that our new religion is formulated, and that the CHURCH OF THE CREATOR is founded.

CHAPTER FOUR

THE SIXTEEN COMMANDMENTS

1) It is the avowed duty and holy responsibility of each generation to assure and secure for all time the existence of the White Race upon the face of this planet.

2) Be fruitful and multiply. Do your part in helping to populate the world with your own kind. It is our sacred goal to populate the lands of this earth with White people exclusively.

3) Remember that the inferior colored races are our deadly enemies, and the most dangerous of all is the Jewish race. It is our immediate objective to relentlessly expand the White Race, and keep shrinking our enemies.

4) The guiding principle of all your actions shall be: What is best for the White Race?

5) You shall keep your race pure. Pollution of the White Race is a heinous crime against Nature and against your own race.

6) Your first loyalty belongs to the White Race.

7) Show preferential treatment in business dealings with members of your own race. Phase out all dealings with Jews as soon as possible. Do not employ niggers or other coloreds. Have social contacts only with members of your own racial family.

8) Destroy and banish all Jewish thought and influence from our society. Work hard to bring about a White world as soon as possible.

9) Work and creativity are our genius. We regard work as a noble pursuit and our willingness to work a blessing to our race.

10) Decide in early youth that during your lifetime you will make at least one major lasting contribution to the White Race.

11) Uphold the honor of your race at all times.

12) It is our duty and our privilege to further Nature's plan by striving towards the advancement and improvement of our future generations.

13) You shall honor, protect and venerate the sanctity of the family unit, and hold it sacred. It is the present link in the long golden chain of our White Race.

14) Throughout your life you shall faithfully uphold our pivotal creed of Blood, Soil and Honor. Practice it diligently, for it is the heart of our faith.

15) As a proud member of the White Race, think and act positively. Be courageous, confident and aggressive. Utilize constructively your creative ability.

16) We, the Racial Comrades of the White Race, are determined to regain complete and unconditional control of our own destiny.

The Sixteen Commandments Defined

1. Secure the Existence of Our Race.

There are some species flourishing on the face of our planet today that have been in existence for over 200 million years. The continued existence of the White Race at this time in its history, on the other hand, is extremely precarious. Unless we take measures drastically different from the criminally irresponsible program we have been pursuing in the past, it is extremely doubtful whether the White Race as such will survive for another two or three generations.

We have observed earlier that the natural enemies of the White Race are the colored races in general, and the most deadly of them all is the Jewish race, in particular. Our decline has not been due to the inferiority of our race in its ability to maintain itself. On the contrary, our superiority in an out and out contest for survival against the colored races is so obvious, that we have allowed this to be used against us, to our own detriment, and towards our own ultimate disaster. Our problem has not been lack of strength, or lack of ability, but the weakness of compassion, the stupidity of bending over backwards to be more than fair to the inferior, and in general, a muddle-headedness, if not criminal negligence, in guarding that which is most precious.

This again is completely contrary to the laws of Nature. Nowhere does Nature say to any fish, plant, bird or animal: in deference to the other weaker, less capable species, hold yourself back and give the inferior species a break; be fair to them; give them a better chance to multiply at your expense and let them crowd you from off the face of the earth.

But this is exactly what the White Race has been doing in its obsession to dispense "brotherly love" to the inferior scum of the world. Now that our backs are against the wall, we will be forced to throw overboard such suicidal thinking. This softheaded, mushy, Christian sentimentality must now be replaced by the eternal, iron fisted laws of Nature.

We must therefore re-orient our thinking completely in this respect. We must not only make sure that our survival on the face of this planet will not ever again be imperiled by our natural enemies, but make deadly certain that it cannot ever be imperiled again. This is the first and the highest law that Nature imposes upon us.

The means for accomplishing this are set forth in the remainder of the commandments.

2. Populate the World.

Nature's pattern for most living things can be briefly summarized as follows: birth, growth, reproduction and death. This is the pattern Nature has ordained for all its living creatures, whether it be the lowliest insect that lives but a day, or the highest order of man himself, who might live his span of three score and ten years. Nature has not meant for any individual of any species to live for long. No indeed, each individual merely plays its roll in being the present link in the long golden chain of its own species. It is Nature's intention that the species should live on and on.

However, the species itself, unless it is vigorous in its fight for survival, will eventually result in extinction. Some species that have adapted themselves well to their environment and in the fight for survival, have lasted for millions of years. In fact, the shark family has existed for at least two hundred million years without undergoing any great changes, a tribute to its marvelous ability to survive. Compare two hundred million years to the short interval that any particular individual of that species exists upon this planet.

It is also thus with the human race, and in particular with the White Race with which we are exclusively concerned. We should remind ourselves that this is Nature's pattern, and remind ourselves of the purpose for which Nature has placed us on this earth. Nature tells us loud and clear that that purpose is to propagate our own kind and thereby perpetuate our species. In the process of the natural selection and survival of the fittest, it tells us to keep improving our species in an ever-upward climb. Nature has never ordained eternal life for any individual, or for any generation.

No, on the contrary, death is certain, but you perpetuate yourself in your children and in the generations that follow. This is the real immortality Nature has in store for you.

You become imbedded in the wonderful blood lines of your race, and as the patriarch or matriarch of your line, have a never-ending chain of descendants that go on, not only for centuries, but for thousands of years and millions of years. That is the possibility of eternal life that Nature has granted us. But only if we are fruitful and multiply, in other words, if we have offspring.

Whether you are a man or a woman, the most important action you will ever take is that of getting married and raising a family. Having children of your own is the most meaningful, the most satisfying, and the most rewarding accomplishment of your entire lifetime. It is the only really permanent and lasting thing that you will ever do. No matter how much money you make, or what fame you might aspire to, all will be erased and obliterated as time goes on. But the resultant consequences of the action you took of getting married and having offspring will go on from generation to generation. It will ring through the ages— not only through the centuries— but through the millenniums and through the millions of years.

Long after any other action that you might have ever taken will have been completely erased from the face of this earth, your descendants will march onward through history. This is only true, of course, if the White Race survives. If it does not survive, not only will your descendants be wiped out with it, but all the struggles of those that have gone before you as well.

Only the present generation can do justice to the past generations and again bring about the future generations. You are the link between the White Race that has gone before you and the White Race that will come after you. If the present generation fails to fulfill its obligations, it will wipe out the hard-earned struggle that the thousands of generations achieved in bringing us to the high level that we have now reached; it will also fail to usher in the future generations that would be carrying that wonderful evolution to ever increasingly greater and higher levels.

The very struggle for existence for any species, and at this stage in history, particularly the White Race, depends on how prolific and how fruitful each and every one of us is in bringing in the next generation. Only by so fulfilling our Manifest Destiny do we achieve a full and rewarding life.

In leading the good life yourself, in meeting your obligations to the past generations that produced you and in fulfilling your obligations to the wonderful generations that will follow you, do your part and have as many children as you can. Remember it is the Manifest Destiny of the White Race to populate the world, or perish.

It is not only a race against time but it is also a race against numbers. If the direction that the world population trend is now taking is not reversed, we are going to be overwhelmed and crushed by the colored races through sheer weight of numbers alone.

Nature's Eternal Religion

It is our manifest duty to overcome this challenge, and to propel humanity to an ever-higher level of evolution. Only the White Race can do this.

Furthermore, it is the moral duty of those members of our race that are above the average in intelligence, ability and physical attractiveness, to make a special effort in having larger than average families. Once the White Race is in control of its own destiny, it will behoove our society to set up certain incentive programs to see to it that the finer specimens of our race are especially encouraged to increase and multiply and further bestow the benefits of their genetic endowment towards the good of the race.

3. Expand the White Race, Shrink Our Enemies.

Practically every species of Nature has their particular natural enemies and some of them have more than others. Whereas the coyote has few natural enemies outside of man himself, the rabbit has a whole flock of predators, pursuing him as fair game for their food and sustenance. Among these are hawks and eagles, coyotes and wolves, bobcats, lynxes and a host of others.

Man, too, has had his natural enemies throughout history, and throughout history each tribe's most deadly enemy has usually been some other tribe of mankind itself. Even before the White Man ever arrived in America, the Indian tribes carried on constant warfare against each other, killing and scalping each other, and taking over the other tribe's hunting grounds. Among the niggers of Africa, constant warfare has prevailed, one tribe killing another, with the victor often ending up eating the vanquished enemy. Evidently it is in the scheme of Nature's natural development of a higher species to have superior races survive and the inferior vanquished and destroyed.

I didn't invent this program. I am merely slating a fact of Nature that has existed from time immemorial. It has been going on constantly, not only in the struggle amongst the races, but also in the struggle for survival among the animal, bird, fish and other kingdoms.

This system evidently worked fairly well and mankind did keep evolving into higher and better types. In fact, by the advent of Christianity the White Man, as personified by the great Roman Empire, was completely supreme and dominant throughout the then known and worthwhile world. Not only that, but had the natural course of events continued, it would have undoubtedly conquered the rest of the world such as India, Africa, China and America, and the White Race would today be completely dominant and supreme throughout the entire world. No doubt it would probably have populated it completely by now. This would undoubtedly have happened, had the Romans at that time only been aware of their precious racial values and continued to keep their race pure.

Sad to say, this development did not continue along natural lines. The

Romans, unfortunately, did not realize the value of their superlative race. The Romans, intelligent as they were, failed to recognize one of Nature's most important laws— that of keeping the species pure. They paid most dearly for their transgressions against this deadly sin.

Working amongst them was their most deadly natural enemy, spread like a virus throughout their empire, ready to disintegrate and dismantle the great Roman Empire and the White Race itself. This deadly virus amongst them was the Jewish population. We have already reviewed elsewhere the havoc the Jewish network wrought amongst the Roman population by introducing and propagating the deadly poison of the "new" Christian teaching that unhinged and demented the Roman mind. Over a few centuries, it induced them to commit suicide, to promote the destruction of their own empire, their own laws, their own religion, and finally, their own race.

Even during Roman times, the Jew, as always, was the first and foremost in the traffic of human slaves. It was the Jewish slave trader, more than anyone, that dragged the slaves from other parts of the world into the Roman Empire. Even in those times the Jew promoted race mixing and mongrelization, which along with Christianity, destroyed the Roman Empire. Tragically, it was never to rise again.

The Jew has long been aware of his capabilities as a parasite to hamper and impair the White Man's mind, and he is ferociously pursuing this course today, as he has over the thousands of years. The Jew, having made huge fortunes over the centuries dragging the black niggers from Africa into America, is now pushing with unparalleled fury the program of race-mixing and mongrelization here on the North American continent. The niggers, with the help of the Jew, are most surely going to destroy the White Race, are going to destroy our civilization, and drag the world down into a mongrelized hell, not unlike that which anybody can go and see for himself in the sub-continent of mongrelized India. Even closer to home we can go to Haiti in a few hours flying time and see before our own eyes what happens to a beautiful countryside when a mongrelized, half-savage mass of scum take over a once beautiful landscape.

We must therefore always keep in mind that: (a) the Jews are our most dangerous natural enemy; (b) the niggers are, next to the Jews, our most deadly menace, one with which we cannot co-exist in the same country, or even on the same continent; (c) all colored races are hostile to the White Race and its natural enemy.

Throughout Nature the laws are quite clear: in order to survive when a menace or danger threatens, that menace is attacked and destroyed. We must therefore make it our prime goal to expunge the Jews and the niggers from America, in fact from all other White areas.

We must also realize that all the colored races are our natural enemies,

Nature's Eternal Religion

that as soon as they are ever capable of over-running us and destroying us, they will most certainly do so. Whether we like it or not, we are forced to take the position that the White Race, like the Romans, must populate the world— or be destroyed.

Again, I didn't invent this situation, nor did I create it. I am merely slating an historical fact and pointing to the inexorable and unbending laws of Nature.

Despite the fact that all the idiotic, whining, bleeding hearts will cry to the contrary, and try to deny this: despite their blabbering about humanitarianism, compassion and brotherly love, what I have staled are the hard cold facts of life and nothing in the world will alter them. It will either be the White Race or the inferior scum of the colored races that will inherit the earth.

As members of the White Race, it is our manifest destiny and our moral duty to make sure that we survive and that the White Race does not perish. At this point in history, the Jews and the colored races are winning victory after victory, and the White Man has been retreating, giving ground, running before an inferior species.

It is a case of the stronger fleeing before the weaker, a phenomena witnessed nowhere else in Nature. Whereas in 1920 the White Race was outnumbered by the colored races in a ratio of only two to one, it is now outnumbered by the colored races in a proportion of seven to one, and a gleeful (Jewish) United Nations predicts that in another twenty years the White Race will be shrunk to the point where they will be outnumbered by the colored races at a ratio of forty-nine to one.

Our unalterable program for the future must be: expand the White Race, shrink the colored races, until the White Race is the supreme inhabitant of the earth.

4. All Benefit to the White Race: The Golden Rule.

This is the foundation of our whole religion: what is good for the White Race is the highest virtue; what is bad for the White Race is the ultimate sin. This is clear and simple. From this solid foundation we can expand and define endlessly as to what is good and what is bad, and this we have done throughout this book. However, if each member of the White Race keeps this clear and simple creed in mind, and uses it as a yardstick in all its action, it will be relatively easy to decide as to what to do in the different situations of life.

Our Golden Rule is: do that which is best for the White Race.

Hold fast to this great principle as you journey through life, and it will sustain you to the end of your days.

5. Racial Purity.

Nature herself, in her eternal wisdom, has decreed that each species keep its line pure and uncontaminated from that of any other near like species. Nature has clearly ordained the inner segregation of each species. There are, for instance, 175 species of woodpeckers, 265 species of flycatchers, and 75 species of larks. There are 258 species of sharks in the ocean. No matter where we look the evidence is overwhelmingly clear that Nature in her infinite wisdom has promulgated this as one of its great natural laws. To violate such a clear and basic law is an outright abomination against Nature. Furthermore, each species, including the human race, has an inborn and an instinctive love of mating with, associating with, and living within the group, of its own kind. Nature has further given each species, and especially the human race, an instinctive revulsion against interbreeding and intermingling with a foreign species, or in the case of the human race, with any alien race.

When the superlative White Race has the great good fortune to be the crowning glory of Nature's own creation, its finest handiwork, we of the CHURCH OF THE CREATOR regard it as the most abominable crime to pollute Nature's finest accomplishment with any of the lower species. It is a major travesty against Nature herself to see the pollution of the White Race taking place throughout the world today. Not only is this crime being perpetrated before our eyes on a wholesale scale, but the White Race is not lifting a finger to prevent its happening. The Jew on the other hand is pouring fuel upon the fire to promote its acceleration.

The White Race must rapidly come to its senses and know these natural truths that even the birds, the Fishes, and every other creature of Nature has known instinctively throughout all the millenniums of their existence.

Racial loyalty is the key to this dilemma. Racial loyalty is racial survival. Mongrelization is racial suicide.

Civilization is a property of the White Race and its most significant characteristic. It is furthermore a living contract ingrained in our race between our yet unborn, our Living, and our Great Forefathers, those who carried the torch and led the way before us.

In our living hands now lies the responsibility of carrying on the noble heritage that is our legacy. We have a contract to bequeath it to our progeny—the White Race that is yet unborn. Not only do we owe the coming White generations the obligation to pass on all the good of the past, but we must strive to contribute further to it during our own time. Above all, it is our holy duty to keep our bloodlines clean and continue to upgrade genetically, so that the next generations will be finer, stronger, more intelligent and more beautiful than any in the past.

Let therefore the White Race rise to a man, close ranks and drive the niggers, the mulattos and the Jews from within our midst. Let us make it overwhelmingly clear that we will no longer, now or ever in the future, ever again tolerate the pollution of this great gift from Nature, the crowning pinnacle of her creation.

6. Racial Loyalty.

We have already discussed in the previous chapters, that contrary to what we have been taught by the conservatives and liberals alike, your First loyalty does not belong to your flag, your country, nor the constitution. Your loyalty, first, last, and always, belongs to your own race, your own kind. Nature tells you this very plainly in her every act as we look around us— your first duty lies in the perpetuation of your own race and your own species. It is a tragic fact of world history that the White Race has been so befuddled and so confused by the Jewish- Christian teaching that they have lost sight of this eternal truth.

It is the unending task of this our religion. Creativity, to impregnate the minds and the souls of the White Race with this great overwhelming fact, to burn it forever into their consciousness, that this great reality is basic to our survival.

Racial loyalty means racial survival.

Nature has endowed us instinctively with this important characteristic for our own protection. She has endowed us with a natural dislike for all other races and a repulsion to keep us from interbreeding with, or intermingling with, or promoting, races other than our own. We clearly see this strong loyalty amongst even the colored and the inferior races. The nigger has racial loyalty for his own kind, the Indians have racial loyalty for themselves, the Chinese have it, and the Hottentots have it. Racial loyalty and racial solidarity is strongest of all in the Jewish race. In no other race is this attribute more abundantly clear than in this parasitic race, and no other attribute than Jewish solidarity has contributed so much to the predominance of the Jew in gaining domination over the White Race and the world as a whole. The Jew may also excel in cunning, in treachery, and in many other base traits, but it is his unflagging racial solidarity that has been instrumental in the enslavement of the rest of the human race. Racial loyalty for the

White Man can and will become his most powerful tool in winning his own freedom and his own salvation.

In the future struggle in regaining control of our own destiny, we must make Racial Loyalty a cardinal issue. We must draw a sharp and distinct line between those who are loyal to the White Race and those who are betraying us. We must force every White Man to stand up and be counted— he is either for us, or he is against us. He will either declare his loyalty to the White Race by deed and word, or he will be branded as a traitor to his race.

Treason to the White Race will be regarded by us as the most sinister crime any person can possibly commit, even more heinous and despicable than treason to the country. We will make the term "race traitor" the most foul and vicious epithet in our vocabulary.

The day will come when the traitors who today are betraying the White Race with impunity will be brought to justice. That justice will be summary and it will be final. Woe unto the traitors to our Race!

7. Preferential Dealings.

Today the Jew has an overwhelming monopoly in business and trade, not only in America, but throughout the world. It is therefore almost impossible to as much as turn around but what you are doing business with some Jewish chain store or some other Jewish outfit, regardless of whether you are buying clothes, or a car, or groceries. It is therefore difficult, if not almost impossible, at this juncture not to do business with the Jews, either unintentionally or otherwise. However, there are any number of transactions in which we do have a choice.

In the professions, for instance, when choosing a lawyer, an accountant, a dentist, a doctor, we certainly can and must avoid having any dealings whatsoever with Jews. Exercise racial loyalty. In selecting a real estate agent, or a contractor to build a house, we certainly can and must give our business to members of our own race and avoid the Jew like the plague. In going to a hardware store or other retail stores that are not part of chain stores, we can certainly select those that are not owned by Jews. We can pretty well take for granted that most chain stores are owned by Jews, or under the control of Jews. In any case, if all White people were indoctrinated with the idea of avoiding business with the Jews, in fact, boycotted them, it would not be long before the White businesses would be supreme. Even the chain stores would be reduced in importance and the Jews driven to the wall.

Whereas this is not the main means of driving the Jew from power and influence, it is nevertheless an important adjunct of our total program of cutting down the Jew and creating racial loyalty amongst the White people. We will thereby further be forging a political and religious force that will drive the Jew from power and drive him from our shores. A part of this program should also be the refusal of the White Man to ever work for a Jew, or a Jewish outfit.

In regards to the nigger, while we are in the transition period where we are not yet united enough to ship the nigger back to Africa, we should immediately institute the policy of increasingly refusing to give any jobs whatsoever to the niggers. We should not employ them as lawn maintenance men, or as maids, or as waiters in restaurants, not even as dishwashers. We should refuse them jobs as cab drivers, ditch diggers, manual laborers, as carpenter's helpers, or any other job.

Some people will argue that they would then automatically go on welfare and further aggravate the load upon the White taxpayer. Unfortunately, this is true, but it is better from our point of view to relegate the nigger to the position of being a completely useless parasite in our society. It is better to have him destroy himself with dope, drink and shiftlessness. It will soon become overwhelmingly clear to the average White person that the nigger is a useless parasite in our society and must be removed. It will then become obvious to the most idiotic bleeding heart that the only thing we can do with the nigger is ship him back to Africa.

A similar policy further should be extended in the presence of goods manufactured by the colored races. Our country at present is flooded with products made in Japan, or from Hong Kong, or in Taiwan, or even in Israel, in factories built with American money. It is much better to buy American made goods in the first place, or preference must be given to those made in say England, Sweden, Germany, Austria, or other White countries.

These are guidelines for the transition period only. Once we are completely in charge of our own destiny, none of these factors will any longer be a problem.

The worst mistake we can make in our thinking is that we can use the nigger as cheap labor. This is the fatal mistake that the White Man has made throughout his history. He has allowed the Jew to drag the nigger into our midst to do the hard manual labor, believing that this was necessary and was cheaper than employing White labor. This was the fatal mistake that the White Man made in India some four thousand years ago. It was the mistake that the Southern plantation owners made in America over two hundred years ago, much to our regret. It is a mistake that the White businessmen and employers are making in South Africa and Rhodesia today.

The fact is, we do not need the nigger. In an age of modern technology, the nigger is completely obsolete. He is even more obsolete today than is the horse and buggy. With the advent of the internal combustion engine for power and the more recent event of electrical power, the last thing in the world the White Man needs is the nigger for cheap labor. The fact is the White Man never did need the nigger for any kind of labor. History clearly demonstrates that whereas the South did employ the nigger as a means of cheap labor, the West was won and developed and built completely without any help from the nigger whatsoever. Even in the northeastern United States, including the New England states, progress and prosperity was certainly not impeded by the absence of niggers.

Today, more than ever, what with the internal combustion engine to provide motor power, with hydro-electric power, with huge steam-electric plants, and with the more recent advent of nuclear power, the nigger is about the most useless, obsolete component in the modern White Man's world we could possibly think of. He is however, a very dangerous, festering, and rapidly spreading cancer in our racial body. A very urgent and drastic operation must be performed and it must be performed soon.

8. Destroy Jewish Influence.

This again is a program to pursue during the transition period while we still have the Jews on our backs. There are many things we can do to help destroy and obstruct Jewish influence, and one of the most effective is to point at and broadcast those things that are Jewish and urge other White people to boycott them. This would include a campaign against the Jewish actors, Jewish books, Jewish politicians, and Jewish public officials. Be active in ferreting out behind the scene Jewish manipulators. Having discovered them, then aggressively spread the word. Arouse the White people. Get them organized in opposing any Jewish activity that rears its ugly head.

People are more effectively influenced by word of mouth and by speech than any other means. It is therefore particularly effective to constantly and continuously expose the Jew, argue about the conspiracy, harangue about his perfidy, and continuously make him the point of contention.

Organize against the Jews, boycott them, expose them. Fight them every inch of the way until we have driven every last vestige of Jewish influence from our land and the parasites themselves from our shores. We will and must expunge the Jews from our midst and cleanse our society from every last trace of the foul Jewish influence that has plagued us for too long.

Victory will be ours. It is inevitable.

9. Work a Blessing.

According to the Jewish Bible, when the Lord drove Adam and Eve from out of the Garden of Eden, he cursed them and said among other things "In the sweat of thy face thou shalt eat bread." The implication here is that man was cursed with work.

This is a Jewish idea. We, of the CHURCH OF THE CREATOR, reject this Jewish idea in its totality.

We believe that work is a blessing. We believe that Nature especially endowed the White Race with certain inherent qualities in its ability to work, to create, and to produce. This is the most outstanding characteristic of the White

Race. It is an endowment that we are particularly proud of and a pursuit that we, of the CHURCH OF THE CREATOR, enthusiastically foster and encourage.

10. Lasting Contribution to the White Race.

Taking a lesson from the pages of Jewish history over the past many thousands of years, we find that the main reason for the success of the Jew in his goal towards becoming master of the world has been his constant preoccupation with the welfare of his race and his unstinted dedication to this cause. It has paid him well personally, and the race as a whole has benefited handsomely.

Jewish success can be attributed mainly to three major reasons.

1) They stick together.

2) They are unanimously dedicated to their race above everything else.

3) They have a far-reaching plan, as they say, "A people without vision perishes."

The Jews are a state within a state. Most of the Jewish wealth generally is poured back into the cause of the Jewish race. The Jews have set up hundreds of foundations to siphon off their enormous fortunes into Jewish-Communist goals. Tremendous sums are sent to Israel, and all of them tax-free. Not only do the Jews themselves send their own money to Israel, but they have set up various power plays whereby they extort huge sums of money from the Gentile nations to send to Israel. To date, more than a billion dollars has been extracted, for instance, from post- war Germany, and sent to Israel as "reparations," but in simple essence it is out and out thievery and blackmail. Imagine, forcing the White German people to pay a billion dollars to a state that never even existed when the alleged "crimes" were supposed to have been committed against the Jews, as restitution for actions that were never committed, from millions of Germans that weren't even born at the time of the alleged "crimes." The American White people, on the other hand, are continually sending aid to Israel, in the form of Falcon Jet fighters, in the form of outright "foreign aid" running to the tune of hundreds of millions a year. However, we should not let this obscure the fact that the Jews themselves give, and give generously, to the state of Israel and to their hundreds and thousands of Jewish organizations in this country. Usually when a Jew dies, he leaves the mass of his vast fortune to the Jewish cause, in one way or another.

According to the Jewish Independent, an economist's newsletter, the average American Jew leaves an estate of $126,000. This is, of course, their reported wealth. The actual Figure is probably a lot closer to half a million dollars. In contrast, the average White Man, when he dies, leaves only a meager estate of something like $2,500.00, hardly enough to bury him. But then we do have a large number of White businessmen who have accumulated a considerable fortune during then-lifetime— fortunes that run into many millions of dollars. And where does their money go when they die? Well, since they haven't particularly planned too well ahead, and haven't really looked for a good cause to leave it to, and even if they had, they would be hard put to find one, usually their wealth, too, ends up in the hands of the Jews. How tragic it is that a man like Henry Ford, who fought the Jews most of his business life, was to create a huge multi- billion dollar fortune, only to have this money fall into the hands of his enemies after his own death, only to be used in perpetuity to promote the Jewish- Communist cause.

Had he personally set up a foundation to further the cause of the White Man in one way or another, put dedicated men in charge of that foundation and transferred a huge part of his estate even before he died, this would not have happened. Furthermore, had there then been a dynamic new religious movement, such as the CHURCH OF THE CREATOR, dedicated to the preservation and promotion of the White Race, this great White American undoubtedly would have left the bulk of his fortune to such a cause.

There now is, and will be forever more, the CHURCH OF THE CREATOR to Fight for, and promote the cause of the White Race. We appeal to all loyal White people who are concerned with the survival of their own kind to make a will and to leave their wealth to our own religion— their own religion, and not let it fall into the hands of the Jews for the promotion of the Jewish cause, the most deadly poison to the White Race there is.

I also suggest that many other foundations could be set up that could be dedicated to the promotion of the White Race. In any case, such foundations or organizations should be well planned and well thought out in advance. Definite action must be taken to insure the estate will go where intended when the time comes. In all further events, I suggest that a man endowed with a considerable amount of wealth should not wait until he dies before he transfers a large portion of his estate to the cause of the White Man. Again, taking a lesson from the Jews, they give and give generously in every fund raising campaign that they undertake in dedication to the Jewish cause. It is not at all unusual for the Jews to have a "Bonds for Israel" drive in Miami Beach, for instance, and in a few days raise $200,000,000.00. In contrast to this, witness the meager response in a fund raising campaign by some Right Wing party to further their cause. Perhaps, of course, this might be due to the fact that the White Man really hasn't been given a worthwhile program, nor a very worthy cause, in the past to which he could really dedicate himself and contribute his hard- earned wealth.

However the time has come and the cause is now here.

There are many other ways that a staunch and loyal member of the White Race can contribute to his own kind, to the White Race, other than financially.

He can, for instance, found a new worthwhile organization dedicated to the cause of his race. He can enter politics and fight for the cause in the political arena. He can write a book that would be of lasting value to his race. There is, for instance, a tremendous need to re-write the history of the human race, placing in true prospective the nefarious influence of the perfidious Jew in the manipulation of the peoples of the world. The Jew has been overwhelmingly influential in manipulating wars and the destruction of nations over the last several thousand years. He has also written the history books of the world. Since his influence has been cleverly deleted from the history books, this major project of re-writing history will take a tremendous amount of research and compilation in order to do it justice.

Another lasting and major project that could be undertaken would be to found an institution for the research and study of White history. Another research institute that would be of tremendous value to the future of the White Race would be to study ways and means of encouraging the increase of the finer specimens of our race and discourage the multiplication of the lower spectrum of our race.

The list of contributions that could be made to our people is almost endless and is only limited by the fertility of our imaginations.

11. Racial Honor.

History has shown that any race, or any nation, that would compromise its honor, soon lost its integrity, and also its freedom. The White Race has always inherently been a proud and honorable race. Pride, self-respect, heroism, have always been the outstanding characteristics of the White Race. It was these attributes that made the White Race the dominant ruler of the world during the period of the Roman Empire. It was when the insidious Jewish-Christian teachings of humbleness and humility; the idea that we were unworthy; that we should turn the other cheek; it was this kind of perverted thinking that brought about the downfall of the Roman Empire and the White Race. We must abolish this nefarious and suicidal thinking from our philosophy and outlook, and once again reestablish those characteristics that are basic to our natural instinct.

We must again cherish and honor such basic virtues as are inherent in the White Race. These virtues are bravery, the willingness to sacrifice one's life for his family, and for his race. These are the highest attributes of a proud and worthy race.

When a man begins to value his life more than the fundamental values of honor and race, then he has taken an overt step towards allowing himself to be enslaved.

Any people or any race which has sunk so low as to throw these cardinal virtues aside for temporary advantages, will usually find that they will usually not only lose their honor, but in the process will also lose their freedom, and often their life.

We must remember that for the White Man the most horrible and the most ugly situation is not the matter of facing death, but being in bondage, being a slave. For the proud White Race this is a catastrophe much worse than death.

12. Up-Breeding.

Nature in her infinite wisdom strives to up-breed and improve the species. This is a never- ending process. It is a natural process that Nature continually strives to further without end. During the last 2000 years this natural process has not only been arrested, but due to the parasitic Jewish manipulation of the White Race, this process has been reversed. Genetically, the White Race has made little, if any, progress from the time of the Romans and the Greeks of classic history.

Now that we have a religion that is of the White Race, for the White Race, and conscious of its value and its destiny, we must take an active hand in its up-breeding. We must work with the laws of Nature. We must help promote the better elements in our race to multiply more abundantly, and discourage the poorer elements in their proliferation. Furthermore, we must see to it that the misfits, the idiots, and the mentally defective are not reproduced at all to proliferate their misery on the newborn generations.

I am well aware that the White Race has been divided and subdivided into different groups. I am well aware that it has been designated into three classifications, such as the Aryan or Nordic, the Mediterranean, and the Alpine. There are many other classifications and branches of the White Race that anthropologists have used. I have studiously avoided using these terms throughout the book, because at this state of our struggle they are preponderantly divisive, rather than constructive. Our main struggle is to unite the White Race, to give it a sense of solidarity, and a common purpose. That common purpose is to free ourselves from Jewish domination, regain control of our own destiny, and populate the world.

Even before we achieve that goal, however, we should be thinking about, and planning for, the up breeding and up grading of our own race.

This does not at all mean that we have to use coercion or regimentation in family planning. Not at all. Without the destructive interference of the Jew, this up breeding would develop within the White Race by natural means, in any case. However, there is much that we can do to help promote such encouragement of selective breeding.

We can do this by the very attitude we inculcate in our religion. If we are overwhelmingly devoted to the survival of the lowest elements of our race, we will encourage down breeding. If our whole philosophy is geared to the up lifting and advancement of our race, we will automatically encourage up breeding. This program can be further encouraged by educational support, cultural support, and even government support. Under the Jewish democracy that we are now living, certainly we can see that the government through a multitude of welfare programs, through the promotion of race-mixing propaganda, the various other nefarious programs, is covertly encouraging the mongrelization and the down breeding of the White Race. It is therefore not hard to see that the very opposite, namely the encouragement of improving, of advancing, and of up-breeding our race can be accomplished just as easily on the positive side. We definitely believe in eugenics and racial health.

This is an important part of the program of the CHURCH OF THE CREATOR. Within a few generations after we have reclaimed control of our own destiny and are well on our way on the program of upgrading, advancing and up breeding our race, the results will be utterly staggering to the imagination. Whereas the White Race has been so superior to any other species on the face of the planet up to this time, with this program inherent in our religion, the future development of the White Race will be a marvel to behold.

13. Sanctity of Family.

In reaping the experience of the lessons of history, we Find that only those races survived that upheld and honored the family. This is so basic that it is almost self-evident, yet in today's rapidly degenerating climate, this basic truth has been almost buried and forgotten. History has shown that when family ties weaken and the family as a unit degenerates on a national scale, then that nation also degenerates and disintegrates.

We Creators believe strongly in family life and the sanctity of the family unit. We believe that it is the basic building block of a nation and of a race. We are proud of the responsibility that the head of the family takes upon himself in caring for his own. This is one of the outstanding virtues of the White Race, in contrast to the nigger, who breeds indiscriminately outside the sanctity of the family unit and with complete irresponsibility.

We therefore regard it as every White person's responsibility to help uphold, protect and promote the sanctity of the White family. But we assume no such responsibility whatsoever for the families of the colored races.

It is in our interest and it is our duty as a race to encourage those conditions economically, socially and spiritually that will aid family building. Our race is only as healthy as are our families, and we hold these two concepts, race and family, as sacred and interchangeable.

14. Blood, Soil and Honor.

Blood means the advancement of our race, the White Race, and keeping it pure. It is our race that has built all civilizations on the face of the earth, that has created culture, progress, civilization and technology. It has conquered all lands and given law and order and government to all peoples. It is the highest virtue of our religion to promote, advance, and expand the White Race. We are strongly committed to the idea of eugenics.

Soil means land. In order for a race to expand it must have room and fertile land. History shows that under cramped conditions the growth of a people stagnated. As an example, the Irish, for the last 1,000 years have never increased beyond 3,500,000 in their homeland. But given more room— more land in America— in which to expand, there are over 20,000,000 Americans of Irish decent in the New World. This is almost six times as many as the population in the land of their origin. This despite the fact that they have been here only a few hundred years.

If the White Race is to survive— and it must survive— then it must grow. To live is to grow. To stagnate is to die, to be overwhelmed by the colored races, our deadliest natural enemies.

In order to fulfill the natural mission Nature has set for us— to grow and to multiply— we must have more and more land for the White Race until the White Race inhabits the world.

We do not want to just control the world— a mistake made by such previous White civilizations as the Romans. No, this would lead to the same disaster as the White Race experienced in Egypt, in China, India, and elsewhere. No, nor do we want to enslave anybody or rule over other inferior races. We do not want any slaves. This would again lead to our mongrelization. We want to follow the same policy as our early American ancestors pursued— we want to populate the land— we want the White Race to exclusively populate the world.

We will either increase, multiply and populate the earth, or we will be pushed off the face of the earth by the flood of the colored races. We much prefer the former, and intend to pursue this policy to its glorious fulfillment

Now we come to that most essential ingredient, honor. No race can remain free if it compromises its honor— pride of race and honor go together. It is extremely essential that we instill in our people the idea of pride of race, that honor is preferable to life itself, and that only a people who jealously guards its honor can be free. Further we must realize that in the intense struggle we are now involved, only the proud and the free can survive.

15. Pride and Confidence.

Having selected the White Race as the crowning pinnacle of all her creations. Nature has endowed it with certain unique characteristics that in combination are the distinctive attributes of the White Race alone. They distinguish the White Man from any other creature.

Some of these characteristics are: his superior intellect; his tremendous creativity and productivity; his restless spirit of adventure and his endless quest for new horizons, be it in the field of geographic discoveries or in the search for knowledge, or in the pursuit of new inventions. The White Man is endowed with outstanding powers of creativity which are manifested in the field of art, sculpture, music, literature, architecture, science, mathematics, technology and in invention. In fact, the field is endless in listing all those activities in which the creativity of the White Man excels.

The White Man in his natural element is the world's greatest Fighter. He is aggressive, he is brave and heroic. Two thousand years ago the White Race, as exemplified by the Romans, conquered the rest of the world in a few centuries. The White Man finds himself in the miserable plight he is in today because he has not followed his natural instincts. He has allowed them to be subdued and subverted by the Jewish-Christian hoax that has blunted, thwarted and deadened those wonderful instinctive attributes with which Nature endowed him so generously in the first place. We, of the CHURCH OF THE CREATOR, therefore implore and command the White Man to again revert back to those wonderful instincts with which Nature endowed him and which made him great in his unequalled past.

It is characteristic of the White Man to always hope for the better and to look forward to an improved situation in his own circumstances, an improvement in the fortunes of the White Race, and an improvement of the world picture in general. It is characteristic of the White Man to be positive in his thinking, in his actions, in his planning, and in his world outlook.

Unlike Christianity, we do not want to present a hypocritical posture of a pious, cringing humanitarian philosophy. We must be honest to our inner-most self just as Nature designed us— tough, aggressive, proud, energetic, creative, productive, and above all, proud and jealous of our ability and of our lofty place in Nature's scheme of the universe. We want to be neither humble nor meek. We mean to be what Nature created us to be— masters of this planet.

Being endowed with these wonderful qualities, it is the duty of the White Man to utilize them to the fullest for the benefit of himself, and his race as a whole. Remember, Nature has selected you as its greatest creation. It has endowed you with all of these wonderful qualities. Utilize them to the fullest. You can and must do no less.

16. Control of our Destiny

To drive the Jew from power and to expel the Jews and niggers from our midst is our foremost immediate objective. Until we have done this, we will not be able to gain control of our own government, of our own affairs, nor of our own destiny. Until we have accomplished this, nothing else really matters, because nothing else will be solved until such time as the White Race reclaims control of its own destiny. We must therefore work relentlessly towards this end.

To achieve this overwhelming goal we must inculcate racial loyalty, we must have a creed of solidarity for the White Race, and we must have a dynamic program embodied in our very religion. This program, this creed, this religion we now have in the CHURCH OF THE CREATOR. The very essence of this program is embodied in the sixteen commandments herewith set forth.

Once we have regained unconditional control of our own destiny, the destiny of the White Race, the solution of all other problems, such as economics, roads, housing, pollution, food supply, education, and a multitude of others, will seem like child's play. Once we regain absolute control of our own destiny, we will already have all those other problems as good as solved. If we don't regain control of our destiny, we will never solve any of our problems, and it will really not make much difference, since we would be on our way to extinction in any case.

We must and we will regain control of our own destiny. We will and we must drive the Jew from power. Victory for the While Race is absolutely certain. The time is ripe now, as the White Race is beginning to realize its creative genius and its awesome power, slowly but surely, with ever increasing awareness. The way to harness that tremendous power for the benefit of the White Race is build the CHURCH OF THE CREATOR on a worldwide basis.

Therefore, be of good cheer! Victory for the White Race is inevitable. Dedicate yourself here and now to join the battle for the survival of the White Race. We will win and we will triumph. The wealth and the beauty of the world will soon be ours, and it will be a magnificent world, a White world.

CHAPTER FIVE

GERMANY, ADOLF HITLER, AND NATIONAL SOCIALISM

In the study of the whole historical movement of the White Race struggling to free itself from under the heel of Jewish tyranny, the name of Adolf Hitler shines forth as the brightest meteor to flash through the heavens since the beginning of history. No doubt the White Race will produce even greater men in the future, but it is my considered opinion that Adolf Hitler stands head and shoulders above any other man as the greatest leader the White Race has ever produced, and as the greatest White Man that ever lived. This may sound as an overly extravagant evaluation, but if so, no man deserved it more, nor did any man come by it more honestly.

The contribution that this great White Man made towards striking a resounding blow for the cause of the White Race and accomplishing a near break-through in smashing the Jewish conspiracy will go down in history as one of the most heroic battles in the history of mankind. When we consider what little he had to start with, what little he had to work with, how tremendous were the obstacles that he had to overcome, the Herculean efforts that were expended, and the heroic fight that was waged, we can safely say without contradiction that in the words of William Shakespeare, "the elements so mixed in him that Nature might stand up and say to all the world, this was a man!"

Indeed, Adolf Hitler was not only the epitome of a man, but he best represented those qualities that shine forth in the White Race— honor, heroism, genius, creativity, leadership, an artistic spirit, and above all, the readiness to sacrifice himself for the good of his race.

But for this one man, undoubtedly Germany would have been overwhelmingly communized in the early 30's. Since Germany is the key and the anchor nation in the heart of Europe, undoubtedly in short order the entire continent would have fallen victim to Jewish-Marxist communism.

Certainly if Hitler and the new National Socialist movement that he founded had not saved Germany, Spain also would have fallen victim to this treacherous cancer. Undoubtedly, the vicious and destructive Spanish Civil War would never have turned out to be a victory for the fighters against Jewish communism. With Spain and Germany gone, in short order a sick and dissipated France, already infected with the Marxist virus, would have succumbed. With Spain, France and Germany on the one side and communist Russia on the other side, it is unthinkable that the Balkan countries of Romania, Czechoslovakia and the others would have put up any worthwhile resistance in the Jewish onslaught to enslave Europe. With the continent gone, the small island kingdom of Great Britain, itself long a citadel of Jewish money power, would shortly have fallen like an overripe tomato. Certainly Fascist Italy would have shortly crumbled, under military invasion, if necessary, and the few other small and relatively weak countries, such as the Scandinavian countries and Greece, would have offered no obstacle whatsoever. So it can be readily seen that if it had not been for the advent of Adolf Hitler, Europe by the 1930's would have been totally crushed in the giant maws of Jewish Marxism.

Undoubtedly by the middle 30's all of Europe would have been in the grip of this fiendish pestilence that we today call communism but is really the Jewish program for the destruction of the White Race and its civilization. Without a doubt, America, who has within its environs more Jews than any other country in the world, and who supplied the money, the material, the production of the armaments of war, certainly, America would not have resisted the final onslaught of this cancer. It is, therefore, fairly safe to say but for the grace of a kindly Providence and the appearance of Adolf Hitler on the scene of world history, today, you and I would be living under a complete nightmare such as has darkened the lights throughout Russia and Eastern Europe today.

But, you might say, Adolf Hitler was destroyed, Germany was utterly defeated, and National Socialism was completely crushed without a vestige remaining.

It is true Adolf Hitler is dead. It is true Germany was utterly vanquished and left a mass of rubble. It is true that National Socialism was eradicated as a political party in Germany. So what has Adolf Hitler done for us— for the White Race?

Well, he has done a great deal. For one thing he has bought us time. As we stated previously, undoubtedly by the end of the 1930's all of Europe and most likely the whole world would be lying crushed and gutted, cowering at the feet of the diabolical Jewish monster— communist Marxism. Adolf Hitler did not die in vain. He died for his beloved White Race, including you and me. He bought us at least 50 years of time in which we could rally ourselves and make a great Final effort to victoriously crush the monster that is now still clutching at our throat.

Yes, he bought us time and he did more than that, he gave us a sense of direction and he gave us a great cause and an inspiring example to strive for. He challenged this vile evil and he showed us all that this monstrous world plague could be challenged and could be overcome. In fact, he came marvelously close to winning the battle in his own time. He gave us hope, he gave us an example, and he gave us an ideology to fight for. In clear lines, he delineated the enemy, and he set forth the goal. He established the first White government that was based on a racial foundation.

Adolf Hitler did not die in vain. From his ashes shall rise a Phoenix right in the heart of America that will spring to life again and take up the battle to save not only America, but to save the White Race for the entire world.

The life story of Adolf Hitler undoubtedly constitutes the most fantastic true romance of any story that has ever been written in the history of mankind. It is a true story, not a fantasy conjured in the minds of storytellers. It is a great epic that has occurred within this present century and we can be proud that it has happened in our own time.

To understand the story of Adolf Hitler we must first of all reach back into the history of Germany itself, and even before that, the story of the German people.

* * *

Anyone who studies the outcroppings of genius in the progress of the White Race cannot help but be impressed by the number of German names that predominate in any such list. Whether it be in the field of music, or in the field of literature, or in the field of chemistry, or mathematics, or in the field of inventions, or in the field of physics, the contributions of genius in all these fields from the German people have been rich indeed. Not only that, but the German people embody all those qualities that are the pride of the White Race— they are hard working, productive, energetic, brave fighters, and above all, tremendously creative. On the other hand, they also possess that fatal flaw that is so characteristic of the White Race— they are so prone to squabbling and fighting amongst themselves, and, furthermore, have a fatal susceptibility to Jewish propaganda.

For centuries not only did the Germans possess the best qualities of the Nordic blood within the White Race, but they were located in the heart of geographic Europe, and therefore, in any European development, were the key element.

Why then, it might well be asked, did Germany lag behind France, Spain and England in the race for colonies, and in fact, in the establishment of a world empire? And the answer lies in its Achilles heel, namely a house divided against itself cannot endure. In no major nation has there been so much divisiveness and so much internal and fraternal bickering as among the German people. Thus it was, until that great leader, Adolf Hitler, came along.

Since the days of the Romans, through the reign of Charlemagne, and for centuries thereafter, Germany has been split into small principalities, dukedoms and kingdoms. Probably not since the days of the fall of Babylon have a people been so infested with Jewish parasites as were the little fiefs, dukedoms and principalities of Germany. Upon these, the Jews continually fastened themselves, and upon their rulers— loaning them money, corrupting their morals and stirring up wars.

Nevertheless, by the 16th century it became evident that the Germans were becoming a major power in the heart of Europe and would by their numbers, their industry and their energy, soon master the continent of Europe, if left unchecked. If there is one thing that the Jews cannot and will not tolerate (if they can help it) it is that a great White people like the Germans unite and predominate in world politics. It was therefore at this time that the Jews promoted what has been known in history as the "Great Schism." The Jew hurled the Protestant Reformation into the face of White Europe, and with it a fratricidal convulsion on an unprecedented scale.

The Jews, who created Christianity in the first place, and dominated and controlled it for the first 1,500 years through the hierarchy of the Roman Catholic church, had thoroughly corrupted the church to the point where the average "believer" was so completely sickened and nauseated by the excesses of the church leadership that he was ready to revolt. The Jews then brought forth a puppet to lead the revolt against the church that was to split wide open the White world all the way from Germany to Sweden to France and England.

Amongst no people were the ensuing convulsions greater than amongst the German people. After smoldering for approximately a century this convulsion burst forth into a flaming struggle among the German people. It was called the Thirty Year's War.

Between 1618 and 1648, a devastating 30 years, the German people hacked each other to pieces and tore themselves apart. This tragic convulsion, when it was finally over, left the German people torn and bleeding, with 5/6 of all their property and buildings destroyed, and the population decimated. When the Treaty of Westphalia finally ended this tragic and bitter fratricide, it was not the German people who wrote the terms of that treaty, but the surrounding outside powers who dictated the terms to the victims.

Needless to say, the perfidious Jew had his hand in it again, and the last thing in the world that he wanted was to see a strong united Germany. What he structured was a resumption of the divided dukedoms and principalities that it had before the suicidal war began, but it was now further saddled with the added problem of being half Catholic and half Protestant. Not only that, but the war had engendered a rich harvest of hatreds amongst the Germans themselves that were not too much unlike those which the Jew fostered between the North and the South of the United States when they plunged our unfortunate country into the Civil War.

This bloody and grueling exercise in self-destruction set the German people back perhaps 300 years in the development of their nationhood, and it cost them world leadership.

This was pretty well the situation of the German people until the advent of Bismarck, who united the petty German states but successfully waged war against the Germans of Austria and soundly defeated them at the battle of Koniggratz in 1866. This battle and the victorious war against the French of 1870— united the German states under the leadership of Prussia, and Bismarck had King William I crowned as head of the German Empire.

Germany was now on its way to unification and a world power, nevertheless, minus the Germans of Austria.

Despite all the time that Germany had lost while the other great nations of Europe were acquiring colonies, Germany was now a world power to be reckoned with and was unquestionably becoming Europe's strongest nation and its leader.

Despite the paramount credit given to Bismarck for uniting Germany, he never came to grips with the Jewish problem as such, and the Jewish power and influence in Germany remained unchecked and unmitigated. Nevertheless, the power and productivity of the German people became manifest, and if there is anything that the Jews did not want, it was that the fine qualities inherent in the German blood should come to the fore and assume leadership of the White Race. With the propaganda control in their hands in Germany, in France, in England and the other countries of Europe, as well as the United States, and with the national hatreds being continually kept alive and fanned with propaganda at will, the Jews were successful in plunging Europe into what is known as the First great World War.

Other things being equal and had both sides been devoid of Jewish power and influence, Germany might have won that war, and in fact, was on her way to doing so. This was not to be, however, since the Jews did not want Germany to win. They did not want a strong White leadership such as the Germans offered. The Jewish control of Germany even during World War I was almost complete. The Minister of War Production was a Jew, in fact, the whole German government was thoroughly riddled with Jewish bureaucrats, and in the spring of 1918, as Germany was pushing forward a victorious campaign to end the war, the Jewish conspiracy brought about a munitions strike at home and sabotaged the whole German war effort.

With the propaganda reins firmly in their control, the Jews then organized a communist revolution in the heart of Germany while the brave German boys were dying in the trenches. The end was not too far in coming. By November a betrayed and Jew-ridden Germany sued for peace while her brave soldiers at the front were still far within enemy territory.

One of those brave soldiers who had been disabled by a poison gas attack, was blind, and in a hospital at the time the armistice was announced, was an unknown corporal by the name of Adolf Hitler.

He tells his reaction when he heard the shattering news of Germany's defeat. "Since the day when I stood at my mother's grave, I had not wept. When in my youth fate seized me with merciless hardness, my defiance mounted. When in the long war years death snatched so many a dear comrade and friend from our ranks, it would have seemed to me almost a sin to complain— after all, were they not dying for Germany? And when at length the creeping gas—in the last days of the dreadful struggle— attacked me too, and began to gnaw at my eyes, and beneath the fear of going blind forever, I nearly lost heart for a moment, the voice of my conscience thundered at me: miserable wretch! Are you going to cry when thousands are a hundred times worse off than you?

And so I bore my lot in dull silence. But now I could not help it. Only now did I see how all personal suffering vanishes in comparison with the misfortune of the Fatherland."

He broke down and cried.

"There followed terrible days and even worse nights— I knew that all was lost. Only fools, liars, and criminals could hope in the mercy of the enemy. In these nights hatred grew in me, hatred for those responsible for this deed."

"There is no making pacts with Jews; there is only to be the hard: either— or."

"I, for my part, decided to go into politics." Who was this man— Adolf Hitler?

This outstanding genius of the White Race, probably the greatest leader the White people have ever had, came from a very inauspicious beginning. He was born of parents in the lower middle class, in a small town on the border of Germany and Austria, but on the Austrian side. It was called Braunau-am-Inn. The date was April 20, 1889.

During his school years young Adolf showed a penchant for being a leader among his schoolmates. He also displayed an avid interest in history and a strong leaning toward nationalism, and loyalty to his own race. He was also blessed with a strong inclination in the artistic fields. By the time he was 12, young Adolf had decided he wanted to be an artist and plainly told his father of his desire.

His father strongly objected to this choice. The conflict that ensued between the two was resolved by his father's death when young Adolf was 13 years old. The family was now in rather dire financial straits, but his mother managed to send him to technical school in Linz. Here his talents for drawing and architecture became obvious.

It was also during this period that Hitler developed a strong feeling for German Nationalism and a strong feel for historical thinking. He says, "The habit of historical thinking which I thus learned in school has never left me in the intervening years. To an ever increasing extent world history became for me an inexhaustible source of understanding for the historical events of the present; in other words, for politics. I do not want to learn it, I want it to instruct me."

When Hitler was 18 years old he went to Vienna to try to begin his professional training towards becoming a painter and artist. He took the required examination at the Vienna Academy of Fine Arts.

To his great surprise he found that he had failed these examinations. The professor who had examined his drawings informed him that his talent lay not in the field of painting, but in the field of architecture. His interest in architecture had been growing steadily in the last few years, but he now realized that in order to take up professional studies in this field, he lacked the necessary educational background.

It was not long thereafter that his mother died and he was now an orphan faced with the problem of making his own living.

Somehow he had to make a living. He had no trade or training in any particular vocation. His future looked bleak.

Nevertheless, bidding his relatives farewell, he declared that he would go to Vienna and never return until he had made good.

"With a suitcase full of clothes and underwear in my hand, and an indomitable will in my heart, I set out for Vienna. I, too, hoped to wrest from fate what my father had accomplished 50 years before; I, too, hoped to become 'something', but in no case a civil servant."

The next four years between 1909 and 1913 turned out to be a time of utter misery and destitution for the strong-willed young man from Linz. These were his most formative years and the years in which he learned the bitter lessons of life from the school of hard knocks.

It was in the metropolitan city of Vienna, 10 percent of whose population at that time was Jewish, that Hitler also began to learn the facts of life about the powerful stranglehold the Jews had on that city in particular, and world influence in general.

He became a voracious reader and read the daily press intensively. It was during this time also that he gained a keen insight into politics and began to detect what the slimy hand of the Jew behind the facade of Marxism was doing to the German people.

He said, "Vienna was and remained for me the hardest, though most thorough, school of my life. I had set foot in this town while still half a boy, and left it a man, grown quiet and grave."

"In this period there took shape within me a world picture and a philosophy which became the granite foundation of all my acts. In addition to what I then created, I have had to learn little; and I have had to alter nothing."

It was also during this time that he thoroughly studied and learned the poisonous effects of the 'Social Democracy' movement in Austria which was a disguised name for Communist Marxism.

He says, "I understood the infamous spiritual terror which this movement exerts, particularly on the bourgeoisie, which is neither morally nor mentally equal to such attacks; at a given sign it unleashes a veritable barrage of lies and slanders against whatever adversary seems most dangerous, until the nerves of the attacked persons break down... this is a tactic based on precise calculation of all human weaknesses, and its results will lead to success with almost mathematical certainty..."

After four years in Vienna, the most dismal years of his life, Hitler left that city for good and moved to Munich in the spring of 1913. He was glad to get out of Vienna, which he called a cosmopolitan "racial Babylon." He felt much more at home, both spiritually and politically, in Munich, since his strong pro-German nationalistic feelings were much more in harmony here than in the Austrian empire of polyglot races. Hitler was at this time 24 years old, and to everyone except himself he must have seemed a total failure.

He had no friends, no family, no job, and no home. He had, however, one thing: an unquenchable confidence in himself, and a deep, burning sense of mission. He also had an intense and abiding love for Germany and the German people. Nobody at that time could have foreseen the tremendous mission that Adolf Hitler was destined to fulfill in his newly adopted land of Germany.

When war broke out in August 1914, he immediately, on the third day of August, petitioned King Ludwig III of Bavaria for permission to volunteer in a Bavarian regiment, and it was granted.

Of this historic turning point in his life. Hitler says: "To me those hours seemed like a release from the painful feelings of my youth. Even today I am not ashamed to say that overpowered by a stormy enthusiasm, I fell down on my knees and thanked heaven from an overflowing heart for granting me the good fortune of being permitted to live at this time."

"A fight for freedom had begun... this time not the fate of Serbia or Austria was involved, but whether the German nation was to be or not to be."

During the 4-1/2 years that Hitler served in the infantry he was wounded twice and received the Iron Cross, second class, at one time and the Iron Cross, first class, the second time. We have already related how at the end of the war he had been gassed and blinded and received the bitter news of the treachery and defeat perpetrated on his beloved fatherland.

It is tremendously important to here recount the tragedy, humiliation, and destruction that was now heaped upon post-war Germany. After the infamous stab in the back that she received on the home front from a munitions strike, a strike that was organized by the Jewish clique in the very heart of the German home front, she was further humiliated, crushed and destroyed.

With Germany crushed to the ground, the Jews then saddled her with a bitter and vengeful Treaty of Versailles, a treaty written and dictated by the Jews so as to enchain Germany for the next 100 years. The fruits of her labors would be plundered by the victors, and particularly by the Jewish international clique.

Upon Germany the Versailles Treaty imposed harsh, dictatorial and draconian peace terms. All of Germany's holdings, her colonies and her territories were taken away from her and divided up among other nations, with Great Britain becoming the prime benefactor. The German traitors, who now were the "representatives" for Germany at the peace table, were made to sign the statement claiming full responsibility for starting the war, and that the war guilt rested upon Germany and the German people. A fantastic "reparations" sum was imposed upon Germany... a sum so huge that it was equivalent to about three times the net worth of all of Germany put together. In order to pay this, and the interest on it, the Germans would be enslaved and in bondage forever and a day.

But the shame and humiliation heaped upon Germany, the reparations, the lost colonies and the war guilt, were only a part of the dire tragedy that now engulfed Germany. At home the Germans were leaderless and helpless, with Jews, revolutionaries and traitors heading up their makeshift government. The rapacious Jew then swarmed in from all parts of the world to loot, plunder and dismember the German Reich, and to perpetrate revolution and destruction upon the helpless people.

In the period immediately following World War I, Germany and its heroic people reached an all time low. Misery and wretchedness, hunger and privation, distress and confusion were rampant throughout the land. Millions upon millions of German people were without work and starving. Thousands died daily of hunger. At the same time the Jews were supplying funds to communist revolutionaries to destroy Germany from within and take it over completely. Jews came in with money from all parts of the world— money they had plundered and stolen from other countries, and rushed into Germany and bought up all of the starving German people's property. Hotels, restaurants, manufacturing plants, and even their homes were bought up by the Jews for a few cents on the dollar. In order to survive, the starving German people had no alternative but to sell their properties, worth a fortune, for a fraction of their real value to these Jews, just in order to obtain enough money to eat. In order to realize just how terribly desperate the conditions in Germany were at this time, it is necessary to go into further study of this deplorable post-war era. These, our White Brethren, were literally living out of garbage pails in order to survive.

Jews owned all the businesses. They had stolen these from the Germans for mere pennies. They had all the good food, all the medical facilities, and the German people were allowed nothing. Many Germans, walking the streets, would stand in front of restaurants, the same restaurants that they themselves formerly owned, and would look inside, hunger eating at their insides. The Jews would sit in the windows of these restaurants, eating food and delicacies, while the Germans were eating garbage. With their usual arrogance, the Jews would hold the food up in front of the Germans looking through the windows, laughing at them, making fun of them, anything to disgrace them further.

There seemed nothing that the German people could do to rectify this at that time. The control of the police and all the courts in Germany were firmly in the hands of the Jews themselves. The Germans could obtain no justice in the courts whatsoever. Jobs were available only to those Germans who did not speak out, but bowed down to the communist Jewish overlords.

Filthy literature was rampant on the newsstands, and young children even were subjected to this type of degradation, something that is now happening right here in America. Newspapers, magazines, lewd movies, obscene literature of all types, were prevalent everywhere. However, no one was allowed to speak out against the Jews. German women were manhandled in the streets, and if they complained, they were arrested by the authorities. Schools and colleges were infested with communist Jewish professors.

All these tragic manifestations and many more that we are facing in the United States today, Germany was totally engulfed with in the period from 1918 until 1933. Unless you worked with the Jews for the destruction of the White German Race, you were boycotted, prevented from obtaining employment, and even from obtaining enough food to sustain life for yourself and your family.

The courts were completely corrupted and in the hands of the Jews. No decision was ever handed down unless the Jews approved of it, or they themselves made it in the first place.

Even the one time wealthy businessmen who had worked all their lives to build their businesses honestly, were deprived of them by the Jews. Many of them were made to work as common laborers, if they were lucky, in the same plants that they had once owned. Conditions were so pitiful and so deplorable that despair clutched at the heart of the German people. White German men and women went to bed at night hungry and starving, praying for a true loyal leader from their ranks that would be able to deliver them from this Jewish nightmare.

Their prayers were answered. A great man did arise from out of their ranks to lead them out of their misery. His name was Adolf Hitler, the same lowly, blind and unknown soldier who had cried in his bunk in the army hospital when the treacherous betrayal and armistice was announced on November 11, 1918.

Shortly after the armistice, a very small group had formed a political party in Munich. They called themselves the German Workers Party. They only had six members. Their problems seemed overwhelming and their future seemed hopeless. It so happened that in 1919 this unknown soldier attended one of their pitiful meetings. His imagination told him that somehow something meaningful could be done with this small beginning.

He joined the party and became party member number seven.

With his great speaking eloquence, undiscovered until now, Hitler began to whip this group into shape. In 1920 the party was renamed the National Socialist German Workers Party, called Nazi for short.

During the next three years, from 1920 until 1923, Hitler and his loyal followers managed with great success to awaken the German people to their racial heritage and their great historic past. We must remember that at this time Germany was rent from one side to the other with communist revolutionaries, Bolsheviks and other Jewish stooges that incited confusion, treason and dissension throughout the land, tearing the German nation apart.

In order for Hitler and his loyal followers to even so much as hold a meeting, they had to battle the communist goon squads to keep their meetings from being broken up. A goodly part of his party organization had to be devoted to fighting with their fists, if necessary, in order to defend their right to speak and their right to hold meetings. This division, called the Storm Troopers, was completely weaponless and had to rely on their fists in order to defend their party's existence. Despite all the precautions they took, hundreds and thousands of them were killed and assassinated in their struggle to save the German race from destruction.

By 1923 the Jews had perpetrated the most treacherous inflation in history upon the German people and it took billions of marks just to buy a loaf of bread. The Jews raped Germany financially and morally. Their Jewish cousins from America swarmed in, and for next to nothing, bought up gold watches, apartment buildings, houses, real estate and completely plundered the German people.

It was at this time that the Nazi party felt that something more desperate had to be done to save the German nation from complete ruin. In November of 1923 they staged a putsch in Munich to take over the Bavarian government, but it was doomed to failure. The Jews still had control of the German army and the militia and they crushed this attempted takeover in short order. Sixteen loyal party members and White heroes were killed in this attempt to save the German Reich.

Hitler escaped death and was saved for a greater destiny by a merciful Providence.

He was brought to trial. In some of his speeches in defense of his party he gave some of the most eloquent oratory that had ever stirred the German people. Nevertheless, with the Jews being in complete control of the courts, he was sentenced to five years in the penitentiary at Landsberg.

Due to the tremendous pressure from the German people themselves, he was finally released on December 20, 1924 after serving nine months. In many respects, this was a blessing in disguise. Because of it, for the first time in his life, Hitler had time to devote himself to setting down the creed and objectives of the Nazi party. This was compiled in his two-volume book known as Mein Kampf. The principles embodied in that classic are to this day a shining beacon pointing the way towards the liberation of the White Race.

When Hitler was released from the penitentiary in 1924, he found his party had fallen apart, was disorganized, and in chaos. The party assets had been confiscated by the courts and these same courts furthermore had forbidden him to so much as speak in a number of the German states. A most difficult task faced him.

Imbued with an indomitable will and a burning zeal to resurrect his broken country. Hitler carried on. Slowly the ban forbidding him to speak was lifted from the different states and Hitler renewed his efforts to reorganize and build the party with an energy that was almost super- human.

Finally by January 30, 1933, his party's efforts were crowned with success and Hitler became the Chancellor of the German Reich.

The multitude of problems that now faced him were colossal and almost insurmountable. He had inherited a country that was completely bankrupt, a country that was saddled with the tyrannical Treaty of Versailles to an interminable future of slavery and bondage. The German people themselves were divided between the followers of Hitler and the Nazi party versus the communists, Bolsheviks, and the Jews, who still had unlimited control over all the property and finances of the country. Germany was without colonies, without credit throughout the world. She was completely disarmed in the face of a hostile world that surrounded her small country, which, after all, was no larger in area than the State of Texas. The country was rent with poverty and disillusionment. Over six million unemployed had hopelessly been staring towards a bleak future. After 13 years of desperate struggle, the lonely unknown soldier of World War I not only became the head of the German government, but he became the leader of the German people.

Far beyond that, he became the symbol and the leader of all White people throughout the world in their struggle against the Jewish monster.

From the time that Hitler came to power in January 1933, a miracle seemed to spread across the land of Germany. In short order the German people again began to have hope and pride and purpose. With his genius for inspiration, organization and leadership, within two years, while the rest of the world was still wallowing in depression and unemployment. Hitler had completely solved the unemployment problem for the German people. Now everybody was working. Great new super-highways were being built. The average worker began to look forward to owning a home of his own. Working people who before could hardly afford to own a bicycle now could afford to own a Volkswagen. Whereas Germany had been completely disarmed and helpless, Hitler again instituted military service, built up Germany's armaments and made her a nation that was feared and respected by her enemies.

The Jews were kicked out of office, out of the courts and out of government. Racial laws were passed prohibiting Jews from being citizens of Germany. It was no longer tolerated that the Jews take up positions in universities and colleges where they could mislead and pollute the minds of the German youth. Jews were barred from the legal profession. They were barred from positions of leadership in theaters, drama and culture; they were barred from positions of leadership in banking, in the news media and in the field of national propaganda. Contrary to the many Jewish lies that have been put out about this period in Germany, the Jews were not physically mistreated. Nor were any of them killed, or jailed, or harmed in any way, other than outright criminals. These were treated the same way as any other criminal, including any one of German nationality. However, with their power shorn, many Jews decided to leave Germany, much to the relief of the German people themselves.

Once freed of Jewish domination and Jewish subjugation, the resurgence in Germany was a miracle to behold. In attributing the reasons for Germany's miraculous recovery under Hitler, most of the credit must be given to Hitler's inspirational leadership. Also his genius for organization and the German people's ability to produce and create were major factors in their recovery.

However, not the least of the actions Hitler took that immediately changed the economic distress in Germany, was the fact that he freed the German monetary system from the interest bondage of the Jewish bankers. Hitler's government issued their own German money— money that was not issued by

Jewish bankers or backed by Jewish gold. It was backed by Germany's ability to produce. It was not subject to the manipulations of the Jewish banks nor the Stock Exchange. It was issued without interest, free of Jewish interest and of any Jewish manipulation. This is something no other country in the world enjoyed then, or enjoys now. This very factor was of tremendous importance in the unprecedented recovery that spread over Germany during the 1930's.

It is not possible to list the multitude of achievements accomplished during the Hitler era of peacetime Germany between 1933 and 1939. To do so would require many volumes of history.

We neither have the space to do so, nor is this our objective in this treatise. I will therefore make a very brief summary listing some of the highlights during this tremendously productive period in the history of the White Race.

Upon achieving the reins of power in Germany, Hitler commenced on a political, economic and social reorganization of Germany by establishing the Nazi party as the only political party, July, 1933; attempting the religious coordination of the Germans, July, 1933 and April, 1935; regulating the national labor and industry, January, 1934; appointing Dr. Joseph Goebbels coordinator of propaganda and cultural life; and by executing recalcitrant party members and dangerous political opponents in the June, 1934, purge. "Mutinies are suppressed," Hitler warned, "In accordance with laws of iron, which are eternally the same." Following the death of von Hindenburg in August, 1934, Hitler united the offices of president and Reich chancellor in himself and assumed the title of Der Fuehrer (The Leader).

From 1933 to 1938 Hitler drove the German Jews from most professions, deprived them of positions of leadership in business, and sanctioned the Nuremberg Laws prohibiting or regulating domestic relations "between Jews and citizens of German or kindred blood."

During the course of the revolution, 1933-1939, Hitler was able to organize, propagandize, and arouse the youth of Germany; to change the national psychology from one of despair to one of confidence in his Third Reich; and to reduce German unemployment by measures which culminated in the four year domestic plan of September, 1936 and a collateral plan for total rearmament.

Since he knew that the Jews would make every attempt to arouse the surrounding nations to crush his new Jew-free, thriving,

German Reich, from the very moment of his rise to power. Hitler commenced an orderly, planned preparation for war, if war should be necessary to defend his homeland and his people. Nevertheless, he held out the hand of friendship in the hope of peace to his surrounding neighbors, who were now being goaded by their Jewish masters to foment war and hatred upon Germany. Hitler reestablished military service in March of 1935 and otherwise scrapped the tyrannical Treaty of Versailles. He proposed peace to the Western powers in May, 1935. He re-occupied and fortified the Rhineland, and repudiated the Locarno Pact in March of 1936. One of his greatest triumphs was the reunion of his homeland, Austria, with his fatherland, Germany, on March 14, 1938.

The uniting of the German people of Austria and those of Germany had been strived for and yearned for by millions of Germans for many generations. The "Anschluss" or political union of Germany and Austria accomplished. Hitler made a triumphal entry into Vienna, the city that had given him nothing but hardship and heartbreak in his early youth. Undoubtedly when he addressed the German people in Vienna, who went wild with enthusiasm and jubilation, it was probably the greatest hour of Hitler's life.

There were still more than three million Germans just across the border in Czechoslovakia in an area called Sudentenland, an area that had been torn from the heart of Germany in the treacherous Versailles Treaty. The Jews now set about persecuting, murdering and tormenting these three million Germans within their clutches.

It was a situation that no honorable German could long tolerate. In September 29, 1938, the premiers of Great Britain and France and the Duce of Italy met at Munich to hear Hitler's demands for the cession of the Sudentenland by Czechoslovakia. By the middle of

October German troops occupied this area and another three million Germans were united to their fatherland. On March 15, 1939 German troops occupied and absorbed the rest of Czechoslovakia, a polyglot of mixed nationalities formerly a part of the Austrian Empire, but artificially carved into a separate country by the treacherous Versailles Treaty makers.

The Versailles Treaty had also far-sightedly laid the seeds for dissension between Germany and Poland by wantonly carving out a huge chunk of land through the middle of East Prussia and ceding it to Poland, thereby cutting Germany in two. We can imagine what this would be like if in our own country here in America a huge corridor were cut out through the middle of Texas severing the lower half and ceding this area, for instance, to Mexico. This is what the treacherous Jews had done to Germany in the Versailles Treaty of 1919. Furthermore, since the Jews in control of the surrounding countries now were going all out to foment hatred and war against Germany, they again applied the same tactics of murder, torture, harassment to the Germans living in the Polish corridor, an area that had for centuries belonged to Germany.

Again, the Germans came to the aid of their fellow blood brothers. In keeping with their national honor, they could not sit idly by and see their German brethren murdered, tormented and tortured just across the border, especially on land that rightfully belonged to Germany.

Hitler did his utmost to try to solve this problem peacefully. When he saw that the Jewish controlled democratic governments wanted to be neither reasonable nor wished any settlement, Hitler gave the Poles an ultimatum. This ultimatum was arrogantly rejected by Poland and on September 1, 1939, Germany's Wehrmacht marched into Poland and utterly crushed the Polish forces and their government in a short period of three weeks.

France and England, then completely controlled by the Jews, as they are in fact to this day, used this excuse to declare war on

Germany, the excuse being that they were duty bound to come to the defense of Poland. The fact that they had no intention of rescuing Poland, and never did, but were solely intent on crushing a Germany which had freed herself from the Jews, was lost upon the rest of the world.

We all know what followed. With the means of propaganda and money, the control of government in the hands of the Jews in the rest of the world, including the United States, one country after another was goaded and tricked into declaring war upon the German people.

Instead of following the example of the German people and letting them help the rest of the White people free themselves from the Jews, the poor deluded White people of the United States, England and France allowed themselves to be used like a bunch of cattle to not only help the Jews destroy Germany and the Germans, but in the end to bring about their own self-destruction.

Again, it is not our purpose here to review the history of World War II. It has been reviewed and written (and distorted) by the Jewish press in a thousand books and tens of thousands of articles.

We all know that Jewish stooges, such as that insane super-egotist, Franklin D. Roosevelt, and that drunken Zionist agent, Winston Churchill, succeeded in lying to their people, tricking their people and goading them into a war on the side that would be to their own worst interests. The German people, with one of the greatest leaders the White Race has ever produced, fought bravely and valiantly. Their glorious exploits will forever be engraved in the pages of history where heroism is recorded. Nevertheless, Germany, who had only a short period of six years to recuperate from financial, industrial and spiritual bankruptcy and a country which in area was only the size of Texas, was able to hold out for 4-1/2 years before it was crushed by the greater part of the rest of the world, including the vast resources of the United States of America and Soviet Russia.

Again we repeat, it is not our objective here to review the history of the tragic Armageddon, this tragic fratricidal war in which White brother killed White brother, one half struggling for their survival and freedom from under the Jewish heel, the other side under the demented influence of their mortal enemy, the treacherous international Jew. It is rather our purpose here to sketch these events in rough framework and to draw our lessons and conclusions from this review.

What lessons can we learn from this powerful episode in history that spanned a period of less than 25 years?

For one thing, we can be tremendously proud that the White Race can produce such a great and magnificent leader as was embodied in Adolf Hitler. On the other hand, we cannot help but be unabashedly ashamed that so many good White people were too stupid to recognize this great genius in their midst. Secondly, we must bow our heads in shame that the White people were gullible enough to allow themselves to be deluded by the treacherous Jew into destroying their greatest opportunity at salvation and freedom from the miserable world pestilence of Judaism.

We can, however, be tremendously encouraged and take heart in the fact that the Jewish power was actually broken within a large area of Europe. In fact, Hitler and the German people came within a hairbreadth of freeing the rest of humanity from the tyranny of the international Jew. Had the hand of fate intervened just a little differently in a number of circumstances, permanent victory could have resulted on the side of the White Man.

For instance, had the timing been just a little later, it is not only possible, but very probable, that the German scientists, in a revitalized and energetic Germany, would have perfected the atom bomb before it would have been possible in a decadent and depression-ridden United States. It was only under the inspiration and pressure of war that the United States could rally itself to undertake such a huge project. Had the war been delayed, say for a matter of only three or four years, it is very possible that

Germany would have had the atom bomb first, and if they had had it first, history would have turned out differently and more favorably for the White Race, and catastrophically for the Jewish race.

Or, had a White leader of similar stature to Hitler arisen during the 30's in the depression- ridden United States, things would have certainly turned out differently for the Jews and for the destiny of the White Race. We did have a few leaders that did show some promise, such as Huey Long in Louisiana— who, by the way, was assassinated by a Jewish doctor— or a Charles Lindberg, who might have led the American people. Unfortunately, Lindberg did not quite have the spiritual fiber.

Or had that miserable drunken Jewish stooge, Winston Churchill, suffered a demise for any one of a number of reasons during the Battle of Britain, the will of the British people might have collapsed and with it the war efforts of the enemies of the German people and their fight for freedom.

Germany, Adolf Hitler, and National Socialism

Or perhaps if the first winter after the Germans invaded Russia in 1941 had not come so unfortunately early and been so tremendously severe, the Germans might have conquered Russia in the first year. Having collapsed Russian resistance, they might have been able to organize the vast natural resources of that country and provided a wide and wonderful base that the rest of the world would then not have been able to crush under any circumstances.

Or some other technical invention might have come forth on the side of the Germans, such as the V-2 rockets, that would have given the Germans an early advantage and lead in the war and decided victory in their favor.

In any case, it is safe to assume that victory could have just as easily come on the side of the White Man fighting for his freedom and turned against the worldwide Jewish conspiracy. The fact is, it almost did, and the last thing in the world the White Race must not fall heir to is the idea that the victory over the Jewish international conspiracy is inevitable. It is our manifest destiny to become supreme throughout the world. We must forever keep this uppermost in our mind with an indomitable determination and an unquenchable passion. The complete victory of the White Man is paramount to his survival. For the White Man it is either: White Supremacy or extinction. The White Man was never created to become a slave to a parasitic race that was never even capable of founding a culture.

Today we have overwhelming evidence from the Jews themselves as to what a major threat they view Hitler's racial philosophy. Nearly 30 years after Hitler's death, it is hardly possible to pick up a newspaper without seeing some snide, disparaging lies about Hitler in print. We can hardly turn on a TV set, but somehow, somewhere, an innuendo, an insulting remark is dropped, a hit-and-run attack is made on Hitler. As in their attack on the Romans, the Jews persistently and forever keep attacking and discrediting that which is best in the White Race. As a result, even today, Adolf Hitler and the Romans rate more abuse and slander from the Jewish smear apparatus than any other targets.

There are, however, some shortcomings in the Nazi philosophy and Hitler's program that we should also recognize and learn our lessons from them.

One of the basic weaknesses of Hitler's program was that it was founded almost completely on the narrow base of the supremacy of the German race rather than the all-inclusive supremacy of the White Race. History quite clearly shows that the British nation had the will, the energy and the genius to build the British Empire, an empire which encompassed approximately one quarter of the surface of the earth. We also know that the French nation produced a great outburst of energy and military success under the leadership of Napoleon. It is also abundantly clear that great geniuses were produced in the field of painting by such nations as Holland, France, Italy, England, Belgium and others. In the field of music we have great opera geniuses in Italy such as Verdi, Puccini,

Nature's Eternal Religion

Mascagni and many others. In the Field of science there are a great many White geniuses who have contributed to the field of chemistry, physics, mathematics, invention and technology from the ranks of the White Man from many nations. In the Field of discovery we have men like Columbus, Captain James Cook and hundreds of others.

In any case, without belaboring the issue, it is abundantly clear that the base should be broad enough to include all the White people in general. While Hitler's appeal was basically directed towards the German people, however, in all fairness to Adolf Hitler, we believe that it was his intention to work for the salvation of the White People as a whole, but unfortunately, in order to get an organized Fighting base constructed, he had to first of all organize the German people. He did do this on a partisan basis which rallied the German people and depicted the British and the French as their past and future enemies. Whether it could have been done in a different way in the short time that he had to prevent the complete subjugation of Germany to the clutches of Bolshevism, today we can only speculate. In any case it is deplorable that the heart and soul of the National Socialist philosophy was based on a narrow foundation primarily encompassing only the German people and espousing Pan-Germanism.

* * *

Ideologically, we, of the CHURCH OF THE CREATOR, part company with National Socialism at this point. We espouse Racial Socialism, not National Socialism. We believe that nationalism is a divisive idea among the White people of the world, not a unifying force. Like religion, it has been used to split the White peoples of the world for centuries, with wars and destruction ensuing. Not only have the French fought the English and the English and French fought the Germans, etc., but during the war between Austria and Prussia even Germans killed Germans, all under the guise of nationalism.

We therefore reject National Socialism and replace it with Racial Socialism. We are not particularly concerned whether a White

Man is an Englishman, a German, a Frenchman or a Norwegian. Our common tie is race, not nationality. The Jew for centuries has been completely indifferent as to whether one of their own was of American, English, or German nationality. The common bond is their race and their blood. Their strength has largely been due to this inbred Racial Loyalty.

Nor are we concerned as to whether a White Man is Nordic,

Aryan, Alpine or Mediterranean. This, too, is divisive and would exclude many of our good White brothers. We therefore speak of the White Race and never of Aryan, Caucasian, etc.

We, too, must think along lines of Racial Loyalty to the White Race. We must never again be caught in the web of nationalism as a divisive wedge used to instigate wars between members of the White Race.

For this reason we base our entire creed on Racial Socialism, not National Socialism. This difference is of major significance. In a following chapter we explore this idea further.

* * *

The second criticism I have of Adolf Hitler and his program is that it was founded on a political base rather than going all the way and building it on a religious base. Hitler really never came to grips with the problem of Christianity, instead, tolerating it and trying to co-exist side by side with it. Nowhere has he ever pointed out that Christianity was a Jewish creation, perpetrated upon the White Race in order to destroy it. While Hitler tried to live and let live as far as the Christian religions were concerned, they in turn fought him tooth and nail. The Catholic church, from its worldwide headquarters in Rome, collaborated with the Jews and with the communists and did everything possible to undermine and stymie the German people's fight for freedom against the worldwide Jewish conspiracy. The Protestant church was no less aggressive and fanatic in their campaign to crush this great racial outburst. Even in Germany itself the Catholic and Protestant churches fought Hitler every inch of the way and used their moral and spiritual influence in dividing the people and setting them against their government. Even during the critical war period the church leaders in Germany committed untold acts of treason against their own people and their government when the latter were engaged in a life and death struggle.

It is overwhelmingly evident that a religion which teaches that the Jews are God's chosen people, that they have a sweetheart arrangement with the Lord, that they are untouchable because the Lord said, "I will curse them that curse thee, and I will bless them that bless thee," is completely untenable with a philosophy of White Racial Supremacy. I therefore believe that Hitler did only part of the job by tackling it from a political and military basis rather than founding a completely new religion that encompassed and united the whole White Race of the world in opposition to the colored races.

Also the fact that he formed an alliance with the Japanese Empire, an empire of the yellow race, is something that undermines the whole concept of White Racial Supremacy.

Again, in fairness to Hitler, perhaps under the pressure of time and expediency, he had no other choice. Perhaps, once he had won the war, and was in firmer control of the resources and the means to carry out further revolutionary changes, he would have come to grips with the churches and their deceitful and hypocritical undermining of the White Race. Perhaps he would have, but at that stage and under those circumstances he was not able to do so.

He did organize the Hitler Youth and inculcate into them a completely new philosophy, namely the philosophy of "Blood, Soil and Honor." Certainly the youth being indoctrinated in the new racial ideas was not encouraged to go to church. In fact, the timing of most of these meetings conflicted with those which they might have spent in church. The priests and pastors were violently jealous of the appeal the philosophy of the Nazi party made upon the youth and that they were losing the youth to the Nazi party.

Had Hitler won the war, and having had more time, I believe it would have undoubtedly resulted in the demise of the Christian churches and the eventual replacement of that suicidal philosophy with a new and a vigorous racial ideology based on the survival and supremacy of the White Race.

Be that as it may, I am firmly convinced that the survival of the Christian religion and the survival of the White Race are incompatible. Either Christianity will survive long enough to destroy the White Race, in which case Christianity will be destroyed along with it, or the White Race will come to its senses, will shake itself free from the suicidal clutches of the Christian philosophy, and found its own religion based upon the purity and supremacy of its great racial destiny.

I first read Hitler's Mein Kampf in the original German when I was 20 years old. I have reread it many times in the English version. Whereas I believe it is one of the great books of all time, I do not believe that it is by any means the complete answer to the problem of America, today, in the 1970's. It has many deficiencies. Some of these are: (a) it is based on a political rather than a religious approach, (b) It empathizes Pan-Germanism, rather than the White Race as a whole, (c) It does not come to grips with Jewish Christianity, a most crucial omission. I have already mentioned these in my review of National Socialism. There are, however, several other factors that make it completely inadequate as a program for the White Race of America today.

In the first place, the book was written in 1924, almost 50 years ago, in a defeated, war-torn Germany, a country in a much different situation than America today. Whereas the cause of the German's problems at that time was the same cause as that of our problems today— namely the International Jew— nevertheless, our situation is vastly different. Whereas Germany in the

1920's was desperately poor and starving, we in America in the 1970's are, superficially at least, enjoying the greatest affluence in the history of mankind. Whereas Germany was a defeated nation saddled with the monstrous Versailles Treaty, this has little or no meaning to the average American of today. Yet in a large portion of his book, Hitler is hammering away at the evils of the Versailles Treaty. Hunger and unemployment were rampant in Germany in the twenties.

Today, in America these issues are irrelevant to the average American worker, nor does he even know what the Versailles Treaty was all about. We, therefore, find that to the average American Mein Kampf is not only hard to understand, but also hard to read, and does not strike fire.

Our problems are vastly different. Whereas, outside of the Jews in their midst, the Germans were racially of one kind. In America the rising tide of niggers is a frightening and ominous reality that every American is aware of. However, with the Jews, liberals and communists cranking out race-mixing propaganda by the carload, the average White American is terribly confused about the solution.

Then there are many other issues— Vietnam, school busing, welfare to the niggers, crime in the streets, and a host of others that plague the average American today that were different from the German Weimar Republic of the twenties, which is the basis of Hitler's book.

Without going into further detail, for the above reasons and others, I feel it is not the correct solution to look towards Nazism as the American program to save the White Race. We need a more comprehensive, far-reaching ideology that is imbedded not only in politics, but in our very religion itself, one that can embrace all the White people of the world, far and beyond the Germans. Furthermore, with the stigma the Jew has placed on the Swastika and Nazism as such, it is a formidable (and unnecessary) obstacle to walk up to the door of a prospective member of the CHURCH OF THE CREATOR, flashing a Nazi armband. You will be shut out before you even start. How much more receptive would be their welcome if instead you talked to them as representing the interests of their own race, the White Race.

I therefore conclude that whereas: Hitler has made a tremendous contribution to the White Race; has shown that a government with a racial base is a great advantage over a polyglot democracy; has exposed the international Jewish network on a world wide basis; has shown the superiority of the leadership principle; nevertheless that neither Mein Kampf not National Socialism are, per se, more than a partial solution for the problems of America today, and the White Race of the world as a whole.

We therefore need, and now have, a more comprehensive creed, one that embraces the total White Race, is predicated on a racial- religious base, and is brought up to date to fit the situation in today's foremost bastion of potential White Power— America.

* * *

In any case, we must now build where this great leader left off.

We must do it now. We have been given an extra reprieve, and because of the sacrifices and the supreme efforts of this great leader and the German people, we have more time in which to accomplish our goal. In the intervening time, what with the churches having turned completely liberal and having debauched and degraded themselves with race-mixing and joining hands with Jewish communism, we now have an excellent opportunity to destroy both these suicidal Jewish philosophies, and build a new religion for the White Race. We can thank Adolf Hitler for the extra time that we have been granted.

On the whole, there are many things that we can be tremendously grateful for to this, the greatest of all leaders of the White Race.

He has given us great inspiration and great hope that this Jewish pestilence can be destroyed. He has alerted the whole world to the fact that there is a Jewish menace and that communism is basically a Jewish creation. He has shown the world that the White Race, too, can unite on the basis of racial bonds and once they have done so, that they can fight like wildcats in defense of their race, their country and their honor. Hitler has shown the world and history the integral value of race itself and that race is the basis of all progress, culture and civilization. He has shown the world the tremendous superiority of the Leadership Principle over the Jewish democratic process. He has demonstrated its superiority not only in times of war but also in the tremendous progress that a bankrupt Germany made during six short years of peace. This remarkable record was clearly demonstrated under the leadership of a White Man, in control of the destiny of a White nation, employing the superior Leadership Principle.

He has shown the way to superior organization in the very form of government itself that is a model for future White governments to emulate. He has forged ahead and given new direction in the field of the arts and culture.

Hitler's National Socialist regime can be regarded as the first real government based on racial principles that the White Race has ever had. Most people are completely confused about Mussolini's Fascist movement and Hitler's Nazi movement. They equate them as being the same, but this is not true.

Both of them were based on the Leadership Principle, and both brought their countries out of the quagmire of Jewish communism. But the significant difference was this: whereas Mussolini's Fascism regarded the State as being the prime consideration.

Hitler said that Race was everything, and the state was merely a vessel for guarding and advancing the best interests of the race.

This is a tremendously important difference and for this reason I regard Hitler's Germany as having the first truly racial government the White Race has ever had.

In summary we can say that Adolf Hitler has bought us at least 50 years of time in which to overcome the worldwide Jewish network. Without his great struggle, undoubtedly the whole world would now be in the iron grip of Jewish tyranny to the same extent that it is now in Soviet Russia. He has made the whole White Race proud of the heroic leadership he gave the German people and the inspiration he imbued them with in their heroic struggle for freedom. He founded a new philosophy which was based on the value of race in a way which it had never before been presented and to an extent which it never before had been promoted. He gave the White Race tremendous encouragement that the Jewish conspiracy can be broken, and will be broken. For these reasons and many others, we can say without reservations that Adolf Hitler was the greatest leader the White Race has ever had, and the greatest White Man that ever lived.

On April 30th at 3:00 P.M., Adolf Hitler was killed in action while defending Berlin from the Mongolian hordes from the East. Contrary to the enemy version, he did not commit suicide, nor did he escape to another country. On May 1, 1945, the German radio broadcast the following message: "From the Fuehrer's headquarters, it is reported that our leader, Adolf Hitler, was killed in action this afternoon fighting in the line of duty to his last breath for Germany, against communism..." He did not die in vain. He and millions of heroic Germans died fighting for our cause in order that the White Race might survive before the diabolic Jewish onslaught.

Not too long before the end, Hitler made this prophetic statement: "Somewhere in a faraway place, a Nazi band is playing Dixie and Swannee River, the blood will run in the streets of America and Great Britain, then my spirit will rise from the grave and the world will know that I was right."

Today, more than a quarter of a century later, the spirit of Hitler is more alive and flourishing in the hearts of millions of militant White racial comrades than ever before in history. With the crimes of the Jews and the niggers becoming more outrageous every day, the White people are fed up and they are ready to fight. They are looking for a leader to take command in the coming battle.

From this greatest of White Men we have received the direction and the inspiration. He spoke these inspiring words:

"When human hearts break and human souls despair, then from the twilight of the past the great conquerors of distress and care, of disgrace and misery, of spiritual slavery and physical compulsion, look down on them and hold out their eternal hands to despairing mortals! Woe to the people that is ashamed to take them!"

Hitler has indicated that he and his people have done their part and the fight will now have to be taken up in the heart of America from here on out. He is holding out his hand to us now, encouraging us onward.

Let us ourselves now take up the fight where he left off— and vow to finish it!

CHAPTER SIX

RACIAL SOCIALISM

In his frantic, unending endeavor to blunt and stifle the healthy, natural instincts of the White Man, the Jew has worked feverishly to confuse us on those prime issues that are vital for our survival. In this category I have already mentioned the havoc he has wrought relative to our ideas about racial loyalty and also our religious orientation.

One other basic idea that the White Man is hopelessly confused about is socialism or collectivism, and I use these words interchangeably. Since this idea has been so terribly abused and confused by the Jews, the Communists and the Kosher Konservatives to the point where they could mean anything, I am going to set forth the position and meaning that the CHURCH OF THE CREATOR gives to the term socialism: to us socialism means Organized Society, period. It does not at all imply state ownership of the means of production, nor does it, in our definition, imply confiscation of private property. On the contrary.

Let us make it crystal clear: we, of the CHURCH OF THE CREATOR are opposed to state ownership of the basic means of production, such as farms, factories, stores, etc. We are for the ownership of private property by individuals. We believe that there is a category of functions that are best performed by organized society as a whole. In this category we place highways, airports, harbors, national defense, law enforcement and many others.

We are in fact not particularly interested in all the dogmatic political terms with which the White Race has been tearing itself apart in arguing the theoretical aspects of each. We are not interested in making a holy cow out of "private enterprise" or "capitalism." Nor are we dogmatically concerned about defending to our dying breath, the much-ballyhooed idea of a "republican" form of government that the Kosher Konservatives are so enchanted about.

All these terms are, at best, theoretical. What we are really concerned about is: what is the most practical and viable type of organized society for the White Man to live in? We come back to that foundation of our religious creed: What is best for the White Race?

In examining the hackneyed political ideas held so dear by the Kosher Konservatives, we find they do not hold up under this basic guide: What is best for the White Race? The idea of a "republic" has broken down before our very eyes in the last two centuries. It was already discarded by the Romans before the first century A.D. It has been an excellent vehicle which the Jews have used to fleece, rob and destroy the White Race. The Kosher Konservatives will argue that it has been converted to "democracy" and it is democracy that is our overwhelming problem. This is, at most, a half-truth. The difference between "democracy" and "republic" is only a matter of semantics. In practical application they both lead to mob rule, to a type of government where the scum elements govern the better elements of the people, with the parasites multiplying and destroying the productive elements.

The essence of democracy (or republicanism) is the two (or more) party system, parties which are always in opposition to each other. This is the Jewish tool of divide and conquer. In practice this means that no matter how clear and urgent the problems, the approach is: division and opposition. Then, after prolonged hassle, no matter what compromised decision is "voted" on, there is an opposing group, hampering, blocking and scuttling the course of action.

The average participant in a democracy has no more understanding of the thousands of complex problems of the affairs of state that the average passenger has in the intricacies of flying the huge jumbo jet which is being piloted by a trained professional.

Without a comprehensive knowledge of the problems he is voting on his vote is less than useless, it is dangerous.

We of the CHURCH OF THE CREATOR believe, not in democracy, but in Racial Socialism, which is teamwork elevated to its highest perfection for the welfare of the whole race, led by its ablest leaders. It combines the best elements of both teamwork and competition. If "team spirit" and rooting for the "home team" are such noble attributes (and they are) then, certainly, having a whole race united in a team effort for their common good is the highest goal we can strive for.

That is what we mean by Racial Socialism as the ultimate in organized society for the White Race.

Let us now also take a look at the term "individual enterprise." It, too, is a theoretical myth and a deceptive fraud. Anyone who has ever played the parlor game "Monopoly" knows what the end result of wide open free enterprise is: before the game is over, one party gains a powerful stranglehold over all the rest, and from then on out, no matter which way the dice roll, when the game is over, he owns everything— houses, land, factories, banks.

This, too, happens in real life. It is easily discernable that, say Standard Oil, left free to play the rules of the game proudly known as "free enterprise" could from the beginning, have driven every other company out of the oil business and acquired the oil business in totality. It could easily have acquired a total monopoly in worldwide oil. It could have owned every service station and gas station in the world through squeeze play and financial strength. It could have then moved into the banking business until it acquired every bank in the country. Left unchecked, it then could have started acquiring manufacturing businesses such as the electrical industries, etc. As its financial powers snowballed, it could then easily have taken over the railroads, real estate, etc., until, in fact, one company owned everything and held every individual at their mercy.

This is "free enterprise" in clear essence, the same "free enterprise" that the Kosher Konservatives just love to prattle about.

Basically this is what has happened on a worldwide basis. Only instead of Standard Oil, it is the Jewish House of Rothschild and the worldwide Jewish banking conspiracy that has a stranglehold on the world. They not only own practically all the physical and financial wealth of the world, but they also own all the governments of the world.

Throughout this book we have referred to this clique as the Jewish conspiracy. Actually it encompasses the whole Jewish race, practicing their religious creed, the Talmud.

It is therefore our conclusion from the lessons of history that neither a "republican" form of government, nor "free enterprise" nor our much-vaunted Constitution is going to save the White Race from mongrelization and destruction.

In order to survive and expand, the White Race must (a) unite, (b) organize, (c) practice racial loyalty, (d) have a religious creed encompassing these same aspects.

Since I have already defined socialism as organized society, it is obvious that to be organized at all the White Man must have a socialist government, which every government has been from time immemorial, in any case. What the White Man must further have is Racial Socialism, that is a government organized with the prime goal of promoting the best interests of the White Race and the White Race alone. It must be based on a racial foundation.

In essence, we, of the CHURCH OF THE CREATOR, believe in a harmonized blending of our Church and our State. We believe our White Society is best served by that combination whereby a race's government and religion blend together in perfect harmony to promote the best interests of our White Race. We believe that "separation of church and state," that much vaunted holy cow in our constitution, is a deceptive fraud and a hoax. One might well ask—how can the same people that go to church and preach "resist not evil," and "turn the other cheek" support a government with huge tax contributions for national defense, and for an ever increasing police forces? It just doesn't make sense. Either you believe in defending yourself, or you don't. How can the same people that spend over a hundred billion dollars a year to presumably have the government defend them from their enemies then go to church and preach "love your enemies?" It is utterly ridiculous. It requires a split personality, a schizophrenic personality to ride on both sides of the fence.

Nor is there any great virtue in having the White people split up and fragmented into a thousand divergent religious camps, each in disagreement with each other, often culminating in religious wars and fratricide, as in Ireland today, and hundreds of religious wars in previous centuries.

We, of the CHURCH OF THE CREATOR, are pursuing the goal of uniting the White Race on the obvious ground that is basic to all, namely— what is best for the White Race— as our cardinal dogma.

We are further bent on harmonizing the goals, objectives and the philosophy of our government with that of our religious thinking. To have these two major forces of our society pulling in opposite directions is sheer idiocy.

We believe in an organized social structure; we believe in a religion that has as its basic foundation the best interests of the White Race; we believe in the total White Race being united in such a religion, rather than fragmented into a thousand conflicting and suicidal Christian creeds; we believe that the government should harmonize with our religious creed and also be based on the same racial foundation. We furthermore believe that such government and such organized society functions best if it is further based on the Leadership Principle.

We call this Racial Socialism.

In order to understand the term socialism we must first of all brush away all the deceptive ideas about this word that have been flooded upon us by the Jews, the Communists and the Kosher Konservatives.

Socialism is not an evil concept as the Kosher Konservatives would have us believe. In essence it means organized society, striving to promote its own best interests collectively. Not only is there nothing wrong with this, but it is the only way civilized man has been able to survive and advance.

Outside of an organized socialist framework, we would not be able to own or protect our property, have highways, form a government, have schools, churches, defense organizations and a hundred other basic requirements. We are all dependent on each other's contributions towards the social structure. We are dependent on thousands of different industries for our existence— railroads, power companies, manufacturing plants, farming, etc. We need the accumulative help of millions of other people to live in today's highly specialized society.

This is what has produced our great civilization, and let me emphasize that we, of the CHURCH OF THE CREATOR are not anti-civilization. We are for civilization, the White Man's civilization.

The fact of the matter is that man is a social creature and like many other species in Nature, he owes his very existence, and in fact his tremendous progress, to the fact that he has been able to organize collectively, that he has been able to so effectively organize a workable society. Socialism is organized society. He has been doing this for so long that it has become deeply ingrained in his instinct by now and he does it intuitively. If it were not for this characteristic of man, he would still be back in the caveman stage of a million years ago where each individual would hump and scrounge for food on his own and live like the present aborigines of central Australia. Even these lowly people have some semblance of social organization.

It was as man began to form and organize a social structure, and organize, divide and specialize in the work and labor that had to be done, that he began his long climb upwards into the higher civilized levels. It was when one man became a shoemaker, another man a tailor, another a farmer, another a schoolteacher, etc., that man began to pull himself up by the bootstraps and become part of the tremendously productive "socialized" society that he is today. Without this division of labor and specialization he would be back at the level of the aborigines we mentioned earlier.

Not only that, but man has a definite spiritual need to belong to his tribe or his group or to identify with his own kind of people, which for the White Man is his own White Race. When the naive conservatives tell you that Collectivism or Socialism is a terrible evil, and that Russia is in the grip of Socialism, they are lying through their teeth. Russia is not at all a Collectivist nation as such. Russia is a vast super slave state under the heel of a tyrannical Jewish dictatorship, the most cruel and hideous that the world has ever seen. A collectivist society is a natural society whereby the natural leaders of the people are just that— natural leaders, leading their people in an organized fashion for their own constructive improvement, not alien slave- masters who have subjugated another race in order to disintegrate and destroy them.

A true and outstanding example of natural leadership and a natural order was the wonderful society in Nazi Germany during the 30's under their natural leader, namely Adolf Hitler. There we had an example of a true German leading his own people, the Germans, and being admired and obeyed by millions of devoted followers. This was one of the finest examples of a people operating under the natural order that Nature has instinctively imbedded in their innermost being, and thereby achieving their full potential in productivity, creativity and racial unity. It is this natural order that brings out the best in a race, and promotes its well-being and eternal urge to advance towards a higher level of existence.

It was a fine and wonderful renaissance of the White Race at its best. It is one of the great tragedies of history that the Jew in control of the overwhelming majority of the rest of the White world was able to smash this outburst of its own realization by the White Race.

In Hitler's Nazi Germany, the individual German owned more private property than he ever did under the democracy of the Weimar Republic. He had more hope, more individual freedom, more opportunities, a higher standard of living. He lived a much happier and a much more constructive life than he did under the Jewish "democracy" of the 1920's, or any other period.

We have already noted earlier in this book particularly in the first chapter, that many species in Nature are social creatures, that is, they live in an organized society. We have observed especially how the bees have a tightly knit and highly organized social structure within which they live. Every bee knows exactly what his function is, they do their job instinctively and their every act helps the colony as a whole. By building the colony and living within it, the bee is able to survive and perpetuate his species. The same honeybee that lives in this type of social structure is by Nature committed to that kind of existence. He cannot do otherwise. If he tried to live as an individual he would die and his species would perish with him.

At this stage of the White Man's evolution, he is in the same position as the organized social- living honeybee. The White Man's natural mode of living is as a member of the tribe, as a member of his larger social group. Were he to live outside of it and live as an individual, again, his society would break down and undoubtedly his race would perish. I repeat, the White Race, having reached the height of excellence that it has, is a highly complex socialized creature whose very inner soul is intertwined in his social structure, in community with the other members of his race. Like the honeybee, Nature has programmed into his very instinct a certain type of society that he fits into and that he must naturally have in order to survive.

Basically this developed from the earlier tribes and grew from there towards higher levels of society which perhaps reached its highest point and culmination in Hitler's National Socialist Germany. It is our purpose to advance further from this high point in the White Man's development.

This natural order has certain inherent characteristics. The first characteristic is racial loyalty— loyalty towards your own people. Nature has endowed each of us with this characteristic instinctively— the urge to keep our race pure. This means that we have a love for our own kind and we have a fierce hostility towards those that would intrude amongst us and endanger our race. Instinctively built into such a social structure, is a high respect for womanhood and the protection of its women. The natural instinct for keeping the race pure incites a fighting hatred in the male to prevent his women from being polluted by males of another race. Not too long ago, if a black nigger raped a White woman, justice was swift and final. He was usually hanged from the nearest tree.

* * *

We, of the CHURCH OF THE CREATOR, firmly believe in the concept of private property and believe that the finest example of a Socialistic White society up to this time was demonstrated by Hitler's National Socialist Germany (which protected private property). Nevertheless, we can demonstrate that even in a society where all property is communally owned, if free from Jewish pollution, it not only can survive very nicely, but can do very well in terms of taking care of its own people and expanding the White Race. We have an example of such in our very own continent as is dramatically demonstrated by a people called the Hutterites.

The Hutterites live in "colonies" of about 70 to 130 souls. There is no private property. All their property is communally owned.

These people have a rather interesting and colorful history. Originating in Moravia in 1528, its members took their name from Jacob Hutter, an early leader, who was burned at the stake by the kind and loving Christian church in 1536. By the end of the 16th century the Hutterites numbered about 20,000 souls. They had certain weaknesses which they still have to this day and it was their weakness of pacifism and disinterest in politics that soon threatened their existence. As pacifists and non-combatants, the Hutterites were victimized by the armies of both sides in the war between Austria and Turkey in 1593. They were plundered, taken captive and many were executed. By 1622 all Hutterites had been driven from Moravia. After several other wanderings they received an invitation from the government of Russia in 1770.

This was accepted by 123 members, who then moved to that undeveloped area to pioneer the farmlands of the Ukraine. This group prospered beautifully for 100 years, until in 1874 they were deprived of military exemption. Once again they felt forced to pack up and leave. This time the entire population, about 800 souls, decided to try again. This time they left for America.

They moved to South Dakota. There, due to the difficulties in obtaining the large tracts of land that they needed, and the easy availability of homesteading for individuals, about half of them abandoned colony life and took up homesteads. The remaining faithful founded three colonies between 1874 and 1877. These three colonies carved civilization from out of the frontier lands, spawned the some 200 colonies that exist today in some of the Western states and western provinces of Canada.

Today these 200 colonies constitute approximately 20,000 members

Racial Socialism

of the Hutterite people. It is most remarkable to note that the original three colonies, numbering only 400 souls, has now expanded and multiplied to over 20,000 members. This despite the fact that the Hutterites practically never recruit new members from the outside. This 20,000 figure is completely due to natural reproduction of their own kind. This means that this fine group of White people have multiplied 50 times their own number within one century.

In studying the life of the Hutterites we find that they live in communal colonies. Each colony grows to a number of about 130 before they divide and form a new colony, a process not dissimilar to the swarming beehive colonies.

Since they do not believe in private property as such, all property is owned by the colony itself. They solely engage in agriculture. This usually comprises a large tract of land which might be either farming or ranching property. They have communal buildings and they all eat together in one large dining room. They are quite religious and each colony has their own preacher.

Each colony also has their own natural leader who supervises and directs the labor and the business of the group as a whole. Each man is assigned his special job and he performs it quite well. Regardless of what kind of job he has, his job is regarded with equal respect and of equal importance to any other. Nobody is paid any wages, but everyone is properly taken care of in all respects.

Anyone is free to leave and divest himself from the colony at any time, but hardly anyone ever does. The members seem happy, healthy and prosperous. Undoubtedly they are as happy, and probably better adjusted to their group and fellow members, and have a better sense of belonging, than does the average American.

Although I would personally not like to live in such a colony, probably because I wasn't brought up that way, and also because I believe in private property, nevertheless, here we have overwhelming evidence that not only can a society that practices communal property ownership survive, but it can flourish and prosper, provided it is not contaminated by Jewish control or interference. This should refute the claim of Kosher Konservatives, once and for all, that it is "socialism" that is the culprit.

The other most interesting aspect of the Hutterite way of living is the observation that in less than a century they have multiplied to 50 times their original numbers. This is most remarkable indeed and it is due, of course, to the fact that they are prolific and raise large families. It is also most noteworthy that despite the fact that

they often raise families of twelve, they are quite capable of feeding, clothing and maintaining this prolific rate of expansion from one generation to the next without having lowered their living standards or the quality of their fine race.

The Hutterites do remarkably well that which Nature has ordained us all to do— to raise a beautiful family of children. They have been most successful in expanding the White Race and populating the land with their own kind. I might add that "their own kind" exemplifies some of the best characteristics of the White Race, intellectually, morally, physically and aesthetically. They prove that the White Race, too, can be as fruitful and prolific as any other.

* * *

Our conclusions on Racial Socialism are summed up with the following observations:

1) The White Race thrives best in an organized society which is socialism.

2) The White Race cannot survive otherwise.

3) The White Man has an inborn natural order that he fits into.

4) The key to such a society is the Leadership Principle.

5) Private property rights are not in conflict with Racial Socialism but an integral part of it.

6) Only through an organized society can an individual adequately protect his property.

7) The White Man thrives ideally under a socialist government, provided he maintains control of his own destiny and protects himself from the destructive intrusion of the Jew.

8) The ideal situation is that combination whereby the religion and the government of a race blend together in perfect harmony to promote the best interests of the race.

9) Keeping the Jew out and keeping the race pure can best be accomplished by having a social structure whose foundation is race.

In the next chapter we will examine the basic underlying concepts of the Leadership Principle.

CHAPTER SEVEN

THE LEADERSHIP PRINCIPLE

There should be no great mystery as to the meaning of the Leadership Principle. It is as simple as it sounds. Yet thanks to all the brain pollution we have been deluged with about "democracy," our great "republic" and other deceptive cliches, the average American is completely confused about this term.

The Leadership Principle is older than civilization itself and goes back to the very beginning of mankind's organized tribal society.

It is as modern as General Motors, The Bell Telephone Company and IBM. The first tribal organization used the Leadership Principle and the above-mentioned industrial giants use it today.

It means simply organized society having a leader at its head to lead, direct and plan the best interests of the whole group. Such leader has authority to command, and on the other hand, must also be totally responsible to the group.

A perfect example of the Leadership Principle is the Kehilla, the Jewish master organization described in a previous chapter. At the head is the "Prince" or the "Sponsor." He has seven powerful Jews under him who take orders from him and pass them down the chain of command to the seven subordinates each has under him. This is repeated in seven echelons, until there are 824,543 subordinates at the lowest level, each supervised and carrying out orders from their immediate superior.

In very short order the idea and the command from the highest leader is transmitted throughout the organization to its lowest level.

The army is organized the same way. Starting with the Commander-in-Chief, there is a chain of command through the generals, to the colonels, etc., down to lowest private. Through such chain of command there is unity of purpose, there is a rapid execution of orders, and therein is exemplified the most efficient and effective organization devised by man.

Let us speculate, for a moment, about the relative merits of two armies, one organized under the above efficient Leadership Principle and the other under "democratic" principles. Let us suppose the sergeants of the latter put it to a vote to each of their companies as to what action they should take. "Boys," he might say, "should we go over the top and engage the enemy, or should we go on a picnic?"

Can you imagine what a useless mob such an army would become? Doubtlessly they would be slaughtered by the enemy who employed the Leadership Principle. It is the same way with the ship of state, or any other organization that departs from this time-proven principle. The Jew espouses "democracy" in glowing terms and deceives us that we are governing ourselves. All the while he knows what a treacherous game he is playing. Skillfully he uses this fraud to divide, confuse and conquer the White Man for his own gain and our detriment. When it comes to his own organizations, he full well knows better and resorts to the Leadership Principle as in the Kehilla.

We have been so terribly confused by Jewish propaganda that the Leadership Principle is synonymous with tyranny and all dictatorships are tyrannies. They point to Adolf Hitler, begin frothing at the mouth about what a terrible man he was.

As we have seen in a previous chapter, this was one of the biggest hoaxes perpetrated upon the White Man since Christianity confounded and confused the Romans nearly 2,000 years ago. Actually Adolf Hitler, ruling under the Leadership Principle, provided the German people with the most constructive, most benevolent, most beloved and most popular government the German people ever had. They had a higher standard of living, had more freedom, and were happier than they ever were under any democracy.

History shows that leaders who are of their own people (in contrast to some traitor fronting for an alien race) are most often dedicated to their people. When Rome changed from the Republican form of

government to the Emperor system, they enjoyed the longest span of peace and prosperity the world has ever known. From Emperor Augustus reign through the next two centuries was known as "Pax Romana," Roman peace, a period of continuous peace and prosperity never again equaled.

Unfortunately, not all the Roman Emperors were good men. The trouble was, as it is today, the Jew was there, in the background, manipulating the intrigues of the court. Nero had a Jewish wife named Poppeai, and so it went.

Nevertheless with all the weaknesses of some of the Roman Emperors (most of them were good men), Rome faired better under the Empire than she did under the Republic, until Christianity took over and destroyed Rome.

What Rome needed and did not have was twofold; (a) she needed a racial religion that would have completely immunized her from the Jew, and (b) she

The Leadership Principle

needed an orderly program of succession.

The latter is not really too difficult to come by and the Jews themselves suggest the format for their "King of the Jews" in Protocol No. 24. He will be well trained, carefully selected by the Elders who decide the line of succession. Such a format, or a similar one, makes sense. Determining the line of succession is by no means an insurmountable problem, as we have so often been told by the Jews themselves.

As the Protocols show, they are masters at employing the effective Leadership Principle for themselves, but work feverishly at preventing the White Race from having any leadership of its own.

It is my conclusion that history has shown from time immemorial that the Leadership Principle is by far the best and most effective organization, not only for government, but also every other type of organization. This whole business of democratic government was invented by the Jews. It results in mob rule, with the mobs being steered by Jewish propaganda and trickery. It results in bickering, in stalemate, in waste, in cowardice and paralysis. People need leaders at their head, not followers who try to appease those that elected them. We can learn something further from the Jews when they say in Protocol No. 10 that programs must be directed from one central mind. If a plan is split into fractional parts from the minds of many, it leaves a confused conglomeration. In this they are right, as experience has proven.

In summary, what the White Race desperately needs today (as it will in the future) are real leaders. Imbued with the Creativity religion, which holds that the good of the White Race as the highest virtue, both leaders and followers will want to combine in pursuing the same constructive path. Organized, united and with a constructive creed and program in its possession, nothing can stop the White Race from reaching the highest pinnacle of success.

Organized and united, the White Race is ten times more powerful than the rest of the world combined.

It is the objective of this book to supply the White Race with the necessary programs and the fighting creed to accomplish what we must— to populate all the good land on the face of this earth. Let all the good leaders of our great Race now come forth and organize their areas. From such beginnings will come the great leaders of our race— leaders who will free us from the Jewish yoke, and then lead us ever onward to ever-higher plateaus of accomplishment and excellence.

CHAPTER EIGHT

FOUNDATIONS OF OUR WHITE SOCIETY

Just as the honey bee has instinctively organized itself according to the pattern Nature has devised for it, and by following it and only by following it does it survive, so also is there a natural order for the White Man's society. If he follows this natural order he will survive and multiply. If he goes contrary to Nature, then Nature will heap retribution upon him and phase him out just as surely as it has the dinosaur, and the dodo, and the thousands of other extinct species.

The White Race, too, has a distinct natural order that Nature has ordained for it. Left undisturbed by such parasitic alien forces as the Jew, the White Man would naturally follow this order.

Basically here are some of the fundamental laws that are inbred and ingrained in the White Race and are inherently its very own:

1. Loyalty and love for its own kind.

Just as every other race has been endowed by Nature with racial loyalty in order to preserve its kind, so the White Man, too, has been endowed with loyalty to his own kind. He, too, has a basic urge to mate only with his kind, and to procreate and perpetuate his own kind. This, of course, is completely in harmony with Nature's law of segregation of the species and its never-ending program to upgrade and improve the species. The fact that the White Race has reached the highest pinnacle of perfection of any of Nature's species over the thousands of years is only one of the many indicators of the powerful urge that the White Man has always had in the past to segregate and to improve his own race.

2. Hatred for alien races and their exclusion from its midst.

Actually these two emotions— love and hatred— go together and are the two sides of the same coin. You naturally love your own kind and defend them at all costs. If those whom you love, such as your own family, your own children, your own wife, are threatened or menaced by an alien race, the hatred that is engendered and called up for their defense is a natural emotion, not only in human beings, but in all species. If a tiger's cubs are menaced, the mother will ferociously defend them. In doing so she is aroused to great hatred and ferocity. Without hatred it is hardly imaginable that she would put up any defense. It is also the same in human beings. Without hatred for the menace that endangers our loved ones, we would hardly be aroused to fight and defend them. Therefore, this idiotic propaganda we are continually told by the liberals, the Jews, and the Christians, that we should not hate, in fact, we should love our enemies, is completely in conflict with Nature and in conflict with our best healthy instincts.

3. Defense of Territory.

Except for the parasites that live on the backs of others, practically every healthy species instinctively realizes and recognizes the need to have a large and adequate territory within which it can live and within which it can expand. It must have land upon which it can utilize the natural resources for its livelihood. Eagles recognize such territory and stake out usually an area of something like 70 square miles for a single eagle family. Wolves recognize this prime law of nature and they too stake out their own territory within which to hunt. A beaver colony has their own pond and if it becomes overgrown they build a dam in a new area and the offspring expands into further areas. Even a meadowlark or a bluebird voices its determination that it has staked out its own territory within which it claims supremacy and admonishes others to stay out.

4. The Leadership Principle.

With this idea and principle goes also the total organization of a structural society. Throughout history the human race as such, and the White Race in particular, has made great progress by virtue of outstanding leaders. Without leaders the White Race falls apart and disintegrates. Under such great leaders as Adolf Hitler, for instance, a people that had suffered tremendous defeat and was being totally destroyed and disintegrated by the evil Jewish parasites, was in short order rallied to a rebirth and regeneration that quickly united the nation. Under his leadership the nation expelled the poisonous parasites that had been undermining and destroying the nation, and quickly began a resurgence that

Nature's Eternal Religion

was the marvel of the century. Under such constructive leadership it began to rebuild itself and in a very few years it again became the most powerful nation on the face of the earth.

5. Chain of Command.

With the leadership principle also extends a chain of command which is exemplified by the organization of an army, or the organization of a corporation such as General Motors, or du Pont, or the Bell Telephone Company, or any one of a thousand others.

It is, in fact, the only sensible and efficient way to organize. All the Jewish propaganda about "democracy" to the contrary, the leadership principle has proved over the thousands of years to be the foundation of organized society. Democracy is nothing other than "mob rule" whereby the Jew has complete control of propaganda and leads and misleads the mob to not only destroy itself, but destroy its nationhood, destroy its country, and destroy its race. Under democracy, where everybody is presumably responsible for everything, and decisions are made by the cowardly vote of a committee, it actually works out that nobody is responsible for anything.

6. Sanctity of the family unit.

Incumbent in the White civilization is the family unit itself which is the basic building block of the whole social structure. If you destroy the family, you destroy the race. The family is the present golden link in the long golden chain of our race. If it is broken at any point in history the whole chain breaks down and is irreparably destroyed. With the sanctity of the family the idea of respect for womanhood is also strongly imbedded. Linked with this concept also is the sacredness of motherhood, which is the foundation of the family unit.

It is to the discredit of the White Race that these sacred ideas have been tarnished in recent years. In the frantic, insane and useless drive to attempt to upgrade the nigger to the White Man's level, we have degraded ourselves and are pulling ourselves down towards his level. Of the multitude of differences between the White Race and the niggers, one outstanding difference is in the type of family life the average healthy White family practices, and the degenerate, practically non-existent family life in the nigger community, which is pointed up by the joke "confused as Father's Day in Harlem."

7. The compulsion toward a racial soul.

There exists within each race which has achieved a homogeny, i.e., a similarity in structure because of its common descent, a certain character or quality that can best be described as soul. It is the very essence of his inner being and it is a common feeling around which racial loyalty can gravitate. Even the lowly nigger has it and talks about his "soul brothers," a descriptive term, loaded with meaning. Of all the races of mankind, the racial soul of the White Man is the loftiest, the most beautiful and the most creative. It is also this quality that every member of the race feels he is a part of and that he is a part of that community spirit. It is the racial soul of a people that makes them stick together and unite. It is this very quality that the Jew has labored so long and tenaciously to destroy in the White Man. It is this quality that must again be reawakened in the White Man and developed to its full potential.

Every human being feels that he must belong to something greater than himself and is most ideally in his own element when he feels that he is a part of a great united racial community. He is most ill at ease, frustrated, and like a Fish out of water when he is placed in a polyglot multi- racial environment. Like other creatures of Nature, people have a herd instinct, a strong inner urge to belong to the tribe. This is a natural instinct and it is one of the basic instincts that Nature has placed within each of us for the

preservation and segregation of the species. The White Man's failure in America and elsewhere today to realize this basic urge has completely disarmed him of his most useful instinct and leaves the field wide open for the Jew's satanic drive to mongrelize and destroy the White Race.

And so in summation we include in the Creed of the CHURCH OF THE CREATOR the basic requirements for the building of a healthy White society. They are as follows:

1) Racial Loyalty

2) Hatred and exclusion of alien races

3) Exclusive Territory

4) The Leadership Principle

5) Chain of Command

6) Sanctity of the Family

7) A Racial Soul.

Without these we cannot build a strong White social order, in fact we cannot even survive. Again, this is not something that I have invented, but these are basic laws that Nature has embedded in the very depths of our instincts over the many hundreds of thousands of years that the White Race evolved to ever-higher levels of existence.

It is part and parcel of our religious beliefs therefore, to foster, nurture and nourish those natural instincts within us, to strengthen them, and thereby strengthen our race and strengthen our White social older.

CHAPTER NINE

THE IMPORTANCE OF LAND AND TERRITORY

Even the most backward savage is well aware of the essential importance of land, room and territory within which his tribe can live and survive. So essential and self-evident is this idea that they will fight and risk their lives in order to either preserve their own, or expand and take over the adjoining tribe's territory. Even before the White Man ever arrived on the shores of

America, the hundreds of Indian tribes constantly fought each other. And what were they fighting for? They were fighting for land, room and territory within which their tribe could hunt and live, could pitch their teepees, and their offspring could prosper and expand. This urge and this knowledge are so basic and instinctive that even the birds and animals are well aware of this basic fact of Nature. In many cases they too stake out their territory. They know that you can only glean so much sustenance from a certain area of land and they mean to stake it out and protect it.

In an earlier chapter we noted how the majestic eagle staked out his territory, lived within it and worked it diligently.

We also observed the wisdom of the wolf family, in the same chapter, of how they stake out their required territory and how they refresh their boundary markers almost weekly. We also saw how other wolf families, too, had their territory and respected adjoining boundaries. They each had the instinctive wisdom to realize that land and territory were basic to their existence. They worked it and they guarded it. Property rights and territory were evidently a serious matter between the wolf families and well organized.

In the cat family, mountain lions will do the same thing. They know they need so much territory to live in and they will stake out their territory and claim it as their own to hunt and provide sustenance for the rearing of their family. Certain types of monkeys not only organize their territory but organize the hierarchy of their tribe. Even birds, when we hear them cheerfully singing what we believe is a song of happiness, are actually declaring to the world that this is their domain and are admonishing intruders to stay out. In the Arctic areas, the lemming, a prolific rodent, on the other hand, has a different solution to the problem. In order to keep the population in line with the territory and the land area available, and to keep this area from becoming overcrowded, they will, every so many years, lead a mass suicidal trek to the ocean and drown by the hundreds of thousands.

The point I am making here is that land and territory are synonymous with population, whether it be animal, bird or human population. Land and territory are basically essential, not only for providing sustenance, but also providing living room. One square mile of land can only provide so much food and fiber for a limited number of people. There are still some people who will deny this, arguing that with increased technology we can go on forever in providing an ever increasing production and that there are no limits in sight. This just isn't true. Not only is there a definite limit to the productivity of the soil regardless of how much technology is involved, but as the population increases, more and more productive land is taken out of production and utilized for home building, cities, living space, highways, roads, canals, right-of- ways, etc. Witness, for instance, the productive orange groves that only 30 years ago existed in Southern California. Now they are practically all gone, all that vast acreage being, by and large, covered with residential subdivisions.

Not only that, but the human population will expand fastest in those areas where there is plenty of room. Empty spaces seem to invite the rearing of larger families. Witness, for instance, the early pioneers in the west. Wherever land spaces were wide open and sparsely settled, the White pioneer had large families. In contrast, city dwellers, especially in apartment housing and areas of heavy density, have relatively small families among the White people. In fact, our best racial stock comes from the rural sections, although many of these sturdy peasants might migrate into the cities later and make their claim to fame and fortune in the cities.

Looking at it from the point of view of whole countries, we find, for instance, countries like Scotland and Ireland, where space is limited; the fertility is curtailed as well. We find that Ireland has a population of about 3-1/2 million and Scotland a population of approximately five million. With the cramped land area available to them these population figures have changed very little over the last 100 years and there are even periods when the population declines. Contrast this for instance, with the number of people of Irish or Scottish descent in America and we find that although they have lived in the new world a relatively short time, racially speaking, yet there are now many times as many Irish and Scottish kinsmen living in America as there are now living in the country of their origin. This all goes to substantiate the fact of Nature that in order for a race of people to survive they need space, room and territory. In other words they need land.

The Importance of Land and Territory

It is an overriding fact that there is only so much usable land in this world and there won't be any more. It is also an ominous fact that the population of the world is increasing by leaps and bounds, and overwhelmingly it is the colored races that are increasing. This is due to the help and aid White technology has given the colored races and due to the fact that the Jew is plundering the White Man and taking food and substance from him and shifting it to the benefit of the colored races. The fact that the Jewish propaganda agencies label this as being philanthropic and humanitarian is beside the point. It is no such thing. It is a criminal act of plunder designed to expand the colored races and shrink the White Race. It does not take any great imagination to project the results into the future.

Unless the White Race wakes up shortly and begins to take its destiny in its own hands, it is going to be crowded into a smaller and smaller living space on the face of this globe. When the White Man has been weakened to the point where the colored races can then finish him off by force, the Jew, having inflamed the colored races with hatred, will then give the signal for the destruction of the remnants of the White Race.

Let us make no mistake about it— the land area of this world and its resources are strictly limited and the time is coming very soon when either the White Race will organize to inhabit the earth, or it will be crowded from off its face by the inferior colored races.

Since there is not now, and there never will be, room enough for both the White Race and the colored races to both perpetuate their own kind on the surface of this earth, I, for one, would much sooner that we survived than they. I am sure no member of the White Race wants to be crowded and finally slaughtered, and thus become extinct If this happens, it will be because we were just too kind, or better, too stupid to fight for our survival.

No, Nature has not created the White Race as its highest and finest accomplishment only to have them destroyed and crowded off the face of the earth by an inferior colored mass. Nor has Nature designated any particular portions of the earth such as Africa for the colored races, or the niggers, or anybody else. The laws of Nature themselves dictate, and the experience of history shows clearly, that land and territory belongs to those that have the will, determination and strength to conquer it, to populate it, and then hold it in defiance of all would-be intruders.

It is a sad reflection on the lack of astuteness on the part of the White Man, or better, on the treacherous cunning of the Jew, who has been in control of world history for the last few thousand years, that the White Man is now crowded densely into a smaller section of the world while the colored races and mulattos occupy the vast majority of the best real estate on the face of the earth. For instance, Africa which is one of the wealthiest landmasses on the face of the earth, is overwhelmingly populated by the inferior black man. The United States, a relatively new country, has a population density 2.3 times as great as that of the continent of Africa.

Or compare the highly gifted and energetic German people who are now crowded into a land area smaller than Texas, whereas the backward Mongolian tribes of East Asia and the Slavic Tribes of Europe and Russia occupy vast areas dozens of times the size of Germany.

Or take the great British people, now crowded in their small island kingdom, bereft of their colonies, even after winning two World Wars. Then, to add insult to injury, the Jews, not only having stripped the great British Empire, are now deliberately shipping hordes of coloreds into the British Kingdom itself, injecting a foul pollution where no pollution had ever existed before.

Yes, our right to the land and territory of the world is the holiest right the White Race possesses. Nature has not only endowed the White Man with the right to possess the real estate of the world but Nature has also endowed the White Man with the intelligence, the energy and the strength with which to exercise that right. It would be a dastardly shame and a dereliction of duty on our part if we fail to realize this, and fail by default to perform our obligation which Nature has clearly pointed out to us. If we fail to do this because we lack the common sense and the courage, we would be committing a most grievous crime against ourselves and our own future generations.

But, some bleeding heart will interject, when you propose such a course, aren't you abandoning civilization and returning to the law of the jungle? To which I reply, no, my dear friend, we are not abandoning civilization. On the contrary, by expanding the White Race and shrinking the colored races we are proceeding on the most certain path for the preservation of civilization. You must remember that it is only the White Race that has created every civilization that has ever existed and when that race in its time and era became mongrelized and died out, civilization died with it. But in any case, we are not nearly as interested in preserving civilization, as such, as we are in preserving and insuring the future for our own kind and for our own race. This is the first, the foremost, and the highest Law of Nature and we would be derelict, when we have the wherewithal to do so, if we would neglect to fulfill the role that Nature and Destiny has ordained for us.

It is most deplorable that these same bleeding hearts who scream to high heaven about the rights and preservation of the niggers and other scum, seem blandly indifferent about the fate of the White Race. They remain totally disinterested when reminded of the fact that in our own generation, the Russians, under the direction of the Jews, drove nine million Germans from their homeland in Prussia and Eastern Germany, a territory that they had occupied for the last several thousand years. Nor does it greatly disturb them

The Importance of Land and Territory

when they are reminded of the historical fact that the Jews during and after the Russian Revolution murdered something like 20 million While Russians, the cream of the intelligentsia and the original creators of art, civilization, industry and enlightenment in the Russian Empire. Nor are these same bleeding hearts greatly disturbed when they are reminded of the recent historical atrocity when the Jews drove 1.5 million Arabs from their farms and their homes and drove them out in the desert, drove them from land that they had occupied for the last two thousand years. This the Jews did without the slightest shred of legality, having no other claim than their lying religious concoctions. They then proceeded to pollute the minds of the White Race to such an extent that the majority of the White people, who should know better, supported them and helped them to commit this historic atrocity.

A cold, hard look at present day facts and Figures should leave no doubt in our minds that the White Race is on a collision course with disaster. Not only are the mulattos and the coloreds rapidly out breeding us (thanks to our generous subsidies of food, technology and medicine) but we are rapidly running out of land and vital resources.

The population of the world is multiplying with increasing rapidity. In 1650 the population numbered approximately half a billion. At that time it was increasing only at the rate of approximately 0.3 percent a year. At that rate it would take 250 years to double. It has, however, been increasing the rate of growth per year ever since. In 1970 the rate of growth had increased to 2.1 percent a year, a rate of increase seven times as great as it was in 1650. At this rate the doubling time is only 33 years.

The world population now is 3.6 billion people, overwhelmingly colored. By the year 2000 the population is predicted to reach a staggering seven billion, with the colored scum overrunning all areas of the world, including those now still predominantly White. In 60 years, at this rate, there will be four times as many people crowding the face of the earth as there are today. Would anyone care to predict their color?

Now let us consider the land resources available, including arable land, fresh water, metals, forests and fuels. At most, there are available on the face of the earth 7.86 billion acres of arable land, recent studies indicate. Approximately half of this land, that is, the richest and most accessible half, is under cultivation today. The other half is marginal land, and will require immense investments of capital input to reach, to clear, irrigate and fertilize before it can produce any food.

According to a recent U.N. Food and Agricultural Organization (F.A.O.) report, opening this marginal land to cultivation is not economically feasible, even given the pressing need for food in the world today. This despite the fact that much of the world today is already starving and undernourished. If only the present world population were fed by the prevailing U.S. standards, we would need 225 percent as much land as is presently cultivated, land that does not exist.

Where will the food come from to feed the hungry hordes of the year 2000?

The answer is that there will be famine and political upheaval, with the strongest fighting for survival. It will be a racial war, and unless the White Race is psychologically prepared to defend its own by force of arms it will be engulfed and overrun.

Not only are we running out of land, we are even more rapidly running out of the raw materials that have built and fueled our increasing technology. The consumption of our vital, nonrenewable resources, such as copper, iron, oil, petroleum, aluminum, lead, silver, mercury, etc., is exponentially increasing even faster than the population explosion. Whereas the population is at present increasing at a rate of 2.1 percent a year, the increased consumption of aluminum is increasing at 6.4 percent a year, copper 4.6 percent a year, petroleum 2.9 percent a year. At this rate, it has been calculated that all the known reserves of aluminum will be exhausted in 31 years, copper in 21 years, and petroleum in 20 years. Whereas we may discover more new deposits, nevertheless, like the arable land, they are limited. Like the good land, new finds are harder and harder to come by, more and more costly to mine, and in any case, strictly limited.

Whereas the above, due to limitation of space, is of necessity, only an incomplete and sketchy analysis of land and raw material resources available on this globe, it nevertheless fairly accurately presents the whole picture— and the implications are overwhelmingly clear: there is neither the land, nor are the raw materials available to sustain the present population explosion for another generation, not even for another 15 years. Something has to give.

The question screams to high heaven: who is going to survive?

The White Race, who has created the present high level of technology, or the colored, the mulattos and the scum?

With the Jew in control of the governments and nerve centers of the world; goading the colored and the niggers to turn on the Whites: spurring them on to multiply even faster; burdening the White Man with more and more parasites on his back, we have reached a highly explosive end of the line. Yet the White Man seems completely oblivious of the danger he is in, nor does he seem to realize that he is the victim designated for destruction.

The White Race acts as if it were drugged and helpless. It remains unorganized and impotent to lift a finger in its own defense.

The Importance of Land and Territory

The lessons from the foregoing are overwhelmingly urgent. They are clear and simple. We must drastically change our whole outlook regarding our role in this world. No longer can we pursue the suicidal role of being the sweet charitable Santa Claus to the colored scum of the world. No longer dare we promote the multiplication of the inferior colored of the world, all of which hate us with a burning passion. No, we must be done with such selfdestructive idiocy.

The White people must take up a new creed and a diametrically opposite policy. We must rally to preserve our own. We must become intensely race conscious, and unite. We must organize. United and organized we are ten times more powerful than the Jews, niggers and coloreds combined. We must save our race.

We must learn from the above that there is just not enough land for natural resources for the White Race and the colored scum to both survive. We must learn the lessons of history that our American pioneers taught us in the eighteenth and nineteenth centuries: to drive the inferior coloreds before us and possess the good earth.

I believe in the spirit of pioneering America. Nature has tapped us on the shoulder and pointed the rest of the way. It is now our overwhelming obligation to proceed. Like our pioneering forefathers, it is our holy duty to acquire for ourselves and our future White generations all the good land and resources of this, our planet earth. The fundamental testament of the CHURCH OF THE CREATOR in this respect for all time is clear and simple: shrink the colored races, expand the White Race, until we populate all the worthwhile lands of this Planet Earth in its entirety. There is no alternative.

CHAPTER TEN

MANIFEST DESTINY

The White Man is a tremendous builder. The few times in history when he has been unshackled and free to do as his inborn nature dictates, he constructs, he creates, he builds empires. Given free rein over a period of time, the creative works of the White Man become truly astounding. One such period was the building of America, and the Winning of the West.

During the middle of the nineteenth century, the majority of Americans were imbued with the idea that it was their Manifest Destiny to conquer and populate America from the shores of the Atlantic to the shores of the Pacific. And conquer they did!

Our doctored history books have given us so much trash about the importance of the Pilgrim Fathers, the Puritans, the Mayflower Compact, and in general, the role of Christianity in the building of America. Our school children and the American population, by and large, as a result, have now become so indoctrinated that practically all of them will rehash this Jewish distortion that America was built by Christians, for Christians, and on Christian principles. A closer examination of history will show that America was built not by Christians, nor on Christian principles, but, on the contrary, was built despite the shackles of Christianity.

Who were the real builders of America? They certainly were not the Pilgrims or the Puritans or other religious zealots, although there were some of these sprinkled throughout the early settlers. Nor was it so much the refugees from religious persecution that made up the bulk of the racial stock who built America, although there were some of these among our early settlers. Basically the people who came over here in large numbers and were the rootstock of America were the best examples of what is great about the White Race. These were people imbued with the spirit of adventure who were looking for a better land and a better opportunity in which to raise their families and to make their fortunes. They were adventurous, aggressive, fearless, energetic, and above all, people with vision and people who wanted to build. They were the same kind of stock that has pushed forward the frontiers of the White Man all over the world in the far-flung continents over the last many thousands of years.

Who were these people? They were the best of our White racial stock that we could be proud of. They were the pioneers, they were the trappers, the hunters, the explorers, the farmers, the ranchers, the railroad builders, and above all, the Indian fighters. They came here from an over- crowded Europe that had been torn asunder and exploited by Jewish financial monopoly and enmeshed in a divisive, strife-torn controversy over the Jewish imposed Christian religion. They were people who were looking for elbowroom and for freedom to follow their natural inclinations and aspirations. In their veins and in their blood was the feeling of a Manifest Destiny to expand and populate the rich new land.

Out of all this emerged the finest and greatest blossoming of White productivity that the world has ever seen. In the "Winning of the West" undoubtedly was demonstrated one of the widest and broadest accomplishments of the human race. In the heroic winning of the West was written one of the most glorious and far- reaching chapters in the history of the White Race, or of any race, for that matter. By sheer dint of courage and labor was built the most productive, creative, powerful and affluent empire the world has ever seen.

Today, America, although the White people in it constitutes less than five percent of the people of the globe, produces as much wealth and substance as all the rest of the world put together. This, in spite of the fact that Americans have been loaded down with severe restrictions and handicaps, such as no nation has ever before known. White Americans have riding on their back 30 million (probably 70 million) black parasites, which are not only a heavy load to carry, but a serious further handicap in as much as throwing gravel into the gears of production. All this production comes from America in spite of the fact that the American people have been forced to subsidize their rivals and their enemies all over the world with foreign aid, technology, loans, products, monetary restrictions, and every other form of shackle that the Jew could possibly dream up. Added to this is the strangling effect of the Jews in our midst, reputedly six million, but probably a great many more.

Without a doubt America today is the basic stronghold of the White Race. For this reason it is under heavy attack by the Jew to have the White American mongrelized and dragged sown into the same snake pit as was India thousands of years ago, South America a few centuries ago, and Haiti 150 years ago. America is the great stronghold of the White Race and it is here that the battle will have to be fought, it is here that the Jew will have to be conquered, it is here that a new world philosophy for the survival of the White Race will have to be formulated and take root.

We owe much to our hearty forefathers who came to a bleak and hostile continent with nothing but their unbounded determination and their native inborn abilities to create and to build. Among these were the early fur traders and trappers, the hunters, and the explorers, restless, energetic and freewheeling, looking for new adventures and ever-wider horizons. With them also soon came the early settlers, the homesteaders, and the farmers. And as they pushed westward the rancher and the cattle barons and their romantic cowboys helped to tame the vast spaces of an ever- onward expanding America. These were in turn followed by city builders, merchants, railroad builders, and entrepreneurs, in the best American sense. As they built this empire, all of them, in one way or another, were Indian fighters.

Since our history has been so badly distorted on the one hand, and since our heroic pioneering forefathers have been mischievously maligned for their policy against the Indians on the other hand, it is of utmost importance that we examine just what the policy of pioneering America was towards the inferior red native, namely the Indian.

There is no question that the White Man was invading a land that was populated by Indians, a race vastly different from himself and decidedly inferior. Although the invasion was a trickle at the beginning, it did not take the Indian long to realize that he was being invaded and deprived of his land. As hostility soon developed, as it must, it did not take the White Man long to realize also that the Indian was his deadly enemy and a dire threat to his existence, to his property, and to the lives of his family

From this developed a bond between the White Race such as had never been experienced in Europe. The White Man realized that he had to stick together to survive, and one of the finest periods of racial loyalty among White People of all different European origins developed. It brought out the best in the White Man—racial loyalty, ingenuity, resourcefulness, and courage. Giving full play to these natural attributes, he pushed steadily onwards, drove the Indian westward and took over his land. Although the White Man was vastly outnumbered, this proved to be no handicap, for when the White Man is united and determined in purpose he can overcome all other forces and all other obstacles. The White Man clearly realized the Indian was his enemy and the motto, "the only good Indian is a dead Indian," became the unwritten law of the land.

It is, therefore, so much garbage to expostulate that America was built on Christian principles. America was not built on Christian principles at all. If the early White American pioneer had followed the dictates of Christian ethics such as, "love your enemies," "turn the other cheek," "sell all thou hast and give it to the poor," "resist not evil," "judge not," etc., and all the other suicidal Christian nonsense, he would never have made it He would have been overwhelmed and killed by the Indians before he ever so much as got a toe-hold on the American continent. No, indeed! America was not built on Christian principles, nor by people that were particularly interested in Christianity. America was built by

Manifest Destiny

the best specimens of the White Race— the White Race exercising its inborn aggressiveness and giving full sway to its superior abilities and competence.

We hear so much nonsense in our modern-day history books, in the movies and in other Jewish propaganda, about how the White Man was perfidious, that he broke treaties with the Indians, how he tricked the Indians, and how he lied and betrayed them. This is, of course, as I have just said— Jewish propaganda— in order to degrade and downgrade the heroic White Man. The White Man just plainly fought and overpowered the Indians and drove them off their land. He did not bargain with the Indians, he did not have to trick them or have to promise them anything, he was out for conquest. He fought the Indian, he defeated the Indian, he killed and slaughtered the Indian and drove him before him as he took over his land. He plainly outfought the Indian and subdued him. It was just simply a matter of conquest, and to accuse the White Man of trickery and chicanery is plainly another lying Jewish trick. The White Man made no treaties with the Indians as such. He handed down edicts, most of which were for containing the Indian in given reservations or areas after he had already been totally defeated in any case. You do not bargain nor make treaties with devastated enemies, you hand down terms, and this is the way the American Indian was managed.

Let us be honest about it. The White European crossed the ocean, invaded the American continent peopled by an inferior red race, and drove westward; he conquered the red man; he took over his land, he killed off most of his opponents, and when he had unquestionably subdued them, he herded them into a shrunken area of then deemed useless land called reservations. No matter how you look at it, it was open, freewheeling conquest, a free-play of the forces of

Nature, it was the White Man at his best. If our forefathers had not done this, there would have been no America— there would, in fact, be no great, strong reservoir of the White Race today. In fact, it is doubtful whether the White Race would still have survive at all.

To better illustrate the thinking and attitude of the White pioneers, the government and the military, as such, let us quote the text of a proclamation by Governor John Evans to the citizens of the Colorado territory in 1864:

PROCLAMATION

Having sent special messengers to the Indians on the plains, directing the friendly to rendezvous at Fort Lyon, Fort Lamed, Fort Laramie and Camp Collins, for safety and protection, warning them that all hostile Indians would be pursued and destroyed, and the last of said messengers having now returned, and the evidence being conclusive that most of the Indian tribes of the plains are at war and hostile to the Whites, and having to the utmost of my ability endeavored to induce all the Indians of the plains to come to said place of rendezvous, promising them subsistence and protection, which, with a few exceptions, they have refused to do.

Now, therefore, I, John Evans, Governor of Colorado Territory, do issue this, my proclamation, authorizing all citizens of Colorado, either individually or in such parties as they may organize, to go in pursuit of all hostile Indians on the plains, scrupulously avoiding those who have responded to my call to rendezvous at the points indicated, also to kill and destroy as enemies of the Country wherever they may be found, all such hostile Indians. And further, as the only reward I am authorized to offer for such services, I hereby empower such citizens, or parties of citizens, to take captive, and hold to their own private use and benefit, all the property of said hostile Indians that they may capture, and to receive for all stolen property recovered from said Indians, such reward as may be deemed proper and just therefore.

I further offer to all such parties as will organize under the militia law of the territory for the purpose, to furnish them arms and ammunition, and lo present their accounts for pay as regular soldiers, for themselves, their horses, their subsistence and transportation, to Congress, under the assurance of the Department Commander that they will be paid. The conflict is upon us, and all good citizens are called upon to do their duty for the defense of their homes and families.

In testimony whereof I have hereunto set my hand and caused the great seal of the Territory of Colorado to be affixed this 11th day of August, A.D. 1864.

S.H. Elbert,

Secretary of Colorado Territory

By the Governor, John Evans

Since the winning of the West and the building of America was one of the most creative and productive epochs in the history of the White Man, we should learn some serious lessons from our own history. If waging war against the colored races, namely the Indians, was so productive a hundred or two hundred years ago in terms of the expansion and well-being of the White Race, and if out of such aggression was built a great wealthy empire, what is the matter with pursuing and adopting such a policy today on a global scale? Why do we pamper and promote the proliferation of the inferior black African in our midst when we have the overwhelming power to rid our beautiful country of that scourge and send him posthaste back to Africa? Why do we not help support our pioneering White Brothers in South Africa and Rhodesia and help him drive the savage black man northward towards the Equator?

Nature herself has endowed us with the inalienable right to survival, the inalienable right to propagate, advance and expand the White Race in the hostile face of all enemies. Let us not forget that the most deadly enemies the White Race has are the colored races. In fact, all colored races are enemies of the White Man.

The best protection the White Man can provide for himself is to expand the territory and the numbers of the White Race on a global basis and shrink that of the colored races, all of which are hostile to us, until this threat exists no more.

As long as the hostile red race had the preponderance of numbers and power, he was a threat and a menace to the White American pioneer. It was not until the White Race by sheer numbers overwhelmingly out powered the Indians that the threat to life and property was destroyed. Similarly, on a global scale the colored races, all of which are hostile to the White Race, and becoming more so every day, are a deadly threat to the very existence of the White Race. If the racial policy of the White Race in America a hundred years ago was such a productive policy for our race, it stands to reason that it would also be an excellent policy on a global scale.

Impossible? Not at all, In fact it is not only possible, it is the only sensible policy the White Race can pursue. Make no mistake about it, the Jews in collaboration with the colored races have marked the White Race for extinction and are rapidly proceeding— and succeeding— in this program.

It is the highest right, the foremost law in Nature, to fight for our survival at all costs! We must secure the existence of the White Race on the face of this planet for all time. And the White Man could easily do it if he united and achieved racial solidarity. Whereas in Roman times, one Roman legionnaire, using his contemporary weapons, such as sword, shield, spear, etc., could perhaps outfight six (or maybe ten) times his number of black savages, today, with the modem technology that is the product of the While Man and the White Man alone, a few trained pilots armed with jet planes and atomic bombs could wipe out any and all opposition from the hostile blacks of Africa, for instance, in no time at all. The fact that our weapons are now also in the hands of our enemy, who could never have conceived or produced them on his own, is a shameful reflection on the lack of loyalty and purpose on the part of the White Race.

Nevertheless, bad as things are today, it is not too late, nor impossible. When the White Race achieves political unity and ideological solidarity, the colored races, due to inability to sustain themselves, will wither on the vine and no nuclear holocaust, with which the Jews are continually intimidating us, will be necessary.

Yes, the handwriting on the wall is clear: White Man, unite or perish! Populate the world or become a mongrelized slave!

Since the black race commits the overwhelming majority of all violent (and other) crimes, it is plain that if we shrink their numbers we will shrink crime. The same principle applies to ignorance and poverty. Therefore, if we want to reduce crime, poverty, filth, slums, and ignorance, the best and most effective program is to shrink the number of niggers in America.

The racial program of the CHURCH OF THE CREATOR therefore, is clearly spelled out: expand the White Race, shrink the coloreds.

This must be our program for all time, not only in America but on a global basis.

Stupidly and foolishly, under the auspices of the Jew and Christian principles, we have been doing just the opposite. In America, as elsewhere in the world, every policy the White Man has foolishly been induced to pursue, whether it be foreign aid, welfare, fiscal policies, taxation, technological aid, medical aid, or one of a hundred other policies, has consistently worked to multiply the colored scum and shrink the base of the productive White Race.

The colored races throughout the world hate us with a passion. Fanned by the worldwide Jewish press, the White Race, polarized in the White American image, is the prime hate target everywhere. Not only is the White Man hated throughout the world, but right here in America itself, the Mexicans, the niggers, the Indians and every other color scum can hardly wait for the day when they can do us in.

Why we should "turn the other cheek," and feed, subsidize and promote the proliferation of the colored scum who hate us, is beyond reason. It is suicide. It is insanity. We owe the colored races nothing. Any one of them will do us in as soon as they have the power. Collectively and organized by the Jew they will have the power in a generation or so, and they will do us in, unless we ourselves unite and organize.

I repeat, united and organized the White Race is ten times as powerful as the rest of the world combined.

Even the apartheid policies of South Africa are suicidal, and even more so, those of Rhodesia, both of which are being attacked as racist. Both countries, although their methods differ, are helping to "farm" a bigger horde of niggers each year. Rhodesia especially, has an insane suicidal policy whereby they are obsessed with "uplifting" the nigger (an impossible project), "educating" him, multiplying him and turning more and more of the government over to these jungle bunnies. The obvious result of this insanity, of course, will be suicidal for the White population. It is as suicidal as feeding and multiplying a horde of rats until they devour you.

Australia has had the most sensible "White only" racial policy of any country in the world. They have, however, been blind to the Jew and the Jew

Manifest Destiny

now owns Australia. This despite the fact the White Man built the continent, but again it is the same old story. However, Australia's racial policy will not save it either, in the final analysis, if the rest of the world goes under.

* * *

Throughout Nature each species endeavors to expand by colonizing into new territory. For example, as soon as the rabbit set foot in the new continent of Australia, it multiplied prolifically until it covered the continent. When the starlings came to North America they rapidly spread across the continent. When the hyacinth came to Florida a century ago it rapidly spread into every canal and waterway that was suitable for its growth. When a weed takes root in a field of wheat, it immediately seeks to enlarge its territory, dispersing seeds to where, if possible, it can take over the whole field, the whole county, the whole country.

This is Nature's program: colonize into new territory and expand to the limit of your abilities— no holds barred.

For thousands of years, the White Race has been colonizing territories and continents, sometimes with great success and also with certain setbacks. During the Roman era it was outstandingly successful. Had the White Race not been stricken with a suicidal, mind-crippling affliction, namely Christianity, it undoubtedly would have gone on and long ago colonized the world. Unfortunately, as history shows, the Romans did succumb to Christianity. The forward surge of the White Race crumbled, the White Race itself went into decay and was almost overrun by the Mohammedan Moors.

In the sixteenth, seventeenth, eighteenth and nineteenth centuries, the White Race again moved forward in a healthy resurgence of colonization that embraced every continent of the world, and as we have just explored, was most vigorous of all in the North American continent.

Now, in the twentieth century, the White Man is again in rapid decline as a poisonous virulent, new Jewish philosophy, communism, is spreading like the plague. Foolishly, the White Man is now retreating, running before inferior scum, shrinking his own and helping his enemies multiply.

Instead of colonizing, White America is being colonized, not only by hordes of black niggers, but all the colored scum of the world. No longer is the White Man colonizing Africa further, but the Africans are colonizing America, the Asians are colonizing America, and the mulattos are colonizing America. Southern Florida is being overrun by the mulatto Cubans. Even that formerly redoubtable fortress of the British Empire, England, is rapidly being colonized by colored scum who are multiplying like rats in her midst. Even the beautiful blonde Swedes, of all people, are having hordes of black niggers shipped in and are not lifting a finger to stop them.

* * * *

The real solution is for the White Man to adopt a sound, clear cut racial policy: The White Race must expand until it inhabits all the good land of this earth; it must consider all colored races its deadly enemies; it must stop giving them aid and assistance of any kind; it must crowd and shrink them from the face of the earth, as it did the Indian in America, only more so.

In order to survive at all, this must be our creed and our testament: it is either them, or us! It is the overwhelming objective of the CHURCH OF THE CREATOR to make sure that the survival of the White Race upon the face of this earth will be secured for all time to come.

We, the White Race, must therefore learn over again the great historic lesson from our illustrious American forefathers. We must project this great productive surge of the White Race on a worldwide basis. We must again, in a planned and deliberate program, resume the colonization of the world which the While Race has pursued for the last several centuries in a more or less haphazard, but vigorous manner. Like the American pioneers, we, the White Race, must now make it our Manifest Destiny to win the world, and populate all the good lands thereof.

CHAPTER ELEVEN

MOHAMMEDANISM - THE POWER OF A MILITANT RELIGION

As we observed in the first chapter of this book, all of Nature and the entire universe is governed by law. The entire universe, including our little world, is governed by the laws of Nature, which are universal, which are fixed, inflexible, and forever the same.

Among these laws of Nature are the laws of survival of the species, which also apply most decidedly to the races of mankind. Many races of mankind have come and gone, and are no more. Some are dying out before our very eyes today. All these species, including the races of mankind, have their own peculiar means of defense and aggression, including the different species of parasites.

Among the races of mankind we have a highly developed species of parasite known as the Eternal Jew. One of the outstanding peculiarities the Jew has developed most highly for his own survival is the art of deceit, conniving and trickery. The Jew is the undisputed master of deceit Being the masterful parasite that he is, he has developed the art of religion as his most powerful weapon to deceive, to control, to enslave, to exploit, to plunder and destroy.

The Jew is not only a "Master of the Lie" and a skillful manipulator of propaganda, but he realized early in his history thousands of years ago what a powerful weapon is religion. Religion is a powerful tool in uniting a race in a common purpose. The Jews achieved this for their own people. They have also used religion to destroy their enemies, and in this respect the most overwhelming achievement in the history of mankind was their invention of Christianity to destroy the Romans.

The Jew, in short, has invented the Old Testament in order to unify his own race, give them a common tradition and purpose and give them a meaningful program with which to plunder and destroy all other races. In order to do the latter more successfully, the Jew also gave some of these other races, especially the White Race, a religion, namely Christianity, whose creed would do just the opposite to their victims that Judaism had done for the Jews. He gave the White

Nature's Eternal Religion

Race a creed that would confuse and confound them, divide, fragmentize and disintegrate them, making them soft prey for the rapacious Jew. The fact that he has actually been successful in this fantastic conspiracy is the best proof possible that he has patiently and carefully planned to bring this about. As to how he has brought this about, we have already piled up massive evidence in the previous chapters, and we will continue to do so in the succeeding pages.

We have also cited that wonderful White civilization of the grandeur that was Rome, how Rome conquered the world and stood supreme and unchallenged. We have shown that Rome had an unprecedented period of 200 years of peace and progress known as Pax Romana when the destructive Judeo-Christian philosophy began to spread its disintegrating virus through the Roman Empire. History tells us that by the year 313 A.D. Emperor Constantine became the first Christian Emperor and at that time decreed Christianity to be the official religion of the Empire. We have seen how the Romans, who fell for this suicidal advice and became fanatic Christians, no longer had the will to defend their homes, their country or their Empire, and that in another century and a half, by the year 476 A.D., the Roman Empire had completely crumbled and fallen apart. We also know that with the advent of Christianity, the White Race, including the ruins of the Roman Empire, and all of Europe, fell into a thousand years of the Dark Ages.

Having heaped this horrible catastrophe on the once proud and powerful Roman Empire, the Jews were not content to leave the White Race there. As they had helped to mongrelize the Egyptian civilization a thousand years previously, they now wanted to make sure that they would mongrelize the whole White Race in Europe and destroy it forever.

In order to do this they concocted a third religion, namely Mohammedanism.

It is more than a coincidence that Judaism, Christianity and Mohammedanism all originate in a relatively small area of Asia extending from Palestine to adjoining Saudi Arabia, or in other words, from Jerusalem to Mecca. Jews, as Benjamin Franklin has pointed out, are Asiatics. This small area, inhabited by Semites, lying east of the Mediterranean and the Red Sea, has spawned three religions, all of which have had an overwhelming and disastrous influence on the White Race.

Whether Mohammed was a Jew or not, history is not too clear. There is so little difference between the Semitic Jew and the Semitic Arab, except for their religion, that it is hard to tell them apart. Mohammed was a Semite, that we know. Before he became the Prophet and founder of the Moslem religion he was married to an extremely wealthy widow who was Jewish. That the Jewish race as a whole had a major part in creating and promoting the spread of Mohammedanism is not only born out by the ensuing events, but is loudly proclaimed by the Jews themselves.

It is our purpose here to show how they welded Mohammedanism into a powerful instrument in order lo further pursue their age-old goal of mongrelizing and destroying the White Race.

We have seen how Jewish Christianity succeeded in tearing the Roman Empire apart and leaving it in shambles, and that by the year 476 A.D. Rome, as such, was no more. But what happened in the next few centuries following the collapse of Rome?

It was during this time that the White Race was probably at the weakest and most disintegrated stage it had been in for thousands of years. The persistent and treacherous Jew did not want to let this golden opportunity pass in dealing the White Race its final deathblow, if possible. So what did he do? He rallied and organized the colored races with a new aggressive and virulent religion that was the very opposite from what he had injected and disseminated throughout the blood stream of the White Race.

Whereas he had conjured up a religion to inflict upon the Romans which told them: to turn the other cheek; to love your enemies; to sell what thou hast and give it to the poor; to resist not evil; and to judge not lest ye be judged, he gave the Arabs a dynamic religion which was the very antithesis of all this.

At the very time when the White Race was at its most confused and disintegrated stage in history, the Moslem religion came out with a fierce and aggressive philosophy that inspired its adherents to conquer and convert by the sword. The followers of this virulent new religion were told that heaven was a beautiful green garden of bliss. Here the soul of the believer, dressed in green robes, lolled on green cushions, enjoyed forgiveness, fruit, wine and service by beautiful maidens described as black-eyed, well rounded of hip and buxom bosoms. The converts were told that if they died in battle they would immediately go to such a blissful heaven. This inspired the Arabs with such fervent zeal that they rushed into battle, caring little whether they were killed or not.

These desert tribes, now fired with such fanatic religious zeal, spread Islam from India to Spain. Egypt, Syria, Asia Minor, North Africa, Spain and Constantinople fell before the advance of the Moslem Empire. The Arab wars swept on victoriously and moved upward from Spain into the heart of France, and might have conquered all of White Europe. It is only by the grace of Providence that in 732 the great White hero, Karl Martel, defeated the Arabs at the Battle of Tours in France, and thereby prevented the conquest of all of Europe.

How different might have been the history of Western Europe had the Moslems conquered! Nevertheless, they did conquer Spain and brought with them the Black Moors of Africa and the Semitic blood of the Arabs. It was not until 1492 that Isabella, the heroic White Queen of Spain, finally drove them out. This was a great year for Spain. Not only did Queen Isabella succeed in driving out the Moors from Spain, but also in the same year she expelled the Jews from Spain, and Columbus sailed for America. Having driven out the Moors and the Jews, Spain then began the greatest and grandest period of her history and the next hundred years can be considered as the golden age of Spain.

Nevertheless, the damage had been done. The almost thousand years of Moorish tenure in Spain and Portugal had permanently contaminated the blood stream of those two unfortunate nations and the lasting damage is apparent in their racial stock to this day. It is my conviction that the Jews had planned to inspire the Arab conquests to sweep over all of Europe and to pollute all the Western nations of Europe with the black blood of Africa. That they did not succeed in this we can all thank our lucky stars and thank Karl Martel, a heroic White Leader, for his historic stand at the Battle Tours.

The Byzantine Empire with its capitol of Constantinople was the surviving eastern half of the Roman Empire after the sixth century. It survived almost a thousand years after the western half, with Rome at its head, had crumbled. The reason why it did survive was that it took a strong stand against the Jewish influence within its empire. It forbade the Jews to have any participation in government, or education, or medicine and in many other fields strictly limited their influence. Nevertheless by 1453, the Turks, who were at this time part of the Moslem Empire, did conquer Constantinople and therewith ended the Byzantine Empire, and with it the White predominance in Asia Minor.

We can learn from this Moslem surge of power what a tremendous influence an aggressive, well-directed religion can have on a scattered and disorganized group of people, even though they be as backward as were the Arab tribes of North Africa and Arabia. Given a religion that united and rallied this amorphous mass of Arab and Bedouin tribes, it laid the foundations for the rise of an Arab Empire. Not only did it build a huge empire that spread as a continuous belt from the coasts of Western Africa to the Philippine Islands, but Moslems are most numerous in North Africa, the Near and Middle East, India and Southeast Asia. They also live in large compact numbers in the Caucasus, Soviet Central Asia, and in China, Even in Europe there are about three million Moslems, living almost exclusively in the Balkan Peninsula.

Not only did Mohammed found a new religion of which the Koran is the holy book, but he built a Moslem Empire, and with it a whole Arabian culture that survives to this day. Islam is followed by one Fifth of all mankind and it is continually making new converts at a rate faster than that of any other major religion.

I cannot emphasize too strongly what a tremendous fountain of energy religion can create when it is matched properly to the people that embrace it. Let the White Race learn this lesson again, and learn it well.

CHAPTER TWELVE

QUEEN ISABELLA— THE INSPIRED CRUSADER

Our debt to the great Queen of Castile and Lyon is hard to measure, but in any case, it is phenomenal. This remarkable woman was possessed of some of the finest qualities that we can be proud of as being characteristic of our great White Race. Even as a child she was endowed with a serene self-possession and had a majestic presence. This was not surprising, perhaps, considering that she was descended from Alfred the Great, William the Conqueror, the Plantagenet kings of England, St. Louis, King of France, and St. Fernando, King of Castile. Like her ancestors, William the Conqueror and Henry II, she was possessed of an iron will, which, once it had marked out an objective, was not easily turned aside. She liked to listen, rather than talk; and when she spoke, it was briefly and to the point.

In order to understand the tremendous accomplishments of this unusual woman, and the tremendous role she played in changing the manifold destiny in the course of history, it is important to understand the times in which she lived. It is also important to understand the several centuries preceding her reign and the jeopardy in which the Mohammedan Moors and the Jews had not only placed Spain, but all of White Europe.

* * *

We have already considered in a previous chapter how the Jews were instrumental in creating and promoting a new religion among the Arabs, and how in their diabolical cunning they were planning to weld a mighty Moslem empire and then use this new battering ram to invade, conquer and destroy White Europe. After the Moslems, by force of the sword, had conquered and converted all the Arab tribes along the northern shores of Africa to the gates of Gibraltar, it was the Spanish Jews who invited the Saracens to cross over into Spain. When in 709 the Saracens finally came, at the instigation of the African Jews, it was the Spanish Jews that were able to open the gates to the conquerors, and were rewarded by being made rulers of Granada, Seville and Cordova. In the new Moslem state, the Jews attained a brilliant height of prosperity and influence.

This the Jews managed to accomplish even after the discovery that they were plotting to bring the Arabs from Africa to overthrow the Gothic Kingdom (later Spain) and even after they were condemned to slavery, and even after their liberation they were repressed by the provisions of the strict Visigothic code. In spite of all this they prospered, and by the beginning of the eighth century they were so rich and powerful in all the principal cities of Spain that they were able to betray that unfortunate country and continue to open the gates further for the fanatic Moorish invaders.

The gradual reconquest by the White Spaniards of the peninsula itself did not particularly disturb the Jews. When St. Fernando recaptured Seville in 1224, he was foolish enough to give them four Moorish mosques to convert into synagogues; he allowed them one of the more pleasant sections of the city for their homes, and demanded only that they refrain from insulting the Christian religion and from making converts among the Christians.

The Jews observed none of these conditions, of course, yet several of the later kings, especially those in need of money, showed them high favor, and Alfonso VIII made a Jew his treasurer.

Here we see this eternal foolish weakness of the White kings, willingly collaborating with their deadly enemies, the Jews, and giving them financial powers to collect the taxes of their subjects. We see this very same sickness in America— in the last decade when we ourselves have had two Jewish Directors of Internal Revenue— one by the name of Cohen and one by the name of Kaplan.

Toward the end of the 13th Century the Jews were so powerful in Spain that they had almost brought the Spanish reconquest of the Moors to an end. There must have been in all of Spain somewhere between four and six million Jews out of a total population of 25 to 30 million, in other words approximately 15 to 20 percent were Jews. There was, furthermore, at this time a program of subversion of the Christian doctrine by a group called the Albigenses, a sect (again created by the Jews) who taught outright self-destruction and suicide as a creed— a further perversion of the brain to speed the destruction of the White Race. Even some non- Jews had themselves circumcised so that they might teach freely (as Jews) this heresy for which they might have been punished as Christians.

Furthermore, the Catholic Church foolishly had always regarded usury as a sin, leaving the field of money lending wide open to the Jews, who thereby had a monopoly as the only bankers and moneylenders. Little by little the capital and commerce of the country passed into their hands. They generally charged

Queen Isabella— The Inspired Crusader

20 percent interest in Aragon and 33-1/3 percent in Castile. During the famine of 1326 they demanded 40 percent interest on money lent to the town of Cuenca to buy wheat. The citizen with taxes to pay, the farmer with no money to buy wheat for his planting, and the burgher held for ransom by robber baron, turned in desperation to the Jewish moneylender, and became his economic slave. By lending money to the kings, the Jews also acquired control of the government. The common people hated them because they often bought from the King the privilege of taxation, and mercilessly wrung all the money they could from the unfortunate citizens.

Now and then the Spaniards reacted in a healthy instinctive way. When things got too desperate the citizens would simply rise up and massacre a good number of the Jews.

In most cases the Pope would come to the defense of the Jews and do his utmost to stop the citizens in their righteous indignation from massacring the Jews— a further proof that Christianity was Jewish in its instigation and continues to be Jewish in its control from the central domination of the Pope himself.

When the Black Death slew half the population of Europe in two years, the Jews suffered worse than the rest, for the desperate populace accused them of having caused the pestilence by poisoning the wells and commenced to slay them all over Europe. There is much evidence that the Jews did, in fact, drop infected people in wells and other sources of water in order to spread the plague and thereby kill off more of the White population.

Pope Clement VI denounced these accusations against the Jews as lies, trying to point out that the plague had been just as deadly in lands where no Jews lived, although this was not easily proved or disproved. He further strongly threatened to excommunicate such people as took part in these massacres, calling them fanatics. Nevertheless, the Spaniards continued to kill the Jews.

In Castile, in 1391, several thousand were massacred. As a result many Jews seemingly embraced Christianity, and became known as Conversos or Marranos. Thus came into being a new class of Jewish "Christians," some of whom were seemingly sincere, but most of whom, while attending Mass on Sunday, secretly continued to attend the Synagogue and to eat Kosher food. Thus, as professing "Christians," the secret Jews were now freed from the restrictions imposed upon their brothers of the Synagogue, and could intermarry with any of the leading families of Spain. Furthermore, a new and highly important field was opened up to them, for as "Christians" they could now become priests, or dedicate their sons to the church to show their "loyalty" to their new religion, with the result that in Isabella's time, they controlled and exploited the Catholic Church in Spain to an astonishing degree.

There were in Spain many Catholic priests who were secretly Jews and made a mockery of the Mass and of the Sacraments they pretended to administer. One such priest, for example, never gave absolution when he heard confessions. The Spanish Catholics naturally resented these sacrileges bitterly, and for good reason blamed the Jews exclusively for the prevalent corruption in the church. In fact, the old Christians, that is the Spaniards, detested

the Conversos even more than the Jews of the Synagogue, whom they at least could identify. Many of these Conversos made a mockery of the sacraments, and when they went to confession, they usually lied to the confessor.

The Jews had Spain under their heel and were having a field day robbing and fleecing their victims.

This was pretty much the situation politically and religiously in Spain when Isabella, at the age of ten, was being brought to the court of her half brother, 26 years her senior. He was now Enrique IV, King of Castile. When Isabella's father had died, Enrique inherited the throne.

* * *

Isabella was a beautiful girl of the fairer Nordic type, with light reddish hair, a determined chin, somewhat too large for her other features, and blue eyes in which there were greenish lights flecked with gold. She received a good education, not unlike the daughters of noblemen in Spain of that period. She had learned to speak Castilian musically and with elegance, and to write it with a touch of distinction. She studied grammar, rhetoric, painting, poetry, history, and philosophy. From her father she inherited a passionate love for music and for poetry, and from her tutors, who had studied at Salamanca University, she had learned much of the philosophy of Aristotle and St. Thomas Aquinas.

When she and her younger brother Alfonso were brought to the court of Enrique IV, they were shocked to see the immorality and the treachery that was going on at the Castilian court. The weak and profligate Enrique was a disgrace to his throne and a traitor to the White Race. Archbishop Carrillo of Toledo accused King Enrique as follows: "The abomination and corruption of sins so heinous that they are not fit to be named, for they corrupt the very atmosphere, and are a foul blot upon human nature." The Archbishop joined other discontented nobles at Burgos in drawing up a series of memorable accusations publicly addressed to the King.

They declared that the King's Moorish guard and others to whom he had given power had "raped married women and corrupted and violated virgins, and men and boys against Nature; and good Christians who dared complain were publicly whipped." They charged that the King had destroyed the property of the Spanish laboring classes by allowing Moors and Jews to exploit them; that he had caused prices to rise unreasonably by debasing the currency; that he had allowed his officials to practice bribery and extortion on a huge scale; that he had made a mockery of justice and government by vicious appointments and by allowing hideous crimes to go unpunished; that he had corrupted the church by casting good Bishops out of their Sees, replacing them with hypocrites and politicians.

To the credit of both Isabella and her brother, Prince Alfonso, it was generally agreed that they walked through this fetid atmosphere of that foul court without contamination, and emerged from it with a lifelong hatred of the prevalent immorality and of its causes, among which they reckoned the influence of Moslems and Jews.

There were many intrigues at court, and revolutions and battle flaring up throughout the kingdom. Isabella's brother, Prince Alfonso, was first in line for the throne. However, when he was fifteen years of age he died suddenly. Some accused King Enrique or his followers of poisoning him, but this is not certain. Isabella became a valuable political pawn and many intrigues were in progress to have her married to various political alliances. King Enrique attempted to marry off the Princess as soon as possible to King Alfonso V of Portugal, who was anxious to obtain Isabella's consent. Another suitor at this time was the Duke of Guyenne, brother and heir apparent of King Louis XI of France. Also determined and intent upon marrying her was a Jewish mulatto of unsavory reputation by the name of Don Pedro Giron who had obtained the King's consent. Fortunately while this lecherous character was on his way, determined to marry Isabella against her will, he became desperately sick and died. Princess Isabella received the news of his death with tears of joy and gratitude and hastened to the chapel to give thanks to God.

Having survived all these, when she was 18 years old she married Prince Fernando, the heir apparent to the throne of Aragon. Don Fernando was a manly youth almost a year younger than she. In their union loomed the prospect of uniting the great kingdoms of Castile and Aragon into one of the most powerful nations in Europe. Many enemies, including her half-brother, King Enrique, fought the prospect of such an alliance. Nevertheless, her marriage, which had been secret, when it became known, became an established fact which King Enrique was powerless to undo.

Isabella's half brother, King Enrique, died on December 12, 1474. Amid the joy and jubilation of her new subjects and amidst great pomp and ceremony, Isabella was crowned Queen of Castile on the 13th day of December that same year. She was then 23 years old, a beautiful and stately figure.

Her husband, Prince Fernando, was not at her side at the time. When he learned the news of Enrique's death and of his wife's coronation, he was in Perpignen, where he had gone early in the autumn to save his father from capture by his enemies.

The Queen and her husband had a strict understanding about their regal prerogatives. Queen Isabella was to be the sole and supreme ruler of the Kingdom of Castile and when Fernando came to the throne he was to be in the same capacity over the Kingdom of Aragon. Many were the intrigues, the gossip, the controversies amongst their followers and enemies to divide the court into two factions, but they were not successful. Henceforth, in most public affairs, they were to act as one person, both signatures on all documents, both faces on all coins. "Even if necessity parted them, love held their wills in unison— many persons tried to divide them, but they were resolved not to disagree."

They could not afford to have differences if they wished to accomplish the gigantic task that awaited them. To bring order out of anarchy, to restore the prestige of the crown, to recover from robber barons crown lands illegally granted them by Enrique, to deflate the currency and restore prosperity to the farms and industries, to settle the Jewish problem, the Moorish problem, the Converso problem— this was a task that seemed impossible for a young woman and a young man with neither troops nor money. France and Portugal were their enemies. Castile was a state of chaos.

The situation was amazingly parallel to that which faced that other great leader, Adolf Hitler, when he inherited a bankrupt, divided and broken Germany in 1933. He, too, had a divided country. He, too, had a nation that was divided within itself, a nation racked by the Jewish problem and faced with a multitude of enemies on the outside.

Although she was unusually fortunate in having a husband that supported her totally in her endeavors, the driving force and the crusading zeal came mainly from Isabella herself.

No sooner had Isabella been crowned Queen of Castile when the country was invaded by Alfonso V, King of Portugal. Fernando and Isabella inherited kingdoms that were without troops and without finances to acquire an army. However, Isabella's enemies had failed to reckon upon her awakening genius. For months she lived almost constantly on horseback going from one end of the kingdom to the other, making speeches, holding conferences, holding court all morning to sentence a few thieves and murderers to be hanged, riding a hundred miles or more, over cold mountain passes to plead with some lukewarm nobleman for 500 soldiers. Wherever she went she stirred into flame the ancient hatred of the Castilians for the Portuguese. While Fernando collected troops from the northern provinces, Isabella assembled several thousand men at Toledo and rode at their head, in full armor like St. Joan, to meet her husband at Valladolid.

By the end of June, 1475, they had assembled a motley host of 42,000 men, poorly equipped and badly disciplined, many of them farm hands and released convicts. Whipping them hastily into 35 battalions, Fernando left Valladolid in

July, and struck southwest to the River Duero. After several months and several battles during which the fighting raged back and forth, Fernando finally put King Alfonso's forces to rout, thereby ending for the time being the threat from Portugal and King Alfonso V's claims to Isabella's throne of Castile.

The victory over Portugal left Isabella undisputed mistress of Castile, but it was a Castile ridden with famine and pestilence, and economically almost beyond repair. No one paid their debts and there was no means of enforcing them to be paid. Disorder was the usual course of events. Peaceful men were not masters of their own property. They had no recourse to anybody for the robberies and the acts of violence they endured.

The chief task that confronted Isabella and Fernando now was to restore respect for law. To do this, Isabella and her husband rode from town to town, sometimes together, sometimes separately, administering justice without delay and without cost to the people. The young Queen would hear complaints, order reconciliations and restitutions, condemn the guilty to death, and ride on to the next place. Within a short time her justice had filled the country with consternation. It was the more terrifying because it was felt to be impartial and incorruptible. A great deal of the corruption was among the wealthy nobles themselves, and, as had been their practice formerly, they offered the Queen enormous sums of money in order to bribe her from enforcing her strict justice. But the Queen preferred justice to money. For instance, when a wealthy noble named Alvar Yanez, who had murdered a notary, offered the Queen the enormous sum of 40,000 ducats if she would spare his life, she emphatically refused and had the head of Yanez struck off the same day. In order to avoid any suspicion of mercenary motives, she had the property distributed among his sons, although there was plenty of precedence in justifying her to have it confiscated.

Isabella and Fernando were only too well aware of the fact that the Mohammedans, who occupied the southern half of Spain, were assembling forces to again invade and conquer the northern half of that divided country. They were also only too well aware that their own forces were scattered, divided, and pitifully weak to meet such an invasion. She knew that there were several other primary prerequisites that had to be corrected before the country could be unified enough to meet such an invasion. The church itself was thoroughly corrupted and staffed with Converso Jews that were in key positions to spread anarchy and confusion during any stress or strain that developed. Her half brother, King Enrique, had given away and forfeited so many crown lands that revenue was almost non-existent for shoring up the royal treasury. They, therefore, felt that two further necessary steps, harsh though they be, had to be taken in order to unite the country and enforce the supreme authority of the Crown.

Since the Catholic Church wielded tremendous power in Spain during

Nature's Eternal Religion

the 15th century, the King and Queen knew that they had to rid the church hierarchy of the deceitful and perfidious Converso Jews who were now posing as Christians, but were ready to sell out the church and their country at the first given opportunity to the Mohammedans.

They decided to institute the Inquisition, and once and for all cleanse the church of this alien group that was neither Spanish nor was it Christian.

Isabella realized that before she could meet the threat of the Moors from the south she had to overcome the enemies within her own country. Among these enemies she could count not only the Jews of the Synagogue, but the secret Jews, the Conversos, who had infiltrated the hierarchy of the church. She knew that it was the Jews who had invited the Mohammedans into the country in the first place, and who had always been considered enemies withinthe gate, sympathizing with, and often lending assistance to, the hated Moors.

Having secured secretly from the Pope two years earlier permission to establish the Inquisition, she and Fernando now proceeded in earnest.

The Jews had not only corrupted and contaminated the Catholic Church itself, but they had also originated and spread the Albigensian heresy. This heresy was teaching and practicing suicide on principle, and the followers frequently smothered or starved their sick, and even put infants to death. Here we see another idea and teaching originated and spread by the Jews that would tend to stifle and destroy the White Race.

It was to meet the questions raised by the Albigenses that the Inquisition was first established. The Inquisition itself never condemned anyone to death. The inquisitors would go to a certain city and summon all heretics to confess within a fixed time, usually within 30 days. Those who did so were treated leniently. A prisoner who was found guilty and refused to abjure was handed over by the inquisitors to the state, which then proceeded against him as a traitor. In practice about two persons out of a hundred accused were put to death. Some were imprisoned. Some were freed. Torture was used as a last resort, but efforts were made to restrict its use.

In the meantime, it became quite evident that the Mohammedans were making a determined attempt to conquer all of Europe. In 1479 Mohammed II, the Grand Turk, advanced by sea to lay waste to the island of Rhodes. When in the next year of 1480 the Knights of St. John at Rhodes repulsed Mohammed II, the latter threw all of Europe into consternation by swooping down upon the shores of Italy. His crews ravaged the coast of Apulia, and on August II, 1480, Mohammed took by storm the city of Otranto in the Kingdom of Naples. Of the 22,000 inhabitants, the barbarians bound 12,000 with ropes, and thus helpless, put them to death with terrible tortures. They slew all the priests in the city. On a hill outside the city, now known as Martyrs' Hill, they butchered many captives who refused to become Mohammedans, and threw their corpses to the dogs.

The apathy of the Italian princes was incredible. Undermined and controlled by Jewish moneylenders, they remained disunited and completely impotent. For example, the King of Naples was at war with Florence, and his son Alfonso, the Duke of Calabria, was 150 leagues away in Tuscany fighting in the Tuscany war. And so it went.

Panic began to sweep over the Spanish kingdoms. Men were asking what would happen if the Turks came from the east and the Moors of Granada took the offensive in the south against Andalusia. Castile was without a doubt on the eve of war, and it would be a war in which she would need every ounce of her strength. And yet there were secret enemies within her gates— enemies who had grown rich upon her wealth in the past and given evidence of their sympathy with the hated and feared Mohammedans. These enemies were the Jewish Conversos in Castile, a nation within a nation.

The landings of the Turks in Italy had sealed the doom of the Conversos.

The first proceedings of the inquisition in Castile were held February 6, 1481. At the same time the Bubonic Plague was raging throughout Spain.

The Conversos were now thoroughly alarmed, and at last began to flee from Seville. Several of the most powerful Conversos met in the Catholic Church of San Salvador to discuss means for protecting themselves. Catholic priests, friars, magistrates, government officials— all of Jewish descent and secret enemies of the Catholic Church and of Spain itself— were present. Diego de Susan, a Rabbi whose fortune was estimated at 10 million maravedis, demanded in a fiery speech that they resist the inquisition by force. They knew they had the main power of the city in their hands and they decided to assemble troops, and to kill their enemies and thereby avenge themselves. By a stroke of fortune, Isabella found out about this plot. The chief conspirators were seized. Susan and his wealthy accomplices were tried before a jury of lawyers. Several of them confessed and were given penances to perform, whereas six of the ring leaders were declared to be impenitent heretics and were turned over by the inquisitors to the secular officials of the town. The six unrepentant conspirators were taken outside the walls of the city, tied to stakes and burned. Susan's execution was three days later.

Thousands of Conversos now fled in panic in all directions, some to Portugal, some to Italy, where the Jews in times of persecution had never failed to find a protector in the Pope.

And so it went from city to city. Even the inquisitors were astonished to find how large a percentage of the Conversos were engaged in undermining the church itself to which they professed allegiance and in intrigues and conspiracies against the crown and the country itself.

Wildly exaggerated accounts of the Spanish Inquisition have been circulated during the past five centuries by writers hostile to Spain and to the Catholic Church. The truth seems to be that in all of Isabella's reign about 2,000 persons, including not only secret Jews, but bigamists, blasphemers, church robbers, false mystics, and other offenders were burned. Public opinion undoubtedly approved of the Inquisition, and Isabella herself always referred to it with pride. Jewish writers in the last five centuries who have dominated our literature have accused Isabella of having brought about the intellectual decay of Spain because of the Inquisition. This, of course, is a great big lie. For the intellectual life of Spain was never more vigorous than in the century after she established the Inquisition. It was the period of her three greatest poets, Cervantes, Lope de Vega and Calderon, the golden age of her literature. It was the period when her finest schools and universities were established, while foreign scholars flocked to Spain and were honored, and medicine and other sciences made their most notable gains. Never were the industries and commerce of Spain so prosperous, and never was order so well maintained at home and prestige abroad as high as during the 16th century when Spain became the head of a new empire that over-shadowed all Europe and the Americas. There is little doubt that the main cause of this great resurgence of Spain was her (partial) cleansing herself of the Jewish pestilence in her midst.

This internal housecleaning came none too soon. The Mohammedans were determined to make an attempt to conquer all of Europe. That wily Moor, Muley Abou'l Hassan, Moslem leader of Granada, had taken by storm the town of Zahara on Christmas day, 1482, and was within 15 miles southeast of Seville. Whether Isabella liked it or not, she was faced with the greatest crisis of her life and as was characteristic of her, she was determined to fight.

Isabella was now resolved to end Moorish domination in the south, no matter how long it might take. What all good Castilian kings had dreamed of doing, what her father had failed to do, and weaklings like Enrique, had neglected to do, she proposed, with the help of her husband Fernando, to accomplish. The King would lead the Spanish host in the crusade, and she, in her magnificent prime at thirty, would be recruiting agent, commissary, purchaser of munitions, field nurse and propaganda bureau, all in one.

It is not my purpose here to review the bloody events of the war that ensued over the next ten years. There were many discouraging defeats and many times when she was on the verge of despair. In fact, the ensuing war was of such a nature that it would have broken many a spirit, but with her iron determination she pursued the war relentlessly. At the same time she pressed the campaign against the Converse Jews. But for the Inquisition and its funds, the prosecution of the war would have been hopeless.

This was the new age of gunpowder and cannon. To wage this war, heavy artillery would be needed, and that must come from France, Germany and Italy.

Queen Isabella— The Inspired Crusader

She did the only possible thing, by confiscating the property of the Converso Jews, she utilized this revenue with which to buy the munitions of war and other supplies needed to wage war against the Moors.

Not only did she wage war against the treacherous Conversos and against the aggressive Moors, but by the time the victory against the Moors was completed she had given birth to her fifth child. Also during those war years Isabella began to study Latin, so that she might understand foreign diplomats without having to depend upon interpreters.

The courage, the zeal and determination of Isabella and her husband finally paid off. After ten years the war was over and on January 2, 1492, the Moorish leader Boabdil came forth, surrendered Granada and handed the keys of the city to King Fernando, who in turn gave them to the Queen, who then passed them on to her oldest son, Prince Juan. Presently the silver cross of the crusade appeared on the high tower of the city of Granada with the flag of Santiago beside it was the first time that the White Race had ruled the city of Granada in 770 years.

The year 1492 was a great year for Spain, for Isabella, and for the White Race. It was the year that the Moors were driven out of Spain. It was the year that Christopher Columbus, under the auspices of King Fernando and Queen Isabella, set out for the new world and discovered America. It was also the year that the royal couple of Spain made a determined decision to rid the country of the other part of that treacherous foe— the Synagogue Jews.

By instituting the Inquisition, Isabella had been mainly concerned with protecting the Catholic Church and driving out the secret Jews from the hierarchy and membership of the church. To a large degree she had been successful in this. However, this had not at all affected the Synagogue Jews, namely, the Jews who stayed loyal to their Judaic faith. She found that they were still ravishing the country to a large degree, betraying Spain to the Moors and the Moslems at every turn, and still in possession of a tremendous amount of wealth and power, all to the detriment of her beloved country. Not only that, but they were continually stirring up the newly converted Converso Jews to acts of sacrilege and offenses against the church.

Bernaldez, the Spanish historian of the time, writes about the Jews: "They, the Jews, live mostly in the larger cities, and in the most wealthy and prosperous and fertile lands— And all of them were merchants and vendors, and had control of the taxing privileges and were the stewards of manors, cloth shearers, tailors, cobblers, leather dealers, curriers, weavers, spicers, peddlers, silk merchants, jewelers, and had other similar occupations. Never did they till the soil, nor were they laborers, nor carpenters, nor masons; but all sought easy occupations and ways of making money with little work. They were cunning people... "

Nature's Eternal Religion

Fernando and Isabella finally decided that the Jews were the ruination of Spain and that nothing would remove the root of the trouble but to drive them from the kingdom. On the last day in March, 1492, they issued an edict ordering all Jews to leave their kingdom on or before July 1st, taking with them no gold, silver, or minted money. On August 2nd, the day before Columbus sailed for America, the Jews had to leave unless they were baptized and converted to Christianity.

About 160,000 Jews appear to have left Spain. Some sailed for Cartagna, Africa and some went to Arcilla and from there on to Fez in the Moorish kingdoms of Africa. Others proceeded to Portugal and were allowed on payment of a large tax, to enter. Some went to Navarre, France, others struggled as far as the Balkans. Some returned to Castile and were baptized. There remained, however a large number of persons of Jewish descent, possibly as many as three or four million, who had been baptized as Christians.

Many of them were received by Pope Alexander VI as refugees in Rome. It seems that the Jews could always count on the Pope to save their neck when things became intolerable in the countries that they had ravaged. This is not too strange considering that the Jews had invented Christianity in the first place, and without a doubt, remained in control of the Papacy in Rome over the centuries that followed. They are, in fact, in firm control of the Catholic Church today, using it as a tool wherewith to blunt and pervert the healthy native instincts of the White Race. For his aid and help to the Jews at this time. Pope Alexander VI, who was born in Spain, was contemptuously referred to in his native land as "The Marrano" and "The Jew."

Queen Isabella lived for another twelve years after the historic year of 1492. During this time many more honors were heaped upon her and she also experienced many heartbreaks within the circle of her own family. I am, however, going to leave the story of Isabella at this point, since her most significant work had now been done.

Her life story stands forth as a blazing epic in the history of the White Race. But for her it is very probable that Europe would have been overrun by the black Moslems of Africa and would today be a bastardized race of mulattos: Her genius, her zeal, and her determination stand as a beacon for all members of the White Race, both men and women, to exalt and to try to emulate. We have much to learn from the history of her struggles, both from what she accomplished, from what she failed to do, and the mistakes she made.

Her accomplishments are a vast inspiration to all members of the White Race and we can be tremendously proud of this great woman. Her life story proves to us that when our White Race seems to have reached bottom, when the Jews seem to have completely destroyed every shred of decency and corrupted the government, the country, and all other institutions, and when things seem

Queen Isabella— The Inspired Crusader

desperate and hopeless, the will, the genius, and the determination of one single person, can in one lifetime, change the situation from the lowest depths of despair to one of grandeur, pride and prosperity. We have seen how Spain was racked with crime, internal division, starvation, pestilence, and direly threatened by enemies within, and also without, her borders. We have seen how corruption had eroded the country from the highest office of the land, the throne, down to the lowest of burgher in the village. We have seen how the black Moors of Africa had conquered and usurped the southern half of Spain and were threatening, not only the rest of Spain, but all of Europe.

At 23 years of age Queen Isabella could hardly have faced a more helpless and desperate situation. Nevertheless, in the next 20 years of her reign, by her indomitable will, her courage and her determination, she conquered all these evils. She overcame them and she restored Spain not only to her highest former grandeur, but brought Spain to new heights never before attained. Not only did Spain reach the greatest heights in her history during Isabella's reign up to that time, but went on in the next century, partially purged of the Jews, to become the greatest power in Europe, to build a mighty empire in the New World, and to bring her art, literature and commerce to heights never before achieved by any other country of Europe.

We have much to learn from her mistakes also. Her greatest mistake was her devotion to the Christian religion instead of realizing the basic value of her great racial heritage. She was able to accomplish what she did, not because of any religious guidelines, but because of the quality of the blood that flowed in her royal veins. Because of her addiction to Christianity she allowed the Jewish dominated Papacy again and again to thwart her determination to take the stringent measures necessary to totally rid her country of the Jewish pestilence. And in this whole question she made the fatal error of regarding the Jews as a religion rather than the parasitic race that they are. She made the fatal mistake of allowing them to deceitfully profess Christianity and in trying to convert them, instead of purging and expunging them from the country. She also made the sad mistake of allowing the Moors, once they were conquered, to remain in Spain, trying to convert them to Christianity, or allowing them to become "peaceful" citizens of her country.

What she should have done is drive every last one of them out across the Mediterranean and back to Africa so that they would not then, nor in future generations, pollute the blood of Spain. She made the unforgivable mistake of allowing three or four million Jews, who deceitfully professed Christianity, but secretly remained Jews at heart, to remain in Spain. She should have exterminated the Jewish problem completely by doing to those Jews that remained Conversos the same as was done to those proven guilty in the Inquisition, or driving them from the realm.

Nature's Eternal Religion

Having gathered the power and momentum to purge and cleanse the country of these treacherous alien elements, the Jews and the Moors, she should have done the job completely and thoroughly. As it was, she allowed millions of these Semites, both Moors and Jews, to remain in her country and contaminate and pollute the blood of the Spanish race further than it already had been.

Centuries of Spaniards have been paying a heavy price for this mistake and today Spain itself is inhabited by a mongrelized race with a heavy Moorish and Jewish contamination flowing in the veins of her people. From this she can never recover.

Despite their pretended conversion, the Jews remained Jews, remaining there to forever betray and conspire with Spain's enemies. In collaboration with the Jews of England and France and the other countries, they endeavored over the next few centuries to stifle and stymie the trade and the expansion of Spain as much as possible, and in numerous cases, betrayed secrets to her enemies through the Jewish grapevine.

To her credit, however, it must be said of Isabella that she did not bring about these conditions. The Jews had heavily infested Spain more than a dozen centuries before she ever came to the throne.

The Moslems had already overrun Spain many centuries before she was ever born, and still occupied half of Spain at the time when she was crowned Queen. But for her determination and her zeal, they undoubtedly would have caused a grave further degeneration of Spain and undoubtedly helped the Arabs and the Moslems to overrun the rest of Spain, and most probably, all of Europe.

Beyond a shadow of doubt, this great Queen did set back and retard the Jewish and Moslem advance by many centuries.

Above all, and this we should note well, she proved to us all what one determined White person can do: by zeal and determination, by organization and leadership, the Jewish power can be broken. She did this in her lifetime, as Adolf Hitler did it in his lifetime.

Let this be a tremendous inspiration to us all. Let us do likewise in our own time, in our own generation.

CHAPTER THIRTEEN

MORMONISM — A BETTER FRAUD

Whereas Mohammedanism is the fastest growing major religion in the world, and also the fastest growing numerically, the Mormon religion, or better termed as The Church of Jesus Christ of Latter Day Saints, is percentage-wise, the fastest growing religion in America today. While not large compared to the major religions, it is claimed that the Mormon church now has a membership of over three million adherents. Whereas it is my opinion that the Mormon religion is a better religion for the White people than Christianity, nevertheless I am convinced that, like Christianity, it is a stupendous fraud and an unmitigated hoax.

There are, nevertheless several important things that we can learn from Mormonism and this is why we are considering it along with the three other major religions. It gives us an answer to the question, namely, is it at all possible to start and propagate a new religion in modern times? The Mormon religion has answered that with an emphatic yes, since it was begun less than a century and a half ago. The other important lesson that we can learn from this relatively new religion is just what makes a religion spread, and what techniques can we use to spread and propagate our own new religion, Creativity.

The Mormon religion was started by a native-born American by the name of Joseph Smith, born in Vermont, 1805. At the age of ten he moved with his parents to the town of Palmyra, New York. In his fifteenth year they moved to a neighboring place called Manchester, and it was here that, as Joseph Smith tells it, he began to see some strange visions and he began to have contact with "angels sent to him by God." By the time he was eighteen he had received several more of these "visions" and "visitations" from the great beyond. In these trances he was told that he would be given some golden plates. He was also to be given a set of transparent rock spectacles called "Urim" and "Thummim" to help him translate the strange ancient Aramaic, Hebrew and Egyptian languages in which the plates were supposedly written.

The angel Moroni "revealed" to Joseph Smith that he had buried the sacred records in the year 420 A.D. in the hill of Cumorah. It was supposedly an abridgement made by Mormon, father of Moroni, from the records of his forefathers, and hence we get the name Mormon.

According to Smith, he then set about "translating" these plates, dictating them from behind a screen to some of his associates.

This may all seem exceedingly strange, and it most certainly is. It reminds me of the alleged story attributed to General Grant when a stranger approached him, shook his hand and said, "The Marquis of Queensbury, I believe?" To which Grant was supposed to have replied, "Anybody that would believe that would be stupid enough to believe anything."

In any case, translated into English, the Book of Mormon, which this new Bible of the Mormon faith was called, was published in the year 1830, the same year Joseph Smith organized the Church of Jesus Christ of Latter Day Saints.

The original plates were then again taken in charge by the angel Moroni and carried away so that no one ever saw them again.

Very convenient.

Smith and his followers maintain that in 1829 Smith was ordained by John, the Baptist, and made an Apostle. On April 6, 1830, the Church of Jesus Christ of Latter Day Saints was established in Fayette, New York, with Joseph Smith as its First Prophet. Members were ordained to go out and preach, and the new belief spread rapidly. A temple was built at Kirkland, Ohio; Missouri became a center; Nauvoo, Illinois was the headquarters for another group. They met popular disfavor and persecution in many quarters, largely because plurality of wives was permitted. Continued persecution drove them further and further westward. Finally Smith was assassinated in a Carthage, Illinois jail on June 27, 1844 and the presidency descended to an aggressive follower by the name of Brigham Young.

To avoid further persecution, the Mormons agreed to leave Illinois, but by some miscarriage of justice, after a part of the Nauvoo settlement had already started to move, the balance was attacked and annihilated. In their 1,500-mile trek to the basin of the Great Salt Lake the Mormons lost another thousand of their followers.

Here, at Salt Lake they dwelt for a time in peace and established the great temple of Salt Lake City. From here on out the Mormon religion spread throughout the world.

Just what does the Mormon religion say? The Book of Mormon is most uninteresting reading, in fact, it is so dull and tedious that it is almost impossible, at least for me, to read through all of it. Certainly I find very little in it that is inspirational.

Although it is supposed to be a 19th century translation of something that the Mormons claim was written by several people over a period of about a thousand years (from 600 B.C. to approximately 400 A.D.) the language is strictly in the 15th century Elizabethan style. Since the Egyptians, Hebrews and Aramaics didn't speak 15th century Elizabethan English, and since the

19th century Americans didn't talk that way either, one wonders why Smith found that such a style of wording, using the biblical yeas and nays, and thees and thous, was a direct translation of something a few thousand years old. Undoubtedly, Smith felt that by imitating the biblical language (King James Version), he would be able to give it a more mystical and religious air, and thereby help make his newly concocted writings more plausible and acceptable. The Book of

Mormon further follows the format of the Christian and Jewish Bible. The story it tells, however, is altogether different.

The Book of Mormon allegedly gives an account of a group of people of the Tribe of Manasseh who left the city of Jerusalem in the year 600 B.C., and some eight or ten years later sailed a ship across the Indian and Pacific oceans to the Western Hemisphere. It then goes on in an exceedingly boring and tedious narration of the trials and tribulations, successes and failures, of the descendants of these people, until finally the remnant of them are exterminated by their enemies in the year 421 A.D. on a hill in what is now New York State, where Joseph Smith claimed to have found their records some 1,400 years later.

In this strange history it also tells of an account of these people in the year 122 B.C. discovering buried records, also on metal plates, which told the story of an earlier migration of another group of people of the Race of Adam from Asia to the Western Hemisphere in the year

2000 B.C. These people supposedly resided in this part of the world until their descendants were wiped out in a civil war in the year 590 B.C.

So here we have a long winded history of two different groups of people who were apparently supposed to be descendants of Adam and who migrated to the Western world in ancient times, one group living here from 2000 B.C. to 590 B.C. and the other group from 590

B.C. to 421 A.D. Just why it was necessary to dream up such a long, dreary story of these people in order to found a new religion, is hard to understand. Although the story is completely different, and the case of characters is also completely different from that of the Old Testament, we find the Mormon church declaring in Point Eight of their "Thirteen Articles of Faith" as follows: "We believe the Bible to be the word of God in so far as it is correctly translated; we also believe the Book of Mormon to be the word of God."

This is like saying I believe in the Bible in so far as it is correct and I also

Nature's Eternal Religion

believe in the theory of evolution, which is more correct.

The two books, the Jewish-Christian Bible and the Book of Mormon are completely contradictory and different. For anybody to say that they believe in both is talking out of both sides of their mouth.

Without going into further details about the Book of Mormon, it is my considered opinion that the stories written therein are the meanderings of a somewhat over-stimulated and unbalanced mind, and do very little to shed light on, or divulge information about, anything. The fact that Joseph Smith gives a signed statement of testament by three witnesses and then further got more witnesses to sign and say that they also saw these plates of gold with engravings on it, does not, to my mind, sound very convincing. It reminds me of the story we have in another chapter in this book telling about the man who tried to pass off the $10,000 check stating over and over again that it was genuine, that it was good, and that he had so many witnesses to back him up. Nevertheless, it all came out of the same set of claims and is not any more genuine than the rest of it.

Be that as it may, this group of zealous fanatics did start a new religion, and in many ways, it at least was better than Christianity. Whereas Mormonism, too, somehow partially polarizes around Jesus Christ, and Moses, and the Jews, strangely, it too, has a watered-down version of the Sermon on the Mount. All I can therefore say of it is that it is a "better fraud," but not much better.

Nevertheless, it seems to me that the average Mormon today is probably more industrious, more law abiding, and more responsible than the average American. Very few of them are living off public welfare and they pretty well manage to take care of their own. Above all, they do not cater to the niggers, as do most Christian denominations. Nor do they promote integration with the niggers. This is all to the credit of the Mormon people and also their religion, regardless of its fictitious foundation.

The thing that is of particular interest to us about the Mormon religion, however, is the fact that it is the most rapidly expanding religion. It is the reason for this expansion that we want to particularly take note of.

The reason is not hard to find. It is the same reason that accounts for the rapid expansion of Jehovah's Witnesses, another strange sect. Both Jehovah's Witnesses and the Mormons are growing rapidly because they pursue an aggressive program of salesmanship, promotion and propaganda, whereas usually when Jehovah's Witnesses appear at the door, they seem to be rather apologetic and somewhat timid in their approach, handing you a copy of their

"Watchtower," the Mormons, in contrast, appear at the same door just bubbling over with confidence and enthusiasm.

Usually in their recruiting and proselytizing campaigns the Mormons

Mormonism — A Better Fraud

will send out two young men as a team. They will appear at your door neatly dressed, smiling, polite and enthusiastic and ask if they could have a few minutes of your time to give you some very important information about their religion. Since they make an attractive appearance, are friendly and enthusiastic, most often they will be invited in. This, of course, is a very, very important step in the program. Once in, they can then take up not only a few minutes, but the next few hours of your time if you are so inclined, and really give you a full-dress sales program of their product: the Mormon religion.

Since the Christian religion is really a product of the ultimate utilization of propaganda at its best, by the use of words and psychology, converting people to the acceptance of fictitious and illusory ideas, we should never forget just how important the aggressive promotion of propaganda is in winning people over to your way of thinking.

Propaganda in itself, like government or the weather, is neither good nor bad. It depends on what kind of propaganda you are being subjected to. Propaganda can be tremendously enlightening, informative, and constructive; or propaganda can be tremendously destructive and suicidal in its effect. Nevertheless, the techniques of propaganda are always the same, whether its direction is for good or evil ends. The thing to remember is that propaganda is a tremendously powerful instrument with which to influence people.

Since we have previously said that religion is necessary for the survival of a people, and that it is especially tremendously important for the salvation of the White people of today, and since we are now in the process of propagating and disseminating our own constructive religion for that very purpose, we should take very good note of the lessons that we can learn from the rise of the Mormon religion. These lessons are as follows:

1) It is most certainly possible to found and propagate a new religion amongst the White people of today and we should be tremendously encouraged thereby. In fact, the people are desperately seeking a new creed that they can believe in, especially the younger generation.

2) The key to the successful dissemination and spreading of such a new religion is by word of mouth, by speaking, by propaganda and employing the proper techniques of salesmanship.

This latter is a whole subject unto itself and I am going to expound further on this in another chapter. Let us remember that regarding propaganda Adolf Hitler said, "Propaganda can make heaven look like hell, and hell look like heaven." Let us never forget that there is nothing so powerful as an idea whose time has arrived, and furthermore, that such an idea will only become powerful if it is skillfully and aggressively promoted by the best and most productive techniques of propaganda.

The time for a new creed— a new idea— for the White Man is now here. That creed is Creativity.

CHAPTER FOURTEEN

CHRISTIANITY AND COMMUNISM - JEWISH TWINS

To hear the Kosher Konservatives tell it, a fierce, intensive battle is raging today between the evil forces of communism and the sacred forces of Christianity. We are led to believe that it is an all out battle between good and evil. We are told that these two forces are the very essence of two poles of opposition— in complete and diametrical conflict.

It is a sham battle. The fact is they are both degenerate products of the collective Jewish mind, designed to do one and the same thing— to destroy the White Race.

If we take a closer look at these two evil forces that have bedeviled and tormented the minds of the White Race for all these years, we find that they are not on opposite sides at all. We find that they are both on the side of international Jewry, doing the job they were designed to do, namely: confuse and confound the White Man's intelligence so that he himself will help the Jew in destroying the White Race.

In comparing the two we find that they are strikingly similar, and not opposites. In fact, there are so many similarities in the two programs and in the philosophy of these two creeds that the hand of the same author can easily be detected. That author is the International Jewish network. They and they alone wrote both the creed of Christianity and the creed of communism.

Both communism and Christianity preach against materialism. Communism designates those productive and creative forces of our society to which we owe in such large part the benefits of a productive White civilization, as "bourgeois." It then lashes out with unparalleled fury at the bourgeois and tells us over and over again that they must be destroyed. Instead of giving credit where credit is due, it slanders and vilifies these constructive and productive elements, namely the bourgeois or the capitalists, as the ultimate in evil.

Christianity tells us basically the same thing. It tells us that it will be more difficult for a camel to pass through the eye of a needle than for a rich man to get to heaven. It tells us that we should "sell all thou hast and give it to the poor," an insidious piece of advice that, if followed, would make us all a pack of roving bums and beggars. It would most surely cause the breakdown of our society. Christianity further tells us "lay not up treasures on earth, but lay up treasures in heaven."

Throughout, the implication is clear. Don't accumulate unto yourself any of the good things in life. If, through hard work, you've already managed to accumulate some wealth, get rid of it, give it away, give it to the poor, above all, give it to the Church, they'll take it, with relish. The net result of this fantastically bad advice, of course, is that it will more easily pass into the hands of the Jews, who do not subscribe to such foolishness. They hope to make fools of us, knowing very well the old saying "A fool and his money are soon parted," is only too true.

The other side of the coin is that the leaders of both Christianity and communism themselves are fantastically materialistic. When we look at the Catholic Church on down through the ages, we find that whereas they were extracting the last mite from the poor widow, the church itself was gathering up and hoarding gold, silver and precious gems in unbelievable quantities. Not only was it taking in and gathering all the gold, silver and precious stones that it could, but it acquired huge amounts of real estate, and the Catholic Church today is undoubtedly the most fantastically wealthy institution on the face of the earth. Even through the Dark Ages when poverty was widespread, mostly because of Christianity itself, we find these huge and fabulously rich cathedrals, built in the midst of poverty, with gold encrusted altars and apses and vaults and columns and walls. The leadership of the Church caused to be built huge and great Basilicas, Cathedrals,

Abbeys, Baptisteries, Mausoleums, Convents, and Churches. Practically all of these were so lavish and so huge in comparison with the meager surroundings of the times, that they flamboyantly stood out as the main repository of all the material wealth— gold, silver and architectural lavishness— of both their era and their geographical location.

The church never has bothered to explain why it was so necessary to have such lavish wealth on display to the worshipping faithful, who were told time and again that it was evil to "lay up treasures." Unto this day, churches are built to be flamboyant, garish and bizarre. Money seems to be no object.

The Vatican, that citadel of "spiritual" leadership, which also preaches, "lay not up treasures on earth," does not practice what it preaches. On the contrary, what it practices is indeed the height of hypocrisy, and the antithesis of spirituality. It goes all out for laying up treasures on earth. It has amassed unto itself a portfolio of 5.6 billion dollars in stocks alone, not to mention all of its real estate, art treasures and other valuables. It enjoys an annual income of 1.5 billion dollars, much of it undoubtedly collected from the "widow's last mite," as well as its vast holdings.

The United States religious establishment as a whole is valued at 102 billion dollars. In 1969, of the 17.6 billion dollars United States individuals contributed to charity (mostly benefiting the niggers), 45 percent, or 7.9 billion dollars was earmarked for religious purposes. Pretty materialistic for a religion that "shuns" earthly treasures and preaches "my kingdom is not of this world."

Likewise, the communist bosses in Russia, practically all of which are Jews, have accumulated unto themselves all the riches of the countryside. While the communist slave laborer is toiling away twelve hours a day and then comes home to a dingy, dirty, filthy, crowded little apartment shared with other families, his Jewish bosses have opulent palaces spread all over the countryside. They drive the best of cars, chauffeur driven, of course, and eat the best of foods. Not only that, but they have the best of planes at their disposal to fly wherever they see fit to govern their slave laborers. These Jewish communist bosses usually also have at their disposal imported clothes and tailors and a galaxy of servants. When they need a rest from running their slave empire, they have private villas on the Black Sea or other choice vacation spots at their beck and call. And so it goes in the Proletarian Worker's Paradise.

Let us pass on to the next similarity. Both communism and Christianity make extensive use of the weapons of terror, both psychological and real. Undoubtedly the most ghoulish and vicious concept ever contrived by the depraved and collective mind of Jewry is the concept of hell. Can you think of anything more horrible than placing millions of people in confinement in a superheated torture chamber and then burning them forever and ever without even the mitigating mercy of allowing them to die? With this piece of "Good News," and "Joyful Tidings,"

Christianity set out to conquer the minds of its superstitious and unreasoning victims. The fact that such a torture chamber was nonexistent did not at all detract from the fact that it was a real threat to those who were made to believe that it was real. To a child, for instance, if you tell him that the Boogieman is going to get him, and he innocently believes you, then the threat is just as real as if a Boogieman actually existed. And so it is with hell. To those that have become convinced that it exists, this horrible threat is just as real as if it did exist.

However, Christianity did not stop with using psychological terror alone. Those who deviated from the official church line were declared as heretics and forthwith burned at the stake.

The idea of using fire in one form or another as a means of torturing their opponents seems to have obsessed these "loving" Christians' minds. According to van Braght's famous Martyr's Mirror, some 33,000 Christians were put to death by other so- called Christians by means of burning at the stake, a grizzly type of revenge. Among my ancestors alone (who were of the Mennonite faith) some 2,000 martyrs were burned at the stake by these ever-loving Christians. One outstanding feature about this burning at the stake business was that they were always White people who were being burned. Never have I heard of a nigger being burned at the stake for his heretical beliefs. Nor have I ever heard of a Jew being burned at the stake for not believing precisely along specified lines of Judaism, even though they did not believe in Christ at all.

Burning at the stake wasn't the only means of torture and death used by these love- dispensing Christians who were so eager lo spread their message of love. During the Inquisition, and other times, all the beastly refinements of torture that the depraved human mind could devise were used to extort confessions and whip the unbelievers or heretics into line. The thumb-screw, water-dip, the iron corset, drawn and quartered, gouging out one's eyes with hot irons, and the rack (slowly tearing limb from body by means of stretching) were but some of the devices used by these ever-loving Christians to spread their gospel of Love. When the communists came along and used physical torture as one of their instruments of conquest, they had very little left to invent but what the Christians had already utilized before them. And this is as can be expected, since it was Jewish fiendishness that designed the means of torture for both.

Nor did the Church hesitate to use wholesale warfare to batter down whole nations that did not submit to their religious dictation. In fact during the 16th, 17th and 18th century the main causes of war were religious dissentions in which one religious group sought to force their beliefs on their opposites by wholesale warfare and slaughter.

The communist record of using wholesale terror, both psychological and physical, is so recent, so widespread and so well known that we need hardly review it here. In Russia alone the Jewish communist regime used terror on a scale unknown before in the annals of history. In order to exterminate the best of the White Race in Russia, namely the White Russians, the Jews slaughtered some 20,000,000. The terror, the killings, the murders that are going on in Russia today defy the imagination of the average White Man's mind. In any case, both communism and Christianity are using, and have used, terror extensively, both psychological and physical, to subjugate their victims. Whereas the Christians excelled in psychological terror, the communists excel in physical terror. But in both cases the Jews were experts in using whatever type of terror best accomplished their ends.

Both communism and Christianity have a book that presumably lays down the creed of their movement. Christianity has the Jewish bible which was written by Jews, mostly about Jews, for the purpose of uniting the Jewish race and for destroying the White Race. The communist bible is Karl Marx's Das Kapital and the Communist Manifesto, written by Karl Marx in conjunction with Friedrich Engels, both of whom were Jews. Both of these Jewish creeds, communism and Christianity, are highly destructive, and when followed, tear down the fabric of the society that has fallen victim to them.

Christianity teaches the evilness of man, that he is a no-good, unworthy sinner, that he is born in sin and that his every instinct is evil. Communism preaches that the productive, creative element of our society, namely the "bourgeois" as they call them, is rotten and evil, and must be destroyed. It can be safely said that any sound, healthy society that turned either to complete Christianity and practiced all of its principles, or any society that practiced pure communism, would soon destroy itself.

Again we want to vigorously point out that contrary to what these Kosher Konservatives are always telling us, communism is by no means the same as socialism or collectivism. The latter are basic constructive elements of any healthy society, but communism is an undisguised Jewish slave-labor camp. Since I have gone into this matter in considerable detail in another chapter, we will not take further space to review this idea here.

Both communism and Christianity preach the equality of man. Christianity preaches that we are all equal in the eyes of the Lord,

whereas the communists preach that we all must become equal in the communist society. The latter argue that the only reason we are not equal is entirely due to environment, and this little quirk of Nature they are going to correct. By the time they get through processing us all in an equal environment, they assure us they will have leveled us all down to where we are all equal. This will only be too true, for the White Race will be leveled down to where they are all equal to a horde of miserable slaves, whereas every Jew, on the other hand, will be a king.

Not only do both communism and Christianity preach the equality of the individual, but they also preach the equality of races, another vicious lie thrown in the face of Nature.

Both creeds have a very tricky dogma that is rather nebulous and confusing, not to say contradictory, in itself. They both, therefore, have set up a hierarchy that interprets what the correct dogma of the day is and everyone is to toe the line or suffer the consequences of an entrenched power structure.

Christianity and communism both have had their schisms. In the case of Christianity, the followers that differed were called heretics and in the case of communism, those that stray from the official line are called deviationists. In the case of Christianity, the Great Schism, of course, was during the Reformation when the Protestant segment developed and broke away from the Catholic

Church. It then proceeded to split and splinter in a thousand different directions from there on out, all to the detriment and destruction of the White Race. The first great split, of course, was when the Byzantine Empire split from the Roman or Western half.

Among the communists there were a number of schisms such as the Mensheviks and the Bolsheviks, and a number of other schisms, before the communists ever came to power. After they did come to power, there were the Stalinist communists and the Trotskyite communists, the latter being vigorously pursued and purged from the ranks. Now we presumably have the Mao wing of the communist party and for a while we had the Tito deviationists, and so on. In any case, the main idea in Christianity and communism is the same: On top of a confusing and impossible dogma sits a tight powerful hierarchy which dictates and interprets what the line of its followers must be, and terror, death and reprisal are the consequences to those who dare to think for themselves.

It is not at all surprising that the archenemy of both these Jewish creeds is Adolph Hitler, because he dared to come out with a healthy, natural social structure that embodied those principles that were in harmony with the natural laws, and with the healthy instincts for the preservation of the White Race. We, therefore, find the Jewish press, the communist press, and Christianity, all in chorus, denouncing Adolph Hitler, and telling us what a terrible, terrible man he was. All perpetrate and repeat over and over again the same Jewish lies about Hitler that the Jews themselves have dreamed up and supplied to their toadying stooges.

The similarities between these creeds go on and on. Both preach the destruction of the present society. They especially zero in on the destruction and downgrading of the more creative and productive elements of society as a whole. Both denounce and vilify the better elements of established society and rejoice at human failures and weaknesses, thereby claiming to prove the correctness of their communist-Christian theory.

The Jews, who are the perpetrators of communism, envision the United Nations headquarters to finally rest in Israel and in particular, in Jerusalem. Christianity too, continuously keeps talking about Zion, the New Jerusalem, and looks to Jerusalem as the Holy Land, its origin and spiritual headquarters.

Both of these Jewish creeds consistently follow policies which are disastrous to the welfare of the White Race. I have already gone into considerably detail about the catastrophic effects of Christianity on the great White Roman civilization. I have also pointed out previously that the Jews in communist Russia killed off 20,000,000 of the best White Russians. However, the programs and policies of both these creeds extend much further than these two major catastrophes of history and to point out how disastrous the effects of both Christianity and communism have been upon the fortunes of the White

Race would require a whole volume in itself. I believe we have scattered throughout this book a mass of such examples that it is hardly necessary to again repeat them here.

Another similarity that manifests itself in both of these Jewish creeds is that both have an incurable ability to put forth a profuseness of verbiage that is extremely vague and beclouded with confusion. Not only is the verbiage profuse, but incredibly lacking in substance. This is an old Jewish trick to confuse and confound the minds of their opposition, the latter being deceived into thinking that all this vast collection of words must have some higher meaning beyond their comprehension.

To further destroy and beat back the opposition, both creeds have developed to a high state the art of hurling vicious trigger words and hate words at their opponents. The Christians developed such hate-trigger words as atheist, heathen, heretic, apostate, blasphemy, pagan, sinner and anti-Christ. The communists have developed a whole stable of similar trigger words, and some of these are Fascist, Nazi, racist, bigot, prejudice, and anti-Semitic. Without anyone really stopping to analyze what each of these words mean and why they should be considered as bad, these words have been developed to a high state of implied evil so that by just merely calling these names, you need not really debate the issues, but mercilessly strike down your opponents without resorting to any debate or reasoning whatsoever.

If the similarities between Christianity and communism seem rather striking, there is a very good reason for their parallel ideology. That reason is, of course, they were both concocted by the Jewish power structure for the common objective of destroying the White Race. Unfortunately, up to this point, both their ideologies have been devastatingly effective. It is partially the purpose of this book and the CHURCH OF THE CREATOR to confront this devastating attack on the mind of the White Race and expose these twin Jewish ideologies for what they are.

Furthermore, I am firmly convinced, and it is my measured conclusion, that the Jews could never have foisted modern communism on a long suffering humanity, had they not First softened up, unhinged and confused the intellect of the White Race with the fallacious snares of Christianity. It is therefore the further objective of Creativity to help straighten out the befuddled thinking of the White Race to where they then can, and will, expunge both of these twin Jewish scourges from the face of this planet.

CHAPTER FIFTEEN

CREATIVITY VS. CHRISTIANITY

In making an analytical comparison between the new, dynamic, militant and vibrant new Creativity religion with the sick and morbid religion of Christianity, we find the philosophies of the two religions in direct opposition to each other. We Creators are tremendously proud of that difference. We are proud to be the enemies of Christianity. We are convinced that our dynamic new religion will pursue and expose Christianity for what it is—a Jewish conspiracy— until all Jewish influence, Christianity and communism are wiped from off the face of the earth.

One immediate difference between Creativity and Christianity that becomes evident is that whereas Creativity is life-oriented, Christianity, from beginning to end, is death-oriented.

The whole objective and purpose of our religion, Creativity and the CHURCH OF THE CREATOR, is to advance the interests of the White Race, the finest creation in Nature's universe. Our purpose is to help promote, preserve, propagate, advance and expand the White Race and finally create a White world of law and order, of beauty and culture.

We believe in leading the good life, we believe in creativity, productivity and advancement. We believe that life should be enjoyed, that every member should utilize the wonderful talents with which the White Race has been endowed. We believe in enjoying the beauties and wonders of Nature. We believe in working productively, in eating well, in living well, and in serving well the interests of our own people.

Christianity, as we have said, is death-oriented. Its whole philosophy is devoted to the morbid pursuit of death. Christ purportedly said, "My kingdom is not of this world." Christianity is only interested in the hereafter world, without offering a shred of evidence that such a world exists. In two thousand years, it has not dredged up the slightest evidence that the netherworld it makes such a fuss about, even exists. While pursuing this morbid obsession of that period after which you are dead, it viciously goes about destroying the only period that has any meaning to anybody— namely your time to live, your time to enjoy the life Nature gave you to live upon this earth. Again, the only time that has any meaning for anybody is that during which they are alive, and the only place that people have ever been known to live is upon this earth. I repeat again, there is not a shred of evidence to the contrary.

Nevertheless, Christianity keeps hammering away at the pointlessness of life, at the futility of it all, at the worthlessness of life, desperately trying to convince you that you would be much better off dead. By so doing it seeks to rob you of the wonderful gift Nature has given you, namely life itself. Christianity teaches that we should "lay not up for yourselves treasures upon earth" but "lay up for yourselves treasures in heaven," which in essence means that you should devote your life to the period when you're dead, a most idiotic and useless pursuit, if there ever was one. Creativity opposes and denounces this kind of suicidal philosophy, and believes that Nature gave us the wonderful gift of life to live it to the fullest, and in so doing to perpetuate our own kind and advance our own race to ever-higher levels.

This is the kind of philosophy we believe in. We are completely in harmony with the laws of Nature and with Nature herself. We are in complete disagreement with the Christian attitude that Nature did a miserably poor job of creating the White Race and that our every natural instinct is bad. We are in complete disagreement and conflict with Christianity when they say that we must remodel those basic inborn instincts and according to the Christian myth become "born again" in a most unnatural and perverted fashion. We Creators believe in working in harmony with the laws of Nature. On the other hand, Christianity is in complete conflict with Nature. Its very philosophy contradicts our basic common sense, it contradicts the lessons of history, and the laws of Nature itself.

The fact that Christianity is in conflict with the laws of the universe and with Nature herself, is not too hard to understand when we realize that it was the Jews who invented and concocted Christianity. Having contrived this whole false ideology, it is also no wonder that they make, and keep reiterating, the preposterous claim that they are God's chosen people. According to these despicable Jews they claim in Deut. 7:6 (and this supposedly is the Lord speaking): "for thou art a holy people unto the Lord thy God: the Lord they God hath chosen thee to be a special people unto himself above all people that are upon the face of the earth."

That any God could choose such a treacherous and despicable perfidious gang of scoundrels as the Chosen People could hardly be believed by anyone. It is doubtful if very many Jews themselves believe this monstrous hoax.

We, of the CHURCH OF THE CREATOR, completely reject this outrageous lie. We believe firmly that the White Race is Nature's finest handiwork and that we were endowed by Nature with the most wonderful attributes that Nature has bestowed upon any of its creatures. We not only believe this because we like to believe it, but we believe it because the evidence is overwhelming that the White Race has been given Nature's highest endowments in intelligence, creativity and productivity. Because of these and many other outstanding attributes, the White Race has produced the finest social structures, the greatest cultures and the highest civilization throughout the history of mankind. It is therefore not wishful thinking for us to say that the White Race is the epitome of creation, but it is overwhelmingly demonstrated by a mass of incontrovertible evidence.

To summarize: Christianity is Jew oriented and believes in the Jews being the Chosen People. In contrast: Creativity believes that the White Race is the Master Race because overwhelming evidence demonstrates this claim.

Furthermore, we Creators believe in breeding up, that is, advancing the White Race to ever higher and finer levels of achievement, beauty and culture. In fact, this is the very heart of our religion. Christianity on the other hand, believes in breeding down, that is, mongrelizing the human species and destroying the better types. Christianity not only believes in destroying the better types of individuals, but also the better types of races. It continually keeps denouncing those that have accomplished something— "it will be easier for a camel to pass through the eye of a needle than a rich man to enter the kingdom of heaven." It keeps promoting and blessing the worst elements of a population: "blessed are the meek," "blessed are the poor in spirit." Creativity rejects this philosophy.

We Creators believe in what the laws of Nature so clearly point out, that the strong and more perfect of the species should survive and propagate more of their own kind, while the misfits, the cripples and the imbeciles should not procreate, but should fall by the wayside. Without a doubt, Christian principles will, in the long run, produce a mongrelized race of misfits, imbeciles, and parasites. In fact it will produce a mass of scum humanity. We aggressively reject their kind of philosophy and their kind of program. We are completely in harmony with the laws of Nature which speak clearly time and time again that Nature desires the survival of the fittest and not the survival and multiplication of the worst elements of its species.

Not only does Creativity believe in promoting the survival and multiplication of the strong and the intelligent, the handsome and the beautiful, but we also believe in prosperity and abundance. We believe that the White Man, having reached the high level of civilization and technology that he now has, should provide his family and himself with all the abundance and wealth that bountiful Nature has bestowed upon him. When the White Man again becomes master of his own destiny and has rid himself of the parasites, the Jews and the niggers that are now riding on his back, we believe that we will have a veritable paradise here upon this earth. We believe that it is possible to have happiness, prosperity and abundance for all of our people, and given free rein, the White Race, when it again inherits the earth, can and will literally be swimming in plenty.

In contrast, the miserable Christian religion believes in depriving man of his property and having him live in austerity and poverty. For the last 2,000 years the Christian religion has been exhorting the White Man to "sell all thou hast and give it to the poor," "lay up not treasures on this earth," and similar nonsense. At the same time it tells him to give, give and give to the Church. While the Church was amassing huge fortunes of gold and silver and everything that was valuable unto itself, it had no compunction whatsoever about the poor miserable people from whom it had stolen the necessities of life.

Whereas Christianity teaches "lay not up treasures on earth, lay up treasures in heaven," we, of the CHURCH OF THE CREATOR reject this idiotic teaching, and propose exactly the opposite. We believe the White Man should do his best to create, produce and lay up treasures on earth for himself, his family and his race. We do not believe in deferring our wealth, efforts and energies to some nebulous hereafter, or some imaginary Jewish heaven. Despite the 5,000 years that the shadowy idea of "life after death" had been floating around, it is significant that not a shred of substantiated evidence has been produced to substantiate it. On the other hand, the evidence is overwhelming that man's life on earth is real, that Nature is real and that Nature's laws are real. Furthermore, this planet earth is the only place man has ever been known to exist and live.

It makes a lot more sense to us to direct our energies toward building a better life in the real world, than forfeiting all for some unknown dreamer's figment of the imagination. We therefore believe that we should enjoy to the fullest the time that Nature has given us to live. We believe we should make the most of it for ourselves and, at the same time, meet our responsibilities for our future generations. We reject the Jewish suggestion that we should forfeit all for a nebulous, non-existent nether land.

Not only does Christianity, with a great amount of success, beat down a man's desire for worldly goods and deprive him of as many of them as possible, but it also sets about to destroy his confidence in himself and undermine his feeling of worthiness. It keeps telling him again and again that he is no good, that he is born in sin, that he is a miserable sinner, that he should be humble and meek. It tells him that he should be tolerant and let himself be pushed around. It tells him to "turn the other cheek" and "not resist evil." In so doing, it tears to shreds his self- confidence and plants within his consciousness a tremendous guilt complex, one that frustrates and destroys his ability and his confidence. No wonder the once proud Roman nation rapidly disintegrated when it embraced this poisonous and destructive "new" creed, which conditioned them into submissiveness.

We, of the CHURCH OF THE CREATOR, reject this miserable and vicious philosophy, this sick and morbid outlook on life, and propose just the opposite. We believe that it is healthy and constructive to have confidence in one's self, in his race and in his future. We do not at all believe that it is a virtue to be tolerant when an outrage is being committed against one's family, or nation, or race. We do not at all go along with the philosophy of "resist not evil" but believe strongly that evil should be resisted with superior force, and that an outrage should not be tolerated, but destroyed. We believe that when there is a threat to ourselves, to our family, or to our race, that we should fight, and that such a threat should be destroyed. Nature tells us instinctively that this is the correct reaction to a threat. We do not believe in tolerating any menace that threatens us. We are thoroughly convinced that this Jewish advice of being humble, meek and submissive in the face of a clear and present danger to our existence is sheer lunacy, and we replace such a philosophy with confidence in ourselves, with an aggressive Fighting spirit to attack, pursue, and destroy any danger that threatens us.

Continuing along this same philosophy, we reject the Christian concept of loving our enemies. Nowhere in Nature is this concept demonstrated and plain common sense tells us that any one silly enough to fall for this kind of stupidity would most certainly be destroyed by his enemies. It certainly places him at a terrible disadvantage. We believe in hating our enemies and we believe that love and hate go together. We believe that if you love your own kind, your own family, your own people, you must automatically hate those that threaten and are a danger to the existence of your loved ones. This again is completely in harmony with the laws of Nature. Even a mother hen will fight to defend her young chicks, and certainly a chicken cannot be considered as one of Nature's most stouthearted creatures.

We repeat, we do not love our enemies. We hate them. It is our purpose to destroy our enemies. In arriving at these philosophies we have not invented anything new. We are faithfully following Nature's laws, and only by following Nature's laws can we survive. Christianity teaches that you should flaunt Nature's laws, that Nature botched her job and completely made us all wrong. Christianity teaches us that all our basic instincts are evil and sinful, that we must completely thwart our endowments and instincts and be remodeled, be "born again" so that we'll act in contradiction and in conflict with Nature's laws. This is, of course, suicidal, and the despicable Jew threw these poisonous teachings into the midst of the White Race in order to destroy us.

Creativity rejects these Jewish-Christian teachings, and, on the contrary, it believes in obeying Nature's laws and obeying our natural instincts. Only a fool can argue that our instincts were given to us by Nature to destroy ourselves. On the contrary.

Nature gave us our wonderful instincts for our own selfpreservation. Like very other creature, we must follow our instincts or else we will most surely perish. We, of the CHURCH OF THE CREATOR, thereof firmly believe in being in harmony with Nature's laws, in being in harmony with our natural instincts.

We believe in the survival, advancement and expansion of our race.

Furthermore, we believe that one of the basic instincts for the survival of our great White Race is to give our first loyalty to our race and to our family. We believe that birth is one of Nature's greatest wonders and we believe that the sanctity of the family should be venerated and protected. In contrast, Christianity openly preaches the breakdown of the family and your race. In Matt.

19:29 Christ purportedly said "And everyone that hath forsaken houses, or brethren, or sisters, or father, or mother, or wife, or children, or lands, for my name's sake, shall receive an hundredfold, and shall inherit everlasting life." What this circumcised Jew is saying is that we should be disloyal to the beloved members of our family and we should forsake them, as well as any land, or houses, or goods that we might have. Instead, we should follow this miserable Jew, who has given us nothing but suicidal advice. All I can say is that anyone stupid enough to fall for this kind of garbage deserves all he gets. How anyone can rate such distorted and ugly advice as being so fantastically wonderful is completely beyond comprehension.

Not only does Christianity teach disloyalty to our loved ones, and to those that are close and dear to us, but Christianity also has a perverted and sordid attitude towards sex, one of the strongest and most beautiful drives in Nature. Throughout the New Testament Christ keeps denouncing sex as being sinful. In fact he denounces even the very thought of it as being an abominable crime. In Matt. 5:28 he says "But I say unto you, that whosoever looketh on a woman to lust after her hath committed adultery with her already in his heart." He is hereby denouncing the natural attraction between the sexes with which Nature has endowed almost every higher living creature.

Creativity on the other hand, believes that love, and the attraction between man and woman, is the most natural thing in the world, that it is a lovely and beautiful emotion. We believe that it is one of the great mainsprings of life and Nature's reward for living. We believe that it is a creative force that Nature has bestowed upon mankind, as every other living creature, to promote the propagation of the species. Certainly without the attraction between man and woman, our race would soon die out. If it were eliminated from any other male and female creature, that species would soon become extinct. We deplore the sinister and sordid Christian attitude towards sex, and on the contrary, take a healthy, positive attitude towards this, the noblest of all passions, that Nature has given to all of its higher creatures. We believe that love, sex and marriage are healthy and noble emotions, that these go together to form a creative force in the uplifting and advancement of the species and the furtherance of Nature's plan. Here again we see Christianity taking a negative and destructive view of the good things in life; a view that would promote the destruction of a race of people; a view that would deny them the enjoyment of the good things in life. Both of these attitudes are typical of the miserable Christian teaching.

Whereas Christianity stifles productivity, destroys creativity and concentrates on "laying up treasures in heaven," in other words concentrating on the death wish, we of the CHURCH OF THE CREATOR believe in a vibrant, positive, healthy, wholesome program. We believe in enjoying life. We believe in creating more life. We believe in advancing life to better and finer horizons. Our program is alive and positive and vibrant. It is not death-oriented like Christianity.

Furthermore, whereas Christianity is vague and contradictory and meanders forever in the land of fantasy and gropes around in an unreal dream world, our philosophy is clear and simple. Our creed is founded on this basic tenet: what is good for the White Race is the highest virtue; what is bad for the White Race is the ultimate sin.

Not only that, but our whole approach to life is based on common sense, the lessons of history and an overwhelming mass of evidence. When we speak about the laws of heredity, we have a mass of positive evidence to back it up. When we speak of the laws of Nature, there is the evidence of the eternal ages to back up our conclusions. When we speak of the values of race and breeding, we have the eternal lessons of history accumulated over thousands of years to verify that which we claim.

Christianity on the other hand flies in the face of reason and common sense. The destructive, suicidal, and moth-eaten advice that the Bible tries to foist upon us, such as "love your enemies," etc., is completely contrary to all reason, contrary to all experience, and contrary to all the lessons of history. Not only that, but it is completely contrary to the laws of Nature and is in complete conflict with Nature.

Furthermore, there is not one shred of evidence to verify most of the long and tortured chapters of both the Old and the New Testament. There is absolutely no historical evidence that the Jews marched through the Red Sea and that it parted its waters in courtesy and accommodation to these abominable parasites. There is absolutely no evidence whatsoever in history that "the sun stood still" in order that these desert tribesmen could kill more of some other desert tribe. There is absolutely no geologic, or historic evidence, that the whole world was flooded in 2348 B.C. How ridiculous! There is not one single shred of evidence that the Jews were descended from Abraham, Isaac and Jacob. There is no evidence whatsoever that they had a special God who made them all kinds of sweetheart promises and assured them that they were the Chosen. There is not a single shred of evidence even that Christ ever lived. He left no letters, no writings, no statues, in fact, no evidence whatsoever. There is no evidence that men such as Methuselah or Noah, lived to be 900 and some years of age. In fact there isn't even any evidence that they ever lived at all.

Not only is there not a single shred of evidence to back up all their lying claims, but they are so outlandish and fantastic and so contrary to the laws of Nature themselves that only a fool with a deranged mind could be persuaded to swallow such trash. The whole impact of this deceptive literature as set forth in the Old and New Testament is to scream at their followers just believe!

believe! believe! Just believe because we say so! Never mind the evidence, never mind the credibility, just believe. And actually there is no more reason for me to believe in this collection of lies, threats, and unfulfilled promises, than there is for me to believe a Hindu's claim that cows are holy. It is the same kind of disgusting deception.

We have therefore swept all this garbage overboard and are starting out anew with a fresh, vibrant, positive and creative religion for the White Race. We call our religion Creativity and our religious organization the CHURCH OF THE CREATOR. We believe it to be worthy of the noble and creative White Race.

CHAPTER SIXTEEN

CHRISTIANITY PECULIARLY VULNERABLE

If we are ever to successfully rescue the White Race from the insane dilemma it now unwittingly finds itself in, there are two basic questions we must properly assess:

a) What is the average White attitude towards Christianity today?

b) After 2,000 years of Christianity, can the White Man's thinking ever again be brought back to sanity and reason?

Let us explore the initial question first.

We all know that Christianity swept the Roman Empire, and in so doing, destroyed it. The downfall of the Roman Empire was then followed by a thousand years of the Dark Ages during which all science and progress was stifled and stagnated, but the Jew- promoted hysteria of "saving souls for Christ" at the same time reached its all time peak. During the Renaissance the White Race began to somewhat regain its senses again and began to look more closely towards Nature and her laws. We find during this time a rekindling of interest in science and an unprecedented flowering in the arts. In fact, the Renaissance period may be regarded as the dawning of a new era in which the White Man again began to partially find his identity. Ever since that time, Christianity, with various fluctuations, up and down, has lost ground. With the dramatic breakthroughs and the fantastic surge in scientific knowledge in the last hundred years, Christianity has lost credulity in the eyes of most White people.

Nevertheless, although most people don't really believe in the teachings of Christianity, the influence still lingers on, and most people think of it as a "good" religion, which, although they don't practice it, they think of it as based on high ideals, and they believe is good for "mankind. When we analyze more closely just who thinks what about Christianity, we find that to probably eight people out of ten it is not too important. Whereas they don't really believe in it, neither do they really understand it, nor do they openly repudiate it. This most obvious fact emerges: the average White individual is just simply terribly confused about Christianity.

There is no phenomenon in history that has so confused, confounded and raised havoc with the White Man's normal reasoning processes as has Christianity.

It is as if a student starting out in mathematics First had a garbled multiplication table drilled into him— two times three equaled seventeen, three times five equaled nine, etc. Until his mind was again straightened out on such fundamentals, any progress such individual could expect to make in mathematics would be forever hopeless— hopeless until such time as his thinking was again brought back in line with realities.

So it is with the Christian indoctrinated White Man. Until he can be delivered from such suicidal idiocies as "love your enemies," "judge not," "sell all thou hast," etc., he is hopelessly enmeshed and in the toil of his enemies.

Even the members of organized churches and those who go to church regularly or irregularly, are confused as to what it is that they believe in. Few people when asked, "Do you really believe in the teachings as expounded by Christ in the Sermon on the Mount?" would not know what Christ purportedly said in the Sermon on the Mount. When their memories are then refreshed and they are asked do you believe in "turning the other cheek;" do you believe in "loving your enemies;" do you believe in "selling all thou hast and giving it to the poor;" do you believe in "resist not evil;" do you believe in "judge not," most of them sheepishly admit that they do not, but, at the same time fail to realize that this is the very crux and essence of Christianity and the so-called "New

Teaching." If they don't believe in that, then they don't really believe in Christianity at all.

Many Americans have rejected church going altogether, but nevertheless, still feel that this is a Christian nation, and rightfully so. Many people who do go to church are tremendously bored by the insipid, repetitious sermons that recite an endless mess of meaningless platitudes over and over again, ad nauseum.

However, they will come back and listen to the same nonsense again Sunday after Sunday, dressed in their Sunday best. They feel that when it's all over they've done their duty for the week, and give very little further thought to the subject matter. Few really ever stop to question what it is that they really believe in, what is the meaning of the Christian teachings and what have these teachings done for them, or for the White Race in general. Most people don't seem to care one way or the other, and going to church is just a formal obligation that they are fulfilling, thinking they have done their good deed thereby.

It can be said categorically that really none of the so-called Christians believe in the teachings that Christ supposedly set forth. If they did, they would in short order destroy themselves, their family and their nation. So, whereas hypocritically most of these church-goers play their part and pretend that they are believers in Christianity, in fact they are not. Even the preachers themselves neither believe in, nor practice, the suicidal teachings embodied in the Sermon on the Mount In fact, it can be said about preachers in general that they are probably the most hypocritical of all human beings. Certainly, whereas they are drawing a salary and freeloading on their flock, they would be the last to sell all they have and give it to the poor. Whereas they preach "it is more blessed to give than to receive" they are the first to have their hand out and persistently urge you to give, give, give and give some more.

Whereas the Jew has, by his persistency, foisted these suicidal ideas upon the White Race over the last 2,000 years, it is amazing how easy it is, when these beliefs are probed and examined, to bring such deluded and indoctrinated people back to life and reality. What took thousands of hours of brain pollution and indoctrination to achieve, can be undone in a few hours, or sometimes in a few weeks.

It is, therefore, the duty of each loyal member of the White Race to reason with his fellow brothers and sisters and bring them back to sanity and reality, to bring them back to their senses, and to free them from the rehash of the Jewish shibboleths to which they have been subjected to so endlessly. In this matter the spoken word is the most powerful influence. It is in this way, as well as with every other means of propaganda and enlightenment, that the White Race can again be set properly on its course, devoted to the propagation, advancement and expansion of its own kind. Thus can the White Race again be reoriented for the duty, obligation and purpose for which Nature in its infinite wisdom created it in the first place.

* * * *

Let us now examine the second question, namely after 2,000 years of Christianity, can the White Man's thinking again be brought back to sanity and reason?

If we look at recent history and examine the sick and dying state of Christianity today, the answer is an overwhelming yes, we can straighten out the White Man's thinking. Actually, this is our main battle— straightening out the thinking of the White Man.

In reasoning with our White Brothers in the need to unite and make common front against the Jews and the colored races, the most persistent argument that always comes up is— "What you say is true, but can you ever get the White people to listen to this kind of an idea?" It is discouraging and frustrating to have this continually come up, time after time, and it is no accident that this argument is used. It is another of these fallacious arguments that is promoted by Jewish propaganda. The Jew's objective is: that if you can get people to think that whereas your idea has merit, but it is hopeless to pursue (because nobody will listen to you), then you will become discouraged and quit the battle.

In combating this idea we must, first of all, label it for what it is. It is Jewish defeatist propaganda. Secondly, certainly people will listen to our dynamic new religion. It is a matter of persistence, a matter of organization and propaganda. When Hitler took on the massive job of reorienting the thinking of the German people in the early twenties, the problems he faced were very similar to what the fighter for White survival faces in America today. The German people at that time were completely befuddled with Jewish propaganda. They were in a defeatist frame of mind. They were completely deluged with communist, liberal and Jewish ideas of Marxism and self-destruction. Nevertheless, once the persuasive power of propaganda was aggressively pushed and promoted and finally organized into a political party with solid aims and programs, the German people listened. They not only listened, but they flocked to the colors of their country and of their race and were united as they never had been before.

Once the Germans realized the value of their race, and once the enemy had been clearly identified, they were more firmly united than any segment of the White race, or White nation, ever before in history. When the crucial test came, they fought like tigers. They fought more energetically and more valiantly than any race or nation has ever fought before or since in history. The fact that the Jew through deceitful propaganda was able to organize the overwhelming masses of White nations in a concerted effort to crush Germany, a country after all only the size of Texas, does not detract from that valiant display of courage and bravery. The fact remains: it was possible to rally and unite the White Race in Germany, it was possible to change their philosophy from the Jewish Marxist dogma to one of racial unity and racial survival.

It is also possible to do this here in America today.

We should remember that it has been done before, that in less than a dozen years the thinking of the German people extricated itself from the morass of Jewish-Marxist philosophy of despair and suicide to one of vibrant self-confidence, heroism, determination and a constructive program of action for survival.

The lesson we have to learn is: persistence and dedication. When we think of what an incredibly difficult problem the Jews had facing them 2,000 years ago in combating the all- powerful Roman Empire and selling them such unattractive and ridiculous selfdestructive ideas as are embraced in Christianity, we should certainly have more confidence in our ability to reeducate our own people to ways of reason and self-preservation. Certainly the Jews faced a long uphill struggle in order to sell such unattractive trash to the Romans. But by persistence, by aggressiveness, by ingenuity, and devilishly skillful propaganda, they did get the Romans to accept their poisonous ideas. It took them over 500 years to do so. We all know that this spelled the downfall of the Roman Empire. How much easier it is today if we used anywhere near similar persistence, dedication and aggressiveness in talking to our White Brothers about a genuine White program for the survival of the White Race. All we have to do is point out the obvious idiocies of the ideas that are being foisted upon us by the conniving Jewish conspiracy. Practically our total problem is straightening out the White Man's thinking. It is simply a matter of pointing out the obvious.

It is all a matter of persistence, a matter of conviction, a matter of how much do you care, a matter of dedication. The time will come when we, the White Race, will have our backs to the wall and will be fighting openly for our very survival. Undoubtedly, the White people will then be eagerly receptive to a program that will save them from destruction. But how much better and how much easier it would be if we became actively motivated to straighten out the White Man's thinking now, to actively engage in a political and philosophical program to reorient the White Man's thinking, to promote our own interests, to promote our own race and promote and assure our survival and well-being, now!

Frankly, the main problem we face is not so much overcoming the Jews and the niggers. That will be easy, as soon as we accomplish the number one problem, and that is straightening out the White Man's thinking. This is our foremost task and this is what this book is devoted towards accomplishing. As soon as this book becomes the common property of the American people, the power of the Jewish conspiracy can be considered as broken for all time.

"All men are created equal" is a dangerous myth. Our people must be firmly rooted in the philosophy of racial survival and advancement. Socialism is organized society. If the White Race isn't worth saving, what is? The work of the CHURCH OF THE CREATOR is to restore the natural instincts Nature gave to the White Race.

CHAPTER SEVENTEEN

FALSE LEADERSHIP

In accordance with the program laid down in the Protocols of the Elders of Zion, the Jew, in his devilish cunning, has concocted a number of organizations that seem to be on the side of the White Man. They come in various guises, such as those fighting "communism." These are undoubtedly the most numerous. There are probably more than a hundred in this category in the United States alone and they profess to be ardently patriotic, Christian, and anti-communist.

At the same time they usually are strongly pro-Jew and pro-nigger. Most of them completely confuse the issue, deploring the symptoms of the disease, rather than identifying and fighting the cause of the disease itself, namely the Jew.

Their ridiculous program, it would seem, is to get together with the Jews and the niggers to fight the Jews and the niggers, an obvious contradiction on the face of it. In so doing, they give a powerful mantle of protection to the Jewish network, the root of all our evils.

By far the largest among these is the John Birch Society, headed by that ardent Jew-lover himself, Robert Welch. Well organized and well financed, a lot of the money coming from the Jews themselves and the rest of it coming from concerned and frightened White people who are looking for some organization to lead them out of the mess they are in, the John Birch Society is doing pretty well. In fact, to misquote (slightly) Robert Welch: "We mean (good) business every step of the way." Whereas the Birch Society claims its fight is against communism, its real purpose is to protect the Jewish conspiracy.

What the John Birch Society really does is act as a collecting organization for all those aggressive and militant White racists that would become potential leadership in the fight against the Jews and the niggers. It then sets about to confuse and befuddle their thinking, conjure up a false culprit, namely communism, and the debilitate the White Man's money, time and energy into numerous useless projects which they are dead certain will never lead to any success. Instead of exposing the cause, namely the Jew, it goes after the effects, and protects the cause. Above all it keeps polluting its memberships' minds with bad news, bad news, a feeling that we are completely surrounded, a feeling of frustration and pointlessness, a feeling that the fight is pretty well lost and pretty well over, but we might as well go through the useless motions anyway. It does an excellent job of debilitating, discouraging, demoralizing, and finally neutralizing the White membership. Finally, they give up the fight and in most cases can never again be recruited into a useful constructive fight against the Jews and the niggers.

I say that— in most cases. It is not true in all cases. I, myself, am an ex-graduate from the Jewish sponsored John Birch Society, being misled in my early naivete into thinking that I was going to be able to do something useful in our fight against the Jews and niggers by joining the John Birch Society. Fortunately for our side, and unfortunately for the Jewish cause, a number of more astute and more capable graduates of the John Birch Society do carry on the fight after they see through the Birch hoax.

Without spending too much further time on the John Birch Society, may I add that the John Birch Society was formed by the Jews in order to collect some of the better potential White leaders, completely mislead them, put up a false culprit and a false program. They thereby hope to protect the Jew and neutralize the battle by White racial loyalists, and destroy their cause. To nobody's great surprise a large number of the chapter leaders, coordinators, and staff of the John Birch Society are Jewish.

Then we have such organizations as the White Citizens Councils and the Ku Klux Klan, who accomplish the same thing as the John Birch Society, but corral those that the Birch Society could not possibly get because the Birch Society completely excludes the racial issue. The White Citizens Councils are seemingly antinigger, but when it comes to pointing the finger at the real culprit, the Jew, they will vigorously protect and shield him from any responsibility in the notorious Jewish plot to destroy the White Race. The Ku Klux Klan goes just a little further than this, and it too seems to be anti-nigger and at times professes even to be mildly anti-Jew.

However, both of these organizations are really a farce and a sham in the fight against the Jewish conspiracy. Usually they will end up with a meaningless flag-waving program, citing their adherence to the Constitution and their Christian principles. Having thereby snookered a lot of White racial loyalists into their ranks and into contributing money to their organization, they will then go all out to support phony political candidates that so much as show a mild "conservative" stance, but are as phony as they are themselves.

The original Ku Klux Klan did a tremendous job a hundred years ago in saving the White Race in the South from mongrelization by the Jews and the niggers, a drive which undoubtedly would have led further to total mongrelization

False Leadership

of America by this time. The Ku Klux Klan of the 1860's was a fine organization that did a tremendous job, and proved once again that the White Man, when his back is against the wall, will fight to save his race. However, the "revived" and new, so-called Ku Klux Klan that was "reorganized" in 1915 is not by any means the same organization, nor does it embody the same principles. Actually the present Ku Klux Klan, from 1915 onward, is an animal of a completely different color. It was organized by members of the Masonic order, which, in turn, was organized by the Jews and is controlled by them to this day. It should, therefore, come as no surprise that the resulting product, namely today's Ku Klux Klan, is another phony front for the Jews to enlist and corral those members of the White Race that would be the dynamic and potential leadership in a real fight against the Jews. It neutralizes those who instinctively have the fighting spirit and healthy instincts to carry on the fight.

It is their purpose to steer these good White people into their organization to again rig them into a phony fight that will insure defeat, neutralize them, and render them useless.

The Klan has a real tricky hooker built into its position. It is presumably against Jews, niggers, and strangely, Catholics. Whereas the first two are racial, and a legitimate target, by declaring its hostility towards Catholics, it opens up a religious split in the White Race itself, thereby negating any good it might have accomplished otherwise. It thereby also lays itself wide open to the criticism of bigotry and enmity of a huge segment of the White Race itself, namely the Catholics. This schizophrenia was deliberately planned by the Jews, of course.

Then, there are the Christian Crusaders, like Billy James Hargis, Carl McIntyre, Dr. Fred Schwartz, and many lesser satellites who are vigorously pretending to lead the Fight against communism in the name of "Christianity." These phonies tell us if only we would all turn to Christianity, why, we would soon conquer this sinful philosophy. To hear them tell it, it's a battle between ideologies, a battle between God and Satan. What they have never explained is why God should be so impotent in a struggle against a creature that reputedly he himself must have evidently created, and why it is that their God continually seems to be losing the battle while his hateful inferior creation continually seems to be winning.

It is not too surprising that Schwartz, himself an Australian Jew, is supposedly fighting the battle against communism in the name of Christianity and under the cloak that he himself, of course, is a "Christian" White Man. Carl McIntyre and Billy James Hargis are not known to be Jews, but it would not surprise me at all if they are not, in fact, undercover "Converso" Jews, grasping leadership in a useless fight that will again drain the White Man of his resources, energy, and time, and lead him down a dead end street. Not only that, but it will lead many concerned White people back into the old snare of

Nature's Eternal Religion

Christianity, where he will completely neutralize himself, and in fact, enlist his forces and energy on the side of the Jews.

It is further no great surprise to me that Billy James Hargis is most ardent in his praise of Israel and organizes endless excursions to Jerusalem and Israel in cooperation with the Israeli tourist bureau. Carl McIntyre has purchased bonds for Israel with money he has looted from his White "Christian" supporters and is now engaged in a project to build a huge and expensive replica of "The Temple of Jerusalem," in other words, the Jewish Temple built by Solomon, at Cape Canaveral, where he now sits on millions of dollars worth of real estate.

Both Hargis and McIntyre have been unusually successful financially, while preaching the Jewish gospel that "it is more blessed to give than to receive" and "lay not up treasures on earth, but lay up treasures in heaven." McIntyre has been successful in financing a thousand or more radio stations across the United States, preaching his deceptive program and in turn reaping and looting millions out of the pockets of the White supporters whom he is misleading.

There are a number of smaller organizations that are successfully following the same formula but are too numerous to mention at this point.

Then there are such organizations that are seemingly anti-Jewish but again strongly pro-Christian, a completely incompatible position, one that is completely self-destructive on the face of it, as it is in practice. One such is the Nationalist Christian Church led by a certain "Dr." Potito. Whereas "Dr." Potito professes to be ardently pro-Hitler, violently anti-Jewish, he again takes those elements of our potential White fighting force that agree in this respect and then through a circuitous route returns these people into the Christian fold. His main line of argument is that the Israelites of the Old Testament were a wonderful, God fearing people and that they did, indeed, have a special sweetheart arrangement with God. He claims that today's Jews are not at all the same people, and in fact, (lo and behold! Would you believe?) we, the White people of Europe and America, are the "real" Israelites! By means of a lot of unsubstantiated and farfetched hocus-pocus he then proceeds to identify the Germans as being the long lost tribe of Judah, the Americans being the long lost tribe of Manasseh, etc., etc.

What this tortured and convulsive reasoning does is (1) it completely confuses the identity of the enemy, (2) it leads a lot of good White racial fighters into the ranks of that suicidal line of thinking, namely Christianity, (3) worst of all, it even makes some of the White people wish they were the Israelites (or the Jews), and by the time they have swallowed all these idiotic concepts and lines of reasoning, or shall we say, of unreasoning, they are so confused and mixed up, that, again, until their thinking is straightened out they are completely useless to the cause of the White Race.

Why anyone would want to be a descendant of the tribe of Judah after reading what a whore-mongering reprobate Judah was and what a treacherous, deceptive, blood-thirsty bunch of cutthroats the Israelites were, even according to their own rendering of history, is beyond comprehension. It is indeed hard to understand why anyone in their right mind would even want to have any association whatsoever with these kinds of renegades, much less want to be a descendant of such scoundrels.

Another variation of this same format is that applied by the numerous Christian Churches themselves, some of which preach the evils of communism, thereby luring a lot of good White people who are concerned about the Jewish destruction of their country, into their church.

As they enter into the membership of their church, being lured into it in the first place because of their opposition to communism, the preacher lulls them more and more into being concerned about the nebulous "hereafter" rather than the obvious destruction of their country and their race. After awhile it becomes less and less important to the recruits to struggle against what by now has come to seem to them as insurmountable odds anyway, and soon they fall prey to the same baited trap as did the Romans.

After going to church long enough and hearing the preacher's brain pollution unsuspectingly being practiced upon them, they become devoted members of the Christian "faith," they begin to love the Jews, and their main concern becomes "saving souls for Christ." Another group of people has thereby been lead down the primrose path of not defending their race, their family, or their country, having fallen victim to the same poisonous creed as destroyed the Romans.

One particularly vicious hooker most of these anti-communist preachers (the vast majority are pro-communist) usually throw into their anti-communist speeches is to really take out after Adolf Hitler, rather than the vicious Jewish agents of communism. By pulling this sleazy trick they accomplish a rather unique feat, namely, that of overwhelmingly impressing their victims with the inevitable forward march of communism, (although admittedly it be evil), and through deceiving them into believing that the cure for it, which Hitler personified, is just as bad, and is they say, actually the same thing as (Jewish) communism itself. A most treacherous deception.

As it must be for lack of space, this is only an incomplete summary of those organizations the Jews have concocted to "lead" us, i.e., lead us into a trap. However, they are typical and are meant to be a warning to the unwary. It is safe to say: if they do not expose the Jew, if they do not stress race as the basic rallying cry; if they do nothing more than deplore and lament, but offer no solution; if they are promoting Christianity; then they are not on our side.

CHAPTER EIGHTEEN

FALSE IDEAS DISSEMINATED BY JEWS

1. "The love of money is the root of all evil."

This oft quoted passage from the bible has been swallowed in total by practically everyone without ever stopping to examine its meaning. When it is examined for what it is really worth, it is found to be patently false. It is not money, nor the love of money, that is the root of all evil, but the root of all evil is the perfidious Jew.

Money is not only a medium of exchange; it is a very necessary and useful tool in the wheels of commerce in our modem civilization. If we did not have such a means of exchange, modern business, progress, and in fact, civilization as a whole, would be irreparably set back and tremendously handicapped. To the average bread-winner and to the average family, the acquiring and earning of money is the means of acquiring security, of obtaining all the necessities of life, such as food, shelter, clothing, entertainment, education, in fact everything required for a decent living. To impugn a man for pursuing a trade, a profession, or business that will earn him the money to take care of himself and his family is about as idiotic as to deny him the right to live.

No, indeed, there is nothing wrong with a man making as much money as he possibly can and providing for himself, for his family and his heirs, to the best of his ability. It is, in fact, those energetic and restless men of ability, (such as Henry Ford) who have created the most and have also given the greatest benefits to our race, to our nation and to civilization.

This whole idea is basically as wrong as so many other quotations in the New Testament which discourages a man from pursuing those natural instincts endowed to him by Nature for his own survival. Among these basic instincts are the will to survive; the basic urge to fight to preserve himself, his family and his property from any direction; the urge to build, to produce, to make, and to improve. The idea that money in itself is evil, or the love thereof, is along the same lines as some of the other bad advice that Christ gave when he said: "Think not of the morrow, look at the lily in the field, it toils not, yet Solomon in all his glory was not arrayed like one of these," etc., or "look at the birds, they toil not yet their heavenly Father takes care of them," etc.

This is all real bad advice. In the first place the birds work hard to do all those things that are required to feed themselves, to build their nests, to raise their young and to perpetuate their species. Those that do not do so, perish forthwith. The lily in the field (and other plants), in their own way, have to compete vigorously against other plants for water and nutrition. If they don't, they get crowded out and are replaced by more healthy and more vigorous plants. All species of Nature, whether they are plants, birds, animals or mankind itself, are in competition with other life. It is the strong, the brave, the vigorous, the courageous, the energetic that survive, while the weak fall by the wayside.

Again this debilitating advice was solely meant for the Gentiles. It was designed to set them back as much as possible; to clear the field for the treacherous Jew who will then have an easier time of it in stealing all the wealth of the world from the White Race and consolidating it in the hands of his own race.

"The race situation is getting so bad in this country I am thinking of leaving the United States and moving my family to Australia in the near future."

Many good White people in this country are thinking along those lines. It is a completely wrong solution to a bad situation.

For years now the White Race has been fleeing before the niggers and the Jews and it has gotten us nowhere. The answer is not to flee but to stand up and fight.

We should be pursuing, not fleeing. We are either going to fight and win the battle in the United States, or we will not win it anywhere. If the best and most race-conscious people flee from this country and leave the rest to mongrelize with the niggers, this wonderful United States of ours will certainly go down the drain. Once the Jews have accomplished that much, you can be sure that they will use the full weight and power of this wealthy country to impose mongrelization in Australia, South Africa or any other part of the world.

No, the answer is not to leave the U.S. The answer is to organize, to unite the White people, to practice racial loyalty, to drive the Jews from power, to ship the niggers back to Africa, and to firmly grasp the reins of power in the hands of a determined, united, raceconscious White government.

2. "Our laws and Constitution are founded on Christianity."

It is amazing, indeed, how many White Americans are laboring under this erroneous conclusion and deluding themselves and others by repeating it in parrot-like fashion. When asked just what Christian principles our laws are based on, they are slumped for answers, and for good reasons. When we examine what were some of the basic Christian principles that were enunciated by Christ in the Sermon on the Mount, for instance, we find such principles as, "turn the other cheek," "love your enemies," "sell all thou hast and give it to the poor," "resist not evil," "judge not."

If our laws were based on these principles we would, of course, have nothing but anarchy and mayhem. If we just take, for instance, the principle "resist not evil," we would have no law enforcement agencies, we would have no Army, Navy or Air Force to defend us from foreign enemies. We would, of course, be completely defenseless and would soon be destroyed. No nation was ever built on such an impossible foundation, least of all America.

Nor was America built on the principle of "turn the other cheek." No, indeed. When, during our early and most constructive years, the White Men from Europe came to these savage and inhospitable shores, they drove back the red man to claim this land for their very own, they did indeed not turn the other cheek. In fact, it was their aggressiveness and their loyalty to their own race in driving back the Indians, and killing them when necessary, to take over their land, that laid the foundation for the building of this great country.

When the White Man then forged onward and westward, he again fought and killed the Indians and drove them from the land. Without a doubt the Winning of the West is one of the most romantic and constructive episodes in the history of mankind. It was the White Man at his best, aggressive, fighting, conquering territory, breaking new land, building homes, building cities, building railroads in new territory and thereby creating a great nation.

No, let us not delude ourselves. There were no suicidal or idiotic Christian principles involved in this great burst of creative and constructive energy that the White Race pursued. It was a glorious example of the free play of the forces of Nature at their best. The White Man, unfettered and uncluttered with a lot of silly ideas about compassion and humanitarianism, fought and drove his way westward and thereby built a great new White nation that today encompasses half the productive strength, and half the wealth, of the world.

As far as our government and laws are concerned, they owe next to nothing to Christianity, but practically everything to the great Roman civilization that preceded us by more than a millennium and a half ago. The very word Republic is taken from the Roman word Respublica. The Republican form of government is modeled strictly from the Roman forms, our law courts are modeled after the courts of Rome, or our European forbearers, who copied them from the Roman model with certain modifications.

In fact, our Founding Fathers, when discussing and debating the form of government to institute, continuously went back to Roman history for experience and example. The facts overwhelmingly point to our judiciary, our congress, our executive, being the benefactors to the great systems of law and government that the Romans had instituted during their epoch in history. That is why we find that anyone who studies for the legal profession today is required to take Latin, since so many of the legal terms used are best stated in the original Latin from which the legal concepts originated. The Romans were, without doubt, the creators of the finest organization of law and government the world has ever seen, and we are blessed to be the heirs of their great tradition and civilization.

We should, therefore, set this matter straight once and for all. Neither is our American government, nor are our laws in the U.S., based on Christian principles. In fact, when all these new Christian principles spread throughout the Roman Empire like a plague, the Roman civilization collapsed. And no wonder, when we consider how devastatingly destructive and suicidal was this new philosophy of "love your enemies, turn the other cheek, judge not, resist not evil."

No, indeed, America was neither built on, nor based on, Christian principles. On the contrary, it was first of all built on the creative energy of the White Race giving free play to its natural instincts, and secondly, its government and laws were built on the experience and rich legacy left us by imperial Rome.

3. "There is nothing you can do about it."

As the Jews push further and further with their various programs for our enslavement, such programs as massive forced busing of our children, higher and more confiscatory taxes, the mongrelization of our White Race, etc., we find our people almost universally throwing up their hands and saying, "There is nothing you can do about it."

This is, of course, another example of the Jew skillfully implanting in our minds the age old military stratagem of: if you can get your enemy to think they are defeated before the battle even starts, then they are as good as defeated. This strategy is as old as the hills, but people are still falling for it.

Despite all the laws and idiotic court decisions, there are many things that you, a White American citizen, can do. The first thing you can do is to take a positive courageous attitude. The second thing you can do is to make up your mind that you are not going to be enslaved and that you are going to fight And the fact is, the situation is far from hopeless. You have many resources available

Nature's Eternal Religion

to you with which to wage the battle. After all, we, the White Americans, outnumber the Jews 30 to 1 and the niggers 7 to 1.

Now just remember that. Furthermore, we have available to us all those tools and means that the Jews, actually a small minority, have used in their favor for our enslavement.

The number of things you can do are almost unlimited and here are but a few suggestions.

1) Form a local protest committee or organization to promote and pursue those political ends that you think are desirable, and in opposition to those that you deem undesirable.

2) Along the same lines, form a political party, or a political organization, to create a power or influence block.

3) Run some good candidates for office, or better still, run for office yourself.

4) Compile propaganda leaflets and literature and get a group to distribute them as widely as possible.

5) Organize and promote massive resistance to such laws as forced busing of your school children.

6) Write letters of protest to your Congressmen and other elected officials. This is probably one of the weaker forms of action you can take.

7) Write letters to the editors of your local newspapers and encourage others to do the same.

8) Form a telephone committee and organize local meetings of protest.

9) Give speeches in protest of those laws that are bad and in favor of such changes as you think should be made.

10) If everything else should fail you still have the right to do the same things as our Founding Fathers did in 1776. If you are being enslaved under a tyrannical government using law and order as a guise, remember that your right to life, liberty and property supersedes all other secondary laws and you have a right to overthrow such tyranny by force if necessary.

Historically when tyrants have sought to enslave them, free men have resorted to force of arms in order to remain free.

Above all the most significant and meaningful action you can take is to organize the CHURCH OF THE CREATOR in your area. Whereas attempting to directly fight the United Nations, school busing, confiscatory taxation and a thousand and one other atrocities the Jews have heaped upon us, might seem the most obvious course to take, it is not, however, the most effective. In most of these things we are fighting the effects instead of destroying the cause.

Let us never forget the cause of most of our troubles and the root of all evil is the perfidious Jew.

Therefore in building the CHURCH OF THE CREATOR nationwide and then expanding worldwide, we are destroying the basic cause of all our problems. As I have said time and time again, the first and most important step is straightening out the White Man's thinking. Once we have accomplished this much, it will be relatively easy to organize and unite the White Race from there on out, and overcoming the Jews and the niggers will be child's play.

So let us proceed. Remember the most effective and meaningful action you can take is to organize a unit of the CHURCH OF THE CREATOR in your area, or join such a group if it already exists. Then go to work and recruit. Preach, promote and disseminate the information, program and ideology contained in this book. Help bring your White racial comrades back to their senses and unite them in the fight for the survival of their own race. It is our common objective— in which you must help— to have one or more copies of this book in the home of every White family in America, and finally in all the world.

We can do it, we must do it, and we will do it. So let us proceed.

5. "The means is as important as the end itself."

Wrong as wrong can be. This bit of nonsense has been probably more strongly promoted by Kosher Konservatives than any other group. Here is what the Jews themselves say about this matter in Protocol No. 15: "How far seeing were our Learned Elders in ancient times when they said that to attain a serious end it behooves not to stop at any means or to count the victims sacrificed for the sake of the end." Whereas we despise the Protocols in total and their objectives, we cannot deny the keen insight into history and human nature that are exhibited throughout the Protocols, lessons deduced from experience and history.

Let us take, for example, the case where we are engaged in a war with the enemy, a war that means either our death or our survival. In such a war all measures are used, as for example: deception, surprise, killing, bombing, destroying the enemy's food supply, destroying their cities, etc. I am not formulating a new theory herewith, but merely stating the facts of history as they have unfolded over the last several thousand years. Yet we find within our own country, when it comes to taking such measures as are necessary for our own survival, the survival of the White Race, we find a multitude of humanitarians preaching brotherly love, compassion, Christian charity, good will, unselfishness, kindness, tenderness, tolerance, generosity, and all the other sops of human kindness, ad nauseam. We soon find our hands so completely tied that we cannot do those things that we should do in order to protect ourselves from the destruction that the Jews have prepared for us.

In matters of survival of the White Race, and in matters of politics, we should use the same cold, clear reasoning as is employed in times of war and forget this nonsense about Christian charity. We must remember that there is no higher law in Nature than selfpreservation and the perpetuation of our species.

6. "Promise just what the people want and make beautiful speeches, then do just the opposite."

The Jews have abused this political ruse so often and for such a long time that it would seem almost self-evident that the White people would catch on. But apparently they haven't. When Kennedy ran for election he made a big issue of arming this country to become so powerful that none would dare attack us. After he was elected he immediately set about disarming us, and leaving us naked and defenseless before our enemies. With the Jew Adam Harmolinski taking over our Defense Department and McNamara playing the front line stooge, this trio soon set about wrecking what inadequate defenses we had at this point in history. This is just one incidence of lying perfidy. There are many others in the few short years Kennedy was in power.

When Nixon was elected he made great promises about his opposition to school integration and busing. However, no sooner had he been elected but he set in motion massive government machinery and massive amounts of the tax payer's money to integrate our schools, bus our children around like a herd of cattle and implement the Jewish program of race mongrelization.

President Johnson was no better. He promised government economy by pretending to be switching off light bulbs in the White House to save the taxpayer's money. Immediately thereupon he launched the greatest spending spree in history (up to that time) and increased the Federal debt and government expenditures beyond anything that had ever been seen before.

These three Presidents are cited merely as typical examples. They themselves did many other acts of treachery that gave the lie to their previous promises. In this they were no different than presidents that came before them. I cite these few examples merely out of thousands of other promises that were made, only to be broken.

We should realize, of course, that this is an old Jewish trick. When Johnson or Kennedy or Nixon performed these acts of treachery, all detrimental to the White Race, they were not acting as representatives of the White Race at all, but as cheap degenerate stooges for the treacherous Jew that was manipulating the country's destiny, using these stooges as front men on the stage to cover up their treachery.

In referring to this, here is their quote from the Eighth Protocol in reference to appointing White stooges to positions in government: "we shall put them in the hands of persons whose past and reputation are such that between them and the people lies an abyss, persons who, in case of disobedience, must face criminal charges— this, in order to make them defend our interests to their last gasp."

7. "All men are created equal."

When the Founding Fathers wrote the Declaration of Independence they were striving for a ringing message that would arouse men to fight and join their cause. The Jews, who were at that time disseminating revolutionary ideas in Europe in general, and in France in particular, were broadcasting the old catch words of "Liberty, Fraternity, Equality." This was in preparation for the French Revolution and other revolutions that they were planning.

America was not immune to this Jewish propaganda and many of these ideas were making headway in America as well. It was, therefore, a great tragedy when our Founding Fathers imbedded, and wrote into the Declaration of Independence the deceptive Jewish catch phrase,

"All men are created equal." This obviously false and idiotic statement has been aggressively exploited from that day on. It has plagued us ever since and been a tremendously powerful weapon in the hands of the Jews, the revolutionaries, the liberals, and the anarchists.

It is so obviously false it would seem no refutation is necessary. But not so. It has been quoted so often by so many of our false leaders, that, like the Sermon on the Mount and so many other ideas that are patently contrary to all reason, it has been accepted by the majority of the White people as being a truism.

The White people should really know better than this. Looking back over their own glorious history, the lesson of the superiority of the White Race over others is so obvious that it should need no explanation.

Not only that, but on the very face of it, even among the same race, men are patently different. Some are highly intelligent, some are tall, some are strong, some are weak, some are idiots. The list of differences is endless. Nor are men ever born in the same stations of life. For instance, a baby born to a millionaire is born into a different station and environment and will immediately have different opportunities for development than, say, for instance, a baby born into a home whose parents are poverty stricken, and of low intelligence. A child born into a musical household, for example, the family of Johann Strauss, would have an altogether different inclination, environment, beginning, and so on, than say would a baby born into a missionary family living among the Indians in the jungles of the Amazon. We could, of course, list endless examples to substantiate this further.

In any case, this false, misleading and untrue statement has been a tremendously powerful wedge for the Jews to drive home their campaign of mongrelization. Upon this false premise is based the second false premise: if the niggers were only given the same opportunity and environment, they would perform the same as the White people. Therefore, we should drive full speed ahead towards a program of mongrelization. The fact that the niggers are inherently inferior to the White Race in intelligence; in mentality; in their lack of cultural creativity; in the fact that they are lazy and shiftless; the fact that their morals are of a completely different and lower level than that of the White Man; and endless other differences of which the color difference is the least—all these are ignored.

The fact is that men are not created equal, are not born equal, do not develop equally. There is a tremendous difference in their contributions to civilization and mankind. We must therefore get back to reality and destroy this false myth.

Nature herself has created all creatures unequal in a million different ways. We proud members of the White Race must remember one thing. Our racial identity is the holiest thing that Nature has bestowed upon us and we must preserve it at all costs.

8. "Don't talk about politics and religion, for politics and religion don't mix."

Whoever has control of the government of a nation, and the very nature of that government, is the most important single fact bearing upon the destiny of that race or nation. Political control determines all other factors such as economics, education, security, progress, culture and just about every other important aspect In the Protocols, the Jews point out that they would like to have the Goyim mind occupied by all kinds of trivialities so that he will never come around to considering the vital issues that affect his destiny.

It is, of course, of utmost importance that we talk about politics, and even more important that we discuss religion. Our life is based on our religious outlook. Then we must make sure that total control is wrestled from the destructive Jews and reclaimed into the hands of loyal White leaders.

Whether or not this is done is also largely affected by the religious complexion of the people. Government is usually a reflection of the philosophy, religious attitude and outlook of the people themselves. It, therefore, behooves us to get our religious thinking straight. We must realize that the preservation, promotion and protection of our great White Race is the most important and most holy cause to which we can devote our lives. We must then translate this outlook into political action and political control of our governments, control vested completely in the hands of loyal racist White leaders. Religion and politics are inseparable, and most vital to our survival.

9. "We are all individuals."

This contradictory idea, strongly fostered by the Jews, is as divisive as it is destructive. The fact of the matter is we are all members of a particular society, striving together for our own total betterment. The whole progress of mankind and civilization can be measured by the increased ability of man to create and build a social organization. From the time that man began to subdivide the different tasks of growing food, weaving cloth, manufacturing, transportation, medical care, etc., from that time on, man began to lift himself by the bootstraps from his jungle existence into a modern, productive society. With this comes the willingness to sacrifice his own interests for the good of his race and is society as a whole. This is one of the remarkably outstanding creative traits of the White Race and this is why he has been able to accomplish so much. Were we to revert to the idea that we are all individuals, with every man for himself rather than fulfilling his obligations to his family, to his local town, to his country, and to his race in general, society as a whole and civilization in total, would soon collapse.

We are by no means individuals. Every act we perform affects our families, affects our community, affects our nation and affects our race. The more we realize our obligations to all the different contracts that we have, the more creative and more effective a society we will build. Should we think of ourselves purely as individuals, we would soon revert back to the caveman stage and wipe out all the progress we have made over the thousands of years.

10. "The only salvation for this nation is a real two party system."

Wrong. The two party system is an ideal Jewish device to divide and conquer. It splits the White vote and gives the Jews and niggers the deciding leverage to win elections. Furthermore, it is basically opposed to the leadership principle and serves to immobilize, divide and fragment the White Race.

Instead of promoting unity and progress, it enmeshes its unfortunate victims in an endless hassle. Two or more opposing factions will bicker and argue endlessly over nit-picking trivialities, usually ending up in a compromise, a stalemate or a deadlock.

The real answer is the time proven system embodied in the leadership principle.

11. "The ballot is the only weapon the people possess."

The ballot is probably the most ineffective weapon the people possess. The people can do a number of things that are more effective from our political point of view. They can form organizations, political and otherwise. They can change the system of government. As a last resort they can overthrow their tyrants by force, if necessary. If threatened with destruction, a race is not only entitled to, but obligated, as the highest right in Nature, to use any means possible to overthrow and destroy their oppressors. The law of the right of survival of the species is the highest law in Nature.

12. "Are you going to condemn all the Jews? There are good and bad people in all races and we shouldn't condemn a whole race."

There might be good and bad people in all races, but if there are any good Jews from the White Man's point of view, they have yet

to be found and identified. To be a Jew means to be a follower of the Talmud, and any follower of the Talmud is a co-conspirator in a vicious program designed to destroy the Gentiles in general and the White Race in particular. To exempt any of the Jews from responsibility in this conspiracy would be like exempting the individual participants in any army fighting against you. Whereas there might be different degrees of involvement in the Jewish hierarchy, different ranks and command posts, nevertheless, all the members of the Jewish race, in one way or another, actively participate in the war against the rest of humanity.

It is rather strange that the same people who are continually offering apologies and exceptions for the Jews, are not at all concerned about the way that warfare has been carried on, say, for instance, in World War I or World War II. When, for example, Hamburg was bombed viciously by the Allied Air Forces who killed 50,000 White people in Hamburg in one night, including old people, women, little babies, children, pregnant women, these same apologists seem to be totally unconcerned about whether perhaps some of those White people were murdered without reason. Nor do we hear any cries of protest when the Allies, under the control of the Jews, launched a vicious three day incineration air raid on the beautiful city of Dresden and burned, cremated and incinerated 300,000 people in one of the most vicious and atrocious massacres in history. Again, these same people seem completely unconcerned as to whether or not all of these Germans (or any of them, in fact) were guilty or deserving of such a horrible fate.

The fact of the matter is none of them were guilty of any crime whatsoever, the only thing the Germans can be accused of is that they had the courage to try to shake off the Jew and defend their race and their nation from the international Jewish conspiracy. For this brave and courageous war the Germans should be highly commended, not condemned.

13. "The phony fight technique."

The Jews are real fond of getting the White Race enmeshed in some silly fight or argument in which they state the issues and the answers. No matter which side you take, both sides are destructive to our cause. Not only do the Jews use this trick to confuse White people and waste their time, bickering and stirring up animosity, but while the White Race is wasting tremendous amounts of energy wallowing in a useless hassle, the Jews feel quite safe that none of that energy will be directed against them.

The Jews are continuously setting up political parties, or opposition groups, that achieve no other purpose than destroying each other, while the Jews walk away with the spoils of war.

In our political system they set up (for instance) the Republican and the Democratic parties. Having thereby set up a so-called "two party system," they then make sure they control both sides. Then they make a big to-do about how wonderful is the two party system, how it exemplifies the American tradition and how it is almost holy. Controlling both sides, either way, no matter who wins, the White people lose and the Jew is the sure winner in every contest

There are so many variations of this phony fight technique that a whole book could be written on it. We will just quote a few examples. Outside of the many political factions that uselessly fight each other in this country we have the phony foreign wars that the Jews have involved us in.

There was, for instance, the Korean War in which the Jews controlled the American forces and they also controlled the North Korean forces. The object was not victory, but confusion and the draining of American resources, financially, in manpower and in world prestige. But above all, the objective was to have the colored races kill as many young White boys in the prime of their manhood as possible, thereby depleting the strength of our White Race. Since the White Goy and America were too stupid to catch on, the Jews made a huge replay of the same action all over again in Vietnam. And so the favorite Jewish pastime of killing White Gentiles goes on at a more murderous pace than ever.

14. "Multiply contradictory and confusing arguments on a thousand issues, all of little importance."

In the Protocols the Jews state that they will confuse and confound the mind of the Goyim with all sides of a thousand different issues. The Goyim will be so confused and lost in a wilderness of contradictory arguments that they will throw up their hands in despair. Jewish control of the communications media gives them an excellent opportunity to pursue this method of mind pollution. The fact that the arguments disseminated are illogical, contradictory and completely ridiculous, makes absolutely no difference. The purpose is to so confuse the White Gentiles that they will be completely paralyzed in pursuing any course of action which might stop the advancement of the Jewish programs.

15. "Jews posing as Gentiles; Jews changing their names."

A chameleon device oft used by the Jews is the trick of changing their names and posing as Gentiles. They are especially fond of picking a real good Anglo-Saxon name, such as a Scotch name, or an Irish name, or one that is unmistakably English, so that they are automatically looked upon as being non-Jewish. A few examples are Douglas Dillon, Douglas Fairbanks and thousands of others. Under this guise they can boldly pursue the Jewish cause with little risk of being detected as one of the so-called "chosen."

16. "Using mulattos with a preponderance of White blood to represent the typical nigger."

There is now a massive drive on to mongrelize the White Race and pump the black blood of Africa into the veins of While America. Every possible program and means is being used. One of the tricks the Jews use is to show these refugees from the jungles of Africa on television interspersed with a group of White people. If an ad is shown in a catalogue or newspaper there is always a group of 2, 3 or 4 White boys and girls and one little nigger in their midst.

However, if they showed the real pure undiluted black nigger, he would be too repulsive for the White American public to accept.

To overcome this, they always select models that are not niggers at all, but mulattos, with a preponderance of White blood in them. In fact, most of them are more than likely three-quarters White or seven-eighths White. These are then passed off to the American audiences as the "typical" nigger. People such as Lena Home, Jim Brown, in the entertainment field, or Senator Brooks in the political Field have more White blood in them than they do black blood and what intelligence (if any) they have, was derived from the White side. The Jews pretend this is a typical black and point to them with pride as proving that the niggers are every bit as capable as the White people. This, of course, is a perversion of Nature and a gross and mischievous insult to the White Race.

17. "Black is beautiful."

This slogan, promoted by the Jews has no more truth in it when applied to people than it does when applied to dirty laundry. The truth is that all the people of the world have not only a high respect for, but envy of, the White Race.

The desire among the colored peoples of the world to be lighter skinned is almost universal. Thus, many aborigines paint themselves White. The peoples of India have developed a rigid caste system in which the distinction is the lighter the skin the higher the caste, and the darker the skin the lower the caste. Not only that, but many colored races have blue-eyed Gods as their idols. Even the Japanese design their dolls with White faces and blue eyes, both of which are typically un-Japanese.

Black niggers, both here and in Africa, who are social climbers, consider it the height of their ambition to marry a White woman and some Jewish outfit in this country is constantly milking the blacks by selling them some sort of a pomade guaranteed to whiten their skin.

It is ironical that the people of the White Race have had their brains so polluted with Jewish racial lies that, of all the peoples of the world, they are the least aware of the great outstanding worth of their White racial heritage. Nevertheless, the colored races of the world are fully aware of what they have not and are not

18. "The policy of reversal."

This refers to the shifty Jewish trick of making things not only appear different from what they are, but of making them appear exactly the opposite to what they are. For instance, the Jewish controlled government of Russia is portrayed as being anti-Jewish and persecuting the Jews; Jews themselves are the most fanatically racist minded people on the face of the earth, yet are portrayed as being violently against racism. Racial integration of our schools, which is actually destroying the White Race, is being publicized with great fanfare as getting quality education to everyone. Increased income taxes, which fan the flames of inflation, are portrayed as a means of stopping inflation. The number of tricks the Jews have up their sleeve in this field is almost endless.

19. The Jews are the "Chosen People."

This is one of the oldest hoaxes in history that the Jews have successfully perpetrated on the White people by foisting their Jewish Old Testament upon the religions of the White people.

The Old Testament, written by the Jews themselves, keeps pounding away at the theme that they have a special contract with God. They claim that God just smiled benevolently on the Jews while they went about their dirty business of slaying, looting and murdering all other tribes. That the White Race should have incorporated this treacherous Jewish history embodying the "Chosen People" hoax as part of their own religion is one of the great perversions of Nature and one of the strange tragedies of history. For this stupid mistake the White Race has paid dearly.

20. "The use of pollsters to confuse what is passed off as popular public opinion."

Having a complete monopoly of the propaganda media, the Jews set up public opinion polls to tell the people what their opinion is.

After they have thoroughly doctored and rigged these opinions to conform with their version of what public opinion should be, they then give these polls wide and universal publicity. They thereby create the illusion of support for their myriad of extremely unpopular Jewish programs. On the other hand, the illusion is created that there is no support for those policies that in reality would benefit the White Race. These phony opinion makers will always show Jewish ideas more popular than they really are and will show White racial ideas to be less popular than they really are.

Thus various Jewish ideas such as foreign aid, race mixing, high taxes, gun control, legalized pot, etc., will be shown to be popular, or at least gaining in popularity. On the other hand, such White values as morality, segregation, repatriation of the nigger to Africa; White Racial unity; self-reliance; aversion to pot, promiscuity and pornography, will be shown as old-fashioned and square. The Jewish press will portray them as something the young people are abandoning, and in general, they will be portrayed as being unpopular and steadily losing ground.

False Ideas Disseminated by Jews

This deceitful Jewish tool also is a powerful weapon for helping swing elections in their favor. Unfortunately, too many White people have had their brains so polluted with Jewish propaganda as to be unable to see through these phony pollsters. Too often they will vote in the direction the Jews tell them is the popular so-called opinion of the day.

21. "Phony labels and smear trigger words."

The all-pervasive Jewish propaganda networks, in short order, build up certain words that heap hate, contempt and derision upon those who are tagged with these loathsome labels. By means of massive repetition, people automatically associate evil and malevolence surrounding anybody tagged with these trigger words, without reasoning what the real meaning might be behind them. The word "racist" is such an example, whereas the real meaning of the word should be someone that practices racial loyalty, a noble attribute, indeed. Yet today, because of Jewish propaganda efforts, it is regarded by millions as a description to be shunned and detested. Another word is the term "Nazi." Since the Jews well realize that the program as set forth by Adolf Hitler in National Socialist Germany was a serious threat to the Jewish conspiracy, they want to frighten everybody away from even looking into, and studying the cure. Hence the massive smear campaign against Hitler and the Nazi philosophy. Nearly 30 years after his death, the name of Adolf Hitler is still the most hateful phrase in the Jewish lexicon.

In the religious field we find similar ready-made trigger-smear words. The word "atheist" is such a term. Instead of open- mindedly considering the evidence and allowing the free play of common sense and reasoning, such a sound rational course is battered to the ground and short- circuited by the massive use of name calling and smear words. Some others are the words "antiChrist," "godless," "blasphemy" and "heresy."

On the other hand, when the Jews seek to promote a deceitful destructive program that plunders and cheats the White Race, they dress them in glamorous, high-sounding labels, usually garnished with a flavor of humanitarianism. The United Nations, a plan of Jewish world government, designed to enslave the Gentiles of the world, is such a phrase. "Making the world safe for democracy" is another such phrase. What these programs really mean is: fighting destructive world wars in which one coalition of White nations destroys another group of White nations. Thereby they insure the advancement of Jewish control over their victims, and insure, furthermore, that the Jews will be able to plan another such deadly war.

Another is "racial brotherhood" which really means that while the Jew is mongrelizing the White Race he wants to make sure that there will be no

393

resistance and no opposition. Other such deceptive labels are "urban renewal," "inter-denominational faith," "desegregation," and "moderates."

22. "Cry persecution."

Throughout their history the Jews have used the cry of persecution with admirable skill. Being extremely parasitic in nature, they will bore into the host nation in which they live, plunder it dry, destroy its morals, undermine its government and finally pull down its foundation, leaving it a wreck and a shambles. When the peoples of such a nation finally wake up and become aware of their oppressor and thereupon take action to throw this parasite off their back, the Jew then raises up a loud cry of persecution. He manages to make the defending nation seem to be the culprit, rather than the parasite. Usually this will evoke the sympathy of the neighboring nations, who will then, in sheer stupidity, unwittingly come to the aid of the Jew. The recent example of this happening to the heroic German people is by no means the first nor the last in the history of Jewish duplicity. The same thing has happened to Egypt, to Babylon, to Persia, and recently to the Arabs in Palestine.

23. "In order to get elected it is necessary to cater to the nigger vote."

It is most pathetic as to how many people have been tricked into swallowing this Jewish lie. Most of the time we are given no choice between candidates, but only a choice of the lesser of two evils. The Jews see to it that the stable of candidates that they field is always such that all are espousing policies detrimental to the White Race and advantageous to the Jews and the niggers.

The White Race still constitutes the majority of the population of America. If we ever did get a good and courageous candidate who came out with a platform that clearly and loudly championed the cause of the White Race, such candidate would be elected by a landslide.

Through either stupidity or cowardice, or both, we have never had such a candidate appear on the public scene, or at least not with enough energy to be heard by many people.

It is our duty to field not only one such candidate, but a whole army of such candidates, working in coordination, all across the land, under the unifying banner of the CHURCH OF THE CREATOR, with a clear and far-reaching program of expanding the White Race and shrinking the colored races, driving the race traitors from power, and grasping control of our destiny into our own hands.

24. "Driving the Jews from power would result in a tremendous blood bath."

This is not necessarily true at all. The German people drove the Jews from power in their own land with very little loss of life, very little bloodshed, and practically no turmoil. They did it legally and they did it by means of the ballot. Contrast this with the tremendous misery and bloodshed that ensued when the Jews took power in Russia. During that terrible catastrophe the country was torn from one end to the other, agriculture and industry were destroyed, famine ensued, and over 20 million of the best White leadership in Russia were murdered.

We, of the CHURCH OF THE CREATOR, believe that we can first of all save America and that the White people can regain control of their own country by legal means. We can do this without much bloodshed if we follow the program laid down in the creed of our new religion.

The first and foremost problem is to straighten out the White Man's thinking, as I have said so many times before.

However, should struggle and bloodshed become necessary, then we, too, must pay this price and use this means. If necessary, we must, and will, invoke the highest law of Nature. We must and we will use all means and every means necessary to insure the survival of our race.

If we don't drive the Jew from power, it is almost certain that a gigantic blood bath will ensue in which 60 million of the best White Americans will he murdered.

25. The "Christ is (is not) a Jew" — confusion.

This silly argument has become one of the favorite pastimes of the Kosher Konservatives in recent years. I have read countless arguments pro and con on this subject from people like Gerald L.

K. Smith and many others who should (and undoubtedly do) know better.

This is such a tricky and meaningless argument, yet one that gets a lot of simpletons, who should know better, booby-trapped into believing that if we could only prove by some devious means that he wasn't a Jew, that, per se, would vindicate that he was something great and special.

In the first place, there is not a shred of evidence that such a man ever existed, and overwhelming evidence that he did not exist I have gone into this more thoroughly in another chapter entitled Christ's Existence not Substantiated by Historical Evidence.

However, if we were to take the Jewish scriptwriters, who wrote the New Testament, at face value, then it is overwhelmingly clear that the Jews are telling us that Christ was one of theirs. In the very first chapter of the New Testament, namely in Matt. I, it gives the supposedly full lineage of Jesus Christ from Abraham, Isaac, Jacob on down to those whoremongers of Judah, David, Solomon, and others, to Joseph, the father of Christ. Furthermore in Luke 2:21, it says plainly that Christ was not only a Jew, but he was a circumcised Jew.

Going still further, it makes very little difference whether he ever lived at all, whether he was a Jew, or whether he was not a Jew. Any way you slice it, the Christian teachings are bad suicidal advice and the Christian religion is bad news for the White Race. History has shown that it destroyed the great and beautiful Roman civilization. We only have to read the Sermon on the Mount (Chapters 5, 6 and 7 in Matthew) to find out the nature of the suicidal advice that destroyed the Roman Empire when it embraced Christianity.

26. "The White people are the true Israelites."

This argument is really treacherous and seems to especially hook those people that want to be Bible-believing Christians, and at the same time have discovered what an evil race of people are the Jews. Since their bible tells them that the Israelites are the "chosen" people of God and that it would be absurd for God to choose such an obviously evil, treacherous, and perfidious race as the Jews, therefore, by some twisted rationalizing, if they could only put themselves in the place of the Israelites, it would make the whole biblical mess more acceptable. Consequently, when somebody comes along and offers them a ridiculous cock-and-bull story that we, the White Race, are really the true Israelites, they jump at this nonsense like a fish at a baited hook.

The whole proposition is so ridiculous that it is hardly worth repudiating here again. However, I will bring up a few salient points that should demolish this silly nonsense once and for all. In the first place, it is only the Jews that practice circumcision, and this is their brand and their trademark. It has been historically so from time immemorial. Secondly, it is part of their own creed, as they have stated was set forth in God's "covenant" with Abraham. Thirdly, the Jewish Bible makes it quite clear that Christ and the Apostles were Jews, Fourthly, when you read what kind of murderous, whoremongering, treacherous scoundrels were their "great" Patriarchs and so-called "men of God" such as Judah, Abraham, David, Solomon and many others, the question arises—why would any self-respecting White Man in his right mind even want to be a descendant of such shabby and disgraceful scum?

27. "But we are human beings, not animals."

This shallow and meaningless argument comes up most often when talking about how Christianity, with its suicidal teachings, not only violates common sense, but also the laws of Nature. To love one's enemies, to turn the other cheek, to resist not evil, to give away everything you have, and other such nonsense is completely contrary to the laws of Nature. Nowhere else in Nature's realm do we find any creature practicing such obvious means to its own self-preservation.

When I have pointed this out, I have often met with the silly argument that we are not animals but human beings. When asked just what this is supposed to mean, it is hard to get a clear answer from these people, but evidently they mean to infer that we are immune from the laws of Nature the other creatures are subjected to. We are evidently supposed to be exempt from the laws of Nature because, they say, we were given the ability to think and reason, that we have a soul, that we have everlasting life and many other such non-sequitur arguments.

The facts of life are somewhat different from what these arguments would imply. The fact is that we are a creature of Nature, just as is any other of the millions of Nature's creatures that inhabit the face of the earth. We most certainly are not immune from any of the laws of Nature. If there be an idiot who thinks we are, for instance, exempt from the laws of gravity, let him try and jump off a 20 story building and see how exempt he is.

Whereas it is certainly true that we have a higher intelligence than other creatures of Nature, this in no way whatsoever immunizes us from any of the laws that govern the universe. We are born just like the other creatures, we procreate just like the other creatures and we die along with the rest of them. We must eat and drink and breathe just like the rest of the creatures of this universe. The laws of heredity apply to us just as rigidly and just as relentlessly as they do to horses or cats or rabbits. If there are some misguided dreamers who would rather think otherwise, that is their problem.

I didn't invent the laws of Nature, nor the laws of gravity, nor the laws of heredity, nor did I invent the realities of life and death.

That is the way it is, that is the way it always will be, and those are the facts of life.

In any case, it is when we foolishly deviate from the laws of Nature that we run headlong into trouble. It is when we no longer trust our own intellect and reasoning and begin to have our minds unhinged by unreal, unsubstantiated, and unnatural teachings, that we begin to reap havoc with our own lives and imperil the existence of our own race. We cannot escape the conclusion that we are, indeed, a creature of Nature, as are all others. Although we are the highest creature of Nature, we are nevertheless subject to each and everyone of Nature's laws, no less, no more so, than any other creature.

28. "You shouldn't take the Bible literally."

Many a time when I have cornered someone in a debate about the impossible and contradictory tenets of Christianity, they will try to weasel out with the expression, "Well, you shouldn't take the Bible literally." Evidently they are inferring that the Bible doesn't really mean what it says, and doesn't say what it means. This, again, in itself, is a strange and idiotic non sequitur argument. If the Bible is such a great piece of literature and is the divine word of God, certainly Christ and/or God, with all their supposedly infinite wisdom, were capable of expressing themselves clearly and explicitly. The fact that the Bible is just saturated with contradictions, with a vast collection of vague and meaningless phrases, is, in itself, the best indication that it is, of course, not the word of God or any such thing.

In any case, if I, as a businessman, were to write a contract selling a piece of land, and then, when it came time to deliver deed and title, blandly stated to my customer, that, well, of course, you shouldn't take what it says there too literally, I would, of course, be accused of being a liar and a cheat.

If we can't take the Bible literally and it doesn't mean what it says and say what it means, then what does it mean, if anything? Since the so-called "Good Book" makes such a big issue of "truth," we can, of course, judge it by its own standards. If it isn't telling the truth, if it doesn't mean what it says, and if it doesn't say what it means, then it is, of course, lying.

29. "The term western civilization is a misnomer."

Not too many people have caught on to this tricky little bit of deceptive Jewish dialectics. The term "Western Civilization" has come into such general use that everybody takes it for granted without analyzing the hidden deception. The civilizations that the world has witnessed over the last 6,000 years (including today's civilization) are not at all "Western" as such, but are White civilizations. Everywhere that civilization has appeared it was created by the White Man, as we have explained in greater detail in another chapter.

And so it is with today's civilization. Whether the White Man resides in Europe, or in the United States, or in Australia or whether he gets a foothold in Hong Kong, or in India, or in China, he builds a civilization. We should therefore make the important distinction that civilization has nothing to do with Western or Eastern hemispheres as such, but is strictly the creation of the White Race. Therefore, by calling it Western Civilization, the Jew has robbed the White Man of his due credit and confused the origin of the creator of our civilization. Civilization is exclusively the product of the White Man, and no other.

30. "There are good Jews and bad Jews."

In discussing and debating the merits and demerits of the Jews, I have had a lot of so-called intellectual sophisticates come up with a barrage of confusing distractions about good Jews and bad Jews. Some will make the silly claim that the present day Jews are not the real descendants of the biblical Jews. The inference being that the biblical Jews were, of course, God's "chosen" and were good guys, but today's Jews have been mongrelized from the Khazars and are a different breed of Jew, admittedly bad.

Others will make the distinction between the Kikes and the good Jew. Another distinction that comes up repeatedly is that there are the communist Jews and the non-communist "good" Jews.

Another distinction is the Zionist Jews and the non-Zionist Jews, the latter evidently, are supposed to be all right The list seems to be endless and the only effect of it all is to get the Jew off the hook and to confuse the issue.

Getting back to the biblical Jews, or Israelites, the Old Testament says very plainly that they all practiced circumcision. Whatever new blood they have taken into their race over the thousands of years, the fact is the practice of circumcision is their brand or trademark today, as strong as ever. Whatever changes there have been in their blood, they have strictly kept their loyalty to their race, their dedication to their deadly conspiracy of world domination and the destruction of the Gentile. They practice racial loyalty today as fervently as they ever have. Their conspiracy for the destruction of the Gentiles has not changed.

It is, therefore, completely pointless to waste any time about the finer distinctions as to which are Hebrew Jews, or which are Khazar Jews, or Sephardic Jews, or any other kind of Jew. As far as the White Man is concerned in his fight against the Jew, a Jew is a Jew, and everyone of them is a mortal danger to our existence. They're all bad Jews, Every Jew has been indoctrinated from his childhood in the principles of Talmudism and his main obsession throughout his life remains to destroy the White Race.

Therefore, let us never forget that all Jews are our enemies and to distinguish between one type of Jew and another type of Jew is as useless as distinguishing between different types of rattlesnakes. If you have been bitten by a rattlesnake it makes very little difference what his genealogy is, whether he is a diamondback or a sidewinder. They are all poisonous.

31. "We are here to help others."

This is another one of those insane so-called Christian principles, that has had a devastating effect on disintegrating the White Race.

What it really means is that unless you are helping somebody else that is less fortunate and more useless than you are, you have no particular purpose in being here. This idea is, of course, silly and contradictory on the face of it.

A very good question that even a little child might ask is— then what are the others here for? The answer obviously is— nothing, and they are perfectly useless. The further conclusion would then be that our only purpose is in helping to promote and expand the useless, and in most cases of so-called Christian charity, this is absolutely true. The whole principle of Christian charity is to proliferate the scum and the colored races, and to destroy the productive element of our society, especially the White society.

We of the CHURCH OF THE CREATOR completely reject this nonsense. We go back to the source of all truth, namely the laws of Nature which say that we are here to propagate, advance and expand our own species, our own kind. We believe that in so doing we are fulfilling the highest law of Nature and the highest law of the universe. It is neither good nor charitable to keep promoting and proliferating the lowest elements of our own race, but it is absolutely suicidal and a perversion of the laws of Nature to help promote and proliferate the colored races, who are, by their own volition, our enemies.

We believe in going back to the basic principles of our creed and our religion, namely pursuing that which is good for the White Race. In so doing we are also in harmony with the highest law of Nature. This law plainly tells us that we should converge our efforts on the goal of propagating, preserving and advancing our race, at the same time opposing and destroying those elements that are a threat to us.

32. "If we would only develop more understanding between the races, we would all get along beautifully."

In their zeal to pursue "understanding" many White do-gooders who join the Peace Corps, the communist party, and many other liberal-Jewish organizations, have heaped a tremendous amount of damage upon their own race. Because they have not been able to see through this Jewish deception of so-called "brotherly" love and understanding, they have become exceedingly useful tools in the hands of the Jews.

The fact of the matter is that those people who have had the least do to with the niggers are most easily duped into promoting the race mixing program instituted by the Jews. It is those people that have had to face the realities of life by having to work with niggers; have had their own neighborhood invaded by an influx of niggers; those who have had the unpleasant experience of seeing these refugees from the jungle at first hand, that become rapidly cured of any Utopian ideas of race-mixing. On the other hand, it is usually some wealthy White do- gooder, who, in many cases never really had to work for a living but inherited his money, and who more or less lives in an insulated ivory tower type of existence, that becomes the most ardent of bleeding hearts, promoting the Jewish program of race mixing.

The better you know the niggers, the more you understand them, the more you know and understand the Jews, the more you realize their true nature. The more you understand them the more you realize what a deadly threat they are to the existence of the White Race. The more you understand them the more certain you become that they really are your enemies.

33. "Separation of Church and State."

The Kosher Konservatives keep telling us again and again what a wonderful Constitution we have. They especially remind us how "wise" were our Founding Fathers for insisting upon the separation of church and state.

Upon examining this concept closer, I fail to see any great merit in separating these two important pillars of our social structure. It does not make too much sense to have the same group of people supporting the defense of their country with military service and tax dollars and then go to church on Sunday and preach "resist not evil," "turn the other cheek," and "love your enemies." It does not make any sense to spend billions on educating our children and then teach "judge not" in Sunday school, telling them to abandon their good sense and judgment.

Nor does it make any sense for the government to promote business and prosperity when the same people who support such government preach sell all thou hast and give it away.

Nor is there any great merit to have most of the White people of America divided into a thousand different factions religiously, when we should be united in a solid front against our mortal enemy— the perfidious Jew.

I believe that a far more ideal situation is that combination whereby the government of the White Race is blended in perfect harmony with its religion, rather than in conflict with it. A religion should unite a race and not divide it,

Nature's Eternal Religion

and only upon a unified racial religion can the solid foundation of an enduring government be built. Once we have religion, government and race all blended in a unified philosophy for the welfare of our race, we will have secured the future of the White Race for all time to come.

34. The "We can't win" phobia.

Probably one of the toughest problems I have encountered in leading the White Man back to sane thinking, is overcoming his defeatist attitude. Countless times I have heard "Yes, I agree with everything you say and I'm 100 percent with you— but can you convince the rest of the White people?"

This is, of course, negative, defeatist thinking, and is not to be tolerated.

If you are in a paddleboat, a mile offshore and sinking, you don't just sit there and contemplate what your chances might or might not be. You do the only sensible thing— you start bailing and paddling for land as if your life depended on it— which it does.

The situation of the White Race is very similar. Rather than idly contemplate odds, we must dig in right now and aggressively pursue the fight to straighten out the White Man's thinking. This is our main problem. If you believe in the program as set forth in this book, then a hundred million other White people can also be convinced, provided you start spreading the word today.

Once we have straightened out the White Man's thinking our problem is as good as solved. The problem of overcoming the Jews and the niggers, and regaining control of our own destiny, in fact all other problems will seem like child's play in comparison.

35. Love and hate.

Hate is a normal healthy emotion with which Nature has endowed all of its higher species. It is a fundamental and vital emotion necessary for the preservation of the species. To emasculate the White Man of the ability to hate those that are a threat to his existence is like de-clawing and de-toothing a tiger and then throwing him back into the jungle to fend for himself.

Defenseless, such a tiger would perish miserably in short order.

So it is with the White Man. If his healthy instincts are tampered with and he loses his ability to hate and fight those that would destroy him, he is left naked and defenseless before his enemies. The perfidious Christians who so loudly proclaim their abhorrence of hate, themselves practiced hate to the ultimate.

False Ideas Disseminated by Jews

When someone disagreed with their "belief or "creed," they branded them as heretics and had them burned at the stake, hanged or otherwise destroyed. They hated fiercely, and, one way or another, made short shrift of their enemies.

Love and hate go together. If you are willing to protect those you love, then you must hate those that threaten their security and existence. Most great movements in history are built on hate— hate for the enemy— hate for a dire threat. There is nothing that unites a group more firmly than hate for a common enemy. Nor is there anything that spurs them on to determined action more decisively than hate.

36. Juggling figures and statistics.

According to the 1970 census, the United States, as of April 1, 1970 had over 203 million inhabitants. Of this number, it claims approximately 11 percent are black and three percent are Jewish.

From this it would appear that the rate of growth of the nigger population had remained approximately the same as in previous years and that the blacks were not increasing any faster than the Whites.

The evidence from many sources convinces me that the government is deliberately lying to us in order to cover up the true facts. This, I am convinced, they are doing in order to lull the White people into a false security. They want to deceive us into believing there is no racial time bomb ticking away in our midst. One does not have to be an especially astute observer to note that the black unmarried broodmares, subsidized by public welfare, are breeding uncontrolled.

They are having as many as 12 to 16 illegitimate black bastards each, and a black population explosion is in our midst.

The fact is the niggers are breeding like rats, whereas the White families are conscientiously and deliberately suppressing their own reproduction to one or two children per family.

I therefore am convinced that the black population is in reality, probably at least three times as large as the government would like to have us believe. I have no way of telling, but I would guess that the truth would be nearer 35 percent of the population in America is now black, in other words approximately 70 million out of the 200 million, instead of 11 percent or 22 million.

Likewise, I believe that the Jewish population is much higher than the (Jewish) government would like to have us believe. Instead of being infested with only three percent (or six million) Jews, I would guess the correct Figure would be close to 20 million Jews in America.

Nature's Eternal Religion

On a worldwide basis, the Jews give us a variety of figures regarding their own numbers. Oft quoted Figures are 18 to 20 million. Again I believe that these Figures are kept deliberately low in order not to alarm the White Gentiles. Again, I have no way of telling, but I would suspect that there are at least 80 million Jews infesting the face of our planet.

In sum total, what with Filipinos, Puerto Ricans, Mexicans, niggers, Jews, Indians and mulattos breeding and multiplying at an ever increasing rate in the country built and founded by White Europeans, I would say the White population of the United States today is down to approximately 50 percent of the total and shrinking rapidly in relation to the colored scum.

It is therefore high time that we the "dispossessed majority" took action to save ourselves from being dispossessed of our land, our property, and our country. To this end we Creators are dedicated, not only in America, but on a worldwide basis.

37. Real estate vs. stocks and bonds.

There are thousands of different ways of investing money. However, basically there are only two major avenues— either in real estate, or in stocks and bonds.

When you invest your money in stocks and bonds, you are basically a spectator, trusting to the management of the corporation (and payment of dividends thereof) to some other party, or parties, who are in control.

In most of the major corporations of America (and the world) today, that control rests in the hands of Jews. When you buy land or improved real estate, you yourself are in control. In fact, you have a monopoly on that portion of the world that you own. It is unique and it is irreplaceable. In the Final analysis, all our wealth rests on land, on real estate.

In the last ten years, whereas in the stock market the Dow-Jones Industrial average has gone up only 18 percent, the average price of land (acreage, city lots, resort property) in the United States has soared 95 percent, a rise three times as great as the general price level, and Five times the Dow-Jones Industrial increase. In many select areas, such as Florida, land has done much better.

Whereas stocks can be maneuvered up and down daily, with the Jewish owned Stock Exchange manipulators reaping profits on both the up and the down movements, land relentlessly appreciates in an ever upward spiral.

Not only are the Jews in complete control of the Stock Exchanges of the world, but they control or own most of the shopping centers and key real estate in the major cities. However, vast quantities of tremendously valuable real estate are still in the hands of White Gentiles. It is therefore the relentless goal of the Jews to drive the Whites from the ownership of all land and improved real estate. Whereas stocks and bonds (which often can become worthless) are highly touted as "Securities," there is a vicious and unending campaign to discourage (the Whites) from owning real estate. This they do by propaganda, taxes, financial manipulations, and dozens of other devices. They have spelled out this goal of depriving the White people of their land in the Protocols.

It is therefore the experience of my lifetime that the White Man should strive to acquire, as early as possible, all the land and improved real estate he can and keep its possession in his family. They don't make any more land.

Likewise the White Man should band together to boycott the Jew in business; he should, if possible, go into business for himself; having built up a thriving business, he should never, never sell out his business, but pass it on to his own family. In no case should he ever sell either his land, or his business, to a Jew.

CHAPTER NINETEEN

RESPECT FOR WHOSE LAW AND ORDER?

The White Race has many strengths and fine attributes that are to be admired. One of these is our genius for law and order.

Wherever the White Race goes, it seems to have the urge to organize its society and to institute law and order. We know that the Romans were great organizers, and that they were great lawgivers. Whatever country they conquered or whatever people they subdued, they instituted suitable laws and created organized government. Basically, this is the cement of civilization, and we can hardly think of civilization and progress without the underlying factors of good government, an organized set of laws, and a police force to see to it that these laws are kept. This is all well and good and the White Race can be proud of its inborn characteristic trait of promoting organization, government, and law and order.

Nevertheless, "law and order," in the hands of the enemy, can be used to destroy a people. If the laws are so framed as to rob the White people, and shrink their reproduction, in fact so designed as to mongrelize and destroy the White Race, then we have a different situation. Then we are obligated to invoke the highest law of Nature, namely the survival of the species.

This is the situation in America today, and in fact, all over the world, with the Jews legislating and enforcing "law and order."

In Russia, too, law and order has been established to the nth degree. If anybody so much as opens their mouth about the Jews, they are shot. Even for such crimes as petty theft the offenders are shot without the benefit of a trial, courts or judges. As a result there is very little so-called "crime" in Russia. The fact is, the criminals are in charge of the government and the law enforcement machinery, and they commit crimes on a massive scale of the most heinous dimensions. Furthermore, the Russian people are completely enslaved and subjugated by the Jews, who have control of all the wealth, all the means of propaganda, the government, and above all, control of all the guns. The Jewish slave drivers are enforcing "law and order" and it is pretty clear to everybody that their use of law and order is grinding the Russian people into destruction. Let us heed, therefore, once and for all, that law and order as such is not the ultimate goal of the White Race, but survival of our species is the highest law that Nature has set before us.

There have been many times when this noble trait of the White Race has been cunningly utilized by the Jew as a powerful weapon to destroy the White Race. We are in such a period of history today, when blind subservience to law and order by the White Race is helping to destroy us. Under the guise of "law and order" the Jews are causing us to commit suicide.

I would like to remind my White Brothers and White Sisters that 200 years ago Americans were being subjected to tyranny and repression by the British Government (which incidentally was then, as now, in the hands of the Jew). However, the White patriots of that day were not as badly afflicted with brain pollution as are we of the present generation. Being above all men who valued their freedom, their possessions, and their country, they chose to defy "the law of the land" when it was used as a pretext to repress the White majority.

I believe this suggests the answer to the question of what do you do when "the law of the land" is being used to destroy you. And I believe the answer to this is plain— as it has been throughout history. There is a higher law which Nature employs constantly, and which, in fact, all races have utilized when they were threatened with destruction. This higher law is the Law of Survival, and we, the White people of America, should now realize that we are in such a position. We must now be prepared to defy the criminal actions of any madmen trying to destroy our racial existence. We must again remember, once and for all, that the highest law in Nature is the law of survival of the species at any cost.

I am certainly all for law and order and I am all for a good government, provided the law and the government is there to protect the interests of the White Race and provide for its survival and its advancement. If it does not do this, then it is not our government. Then it is our enemy, regardless of whether or not the puppets who are fronting for that government seem to be White Men. Let us never be fooled by the fraud of White stooges, manipulated by Jewish hands, who are heading up our government. It is still a Jewish government. We are only too painfully aware that the Jews at all times have been able to solicit White traitors and front-men to expedite their dirty work.

When we look at the powerful establishment that rules over our lives in America today we must ask ourselves— just whose government is this? Who is it that through so-called legal taxation robs us of exorbitant sums of hard warned money to the tune of several hundred billions a year? Why, it is the Internal Revenue Service in the hands of "our" government. Who is it that orders and enforces the busing of our children like a truckload of cattle into the black jungles in order to hasten the mongrelization of the White Race? Why, we all know that the Federal Government under the guise of H.E.W. and with the collaboration of the Jewish controlled courts, pushes, promotes and enforces this abominable crime. Who is it that promotes the multiplication and proliferation of the niggers in our midst? Again it is our "duly elected" government that robs the working White Man and woman of billions in hard earned savings and transfers it to the black animals and thereby promotes the spread of crime, anarchy and decay that are tearing the heart out of all our formerly lovely big cities.

Who is it that robs the White citizens of America of our hard earned money and squanders it abroad to the alien races to promote the expansion of niggers, of other colored races such as Chinese and Hindus, and our Jewish communist enemies such as Israel, Yugoslavia, Russia and dozens of others? Again it is our so-called "constitutional" government, supposedly the "Finest creation in the history of mankind," so we are told.

Who is it that is deviously robbing us of our constitutional right to keep and bear arms? Again it is "our" government that is doing this to us in order to more easily enslave us. It is significant that whereas the sponsors of these gun bills are usually good sounding Anglo-Saxon names, there are always Jews behind these facades that do the manipulating. Take for instance the infamous New York Sullivan law. It bears a good old Irish name, the name of Big Tim Sullivan, Tammany Hall leader and New York State Senator, who evidently was tricked into supporting the bill in good faith. However, it was conceived by a couple of Jews, one by the name of George P. LeBrun, actively assisted by two other Jews, Dr. Solomon Baruch, the father of Bernard Baruch, and another Jew by the name of Nathan Strauss. We also are aware of the Dodd Gun Bill and we know that Senator Dodd was not a Jew. However, it was one David Martin, alias Isadore Levine, a Russian Jew, born in Canada, who put the bill together and promoted it, with Senator Dodd fronting for it. Again this is "our" government that is disarming us in order to better and more easily enslave us.

Who is it that protects the niggers when they burn down our cities, when they rob and loot and pillage and rape? In the olden days if such atrocities had been committed, the citizens would have been outraged to the point where they would have grabbed their guns and shot the anarchists dead in their tracks. But not today. Today these lawless savages and criminals are duly protected by "our" police force. In fact, I have personally seen on television these looting criminals smashing store front windows and carrying out television sets and other major appliances right in front of a police officer who stood by, meekly condoning the crimes committed under his nose.

Who is it that hosts, wines and dines our foreign enemies such as Khrushchev, Kosygin, Golda Meier of Israel, and other foreign enemies that come to infest our shores with their "state visits"? Again it is the deceitful Jewish government in control of our fair country, and I must say most emphatically it is not "our" government.

Can we, as true and faithful members of the White Race, then, be loyal to such a treacherous establishment that has usurped the power of government in order therewith to more readily destroy us? Are we in good conscience duty bound to obey such a treacherous tyrant who is using the law as a weapon to exterminate the White Race? The answer to both of these questions is a most emphatic, resounding No! When traitors and enemies have usurped the government, the courts of the land, and the law enforcement agencies, in order to commit genocide on the White Race, then the time has to come to invoke Nature's highest law that supersedes all others— and that is the Law of Survival. Such a time is now at hand.

As long as our governments are Jew-controlled, we, the White People of the world must face the stark facts of life: the so-called governments now in power, despite all their "legal" trappings, are nothing but the strong-arm enforcement agencies of the worldwide Jewish network. Such governments are our most implacable enemy, and will be until the day the White Man gains control of his country's government. The White People owe such governments no loyalty whatsoever, only their utmost hatred and enmity. We must therefore oppose this arm of the Jewish conspiracy as relentlessly as its other major tentacles. We must, in fact, fight it more vigorously since it heaps more injury on the White Man; robs him of a greater part of his hard- won earnings and more ruthlessly forces integration upon him than any other organization in existence.

We must therefore bend all our efforts to the day when we will forcefully wrest government, all governments, from the hands of the Jews and again place it firmly in our own hands, the White Man's hands.

What then can we do? One of the first things we must remember is that we must never, never give up our firearms at any cost, law or no law. We must remember that the Jew is not really interested in law and order as such, he is interested in smashing the weapons from out of our hands so that he will more easily be able to overcome us. We must, therefore, never, never compromise our position to be able to defend ourselves, our homes and our families. Any risk by our people in keeping their guns is far less than that of surrendering them in order to "obey the law." There are many other means at our disposal for our own defense, and for wresting the government and the courts from the hands of our enemies. Insofar as we are aware of "law and order" being used against us to destroy us, it is our every right, in fact, it is our duty, as members of the White Race, to resist them in every way possible, to resist them passively and actively.

We are well aware that the courts are almost exclusively in the hands of Jewish judges or White traitors who are controlled by the Jews. We know that

Nature's Eternal Religion

J. Edgar Hoover, who was at the head of the F.B.I., was a stooge who did the bidding of his Jewish masters and who has written some very favorable things about the B'nai B'rith in his book. We are also well aware that unless he was their man, he most certainly would never have lasted some 45 years in such a sensitive post as head of the F.B.I. We also know that the F.B.I. is used mainly as a club to harass those White people who are fighting the communists, the niggers and the Jews. It is glaringly obvious that the F.B.I, is the strong-arm of the Jewish Conspiracy to enforce integration wherever there is any difficulty in this matter. Should we then collaborate with this Jewish strong-arm? The answer again is overwhelmingly No, under no circumstances.

In the olden days when there was breakdown of law and order and people were no longer safe, they resorted to taking the law into their own hands. In many of the frontier towns of the West when the criminals became intolerable, the citizens formed vigilante committees. Here is how Webster defines a vigilante committee: "a volunteer committee of citizens for the oversight and the protection of an interest; especially a committee organized to suppress and punish crimes summarily (as when the processes of law appear inadequate)." The time is rapidly approaching when we are going to be faced with a breakdown of law and order, when the White man, woman and child is going to be at the mercy of fiendish criminals and the Jewish law enforcement agencies are not going to lift a finger to defend them; at the same time we are going to be faced with a situation where the White Man is going to be dealt with harshly when he tries to defend himself from the beastly savagery of the niggers. We are therefore going to be forced to resort to the highest law of Nature and that is to defend ourselves and invoke the Law of Survival of the species. We might even be forced to defend ourselves from guerrilla warfare, in which the color of our skin will be the uniform designating which side we are on. Let us have imbued within each and everyone of us a strong and overwhelming loyalty to our own White Race.

In the meantime we should work feverishly and aggressively to organize politically, to distribute literature on behalf of the White Race, to promote and foster White solidarity, and to get control of the government and political machinery of the state by legal means if possible. If this is not possible by legal means, then we must resort to the same means as our forefathers used two hundred years ago to defend their liberty, their property, their homes and their families.

In any case, the key to all these actions is first of all the distribution of propaganda and enlightenment, and secondly organization. In order to do this we must First of all have a religious conviction, we must have a philosophy and a program.

We must have purpose and direction. We must have leaders. To supply the fundamental underlying creed for all these things, is the objective of formulating the new religion that we are herewith expounding, namely the creed of the CHURCH OF THE CREATOR.

CHAPTER TWENTY

FACTS, MYTHS AND LIES

If a man came to you and told you that he had just seen another man jump over a building fifty feet high, from a standing start, unaided by any mechanics or tricks, what would you think?

Undoubtedly, you would be surprised, for nowhere in your experience could you recollect a man jumping over a fifty foot building. Perhaps you had witnessed a jump of five or six feet at athletic events, and perhaps even as much as seven feet, if you had witnessed world champions in competition. But fifty feet? Never had you seen such a feat with your own eyes. Nor had any of your friends witnessed such an unbelievable performance, nor had you ever even read of such a thing.

You had never before seen the man that relayed this story to you. Until he told you this fantastic yam you knew nothing about him and had no reason to regard him as either honest or dishonest. Having told you that he personally saw a man jump over a building fifty feet high with one leap, you now have a choice of a limited number of conclusions:

1) That a man did leap over a fifty-foot high building, and a miracle had been witnessed by the man telling you the story.

2) That the man is dishonest and he is lying to you.

3) That the man is mistaken, but honestly thinks that he saw another man leap over a building fifty feet high. There could be a number of reasons as to why he is mistaken, but it hardly makes any difference as to what they might be— his mind may be deranged, his eyesight poor, his judgment bad. It makes no difference, if he is badly mistaken, what he is telling you is not a fact.

In trying to decide which of these three alternatives you would choose, you would probably follow a logical sequence something like this: "Well now, the best high jumper in the world has cleared barely seven feet, therefore, it would have to be a fantastic miracle to have anybody jump fifty feet into the air.

Since I have never seen any miracles happen, and even the ones I read about are of most questionable nature, I would definitely rule out the first alternative."

Fine, that leaves the other two. He is either lying to you or he is mistaken. You consider the possibility of him being mistaken and probably conclude that unless he is a complete nut he can't be that badly mistaken. Then you consider how many lies are told every day, and the most obvious conclusion is that the man most likely was lying to you. You hear lies and exaggerations every day— from people directly, or on radio and television, newspapers, courtrooms, political speeches, practically in any sphere of activity. Therefore, it would be only commonplace if the man told you a lie. Certainly a million times more likely than that he had witnessed a miracle.

Of course, there is still the other possibility that he was honest, but a nut— mentally deranged. There are hundreds of thousands of such people in the world too— but not nearly as many as there are liars. However, since you had no stake in the matter, you would undoubtedly quickly come to the obvious conclusion that No. 1: No miracle happened, the man did not see anybody leap unaided over a fifty-foot building. No. 2: He did not tell you a fact, and was obviously lying. No. 3: Although unlikely, he might be off his rocker.

But supposing you had an important stake in the matter of whether another person is telling you the truth or note. Suppose you were at a service station getting your car filled with gas, and a man come to you and said: "I would like to buy your car. Here is my check for $10,000.00." Well, you hadn't thought of selling your car, but you think a minute and figure, "Well, I only paid $3,000.00 for it when it was new. Now that I've driven it a couple of years, it certainly isn't worth more than $1,000.00. And he wants to pay me $10,000.00— this is too good to be true."

The next obvious thought undoubtedly is: "I don't know this man from Adam. I wonder if his check is any good." This thought would occur even to the most naive yokel under the circumstances. Even the average person would reason that whereas it is a wonderful deal on the face of it, if he turned the car and title over to this stranger, he would have lost his car and received nothing in return— if the check was bad.

So you turn to the stranger and say, "I would be glad to make the deal, but how do I know the check is any good?" And the stranger says to you, "Why, This check is good." So obviously you can't have any doubt about this check honestly being worth $10,000.00. Furthermore, there was my friend, John Smith, who will vouch that my check is good. He isn't here now, but he told me so yesterday. Then there is my brother and my father and my mother. They will all tell you that I am honest. So you see there is really no reason why you shouldn't turn over your car to me."

You are still not convinced. In fact, you are now more skeptical than

Nature's Eternal Religion

ever. You consider the evidence. The face of the check says in writing that it is a good check. But if the same man wrote it on the face of the check as signed it, the whole check is just as phony as if he had not written the additional blurb on it. Then there are those other people he mentioned as references. Now, if you, yourself, had talked to these other references, and they vouched for his Financial situation and his honesty, although it would not necessarily prove it to your satisfaction, it would certainly add some weight to the worth of the check. However, since they are not here for you to check with personally, all you really have is the same man's word that those references would vouch for him. In summing up the evidence, the signed check, the writing on it, saying it is a good check, the references vouching for the man's honesty are all dependent on the same source. If he is dishonest the check is no good, the writing on it is worthless and the witnesses are fictitious.

However, at this point you don't necessarily throw such an obviously good deal out of the window. You would love to make such an enticing deal where you would get $10,000.00— for a car worth only $1,000.00. You are being shrewd. You are suspicious of the wonderful offer, but you don't know that his check is bad either, and he may want your particular car for reasons that are immaterial to you. So rather than just drop the deal at this point you call the bank on which the check is drawn. The bookkeeping department tells you there is no such an account. Now you are reasonably certain that the man is a phony and even writing on the face of the check "This check is good," didn't prove a thing. You tell the man to be on his way and peddle his fish elsewhere. You used shrewd judgment Before you parted with your car you didn't take some stranger's word for it, written or verbal, that he was telling you the truth. You wanted outside sources. You wanted independent verification. You did not accept claims that went round and round in the same circle. Even the fact that you were talking to him face to face, here and now, was not sufficient proof.

Now, nobody wants to lose a car, because it is a thing of some value. But it can be replaced, and as it inevitably wears out in a few short years, it will be replaced. There are a lot of things that are more important than a car.

Certainly one of the most important is the course and direction of one's life, and there is nothing that shapes and warps that direction more decidedly than a man's upbringing and his religion.

When it comes to the particular religion a person anchors and polarizes his life around, it seems that less care and judgment is used than in buying or selling a car. In fact, probably less care and judgment is used than when buying a pair of shoes. Most people gravitate to some religious affiliation or other more by emotion or circumstance than having used one ounce of logic in arriving at their choice.

Practically all White people are associated, more or less, with some particular division of the Christian religion, or their parents were, or many of their friends are. In any case, their upbringing was, in some way or another, influenced by a Christian background. This overwhelming fact will shape their career, their environment, their marriage, their education, and particularly their attitudes and thinking throughout their life. Although they may not be particularly religious themselves, the full impact of the religious atmosphere shaping their life from beginning to end will generally not escape them.

Most White people, religious or not, (and most are not) will accept the myths, lies and stories set forth in the bible as being the truth, although they haven't taken the slightest pains to check any of the ideas, theories, philosophies or teachings against any hard evidence whatsoever. The bible, like the man with the check, keeps "verifying" itself. Peter claims that Paul said so and Paul says that Peter said so and that John said so and that Matthew said so and that James said so. However, all these people have been dead for a long, long time (if they ever lived at all) and nobody's uncle or great-granddaddy or great-grand uncle has personally had any contact with them.

Nor do any of these so-called "miracles" that so seem to fascinate us verify or check with any experiences that we have had, nor do they check with scientific facts, or scientific possibilities, nor do they check with experiences that other people have had. Nor do these "miracles" conform with the laws of Nature. It is all again a matter of it coming from the same source, the same book, vouching for itself and saying that so and so confirms it and so and so witnessed it, but it all comes out of the same pages.

Furthermore, they are pages that were written by people unknown and not necessarily even by the people whose names are attached to them. We know little or nothing about these people, except what the bible says. We don't even know if most of them lived at all. In any case, the writers are many and of unknown origin, and who knows who put the whole vehicle together? All we really know, is that it was collectively written by Jews, a people whose faculty for deception is unlimited.

We know for a fact that nobody in fighting some desert tribe could implore the "sun to stand still." This implies the earth would stand still on its axis for ten hours so that they would have more daylight within which to finish their bloody slaughter (Joshua 10:12).

When one considers the vastness of the earth and Nature's laws by which it rotates about its axis, such an idea is so idiotically ridiculous that its hardly worth considering. Yet this is what the "good (Jewish) book" says and this is what many people will blindly accept.

Nor has anybody in the last hundred years, or in the last thousand years or any other period of history, actually really witnessed a horde of people escaping through something like the bottom of the Red Sea, with those waters voluntarily parting to let them through, then collapsing upon their pursuing enemies. Nor has anybody seen any of dozens of other "miracles" happen that are so vividly described in the "good book." It is completely contrary to all the immutable laws of Nature. It is contrary to common sense, to any of the real life experiences that any one has witnessed. It is contrary to anything anybody else they can trust has told them they themselves have witnessed. Yet people will foolishly accept these kind of stories and readily become apologists in explaining in some circuitous fantastic way and torturing their reason in order to make it possible that "it could have happened," and, they will usually add that undoubtedly it did.

The fact of the matter is people today (as they have for thousands of years) are flooded by more myths, lies, untruths, than they are privileged with the truth. Unfortunately for the average person, it is not easy to discern and differentiate that which is a fact, that which is a lie, that which is truth and that which is a myth.

The crux of this chapter is that the White Race, the most intelligent creatures on the face of the earth, has been incredibly naive and gullible when it comes to accepting the collection of myths, lies and fables as set forth in the Jewish bible. Whereas in purchasing a house, for instance, they will insist on evidence— evidence of title, validity of the signatures on the deed, notarization of those signatures and even insist on a Policy of Title Insurance. Yet when it comes to their religion the same people will throw overboard every vestige of sense they were born with. Blindly and stupidly they will accept contradictions, bad advice, lies, violations of the laws of Nature, all in the name of "faith." Without checking who wrote these biblical myths, what is the evidence, does it seem reasonable, they completely abandon the judgment and the experience of a lifetime. They swallow wholesale this Jewish collection of myths, lies and bad advice, with the most disastrous consequences to themselves, to their children, and to their race.

Yet, to live is to make decisions, and in order to make decisions a person must come to conclusions. In order to arrive at good logical conclusions we must use valid evidence. The essence of good judgment is being able to sift and to weigh the information that is available to us, determine that which is valid and that which is not, and weigh the importance of each. This may not be easy, but it is essential. This subject is crucial, and we want to look into it further in the next chapter.

CHAPTER TWENTY-ONE

EVIDENCE, JUDGMENT, CONCLUSIONS AND DECISIONS

We have all heard a great deal and read much about court cases, and many of us have undoubtedly witnessed such cases being dramatized before our eyes. Most of us have undoubtedly seen such court scenes on television and some of us may even have been participants in real court cases.

In such cases we see a classic example of decision making in action. If it is a criminal case, the jury has to make a decision whether the alleged culprit is guilty or innocent. They are usually instructed by the judge that if the case has been "proved" beyond a shadow of doubt to charge the defendant as guilty.

Here is where we run into difficulty, for in the first place there is no such thing as "absolute proof." There is only evidence— and evidence comes in all shapes and forms. There may be scanty evidence, or there might be massive evidence. There might be overwhelming evidence, there might be fair evidence, there might be no evidence, there might be questionable evidence, there might be only hearsay or the evidence might be damning. It is in evaluating such evidence where the problem arises. Here is where good judgment comes into play.

It is extremely educational to hear the two sides of a case being argued by two competent, though usually less than completely honest, attorneys. After one side has made a fervent and eloquent presentation, paraded all their witnesses and overwhelmingly "proven" their side, we are convinced that this is the way it is. Now, however, comes the other side. The opposing attorney is equally glib, equally eloquent, and equally persuasive. He, too, has an impressive array of witnesses all confirming their side of the story. So who is right?

It is here that the intelligent and discerning jury or judge must sift and weigh each piece of evidence, the plausibility and character of the witnesses involved, the relative weight and importance of each piece of evidence presented. Furthermore, he must, like a detective, put all the pieces of the puzzle together and weight this in the balance against his own experiences and his

Nature's Eternal Religion

own judgment and then come to a conclusion, or better still, come to many conclusions, all of which gathered together are finally solidified in reaching a decision.

It is similar throughout the entire journey of life. A person is forced to make decisions constantly, some petty, some important and some that are of such major importance that they will determine the future course of the rest of one's life. The process is very similar to what we have already described in the court case in reaching these decisions.

Probably the worst situation to be in is to be confused and undecided. Some people arc perpetually confused and undecided in some areas, especially their religion.

The White Race is terribly confused about Christianity. The White Man's concepts are extremely hazy about the myriad of contradictory claims and bad information foisted upon him by this tricky religion. On most questions, he has not thought it through nor has he seen through this hoax. He has reached no conclusion, no decision.

As long as a person is undecided about a vital question, he is confused. He remains paralyzed from taking constructive action on such vital question or problem. He remains stymied and undecided. Not suspecting that Christianity has given him a mass of bad information, the average White Man remains confused and paralyzed on this issue for the rest of his life— a most miserable position to be in. Remember, confusion is a paralyzing poison. To remain in a state of confusion is to be de-activated, to be doped.

We cannot escape making decisions. Even to avoid making a decision is a decision in itself and the results can be just as disastrous as making a bad decision. Let us imagine, for instance, you're speeding along on the highway at 60 miles an hour and suddenly a slow truck pulls in ahead of you from a side road. Whether you like it or not you are faced with a decision. Either you can slam on the brakes, if that is what your judgment tells you to do in order to avoid hitting the truck, or you can swerve to the side and probably run into the ditch, or you can avoid making any decision at all and just keep on going and slam headlong into the rear of the truck. In the latter case, avoiding making a decision was a very drastic decision indeed, and a very disastrous one.

So it is throughout life. Decisions are thrust upon us daily and we cannot avoid making them. Therefore, it behooves us that we become adept at making decisions, and most preferably, making good decisions. In fact, the mark of a man of good judgment is one who can, of course, make good decisions. Not only is it a mark of good judgment, but it is also a mark of good character for a man to be able to make decisions, preferably good decisions, and stick with them and carry them out.

In making good sound judgments and correct decisions nothing is more important than having good evidence and good information. This is the essence of good decision-making. Of course, if, in each case where we were forced to make a decision, we had all the evidence that could possibly be obtained, and if all the evidence was absolutely correct and undisputed, then, decision-making would be relatively easy. Unfortunately, however, this is not the way it happens in real life.

In most cases, unfortunately, the evidence and the information is rather scanty and incomplete. Much of it is unverified and unsubstantiated. Not only that, but in many cases it is conflicting and confusing. Let's take the case, for instance, of a young man, as he grows up. He reaches an age where he must make a decision about what career he will train for and pursue. There are, of course, endless factors to be considered. There are factors of whether or not he would like that kind of work; whether or not his capabilities and talents lie in that line; whether or not the remuneration would be adequate for the standard of living to which he would like to become accustomed; whether or not world conditions might change so that his trade, avocation or profession might suffer a drastic change; and so on. No matter how exhaustively he studies each one of these different questions, and tries to pursue each path to its bitter end, presumably, he will never have all the information and all the conclusive evidence needed to make an absolutely infallible decision.

The same thing would be true in making the decision as to whom he is going to choose for his mate when he decides to get married. He could, of course, spend the rest of his life sifting, weighing and pursuing further details of evidence to help make up his mind and finally die of old age and a bachelor in the process.

And herein lies the true secret of decision making, that is: to know what information to seek, what evidence is important, what evidence is plausible and what is not, when to pursue the search further for more evidence and details, and when to decide that sufficient evidence is on hand to make an intelligent judgment and upon that judgment to come to a decision.

Undoubtedly, in many cases, as for instance the truck in the path of your speeding car, you cannot wait forever to make a decision with the evidence at hand. In some cases, on the other hand, hasty decisions are made when they need not be made at all at that time. A person might easily have waited and not burned their bridges, instead leaving options open, depending upon the unraveling of further events.

A suggested guide, therefore, in decision-making is:
1) Don't let a decision be made for you by default, since in some cases, time is of the essence and a decision must be reached within a specified time. In such cases it is much better to make a decision,

even though there may be danger of making a wrong decision, than making no decision at all. There are many times in our life when the worst decision we could have made is to have defaulted by making no decision. Therefore, make your own decisions, or someone else will make them for you.

2) Decisions should be based on evidence, the best possible evidence you can obtain. They should not be based on garbled thinking or wishful thinking.

The fact that the majority is agreed on the acceptance of a certain concept should not influence our decisions. The majority has been (and is today) wrong about many things. For instance, in the middle ages most of the people of Europe believed that the world was flat, not round. The majority believing so did not make it flat. It was just as round then as it is now. The overwhelming majority was just simply wrong. They are mistaken today about many other things— including the Jews and about Christianity.

Even in matters of the emotions, such as love, marriage, hate, preference, these, too, are pieces of evidence and should be weighed and analyzed with the same objectivity as any other evidence. Honest emotion is also a factor in decision-making. There is a vast difference between making a decision on what your emotions are about something, and basing a decision merely on the fact that you don't have a hunch or a feeling that such and such is so when you really don't have any information or reason to back it up.

Insist on all the cold hard evidence that you can get about a question. Don't settle for unfounded hearsay, stories, myths and even outright lies. Herein lies the important criterion— being able to differentiate between substantiated facts and those that have, many times, generally been accepted as facts, but are really based on myth.

Be able to distinguish in your own mind that which you know, and that which you believe, but don't really know. It is remarkable how many people cannot distinguish one from the other, confuse one with the other, and make decisions as readily on the basis of things that they don't know as they do on things that they do know. Again the significant criterion is evidence. It is a matter of distinguishing between fact and fancy, reality and unreality. It is therefore of tremendous importance to draw a clear distinguishing line between that which is a presumption, an allegation or a commonly accepted belief on the one hand, and a firmly substantiated fact on the other hand.

We, of the CHURCH OF THE CREATOR, deem reality as a thousand times more important than the realm of fantasy as a basis for our conclusions and decisions.

In attempting to make judgments about religions, past and present; in finding better ways and means of spreading Creativity; in making decisions in life in general; and especially in pursuing the fight for the survival of our race, we might do well to keep these ground rules in mind.

CHAPTER TWENTY-TWO

MY OWN SPIRITUAL AWAKENING

My parents were members of the Mennonite religion, a Protestant sect originating in Holland during the middle 1500's. This faith was founded by a man named Menno Siemens, who, like Martin Luther, broke away from the abuses of the Catholic religion of that time, and was originally a Catholic priest.

The Mennonites were severely persecuted by the ever-loving and broadminded Christians of the times, both the Catholics and the Lutheran Protestants. As a result, a large number of them were dispersed to several of the neighboring countries, some settling for a while and then being driven further again. My ancestors originally came from Holland, and then moved to Prussia, where they settled for several generations. Due to hostility from the government, a large group of these moved into the unsettled area of the Ukraine, Russia. The year was 1804. There, like many pioneers that settled the West, my ancestors pioneered the wild steppes of Russia. Within a generation or two they were doing well and were becoming rather prosperous in comparison to the Russian peasants. By the beginning of World War I this particular small colony had grown to 58 small towns comprised of about thirty thousand souls.

They were a hard working and frugal type of people, intensely religious. They took good care of their own. By the beginning of World War I they had become an extremely prosperous island in a rather backward sea of peasants in that part of Russia. Their farms, their standard of living, their general well-being, and their educational level, was far above that of the Russians themselves. The Mennonites kept their native German language, they ran their own schools, and neither fraternized, socialized, nor intermarried with the Russians. In fact, they would no more think of marrying a Russian than the White Man in America would think of marrying a nigger.

Their prosperous and peaceful existence was shattered with the Russian revolution when a hellish reign of terror burst loose upon them. They hardly knew what hit them. Suddenly they were overrun by the revolution, were pulverized, robbed and looted. Many of them were murdered. Like millions of

My Own Spiritual Awakening

other Russians, many of my people starved to death in Stalin's brutal program of forced famine. One of my own earliest recollections of this time is hunger and starvation.

By 1924 the situation stabilized somewhat and my father decided to take advantage of the situation to migrate.

We moved to Mexico. I think things were a little too wild for my mother there and just too uncivilized. In any case, by the end of 1925 we moved to Herschel, Saskatchewan, Canada, where some of my dad's relatives had preceded us by a year.

I started going to public school that winter. I was eight years old. We were pretty destitute and my clothing situation was less than adequate. As I remember it, I nearly froze to death that first winter. On top of that I couldn't speak a word of English. Things were rather rough.

Nevertheless, by the time I was twelve I had learned to speak English fluently and I had finished the first eight grades.

Mennonites as a whole are quite religious. I personally was brought up in a fairly religious home and received a rather thorough grounding of bible studies at Sunday school. The Mennonites had no sooner settled at Herschel, when one of their first acts was to build a community church. We went to it regularly.

My mother's religious influence upon me was strong and I was somewhat troubled by the ideas of heaven and hell, but not overly so. In my thirteenth year I had the opportunity to go to a German English Academy away from home, where I took the tenth grade. Besides taking all the full regular tenth grade curricula we were loaded down with extra German language subjects and religious instruction.

It was at this time that my religious thinking began to crystallize somewhat.

One of the things that I particularly remember from this period is a nineteen-year-old fellow student who was taking the eleventh grade. He told me that he had been quite a rousing reprobate and sinner in his teenage years, but now he had gotten religion. He told me that he was now converted, and not only that, but he was born again, and gee, wasn't it all wonderful. As these newly converted sinners always do, he did his utmost to try and have me converted also. I strongly resisted his effort.

The thing that he was particularly stressing was how wonderful it was, what great peace of mind he now had since he was born again in Christ, etc. Since he lived just a door or two down the hall in the same dormitory as I did, I had plenty of opportunity, of course, to observe his activities during the entire school year.

It soon began to appear to me that he did not have nearly as much peace of mind as he professed to have. In fact, it seemed like he had a lot more worries on his mind than did the rest of us. I observed that throughout almost the entire day his conscience was being racked by the question of sin.

I remember particularly one cold blustery Canadian winter night, at about one o'clock in the morning, his conscience began to get the best of him. The story came out that during the day he had told some friends, to whose house he had been invited, that he brushed his teeth up and down. As he lay in bed, his conscience began to nag him. He had lied to them. He really brushed his teeth crosswise.

So heavy did this weigh on his conscience that he got up in the middle of the night, jammed open the icy double storm-windows, crawled out, and walked two miles to his friend's home in the middle of the night. There he rapped on the door, and awakening them out of their sound sleep, confessed to them that he had told them this dreadful, shameful lie.

This episode, among many others, did not at all convince me that these so-called born again Christians went around with more peace of mind than did any of the rest of us. On the contrary, it convinced me that they were guilt-ridden and conscience-stricken over trifles. I observed further that they were encumbered with a series of mental blocks in their normal thinking that severely interfered with their solving the problems of the day.

From there on out my interest in religion became less and less personal and more and more academic. When I was seventeen I first entered the University of Saskatchewan. One of the subjects that I studied that first year was Ancient History, covering most of the older civilizations. It was during this period that it became clear to me that there were a vast number of religions other than Christianity on the face of this earth. I realized that many had come and gone, and thousands of varieties of religion were still floating around today.

It began to put Christianity in a different perspective. It seemed to me that Christianity was just another man-made religion, albeit one of the major religions.

I began to look at the concepts of Christianity from a more analytical point of view, i.e. just what did it say, just what were some of its ideas and what evidence was there to substantiate these claims. Nevertheless, for me religion remained for decades an unresolved puzzle. For a long time thereafter I pursued the normal course of getting an education, getting married, and establishing myself in a business. Religion as such was of minor importance and I seldom ever went to church. I never did join the Mennonite church.

When I was in my middle thirties I was somehow influenced to join a

Presbyterian church and began to attend somewhat more regularly, although with very little enthusiasm. The fact was I was immensely bored in church and could hardly wait to get out after hearing the same nonsensical platitudes repeated over and over again, ad nauseum.

One day I discussed with my minister some of my ideas about religion and some of the questions I had in my mind. I told him that the whole thing didn't make much sense to me. In the first place if God was such a loving God, why is it that he would create all these millions of people who according to the rules and regulations laid down in the bible, by and large, were all going to go to hell. I told him the whole thing seemed absurd to me. He was one of these liberal preachers also in his middle thirties at the time.

What he told me came as a surprise to me. He said he had no way of answering that question, and if that was my belief, I should stick with it. He confessed that he was pretty unsure about the whole thing himself. Not much to my surprise, a few years later he left the ministerial profession and began to earn an honest living.

In the early 1960's, then living in Florida, I became more and more concerned about the shameful way in which this country was being destroyed by the Jewish-communist conspiracy. When I was twenty years old I had already read Adolf Hitler's Mein Kampf. I was well aware of the Jewish role in the communist conspiracy, but like most Americans, I was occupied with taking care of my business activities and taking little or no part in the political affairs of the country, abdicating those to the scoundrels and the traitors. Nor did I know any activity or organization that I could turn to in order to do something, despite the fact that now I was becoming most desperately concerned.

It was at about this time that I first heard of the John Birch Society. I understood that they were "fighting communism." After spending five dollars sending for an introductory packet and reading their literature, I decided to join.

For six years I labored assiduously and energetically within the confines of the John Birch Society before it began to dawn on me what the real nature of the Society was. In any case, I recruited dozens of members; for several years I headed up a speaker's bureau sponsored by the Birch Society; I even opened an American Opinion Bookstore which sold, distributed and promoted books sponsored by the Society. In order that I could devote more time to this activity I even closed up my real estate business. In 1966 I was impatient with the Society's program of "education is our only weapon" and I ran for the State Legislature.

It was at this time that I began to notice that something was curiously wrong with the Birch Society. Instead of wholeheartedly supporting somebody who openly came out as a Birch member and ran for public office, I noticed instead their support was going to some phony that wasn't even a member and whose program would lead them down a dead end street. I furthermore noticed that the Birch members were the most pessimistic of all my supporters in prognosticating my chances of being elected. When I did get elected, they were the first to throw cold water on the event by coming up with such lame rationalizations as, well anybody could have done it in this election year, and it was probably a fluke, etc.

When I got to the Florida State Legislature and began to propose some radical opposition to the Jewish controlled Supreme Court and other matters, the Republican Party, on whose platform I had run, turned solidly against me and in the ensuing fight that developed I received next to no support from the Birch Society itself. It was at this time that the Supreme Court ordered a reapportionment election. In the next go-around I was defeated.

My multitude of labors and strenuous efforts had accomplished little, both in the political activity and in the framework of the Birch Society. I came out of it, however, poorer in the pocketbook, but richer in experience.

I had learned two things: (a) that it is impossible to accomplish anything within the framework of the old political parties, and (b) that the John Birch Society was a phony.

However, I continued to stay in the Birch Society for some time thereafter, with the feeling that perhaps I was at least doing some good. The more I looked into it though the more it began to dawn on me that the whole Society was a smoke screen for the Jews. It began to become clear to me that their whole effort was designed to scatter the efforts of their members on a myriad of ineffective projects, keep them busy, keep them paying, but never, never let them so much as get to the root-cause of it all— the perfidious international Jewish network.

In 1969, after six years, I sent in my resignation to Robert Welch, the founder of the Birch Society, and demanded back my $1000.00 life membership that I had so foolishly given them a few years earlier. Of course, the chances of this Jewish outfit refunding my thousand dollars were next to nil. Instead I got a many paged letter from Welch giving me a lot of double talk and what a big mistake I was making in accusing the poor little innocent Jew of being behind this whole big communist conspiracy.

This was a rather important turning point in my life. Whereas I had been somewhat aware of the whole Jewish conspiracy for most of my life, I had been diverted by the Birch Society and had pushed those ideas into the background. Now I began to realize that the Birch Society itself was just another Jewish program to confuse the White people regarding both the cause of the conspiracy, and the cure thereof. I realized that the Society was something like a research group pretending to find the cause of yellow fever. Every time the researchers came to the inevitable conclusion that it was carried by the mosquito, the Top Brass would protect the mosquito, throw out the researchers, and start out all over again with a new team.

Now I began to realize that the whole basis of this age-old struggle was race. It was the Jewish race using all the weapons at its command, and it did have a huge arsenal to destroy, mongrelize and enslave the mongrelized product of the White Race.

At this time I had not yet suspected that their most powerful weapon of all was their skillful use of Christianity on the White Race.

I decided to form a new political party polarized around the issue of the White Race. This I did, and formed the Nationalist White Party.

I had the immediate hostility of the Birch Society, which did not at all surprise me. What did surprise me now was I found that the strongest opposition came not from the Jews (as I had expected) but from the Christians. Every time we would discuss the issue of race, somehow or other Christianity and Christian principles would crop up so that in the end we wound up in a hassle about religion rather than trying to get down to the basic issue of the struggle against the Jews. This despite the fact that I had taken a pro- Christian stand. Continually I was told that the Jews were God's chosen people; that the niggers, too, were God's creatures; that racial discrimination was un-Christian, that "our Savior" was a Jew, the bible said "I will curse them that curse thee, and bless them that bless thee," etc., etc.

This was a surprising new development. Whereas up to this time, I had regarded Christianity as something rather innocuous, and perhaps a time-consuming nuisance, it now suddenly hit me like a bolt out of the blue that Christianity was one of the most powerful weapons that the Jews had in their arsenal.

Now I began to study the bible all over again and particularly focused on the Sermon on the Mount. To my surprise I found that it contained nothing but real bad, suicidal advice. Whereas before, I had heard and read all the bits and pieces of it, it had never occurred to me to examine what this kind of advice would do to a nation and to a race. Now I began to realize that such suicidal advice as "turn the other cheek," "love your enemies," "sell all that thou hast and give it to the poor," "judge not lest ye be judged," and "resist not evil," was real suicidal advice.

I now dug deeper into it and I found that the so-called Apostles, as well as the man purported to be Christ himself, were all of Jewish origin. Strangely, though, they had never sold their suicidal ideas to the Jews— on the contrary, they had sold it to the greatest civilization of ancient times, namely the Romans.

Then a lot of other things began to fall into place. Looking at Roman history it became clear to me that whereas Rome had established a great civilization, had conquered the world, was completely supreme, that when

Christianity hit it like a plague, it began to crumble and fall apart. And after studying the underlying suicidal ideas that Christianity had perpetrated upon the Romans, I could easily understand why the Romans no longer cared to defend their Empire, nor to meet their earthly responsibilities. It became clear to me why the whole great White Empire disintegrated under the influence of this new Jewish poison.

I now felt like an excited detective who unexpectedly had stumbled on the greatest mystery, the most sinister conspiracy in the history of mankind. I began to look more and more towards the eternal laws of Nature for the solution. I began to study the Old and the New Testament with feverish and renewed interest. I studied the history of the races— the great White Race, the Jews, the niggers.

I traced the rise and decline of civilizations. Like a detective, I began to feel that all the pieces, at last, were beginning to fall into place.

The more I dug into this, the more all the mosaic pieces began to fit together. I began to get a multitude of answers to questions that had eluded me throughout my life. Studying Nature's laws, studying religions and studying history and adding this to the experiences of my own lifetime, I found that I had finally made a breakthrough. My search had been rewarded by a multitude of answers— including the big one— namely, what is our purpose in life.

The more I studied the Jewish plague, Christianity, religion, and the laws of Nature, the more compelling the solution thrust itself upon me. I suddenly realized that I had achieved a devastating breakthrough that was sweeping in its implications, compelling in its simplicity, and so overwhelmingly obvious that I wondered why I hadn't seen the picture a long time ago.

It became abundantly clear to me that what the White Race needed was a completely new approach to the whole problem of extricating itself from the sinister Jewish conspiracy. And in order to get this new approach it seemed overwhelmingly clear that what the White Race really needed was a new religion, a new philosophy of life and a new Weltanschauung. It also occurred to me that my whole life experience had taught me and prepared me to do this fundamental job, namely, of formulating the new religion that was so necessary to the survival of the White Race. It also became overwhelmingly clear to me that to found a new party based on race while trying to coexist with Jewish Christianity was impossible. Every weapon that we needed in such a struggle was already undermined and neutralized by the basic concepts of Christianity itself.

I began to discuss my ideas with friends. In short order, it seemed that they too could see the picture when it was laid out to them. Even some former "born again" Christians, to my surprise, did a complete turn about, and became exceedingly hostile to the Christian religion with which they had been duped

My Own Spiritual Awakening

and were won over wholeheartedly to the doctrine of loyalty to their race.

I argued and debated with Christian preachers. To my further surprise, I found them completely at a loss to explain he numerous basic questions I threw at them, and usually they became hopelessly trapped in their own set of lies.

I corresponded with former Kosher Konservative friends of mine and they, too, either conceded my position on Jews and Christianity, or were hopelessly driven to the wall.

It was then I decided to compile my creed into a book. I decided to formulate a new religion for the White Race that would lead it out of the quagmire of Jewish entrapment, out of despair and

degradation, and into the bright light of greatness, to the heights of the wonderful destiny that Nature herself, in her great wisdom, had destined for this magnificent race.

CHAPTER TWENTY-THREE

GUIDEPOSTS ALONG THE PATH OF LIFE

No matter which way we turn today, we are engulfed by the influence of the all-pervading mass media, pounding in upon our minds. Especially with the advent of television, the White people of America are artificially flooded with an avalanche of suggestions and advice. Add to this the tremendous amount of indoctrination and brain pollution our young people receive during kindergarten, elementary school, high school and university, it is no wonder that confounded and bedeviled as the present generation is, it knows neither the purpose nor the meaning of their whole lives, nor do they even know their own identify. They don't know who they are, they don't know where they are going, they don't know what to do, and they don't know what their life's purpose really is.

Lacking purpose and direction, they are easily led by the nose into some hare-brained "cause" which serves neither them, nor their own people.

The trouble with all the "education" and advice that the younger generation of today is getting is that it is mostly all bad, and it is meant to be bad. Their brains are purposely being polluted by the Jewish network, which has complete control of education, as well as the propaganda apparatus. Despite all the filthy bedraggled longhaired hippies we see on the roads, in the parks, and all over the country today, most of these young people are inherently good, and would like to have some meaning in their life.

They are more to be pitied than censured, and are really victims rather than culprits.

They are a lost generation because they have been robbed of their most meaningful purpose in life which Nature has in store for each generation. What this young generation is looking for today, as they always have, is a meaning in life, something they can dedicate themselves to with the enthusiasm and the zeal that is such a wonderful thing in young people. They desperately need goals, they need direction, and they need worthwhile ideals. Without these a person is like a ship at sea: without a rudder and without a captain, aimlessly flapping its sails in the wind and subject to running aground on the First shoal that it encounters.

I would have given anything if, when I was a youngster, my father could have given me some of the advice that I have come by over a lifetime and only through the school of hard experience. How wonderful it would have been to have had from my earliest youth a sound basic philosophy that could have sustained and given me direction throughout my lifetime. Unfortunately, it was not until well after my 50th birthday that I had finally been able to realize the meaning and purpose of life. Unfortunately, most people can live to be 90 and go to their grave without ever having solved this important riddle.

How much more fortunate and how much more valuable it would have been to me if, during my college years, I would have had a thorough education on the detrimental Jewish influence on our civilization and its disastrous effect on the White Race, instead of receiving the usual run of liberal college education that I did, along with thousands of others. How much more meaningful it would have been to my life if, during my early boyhood years, instead of going to Sunday school and learning a rehash of all the old Jewish shibboleths, I would have been told about Racial Loyalty, and where my duty lay.

I therefore feel myself obligated to address first and foremost the young people in the teenage group, who are just starting out in life and are in their most impressionable years, in a period when their direction is most easily influenced either for the good or for the bad.

First of all, I would like to address myself to those young boys who are just entering high school and have the whole wide world before them— a world they can easily conquer, or a world that will cruelly crush them.

One of the first things I would suggest to you is that you take stock of your abilities. Find out what your I.Q. is and try to analyze yourself as to where your best abilities lay. Start seriously thinking about what you want to be in life. Whether or not this is what you finally do become is beside the point. Whether at present you make it your goal to become a professional baseball player but later turn out to be a businessman instead— that is perfectly all right.

The fact is that my own goals and objectives as a teenager ran through many stages. I remember that when I was twelve I wanted to be a professional baseball player like Babe Ruth. When I was fourteen I wanted to be a cowboy and have a ranch. When I was sixteen I wanted to be a boxer. When I was eighteen I wanted to be a movie star, a schoolteacher, a lawyer, and finally an engineer.

I did become a schoolteacher and an electrical engineer. In fact, I even invented an electric can opener and received several patents on it, but it so turned out that my lifelong calling was in the real estate business.

Now I don't suggest that you change your goals and objectives as much as I have, but the point that I am making is that it is of utmost importance that you have a goal, or goals, before you, goals that you set that you want to conquer and that you want to strive for at all times. Not only must you have goals, but they must be good, worthwhile goals, rather than some far-off idiocy like saving a few whooping cranes that might be left, or jumping on the bandwagon of some phony Jewish mania of the moment.

In order for your goal to be worthwhile it should be something that you feel you would like to do, and something that you feel would be useful in your earning a good living for yourself and supporting a family that you undoubtedly will have later. You should also think in terms of what you can do to make some meaningful and lasting contribution to your own people, namely the White Race, something that will be of lasting benefit and an eternal credit to you personally. Remember that Nature put you on this earth so that you will be a link, an important link, in the perpetuation of your own species, your own race, namely the White Race.

I would further suggest that you enjoy yourself while you're young, as in fact, you should do throughout your whole life. Regardless of all the Jewish suggestions that are thrown your way regarding some of the baser amusements, I would suggest that you will find your greatest enjoyment in the exploration of Nature, in hiking the mountains and fording streams, in fishing and in boating, and in camping in the forests.

I would also suggest that you engage vigorously in the field of sports and become as proficient as you can in several of them, whether it be swimming, or tennis, or whatever you might be interested in. If you are interested and proficient in several at the same time, all the better. It is some of the finest training you can receive. It is always good to remember that a sound mind can usually only exist in a sound body, and that it is as important to keep your body clean and strong and healthy, as it is to keep your mind exercised in intellectual learning.

It is also important to learn to box and to fight and to defend yourself in the hostile and torn world through which you will undoubtedly have to fight your way. It is a good idea to become proficient in the use of firearms and guns and become an excellent shot. You may some (lay have to defend your home and your street from a band of marauding niggers, rioting and on the rampage. You might have to resist by force of arms a Jewish takeover, as happened in Russia.

Learn to appreciate good music and to distinguish good music that has stood the test of ages from the rash of trash that is dished up to you through the Jewish radio networks, records and television, ad nauseum. Learn to hate the niggerized bang-bang of jungle noise that is now becoming so common, noise that is completely devoid of melody, harmony and devoid of beauty. Be vocal and outspoken about making your preferences and dislikes known. As in all things, learn to distinguish the good from the trash. Learn to distinguish good art from bad, good literature from trash and pornography that is becoming so common these days.

Not only is it good to become discriminating in music, in art and in literature, but above all, be discriminating in your choice of friends. Associate only with those that will be an inspiration to you towards higher goals and greater achievements. Don't waste your time with those that would drag you down to their low level.

The Jewish bible has told us for so many centuries that we should be meek and humble. I say that this is completely wrong and completely contrary to Nature. Anyone who achieves anything in life must have pride of accomplishment. Pride and confidence in one's self is one of the first prerequisites in winning distinction and becoming a success.

Therefore, first of all take pride in yourself in what you are, in what you think you can become, and in what you think you can do. Take pride in your dress and in your grooming. Be neat and clean and tastefully dressed no matter what you happen to be dressed for. Take pride in your speech, in keeping it clear and cultivated and articulate. Take pride in your family. Be proud of your achievements without being arrogant, and develop the desire to excel, the desire to win. Take pride in your hometown. Above all take pride in your race, be proud to be a member of the great White Race which you have the great good fortune to be a part of, and will bear the responsibility of perpetuating in the future.

In your studies and in the decisions you make, in the activities that you choose, learn to distinguish between what is important and what is trivial. Waste no time with the trivial. Give a great deal of time and attention to that which is important. It is amazing how many people have never learned this one important fact in their lifetime.

The ability to distinguish the important from the trivial, and act thereon, more than any other one thing is the outstanding characteristic of a successful man.

Next, my dear young friend, I would advise you to dream big dreams. You have your whole lifetime ahead of you and at this stage your abilities and potentials are completely unknown, untapped and untested. Remember, Nature created you as a member of the great, proud White Race. You are endowed with the highest intelligence, finest reasoning powers that Nature in her wisdom has seen fit to give to any of its millions of creatures. Use the intelligence that Nature gave you, use those reasoning powers, and above all, use your common sense, which is really not at all so common.

Not only has Nature bestowed upon you, as a member of the White Race, the Finest intelligence, but Nature has also made you the most creative and the most productive creature on the face of the earth. I say, therefore, put all that creativity, intelligence and productivity to work for yourself, for the family that you will undoubtedly later found, and for the benefit of the great White Race that produced you.

Dare to dream big dreams— dare to be great. At your age your potentialities are untapped and unknown. Who knows what a great niche history might have waiting for you in its future pages? Remember that besides ability, the main ingredients of greatness are purpose and perseverance. Above all, have confidence in your self. If you don't, nobody else will.

With these thoughts in mind there is no limit to the great things you can accomplish, and you undoubtedly will.

* * *

Advice to Boys of College Age

If you are approximately around the age of 20, you are at a crossroads where you will have to make many decisions which will irrevocably shape the pattern for the rest of your life.

One of the first things that a boy just having finished high school has to decide upon is whether or not he is going to go to college and get a college education, and if so, what profession or avocation should he pursue. Also, by now he has found out about girls and is probably deeply involved in a love affair. The thought of marriage has undoubtedly crossed his mind by now, or at least it should have.

Let's take these items one by one. First of all, let's talk about college educations.

I personally not only went to college and earned two college degrees, one in Arts and Science and the other a Bachelor of Science in Engineering, but I also obtained a Teacher's Certificate and taught school for two years, so I have some background in the educational field. Looking back on this 30 years later, it is my considered opinion that I wasted much of my time in the so- called halls of learning.

Much of the so-called knowledge that was dished out to me was trivial, and much of it was useless. Throughout his college years the young student has inculcated and impregnated into his impressionable mind many ideas that are not only wrong, but are outright harmful and dangerous to himself, to his country and to his race. These ideas, of course, are deliberately foisted upon him by the Jewish network in order that they may more easily destroy and enslave the White Race. It is not my purpose here to make a list of all the wrong premises and harmful ideas that were being disseminated in the colleges of my day and from what I can visibly see, it is much, much worse today. In fact to make a full catalogue of all the bad information and the poisonous idiocies with which our young people's minds are being polluted in the colleges today would take the bigger part of this book. This book is, in large part, all about undoing the damage that the Jews have done, not only in the colleges but also in all the other fields of activity in which they have perverted the minds of the White Race.

I would, therefore, say that college education, per se, has been highly overrated. In fact, our colleges are turning out a flood of over-educated fools who are too good to do an honest day's work, and not capable of fulfilling the jobs for which they mistakenly think the world will be begging them when they graduate. Most of such jobs neither exist, nor is there any need for them.

If a young man would have taken the same $15,000 to $30,000 investment that he spends (or his parents spend) on a college education, and used those same four, five or six years to get started in a meaningful business, in most cases, everybody would have been far better off.

If, therefore, you are not particularly a brilliant student, I wouldn't worry about it at all. College is not for everybody, by any means.

In fact, the Jews have dragged our colleges down into the muck and the mire to where they now have become centers for brain pollution rather than education. I would say that a great many more good kids are ruined in our present day colleges than get a positive benefit from them. This, too, the White Man must correct when he again assumes control of his own destiny.

If you are an outstanding student, and you want to pursue some profession like becoming a doctor, or a lawyer, or a teacher, or an engineer, then it is imperative that you go to college and obtain the required degrees, this in spite of the fact that you are subjecting yourself to a tremendous peril in having your mind polluted by an avalanche of false premises. However, if you have thoroughly studied this book and further studied the Jewish problem, and keep reviewing that knowledge at all times, you could not only become pretty well immune to Jewish propaganda, but you might even be able to help rescue some of your fellow classmates. In no case, however, should you forget that propaganda is a subtle and powerful tool and that if you will spend four or six years in the Jew-polluted "Halls of Learning" it will require a strong character and a firm purpose not to become contaminated with their filth.

Unfortunately, those people who lightheartedly dismiss the thought that they may be vulnerable, are usually the easiest victims. In any case, if you have read this book, you will be much, much better fortified than the average young man who ventures into this Jewish jungle of mind manipulation.

Therefore, I say that if you do go to college, go only because you have to have those degrees in order to pursue that profession about which you have already made up your mind.

If you haven't made up your mind as to what you want to become at this stage, I would suggest that you do not go to college. There are many tremendously successful businessmen that never did go to college. Some of our most outstanding multimillionaires like Henry Ford and H.L. Hunt, etc., never set foot in a college during their younger days. Even Thomas Edison, one of our greatest inventors, never went to college.

If you have no profession in mind, and book learning does not particularly appeal to you anyway, I would suggest that you forget about college, at least for the time being, and try to think of different lines of endeavor that you might be interested in. Think of the different types of businesses that there are and pick out some particular one, or ones, which you think you might become interested in being a part of.

Think of being in business for yourself someday, of owning your own business enterprise. If you really have something on the ball, have drive and ambition, there is no reason in the world why you can't have a large and flourishing business of your own before long.

The question is: How do you get into business? Undoubtedly, you can't just plunge into a business without money and without experience. No, of course you can't. Therefore, the way to start is to start at the bottom. Get a job, no matter how lowly it is, in the business you have zeroed in upon. While you are working at this, you will be doing several constructive things: You will be gaining experience; you will be earning a living for yourself; and you will also be testing yourself as to whether you have the ability and inclination for that particular type of business. It is remarkable how many young boys started out as a bus boy or a floor sweeper for a corporation and ended up being its president. But even if you never take over the particular business in which you learn the ropes, so as to speak, after you have acquired the basic experience and you have the determination, you can always leave that business and start a similar business of your own in a small way, building as you go along. For instance, the founder of many a large contracting and building business usually started out as a carpenter working for somebody else. Many an owner of a large and successful restaurant started out as a cook or a dishwasher as a kid working for somebody else. The owner of many a large real estate enterprise often started out as a green salesman working for somebody else. The owner of many a car dealership started out working as a car salesman for somebody else.

They say there are something like 32,000 different kinds of jobs and businesses that a person can engage in. Whether this figure is correct or not, I do not know, but I suspect that there are probably many more, actually. In any case, with today's tremendous expansion of specialization, there are more opportunities for ingenuity and resourcefulness than there ever were before. It is not at all true that the day of the self-made man is over. I say that opportunity was never better.

There are many satisfactions as well as a lot of responsibilities in owning your own business. It is true, you may work as hard, or harder, than if you worked for somebody else, but at least you know you're working for yourself, and I've always said that if you are worth a certain amount to somebody else, you are worth twice as much to yourself.

I have also worked for a large corporation. In fact, immediately after I graduated from electrical engineering I went to work for a large corporation in Montreal, a corporation that had somewhere around 10,000 employees scattered throughout the country. I was employed as an electronic engineer. It is my recollection and my experience that working for a large corporation is one of the worst things you could do. It has a tendency to stifle a man's imagination and ambition, not to mention his sense of independence.

In a following chapter, I am going to dwell more thoroughly on the advantages of being self- employed. Suffice it to say that the advantages are many, and the idea of security with a big corporation, which is the big lure for many a young executive- minded graduate from college, is a snare and a myth.

I would suggest that besides trying to become established in a business of your own, you start acquiring real estate, property and land as soon as you possibly can. More people have made money in land and real estate than they have in oil or any other business.

As I mentioned previously, if you are around the age of 20 you will undoubtedly be thinking of getting married, or at least you should be. If you have found the right girl I would say: don't waste too much time in getting married and getting established. Nature says that you are ready to start reproducing your own kind when you are 15 or 16 years old. The way our society is set up at this time, this does not seem too practical, but I would say that it is a travesty against Nature to prolong and delay this important stage in life for ten years after Nature said that you were mature and ready. If you are 20 and you are so inclined, I would say go ahead and get married, whether you are financially capable at that time or not It is amazing how responsible and capable a young man soon becomes when he gets married and is faced with the responsibilities of establishing his own household.

Undoubtedly, one of the most important steps in life that you will ever take, if not the most important step, is getting married. A good marriage is one of the most gratifying and one of the most meaningful actions that you will ever take in your life. You are thereby fulfilling the meaning and purpose of life for which Nature created you in the first place, namely that of perpetuating your own species and becoming a link in that long golden chain. It makes you the patriarch of a long line of descendants of thousands of real people who would never have lived at all if it hadn't been for you founding the line!

Think of it! Long after any material thing you may have done is completely obliterated, the line of human beings that you are responsible for will keep multiplying and marching on into history. Raising a family of handsome, bright, lovable and enthusiastic children is the most rewarding and enjoyable responsibility you will ever undertake in your life. The children you will raise will undoubtedly be the most significant and meaningful accomplishment of your whole life. In fact, when your life span has run its course and you come to reflect on the long and varied path of your years on this earth, you will find the children which are now multiplying into grandchildren, are not only your overwhelming and abiding interest, but the only real permanent thing that you will leave behind you when you depart from this world. The ramifications of your having founded a family and raising a number of children, who in turn will do likewise in their generation, is tremendous and unending. The offspring that will echo into the future untold generations is practically beyond comprehension. I therefore repeat, the most significant, meaningful and lasting thing that you will ever do is when you get marred and start raising a family. And may I say that in doing your part in promoting and propagating the White Race, have a good-sized family, have as many as you can.

In planning for your family and in planning for your business, think ahead. Set up goals. Think of where you want to be five years from now. Think of where you want to be, and what you want to be, ten years from now, twenty years from now, thirty years from now. Have a concrete plan of action, the more detailed the better. Set it down on paper. This will help to reinforce it in your mind and it will also be there to jog your memory to keep you on the track. Discuss these plans with your wife, if you are married. Determine to have the finer things in life for yourself and your family. Decide that you will have a nice home, live in a good neighborhood, and that you will lead the good life. Then go to work and accomplish it.

While you are doing so, enjoy yourself. Take vacations regularly. Plan to have hobbies and interests outside of your business. The White Race is going to have a tremendous fight on its hands in your generation to win back their own independence and wrest control of their destiny back into their own hands. Plan to participate in that great fight and do your part. One of the most important lessons you will ever learn in your life is not what the regular colleges would give you, but to learn the true nature of the Jewish conspiracy and what you can do about freeing the White Race from this overwhelming tragedy. It will be the most useful accumulation of knowledge that you will acquire in any field. Not

Guideposts Along the Path of Life

only will it help you in participating in the White Man's struggle, but it will help you in your business, it will help you in your family relations, and it will help you in the upbringing of your children.

Learn to become a good public speaker. In fact, this is something you should have already started learning and participating in when you were in high school. The benefits of being able to express yourself and to speak well in public are so beneficial from every aspect that no young man who wants to get ahead can afford to ignore this important part of his education.

Remember in your business activities and contacts to boycott the Jew and at all times, to favor your White racial comrades. Be discriminating and be loyal to your own race. Despite the fact that the Jew at present seems triumphant and the future may seem black, never become pessimistic. Things can change quickly and they can sometimes quickly change for the better.

Witness how quickly the situation changed in Germany. When the Germans were completely downtrodden and completely demoralized, a great leader came along and rallied the German people. They did overcome the Jew and they did gain control of their own destiny in short order. In no time at all where there had been poverty, hunger, discouragement, and tyranny, the country was suddenly changed into that of vibrant optimism, prosperity, order, productivity and creativity. All this was achieved through will, determination and a positive program. Therefore, I suggest that you keep a buoyant, enthusiastic and aggressive attitude towards your work, your projects and your enterprises at all times. Be optimistic, as well as realistic, and after careful preparation and planning, expect success. Be success minded. The old saying "If at first you don't succeed, try, try again," well applies here also.

Don't get suckered into the useless and debilitating habit of smoking or drinking, and of course, avoid like the plague the suicidal drug kick that the Jew is promoting so widely at this time. These drugs, whether they be tobacco, alcohol or the mind destroying drugs, are all Jew promoted, they're being promoted to destroy the White Race and at the same time make these scoundrels millions in profits. If, unfortunately, you are already well into one of these habits, make up your mind to get out of it, period.

I personally started smoking regularly when I was 26 years old, for no good reason that I can now remember. However, by the time I was 40 I came to the conclusion that it was a filthy, useless habit, one that really wasn't giving me any satisfaction and one that I could well do without I therefore decided one day to quit without any ifs or buts. Having made up my mind, I extinguished the last cigarette and have never touched another since. So it can be done. It just takes a firm resolve and once this has been achieved it is not really very difficult.

In any case, young man, you have now reached the stage where the twig has long been bent and some of the things that you now do are beginning to shape the permanent tree. I would suggest that you give full play to those great qualities with which the White Man has been blessed, namely creativity, daring, productivity, aggressiveness and a freewheeling spirit of adventure. At all times uphold your self-respect and your honor. Be a credit to the great White Race of which you are a part. Acting within the framework of those instincts with which Nature endowed you, you will lead the fullest and the most rewarding life possible.

* * *

We now come to the fair sex— that most beautiful of all creatures in Nature's realm. In suggesting advice to young girls of high school and college age I would say much that has already been given to the boys also applies to these young ladies, but there are several important differences. And it is these differences that I want to point out.

Such habits as neatness of dress, good grooming and, in general, presenting an attractive appearance is, of course, even more important to girls than to boys. After all, whereas it is desirable for boys to be masculine, capable, and handsome, girls on the other hand are the beautiful sex, in fact from a man's point of view, the most beautiful creature in Nature's universe. The caliber of man she will attract will therefore depend much on her natural beauty and also what she further does to enhance that natural beauty.

This, of course, she can do by keeping fit and trim, in good physical condition, keeping a good complexion, by following a wholesome diet, and other means. Not too many boys are attracted by a fat, slovenly looking girl.

One of the worst habits teenagers have developed these days is that of bad eating habits. Many bad complexions are directly a result of this. As far as being fat and overweight is concerned, there is really no good excuse for anyone to get into that shape. Whereas there are a few people who cannot gain weight, everybody, but everybody, can lose weight by just cutting down their eating to the point where they reach the desired weight Even fasting for a week at a time, if necessary, will not hurt anyone. In fact, it may do a lot of good.

Many of the items such as strength of character, not smoking, avoiding alcohol and drugs, apply equally to you girls and there is no need for me to repeat all these details. Your own good common sense will tell you what to do, and the important thing is to use your common sense.

This also applies in using care and discrimination in selecting your friends, whether they be boys or whether they be girls.

The main point of departure, however, from the advice that I have suggested to the boys is when it comes to the matter of choosing a career. In the present Judaized times, when the younger generation is so adrift, without ideals

Guideposts Along the Path of Life

or goals, it seems that one of the false goals that are thrust at you is that every girl should seek a career.

In stampeding every girl into higher education, going to college, spending years and years in doing that which is completely unnatural, namely cramming and stuffing volumes of useless information into their heads, you are not deriving benefits, but you are being banned.

The most rewarding, fulfilling and natural thing you can do is to become a mother and rear a family. Again Nature says that when you are 15 or 16 you are ready. Again, unfortunately, because of our present economic and social structure this may be a bit early for practical reasons. When a girl is 16, 17 or 18 years old, her love interest is at its peak and it is an abomination against Nature for her to spend the next five or six years going to college stuffing, for the most part, information into her mind that she will never again use and will, by and large, soon forget.

I am convinced that the present artificial obsession with college is part of the Jewish program to delay the marriage of young White couples, and thereby again cut down on the propagation of our race.

By means of all this flood of propaganda from movies, TV, magazines, etc., a young girl is given the impression that unless she has a career of her own, she is a failure. She gets the impression that it is better to have a career than a marriage, or that she can quite easily have both a career and a marriage.

Both of these premises are patently false.

If we look at some of these career women that have had even unusually successful careers, we find, by and large, that they lead rather strained, unnatural and unhappy lives. Many of them, as they become a little older, become increasingly aggressive and independent, and with their sexual drives either suppressed or perverted, soon become totally unfit as a marriage partner. If they are married and also have a career, the stress and strain of battling in a man's world makes them rather poor wives, and not only that, but poor mothers, if they have any children. Usually such women have few, if any, children. Anyway you look at it, a career for the woman has a damaging effect on her family life. It is bad for her, it is bad for her husband and it is bad for her children, if she has any.

Unfortunately at present, under the Jewish domination of our White society, due to high taxes and many other types of Jewish robbery, many White wives have to work to make ends meet.

But when the White Race is once again master of its own destiny and throws the Jews and niggers off its back, it will not be necessary for any White wife to have to go to work. She will be able to enjoy the natural role for which Nature created her— being a wife, a mother and a homemaker.

It is the man's duty and obligation to provide for the family, and it is a woman's privilege to take care of the home and raise her family.

It is therefore my considered suggestion to girls in this age group to keep the paramount goal in mind— that she will become a wife and a mother, that this is where her great good fortune lies, and not in a career. A girl would therefore do well to cultivate those studies and those pursuits that will help her in her future role as such, rather than pursuing higher mathematics, physics and chemistry. Along the lines that would make her more attractive as a wife and a future mother would be the study of music, the study of cooking, the study of good literature, the study of home decoration, developing a good taste in the lines of furniture,

clothes, art and entertaining. Of major importance in enhancing your desirability as a marriage partner is also the development of the social graces such as learning to sing, learning to become a good dancer, and most important of all having a cultivated manner of speech and being a good conversationalist. One of the finest assets either a boy or girl can have is being able to speak well and interestingly. Most of the things I have been talking about are not learned at college and do not require a college education as a prerequisite.

Many girls go to college with the idea that they are thereby going to have a better opportunity of catching a husband because they will be in the company of boys who are college students. They believe that they will thereby be able to select a better type of husband. This may or may not be true. If that is your purpose in going to college, however, be sure that you are honest with yourself, that you admit this is your purpose. Then go about the job with that objective in mind. Keep in mind also, however, that if you do go to college that the sane and sensible outlook on life that you entered college with may be seriously impaired. So, also, may your morals and your sense of direction be thoroughly confused by the profusion of Jewish propaganda that you are going to be engulfed with. It is a calculated risk you have to take and usually going to college for this purpose is a poor risk.

In general, I would like to add this for both the boys and girls: remember the prime purpose for which Nature placed you upon this earth— to propagate your own kind, your own species, to multiply and expand the White Race, to fight for that Race in the face of a hostile world, come what may. To do this means to get married, to raise a family and for the husband to earn a good substantial living. The more substantial the better.

And here I would like to point out another little piece of advice that is being trampled in today's rush of false meanings, and that is the much bantered slogan of today's youth, namely, that "money isn't everything." Of course, money isn't everything, but the implication seems to be that it is nothing, and this is not so. No matter how you slice it, the kind of income that the head of the house can bring home to his family is in large part the determining factor of many important things. It will determine the kind of neighborhood you live in, the type of house you have, the kind of clothes you wear and the quality of the food that you eat. It will decide the amount of time you can take off for traveling the world, the amount of time off you can take for amusements, for having fun and for recreation. So don't be fooled by this liberal line so many of these college kids are passing along to the effect that "money isn't everything," decrying "crass commercialism," and a lot of other similar nonsense. Most of these empty-headed fools come from an environment where they never had to do a lick of work. Were they thrown out on their own, and had to provide for themselves, they would find that the realities of life would soon shatter such nonsensical ideas in no uncertain terms.

In summary, I suggest that you be proud of your great good fortune to have been born a member of Nature's elite, her Crowning Glory, the great White Race. You have been endowed by Nature with many outstanding talents. After making a thorough assessment of your abilities, waste no time making the most of them.

Plan ahead. Set goals. Be confident, aggressive, creative, and constructive. Assert yourself. If you are sure of your ground, let yourself be heard from.

Dare to be great. Be idealistic, yet realistic and practical at the same time. Remember that as a young person, you have one precious asset that we older people cannot buy at any price—time. Make the most of it.

Above all, be proud of those wonderful White ancestors that produced you and made it possible for you to live at this exciting time in the history of our race. Vow that you will not only carry on your great White heritage, but that you will do your part in helping raise it to ever greater heights of excellence.

CHAPTER TWENTY-FOUR

THE ADVANTAGES OF BEING SELF-EMPLOYED

In the previous chapter I mentioned ways and means by which young people might get into business for themselves. I also mentioned some of the many advantages of being self-employed. Since this is rather a broad subject and involves more than just young people, I want to cover the ground a little more thoroughly in this chapter.

It is important in the White Man's struggle to regain control of his own destiny that he own and gain control of as many businesses as possible. At present the Jew overwhelmingly dominates the business field, as he does so many other nerve centers of power. I believe the advantages of controlling your own business have not been clearly pointed out to the White Man before, since most of the propaganda that we read is written by Jews. They know the importance of owning businesses, and far be it from them to encourage the White Man to go into competition with them any more than they can help it. Using deception to the utmost in both education and in propaganda, they keep talking about jobs only.

One of the attributes of having your own business is the healthier mental attitude that you thereby achieve. Certainly having your own business generates more pride and confidence in yourself than being an employee under the direction of somebody else. There is the story of the little old man who had a newsstand in some big city and spent practically all his time at that store. When asked why he spent so much time there he replied, "It is all mine and I can do as I please. I get more pleasure out of running my own little store than I do anything else. That's why I spend so much time here." When you build your own business you are in a way a creator, you are doing a creative job of building and fashioning a living organization that is not only productive, but also profitable. As the business expands and gets larger, there is a definite satisfaction attached to it that you are a productive and creative segment of our society. As a pillar of the community, in owning a business you carry a great deal of prestige and respect, something that you have justifiably earned.

Certainly the income you can make from building and expanding your own business is, in most instances, far superior to what you could earn by putting in the same amount of time and effort working for somebody else. I have always said that certainly you are worth twice as much to yourself than to the company you may be working for. Statistics show that the self-employed businessman certainly makes a much better income that the average employee, and in thousands and hundreds of thousands of cases the sky is the limit. Without a doubt your chances of becoming a millionaire working for someone else are very slim, whereas most businessmen that did become millionaires did so through owning their own business.

We hear so much about the advantages of working for a big corporation and one of those most frequently cited is the retirement pension that you might get when you have faithfully and dutifully worked for the company for the last forty years, and when at sixty- five you are finally put out to pasture. Living as I did in south Florida on the Gold Coast and witnessing a large number of retirees, I would say that the prospects awaiting you when you are retired from a large company are not nearly as rosy as many have assumed over all these years. For one thing, a man, as he gets older, likes to taper off in his working activities, but he does not necessarily want to quit altogether. When you work for a big company and you are approaching sixty or sixty- five, you are presumably in a high salary bracket. Therefore the company does not want to, nor can it afford to, have you slow down and produce less than you used to. In fact, because of your higher salary, they expect you to produce more than you did before and assume more responsibilities than ever.

Then finally comes the day when you reach sixty-five and you retire. The cutoff is sudden and drastic. Frankly, many businessmen who have been with a large company over the most active forty years of their lives find the sudden change quite a shock. It is not the rosy enchantment they had expected. To many it is a hard adjustment to make. In many cases they feel lost and don't know what to do with their time. Too often, shortly thereafter, instead of enjoying what they thought would be their golden years, their health fails and they die. In many cases the biggest contribution towards the failure of their health was the psychological change.

It is different if you have your own business. Most men who went into business on their own when they were in their early twenties will have built a substantial business in forty years, often in less than ten years. By the time they reach sixty they are usually wealthy and independent. They have their chain of command and management pretty well established so that they can come and go as they please, they can work as little, or as much as they want to, and their business carries on. Invariably they prefer to stay in the management of it long past the age of sixty or sixty-five, in fact many of them stay in it in their seventies and eighties and enjoy every minute of it.

Another advantage that self-employment provides is family stability. When you work for a large company, they seem to have a nasty habit of moving you every few years to a different plant somewhere across the country, thus uprooting you from your established home, from your friends and from the many contacts that you have established. This includes a break from your clubs, from the schools your children go to, from your home and many other long established contacts you have made. In the case of the established business, not only does the family have an opportunity to sink down roots in their own area, an area usually of their choice, but these roots are many times perpetuated for two or three and more generations.

Such stability is further reinforced by peace of mind that you need have no fear of being laid off. You are in charge and you are in control of your fortunes and your destiny. You do not have to be afraid of your boss hiring one of his relatives to replace you. You have peace of mind that you need not be a victim of political maneuvering or, that you may lose your job because somebody else, who wanted it, buttered-up the boss in your absence. When you own your business you are the boss and your job is whatever you make it and it lasts as long as you want it to. You can work at your own pace and you can shape your job so that your talents can be utilized to the best of their ability.

When it comes to taking vacations you have several advantages.

1) You can choose the time according to when you want to go.

2) You can expand it to whatever length you want.

3) You can take as many as you want throughout the year, providing of course that you are still taking good care of your business.

4) You can plan your vacations in such a way that they can be written off as a business expense. For instance, you might want to go to Hawaii and set up a dealership there, or establish a business outlet, or negotiate a deal. In any case, the opportunity to mix business with the kind of vacation you want is almost unlimited. Not only can vacations be treated in this way, but in many cases you can also combine recreational activities with your business. For instance, you might want to join a yacht club or a country club and charge it off as a business expense. This you might be able to do because you might be utilizing such memberships as a valuable means of establishing business contacts.

Another gratifying advantage of having a business of your own is that you can very often train your own children to take over the management and thereby transfer to the next generation, namely your own children, the family business, while you yourself, nevertheless, still keep an active hand in the control of it. Thereby, it becomes a family enterprise that you can see growing and expanding, something that is perpetuated into future generations. This can be a most rewarding satisfaction indeed. By so doing, you establish closer family ties and a wider community identity. You have the assurance that upon your death your business will not be usurped by some grasping Jew, but will already be firmly in the hands of your children, who have, over the years, been trained in its management

By owning your own business you can make many contributions to your community. You can establish scholarships, you can sponsor a boy's "Little League" baseball team, you can pursue research in technology in certain lines that interest you, or you can pursue any other of a dozen different outlets.

Financially, you are flexible in so many different ways that you are not in a salaried job. Should we have a drastic inflationary rise, the value of your business, the real estate that it is on and buildings all increase accordingly. As your business progresses you are continually building up the equity of the business itself, something that is not necessarily subject to the confiscatory income tax that wages and salaries are plagued with.

In many other ways your position is much more flexible. You can sell your business if you want to, should that become desirable; you can borrow money on it; many times you can lease it and still keep it; or you can will it to your children, or anybody else, for that matter, if you should so desire.

Many successful businessmen have sold their business to some huge corporation, for millions. They have then been given the management of it at a handsome salary. However, I don't particularly recommend this, since the buying company is probably in the hands of Jews, and the White Race loses again.

Many people are, of course, afraid to start a business because they feel that there is too much risk involved. This is not good thinking. After all, everything is a risk. To live at all is a risk. When you take a job with some big company you certainly are involved in the risk of losing that job. If you start in business when you are still in your early twenties or even under twenty, and start with very little, you cannot be hurt too much in the trials and errors that accompany the early founding of a business. Even if you go broke you haven't lost too much because you probably didn't have too much to start with, and you're still young. Many of the most successful businesses have been established after the founder learned from the experience of going broke in one or more unsuccessful enterprises. But in most cases, once you have the business established, the chances are that you will not only be able to keep it, but expand it, and perhaps become tremendously wealthy.

A common fallacy which persists even to this day is that most businesses were very vulnerable and went broke during the depression. This just isn't so. The First thing the businesses did was to lay off many of their employees. In some cases small businesses let all their employees go but they stayed and ran the business. When I look back to the small country town back in Saskatchewan during the depression (I was a teenager), I remember that practically none of the small businesses in that town went broke. There were two grocery stores there and they both stayed in business. They didn't keep any outside employees but they had the whole family working the store and continued in business as usual. I remember that a machinery dealer that was in business before the depression kept right on going. He didn't need any employees but he kept his business and ran it himself. I furthermore remember a small gas and oil business that was in existence before the depression and it kept right on going and never faltered.

And so it was with most of the other small businesses that were there. They all stayed in there and kept on going, although some of them with somewhat reduced profits. Nevertheless, since everything else that they had to buy also cost less, they were in many ways no worse off than they were before. However, men that had jobs before the depression and lost them were much worse off and had a miserable time finding work to keep their families in groceries.

My dad, who was a wheat farmer at that time, managed to keep his family in groceries during the depression. We had little or no money, but we had plenty to eat. Living off our own beef, hogs, chickens, vegetables, etc., we ate well. Somehow, he managed to hang on to the farm throughout the depression, and before he died, turned the farm over to my oldest brother.

Despite the fact that he had only come to Canada a short three years before the depression struck, he managed to build up a thriving farm, in fact was running three farms by 1929. When the depression did come, he managed to hang on, having a home for his family, employment for his family, and plenty to eat for his family. Being a farmer, he, too, had a business of his own to rely on.

In conclusion, it is my experience that those people that have had a business of their own were not only better off during the depression than were the employees, but when the post-war expansion came along they were in an excellent position to take advantage of it, to expand and become a large and thriving business. Many of those who before the war were only in shoestring operations expanded into huge multimillion dollar corporations after the war.

In any case, it is my observation and conclusion that we need a lot more White gentiles going into business for themselves, to acquire control of the businesses, to acquire land and real estate and drive the Jew from this field in which he has had a monopoly for too long. If we, furthermore, practice racial loyalty amongst ourselves, if we help promote business preferences amongst our White racial brothers to the exclusion of all Jews, we would, without a doubt, soon drive these parasites from the field.

It should be our determined objective to do just that as one of the many phases of the White Man's drive to throw the Jew from off our back, and again

gain control of our own business, our own destiny, and our own government.

CHAPTER TWENTY-FIVE

HORATIUS AT THE BRIDGE

The Romans were a brave and noble people. In the Golden Age of classical history they were supreme. The White Race can be eternally proud of what the Romans accomplished. Our debt to them is overwhelming. We can learn a great deal from what they built. We can also learn much from their failure to protect their wonderful race from disintegration.

For several centuries after the founding of their settlement, the Romans were but an inconsequential people, holding out amid constant struggles, a very small portion of Italian territory. From about 350 B.C. on, however, their territory expanded rapidly. Within a century they had conquered the whole peninsula of Italy. By the beginning of the Christian era, Rome was master of all the lands bordering on the Mediterranean, virtually, that is, of the then known world. The Roman Empire thus established in all its glory and grandeur lasted another five centuries.

It was not brought to ruin by the Vandals and the Huns, who, we are told invaded it. No, not at all. It was disintegrated from within as by a cancer— a cancer produced by the Jews. The name of the cancer was Christianity.

Christianity emasculated the virile Roman. Christianity transformed the heroic fighting Roman, feared by all the world, into a spineless whimpering milksop. Whereas the so-called "pagan" Romans built a wonderful civilization and a powerful World Empire, the "Christian" Romans pulled the whole framework down into a degenerate shambles, plunging the White Race into a thousand years of the Dark Ages.

Nevertheless, this greatest of all ancient civilizations lasted for a thousand years, and when it crumbled, the civilization that was Rome was a predominant influence over Europe for another thousand years. It still greatly influences our civilization today.

The White Race, in fact, is deeply indebted to the Romans. We can be exceedingly proud of being racial brothers of these great people.

Horatius at the Bridge

This supremacy of the Roman people was based on certain qualities which we find them possessing from the very beginnings of their history. The Romans were resolute and tenacious, strenuous and indefatigable; they were daunted by no reverse or misfortune, and never admitted defeat. They were conspicuous for their self-denying patriotism and their strong sense of discipline and duty. They were clear headed, businesslike and efficient, and finally, they were not a mere fighting race, but one gifted above all other nations with a genius for consolidating and organizing, and for the framing and administering of laws.

Roman law, Roman organization, and Roman institutions persist to this day over most of continental Europe. The very laws and government of the United States are based on Roman precedent and Roman models. When in the Middle Ages the power of the once great Roman Empire passed to the Jewish Christian Church, the latter usurped the Roman genius for organization, discipline and government for its own benefit.

We must for all time learn the weakness of the Romans that enabled the Jews to bring it crumbling down in ruins. The Romans failed to realize the integral value of race, in not only building, but also in securing, civilization for the future. Had the Romans built their government and their religion on a racial base, the Jews would never have had a chance. Had the Romans then had a solid racial religion such as we of the CHURCH OF THE CREATOR have set forth, history would have turned out differently. The Jew would long ago have become extinct and the great White Race would today inhabit the total world.

Whereas, it is not my objective here to review the glorious history of the Roman civilization, I do want to spotlight the essence of the Roman spirit as set forth in an epic by the English poet, Lord Macaulay. This spirit is beautifully and nobly expressed in his heroic narration of Horatius at the Bridge. It is part of his work The Lays of Ancient Rome.

It tells about the time when in her early history Rome was beginning to show her future genius, and the caliber of her men. When an overwhelming army led by their enemy, Lars Porsena of Clusium was descending on the City of Rome, the city fathers realized that Rome was doomed unless the enemy could be stopped from crossing the bridge into the city.

They decided that the bridge must be cut down. But time was too short, unless the approaching army could be held at bay long enough to destroy the bridge. They called for three volunteers to stand off the army of thirty thousand while the bridge could be hewn down. The bridgehead had to be defended on the opposite side of the river Tiber, so that none of the enemy could so much as set foot on it.

Horatius volunteered. In so doing, he expresses a basic creed that we of the CHURCH OF THE CREATOR must also make our own.

As Lord Macaulay's epic so dramatically sets forth:

Then out spake brave Horatius, The Captain of the Gate:

"To every man upon this earth Death cometh soon or late. And how can man die better than facing fearful odds, For the ashes of his fathers, And the temples of his Gods."

This heroic epic then goes on to tell how Horatius, with two brave stalwarts, held the bridgehead until the bridge was cut down; how he stood his ground even after the city fathers called to him and his two comrades to re-cross the tottering bridge before it collapsed; of how he finally, alone, stood his ground while the bridge fell, then slowly and contemptuously turned his back on the enemy, dove into the river Tiber, armor and all, and swam to the opposite shore.

It is his heroic six-line speech, however, that we Creators want to make part of our own creed. We must make it part of our religious conviction: it is better to die fighting for our race, for our White

Race, than to surrender to the enemies of our race; it is far better to die a hero, than be a coward and a slave. We must realize that Nature never intended for any individual to live forever, and since die we must, the greatest honor and the highest dedication we can bestow upon our people, our race, is to fight to preserve it at all costs, or die in the attempt.

CHAPTER TWENTY-SIX

LATIN— CIVILIZATION'S FOREMOST LANGUAGE

The communication of ideas through language is the principle ingredient that builds civilization. Of all the thousands of languages to come and go, threading through the civilizations of mankind, undoubtedly the culmination was already reached two thousand years ago with the formulation of the Latin language.

This is not to say necessarily that the greatest literature was written in Latin, but that the language itself must be considered first and foremost among the languages of mankind even to the present day. Latin literature itself probably reached its golden age and its peak during the time of Cicero, Caesar and Pompeii and the literary language, and in general, written Latin remained fixed at the stage that it had reached about 50 B.C.

The sounds and the forms of Latin make it one of the most sonorous and stately of languages; and the nature of its syntax gives it a compactness and precision that no modern languages possess, making it an admirable instrument for training in exactness of thinking and conciseness of expression. Moreover, knowledge of Latin is the key to one of the great literatures of the world. Not only are some half dozen of the Latin writers among the immortals of mankind, but the influence of Latin writings on the growth and character of our own English literature has been as continuous and as profound as the influence of Latin upon our English language.

During the first and second century A.D. when Rome had conquered most of the then known civilized world, Rome and its language, Latin, spread its influence throughout all this territory, carrying with it the great prestige of Roman culture, administration and its laws. It was Latin that remained the language of the church, of diplomacy, and of culture in general, during the whole of the middle ages. Then with the coming of the Renaissance it became once more the language of poetry and of learning, threatening to even overshadow the newborn Romance languages.

During the long centuries of Roman supremacy in Europe, Latin came to have a peculiar preeminence which no other language has ever enjoyed. French, Italian, Spanish, Portuguese and Romanian are merely the modern representatives of Latin as it was spoken in various parts of the Roman Empire, hence they are known as Romance Languages. Moreover, all through the Middle Ages and down to quite modern times, Latin was the language of learning and diplomacy; an educated man in any part of Europe knew Latin as well as his own language, and both wrote and spoke it freely. It was for this reason that the philosophical and scientific works of such men as Bacon, Newton and many others were written in Latin, not in English.

So basic and so important is the Latin language even today that most of the basic legal terms used in English and American law, for instance, are expressed in Latin. The names of species in zoology and botany are today expressed in Latin, making the names universal, no matter in what language they might be referred to. Furthermore, modern medicine is filled with Latin designations for different drugs, terms designating muscles, bones, nerves and other parts of humans, plants and animals. The different species of animals, birds, insects, are expressed in Latin.

It is indeed a universal language and may be truly designated as the foremost language of the White Man's civilization.

Not only did the Romance languages derive directly from Latin, but even the Germanic and Anglo-Saxon languages have a great percentage of their rootstock of words originating from the Latin. Taking this, together with the Romance languages, the influence of the Latin language as developed by the great Roman civilization is overwhelming. We owe much more than has been credited to this outstanding language.

I, therefore, believe that the teaching and study of Latin in our schools should be more emphasized and expanded. Instead of

studying and promoting half a dozen or more foreign languages in our schools, most of which are a waste of time because they are usually soon forgotten and never used again, it would be much more beneficial to make a thorough study of Latin a universal study by all the different White nations of the world. In this way, rather than having to learn English, German, Spanish, French, Portuguese, Italian, Greek and numerous other languages when traveling abroad, the knowledge of just one extra language, namely Latin, would be sufficient. By this means, if the English, the Germans, the French, the Scandinavians and all the other White countries taught their children an excellent Latin from early childhood as a second language, then the White Man would have a universal language he could converse in, no matter which country he traveled.

Since we do not promote the participation of the colored races in our future history in any case, we are not particularly concerned whether they adopt this measure or not.

But it would certainly be a great help and a decided advancement for the White Races to have a universal language in which they could all converse, and one which would be understood by every White individual. Not only would this give us all a better understanding of the common White heritage we owe the great Roman civilization, but it would also further help to forge a common unifying bond between all the White peoples of the world.

A common language is a unifying element among people. A language difference is a divisive factor.

For instance, in some countries such as Switzerland, the country is divided into four languages; German, French, Italian and a small percentage of Helvetic. As a result the Swiss are burdened with learning four languages just so they can converse with their own countrymen. Despite the fact that will try to deny it, it presents a problem and it is divisive. The question comes up continually— is such and such a German Swiss, a French Swiss, or an Italian Swiss? Or is he a Helvetian Swiss? Secondly, what language should a restaurant menu be written in, or a traffic sign, or a government announcement? The problems are endless and needless. If the Swiss had a common language these problems would vanish.

In Belgium we have a fine White people divided by religion, and divided by language. One group of Belgians speak Flemish, another group speak French. Because of both the difference in language and the difference in religion, these groups have been continuously at each other's throats for generations. They are bitterly divided today, when the cause is needless, and the difference artificial.

In Canada, the Jews have seen to it that the French speaking Canadians and the English speaking Canadians were sure to pursue their language differences by making that country bilingual, when English would easily have been established as the official language when the British conquered Canada over 200 years ago. But no— it had to remain bilingual as a festering sore for the last two centuries until now it is possible to use language as a revolutionary tool for partitioning French (White) Canada from British (White) Canada, with bitterness, strife, bloodshed and hatred ensuing.

Even in our own United States, when I was last in Puerto Rico, I noticed that unusual efforts were made to promote Spanish in that American territory. Traffic signs, street signs and every other official designation were not bilingual, but Spanish. The Jews want to make sure that this divisive element is not phased out (which it easily could have been) but nurtured and promoted. And so it goes, around the world.

In short the Jew uses every tool of division he can to split the White

Race— language, religion, nationality, age difference, sex deference and dozens of others. Since Latin is so obviously the language that best expresses the common bond and heritage of the White Race, the Jew has, especially in the last 30 years, been extremely aggressive in trying to phase out Latin peruse. It is now

no longer a prerequisite for law, or for medicine in most colleges, and despite the fact that it is the most illustrious and significant language in the White Man's heritage, it is now always referred to as a "dead" language. As the Jews did to Germany, Adolf Hitler and the White Race in general, no opportunity is allowed to pass without heaping ridicule and contempt upon everything that is Roman and Latin.

So I say, let us not only preserve Latin as our priceless heritage, but let us realize what a tremendously valuable asset the White Race has even today in this noble language for our own unification throughout all the lands of the world. There is no question about it, whereas language differences are divisive, a common language is unifying. I therefore suggest that after we have established Latin as the second language among all the White peoples of the world, we proceed from there. As the decades and generations proceed we should then promote this foremost language of the White Man's civilization to become the primary language, keeping the regional languages as a secondary language.

By choosing Latin as the common ground, instead of, say, English, German, French or Spanish, we would avoid the partisanship and opposition that would ensue should we try to settle upon one of the leading modem languages.

Therefore, in the interest of unanimity; in the interest of convenience and practicality; in the interest of unifying the White Race; and, above all in the interest of preserving our wonderful Roman-Latin heritage, I suggest we now promote the historic Latin language until one day it again becomes the common bond and the universal language of a regenerated White Race.

CHAPTER TWENTY-SEVEN

ROAD TO GREATNESS

Anyone who is for eliminating and rooting out the very causes of crime, poverty, disease and ignorance, must of necessity also be for the shrinking of the colored races. Anyone who is for the promotion and advancement of civilization and culture, peace, plenty and prosperity, must of necessity be for the advancement and expansion of the White Race. Our religion, Creativity, is for both of these goals, namely the shrinking of the colored races and the expansion of the White Race, not only because it is highly desirable, which it is; we are overwhelmingly dedicated to these goals because Nature has bestowed upon us the manifest calling to expand our kind to the limit of our abilities and to populate the world with our own. We are committed to this program because it is implanted in our very instinct and in our very soul to do so.

Nature not only grants us every right to expand our own kind to the limit of our abilities, but tells us that this is the very essence of our mission in being here upon this earth.

There is another overriding reason why we must expand the White Race to the limit of our abilities. If we do not, the colored scum not only will, but is, expanding at a frightening rate. They not only will annihilate us and crowd us from the face of the earth, but they are doing so, here and now, right before our eyes. They are only able to do so with our help and our acquiescence. They are doing it with the complicity of the Jew in conjunction with our own blindness, or better still, our own criminal stupidity.

When we look at the crime statistics we find that more than 85 percent of all violent crimes in the United States are committed by the niggers, who constitute (we are told) approximately 12 percent of our population. Another disproportionate number of crimes of violence is committed by Puerto Ricans and other mixed breeds that the Jews have deliberately dragged into this country in large numbers. When it comes to the more sophisticated crimes, such as fraud, swindle, forgery, organized crime and prostitution, we find the majority of these crimes are either committed directly, or instigated, or managed, by the International Jew. Even those crimes of which the White Man is accused, if investigated in depth, it will be found that somehow the Jew dragged the White Man into it one way or another, either through his promotion of alcohol, or his pornography racket, or his organization of the dope racket, or one of the many other organized forms of crime at which the Jew is so adept. In any case it can be safely said that the incidence of crime for 100,000 niggers, or 100,000 Jews is at least 20 to 30 times as high as it is for the same number of White people. If further, the Jewish influence, both through his organized crime and degenerate propaganda, were totally eliminated from the White Man's society, it would be quite safe to say that crime as such would vanish as a problem of any importance, and, in fact, would be a rarity, rather than the overwhelming plague that it has become today.

The same conclusion can be reached in regards to poverty, disease and ignorance. If we were living totally in a White society, completely purged of Jewish influence, these problems, too, would be as good as solved.

With the Jewish stranglehold that now seems to overwhelm the White Race, these problems will never be solved. On the contrary, they will get worse and the White Race will be utterly destroyed unless we break that stranglehold. We must, at all costs, free ourselves from this tyrannical Jewish domination, and wrest control of the White Man's destiny from the Jew and again place it in the firm hands of the White Man himself.

In this book we have already set the goals, spelled out the objectives, and built an eternal Creed around which the White Man can rally forever. The purpose of this chapter is to discuss and suggest the means of achieving these great and eternal goals.

How do we go about this? The answer lies with you, my dear White brother or White sister. What better person in the world is there than you who are reading this, to grasp the problem, dedicate yourself to it and start to work right now? The goals can and must be achieved. It is a matter of life and death.

The key words in this mighty struggle are: dedication, propaganda, and organization. I repeat: dedication, propaganda, and organization.

One man, or one woman, working for a cause, can do much in a lifetime. With others helping him, or her, they can do a great deal more. Thousands working together in unison towards a common goal, organized and dedicated, can become a tremendous and overwhelming influence. Millions of White people working as an organized force towards a united cause, can and will become the mightiest force on the face of the earth. There is nothing that can stop them. Not only is there strength in numbers, but there is a tremendous strength in unity and in having a dedicated goal. It acts as a huge battering ram that no disorganized force can resist.

Organized and united the White Race is ten times as powerful as the rest of the world combined.

Throughout this book we have already discussed how tremendously important are dedication and loyalty to one's own race. Beyond a shadow of doubt, these are the first and basic elements that we must have in order to start rebuilding our White society and again gain control of our own destiny. Since I have emphasized this throughout the book, I will not dwell on this tremendously important element at this time but I do want to emphasize further the key importance of propaganda.

Whereas the Jew full well knows the value of propaganda, most White people shun the very term, as if it were something corrupt and unclean. This is a completely nonsensical attitude, and we must not allow ourselves to be prejudiced against using this most important and powerful tool. Propaganda as such is neither good nor bad, depending on how it is used. It is like the word "government" which can be good, bad or indifferent. Or it is like the words "religion" or "politics" or "money." None of these words are necessarily good or bad in themselves. Properly used they can be of tremendous influence for the good. In the wrong hands (such as for instance the Jew's) they can be powerful tools which can do us a great deal of harm. In short, propaganda is like fire, depending on how it is used, and by whom, as to whether it will be destructive or whether it will be highly constructive.

Hitler has truthfully said that propaganda can make heaven look like hell, and conversely, hell look like heaven. The Jews have overwhelmingly proven this to be true. They have made communist Russia, which is a hell-state, a super-slave state, look good in the eyes of most Americans by the overwhelming and widespread use of propaganda. At the same time they have made Hitler's Nazi Germany, a period of great constructive activity for the White Race, a resurgence and blossoming of culture and prosperity, appear as a fiendish slave-state in the eyes of much of the rest of the White world. It was propaganda in huge quantities foisted upon the minds of the White people of America that drove them to war against their own best interests, and helped the Jews smash the White Man's struggle for retaining control of his own destiny.

Had, for instance, the propaganda of the 1930's in America been in the hands of people who were dedicated to the interests of the White Race, and had they exposed the nefarious Jewish conspiracy instead of lying to the White people, I am sure that the White people of America would have joined the Germans in cleaning house.

So, from this one instance alone we can see that propaganda is like the hand on a throttle of a huge and powerful locomotive. That hand can, with very little effort, make that powerful locomotive go either backwards or forwards. It is the hand on the throttle that decides. So it is with propaganda. The Jew has known for thousands of years the tremendous power that he controls if he is in charge of the propaganda apparatus. It is for this reason he has always gravitated to the nerve centers of power and first of all gained control of the news media. Once in control of that means of propaganda, he feels relatively secure, because he knows that without any competition, he can manipulate, poison, direct and confuse the minds of his Goyim victims at will.

At present the White man is almost entirely stripped of any widespread means of propaganda. Even those we seem to think are in the hands of the White Man, are, by and large, manipulated in the background by the same foul culprit— the Jew.

Are we then entirely helpless in this respect? No, we are not. One of the most powerful means of transmitting ideas is the spoken word. Word of mouth. This the Jew cannot control, at least not at this time in America. You can and must take advantage of every opportunity to talk about the creed and program of the White Race as summarized and contained in this book. But that is only the starting point. Not only can you talk up the White Man's program, but you can distribute large quantities of this book itself and give your White racial comrades an opportunity to read and see the logic of the whole program for themselves.

Skill in the use of propaganda is of the utmost importance. It is a grave mistake to try to promote too many issues at one time. The real genius of a successful politician is to keep hammering away on just a few points at the most, at the same time approach it from a thousand different angles, always reaching the same conclusion and hammering away like a battering ram at the same vulnerable target. In no case are the masses of the people able to sustain a concerted drive against a multitude of fronts. To try and do so is only to confuse the issues and to scatter the energy needed to batter down the enemy. Propaganda should not be like a scattering of buckshot, but should carry the wallop of a Magnum high-powered rifle bullet.

Furthermore, propaganda must be aimed for the masses, not for the few intellectuals. It is the masses that are the powerhouse of our drive for racial independence and supremacy and therefore this whole religious movement must be aimed for the masses. It is, furthermore, a mistake to talk in lofty intellectual circles above the heads of the people whom you are trying to reach.

The more simple and the more powerful you can keep the issue or the issues, the more effective will be the impact. In this regard repetition is a key to driving home the point In this book I have used repetition over and over again of many of the key issues and done so intentionally to emphasize those things that are most important, approaching the issue from many different angles in order to arrive at the same conclusion. If the unimportant and the important were mentioned with only the same infrequency, the average listener or the average reader would not discern from your presentation what is important and what is trivial.

For instance, at this time, the Jews are hammering away at ecology, repeating over and over again the importance of ecology without really saying anything much that is new. The very fact, however, that it is given so much time and so much repetition and so much emphasis impresses upon the average listener that it must be of utmost importance and after awhile he begins to accept it as a fact. The fact that the Jews are putting over a fallacious and fictitious idea for the devious purpose of controlling more of your land and more of your business activities, is beside the point. The average person, listening to the ecology propaganda day after day, soon begins to be swept up with the propaganda, becomes convinced of its importance, and soon begins to make the issue his very own.

So it is with the tremendously important issue of race that we are now faced with in hammering home into the consciousness of our own people. We must keep repeating the issue again and again and again, we must keep hammering away at it. We must approach it from a thousand different angles until the White Man realizes the true issues of his fight for survival that he is now embroiled in, one from which he cannot escape.

The first place to begin is to form a Church group of your own, that is, a CHURCH OF THE CREATOR. Christianity says "where two or more are gathered" is a good unit to start with. We can't help but agree with most of the propaganda procedures and methods that Christianity has used and perfected over the last some 19 centuries. Nobody can really argue with the effectiveness of their methods. After all, they had a most difficult and unattractive product to sell, and the fact that they have sold it so successfully speaks highly of the effectiveness of their sales methods. We would do well to examine their methods and get the benefit of the 19 centuries of experience they have acquired. These are now available to us in the means of organizing a Church of our own.

We can learn much from the means they have utilized in so successfully spreading their doctrine.

Certainly the number of Christian Churches that are springing up even today in America and the ease with which it seems they can raise money to build these tremendously costly and bizarre church buildings for a completely pointless and unrealistic cause, should be of encouragement for us, the White Race. It should make us realize that we can do better in promoting and spreading a much more worthy cause— namely the survival of the White Race. Therefore, we too can organize, we too can gain members, we too can raise money, and we too can build meetinghouses for the assemblage of the loyal members of our race.

Since some religious sects are more successful than others, let us learn

Nature's Eternal Religion

from the more successful. At this point in America the Mormon religion is spreading the fastest, as we have already stated in a previous chapter. Let us therefore remember and review what the Mormon technique is.

After you have founded the nucleus for a Church group, starting with as few as possibly two or three, give yourselves a specific name to distinguish your particular CHURCH OF THE CREATOR from that of another group. Start out with a headquarters and a mailing address which might be your own home or it might be a building or a hall that you can rent. Having done this much, start recruiting. We will remember the Mormon technique of recruiting was to have two young men, neatly dressed, go from house to house, with a cheerful and inviting line of entry to engage people in conversation, and if possible to gain entrance to their living room, where they can discuss their particular religion further.

This is very important. Getting accepted and getting entrance whereby you can then further discuss at leisure the tenets of your particular belief is a first, but a very important, step. From there on out you have so many issues that you can more or less choose from to probe the White brothers and sisters to whom you are speaking. Today, with the average White family's children being bused away into a nigger district; or the niggers being bused into their district; with White neighborhoods being encroached by the blacks; with taxes and welfare being heaped on the backs of the White worker; with blacks being promoted into jobs that were held by Whites, there are a dozen different issues that worry and weigh upon the minds of the average White family in America.

It is your task to probe and find out just which of these issues strike fire with the person or persons with whom you are speaking. Having found that issue, it is then paramount to explore it fully and to suggest the solution to those problems. And in one way or another the solution will be in joining with the other White racial comrades in a common cause under the leadership of the CHURCH OF THE CREATOR and in organizing further from there. Therefore, when you find those who are interested in joining into the White community, invite them to your next Church meeting— meetings that should be held at a regular time each week.

From this small and inauspicious beginning build a huge and mighty church in your neighborhood. It is our objective to have built a hundred thousand such temples for the preservation of the White Race across this great land of ours, and from there on out throughout the world. I am convinced that if only one tenth of the time, energy and money were spent in the promotion and spreading of the White Man's religion, namely Creativity, that is now spent on barely keeping alive the sick and morbid Christian religion, that our religion would spread like wildfire. I believe that if less than one tenth of the effort were spent in exposing Christianity for what it is and explaining our new vibrant and dynamic religion, that Christianity would soon wither on the vine and Creativity would triumph throughout the White world. This is our goal and our objective.

Since our program is so revolutionary and so basic and requires a reorientation in so much of the confused thinking that now clutters the mind of the White Race, it is of utmost importance that as many prospective recruits to our Church be given the opportunity and be induced to read this book. Therefore, constant campaigns to distribute and disseminate this book should be launched not only in your neighborhood, but in areas where you think there is fertile ground. With so many White parents alarmed and seething with rebellion against the forced integration and mongrelization of our White Race, the opportunities for promoting and distributing this book are endless.

In the distribution of this book, again the house-to-house method is one of the best. Again, going in pairs, either two men making an attractive presentation, or a man and a woman, going house to house. Try to either sell the book after some favorable discussion, or, if the prospective recruits are hesitant in buying it, make them an outright gift of it. Another alternative is to let them borrow the book and let them read it for themselves with the idea that you will check back and see whether they would wish to buy it later. In any case, avail yourselves of a thousand copies of this book and start distributing them.

That this might mean a considerable sacrifice to some, is undoubtedly true. However, when you consider of how much money the Jews are robbing from you constantly, year after year after year, such sacrifice is a tremendously good investment, one that must be made. Remember what the Jew does. He gives and gives generously to his many racial causes. He keeps plowing back his earnings in one way or another to again benefit his race, which in turn rewards him handsomely for his dedication and loyalty. In any case, remember, when this book at last becomes the public property of the White Race, we can consider that the back of the Jewish conspiracy will have been broken forever.

One of the most important aspects of gaining recruits and in the use of propaganda is the ability to effectively speak in public.

Hitler says that all great movements have been promoted by the power of the spoken word. It therefore behooves you to learn to speak well. Not only is it important to become a good public speaker, but it is important to become a good debater even in small circles or in a contest with a single individual. One of the best organizations that I know of that you can join quite easily and rather inexpensively to learn to speak well is an organization called Toastmasters. Not only will this give you an opportunity to immediately learn to improve your speaking techniques, but you will have an immediate platform from which to test some of your ideas and your speeches, as well as to make a number of new contacts, most of which are quite articulate and certainly above average in intelligence and in ability.

Nature's Eternal Religion

I personally joined Toastmasters back in 1965 and within a year I had gained enough confidence to enter the political field and run for the State House of Representatives, which I successfully won in my first try.

As you get further organized, the use of handbills with brief and catchy slogans announcing your meetings are very effective.

These can be distributed on a house-to-house basis, or at shopping centers, or football games or other areas wherever a large number of people can be contacted with a minimum of effort.

Another effective device is the use of the recorded telephone message with a number to call that can be advertised by word of mouth, by cards, by handbills and by advertising. This telephone message should be changed every week. A schedule should be set up and the message itself should inform the listener when the message changes so that he can call and listen again to the new message.

One of the most fertile Fields to disseminate and spread the inspiring and dynamic new religion is amongst those who today seem to be most hopelessly enmeshed in the Jewish network. This group is the young people of today, especially the college students. When we see all the Jewish perversion that our young people have fallen prey to, we are too inclined to blame them for their transgressions and write them off as hopelessly lost. This is completely erroneous. These young people who have become hippies, who have become Marxists and revolutionaries, are much more to be pitied than censured. They are victims rather than culprits. They have had the full fury of the treacherous Jewish conspiracy unleashed upon them, with absolutely no guidance and no defenses provided for them by their parents or their elders. Basically and underneath, these people are fine idealistic White loyalists, with their instincts still very much alive and receptive to a goal and an ideology they can follow and one they can believe in. They have been so thoroughly duped and misled and deceived by their elders with all this hypocritical Christianity, they are overwhelmingly confused by all the contradictory bad advice they have received. With no goals to strive for, no objectives to follow, with no particular future to work for, they have thrown it all overboard and rebelled. They have rebelled, but they don't know what to replace it with. They are desperately searching, groping in a vacuum.

I therefore believe that especially on the college campuses our new religion, based on the laws of Nature, based on common sense, and on the lessons of history, and above all based on their own good healthy instincts, will catch on and spread like wildfire. I therefore believe that our greatest emphasis should be with the young people, and especially those that are now roaming the college campuses, aimlessly searching for what they know not. I believe here is the most fertile and most significant field of endeavor where we can really sow the seed.

Therefore, the utmost effort should be directed towards forming college groups, college clubs, based on the advancement and

promotion of the White Race, and founding Church groups amongst the students that they themselves can lead and expand.

Another tremendously significant project that can be undertaken by dedicated loyal White people with means is to start a private school or a private university that is based on the principles of the CHURCH OF THE CREATOR. This is no more difficult than say, starting a Catholic School or Catholic University or a Methodist College or a Baptist School. Certainly the need for such a series of schools is overwhelming, and the good that could be derived from such would be everlasting. With our so-called public schools being mongrelized and becoming dens of iniquity and crime, the need for schools based on the preservation of the White Race and loyalty to the White Race, is overwhelming and urgent.

As a further offshoot of this same idea, training schools for leaders in the White movement and leaders for our Church must be formed. This would be along the same lines as the theological schools the Christian churches now use to train their preachers and ministers. In the same way we must have schools to train our leaders and our missionaries to promote, disseminate and advance our philosophy and our Race.

We also need bookstores which stock books that expose the Jew and promote Creativity. In this line of endeavor we also need a number of creative writers that will re-write history of the last several thousand years taking into account the Jewish influence and perversion of our White history, of our thinking, and of our religion. If you are editorially inclined, you could probably start a newspaper that would disseminate the ideas that our new religion is based upon. Certainly the Jews have done this very effectively in publishing and disseminating communistic newspapers, liberal newspapers, and, in fact, mostly every newspaper is tinged with these ideologies, being covertly or overtly disseminated throughout their pages.

As I have mentioned before, most great movements are spread by the power of the spoken word. This is still as true today as it ever was and what our religion and our movement desperately needs is a great number of well-trained speakers who will go out into the field and deliver our message as missionaries for our dynamic new movement. Therefore, one other thing that you could do is to form a Speakers Bureau that will help train and inform articulate and dynamic young speakers to go out and spread the word. The John Birch Society has done this very effectively and a study of their methods could be a constructive guide as to what we can do in sending out missionaries to spread our own dynamic and revolutionary new ideas.

If you are at that stage of life where you are about to choose a career or a job, it would behoove you to go into such fields in which you could take advantage of being a missionary for our cause. If you choose an occupation such as being a writer for a newspaper, or an advertising agent, or an author of books, or a publisher, or in any field that has to do with public information, you can be in a key position to disseminate the ideas with missionary zeal.

The foregoing are a number of ways and means that you can start today to launch this tremendously important revolutionary new religion. No one person will do all of these things.

In fact, if you choose one or two or three you will be doing well. But in any case, it is a guide to start you thinking as to what you can do to start putting into action that about which you have been reading and about which you have been thinking. This is by no means a complete list nor is this the end of the activities in which you can engage. It might behoove you to sit down and make a list of other activities that you could successfully promote and start your own program.

In any case, this is a beginning and a guide. It is urgent that you start now and put your shoulder to the wheel. Remember, ideology without action is sterile. We must act. There is no time to lose and there is no better time to start than right now.

CHAPTER TWENTY-EIGHT

OUR BRILLIANT FUTURE

The most exciting, the most dynamic, the most wonderful and beautiful years for the White Race lie ahead of us.

In the next few pages I am going to prognosticate what I see ahead for the future of the White Race after it has accomplished its goals of populating the world. I am envisioning a world in which the niggers, the Jews and the colored races are no longer in our midst to debilitate us, plunderer us, to harass us, or to plague us. I am looking forward to the time when the White Race will be able to exercise its wonderful productive and creative genius without having upon its back all the leaches that now suck the very lifeblood from out of our veins. When I contemplate the coming of this wonderful era, our future looks rosy beyond anything that has ever been imagined before. In fact, a heaven on earth would not be too expansive a description of the exciting future that awaits us.

When the White Race has expanded to where it will populate all the worthwhile land of this Planet Earth, we will see an up breeding of the White Race instead of the down-breeding that has been going on for the last 2,000 years, and we will see a Super Race emerge that will be a pride and a joy to behold. I believe that within the next century after the White Man has accomplished his primary goal of populating the world, we will find the average White man or woman as being handsome, athletic in build and unusually healthy in mind and body. The average man will be handsome and manly looking, in fact more so that the average movie star of today. The average White woman will be tall, possessed of a beautiful feminine figure and exceedingly beautiful in appearance.

I furthermore predict that the average intelligence will rise considerably as the White Race embarks on its program for improving and advancing itself. Whereas today a man with an I.Q. of 150 is considered to be a rare genius and occurs roughly once in 5,000, I foresee that in a hundred years from the time the White Man has gained control of his own destiny, a genius of this caliber will be considered quite commonplace. Furthermore, we can expect to have super- geniuses with I.Q.'s of 200 and more, leading our Race into fields of technology and science and culture to heights that can hardly be dreamed of today. Mathematics, Chemistry, Physics, Science, Technology will break through to dizzying new heights that we can hardly visualize today.

Finer music will be written than has ever been written in the past. Art and sculpture, architecture, freed from Jewish influence, will reach far superior standards of beauty than have ever been achieved before, even far out-distancing that achieved by the Greeks and the Romans in Classical civilization or during the time of the Renaissance. We will have many geniuses of the type exemplified by Leonardo da Vinci or Michelangelo, or Rembrandt, and we will, in fact, have super-geniuses that will far surpass anything that the best of the White Man in the past has ever achieved.

Not only will the future White Man be a superior species in health, but with no more of the niggers and the colored races in our midst to spread disease. Filth and pollution amongst us, the former incidence of disease will be greatly reduced by several factors: a healthier specimen of individual; superior nutritional technology; the absence of slums, filth and degeneracy.

With the passing of the niggers, the Jews, and the scum from our midst, I further foresee the White Race, in a very short space of time, will have completely eradicated poverty from throughout the land. Not only will there be no masses of colored freeloaders riding on our back to pull down our standard of living, but we will also have gotten rid of the Jew who has been robbing us of more than three quarters of our wealth through sheer chicanery, coercion, and plunder.

Furthermore, the White Man's organization will be so much superior, so much more productive and so much more creative, and the White Man, then having very few ignorant and indolent drones amongst his own kind, poverty as a problem will have been completely eradicated in our society. In fact, when we have populated the world and have at our disposal the wealth and resources of the whole wide world with which to create, build and produce for ourselves, we will literally be swimming in wealth. It is not only possible, but entirely probable, that every White family will be able to afford a beautiful large home in attractive, clean surroundings. It will be possible to have all the fine clothes, books, good food and whatever else they desire, entirely within their reach and at their disposal.

Why do I predict such a bountiful future? Because this goal is not only entirely possible, but inescapable when the White Man is free lo exercise his tremendous creative and productive abilities for his own use. With even more advanced, capable generations coming up, providing for himself and his family will be a breeze for the White Man of the future. Instead of most of the White Man's energy and productivity now being siphoned off to the parasites that

Our Brilliant Future

ride on his back; his energy being dissipated in destructive wars and in-fighting amongst the White people themselves; all of the creative productivity will in the future will go towards his own benefit.

We will, for instance, have no more warfare between the different peoples. The White Race, when it has made the Creativity religion its very own and eliminated the destructive Jewish influence from its midst, will also have eliminated Jewish instigated warfare.

Being united in the one common purpose of advancing itself, it will no longer have the slightest reason to carry out suicidal warfare against itself, and there will no longer be any threat from the colored races against whom to wage any kind of warfare. In short, the tremendously destructive and debilitating consequences of warfare that the Jews have manipulated the White Race into, generation after generation, century after century, will be entirely eradicated. It will no longer be one of the many evils that now so tragically plague us.

When you think of the tremendous cost to the White Race in terms of wealth, material, energy and in blood that the Jewish instigated wars have cost us in the past and when we consider that all this effort can instead be directed for our own constructive benefit, the very idea itself is staggering. Nevertheless, this is what we can do, when the White Man embraces the religion that we are now founding, a religion that teaches him to unite and create and produce for his own benefit, and teaches him to demand and exercise control of his own destiny.

Not only will we be rid forever of the destructive and debilitating wars that the Jews have manipulated upon us, we will no longer have to support a huge expensive and nonproductive war machine as we are today. Furthermore, our astronomical welfare costs, which are now being wasted on the parasitic nigger of today, will also be entirely eliminated. These two factors alone, coupled with the absence of Jewish plunder, I feel confident, will lower our taxes to a fraction of what they are today. I predict that taxes will be reduced to where they will be less than ten percent, perhaps five percent, of what they are at present. Considering further that crime will be reduced to where it will be less than one percent of what it is today, it is not hard to imagine where the present huge costs of government, (with warfare and welfare eliminated) will be a small fraction of the burden that it is today. The White Man will then be in a position where his creativity and productivity can benefit those who have worked for it - namely the White Man himself.

The whole effect of this will be accumulative. With crime reduced to one percent (or less) of what it is today, the nonproductive cost of maintaining a huge police force will shrink accordingly. The streets will again be safe for men, women and children, day or night. Most of the bureaucratic controls that businessmen and the average citizen in general is plagued with, will be eliminated. No longer will we need armies of bookkeepers and paper-shufflers in and out of government to debilitate and harass our every move.

The White Man can again, in fact, will be encouraged, to do that which he does best— create and produce.

With the imbeciles, idiots and morons being culled out by the simple process of not being allowed to breed and multiply their misery, mental problems, too, will be shrunk to a rarity, rather than the mushrooming phenomena it is becoming today. Our whole approach will be to prevent the reproduction and multiplication of mental and physical defectives. These must and will be culled out as Nature dictates. Rather than keep every deformed and defective alive at all costs, to breed again and to multiply, our approach will be to bring only healthy and intelligent children into the world, as far as possible. This is what Nature tells us to do.

I can foresee so many tremendous and beautiful advantages accruing to the White Race once he is on its way to advancing itself that the list is almost endless and it is staggering to the imagination.

We have already mentioned that we would see the end of warfare and internecine strife. Crime and poverty would be practically eliminated. With the niggers no longer in our midst, there would be no slums. In fact, if you have visited some of the beautiful and clean cities in Germany, in Switzerland, you have a small insight as to the beautiful cities and the beautiful rural landscape that we can expect when the White Man has again found himself. Cities will be clean, with beautiful parks interspersed at frequent intervals. Streets will be lined with trees and flowers in abundance, with everything neat and clean, as we have already experienced in many of the all-White countries of Europe today, such as Holland, Switzerland and Germany. Only with the future White Race, having rid itself of the Jew, this trend towards beauty and cleanliness will be accentuated and will far exceed anything that we have today.

Furthermore, we will no longer be plagued and drained of our resources by having to send "Foreign Aid" out of our midst because we will no longer be shipping a tremendous amount of our hard earned money to countries like India, where it has been going down a rat hole. In fact, the White Nations of the world, being amply supplied with the land of all the different continents, and with the inherent wealth of these natural resources, will be doing fabulously well on their own. There will be very little need for any trans-shipment of aid. Prosperous trade will instead be the order of the day.

Not only will we have a clean and prosperous environment, but there will no longer be any racial strife. We will all be of the same race and speak the same language. We will all have learned through our new religion to honor, respect and promote that race and promote each other. We will have learned the lesson of Racial Loyalty, Racial Solidarity.

Our Brilliant Future

Furthermore, with the advanced technology, with the finer, more capable and more intelligent type of people to take advantage of that advanced technology; with the resources of the world at our disposal, we will be literally swimming in wealth without having to probably work nearly as hard as we do today. I can foresee that whereas the White Race is productive and creative; whereas the White Man is a builder and a worker; nevertheless, he can, with less work than he is exerting now, accomplish all this and still have ample time for leisure and enjoyment. I therefore foresee a great expansion of our recreational endeavors. I can see where the White people will be spending more time doing those things that interest them most. They will be spending more time at sports and athletics. They will be spending more time on cultural projects, music, an, sculpture and many other creative activities that have not even been invented today.

With the White Man's productivity so greatly increased and being rid of all the freeloading parasites, every White Man will be in a position where he can easily found and support a family. He will be able to do this at a younger age, as Nature says he should. With the parasitic Jews and niggers no longer riding on his back, not only will the standard of living be much higher, but the wife of the couple will no longer need to go to work to help make ends meet financially. She will be free to do that which Nature has fitted her for—to be a wife and mother, to take care of her family and to build a happy home. She will have time to devote to arts and crafts, to music and to cultural pursuits. The whole family, in fact will have more time and means to devote to such higher pursuits as well as other recreational enjoyments.

I foresee the White Race celebrating many national holidays and activities that will honor their great leaders of the past. They will exalt and pay tribute to those geniuses who have brought the White Race to the high state of achievement, prosperity and well being that they will then enjoy. I foresee many rallies and parades and cultural activities that will honor and elevate the White Race as a religious celebration. The Nuremberg rallies of the 1930's under the leadership of that great White Man, Adolf Hitler, are a typical example of the kind of celebrations the White Race will enjoy in the future centuries.

These kind of festive rallies are a soul-rewarding activity of tremendous benefit to our people. It is the kind of cement that helps to unite and bind the people together toward common objectives that aim for higher and greater goals, and at the same time the participants reaping a psychological reward that is a needed stimulant for the individual.

With all this, I predict, will also come a technological explosion the magnitude of which is hard to imagine. Although this huge technological advancement will come naturally because of the superior creative genius of the White Race, this is not nearly as important to our welfare as will be the cleansing of our race, and the White Race being in control of its own destiny.

Nevertheless, with the White Man being in control of his own destiny and having the innate and inborn desires to improve and advance his own kind, combined with the technological advances that he is so capable of, this will truly create a heaven on earth the likes of which the world has never before seen. Unlike Christianity, which predicts fire and blood, plagues and suffering, hell-fire and destruction, I am buoyantly optimistic of the White Man's future and predict great and wonderful things to come. I predict them because they are inevitable for the White Race.

Being so highly endowed with creativity, intelligence, productivity and the genius that is so characteristic of the White Race, all we really need is to rid ourselves of the parasites that have crippled us in the past, and take charge of our own destiny.

When that day comes, our future will not only be bright and beautiful, it will be dynamic and exciting beyond anything that mankind in the past has ever even imagined.